THE

ETYMOLOGY

OF THE

WORDS OF THE GREEK LANGUAGE

IN ALPHABETICAL ORDER,

WITH THE OMISSION GENERALLY OF PLANTS
AND SOMETIMES OF THE MORE UNCOMMON ANIMALS.

Si quid novisti rectius istis,
Candidus imperti : si non, his utere mecum.

LONDON:
LONGMAN, GREEN, LONGMAN, AND ROBERTS.
1860.

3d4. b.10.

Works by the same Author.

A MANUAL of LATIN ETYMOLOGY. 2d Edition, price 4s.

The PRIMITIVES of the GREEK·LANGUAGE, Explained so as to fix themselves on the Memory. 2d Edition, price 4s.

ELECTA ex OVIDIO et TIBULLO. As used at Eton. With English Notes. New Edition, price 6s.

The THIRD GREEK DELECTUS, with English Notes. Price 15s. 6d.

The SECOND GREEK DELECTUS, with English Notes and Lexicon. New Edition, price 9s. 6d.

The SECOND LATIN DELECTUS, with English Notes. New Edition, price 6s.

GREEK EXERCISES. New Edition, price 6s. 6d.; and a Key, price 3s.

EPITOME SACRÆ HISTORIÆ, with English Notes. New Edition, price 2s.

London: LONGMAN, GREEN, LONGMAN, and ROBERTS.

[*Price, stitched, 3s. 6d.; bound, 4s.*]

PREFACE.

This little Work corresponds to that of another by the same Author, entitled "A Manual of Latin Etymology." The two together contain a great mass of information on the origin of the words of the Greek and Latin languages.

It may be asked, Why a special book for Etymology? Why not leave this to the writers of Lexicons and Dictionaries? But in truth derivations cannot be treated of fully and adequately in such works. Etymology requires the consideration of various, and often of conflicting, thoughts and conjectures, and frequently demands various observations and illustrations with a view to establish or corroborate, to build up or confirm; and these are often incompatible with the dimensions and numerous purposes and objects of a Dictionary, which cannot therefore give the necessary room to Etymological discussion. Besides, Etymology is a study in itself, a subject of its own: it forms a separate department of Philology, and should receive its distinct and separate attention, unmixed with other matter. Accordingly, the Author hails with much satisfaction the appearance of Mr. Hensleigh Wedgwood's English Etymology, which he hopes will meet with extensive encouragement. Not that instances in former times are wanting of similar attempts in Etymology: for we have the valuable labors of Lennep, Voss, Becman, Martin, Menage, Wachter, Tooke, and others, all in the same direction.

Yet it is willingly conceded that the Lexicons have been constantly consulted by the Author, and that they have greatly enriched his pages. In particular, the valuable Lexicons of Dean Liddell and Dr. Donnegan have supplied a great deal of useful matter; their works being fraught with rich stores from Schneider, Passow, Pott, Buttmann, and other continental etymologists. Nor has the author left unconsulted the Lexicons or Indexes of Stephens, Scapula, Constantine, Damm, Hederic, Schleusner, Parkhurst, Ewing, Jones, Wright, Grove and Ormston: while the etymological labors of the distinguished writers first mentioned, as well as those of Valckenaer, Hemsterhuis, Casaubon, Brunck, Heyne, Hermann, Hoogeveen, Bos, Matthiæ, Forcellini, Jablonski, Bochart, Reland, Sturze, Dahler, Gregory, the Blomfields, Toup, Bp. Burgess, Webster, Todd, Jamieson, Dunbar, Dalzel, Major, and of others on a smaller scale and in narrower spheres, have contributed their share in making this work what it is. We have, in fact, in these pages a goodly result of the labors of scholars of the first talent and celebrity.

The author has endeavoured to give the reader a fair exhibition of the claims of the Oriental and of the old European Languages to the origination of Greek words. This undoubtedly will make his Work more varied, more interesting, more impartial, and more perfect.

GARVESTON RECTORY,
   Norfolk, 1860.

Greek capital letters are used when a word seems a decided Primitive or unusually doubtful.

† is prefixed to such words as are avowedly obsolete or of only supposed previous existence.

R. is short for ' The Root,' or ' The Root is —'.

GREEK ETYMOLOGY.

A.

A, Ἀ, ah! ha! and
Ἀ, Ἀ, ha ha! aha!—From the sound. Found apparently in all languages.

Ἀ-, not.— For Ἄνευ, whence ἀν-, as in Ἀν-ώνυμος. (2) For Ἀπὸ, as Ἀπό-μουσος. So Lat. ab-sonus. (3) For Ἄτερ.

Ἀ-, much; as in Ἀ-τενὴς, Ἀ-τενίζω. (Other instances in new Steph. Lex., pp. 10, 11, note.)—For Ἄγαν. (2) For Ἄδην. (3) For Ἄρι. Ἀ- appears often to be merely euphonic, from much use of it. Note our A-rise, A-wake.

Ἀ-, together.— For Ἅμα; as in Ἀ-λοχος.

Ἀάζω, to breathe out.—R. †ἀω, redupl. of †ἄω, †ἄσθην, whence Ἄσθμα, a panting, and Ἄημι.

Ἀάσκω (as Ἠδάσκω), Ἀάω, ἄασα, to injure.— Formed like Ἀἄζω, redupl. of †Ἀω, to breathe, breathe upon, dry up, scorch, blast. So Hermann, in new Steph. 1296. Thus, ' He shall blow upon them, and they shall wither:' (Isa. 40. 24.. and vs. 7.) See Ἄζω.

Ἄατος, insatiable.— From α, and †ἄω, †ἄται, allied to ἄσαι, to satiate, in Homer. †Ἀω is to breathe, to breathe hard, as in Ἄσθμα; then, to be tired, satiated. (Hermann, in new Steph. 1295.)

Ἀβακέω, to be speechless.—From α, βἄζω, βέβαχα, to talk. So, Ἀστρό-βακος is an astrologer. K, as, πεφύλαΧα, φυλαΚή: so, μαλαΚός.

Ἀβάλε, Ἀ βάλε, Βάλε, oh that!— Properly said of one wishing to change his lot: Βάλε, as Ἄπαγε, Apage, away with it! (2) Hebr. and Chald. abal, to mourn.

Ἄβαξ, -ακος, a slab, counter, geometrical table, board. —The Etym. M. says, 'as hung on a wall, without legs to rest on.' Ὁ μὴ ἔχων βάσιν, one that has no base or pedestal. This βάσις is allied to Βέβαιος, firm, and (through βέβακα, βέβακται) to Baculus and Βάκτρον, a staff, as well as to this Ἀ-βαξ, ἄ-βακος.

Ἀβδηριτικὸς, silly, like the people of Abdēra in Thrace.

Ἀβέλτερος, silly, stupid.—Dunbar says : ' Βέλτερος, better, is for Βελώτερος, from βέλος. Hence Ἀ-βέλτερος, rude in [βέλος] arms.' Then, rude generally. Rather, as we say, ' He knows no better.' In another sense we say, ' He is no better than he should be.'

1

Ἀβλεμὴς, feeble, powerless.—Ldd. and Dnn. from α and βλεμεαίνω: Or allied to it: Not acting with spirit and vigour. (2) For †ἀπο-βλεμὴς (like ἀρτΕΜΗΣ), from †βλέω, βάλλω: answering to Ab-jectus, Abject, cast down, prostrate. So Re-missus, Remiss. See Βληχρός. Or α, not: Not hitting the mark.

Ἀβολέω, to meet with.— R. α for ἅμα, †βολέω, βάλλω: To strike on a person. So Ἀντι-βολέω.

Ἄβρα, or Ἅβρα, any favourite female slave, gen. explained ' delicate ;' fem. of ἁβρός. (2) Kuhne from Hebr. EBR, a Hebrew woman: such being treated as slaves by the Pagans.

Ἁβρὸς, tender, soft, gentle.—Ldd. from ἅβα, Dor. of ἥβη, youth. (2) Like Ἀπαλὸς, from ἅπτομαι, to touch. B in aor. 2., as καλύΠΤω, ἐκάλυΒον. Soft to the touch.

Ἁβροτάζω, to miss.— Prop. to miss one's way in the ἀβρότη, night. (2) We find ἤμβροτον, ' by transp. and insertion [of β as in μεσημΒρία], for ἥμαρτον, †ἥμβρα-τον,' says Blomf. on Matthiae. Some then to this refer Ἀβροτάζω, i. e. ἁμαρτάνω, to miss ; and Thiersch from α, †μορτὸς, †μορτὸς, †βροτός, from μείρω: To miss one's PART.

Ἀβρότη, night.— From α, βροτός : When no men are abroad. Homer has ἀβρότη νύξ.

Ἀβρότονον, southernwood.— R. ἁβρὸς, delicate, τόνος, sinew. ' The leaves of this plant, slender as they are,' &c.: Mrs. Loudon. ' Quia ἀβρῶς τείνεται [τέτονε]': Voss. Etym. Lat.

ἈΒΥΡΤΑΚΗ, a sour sauce of leeks, cresses, capers, pomegranates, &c.—' A foreign dainty, and therefore it seems a foreign word,' says Lennep. Yet, as Βάλανος and Γάλανος, Βλέφαρον and Γλέφαρον, Βέφυρα and Γέφυρα, σίβυνος and σίγυνος, are found, ἀβυρτάκη might be for ἀγυρτάκη (as ἐριθΑΚΗ, δαιΑΚΗ, μανδΑΚΗ, παρδΑΚΗ), from ἀγύρτης, a gatherer, collector. (2) Reland from Persian aber, fruit-preserve, tag, pomegranate.

Ἀγαθὸς, good.— R. ἄγαμαι : Which is admired, or to be admired. In form, as γνάΘΟΣ. (2) Lenn. from ἄγω, ' to lead, be superior :' Dalz. from ἄγω, ' to drive off booty.' See Ἀρετή, Ἀρείων. So ψἀμΑΘΟΣ, in form.

B

Ἀγάλλω, to make splendid, adorn. Ἀγάλλομαι, to make oneself gay, pride oneself, exult.— R. a, much, †γάω, γάνος, brightness, gaiety ; γαίω to be proud of. So Ψάω, Ψάλλω.— Allied by Todd to Celt. gae, our gay. (2) Some derive Ἀγάλλομαι from ἄγα, ἄγαν, ἄλλομαι, to leap : as Salto, Exsulto, Exult. (3) ' Chald. gela, to shine :' Mrt.

Ἄγαλμα, -ατος, a splendid ornament ; an image of the gods, as richly ornamented.— R. ἀγάλλω, ἄγαλμαι.

Ἄγαμαι, Ἀγάομαι, Ἀγάζομαι, to wonder at, admire envy.—Valck. from ἄγω, †ἄγημι, ἄγαμαι : I am led or attracted to an object. Or, I am carried away. Cicero : ' Totos ad se convertit et rapit.' Compare Ἀγῆμα from Ἄγω, Δύναμαι from Δύνω. (2) R. ἄγη, wonder, allied to αὐγή, splendour : To be splendour-struck, dazzled. Or to ἄζομαι, to stand in awe of, as πλάζω, ἔπλαΓον. See Ἄγος. (3) From a, much, and γάω allied (like Γαμψὸς to Καμψὸς) to †χάω, χαίνω, ' inhio,' ' to admire or to be astonished at' (Dnn.). Thus Virgil : ' Tenuitque inhians tria Cerberus ora,' amazed, stupefied. Horace : ' Hunc plausus hiantem corripuit.'—Thus Thiersch from Root ΓΑΓ, Germ. gaf-fen, to gape at.

Ἄγαν, very much, too much.—For κατ' ἄγην, with wonder, ' mirum in modum.'

Ἀγανακτέω, to be grieved or aggrieved.— R. ἄγαν, ἄκται (whence Ἀκτή), p. p. of ἄγνῦμι, to break : To be much broken in mind and spirits. Cicero : ' Animo fracto et afflicto.' Ezek. 6. 9 : ' I am broken with their whorish spirit.' Psa. 69. 20 : ' Reproach hath broken my heart.' Acts 21. 13 : ' What mean you to weep and to break my heart ?' (2) R. ἀγα- (as in Ἀγα-κλυτὸ) νάσσω, νένακται, to compress. As Στένω from Στενός. (3) R. ἄγαν, ἄχθομαι, I am out of spirits. For Ἀγαναχθέω.

Ἀγανὸς, pleasing, mild, gentle, kindly.— R. a, much; γάνος, gladness, pleasure.

Ἀγαπάω, to be pleased or delighted with, regard, love, acquiesce in, content oneself with.— Valck. from ἀγα- for ἄγαν (as in ἀγα-κλεὴς), and a root †ΠΑΩ, which he supposes to have meant to pay attention to, as in Ἑμ-πάζομαι, Πατήρ, Παῖς, and Latin Pasco, pavi. (2) Soft for ἀγαφάω, from ἀγα-, ἀφάω, to handle : To caress, fondle. (3) Lennep from ἀγάπη, this from †ἀ-γάω, ἀγάομαι, to admire, respect. See πόρΠΗ. (4) ' Hebr. agab, adamare ; and Arab. placēre :' Mrt.

Ἀγανὸς, illustrious, noble.— R. †ἀγάω, ἀγάομαι, to admire. (2) Allied to Γαυρός.

Ἀγγαρεύω, to press into the public service, as did an ΑΓΓΑΡΟΣ, a Persian mounted courier. A Persian word.

Ἀγγέλλω, to bring a message.—†Ἀγαγέω (from ἄγω, ἀγαγὼν), to bring, †ἀγγέω, ἀγγέλλω, as Ψάω, Ψάλλω. See Δι-άκτορος. (2) R. ἀνάγω, †ἄγγω, bring back. (3) R. ἄγγελος, this from ἄγγαρος above.

ΑΓΓΟΣ, Ἀγγεῖον, a vessel, jar, pail, pan.— Many

refer this to Hebr. aggan, crater. (2) R. †ἀγαγέω, †ἀγ-γέω (as in Ἀγγέλλω), from ἄγω : a vessel for carrying things in, or which carries anything in it.

Ἀγείρω, to bring together, assemble.— R. ἄγω, συν-άγω. As †φθέω, φθΕΙΡΩ ; κείω, κΕΙΡΩ ; ἱμΕΙΡΩ. Ἄγημα is found, as from †ἀγέω. (2) ' Hebr. agar :' Mrt.

Ἀγέλη, herd, drove.— R. ἄγω, as Drive, Drove. So Νέφος, Νεφέλη.

Ἀγέρωχος, glorious, noble ; vainglorious. proud.— R. a, much, γέρας, reward : Having much reward. Some add ἔχω, ὄχα, to have. (2) Lenn. from ἀγείρω, ἀγερῶ, to collect, i.e. a multitude about one, 1. as Honoratus, 2. as Ostentator, Ἀγύρτης.

Ἄγη, from ἄγαμαι ; astonishment, &c.

Ἀγινέω: a form of Ἄγω. As Βινέω, Ὀρίνω.

Ἅγιος, sacred, holy ; cursed, as devoted to the gods, Sacer.— R. ἄγος.

Ἀγκή, Ἀγκάλη, Ἀγκοίνη, an arm ; Ἀγκαλὶς, arm-ful ; Ἄγκιστρον, hook ; Ἄγκος, valley ; Ἀγκύλος, crooked ; Ἀγκύλη, arm, knee, hook, hilt ; Ἀγκὼν, arm, angle of a wall, arm of the sea ; Ἀγκῦρα, an anchor.—All these evidently point to one root, which seems to be ἄγω, ἄγσω (ἄξω), †ἄγκα, to bring (round), like περι-ηγὴς, curved : and Steph. explains περι-άγνῦμι ' contorqueo.'—Or, as Ὀκλαδὸν, on bent knees, is from κλάω, to break, (as the knees seem broken,) so ἄγω here and in Περι-ηγὴς is the same as ἄγνῦμι, to break. And Liddell explains ἄγα ' to flow in a winding course.' See, too, Ἀγοστός. So Lat. suffrāgo, the joint of the knee, from Suffrango. (2) The Ed. Rev. compares uncus and Sansk. ancus. So Ὄγκος.

Ἀγκύλη, ' a hook, loop ; arm or knee from its bend-ing ; a javelin thrown by a strap bended round the mid-dle ; a sort of cup ; a handle, thong ; Ἀγκυλαι, arms of a sailyard :' Ewing.— R. ἀγκύλος in the last.

Ἀγλαὸς, splendid.— R. ἀγάλλω, ἀγαλῶ, (ἀγλαῶ,) to adorn. Allied to Αἴγλη, brightness. (2) R. a, γλάω, γλαυκός.

Ἁγνὸς, like Ἅγιος, from ἄγος.

Ἀγνύθες, stones hung by weavers to the warp.— As Saxum, from ἄξον or ἄξω, a Cretan word for Rock, (Steph. 1060) means Broken, from ἄγνῦμι, ἄξω, to break, so ἄγνυθες. And so Rumpo, Rupes. (2) Or from ἄγω, as Κατ-άγω, to spin, i.e. draw out, and Κάτ-αγμα, wool spun out. ' The slender silk to LEAD :' Marmion.

Ἄγνυμι, Ἄγω, to break.—Ἄγω, to lead, is also to drag by force ; (just as Ῥυστάζω, to drag, from ἐρύω, ῥύω, to draw :) hence then to ·hurl violently, to break. So Ὄρω, Ὄρνῦμι.

Ἀγορὰ, assembly, council, market.— R. ἀγείρω, ἄ-γορα.

Ἀγοράζω, to buy in an ἀγορά.

Ἀγορεύω, to harangue in an ἀγορὰ of the people.

Ἄγος, εος, religious awe ;—crime, as calling it forth ;— curse invoked by crime, as Sacer is ' cursed.'—Ἄγος and Ἅγιος are from ἅζω, to stand in awe of, as πλάζω, πλάζιος. .

Ἀγοστός, the hand clenched, grasp, elbow.—From ἄγω, to curve, as fully stated in Ἀγκή.—οστος as in ἀκΟΣΤΗ. Some add ὀστᾶ, the bones : for there περιάγονται τὰ ὀστᾶ τῶν δακτύλων : Etym. M.

Ἅγρα, booty.—R. ἄγω, to carry off. Polyænus : τὴν λείαν ἄγειν. So Ἕλωρ from †ἕλω, εἷλον.

Ἅγρει, come on !—R. †ἀγρέω, from ἀγείρω : Collect yourself, as in Ἀγρυπνος. Homer has Ἀγρόμενοι. (2) Come on to the ἄγραν. prey.

Ἀγρεΐφνα, or Ἀγρίφα, a harrow.—Perhaps from ἀγρέω : from its seizing and dragging the clods along like so much ἄγραν, game. (2) Dnn. from ἀγρός ? (3) Allied to our gripe. See Γράπος 2. (Very rare.)

Ἀγρός, a field.—As belonging to an ἀγός, chieftain. Thus Regio from Rex, Regis. (2) R. ἄγω, ' prey, wild beast,' (Wr.) ' All sheep and oxen, yea, and the beasts of the FIELD,' (Ps. 8. 7) where Poole says, ' The wild beasts.' (3) Sax. acer, Germ. acker, Irish, acra, our acre formerly an open field : agr, akoro, Hebr., Syr., Arabic, a field. (Webster. Todd.)

Ἀγρυπνος, wakeful. — R. ἄγρω, (ἀγρόμενοι, Il. η. 332,) like ἀγείρω, ἀγερῶ : ὗπνος : Collecting oneself (se colligens) from sleep. ' It seems formed from ἄγρω or ἔγρω :' Blomf.

Ἀγρωστις, grass.—As everywhere growing in the ἀγροῖς, fields :' Forcell. (2) Allied to Γράστις, grass.

Ἀγυιά, a way, street.—R. ἄγω : ' Quà te ducit via,' Virg. We say, ' Where will this road lead me ?' And the Greeks said, 'Η ὁδὸς φέρει.—So in form ὀργΥΙΑ.

Ἄγυρις, an assembly, ἀγορά. Τ, as in ὀνΤμα.

Ἀγύρτης, a collector of an ἄγυρις.

Ἀγχι, Ἀγχοῦ, near.—' Ἀγχὶ is dative of †ἀγξ, the bend of the arm. So Ἐγγὺς is ἐν ὕῃ :' Blomf. Allied to Ἀγκὴ, the arm. ' I'll be at thy elbow :' Shaksp.

Ἄγχω, to bind hard, compress, strangle.—R. ἄγω, †ἄγωσω, †ἄγκα, for συν-άγω, to draw together, Lat. ' ad-duco,' to draw tight.—Or (as ἔΓχος for †ἔχος, and λαΓχάνω,) from ἄγω, ἄχα (ἦχα).

ΑΓΩ, †ΕΓΩ,(whence Ἐγείρω, Ἐπείγω, and Ὀγμός,) primitive verbs, to carry, lead, bring, drive.— Parkh. from the Hebrew.

Ἀγών, a solemn assembly, combat, contest, struggle, lawsuit.— From ἄγω, συν-άγω, to bring together.— Or in the sense of ἄγειν ἀγῶνα, to celebrate a combat. (2) A gathering of ἀγοί, chieftains. (3) ' Hebr. agen, to fatigue :' Wr.

Ἀδάξω, Ἀδαχέω, ' to sting, cause an itching : perh. from a, †δάκω, †δάξω, to bite :' Ldd. See Δάκνω.

Ἀδελφός, a brother.— R. ἀ, δελφὺς, womb : One of the same mother with. 'Ἰῆς ἐκ νηδύος ἦσαν, Hom.

†Ἀδέω, fut. ἀδήσω, to satiate, fatigue.— Allied to ἄδην, to satiety, ἄσω, to satiate.

†Ἀδέω, Ἀνδάνω, to please.—Allied to ἁδέω, to satiate, satisfy. That is, to give satisfaction to any one, to please. We say, ' I received great satisfaction from it :' and,

3

' He was full of compliments,' from Compleo, to fill. Hemsterhuis says : ' The use of the Soft and the Aspirate was formerly promiscuous.' So Ἅρω, Ἁρμόζω : Ὅρω, Ὁρμάω : and see Ἀκλάος. (2) ' Hebr. hadah, to be glad :' Mrt.

Ἀδήμων, ill at ease. Ἀδημονέω, to be ill at ease.— ' Perh. akin to Ἀδέω, Ἄδην :' Ldd. Ἀδέω, ἄδημαι, is to fatigue. Compare Γέμω and Gemo.

Ἄδην, Ἄδδην, abundantly, to satiety.— As Βάδην, Στάδην, from †βάω, †στάω, so Ἄδην from †άω, †ἄται, whence Ἀ-ατος, insatiable, ἄσω, to satiate.

ΑΔΗΝ, -ένος, a gland ;—glandular swelling. Very rare : a medical word. — Perhaps allied to Ἀδινὸς, compressed, thick.

Ἄδης. See Ἀΐδης.

Ἀδινὸς, abundant, crowded, oppressed, compressed, thick, incessant, vehement, loud.— R. ἄδην. So ἀληθΙΝΟΣ.

Ἀδρὸς, ' much, great : from ἄδην [as κυδΡΟΣ] :' Mart. Some add, stout, fat, strong. See Ἀδινός. (2) Hebr. ader, strong, ample, magnificent.

Ἄδω, for Ἀείδω.

Ἀεθλος, Ἄθλος, combat, conflict, labor and toil.— From a, much, ἐθέλω, †θέλω, to be willing. Homer : ΕΘΕΛΕΝ δὲ πολὺ προμάχεσθαι ἁπάντων. And : Οὐδ' οὐκ ΕΘΕΛΟΝΤΑ μάχεσθαι. Thucyd.: Νομίσατε εἶναι τοῦ καλῶς πολεμεῖν τὸ ΕΘΕΛΕΙΝ. (2) As Ἄεμμα for Ἄμμα, Ἄθλος came first, from a, much, ἄλάω, to bruise, beat.

Ἀεί, Ἀιεί, Ἀὲν, Ἀὲς, Ἀὲ, in uninterrupted succession, always. — Elegantly derived by Lennep and Dunbar from ἄω, to breathe : the duration of time being shown well by the continual movement of breathing. As also in Ἀῶ, which see. We say, ' So much time transpired :' ' At the expiration of the time :' from Spiro. (2) Our aye, (' For ever and for aye.') Sax. aa, Goth. a, Mœs. Goth. aiw.

Ἀείδω, to sing.— From a, much ; εἰδῶ, to know. Thus Theocritus has πολύ-ἴδρις ἀοιδός. Horace : ' Citharæ sciens.' Spenser : ' And bards that to the chord Can tune their voices cunningly,' i. e. knowingly. Theocritus has : Ὁλθια ὃσσα ἸΣΑΤΙ, πανέλθεα ὡς γλυκυφωνεῖ ! Dalzel says on Pind. Ol. l. 15, ' Σοφοὶ here are poets, as elsewhere in Pindar.' (2) ' Hebr. yada, to confess, praise :' Pkh.

Ἀείρω, Αἴρω, to raise. — R. ἄρω, prop. to draw, whence Ἀρύω, to draw up, Ἐρύω, to draw. (2) To take up into the ἀέρα, air. (3) ' Hebr. arim, sustulit :' Mrt.

Ἀελλα, a whirlwind.—R. †άω, ἄημι, to blow, as θάω, Θύελλα, Lat. duELLUM. (2) R. a, much ; ἕλλω, to roll. Ἤντερ ἀελλαι ΕΙΛΕΩΣΙΝ, Hom.

Ἄεμμα, same as Ἄμμα.

Ἀέξω, Αΰξω, Αὐξάνω, to increase.— R. ἄγω, ἄξω, to carry (forwards): ἀγείρω. Ἀέξω, like Ἀέμμα. Φέρεται is ' advances ' in Œd. T. 501. ' Pro-dūcas sobolem :' Hor., multiply. (2) Our verb wax, Sax. weaxan,

Germ. *wachsen*, Sw. *vaxa*, Lat. *augeo, auxi*.

Ἄεσα, I slept.— R. †ἄω, ἄημι, to breathe; here to breathe hard, as in sleep.

Ἀετὸς, Ἀιετὸς, an eagle. — From Ἀέσαι, to rush, (in Hesych.): prop. to blow, pant, ἀΐσσω. Pf. p. ἄεται. (**2**) ' Hebr. *aī*, to fly:' Dr. Valpy.

Ἄζα, dryness, the white mould on dry things, soot, &c.— R. ἄζω. So Αὐχμὸς and Αὐσταλέος. (**2**) ' Hebr. *az*, to burn:' Wr.

Ἀζηχὴς, hard, rough ; also, unceasing, excessive. — R. ἄζω, to dry, ἠχὴ, sound. Homer has Ἀδον ἄυσεν, and Virgil, ' *Aridus* audiri fragor,' where Servius says, ' *Aridus* means, very much.' Some simply from ἄζω. (**2**) Α, ζα, ἠχή. (**3**) Α, ζα, ἔχω, to hold on : *con-tinuus*, unceasing.

Ἄζος, for Ἄοζος.

Ἄζω, to dry, parch.— R. †ἄω, ἄημι, to blow upon. Haggai 1. 9. See Ἀδσκω. (**2**) R. α, ζῶ ?

Ἄζω, Ἄζομαι, to stand in awe of.— R. †ἄω, ἄημι, to breathe hard, pant, palpitate. Spenser : ' Yet might her heart be seen to pant and quake.' The aspirate expresses better the panting. Compare Αἱρέὼ. (**2**) As Γαῖα, Αἶα ; Φημί, Ἡμί ; Φεῦ, Heu ; If, for Gif ; so Ἄζω for Χάζω, to give way, retire.

Ἀηδὼν, the nightingale.— The same as ἀειδὼν, from ἀείδω. ' Thee, chauntress:' Milton.

Ἄημι, to breathe, blow.— R. †ἄω, †ἄσθην, whence Ἀσθμα, asthma. See † ἌΩ.

Ἀὴρ, aër, the air :— thick air.— R. †ἄω, ἄημι, to blow, breathe. So αἴθω, αἰθHP. As ' thick air,' it may be prop. ' exhalation, vapor.' (**2**) ' Hebr. *ar*, to flow:' Dr. Valpy.

Ἀησυλος, thought the same as Αἴσυλος. Better Heyne, from α, not, ἥδομαι, ἥσομαι : Not easy to be pleased, rough-tempered, &c.— Some for †ἄσυλος (See in the next), from ἄτω, ἄσω, to hurt, ἀτάω.

Ἄησυρος, light.— Lengthened from ἄσυρος from α, σύρω, σύρῶ : Easily drawn. (**2**) For ἀερό-συρος, drawn by the air. Horace : ' Cinis aridus *ventis ferar*.' (**3**) R. ἄησις, a blowing. Easily blown about. (**4**) Valck. reads ἀεί-συρος.

Ἀήτης, Ἄημα, a blast.— R. ἄημι, to blow.

Ἄητος, ' prob. from ἄημι : orig. stormy, and so violent, terrible :' Lidd. (**2**) For Ἄατος, insatiable. (**3**) Lengthened from ἄτω, ἄσω, to hurt, ἀτάω. See Ἀήσυρος.

Ἀθάρα, Ἀθήρα, pottage, porridge.— R. α, much ; θέρω, ἔθαρον, θερμαίνω, to heat, warm. See ΘἈρσος. (**2**) ' An *Egyptian* word:' Jablonski. And so says Pliny.

Ἀθέλγω, to suck, to milk — From α, much ; ἔλκω, to draw, as Θ in Θάμα from Ἅμα, Θάλασσα, Θειλόπεδον, and Θέλγω. Bacon : ' The crown had *sucked* to hard and now being full was like to *draw* less.' Horace : ' Pocula arente fauce *traxerim*.'

Ἀθερίζω, to think slightly of.— Prop. to care for it no more than for an ἀθέρα, spike of an ear of corn. We say, ' I don't care a fig for it.' (**2**) ' Better perh.

from α, θερίζω, to reap : or with Schneid. from α, θέρω, θεραπεύω :' Dnn.

Ἀθερίνη, a small bony fish.— Referred by Dnn. to ἀθὴρ, έρος, the awn of an ear of corn.

Ἀθὴρ, g. ἀθέρος, the awn or beard of an ear of corn. —Some from α, intens., θέρω, as Ἀrista (like Ἀrena) from ἄreo : It being dry, compared to the ear itself. Forcellini says that Arista is used ' pro herbis *aridis* inutilibus.' (**2**) Aspir. for †ἀτὴρ, †ἀτέρος, from α, τείρω, τερῶ, from its sense in its derivatives ' τρέω, τράω, τιτράω, to transpierce, τρόω, τιτρώσκω, to perforate :' Dnn. As being sharp and prickly.

Ἄθλιος, wretched.— R. ἄθλος, a struggle.

Ἄθλον, the reward of the Ἄθλος.

Ἄθλος : in Ἄεθλος.

Ἀθρέω, to look attentively at.— R. α, much ; θεωρέω. (**2**) R. α, †τρέω, τρῆμα ; to perforate (with the eye). Observe Τορὸς from Τορέω.

Ἄθροος, gathered together, crowded.— R. α, θρόος, noise of a tumult.

Ἀθύρω, ἀθύρω, ' from α, [or ἀπὸ,] θύρα, to sport, play as children do out of doors :' Ewing. So Ἄθυρος is open, Ἀθυρόγλωσσος, Ἀθυρόστομος, ' having a mouth without a door, garrulous :' Ewing. (**2**) Dnn. compares it with Θύω, to move rapidly. As ττΤΡΩ.

Αἶ, alas ! oh that ! if.— From the sound. (**2**) Properly ' If' : Cretan for Εἰ.

Αἶα, for Γαῖα. As our If for Gif from Give.

Αἰάζω, to bewail.— Seneca : ' Sonuistis *aī, aī*.' So Οἴζω, Οἱμώζω, Ὀΐζω.

Αἰάνης, -νος, ' prob. from αἰεί : everlasting : hence irksome, then painful :' Ldd. (**2**) From αῖ, alas : αἰάζω.

Αἰβοῖ, ' *bah* ! exclam. of disgust or astonishment : Αἰβοῖ Βοῖ of laughter :' Ldd. From the sound. So ' Ιαιβοῖ αἰβοῖ : *bah* ! *bah* ! (**2**) ' Hebr. *aboi* :' Mrt.

Αἰγανέα, a hunting-spear for killing (αἶγας) goats. (**2**) R. αἴσσω, αἶγον, to rush on (with). Eurip. has Ἦσσον δὲ λόγχαις. Or which you make to rush forward. (**3**) ' Coray supposes from Hesych. a form ἀγανέα. R. ἀκὴ :' Dnn.

Αἴγειρος, a black poplar.— From its vibrations, from αἴσσω, αἶγον. As Κορυθ-άϊξ. So Pōpulus from Παιπαλῶ (Æol. Ποιπαλῶ), fut. of Παιπάλλω, to shake.

Αἰγιαλὸς, a shore.— R. αἴσσω, αἶγον, to rush ; ἅλς, ἁλὸς, the sea: On which the sea springs. (**2**) For ἀγιαλὸς, from †ἄγω, ἄγνῦμι, to break, and ἁλός : Like Ἀκτὴ, and Ῥηγμὶς from ῥήσσω. The Ι seems often inserted: see on Αἰγανέα, Αἰγωλιὸς, Αἰκάλλω.

Αἰγιὰς, Αἰγὶς, ' a white speck on the pupil of the eye, giving a supposed resemblance to the eye αἶγὸς of a goat : —the pith of pine, from the same resembl. in the horizontal section :' Dnn.

Αἴγις, a storm.— R. αἴσσω, αἶγον, to rush.

Αἰγὶς, a shield.— As made of αἰγὸς goat's skin. So Galea from Γαλέα ; and Ἰκτιδέη. (**2**) R. αἴσσω, αἶγον, to rush (with).

Αἴγλη, brightness.— Like ἀγλαὸς, bright, from ἀ-

4

γάλλω; or from α, γλάω, γλαυκός. (2) R. αἴσσω, αἴγον: From the dartings of light. (3) For ἄγλη from †ἄγω, ἄγνῦμι, to break: the refraction of light.

Αἰγυπιὸs, a vulture.—For αἰετο-γυπιὸς, compound of eagle and (γὺψ, γυπὸς) a vulture. As Αἰπόλος is Αἰγο-πόλος. See Ἀετός. (2) For ἀ-γυπιὸς, where α is nearly quiescent: as in

Αἰγωλιὸς, an owl.—For ἀγωλιὸς, allied to Γωλεοὶ, holes. See above.

Ἀΐδης, Ἅδης, Ἀϊδωνεὺς, the grave; Pluto.—Generally referred to α; ἴδον, video. The unseen world, or, Where is no seeing. Hesiod has adjective Ἀϊδής. Ἀΐδηλον Ἅδαν, Soph. Ἀθήνη Δῦν Ἄϊδος κυνέην, ΜΗ μιν ἸΔΟΙ Ἄρης: Homer. 'Here their prison ordain'd in utter darkness:' Milton. 'The use of the Soft and of the Aspirate was formerly promiscuous,' says Hemsterhuis.

Ἀΐδιος, eternal.—R. ἀεί. So Μὰψ, Μαψίδιος.

Αἰδοῖα, et Αἰδὼς, à sequenti, ut Veretrum à Vereor, Pudenda à Pudet.

Αἰδὼς, shame, modesty.—R. α; ἴδον. Not permitting us to look up or at a person. Watts: 'At Thy foot asham'd I lie: Upwards I dare not look.' So Psalm 40. 12. Eurip. Orest. 454, 5. Soph. Phil. 929. Æsch. Pers. 700. Aristophanes: Εἶτα δύνασαι πρὸς ἔμ' ἀποβλέπειν; Αἰεί: in Ἀεί.

Αἰζηὸς, Ἀζηὸς, vigorous, lively.—R. α, much, ζέω, ferveo. 'Fervens juventâ.' (2) R. α, ζάω, ζῶ: Full of life.

Αἴητος, the same as Ἄητος.

Αἰθάλη, embers, black cinders, soot.—R. αἴθω, to burn.

Αἰθὴρ, Αἴθρα, clear sky, pure air.—R. αἴθω.

Αἴθουσα, a corridor, 'looking E. or S. to catch the sun: masc. αἴθων:' Ldd.

Αἴθυια, 'cormorant, diver: prob. from [or allied to] αἰθύσσω, to move suddenly or rapidly:' Dnn. (2) 'R. αἴθω: Flame-colored:' Mrt. Much as ἀγΥΙΑ.

Αἰθύσσω, to put into rapid motion, stir up, kindle;— move rapidly.—For †ἀθύσσω, from α, δύω, δύσω, to rush. (2) But as well from αἴθω: 'To break out as a flame:' Ewing.

Αἴθω, to kindle, burn.—From †ἄω, †ἄσται, to shine, whence Ἀστὴρ, Ἄστρον, a star. †Ἄω, †αἴω, †αἴθην. So γήθΩ, νήθΩ, &c. The ι, not found in †ἄω, is found n various senses of words formed from it, αἰσθω, Latin αἰο, ἀῖσσω.

Αἰκάλλω, to flatter, wheedle.—As αι in Αἰζηὸς, for †ἀκάλλω: R. α, καλός: To say pretty things of. Horace of a flatterer: 'Clamabit, PULCHRE, bene, rectè.' So Καλλύνομαι is to extol one's self.

Αἰκὴ, rapid motion.—Allied to Ἀΐσσω.

Αἰκία, for Ἀείκεια, from ἀ-εικὴς: Unseemly conduct.

Αἴκνον, Αἴκλον, the Lacedemonian evening meal.— From α for ἅμα; ἵκω: A coming together spec. in the evening, an evening (meal), as Cœna is Commons from

5

Κοινά. Αἴκλος was 'of the evening,' the time of meeting.

Αἴλινος, a mournful dirge.—From Αἲ Λίνος, Ah Linus!

Αἴλουρος, Αἰλέλουρον, a cat, weasel.—R. αἰόλλω to move or turn, οὐρὰ the tail. Or α, ἕλλω, ἰλλω.

Αἷμα, blood.—The Etym. M. well from αἴθω, to burn, pf. p. †αῖμαι. 'The ancients,' says Damm, 'if they were ignorant of its motion, were not ignorant of its heat.' To quote again from Hemsterhuis: 'The use of the Soft and the Aspirate was formerly promiscuous.' So Ἄρω, Ἁρμονία: Ὅρω, Ὁρμάω.

Αἱμασία, Αἷμος, 'a thorn bush or brier, quicket edge:' Dnn. Also, a coppice: a stone wall.—Not badly, though in a homely manner, referred to αἱμάσσω and αἷμα: As fetching blood. Compare Ἁρπέζα. Then 'a wall' would proceed from the general sense of a 'hedge.' See on Ἀκτὴ 1.

Αἱμύλος, wily, wheedling, deceiving.—Like αἵμων, knowing. (2) R. αἷμα: 'Warming the blood, causing it to thrill, soothing, flattering:' Ewing. Lively, sharp, &c. would in some way resemble our Sanguine from Sanguis. (3) Dnn. allies it to Αἱμὸς, as anything pointed, sharp. Above.

Αἵμων, 'the same as δαίμων, knowing, skilful:' Ldd. — But perhaps, as Αἰσθάνομαι 'to perceive' from †αἴσθην a. 1. passive, so Αἵμων (aspirated) from †αῖμαι pf. pass. of αἴω.

Αἰνίσσομαι, to speak by αἶνος fable, teach darkly, hint.

Αἶνος, tale, story, proverb, fable.—From †αἴω, Latin ΑΙΟ, αὐω, to speak. 'From †ἄω to breathe: use my breath audibly, say:' Ewing. So Fabula is from For, Fāri.

Αἶνος, praise.—From †αἴω, to speak, as above. 'What is SAID for a person, in his praise.' So Παραινέω is to exhort, i. e. speak to.

Αἰνὸς, painful, grievous, terrible.—From αἶ, alas! Or from αἰανός.

Αἴνυμαι, to take.—R. αἴρομαι, †αἴρνυμαι, as ὅρομαι, ὅρνυμαι. (2) R. ἀνὰ, up: To take up.

Αἴξ, αἰγὸς, a goat;—also a storm, wave, meteor.— From αἴσσω, ξω, to spring up; we say to caper.

Αἰξωνεύομαι, to revile like the Æxônes, the Cecropian tribe.

Αἰόλλω, to shift to and fro, change. Αἴολος, easily turning, varied, versatile, nimble.—Εἰλέω was to roll, (Steph. 3570,) ἔολα, and ἀελλέω (3577) to roll, to vary; whence †ἀολέω, αἰόλλω. Allied is Ἀολλὴς collective; Ἄελλα a storm; &c.

Αἰονάω, to wet, sprinkle.—For ἀονάω, from †α, ὀνάω lengthened from νάω (as Ὀκέλλω for κέλλω, and Ὀδαξέω,) to flow: To cause to flow, pour.

Αἰπόλος, goat-herd.—For αἰγο-πόλος; αἴξ, πολέω.

Αἰπὺς, high, steep.—As we find Πέπτω and Πέσσω, Λίπτω and Λίσσομαι, Ἐνίπτω and Ἐνίσσω, Ὄπτομαι and Ὄσσομαι, so might be †Αἴπτω and Αἴσσω, to spring up. Now from Θρώσκω, to leap, is Θρωσμὸς, a high place, mound, so, from †Αἴττω could be Αἶπὸς, high. See Αἴψα, Αἴφνης.

Αἶρα, a hammer, mallet.—R. αἴρω, to raise.

Αἱρέω, to seize, destroy.—Allied to Αἴρω, to raise, take up. The Asp. may mark emphasis.

Ἄ-ῑρος Ἶρος, unhappy Irus. As Δύσ-παρις, Dysparis, unhappy Paris.

Αἴρω, for Ἀείρω.

Ἀΐς, g. Ἀΐδος, the same as Ἀΐδης.

Αἶσα, one's due or right, portion, lot.— From α, much; Ἴση equal: An equal share. Horace: 'Æquâ lege necessitas Sortitur insignes et imos.' (2) As Γαῖα, Αἶα; Λεἶβω, Εἶβω, so for †δαῖσα from δαίω, σω, to divide.

Αἴσακος, a myrtle branch handed at table as a challenge to sing.—R. ᾄδω, ᾄσω i.e. αἴσω, to sing. (2) 'Held by him to whom the αἶσα lot fell to sing :' Dnn.

Αἰσάλων, a hawk or small falcon. — 'R. αἴσσω : from its rapid flight :' Dnn.

Αἰσθάνομαι, to perceive, understand.—R. ἀίω, ἀίσθην.

Ἀΐσθω, to breathe out, expire.—R. †ἀω, ἄσθην whence Ἀσθμα; ἀίω, ἀίω, ἀίσθην.

Αἴσιμος, destined; according to what is due and fit. —R. αἶσα.

†Αἰσιμόω, Ἀν-αισιμόω, to use up, spend, consume, wastes.—R. αἶσα': Dnn. Prop., to do with anything what is αἴσιμον, fitting, to put to fit and proper purposes, rite et jure tracto.

Ἀΐσσω, Ἀΐσσω, to make to rush, to rush, bound.— R. †ἀω, to breathe, pant, †ἀίω, ἀίω, ἀίσω. See αἴω, ἀίσθω. Observe Ἀἰκή.

Ἀἴστος, unknown.—R. α; †Ἴστος, allied to Ἱστωρ, Ἱστορία, &c.

Αἰσυητήρ, Αἰσυμνητήρ, a regulator, president.— As giving to each his αἶσα due. 'Justi honestique moderator :' Hemsterh.

Αἴσυλος, unjust.—R. α; Ἴσος, as In-æquus, Iniquus.

Αἶσχος, Αἰσχύνη, shame, disgrace. — Like Αἰκία for Ἀ-είκεια, unseemly conduct : Σ, as in ἔΣχον, ἔΣπον, ἔΣκω. For αἶσκος, or the X from εἴκω, εἶχα. (2) R. α, Ἴσχω : Unrestrained conduct, uncontrolableness. 'Clodii furores nullis legibus fromare poteramus :' Cic.

Αἰτέω, to beg, ask.—From α, Ἴται, pf. pass. of εἶμι, to go, whence Ἴτης, Ἰτέον: To go much about; i.e. begging. Homer: 'ΙΜΕΝ ΑΙΤΗΣΩΝ. So Ἴκω, Ἰκέτης, Ἀφ-ικτωρ; Ambi-eo, Ambio. Livy: 'Circum-ire supplex.'

Αἴτης, a lover, intimate. — R. α for ἅμα, Ἴται as in Αἰτέω : As Com-es, Com-itis, from Com-eo: Who keeps company with.

Αἰτία, a cause, motive; from αἰτέω to ask (the cause) :—a cause at law, an accusation, in which one is asked a reason of his conduct. Compare Causa and Ac-cūso.

Αἴτιος, accused, culpable. Αἴτιον, Vitium, fault.— Above. ' Who is asked or questioned :' Dr. Major.

6

Αἶτος in Pind. Ol. 3. 30 is explained ἐνδιαίτημα by Eustathius, which is from δίαιτα. Hermann needlessly alters the word. Indeed the Latin ÆDES seems to come from it. Αἶτος is like Ἀ-δυτον, Adytum, and is from α, not, Ἴται pf. p. of εἶμι, whence Ἰτέον. See Αἰτέω.

Αἴφνης, Ἐξαίφνης, Ἄφνω, suddenly.—R. ἀ-φανής : In an unforeseen manner. (2) R. ἄπτω, ἅφα, to connect : As Cōntinuò, immediately, from Con-teneo. See Ἐξαπίνης and Ἄφαρ. (3) Allied to Αἴψα.

Αἰχμὴ, point of a spear.—a spear.— For ἀχμὴ from ἀκὴ, a point : and allied to ἀκΑΧΜένη, pointed. (2) R. αἴσσω, αἴχμαι : To rush with. Eurip.: ΉΣΣΟΝ δὲ λόγχαις. Or, which is shot or darted: Ἔγχος ΉΙΧΘΗ παλάμηφιν, Hom.

Αἴψα, forthwith.—For ἅψα (as αἴφνης,) from ἅπτω, ἅψω, to join. As Continuò, forthwith, from Con-teneo, Contineo. See Ἄφαρ. (2) From obs. †ἀΐττω, (mentioned in Αἰπός,) ψω, αἴσσω, to spring, rush.

'Αΐω, to breathe out.—R. †ἀω, †ἀίσθην, ἀσθμα. See †Ἀ Ω.

Ἀΐω, Αἰσθάνομαι (through ἀίσθην,), to perceive, understand, feel, hear, observe see.— From breathing (See above,) the idea was carried to the properties of breathing things. Cicero has 'spirabilis animus.' Compare Anima, breath, and Animus, the mind; Ψυχὴ, breath and the soul; Πνεῦμα, the wind and the spirit.

Αἰὼν, duration, space of time, time, an age, life-time, life.—R. ἀεὶ ὢν, being in uninterrupted succession. Or simply from αἰεί. See Aristotle on Heaven 1. 11.

Αἰὼν, ἡ, marrow, spinal-marrow.— I suppose as the element of life. Above.

Αἰωρέω, to lift up. — R. ἀείρω, ἄορα.

Ἀκαδήμεια, 'the olive-grove of Academe, Plato's retirement,' says Milton. From one Academus. Some however say from ἄκος, δήμου, 'cure of the people.'

Ἀκάζω, to sharpen, point, edge.—R. ἀκὴ, a point.

Ἄκαινα, a pointed crook or rod. — R. ἀκὴ.

Ἀκακία, the thorny acacia.— Redupl. from ἀκὴ. As Ἀγαγών.

Ἀκαλήφη, a nettle.— Quaintly, though perhaps truly, deduced by Stephens from α, καλὴ, ἀφή : Not good in the touch. A 'Noli-me-tangere,' a 'Touch-me-not.'

Ἀκαλὸς, 'peaceful, still : from ἀκὴν, like Ἥκαλος :' Ldd. See Ἀκέων.

Ἄκανθα, a thorn.—R. ἀκὴ. †ἀκαίνω, †ἀκάνθην.

Ἀκανθίς, thistle-finch. — Feeding on the flour of ἄκανθαι, as Carduēlis from Carduus.

Ἄκανθος, the acanthus.—R. ἄκανθα. The 'acanthus spínōsus' is landed by Loudon.

Ἄκανος, 'same as ἄκανθα: hence a kind of thistle, and the prickly beard of some fruits :' Ldd.

Ἄκαρι, a mite.— R. α, κείρω, ἔκαρον : Too small to cut. As Ἀ-τομον, Atom.

Ἄκασκα, gently.—For ἄκακα, (as ἔΣχον,) redupl. of ἀκᾶ in Ἀκέων.

Ἄκατος, a pinnace: — drinking-cup, prob. like a boat.

— R. ἀκάζω: From its pointed prow.

'Ακαχίζω, to grieve.— Redupl. from ἄχος, pain.

'Ακέομαι, to heal: oft. to mend clothes.—' Most prob. to cure, i.e. to *quiet* pain, R. ἀκὴν, *silently*.— Damm from α, [†χάω,] χαίνω, to close (a wound), [See Buttm. in Next.].— From the later meaning, to mend clothes, came the erroneous deriv. from ἀκὴ, a needle :' Dnn.— Yet it may be originally, ' to sew up WOUNDS with the ἀκὴ needle.'

'Ακέων, silent, pensive, soft : 'Ακᾶ, 'Ακᾷ, 'Ακὴν, gently, softly.— Hemsterh. from ἀκὴ, a point : ' In pungent or poignant grief.' (2) As ἵλαον ἵλεων, so Buttm. makes ἀκέων for ἄκαον, ἄ-χαον : Not opening the mouth. (Isa. 53. 7.)

'ΑΚΗ, 'Ακὶs, a point.— Perh. from α, †κέω, κεάζω to split : or †κάω, †χάω, χαίνω, (See 'Ακέων,) whence σχάζω, to scarify. I.e. an edge made for splitting or scarifying, &c.— Or it may be a Primitive.

'Ακὴν. In 'Ακέων.

'Ακιδνος, weak, feeble.— As ἀλαπαΔΝΟΣ; from ἀ, κίω, to go : Unable to move forward. So "Ακιρος. Much like "Α-κίκυς.

'ΑΚΙΝΑΚΗΣ, a scimitar. Called by Horace ' *Medus* acinaces,' and prob. a *Medish* word. Some offer ἀκὴ as the root, but ?

'Άκινος, a grape-stone.—' Perh. from its sharp taste : from ἀκίς : Puugent, *acer :*' Lenn. See 'Ακή.

'Ακιρὸs, 'same as 'Ακιδνος :' Ldd.

'Ακκίζομαι, I seem not to wish what I much wish, I coquet.— From a senseless woman called *Acco.* (Schol. on Plat. Gorg. 113.)

'Ακμὴ, a point, highest point, crisis. Like 'Ακή. 'Ακμὴν, at this *point* of time, now. Others understand it ' very,' i.e. at the highest point.

'Ακμηνος, hungry, fasting.—' Brought to a crisis (ἀκμὴ) of distress :' Ewing. Or, At the edge of appetite. Thus 'Ακμάζει is, It is high time to do any thing. Indeed Hesych. explains 'Ακμὴ by fasting. (2) From a, †κμέω, whence πολύ-κμητος : Worn with toil, exhausted, faint. See on 'ΑμεννΗΝΟΣ.

"Ακμων, an anvil.— R. a, κάμνω, †κμέω : Much belaboured with blows, or much laboured at. Homer has πολύ-κμητος σίδηρος.— Or a, not : Unwearied with blows. So 'Ακμὴς is unwearied.

'Ακνηστις, the dorsal spine.—' From a, κνάω, ἐκνήσται: Which brutes cannot scratch :' Steph. and Wbst. (2) Ldd. allies it to "Ακανος, †'Ακνος. ?

'Ακολος, a mouthful of bread.—' From a, κόλον, food : where a is ' scarcely, if at all,' as in 'Αδύνατον Heb. 6. 4 (Schleusn). (2) ' Hebr. *akel*, to eat up :' Wr.

'Ακολουθέω, to follow.— Plato from a for ἅμα, κέλευθos, a way. Κελεύθω is mentioned in Steph. 4845; (pf. m. κεκόλευθα). (2) Some compare it with Lat. *côlo.* ?

'Ακόνη, a whetstone— R. ἀκὴ, an edge ; as Βέλος, Βελόνη.

'Ακος, a cure. See 'Ακέομαι.

7

'Ακοστὴ, barley.— R. ἀκὴ, a point : Pointed, prickly. As Hordeum from Horridum, †Hordum, bristly. See 'Αγοστός.

'Ακούω, to hear.— R. ἀκὴ. Much as Lat. *acuo*, to sharpen (the ears) : to be sharp in hearing. We say, To *prick up* one's ears. Horace has ' aures *acūtas*.' Cic.: ' *Erigite* aures vestras.' Apollonius : 'Ορθοῦσιν ἐπ' οὔασιν. So 'Ακροάομαι from 'Ακρος. (2) From a, intens., κοέω to hear.

"Ακρα, promontory, citadel.— R. ἄκρος.

'Ακρατίζομαι, to breakfast.— For this meal consisted of bread steeped in ἄ-κράτον, unmixed wine.

'Ακρέμων, (like 'Αρτέμων,) ' the extremity of a branch; — a branch : from ἄκρos :' Dnn. ' From ἄκρos : strictly, a bough ending in smaller branches and twigs :' Ldd. ' An *uppermost* branch,' Isa. 17. 9. ' The *highest* branch of the cedar,' 17. 3. ' The *topmost* bough,' Young's N. Th. So Dr. Jones here : 'As being the highest branch.' (2) R. a, much, κρεμάω : From branches hanging down or over.

'Ακριβὴs, exact, accurate, strict.—' Usually derived from ἄκρos :' Ldd. ''Ακρος and [†βάω,] βαίνω :' Ormst. Going to the height or top of a thing. Milton has ' From the *height* of this great argument.' (2) From a, much ; κρίνω to judge. B, as in τρίβω.

'Ακρις, a locust.—' A common name to all locusts, from ἄκρα, a top : As feeding on the tops of ears of corn and plants :' Schleusn. (2) R. a, κείρω, κερῶ.

'Ακροάομαι, to listen to.— Fully represented in 'Ακούω.

"Ακρος, extreme, upmost.— R. ἀκὴ, a point. (2) From a, euphon., κάρα, (κρᾶ,) the head.

'Ακτάζω, to feast well. Plutarch says : " What do people mean when in inviting each other to fare pleasantly they say, 'Ακτάσωμεν to-day ? Is it not that a dinner παρ' ἀκτῇ is the pleasantest kind of dinner, as indeed it is ? " ' In *actâ* jacēbat ebrius :' Cic.

'Ακταίνω ' seems a form of ἄγω, (ἄκται,) to put in motion, raise, support : — move rapidly, be active :' Ldd.

'Ακτὴ, a shore ; — any raised place.— R. ἄγνυμι, ἄκται, to break : From the breakers. Or a broken shore. So 'Ρήγνυμι, 'Ρηγμίν.

'Ακτὴ, corn.— As above : Broken or bruised by the flail or mill.

'Ακτὶs, a sunbeam.— As above : Broken or refracted ; ' a fragment of the sun,' says Ewing.

'ΑΚΤΛΟΣ, acorn.— The Sax. *ac* is our *oak*.— Unless, (as 'Ακρέμων from ἄκρος,) from ἀκὴ, the extremity. (2) ' Hebr. *akel*, to eat :' Wr.

'Ακωκὴ, a point.— R. ἀκὴ, as 'Αγωγή.

'Ακων, -οντος, a javelin.— R. ἀκὴ : Pointed.

'ΑΛΑΒΑΡΧΗΣ, a Jewish magistrate.— A foreign word : (Sturze in Steph. cLxix.) Some read 'Αραβάρχης, a governor of the *Arabs.*

'Αλάβαστρον, alabaster stone : — a box of it.— From a ; †λαβῶ, λαμβάνω : Difficult to handle from its smoothness.— Some say from an alabaster box having *no* λαβὰs handles.

'Αλάζων, ' from ἄλη, a wandering : A vagabond, false pretender, quack, swaggering :' Ldd. (2) From a, λά-ζομαι : One who takes too much on himself, *assumes*.

'Αλαίνω, 'Αλάομαι, to wander. — R. ἄλη.

'Αλαλαί, exclam. of joy : 'Αλαλή, a loud ry, war-cry : 'Αλαλάζω, to raise the ἀλαλή. — From the sound αλ-αλ. See 'Ολολύζω, 'Ελελεῦ, 'Ελελίζω. (2) From the Arabic *AL-AI*, God, God ! or Hebr. *EL-EL*.

'Αλάλκω, the same as 'Αλέκω, †ἄλκω.

'Αλαὸς, ' not seeing, blind :' Ldd.—R. a, λάω, to see.

'Αλαπάζω, the same as 'Λαπάζω.

"Αλας,"Αλς, ἁλὸς, salt :— the salt sea.— R. ἄλλομαι, †ἄλλω, †ἁλῶ, to jump up. ' *Saliente sale*,' says Ti-bullus ; ' *saliente* micâ,' Horace.— But some think the sea the first meaning, from the springing waves : as 'Αΐξ, ἀΐσσω. (2) Welsh *halen*, Germ. *salz*, Russ. *sol*, our *salt*.

"Αλαστος, 'Αλάστωρ :—Bp. Blomfield says : ' From ἄλη error is 'Αλάζω to deceive ; 'Αλάστωρ who leads into error : 'Αλαστος, led into error ;—[leading into error,] pernicious.'—But others from a, †λάθω, †λέ-λασται, λανθάνω. Thus Liddell : '"Αλαστος, not to be forgotten or forgiven, insufferable : — unceasing : — abominable, accursed. 'Αλαστέω, [not to forget,] to be implacable, bear hate. 'Αλάστωρ, [who does not forget,] an avenger : — also accursed.'

'Αλγέω, to grieve, feel pain.— R. ἀλέγω, to care about.

"Αλδω, -έω, -αίνω, "Αλθω, to cause to thrive or grow, increase.— Damm thinks it a lisping form of ἄρδω, to irrigate, as κλίβανον for κρίβανον. (2) Allied to "Αλις, abundantly : To cause to be abundant or luxuriant. The Lat. *ALO* is very observable. Δ, as ἔλΔομαι, μέλΔω. (3) R. ἀλέα, the heat of the sun.

'Αλέα, 'Αλέα, heat of the sun.— As 'Αλίω is the same as Εἰλύω, as 'Αλεὶς is referred by Ldd. to Εἰλύω, as 'Αλίσκω and "Ελω Εἶλον are the same, so 'Αλέα, 'Αλέα are referred by Dnn. to "Ελη, the shining of the sun. (2) Wright from ἥλιος, Dor. ἅλιος, the sun. (3) As from αὖος or αὖω is Αὐαλέα, so from obs. †ἕω to shine, (whence 'Αστήρ, 'Αστρον, Αθω, Αὐγὴ,) is †'Ααλέα or 'Αλέα.— Or 'Αλέα for Αὐαλέα, dry, burnt up : Used actively.

'Αλέα, an avoiding, escape : 'Αλεείνω, to avoid, escape : 'Αλεύω, to remove, keep from, ward off : 'Αλέομαι, to escape : 'Αλύσκω, to avoid, also to wander about. All these are allied to "Αλη a wandering away, roaming off, deviating, declining. See however on 'Αλέκω.

'Αλέγω, 'Αλεγίζω, ' to regard or count : usu. derived from a copul., λέγω, to count. Also, to regard, heed, have a care for :' Ldd.

"Αλειαρ, wheaten flour.— R. ἀλέω, to grind.

'Αλεὶς, collected, drawn together ; — shrinking.— ' Belonging to Εἴλω :' Ldd. Convolūtus, conglobātus. See 'ΑΛΕΩ.

"Αλεισον, a carved cup.— R. a, not, λεῖον or λισσὸν, smooth. Asperum signis. (2) Allied to 'Αλλέω to roll :
8

i.e. rolled round, as the Etymol. M. explains it περι-φερές.

'Αλείτης, who leads or goes astray.— See 'Αλιτέω.

'Αλείφω, to oil, anoint.— R. a ; λειῶ, to smooth ;— allied too to Λείβω to shed, Λίπος, fat, oil.

'Αλέκτωρ, the cock.— Akin to 'Αλεκτος : The sleep-less : from λέγομαι, λέλεκται, to lie down. Others, as not suffering us to lie in bed. Gray : ' The cock's shrill clarion ... No more shall wake them from their lowly bed.'

'Αλέκω, 'Αλέξω, -έω, to ward off, defend.— Allied to 'Αλεύω in the 2d 'Αλέα. Yet ' to ward off' may flow from collecting or coiling oneself up. Virgil : ' Sub-stitit Æneas, et se collēgit in arma.' See 'ΑΛΕΩ.

'Αλέομαι : in the 2d 'Αλέα.

"Αλευρον, like "Αλειαρ, from ἀλέω.

'Αλεύω : in the 2d 'Αλέα.

'ΑΛΕΩ, 'ΙΛΕΩ, "ΕΛΛΩ, "ΕΑΛΩ, "ΕΛΩ, 'ΑΛΙΩ, "ΙΛΛΩ ΕΙΛΩ, "ΕΙΛΩ, ΕΙΛΕΩ, &c. seem to have been Primitives and all allied, and to have orig. meant to drive, but espe-cially to drive round, coil, roll : — to wind round, wend or wander round about : — to encompass and so drive into a corner, hem in, take : — to drive round in a mill, grind. These meanings are not however common *in use* to them all.—' Hebr. *eel*, to move quickly :' Wr.

"Αλη, a wandering.— See 'ΑΛΕΩ.

'Αληθής, without reserve, open, sincere, true.— R. a ; λήθω, †λαθέω, *lateo*, to elude notice : One who does not elude observation, open. Or manifest, clear, certain.

'Αλὴς, 'Αλὴς, crowded : as 'Αλεὶς.

"Αλθω, to cause to grow, — to heal.— R. ἄλδω, ἄλ-θην, to cause to grow, nourish, strengthen.

'Αλίβας, sapless.— R. a ; λίβἀs, a dripping. ' Without vital moisture,' Dnn. Compare Λίπος, fat.

'Αλίγκιος, alike.— For ἀλίκιος (as λαΓχάνω, κίΓ-κλος) : and, as 'Αζηχὴς is thought by some to have a double compound a, ζα : so Damm brings ἀλίκιος from a, λα, and †ἴκιος like 'Ικελος, Εἴκελος, from εἴκω, to be like ; and as Αλκία is 'Α-ίκεια, 'Α-είκεια. (2) Lenn. from †ἁλίω, ἀλίσκω, *capio* : Capax, holding (so much), of such and such capacity or dimensions. He compares 'Αλίγκιος with "ΗΛιξ, ικος, equal in age. And Blomf. says : ' It seems to come from "ΗΛιξ.' (3) As our Like prop. means ' even, smooth,' (Webster,) so †ἀλίκιος from a ; †λίω i.e. λειῶ, to smooth, whence Λισσὸς and Λιτὸς, smooth, plain : †λίω, †λίλικα. See Λίμνη, Λιμήν. (4) From a, λίζω, λέλιχα, to graze, scratch : Not grazing against, not jarring, i.e. agreeing. Or a, together, λίγ-γω, γξω : ' Non absonus stridore,' Greg. (5) Allied to our *LIKE, ALIKE* ;—*lic* Sax., *liik* Dutch.

'Αλιεὺς, a fisherman.— R. ἅλς, ἁλός, the sea.

'Αλίζω, to assemble : — from ἅλης or ἀλεὶς. Also, to salt, from ἅλς, ἁλός.

'Αλινδέω, to roll, as 'Αλίω. And to wander, as 'Α-λάω. So Κυλίω, Κυλινδέω.

"Αλιος, ' of the sea, ἁλός : — as the sea is a watery waste, "Αλιος is vain, fruitless :' Ewing. As Homer :

ἀ-τρυγέτοιο θαλάσσης. (2) R. ἄλη, a wandering : Wandering from the mark. So 'Ηλὸς, 'Ηλίθιος.

Ἅλις, in abundance, enough.— R. ἁλής, crowded.

'Αλισγέω, to pollute.— Allied to 'Αλίω and 'Αλινδέω to roll : (In form as Μισγέω.) : To roll in the mire, wallow. Jeremiah : ' Wallow thyself in ashes.' So Volutābrum from Volŭto.

'Αλίσκομαι, to be taken.— R. ἁλίω, to roll round, encompass, hem in, take. 1 Sam. 23. 26 : 'Saul and his men *compassed* David and his men *round about*, to take them.' See 'ΑΛΕΩ, and 'Ελω, Εἶλον.

'Αλιτέω, 'Αλείτω, to sin, transgress.— R. ἄλη, a wandering : to wander from the way, to err like lost sheep. So 'Αλαίνω and 'Αλητεύω to wander. (2) Thiersch curiously from α, λιτή : ' Who prays not, godless.'

'Αλίω to roll.— See 'ΑΛΕΩ.

'Αλκαία, a lion's tail.— 'R. ἀλκή : From the fury [or power] with which he lashes it about :' Ldd.

'Αλκεία, a poisonous plant.— R. ἀλκή, force ; as Arsenic is 'Αρσενικὸν, masculine, powerful.

'Αλκή, strength.— R. ἀλέκω, ἀλάλκω : The power of warding off. (2) R. ἄλδω, ἄλκα, to strengthen.

'Αλκύων, a kingfisher.— R. ἅλς, ἁλός, the sea ; κύω, to bring forth. ' It is said she breeds in the sea, and that there is always a calm during her incubation :' Todd.

'Αλλά, but.— Neut. pl. of 'Αλλος : (Quite) otherwise. So Latin Cæterŭm.

'Αλλᾶς, a sausage, pudding.— R. †ἀολλήεις, †ἀολλῆις, †ἀολλᾶς, like 'Αργᾶς. Allied to 'Αολλής, 'confertus,' which from 'farcio', whence ' farcĭmen, a sausage.' So 'Αλεῖος is ' coactus in unum, confertus.' (Steph.)

'Αλλάσσω, to make ἄλλο other than it is, change. So to Alter from Alter. See 'Ανάσσω.

'ΑΛΛΗΛΟΤΙΑ, *Hallelujah* : Made up of *Hebrew* words, ' Praise ye the Lord !'

'Αλλομαι, to leap, spring.— Allied by Lennep to 'Αλίω to roll, 'ΑΛΕΩ and 'Ελλω. ' Versor huc illuc motu *volutorio* :' Lenn. Agreeing with the preliminary tossing of the body, especially in vaulting.) As 'Αίσσω, to spring, from †ἄω, to breathe, pant ; so from ἄω (See 'Αζω,) might be †'Αλλω in this sense, as Ψάω, Ψάλλω ; †Βάω, Βάλλω. (3) ' Arab. *halla*, to impel, shoot :' Wbst. ' Hebr. *eel*, to move quickly :' Wr.

'Αλλος, other, another.— Allied to Αἰόλος various. Compare ἴλλω, ἵλλω. (2) 'Welsh *all*, other : Irish *aile, eile* : Armoric *eel, all, eguile*,' &c.: Wbst.

'Αλμη, salt-water : ἅλας.

'Αλοάω, to thresh in an ἅλως or ἁλωά.

'Αλοξ, 'Αῦλαξ, 'ΩΛΞ, a furrow.— Like an Αὖλὸς, pipe. (2) R. ἔλκω, ὅλκα, to draw on : whence †ὅλκς, ὅλξ, g. ὅλκος. But the A in 'Αλοξ ?

'Αλοχος, a wife.— R. α, together, λέγομαι, λέλοχα, to lie down, allied to Λέχος. So 'Α-κοίτης.

'Αληνὸς, ' cherishing, pleasant : perh. for Θαλπνὸς, (Ewing,) from δάλπω : as Γαῖα, Αἶα ; Λείβω, Εἴβω. (2) For †'Αλφνὸς from ἄλφι, corn : Nourishing. (3) R. α ; ἔλπις : To be hoped or desired.

9

'Αλς, ἁλός : See 'Αλας.

'Αλσος, a grove, thicket.— R. ἄλδω, σω : 'A place *grown* with trees :' Ldd.

'Αλτῆρες, weights held in jumping.— R. ἄλλομαι, ἅλται.

'Αλτις, a sacred grove.— R. ἄλδω, ὕλται, as 'Αλσος.

'Αλυς, indolence or listlessness.— R. ἄλη. ' Idle vagrancy :' Dnn.

'Αλυσις, a chain.— Usually from α ; λύω, σω, to loose : Indissoluble.— But the Aspirate points to ἀλέω or ἀλύω, εἰλύω, to roll or wrap round.

'Αλύσκω : in the 2d 'Αλέα.

'Αλύτης, a lictor who kept order at the games :— R. ἀλύω. ' For he had to wander about continually among the crowd :' Hemst.

'Αλύω, to wander in mind : to be beside oneself in sorrow or in joy :—Allied to 'Αλαίνω, 'Αλδομαι. (2) R. α, much, λύω, as in ἐκ-λέλυμαι.

'ΑΛΦΑ, *alpha* : Hebr. *aleph.*

'Αλφη, gain of prostitution.— R. ἄλφω.

'Αλφιτον, 'Αλφι, pearl barley.— R. ἀλέω, to grind (as 'Αλευρον,) whence †ἀλέπτω, (as ἐρΕΠΤΩ, and χαλάω, χαλΕΠΤΩ,) †ἄλεφα, †ἄλφα. So, Ψάω, Ψῆϕος. (2) Nor does Hemsterhuis think it absurd to deduce it from ἄλφω, to find : ' A great *find* among raw meats': ' The *invention*, by excellence : barley-meal being the first in use :' Dnn.— Some from ἄλφω, as explained ὠφελῶ by Hesych.: from its immense utility. (3) R. †ἄλφος, Lat. *ALBUS*. See 'Αλφος. Homer has λευκὰ ἄλφιτα. (4) From α, λέπω, λέλοφα : As peeled wheat.

'Αλφος, the white leprosy.—'Among the ancient Greeks ἄλφος was white, whence *albus* :' Hemst. That is, ' white as ἄλφι, ground corn :' Scheide.

'Αλφω, 'Αλφαίνω, to yield, procure, get, find.— Lennep allies 'Αλφω to 'Αλδω and 'Αλθω, to cause to grow, to increase. (2) Allied to 'Αλίσκω, 'Αλίσκομαι, and 'Ελω, εἶλον, to take. (3) From ἄλη, a wandering about, i. e. to seek and find. Φ as in ψάω, ψῆϕος ; στέϕω.

'Αλωή, the same as 'Αλως.

'Αλώπηξ, a fox :— a falling off of the hair, as in the mange of foxes :— pl. the deep-seated muscles of the loins, perh. from the deep coverts of foxes. See on 'Ελειὸς.— R. ἄλη, fraudulent. (2) R. α ; λέπω, λέλοφα, to take off the bark, to peel. ' Qui callidè cibum *decorticare* novit :' Lenn. (3) ' For ἀλώφηξ, a devourer of the vineyard : from ἄλως, φάγω, ξω :' Ewing.

'Αλωπὸς, fraudulent.— R. ἄλη, a leading into error (Æsch. Ag. 194), and ὣψ, ὠπός : or -ωπος is a termination.

'Αλως, a threshing-floor, corn-floor, granary, vineyard, area, *halo* round the sun and moon. And 'Αλωή. And 'Αλοιάω, to thresh.— R. ἄλως, ἀλώ, to grind, bruise, pound. Some ally it to 'Αλίζω to collect (the corn) : 'Αλής, drawn together. (2) As a vineyard, orchard, corn-field, Dnn. allies it to obs. †ἄλω, *alo*, ἄλδω, ἄλσος.

C

῞AMA, 'AMᾶ, at one and the same place or time together with. Lennep compares 'Αμὸs, one; making 'Αμᾶ the same as ἃμἀ. Then 'Αμάω, to gather into ONE. —' The Syriac AM, with :' Mrt. ' Hebr. om, together :' Wr. Seen in Emma-nu-el, WITH us GOD.

῎Αμαθος, sand.— For ψάμαθος, as Αἰα for Γαῖα. So ῎Αμμος for Ψάμμος. (2) R. ἀμάω, ἀμάθην, to accumulate. ' Cumulos malè pinguis arēnæ :' Virg.

'Αμαθύνω, to level with the ἄμαθος sand, destroy.

'Αμαλδύνω, to make ἀμαλὸν soft, weaken, dissolve, destroy.

῎Αμαλλα, a bundle or armful of corn.— R. ἅμα, together: as ἀελΛΑ, ϑνελΛα. Or R. ἀμάω ' to gather, grasp', Ewing. So Dnn. (2) R. ἅμα, ἀλεὶs, collected. (3) ' The Hebr. alem :' Wr.

'Αμαλὸs, 'Αμαλὸs, soft, tender, weak.— R. ἅμα, as from ὁμᾶ together is 'Ομαλὸs, even, level, smooth. (2) R. a; μαλὸs, = ἀμαλόs. (3) ' Hebr. amel, weak, languid :' Oger and Wr.

'Αμάμαξυs, a vine trained on two poles.— Redupl. for ἄμαξυs, (Dnn.) from ἅμα, ἄξων a board, plank. See the latter part of the next.

῎Αμαξα, a heavy waggon :—some say in which all the goods of a family are carried, from ἅμα, ἄγω, ἄξω : (Horace : ' Quorum plaustra vagas rite trahunt domos :' ' Easily transported from place to place,' says Adam Smith :) But Pott from ἅμα, ἄξων : ' Of two axles, i.e. four wheels.'

'Αμάρα, a dike, trench.— As ψαφΑΡΑ, μνσΑΡΑ; from ἀμάω, to collect : A collection, reservoir, of water. (2) R. a, μείρω, †ἔμαρον : a dividing off. (3) 'Arabic Amara, fluxit :' Scheide. (4) Mrt.'s ἅμα, ῥέω ῥῶ is hardly worth mention.

†'Αμαρτέω, 'Αμαρτάνω, to miss, fail, go wrong, err, sin.— R. a, ὁμαρτέω, ' to equal in speed', (Ewing) : Not to keep up with. But not only is there 'Ομαρτῇ, but 'Αμαρτῇ. Better still then from a, †ἀμαρτῇ. (2) Buttm. neglects the aspirate, and brings from a; μείρω, μέμαρται : To be without one's μέροs share. (3) R. a; μάρπτω, to seize : soft for ἀμαρπτέω. (4) Some compare 'Αβροτέω, 'Αβροτάζω : which see.

'Αμαρύσσω, to glitter.— R. a; †μαίρω, †μαρῶ, μαρμαίρω, to glitter : So ΜΑΡαυγέω.

'Αμαίs. See in 'Αμίs.

'Αμαυρὸs, obscure, dark, black.—' R. a; μαίρω, [μαρῶ,] to shine :' Ewing. Υ addded as in our moUntain. Compare 'Αφαυρόs. Dnn. takes a as euphonic, as Γαῦρος, ῎Αγαυρos. Note that Φαιὸs from Φάos is ' duskish.'

'Αμάω, to gather ἅμα together, to grasp in the hands, spec. the stalks of corn in reaping, then to reap. (2) ' Hebr. om, to gather :' Wr. See on ῞Αμα.

῎Αμβη, ῎Αμβων, a brow, brim, boss.—' Prob. from ἀμφ—, amb—, and so :' ἀμφορεὺs, amphora :' So says Liddell on ῎Αμβιξ, and equally true is it of ῎Αμβη, ῎Αμβων. (2) R. †ἀμβάω, †ἀμβῶ, ἀμβαίνω; what mounts on high.

῎Αμβιξ, ικος, a cup, beaker.— See in ῎Αμβη. (2) ' Arab. abiq :' Mrt.

10

'Αμβλέω, 'Αμβλίσκω, to miscarry in the birth.—For ἀνα-βολέω, ἀμβολέω, to throw or cast off, reject. (2) R. ἀμβλύs : ' To make blunt, weak, abortive :' Jones.

'Αμβλὸs, blunt, dull.—As B is added for euphony in μέμΒλεται, μέμΒλωκα, so Dnn. thinks in ἀμΒλὺs, from a, μῶλυs, dull, (ἀμῶλυs, †ἀμλὸs, ἀμΒλύs;) or from ἀμαλὸs, †ἀμλὸs, weak : ' better,' he says, ' for 'Αμαλδύνω and 'Αμβλύνω have nearly the same sense.' (2) R. ἀμβδλλω, †ἀμβλέω, so that ἀμβλὸs is Re-missus, Remiss, slow. See 'Αβληχρόs. (3) Mrt. from Hebr. ambul, weak.

'Αμβρόσιος, immortal.— For ἀβρόσιος (as λαΜβάνω, ἀΜφασίη,) from a, βροτόs. As 'Αφροδίτη, 'Αφροδίσιος.

'Αμβροτεῖν. See in 'Αβροτάζω. M added as above.

῎Αμβων. See ῎Αμβη.

'Αμέθυστος, amethyst.— R. a, μέθυ : ' Because it comes very near to the colour of wine. So Pliny. And not, as Athenæus says the ancients believed, from its keeping off drunkenness :' Schleusn.

'Αμείβοντες, prop. ' crossers', ' alternaters', rafters crossing and meeting each other : from

'Αμείβω, ('Αμέ̄ω is allied,) to act or give in return, move by returns, give in change, exchange, barter. Midd., alternate with another's discourse, reply.— From ἅμα, together with. Its form as Στείβω, θλίβω, Τρίβω. (2) Bp. Burgess from a, obs. †μέω, Lat. meo, to pass from one place to another.

'Αμείνων, better.— Fischer says for ἀμενίων, from a intens., μένος, inclination : More to our mind. Or, which is the same, from †μένω, μέμονα, μενεαίνω, to long for.

'Αμείρω, to deprive one of his μέρος share : a intens.

'Αμέλγω, to press out juice as honey or milk, to pluck fruit.— Some from ἅμα, ἕλκω, (as in 'Αμαξα,) to draw the parts together. (2) Some simply from ἅμα, rest being a termination : or from a, †μέω, Lat. meo : To make to pass out. See the latter part of 'Αμείβω. (3) As μέλοs and μέροs are identified, so ἀμέλγω and ἀμέργω below. (4) Our word milk, Dutch melken, Sued. miolka, Russ. melayu, &c. are allied.

'Αμενηνὸs, ' faint, feeble. Derivation uncertain :' Ldd. Yet others derive it undoubtingly from a, μένοs, or direct from ἀ-μενὴs weak. Compare τιθΗΝΟΣ, ἀκμΗΝΟΣ, Lat. terrENUS, serENUS, septENUS.

'Αμέργω, to pluck or pull.— R. a for ἀπὸ, μέρος : To pull the parts asunder. As 'Απομερίζω, ' to divide, separate,' Dnn. See below.— Or at once as μερίζω : especially as O seems a compound in the kindred †'Ομόργω, 'Ομόργνυμι, and to answer to A intens. here. (2) The same as 'Αμέλγω.

'Αμέρδω, to take ἀπὸ away from another his μέρos portion. As 'Αμείρω.

'Αμεύομαι, the same as 'Αμείβω.

῎Αμη, a rake or harrow, as gathering within its teeth stones and clods as it passes ; from ἅμα or ἀμάω.— Also a scythe or sickle, clearly from ἀμάω.— Also a mattock or pickaxe, answering to the explanation of ἀμησάμενος in Schol. Hom. by συνελῶν χερσὶ, grasping with the hand : As being grasped. So a spade or shovel.—Also a water-bucket, but this seems to agree better with 'Αμὰς or 'Αμὶς which see.

'ΑΜΗΝ, verily : a *Hebrew* word.

"Αμης, ου and ητος, 'a preparation of milk for the table, prob. by coagulation :' Dnn.—From ἀμάω ; ἀμησάμενος meaning συναγαγών. (Schol. Hom.) Just as Coagulate from Co-ago. Some say from its being a medley : an omnium-gatherum. (2) R. ἄμητος : A harvest cake.

"Αμητος, harvest.—R. ἀμάω, ἀμηται.

'Αμιθρέω, ' transp. from ἀριθμέω ;' Dnn.

"Αμιλλα, a contest.—' From ἅμα [much as ἄελλα, θύελλα,] nothing to do with ἴλη :' Ldd. "Ιλη would make one Λ, as in "Ομ-ιλος. Some add ἴλλω, to twist, fold, as in wrestling.

'Αμιναῖος, relating to *Aminæa*, a part of Campania famous for its wine.

'ΑΜΙΣ, a chamber pot :— also a boat, and so 'Αμάς. — Perhaps ἀμ here is short for ἀμφ— or †ἀμβ—, as Am-jicio, Amicio is for ambi-jacio, as Am-plector, as An-hēlo for Am-hālo, and as 'Αμ-φορεὺς for ἀμφι--φορεύς. Allied, if so, to "Αμβιξ. For ἀμφ' the Dutch is om, Germ. um.

"Αμμα, a fastening.—R. ἅπτω, ἅμμαι.

"Αμμος, sand, for Ψάμμος, as Γαῖα, Αἶα.

'Αμνάμος, an offspring or descendant.—Allied by Ldd. and Dnn. to 'Αμνὸς, a lamb. (Very rare.)

'Αμνίον, a bowl in which the αἷμα blood of victims was caught, for αἱμνίον. But some say the blood prop. ἀμνῶν of lambs.

'Αμνίον, the same as 'Υμνίον, 'Υμένιον, from ὑμὴν, ὑμένος. Prob. by corruption.

'Αμνὸς, a lamb.—R. ἀμενὴς, weak, †ἀμνὴς : Or from ἀμενηνός.—Or μένος here is fury. ' *Placidum* pecus ', Ovid.

'Αμολγὸς, ' prop. milkingtime, from ἀμέλγω : hence, morning or evening twilight, the first or the latter part of the night. Schneider cites Il. χ. 28 μετ' ἄστρασι νυκτὸς ἀμολγῷ, where twilight, he says, does not apply ; but it seems not incompatible with the early part of the night :' Dnn.

'Αμορβὸς, ' a companion, follower ; herdsman, shepherd.—R. ἅμα, ὁρμάω : to which belongs 'Αμορμὸς, the same :' Dnn. Or ἅμα, †ὅρω, ὅρομαι.—Some also read 'Αμορβὸς for 'Αμολγὸς above, ' darkness' : the Schol. on Nicander taking it for ἄ-μορφος, ' without form and void.' B, M, Φ are equivalent letters.

'Αμοργὴ, olive-lees.—R. ἀμέργω, ἀμοργα.

'Αμοργὶς, fine flax from the island of *Amorgos* in the Sporades.

'Αμὸς, one : See in Αμα.—Also for 'Εμὸς. And "Αμος for 'Ημος.

"Αμοτον, insatiably.— Blomf. says : ' From †μάω, to fill, cram, was μοτὸς lint : which was applied to hollow

wounds to fill up the flesh : and "Α-μοτος, which cannot be filled up.' Like "Α-πληστος. "Εμμοτος also is found. Isaiah 1. 6 : ' The wounds have not been *closed up*.' Justin: ' Sanguis aliter *cludi* non posset.' (2) R. α, and an obs. word allied to μετρέω, Lat. *metior*. Like *im-mensus*.

'Αμπελος, a vine.— R. ἀμπὶ = ἀμφὶ, as in 'Αμπίσχω : As creeping about with its branches. (2) R. ἀνὰ, πέλω. ' It supports itself on something and so moves up :' Damm.

'Αμπλακέω, to miss, err : for 'Απλακέω, (as λαMβάνω,) from α, much : πλάζω or †πλάω to wander.

'Αμπρον, used, says Liddell, only by the Grammarians as the root of 'Αμπρεύω, to draw along, drag, for ἀναπορεύω. So 'Αμπονον for ἀνὰ πόνον, and 'Αμμιγα.

'Αμπυξ, πυκος, a band or fillet, head-band, cover of a cup, anything round as a wheel.—All derive from ἀμπέχω to hold round : but certainly from ἀνὰ, πύκα or πυκάζω to make close and cover up.

"Αμπωτις, the ebb.—R. ἀνὰ, πότος, πόσις : A drinking or swallowing up.

'Αμυγδαλῆ, almond.— As 'Απομαγδαλιὰ from ἀπομάσσω, so our word from ἀμύσσω ; ' The bark is like skin lacerated by the nails :' Lenn.

'Αμύδις, the same as "Αμα. So "Αλλα, 'Αλλυδις.

'Αμυδρὸς, dim or dark, indistinct as letters.—R. α, μυδάω, to be putrid from damp.

'Αμύκλαι, shoes worn by the people of *Amyclæ* in Laconia.

"Αμυλον, ' fine meal, prepared more carefully than by common grinding :' Ldd.—R. α, μύλη, mill.

'Αμύμων, irreproachable.— R. μῦμαρ, or allied.

'Αμύνω, Μύνομαι, to ward or keep off, repel, defend, (as Lat. de-fendo has both senses,) help, fight for.— Lennep says : ' Μύνομαι, to make pleas and pretexts ; from μύω, to shut, cover : hence 'Αμύνω.' (As Θύω, Θύνω.) The sense of shutting oneself up leads to that of securing and defending oneself, warding off, &c.

'Αμύσσω, to lacerate.—R. α ; †μύσσω allied to Μυστίλλω, and to Μύτιλος, mutilated. (2) ' R. αἷμα, ἀμάσσω : To draw blood, wound : or αἷμος, a thorn :' Dnn. Compare 'Αμνίον.

"Αμυστις, a large draught taken without closing the lips, from α, μύω, μέμυσται.

'Αμφασίη, speechlessness.— As ἀΜβρόσιος ; for α, †φάω, φημὶ, to speak.

'Αμφὶ, around, about.—R. ἅμα, for ἄμφι, as νόσΦΙ, ΐΦΙ. Allied to 'Αμφω, both; 'Αμφὶς, on both sides. One thing or person ἅμα with another. So the Proverb: 'Αμ' ἔπος, ἅμ' ἔργον. Homer : Σὲ ἅμα καὶ Ἐμ': i.e. you and me *together*, *BOTH* you and me. From the sense ' on both or many sides ἅμα together', is ' around, about.' (2) The Latin *amb-*, Sax. *amb*, *emb*, *ymb*, Dutch *om*, Germ. *um*.

'ΑΜΦΙΑΣ, a Sicilian wine of very moderate quality. —Can it be from ἀμφὶ ' between, in the middle', (Dnn.): Middling? Compare "Απιος. (Very rare word.)

'Αμφιτρίτη, *Amphitrīte*, prop. the sea: ἀμφί, †τρίω, τρίβω, (Lat. *trīta*): The sea wearing the shore. See Ακτή, 'Ρηγμίν.

'Αμφω: in 'Αμφί.

*Αν, if.— For ἐάν. (**2**) Our old *an:* ' *An* it please your honor.' Webst. refers to *an* in Arabic, Samaritan, Chaldaic, Irish.

*Αν, from meaning 'if ', is often merely a particle of doubt, conjecture, contingency. Sometimes custom, as we say, ' He *would* get up of a morning and walk six miles.' 'Αν-, not, for 'Ανευ.

'ΑΝΑ, up, upon, over, through, by means of, in course of. Also as we say *Per* annum, as Two by two, Year by year, &c.— Goth. *ana*, Germ. *an*, our *on*.

'Ανα-, back, back again, again.— If we go higher *UP* into time, we go back. Above.

'Αναβρόχω: See in Βρόγχος.

'Ανάγκη, necessity.— Redupl. (as *Αλαλκε) from †ἄγκη, from ἄγχω, to press tight, as δέΚομαι and δέΧομαι, φυλαΚή and πεφύλαΧα. (**2**) Allied to 'Αγκύλος, bent: Which is not to be bent, inflexible. (**3**) R. ἀνάσσω, ξω, χα, to be master over.

'Αναίνομαι, to refuse, reject.— R αν, not; αἰνῶ, to approve. (**2**) R. αν, †αἴω, Lat. *aio*, as Nego is Ne-aio Ne-ajo. (**3**) Buttm. from ἀν-, not, simply. (**4**) Thiersch from Germ. *nein*, no: with A.

'Αναισιμόω: See Αἰσιμόω.

*Ανακες, the same as *Ανακτες, kings, spec. applied to Castor and Pollux. Compare 'Ανακῶς. Formed from ἀνάσσω, pf. act. ἄναχα, as φυλαΚή from πεφύλαΧα.

'Ανάκτορον, a palace ἀνάκτων of kings, a temple. So Basilica from Βασιλεύς.

'Ανάκωλος, ' shortened, short, from κόλος. Also, a long and flowing robe; from the term ἀνακεκολπωμένος in explan. of ζειρά, it may have been worn *tucked up*, and so appeared SHORT:' Dnn.

'Ανακῶς, carefully: i.e. in the manner ἀνάκων of kings or overseers.

'Ανακωχή, Διακωχή, Κατακωχή, stay, cessation, truce.— ' The more analogous form from ἀνέχω, ἄνΟχα, is ἀνΟκωχή as written by some Grammarians:' Ldd. In Homer is συν-Οκωχότε. (**2**) For ἀναγωχή, &c. from ἀνάγω, &c. to withdraw: as we find καταγηΟχα.

'Αναλίσκω, 'Αναλόω, to spend, consume. — R. ἀνὰ, ἁλίσκω, to take up, as Sub-emo, Sumo.

*Αναξ, a king, ruler.— R. ἀνάσσω, ξω.

'Αναξυρίδες, trowsers worn by Eastern nations.— For ἀνα-συρίδες, from σύρω, as being drawn up. Drawers. So Eustath. (**2**) ' A *Persian* word:' Ldd.

'Αναπαριάζω, to break faith like the *Parians*.

'Αναρίτης: See Νηρίτης.

'Αναρριχάομαι, to clamber up with hands and feet.— R ἀνὰ, ἀρρίχη, a basket which they used (ἀνιμᾶν) to draw up by ropes (Suid.). This verb ἀνιμᾶν is explained by Liddell ' to draw up, strictly by straps; intrans. to *mount up*.' (**2**) Some from ἀράχνη, a spider. ??

12

'Ανάσσω, to rule, reign : to be ἀνὰ over others. As 'Αλλάσσω.

*Αναυρος, ' *Anaurus*, a river in Thessaly: hence applied to any torrent:' Ldd. Yet prob. from *a*, much, νάω, to flow. As Αὔρα from †ἄω to blow. See ἀμ-ΑΤΡΟΣ.

'Ανδάνω, to please.— R. ἀδέω, as †μαθέω, μαΝθάνω.

*Ανθηρα, ων, any raised banks or borders, flower beds, edges of rivers, earth dug up, trench or canal. — R. ἀνθέω, (ἀναδέω,) ' to surround with, crown with', Dnn. (**2**) Some say for ἄνθηρα from ἄνθος: as

'Ανθράχλη, a coal-pan. — ' Plainly akin to ἄνθραξ:' Ldd.

'Ανδρίας, the statue ἀνδρὸς of a man.

'Ανέδην, negligently, loosely, confusedly.— As Στάδην, Βάδην. R. †ἀνέω, ἀνίημι, to remit. So 'Ανειμένως. And *Ανετος and *Ανεσις.

*Ανεμος, wind. — As *Ανετος, let loose, from †ἀνέω, ἄνεται, ἀνίημι, and *Ανεσις from ἄνεσαι, so ἄνεμος from ἄνεμαι pers. 1. as ψαλΜΟΣ from ἔψαλμαι: Air let loose. ' Wind was not ill called by the ancients a swifter course of air:' (Dr. J.). Says Homer, Ζεφύροιο ἄητας 'Ωκεανὸς AN-IHΣI. (**2**) ' For ἄεμος from ἄω to blow:' Dnn. Why N ?

'Ανεμώλιος, light, empty or useless as the ἄνεμος wind. So 'Υπ-ηνέμιος is used. And 'Εξ-ανεμόω is to render void. Ovid: ' *Levis* es multòque tuis *ventosior* alis.' Shaksp.: 'They pass by me as the *idle wind*.' Isaiah 41. 29: ' Their molten images are *wind* and confusion.' 26. 18. and Eccles. 5. 16.

'Ανερείπομαι, to snatch up and carry off.— Allied to 'Ερέπτω.

*Ανευ, *Ανις, apart from, without.— R. †ἀνέω, ἀνίημι, to let go at large, let *alone*. Bp. Butler says : ' Sinè from Sino, I let alone. It signifies being [or doing] without a thing.' Indeed 'Ανίημι is ' to give up, omit, neglect', (Dnn.) (**2**) Hebr. *AYN*, without.

'Ανέψιος, a cousin, relation.— For ἀνΑψιος, (E as νημΕρτής,) from ἀν-άπτω, ἀν-άψω: One who is joined to or connected with another. A connexion. 'Αν- is ' back', as Re in ' Re-lative.' (**2**) R. ἔπομαι, ἔψομαι, ' to belong to, attach to:' (Ldd.)

*Ανεως, speechless.— As Λεώς, Λαὸς, so *Ανεως for Αναος from ἀν-, not, †ἄω, αὔω to call upon, Latin *AIO*.

*Ανη, completion; from the verb *Ανω.

'Ανήνοθε, 'Επ-ενήνοθε, Κατ-ενήνοθε, used in this way, ' The smell of the fat came forth ', ' The blood flowed warm from the wound', 'Such oil as comes forth on the Gods', ' The hair flowed down the shoulders.'— From ἀνθέω, ἐν-όθω, to move, quiver, tremble: with ἀνα-, ἐπ-, or κατ-. (**2**) Buttm. simply from ἄνα, through an obs. †ἄνθω, as *Ανρομαι from 'Αντί: To be upon. (**3**) R. ἔθω, ὄθα, to be wont to do or to be. (**4**) R. †ἔθω, obsol. from †ἔω, †ἔθην, εἰμί, to be.

'Ανὴρ, a man, a husband.— R. ἀνὰ, up, as ἀΗΡ, αἰθΗΡ. *Above* other animals: *Above* the wife. 'Thy husband is thy head, thy sov'reign:' Shaksp. (**2**)

' From ἄνω, to perfect. "Ανθρωπος is a man in general: ἀνὴρ the male sex, a full-grown man, a brave man, a term of respect: in *perfection* of sex, age, faculty and honor:' Ormst.

'Ανθερεὼν, the chin, ' the ἄνθος flower of manhood', Dr. Jones. ' Prima genas vestībat FLORE juventa', Virg. Or from ἀνθέω to flourish, 'used by Homer of the sprouting of the beard': Ldd.

'Ανθέριξ, supposed put for ἀθέριξ, (as μαΝθάνω,) ' from ἀθὴρ, ἀθέρος: the beard of an ear of corn, and the ear itself:' Ldd.

'Ανθεστηριὼν, an Attic month. Macrobius says that *April* is so called ' ab eo quòd eo tempore cuncta florescant': from ἀνθέω. ' Passow and others with better reason say *November*: from ἄνθος, στερέω, as the month when flowers disappear:' Dnn.

"Ανθος, a flower.— R. ἄνω, ἄνθην, to perfect: The perfection of a plant. (2) Buttm. from ἀνά: ἄνθος thus being prim. the sprout or growing point or summit. (3) Thiersch from 'Ανήνοθε.

'Ανθραξ, ακος, a coal: — carbuncle, the gem and the ulcer, as this is from Carbo.— For ἀθραξ (as ἀΝθέριξ,) from θέρω, τέθαρκα, τέθρακα, 'to make hot, burn.' (Ldd.) Thus Carbo is ' a *burning* coal ', (Forcell.) (2) R. ἄντρον, ἄντραξ, ἄνθραξ, (see ἄνθρωπος): The produce of dug caverns. (3) Lenn. from ἄνθος: from the florid color of burning coal. ' *Virens* in Ætnâ flamma', Hor.

'Ανθρήδων, 'Ανθρήνη, the hornet.— Lennep from its frequenting ἄνθη flowers. (2) For 'Αθρήδων, 'Αθρήνη, (as ἀΝθέριξ,) from α, θέρω, whence θερμὸς, 'hot, hasty', (Ldd.) As irascible, ' waspish.' Acc. to Plautus's phrase ' Irritare crabrōnes.'

"Ανθρωπος, a man.— Soft for "Αντρωπος; R. ἀνα-τρέπω, ἀνατέτροπα: Turning his face upwards. Ovid: ' Pronaque cùm spectent animalia cetera terram, Os homini sublīme dedit, cœlumque tuēri Jussit, et erectos ad sidera tollere vultus.' (2) R. ἀναθρῶ ὦτι, to look up with the face. Plato says, 'Αναθρῶν ἃ ὄπωπε. (3) Buttm. simply from ἀνά, up. But?

'Ανΐα, ' bane, kill-joy, sorrow, grief:' Ldd.— R. ἀνά, up: A state of 'suspense which' from 'suspendo', to hang up: and Gr. αἰθρησις. "Εως πότε τὴν ψυχὴν ἡμῶν ΑΙΡΕΙΣ; Jo. x. 24. ' Care which hangs the mind in suspense', Wilkinson's Prayers, p. 177. 'Ανΐα as Πενία. (2) Something ἀν-ίατον, incurable. (3) ' Hebr. *aniah*, sadness:' Oger and Mrt.

'Αννιβίζω, to side with 'Αννίβας, *Annibal.*

'Ανοίγω, Οἴγω, to open.— R. ἀνά, †οἴω, οἴσω, οἶκα, to carry up, sc. the latch. Γ, as τμήΓω.

'Ανοπαῖα, ' some from ἀν, †ὄπτομαι: Unnoticed like a bird. Some read ἀν' ὀπαῖα, up to the ὀπὴ hole in the roof, up the chimney. Some understand it as an eagle, &c.:' Ldd. ' Some read παν-οπαῖα:' Dnn. (2) ' Hebr. *anophe*:' Wr.

"Αντα, 'Αντί, "Αντην, so as to face, opposite, before. — Allied to 'Ανά, up. We say, To go UP to a person.

13

Dunbar from ἀνά supposes ἄντς, ἄντὸς the upper part of the body, the face: κατ' ἄντα, ἐν ἀντί. (2) Jamieson quotes the Goth. and Germ. dialects, *anda, ande, and, ante, ant, ent, ont.*

'Ανταῖος, opposite: and

'Αντάω, 'Αντίάω, "Αντομαι, to meet, go before, go up to, beg.— R. ἄντα.

'Αντί: See "Αντα. Also ' in exchange for': one thing being set before or against another.

'Αντικρὺ, -ὺς, over-against;— straight on, directly;— before, openly;— straight through.— R. ἀντί, ἴκω. As ἀ/Τήλιος. (2) R. ἀντί, κάρα, κρά. (3) 'Αντί, κρούω: Striking against.

'Αντίος, opposite. — R. ἀντί.

'Αντλέω, to drain the ἄντλος bilge-water from the hold of a ship;— drain out the cup of woe, endure grief.

"Αντλος, ' the bilge-water in the sink of a ship's hold, the sink itself, the bottom of the hold, a ship's pump; a vessel for drawing water:' Dnn.— Clearly, like 'Ο-τλος, from τλάω : with ἀνά. ' What sustains a burden placed on it:' Lenn. ' Or, passively, what is borne or raised up:' Scheid. 'Αντλέω probably came first.

"Αντρον, a cavern.— R. †ἀνα-τρέω, †ἀντρῶ, to perforate: A natural perforation. 'Αμφι-τρῆτος αὐλίου, Soph.

"Αντυξ, -υγος, ' anything rounded or curved, as the rim of a round shield;— the rail or high rim of a chariot;— the chariot;— the frame [bridge, Dnn.] of a lyre;— orbit of the planets;— the breasts:' Ldd.— Soft for ἄμτυξ for ἀμφίτυξ, as 'Αμφορεὺς for 'Αμφιφορεύς: from τένυξαι, τέτυξα, from τεύχω to frame. (2) From ἀνά, &c.: A frame made on the *upper* part of a thing. 'Αντυγες, ' quæ sellam curūlem *superne* ambiant:' Hemst. So Καταῦ-τυξ.

"Ανω, upwards.— R. ἀνά.

'Ανω, 'Ανύω, 'Ανύω Att., 'Ανύτω, 'Ανύτω Att., to complete, accomplish.—'A kindred word with 'Ανά:' Buttm. I.e. to go through, per-ficio.

'Ανώγαιον, -γέων, anything ἄνω above γέα ground, upper-floor.

'Ανώγω, to command, order.— Matthiæ from ἀνάσσω, (explained κελεύω by Hesych.) ἄνωγα, as ἀρήγω, ἀρΩγὸς: ἀγΩγή.

'Αξίνη, battle-axe.— As 'Τσμίνη. ' R. probably ἄγνυμι, ἄξω, to break:' Dnn. ' They *break* down the carved work with *axes*:' Psalms. (2) R. α, †ξίω, ξίφος, ξέω. (3) ' Sax. *eax*, Swed. *yxe*, Ethiop. *hatsi* an axe, Arab. *hazza* to cut:' Webst.

"Αξιος, worth so much; from ἄγω, ἄξω, to weigh so much;— worth its price, reasonable, cheap;— worthy, deserving, proper, &c. (Compare Job 28. 16: ' Neither shall silver be *weighed* for the price thereof.' Gen. 43. 21: ' Our money in full *weight*.') "Αγω is also to think, estimate, as Lat. *duco*: thence could be the sense ' estimable, worthy,' &c.— Parkh. explains ἄγω to draw down the beam, Ormston to bring to market or to a standard.

'Αξιόω, to judge ἄξιον worthy;—or worthy to be done, deign to do;—worthy to obtain, so desire, beg, ask;—worthy of credit, so believe. (**2**) Webst. compares our *ask*, formerly pron. *ax*, Sax. *axian*, Germ. *heischen*, &c,

"Αξων, axle-tree, wheel, polar axis. "Αξονες, wooden tablets of the laws, made to turn on an axis.—R. ἄγω, ἄξω: which drives the wheel round, or round which it is driven: or simply as carrying the weight. ' Valido *nitens* sub pondere faginus *axis* :' Virg. (**2**) 'Sax. *ax*, Germ. *achse*, Dutch, *as*, Russ. *os* :' Wbst.

· 'Αοζέω, to wait, serve. "Αοζος, a servant, attendant. —The same as δοσσέω, as our glaSS, glaZier ; EliSSa, EliZa. (**2**) Ζέω, †οζέω, (as 'Οκέλλω,) δοζέω: Compare Αίζηός. To be ardent.

'Αοιδὸς, a singer : ἀείδω.

'Αολλής, collected, crowded, like 'Αλής.—R. a, ἔλλω, ὄλλα, 'to roll together', (Dnn.) Compare Αἰόλος.

"Αορ, "Αορ, 'a sword, i.e. a hanger, from ἀείρω, [ἄορα]:' Ldd. (**2**) R. †ἄω, ἄστρον, to shine. ' Micat ensis', Virg.

"Αορες in Od. 17. 222 is thought by some to be tripods, 'having ears by which they may be raised:' Schol., Hom., from ἀείρω. But Ldd. thinks it only heterogen. for ἄορα: ἄορ being neuter.

'Αορτὴ, the aorta, great artery. And the lower extremities of the wind-pipe, from ἀείρω, ἄορται, 'as hanging into the lungs:' Dnn. As

'Αορτήρ, a belt to hang anything on. As above.

'Αοσσέω, to help, aid.—R. a, ὄσσα: To come readily to the sound of a sufferer, as Βοη-θέω. See 'Αοζέω.

'Απᾶδις in Pind. Pyth. 1. 161. Heyne: ' Pauw thinks that ἦπας or ἦπις meant ἧπαρ, and conjectures 'Απᾶδας or 'Απῖδας. Rightly, only read ἀπῖδας Doricè.' Ldd.: ' Some good MSS. give ἐλπίδας which Böckh adopts.'

'Απαί, as 'Από. So Παραί, 'Υπαί.

'Απαλὸς, tender, soft to the touch.—R. ἄπτω or †ἄπω, Lat. *apo* and *apio*: mid. ἅπτομαι : Easy to the touch.

"Απαξ, once, only once, once for all.— Pott from a for ἅμα, †πάγω, †πάξω, πακτόω: Close and joined together. We say, ' A long pull, a strong pull, and a pull altogether.' So Δι-απ-πάξ. Like Δάξ, Λάξ, Πὸξ, 'Επιμίξ. (**2**) From ἄ-πας, as 'Απρίξ from πρίω.

"Απας, for ἁμα-πᾶς.

'Απατάω, to mislead, beguile, 'deceive. — Usually thought put for †ἀπο-πατάω, to lead from the πάτος, path. (**2**) R. ἄπτομαι, †ἀπῶ, Lat. *apo*, *apio*: To touch, touch gently, caress. See †'Απαφάω.

'ΑΠΑΤΟΥΡΙΑ, an Athenian festival.—Some from ἀπάτη. Budæus calls it ' *fallaciarum* solemnitas Athēnis.' Some from a (ἅμα), πατήρ: Where fathers met together to register their sons. Or where the ἀπάτορες were registered. But ?

14

'Απαυράω, to derive good or evil from, to take from. — R. αἵρω, ἀρῶ, †αὐράω as λαΤω from †λάω, †λαβῶ. So 'Επαυράω.

†'Απαφάω, 'Απαφίσκω, the same as ἀπατάω: redupl. of ἀφάω, (as 'Αλ-αλκε,) from †ἄφα, ἄπτομαι, to touch, caress.

'Απειλέω, to threaten, boast.—R. ἀπὸ, εἰλέω to roll : i.e. roll the eyes about in a threatening or vaunting manner, (Compare Βλέπω from †Βλέω). Virgil: ' Dicentem aversa tuētur, Huc illuc *volvens* oculos:' ' Flammea *torquens* Lumina:' ' Ardentes oculos *intorsit*, graviter fundens.' So Jacto from Jacio: To throw oneself about.— But

'Απειλέω, to hem in, crowd together.—R. εἰλέω. See 'ΑΛΕΩ.

'Απέκιζαν, they lost: from †κίχω, †κίξω, κιχάνω: and ἀπὸ denies: They failed of coming to. Brunck makes it ' depulerunt', i.e. they made to go off.

'Απελλαί, places of assembly : 'Απειλλάζω, to meet in such.—Allied to the 2d 'Απειλέω: from †Ελλω, ἔλσω. Comp. ἀολλής.

"Απελος, ulcer : 'from a, πέλος, *pellis*, [φελλὸς]: Not yet skinned over:' Ldd. (**2**) From a, intens.: πελὸς, livid.

'Απήνη, waggon, car.—R. ἄπτω, †ἄπω, Lat. *apo*, *apio*, like εἰρΗΝΗ, σεΛΗΝΗ: Fastened to mules. ' Bind the chariot to the swift beast ', Micah 1. 13. The Schol. Pind. explains it ἅρμα ἐξ ἡμιόνων ζευχθέν. Or the reverse, as ' Tie the kine to the cart'. 1 Sam. 6. 'Υπ' ἀμάξησιν βόας ... ζεύγνυσαν, Il. ω. 782.— Even as well joined together, as ἅρματα κολληθέντα. And see "Αρμα.

'Απηνής, unbending, unyielding.— ' R. ἀπὸ, ἐνηής, mild:' Dnn. (**2**) Usually from ἀπὸ, ἡνία, bridle: Breaking from the bridle, unbridled. Lat. ef-frænis.

'Απιος, far away ἀπὸ from. So 'Αντὶ 'Αντιος, Περισσὸς, ξυνὸς, Πρόμος.

'Απίτης, perry. — From 'ΑΠΙΟΝ a pear.

'Απλακεῖν. See 'Αμπλακέω.

"Απλετος, immense.—R. †πλέω, *im-pleo*, *re-pleo*, *com-pleo*, πλήθω : Not to be filled up.

'Απλοῖς, 'Απληγὶς, a single cloak, not worn double; from ἁπλόος, ἁπλόη, ἁπλῆ.

'Απλόος, simple. — Blomf., Dnn., &c. from a, πολέω, †πλόω, to turn, allied to πλέκω to fold. Without a fold, as Simplicis is Sine-plicâ. So Δίπλοος, Τρίπλοος, two-fold, three-fold. For the aspirate see on 'Αδέω. (**2**) R. ἅμα, πέλω, †πλέω: What is all together, plain, level, as 'Αμαλός.

'Απὸ, from.—Allied to "Απτω, †'Απω, Lat. *apo*, *apio*, *apto*: Thus, He came from such a stock, It flowed from such a source, He came from such a place, mark clearly a *joining* on both. So Οἱ ἀπὸ τῆς στοᾶς, those belonging to the Porch, the Stoics. (**2**) ' Hebr. *ab*, first original:' Pkh. (**3**) ' Engl. and Sax. *of*, Germ. *ab*, Sw. Dan. Dut. *af* :' Wbst.

'Αποέρξειε Il. φ. 329, should force or hurry away. —

—An active form of Ἔῤῥω: To make to go under an
evil omen. (**2**) From †ἔρω, ἐρύω, ἐρύσω, ἔρσω, to
draw, drag. (**3**) From ἔργω, to keep apart, Æol. fut.
ἔρσω for ἔρξω. (**4**) From ἔρδω, σω: To do away
with.

Ἄπος, labor, tiredness.— An uncertain word in Eur.
Ph. 865. Hesych. and Valck. read αἶπος, toil: Porsen
κᾶπος, for which however ἄπος might be written, as Αἶα
for Γαῖα, Εἶβω for Λείβω. But from αἰπὺς, high, could
be αἶπος, just as Arduus, Arduous, laborious, from ἄρδην,
lifted up. And αἶπος might be ἄπος, ἄπος.

Ἀποφώλιος, explained by Hesych. vain, useless, by
Eustath. untaught, ignorant.—Ldd. from ὄφελος,
profit. Ω, as O in ʼοφΟλὸς a collat. form of ὄφΕλός.
(**2**) But perh. from †ἀποφάω, †ἀποφῶ, ἀπόφημι, (in
form as Ἀνεμώλιος, Ἀπατήλιος :) Fainting, exhausted,
weak, (as Ἀπεῖπον, Ἀπερέω, Ἀπαγορεύω,) then weak
in mind. It is explained too 'monstrous', i.e. 'in-
fandus,' ' ne-fandus,' i.e. 'not to be SPOKEN.' (**3**)
Some even go to φωλεὸς, a cave: 'Hidden, ineffectual':
and Dr. Jones, as the religious mysteries and lessons of
philosophy were often taught in them. ? ?

Ἄππα, like Ἄββα, Πάππα, Ἄπφα, Ἀπφὺς, a term of
endearment. Common more or less to all nations apparently, natural sounds.

Ἀππαπαῖ παπαῖ παπαιάξ, Ἰαππαπαιάξ, exclamations
of admiration. These from the sound.

Ἀπρίξ, firmly.— R. α, πρίω to cut off.

ʼΑΠΤΩ or †ʼΑΠΩ, (Dnn.), preserved in Lat. APO,
APIO, (Forcell.) to join, fasten. Ἅπτομαι, to join
myself to, touch.— 'Hebr. APP, to bind close:' Pkh.

Ἅπτω, to set fire to: i.e. to join to or touch with fire.
Above. Thus ἅπτομαι is to touch, and we say Touch-
wood. 'De cœlo tactas quercus', Virg. ' Tactum de
cœlo Capitolium', Sueton. 'And touch'd Isaiah's hallow'd lips with fire': Pope. (**2**) 'Hebr. APH, to heat
through :' Pkh.

Ἀπύω, ' for Ἠπύω,' Dnn.

Ἄρα, Ἄρ, Ῥα, a particle joining or connecting sen-
tences, i.e. then, therefore, hereupon, surely then, &c.
And Ἄρα, whether then? this perh. for ἦ ἄρα.— R.
ἄρω, to join.

Ἀρά, a prayer; — prayer for evil, curse; —evil im-
precated.— R. αἴρω, ἀρῶ : 'Men should pray, lifting up
holy hands', 1 Tim. 2. 8. 'When I lift up my hands',
Psa. 28. 2. 'With lifting up their hands', Nehem. 8. 6.
So Gen. 14. 12. Horace Od. 3. 23. 1. (**2**) R. ἄρω, to
join i.e. words together, as Εἴρω and Ἐρέω, and Sermo
from Sero : (compare Ἔπω ;) An address to heaven.
So ʼΕΠΟΣ εὐξαμένοιο Il. π. 236. In Œd. C. 1655 ἐν
ταὐτῷ λόγῳ, 'eâdem prece' Brunck. (**3**) In the sense
of curse, ἀρόομαι from α, ῥάζω, to snarl at. (**4**) Hebr.
arar, he cursed.

Ἄραβος, rattling, clashing, gnashing of teeth.— Pott
says : ' Hence prob. ἀράσσω.' Rather, ἄραβος is allied
to ἀράσσω. So τάρΒΟΣ, τύμΒΟΣ. (**2**) 'Roar of a
cataract : Hebr. ARBH :' Dr. Jones. 'Arabes,' Wr.

15

Ἄραβος, rumbling of the stomach, beating of the
pulse.—'Akin to Ἄραβος :' Ldd. So κέλΑΔΟΣ.

Ἀραιὸς, thin, rare, porous, spongy, light, weak.— R.
α, ῥαίω, to break : as Fragilis, Frail, from Frango. So
Τέρην, tender, from Τείρω, Τερῶ.— Dnn. explains ῥαίω,
' to destroy by bruising': and Forcellini explains Per-
tusus by Perforatus, well agreeing with the sense ' porous.'
(**2**) 'R. ἀρύω, haurio : Exhaustus': Greg. Sucked up,
drained, ' spongy.'

Ἀράσσω, Ῥάσσω, Ῥήσσω, to strike, beat, knock, dash.
— Allied to ῥαίω to break, and †ῥάω whence Ἄῤῥατος.
(**2**) ' Hebr. aretz, to agitate :' Wr.

Ἀράχνη, -ης, a spider.— R. ἄρω, ἄχνη : That pre-
pares and adjusts the fine down of its web :' Lenn.
Justified by the derivative Ἀράχνιον, 'a downy substance like spiders' webs on grapes and olives'. (Dnn.)
(**2**) Hebr. arag, it weaved. 'Weaving spiders', Shaksp.

ΑΡΒΗΛΟΣ, a shoemaker's knife.— Q. ? (Only in
Nicand. Ther. 423.)

Ἀρβύλη, a strong half-boot : written also Ἀρμύλη,
(See on Ἀμορβός,) thus justifying Liddell's belief that
it is akin to ἄρω, ἀρμόζω, as fitted to the foot, or ex-
quisitely made. So Ἀρτὴρ is a kind of shoe. Euripides
has : ἀρβύλῃσιν ΑΡΜΟΣΑΣ πόδα.

Ἀργαλέος, troublesome, painful.— For ἀεργάλεος ; R.
α, ἔργον : Causing much trouble.

Ἀργίλοφοι, 'prop. the feet of sheepskins, and these
are [ἀργοὶ] useless': Schol. Aristoph. ' I.e. λόφοι ἀρ-
γοὶ, tops or ends which are useless :' Dr. Jones.

Ἄργεμος, white speck on the eye.— R. ἀργός.

Ἀργέστης, the S. wind, ' clearing, brightening, as
Horace's Notus albus, detergens nubila cœlo :' Ldd.—
As above.

Ἀργῆς, some serpent, ' from its rapid movements, or
white color:' Dnn.— R. ἀργός.

Ἄργιλλος, white clay. — From

Ἀργὸς, white.— As Μάω, Μαργός, and †Λάω, Largus,
so †άω, (to shine, whence Ἀστὴρ, Ἄστρον, Αὐγὴ,)
ἀργός. (**2**) See the Next.

Ἀργὸς, 'swift, swift-footed : for all swift motion
causes a glancing, flashing or flickering :' Ldd., thus
making 'white' the first sense. But Ἀργὸς may mean
quick, rapid, flashing, from α much, ἔργον: compare
Mico' to ' move fast, brandish' and to ' shine.'— Above.

Ἀργὸς, idle, useless : ἄ-εργος.

Ἄργυρος, silver.— R. ἀργὸς, white.

Ἄρδα, dirt, filth.— 'R. ἄρδω :' Dnn. Just as Forcellini defines Lutum ' terra humore soluta, ἃ λύω
solvo :' Moistened earth.

Ἄρδην, so as to be lifted up, from αἴρω, ἄρται : — altogether, entirely, i. e. by one lift, or from top to bottom.
So βάδΗΝ, στάδΗΝ.

Ἄρδις, point of a dart, as fitted to the wood, from
ἄρω, ἄρται. So Δ in Ἄρδην and in

Ἄρδω, to water, refresh.— R. ἄρω, ἄρται, paro, re-
paro, to repair, recruit. As μέλΔω. (**2**) Allied to Ἄλδω.
(**3**) As Ἀρδεύω is found, some say ἄρι δεύω. ? ?

'Αρείων, braver, then better, as Virtus, Virtue, is from Vir, prop. manliness.— From "Αρης, "Αρεος, Mars. (2) R. ἄρω, to suit : More suitable.

'Αρέσκω, to please, appease, &c.— R. ἄρω, (as Τίεσκε, Κέσκομαι, Lat. areSCO) : To suit myself to. So "Ηραρεν is ' pleased,' Od. δ. 776.

'Αρετάω, to confer distinction, advantage or success. And 'Αρετή is ' distinction of birth, rank or fortune,' (Dnn.) So Brunck renders 'Αρετὴ decus in Soph. Phil. 1420. See the Next.

'Αρετή, superiority, distinction, chiefly in "Αρης, "Αρεος battle, and so valor, virtue (which from Vir). But perh. from ἄρω : The fitness of anything for its end or object. So 'Αρετή is said of the goodness of plants.

'Αρήγω, to help, ward off ill from.— R. ἄρω, as τμΗΓΩ : To suit oneself to another's wants.

'Αρημένος, worn down, exhausted, hurt.— R. α, ῥαίω, to break, †ῥάω, whence "Αῤῥατος.— Or blasted, from ἀρά, a curse : †ἄρημι.

'Αρήν, ἀρένος, ἀρνὸς, a ram ; ' from ἄῤῥην, a male : ' Dnn.— Also, a lamb, in both genders : Eustath. from ἀρά, a prayer : as in making vows and prayers [or curses] lambs were sacrificed. Homer : Οἴσετε "ΑΡΝ' ἕτερον λευκὸν, ἑτέρην δὲ μέλαιναν.

'Αρης, εος, Mars.— R. ἄρω, to join i.e. in battle. Μάχην συν-ἄπτειν, Xen. Con-seruisse mantis, Ov.— "Αρης, 'Αρετή, "Αρω, seem kindred words :' Dnn. (2) Goth. aur, a weapon.

'Αρητήρ, a priest : ' for they conveyed the ἀρὰς prayers of the people to the gods :' Ldd.

'Αρθμὸς, bond, friendship : and

"Αρθρον, a joint, limb.— R. ἄρω, ἀρθην, to join.

'Αρι—, very.—' Prob. from ἀρεῖον, better :' Dnn. Or for ἄριστα. (2) R. ἄρω, to join one thing to another, and so increase. Compare 'Ερι—. (3) R. αἴρω, ἀρῶ, to raise : Conspicuously, eminently.

'Αρίζηλος, ' Epic form of ἀρίδηλος', Ldd. The converse would be however clearer, as Z is ΔΣ. (2) Some explain it 'Αρι-ζήλωτος.

'Αριθμὸς, number.—' R. ἄρω, to join. A number is a multitude composed of units :' Pkh. 'Αρθμὸς is compared by Dnn.: but there was prob. a word 'Αρίζω.

'Αρὶς, a carpenter's tool.— R. ἄρω, instruo. Horace has Instrumenta artis, for tools. So 'Αρμενον.

'Αριστερὸς, the left, inauspicious.— As, to propitiate the Gods, the Greeks called the Furies Εὐ-μενίδες, (Latin Parcæ from Parco,) and the left Εὐ-ώνυμος, so 'Αρίστερος ·from ἄριστος. We find Ελαχιστότερος, 'Αρειότερος, &c. (2) R. ἀρά, a curse.

"Αριστον, breakfast.— R. ἄρι for ἦρι, at an early hour : The first meal in the morning. ' Prim. the meal taken gen. at sun-rise : aft. the noontide meal :' Dnn. 'Εντύνοντ' ἄριστον "ΑΜ' ΗΟΙ. So Prandium from πρὰν or πρωΐν.

"Αριστος, superl. of 'Αρείων.

'Αρκέω, to be of use, aid, ward off ill :—to have suit-

16

able supplies, to be satisfied.— R. ἄρω, ἄρκα, to suit : like 'Αρήγω. (2) Some compare †'Αλκέω, 'Αλάλκω.

"Αρκιος, sufficient.— Above.

'Αρκτεύω, ' to consecrate virgins to Diana, in atonement for having killed ἄρκτον a bear sacred to her :' Dnn.

"Αρκτος, "Αρκος, a bear.—' For ἀρκετὸς, self-sufficient, as living so long without external nourishment. It will lie a whole year without eating and drinking :' Pkh.— ' From ἀρκέω : it is specially devoted to the defence of its young. See 2 Sam. 17. 8:' Damm. So Prov. 17. 12. (2) For ἀρί-κοτος, rancorous, malicious. (3) Welsh arth, Irish art. But the K shows the Greek prior.

"Αρκυς, a hunter's net.— Eustath. as catching ἄρκους bears. (2) Allied to ἔρκος, an inclosure. Or to ἄρω, ἄρκα (as 'Αρκέω) : As well joined and knitted together.

"Αρμα, a chariot.— R. ἄρω, ἄρμαι, (Compare aspir. in 'Αρμόζω,) : Well joined together, as Homer's ἅρμασι κολλητοῖσι. Or as joined on to horses : compare 'Απήνη.

"Αρμα, as 'Αρθμὸς, union.

"Αρμα, ' a tribute, lit. what is taken up :' Dnn. From αἴρω, ἄρμαι. So "Αρσις is a levy of taxes.

'Αρμαλιὰ, food, provisions.— R. ἄρω, ἄρμαι : As prepared, provided : ' provision.' Compare aspir. in 'Αρμόζω.

'Αρμάτειος, said of a martial strain, sung from ἄρματα war chariots. ' Eurip. uses it of a plaintive ode, .but Plut. of an animating war-song :' Dnn.

'Αρμενα, tackle, rigging : any tools or implements. — R. ἄρω, instruo : Instruments of any kind. Or as Pliny : ' Aptabimus vela et disponemus rudentes.'

'Αρμή, -ὸς, a joining : 'Αρμόδιος, suiting : 'Αρμόζω, to suit ; 'Αρμονία, harmony.— All from ἄρω or †ἄρω, to join.

'Αρμοῖ and 'Αρτι, just now, just before :—now, even now, forthwith. Dative of 'Αρμὸς, above, like οἶκΟΙ. It means the past and the future just joined on to the present. 'Αρμοῖ is also ' exactly as, suitably to ;' "Αρω being ' to suit.'

'Αρνειὸς δἰς, a male sheep, ram.— R. ἄῤῥην, ἄῤῥενος, (ἄρνος).— Also 'pertaining to lambs': R. ἀρήν, g. ἀρνός.

'Αρνέομαι, to disavow, reject, deny, refuse.— R. αἴρω, ἀρῶ, to take away, i.e. put away in disdain, ' scont the idea': as ἵκω, ἱκΝΕΟΜΑΙ. Compare μισθ-ΑΡΝΕΩ. (2) Pott from α, not ; ῥέω, to say. ?

'Αρνεύω, to plunge headlong, dive.—' Prob. from the butting of young rams : from ἀρήν, (ἀρνός,) :' Dnn.

'Αρνὸς, gen. of 'Αρήν ; for ἀρένος.

"Αρνυμαι, to earn, acquire.— R. αἴρω, ἀρῶ, as †"Αγω, "Αγνυμαι. (2) Our earn.

'Αρος, use, profit.— As above : To take up, employ. Or αἴρομαι, to carry off, gain, as ἄροιτο Il. 10. 307. (2) R. ἄρω : Suitableness.

'Αροτρον, a plough : and

'Αρουρα, ploughed land : from

'Αρόω, to plough.— R. ἄρω : to prepare, adapt the

land for cultivation. Compare ἄρΩμα. (2) Allied to ἀρόω, to draw up i.e. the earth. (3) Or to ἀράσσω, to break i.e. the soil. (4) Our verb ear in Isai. 30.24, (whence earth.) Goth. arian, Sax. erian. Martin ' from †ἔρα the earth in ἔράζε, or Chald. ara, the earth.'

'Αρπάζω, to seize.—From αἴρω, ἀρῶ, to take up, αἱρέω: Π, as in μέλΠω, εἰλυσΠάομαι, πόρΠη. Compare the shorter word Ἅρπη. (2) ' Hebr. harepk, to strip:' Wr.

'Αρπαστὸν, ' the game catchball: prop. to be taken or caught:' Ldd.—Above.

'Αρπεδὴς, level with the ground.—R. ἀρι— or ἄρω, πέδον.

'Αρπεδόνη, ' rope for snaring game: twist or thread for cloth: bow-string:' Ldd.—Allied to Ἅρπη, Ἅρπυια, 'Αρπάζω.

'Αρπεζα, found only in Nicander, and variously explained. The foot of a mountain, so thought to be for ὀρόπεζα, R. ὄρος, πέζα: (A, as 'Οστακὸς and 'Αστακός, 'Οῤῥωδέω and 'Αῤῥωδέω,) thorn-hedge, so thought allied to Ἅρπη and 'Αρπάζω to seize, tear:—a loose flint low wall.

'Αρπη, a falcon; a sickle; allied, like Ἅρπυιαι, to 'Αρπάζω. Also an excessive flow of bile, i.e. seizing the body violently.

'Αρπὶς, a shoe, ' allied to 'ΑρΒυλὶς', says Liddell. But the Etym. M. for ῥαπὶς from ῥάπτω to sew. Vice versâ is RApio from †'ΑΡπαῶ, 'ΑΡπάσω.

Ἅρπυιαι, harpies. As Ἅρπη.

'ΑΡῬΑΒΩΝ, arrhabo, earnest-money.—' A Hebrew word in Greek letters': Pkh.

Ἅῤῥατος. See 'Ραίω.

Ἅῤῥην: in Ἅρσην.

'Αῤῥηνὴς, ferocious.—' R. α, ῥὴν, a lamb: Unlike the lamb:' Reiske.

'Αῤῥηφόρος, a virgin who bore the vessels in Minerva's festival.—For ἀῤῥητο-φόρος. As Ido-latry for Idololatry. In-fanda ferens.

Ἅῤῥιχος: in 'Αρσιχος. So Ἅρσην, Ἅῤῥην.

†'Αρς, supposed nomin. of ἀρνὸς, which however is better for ἀρένος.

'Αῤῥωδέω, Ion. for 'Οῤῥωδέω.

'Αρσενικὸν, arsenic.—R. ἄρσην, εν, used for vehement, violent, Philoct. 1455. So ἀνδρειοτέροις θηράτροις Ælian l. 1.

'Αρσην, mas, maris.—' Ab ἄρδω, σω: Quia fœmineos locos rigat et fœcundat:' Damm. Vel ab ἀρόω, ἀρόσω. Communia sunt ἄροσις παίδων, &c. Œd. T. 1497: τὴν τεκοῦσαν ἭΡΟΣΕΝ.

'Αρσιος, fitting, agreeing.—R. ἄρω, ἄρσω.

Ἅρσιχος, a wicker basket.—R. ἄρω, ἄρσω, to join together.

'ΑΡΤΑΒΗ, a Persian measure.

'Αρταμέω, ' to cut in pieces, cut up: Ἅρταμος, a butcher, cook,—a murderer:' Ldd.—R. ἄρω, ἄρται, to prepare sc. for the table; 'Αρταμος like 'Ορχαμος. (2) R. ἄρτος, τάμνω: A bread-cutter, 'Αρτοτάμος. (3) For ἀρτι-ταμέω, as 'Αμφορεὺς for 'Αμφιφορεύς. To cut into ἄρτια equal sections.

17

'Αρτάνη, cord, rope, by which anything is hung up, from

'Αρτάω, to fasten to, hang up.— R. ἄρω, ἄρται, to join to. (2) R. αἴρω, ἄρται, to raise up.

'Αρτεμὴς, sound, safe, well.— R. ἄρω, ἄρται: Well arranged or disposed, perfect, entire.

'Αρτεμις, Diana.—As making women ἀρτεμεῖς sound and whole at child-birth: Hor. C. S. 13, 14. ' As being in ever-blooming health and beauty:' Schneid.

'Αρτέμων, ' the top-gallant sail;— a pulley: from ἀρτάω:' Dnn.

Ἅρτημα, an ear-ring, i.e. hanging ornament: ἀρτάω.

'Αρτὴρ, a felt-shoe.— As well-packed; ἄρω, ἄρται.

Ἅρσον, says Homer, Pack up everything in the vessels.

Ἅρτι, 'Αρτίως: in 'Αρμοῖ.

'Αρτιάζω, to play at (ἄρτια) even and odd. So the word Equinox includes Day as well as Night.

Ἅρτιος, ready, perfect, sound, as 'Αρτεμὴς. Also, even: i.e. having one part suited to another: ἄρω, ἄρται.

Ἅρτος, bread.— R. ἄρω, ἄρται, to provide: Provision: ' For so He provideth for the earth.' Or, to prepare: Prepared flour. Or, Suited for man's sustenance. Or, as Homer: Ἥραρε he refreshed his spirits with food. See 'Αρμαλιά.

'Αρτύνω, to arrange, manage: 'Αρτυτήρ, a Director. — R. ἄρω, ἄρται.

'Αρτύω, to season meat: i.e. to prepare with spices: Above.

'Αρύβαλλος, -Βαλος, ' from ἀρύω: a pot for drawing water;—a bag which drew close:' Ldd. Perh. for 'Αρύβαλος.

'Αρύτηρ, vessel for taking up liquids: from

'Αρύω, 'Αρύτω, to draw up, to draw off.— Allied to 'Ερύω: Ἅρω being prim. to draw. Or from αἴρω, ἀρῶ, to raise.

'Αρχαῖος, original, ancient, going to the ἀρχή.

'Αρχεῖον, senate-house for the ἀρχαὶ magistrates.

'Αρχὴ, beginning;—magistracy. Ἄρχω, to begin, —begin before others, take the lead, hold the first rank, rule.— R. ἄρω, ἄρται, to prepare, make ready, set about. Horace: ' Jam nox inducere terris Umbras ... parabat,' was preparing, was beginning. Χ, as νέω, νήΧω: στενάΧω. (2) ' Hebr. araoh, he disposed:' Pkh.

ἈΡΩ, †'ΕΡΩ, ἊΡΩ, prim. to draw (as 'Αρύω, 'Ερύω,) —then draw together, join, fit, fasten, arrange, adjust, prepare, get ready. Hence Αἴρω, 'Αείρω, &c.—A Primitive.

'Αρωγὸς, helper.—R. ἀρήγω, as ἀγΩγός.

'Αρωμα, spice or herb for seasoning.—' As Ἅρτυμα, prob. from ἄρω:' Dnn. A preparation, properly. See 'Αρτύω. As to Ω, compare ἀρΟάω. (2) R. ἄρι, ὄζω, to smell; ἄσμαι, ἄμαι, as the Σ in σωΣτέος from σώζω disappears in σωτήρ.

Ἅσαι, for ἆσαι. See in Ἅατος.

'Ασαλαμίνιοι, not skilled in naval affairs as the people of Salamis.

'Ασάμινθος, ' a basin, bathing-tub.—R. ἄσις, μινύθω : or ἄσις alone :' Dnn. The latter, much as in Λαβύρινθος.

'Ασβόλη, 'Ασβολος, soot, lamp-black.—R. α, euphon., σβέω, σβόλος, as Βδέω, Βδόλος. Soot from extinguished fires. (2) R. ἄσις, βολή : A refuse of mire and dirt. See the last. (3) R. α, much, and βολή : with Σ, as d-Σφάραγος, ἀσχαλάω, δαΣπλῆς : Rejiculum, Refuse.

'Ασαρον, a floor of mosaic work, not swept with a broom, but rubbed with a sponge.—R. α, σαρόω.

'Ασελγής, wanton, lewd.— For 'ΑσΑλγής, as νημΕρτής : from α, intens. σαλαγέω=βυνέω. (2) Formerly derived from α, and Σέλγη in Asia Minor, whose inhabitants are called by Strabo and Libanius temperate and virtuous.

'Ασση, surfeit.—R. ἄσαι, to glut, in Homer. See 'Αατος and 'Αδέω.

'Ασθμα, a panting.— R. †άω, †άσθην, whence Αΰω, &c.

'Ασιλλα, a frame or yoke over the shoulders to carry things with.—R. α, †σίλλω, (see Σίλλος,) the same as ἴλλω, to twist about : keeping steady, like 'Αστράβη.

'Ασις, mud, slime.—' Such as a swollen river brings with it, prob. from ἄσαι to satiate. I.e., glut, superfluity :' Ldd. (2) R. ἄζω, ἄσω, to dry, as 'Αζα : Mud dried by the sun.

'Ασκάντης, a small bad couch.—'R. α, σκάζω, like Lat. scando, to limp : Higher on one side than the other :' Lenn. (2) Our word askaunt.

'Ασκαρίς, an intestinal worm, always springing up and down : α, σκαίρω, σκαρῶ.

'Ασκεθής, 'Ασκηθής, unharmed, unscathed.— Dnn. from ἀσκέω : ' Taken care of, hence preserved.' (2) Allied to Σκέπω, Σκηνή, &c.: Much protected : with A prefix. (3) Allied to our un-scathed.

'Ασκέρα, a shoe lined with fur.—R. ἀσκέω, to elaborate, as φοβΕΡΑ : and perhaps allied to 'Ασκεθής. See Dnn. above. (2) R. α ; †σκέω, σκέπω, to protect.

'Ασκέω, ' to attend carefully to, take pains with, work skilfully, exercise, practice. Akin to Σκεῦος, Σκευάω, [or Σκευή,] = Σκευάζω, Hesych.:' Dnn. And Σκευάζω is to prepare, construct, fit out. With a prefix. (2) For †ἀσκέω, †ἀξέω. Ξέω and ξύω are to polish, carve. Homer : 'Εἀνὸν ἔξυσεν ἀσκήσασα. (3) Some compare Σκεθρὸς, exact. (4) ' Chald. asaq, exercēri :' Mrt.

'Ασκὸς, a bag, sack, wine-skin.—Allied to Σκεῦος, a vase, vessel, &c. and from †σκέω, σκέπω, to cover, protect. With a prefix. (2) Mrt. from α, σχέω, σχῶ, to hold, as Ion. δέΚομαι.

'Ασμα, a song.—R. ᾄδω, ᾄσμαι, ἀείδω.

'Ασμενος, pleased.— From 'ήδομαι, ἡσμένος :' Dnn. †'Αδω, †ἀδέω, ἀνδάνω, &c.

'Ασπάζομαι, to embrace, salute.—R. α for ἅμα, σπάω : To draw close to oneself. ' Adduxit colla lacertis', Ov.

'Ασπαίρω, the same as Σπαίρω.

'Ασπάλαξ, a mole,—R. α, σπάω : As drawing up the earth. ' Fodēre cubilia talpae :' Virg. Compare Ψαλάσσω.

18

'Ασπαλιεὺς, a fisherman.— From 'ΑΣΠΑΛΟΣ, a fish, or kind of fish. —Some from α, σπάω, to draw (out of the water).

'Ασπετος, unspeakable, unspeakably great.— R. α, ἐπω, ἔσπω, †σπέω, to speak. So "Ασχετος from ἔχω, ἴσχω, †σχέω.

'Ασπιδής, ' round like 'Ασπὶς, -ίδος, a shield : or, better, from α, σπιδής :' Dnn.

'Ασπὶς, a round or oval shield.— Some from ἀπὸ ίς, ἄψις, the circumference of anything. (2) As ἔΣπω, ἔΣχω, λέΣχη, for ἀπὶς from †ἄπω, ἄπτω : Well joined and linked. (3) Hebr. ASP, to gather together.

'Ασπὶς, an asp.—' Perh. from rolling itself up in a spiral form like a shield :' Ewing. And so the Encycl. Brit.

'Ασσα, "Αττα, for ἄτινα, †άττα, then ἄττα, as pluMBer we pronounce pluMMer.—But Matthiæ from ἄ, and σὰ, τὰ, Doric for τι and τινα.

'Ασσάριον, a diminutive of the Roman as, assis, from Greek εἶς one, and like our Ace.

'Ασσον, nearer.—R. ἄγχι, near ; †ἄγχσσον, as Βράχίον, Βράσσον ; Πάχίον, Πάσσον.

'Ασταϰὸς, 'Οστακὸς, a kind of crab.—' R. ὀστέον, a bone :' Dnn.

'ΑΣΤΑΝΔΗΣ, a Persian courier.

'Αστεῖος, urbane, courteous.—R. ἄστυ, urbs.

'Αστεμφὴς, 'Αστεμβὴς, firm.— See Στέμφυλον and Στέμβω.

'Αστεροπὴ, lightning.—R. ἀστὴρ, ἀστέρος : Glittering like a star. So πόρΠΗ. (2) ' Poet. for 'Αστραπὴ :' Dnn. (3) R. α, στερόω, ὀψ, ὀπὸς, or ὀψ, ὀπὸς, as Οἶνοψ : Depriving of the sight.

'Αστηνος, the same as Δύστηνος.

'Αστὴρ, "Αστρον, a star.— R. †άω, †άσται, whence Αΰω to kindle, Αὐγὴ splendor, Αἴθω to burn.

'Αστράβη, pack-saddle, pack-horse.— R. α, στρέφω, ἔστραβον whence στραβός : Not turning over. So ἄ-στραβής, immoveable.

'Αστράγαλος, knuckle, ankle, a vertebra of the neck ; —pastern-bone ;— game with them ;— part of the Ionian volute in buildings.— Allied to Στραγγεύω, to turn, Στρογγύλος, round : with α.

'Αστράπτω, to lighten : to shine :—'Αστραπὴ, a shining.—Allied to 'Αστεροπὴ : from ἀστέρος, †ἀστερόπτω. (2) 'R. α, στρέφω, ἔστραπται, ἔστραφον : from the tortuous appearance of lightning :' Schneid.

'Αστριξ, 'Αστριχος, 'same as 'Αστράγαλος': Dnn., and prob. corruptions of it.

'Αστυ, ἄστεος, a city.— R. α, †στάω or †στάω, στῶ, ἵστημι, to be established : ' Constitūta respublica', Cic. So a State or political body is from Sto, Statum. So Martin compares Germ. stadt. Compare 'Οστέον. (2) An Egyptian word, says Diodorus.

'Ασυφὴς, filthy, impure.—R. α, intens., and σύρω : allied to Σύρμα, Συρφετὸς, refuse.

'Ασύφηλος, vile, 'senseless', (Dnn.) dishonored ; dishonoring, (act.) reviling.—Damn well for ἀσύφηλος, as ἄγΥρις, ὄνΥμα, ἀποπΥδαρίζω : from a, σοφὸς, as ἀτα-τΗΛΟΣ. This agrees with 'senseless' above. Then vile ; and making vile, reviling. (2) 'Arab. *asepel*:' Wr.

Ἄσφαλτος, mineral pitch : a, σφάλλω, ἔσφαλται, as Ἀσφαλὴς, firm : A firm cement.

Ἀσφάραγος, throat, gullet.—Allied to Φάρυγξ. (Ldd.) So δαΣπλὴς and

Ἀσχαλάω, Ἀσχάλλω, to be grieved or vexed.— For ἀχάλλω (as in ἀΣφάραγος,) from ἄχος, pain.

Ἄσωτος, utterly profligate.— R. a, σώζω, as Σωτήρ : Not to be saved.

Ἀτάλλω, Ἀτιτάλλω, (somewhat as Μένω, †Μιμένω, Μίμνω,) to bring up the ἀταλοὺς young :— play as a child, like Παίζω from Παῖς.

Ἀταλὸς, of tender age, delicate.— R. a, ταλάω : Un-enduring.

Ἀτάρ, but, yet, however, nevertheless. — For Αὐτάρ. (2) ' Hebr. *ater*, to obstruct :' Wr.

Ἀτάρμυκτος, fearless.— For ἀτάρβυκτος (as τερέ-Μινθος, τερέβινθος, Βύρμηξ and Μύρμηξ,) from τάρβος, fear. (2) R. τείρω, τέταρμαι, allied to Ταράσσω.

Ἀταρτηρὸς, supposed put for Ἀτηρὸς, injurious, as Ἐπιτάρροθος for Ἐπίρροθος. A in ἄτη is long, but short in ἀτέων Il. 20. 332.— But much better from a, τείρω, τέταρται, to torment, harass. Thus ἀταρτηροῖς ἐπέεσσι Il. a, 223, ' *asperis* verbis', (Clarke). See the last part of Ἀτάρμυκτος.

Ἀτάσθαλος, 'blindly foolish, madly violent : from ἀ-τάω, [ἀτάσθην,] ἀτέω :' Ldd. See ἀτέων in Ἀταρ-τηρός.

Ἄτε, as, since, as if : from ὅστε, for δἰ ἄτε, καθ᾽ ἄτε.

Ἀτέμβω, ' to lead into mischief, distract, distress, tor-ment, deceive ;— to bereave, deprive. Ἀτέμβομαι, to rebuke, reproach.— Damm from ἄτη, ἐμβιβάζω ; but prob. only ἄτη :' Dnn. See the last part of Ἄτη. (2) R. ἀπο-τέμνω, ἀποτεμῶ, to cut off, deprive : (B as Θλίβω, τρίβω,) though ' to Distress' (above) might lead to this sense. And ' Reproach ' may be, ' to tor-ment with words, distract or confound.'

Ἀτενίζω, to look at ἀτενὲς attentively : R. a intens., τείνω, τενῶ, *tendo, attendo, intendo* : To be intent on.

Ἄτερ, Ἄτερθε, apart from, without. — Ἄτερθε short for ἐκάτερθε, apart from, as Τράπεζα for Τετράπεζα, *Lactis* from Γάλακτος, Uncle from Avunculus. (2) ' Hebr. *ater*, to obstruct :' Wr.

Ἀτέραμων, Ἀτέραμνος, not tender, hard.—Allied to Τέρην, tender : with a.

Ἄτερος, the other, ὁ ἕτερος. Strangely formed like ΘΑτερον, which see.

Ἀτέω, to be fool-hardy, i.e. under delusion, from ἄτη. See the next.

Ἄτη, hurt, mischief ;—mental injury, infatuation, delusion, sent as a punishment or a misfortune.— ' R. ἀάω :' Dnn. I.e. from pf. pass. ἄαται, ἄται. See on Ἀάσκω. In ἀτέω, ἀ is rather from †ἀω simply.

19

Ἄτλας, ' who carries burdens, a porter, —the upper vertebra of the neck,—the statue of a man serving as a pillar :' Dnn.— R. a, intens., τλὰς sustaining.

Ἀτμήν, ἀτμένος, a slave.—Bos for ἀτιζόμενος or ἀτε-τιμένος, dishonored. (2) Schneid. for ἀδμένος from a, δαμῶ, δμῶ, *domo*, whence δμώς. ' The grammarians have also ἀΔμὴν :' Ldd. See ἔΤνος.

Ἀτμὸς, vapor.— ' R. ἄζω, ἄω :' Dnn. I.e. †ἄω, †ἄ-ται, ἀάζω : A breathing out. Compare Ἀυτμή. Indeed Ἀτμὸς may be shortened and altered from Ἀυτμή. (2) Hebr. *ATM*, was obscured : Wr. says ' to be burnt up.'

Ἄτρακτος, a spindle, distaff,—arrow.— R. a, τρέχω, †τέθρακται (prop.) or †τέτρακται : As running round : ' *Currite*, fusi': Catull. (2) R. ταρδάσσω, τετράκται, (τέτρακται,) to agitate.

Ἀτραπὸς, a path.— R. a, τρέπω, ἔτραπον : 'A straight path, without turnings :' Steph. We say, It's a long path that has no turning. Dnn. takes a otherwise : ' On which persons go and come.' (2) R. τραπέω, to tread grapes,—suppose then to tread generally. ' Cal-canda via :' Ho·.

Ἀτρεκὴς, exact, strict, upright, accurate.— R. a, το-ρέω, τρέω, †τέτρεκα, to pierce, whence Τορὸς, explicit, accurate ; allied to Τρανὴς, distinct. (2) R. a, and τρέω, to fear : Fearless, upright, &c. (3) Allied to our *trick*, Dutch *treck* : a negative.

Ἄττα, a natural term of respect, like Ἄππα, Τάτα, Τάττα, Τέττα.

Ἀτταλαττατὰ, Ἀτταπαπτατὰ, Ἀτταταὶ, Ἀττατauὰξ, Ἰαττατal, certain exclamations from fancied sounds.

Ἀττανίτης, a cake.— R. ἄττανον, a frying-pan, and this from ἄττω, to make to jump. So

Ἀττάραγος, -χος, a crumb of over-baked bread, ready to jump up, as above. ' Saliente miеâ,' Hor. So

Ἀττέλαβος, a locust without wings, but with springy legs. — R. ἄττω, as above.

Ἀττικίζω, to live or side with the people of *Attica*.

Ἄττω, Ἄιττω, to rush, spring : ἀίσσω, ἀίττω.

Ἀτύζω, to strike with terror, bewilder. — ' R. ἀτάω' : Dnn. See Ἄτη, and ἀτέω there. (2) R. a, †τύω, τι-τύσκομαι, τύπτω, to strike. As Πλήσσω is used.

Αὖ, again, back again, back, in turn : expressing re-petition and reciprocation. ' Seemingly from ἄω, to breathe. It means the act consequent on breathing, i.e. throwing back the breath :' Dr. Jones. The poet Sewell has ' the quick *reciprocating* breath.' Compare 'Aεί.

Αὐαίνω, the same as Αὔω.

Αὐγαίνω, to view and to shine in an αὐγὴ clear light.

Αὐγὴ, splendor.— R. αὔω, to kindle a flame. (2) For †ἀγὴ, (as our moUntain,) from ἄγω, ἄγνυμι, from the *refractions* of the sun, like Ἀκτίν.

Αὐδὴ, voice.— R. αὔω, to call upon, whence Ἀύω, Ἀυτή.

Αὐθέντης, Αὐτοέντης, one who kills with his own hand : and who kills persons of his own family.— R.

αὐτὸς, and †ἔνω for φένω, (as Αἶα for Γαῖα,) to kill: whence some derive 'Εναίρω. (2) As Χαλκεντὴς is armed with ἔντεα weapons, so Αὐθέντης armed against himself. (3) As νημΕρτὴς, for αὐθΑντης from ἄνω, ἀνύω, to despatch: Despatching himself or his own friends.

Αὐθέντης, one who acts from his own authority.—'R. αὐτὸς, εἶς, ἐντός:' Dnn. 'Qui seipsum *mittit* ad negotia:' Mrt. (2) For Αὐθάντης, as at the end of Αὐθέντης above: Himself despatching.

Αὖθι, there: for Αὐτόθι, in that very spot.

Αὖθι, Αὖθις, again, back, αὖ: as 'Αλλοθι. Comp. πολλάκι, παλλακIΣ.

Αὐλαία, hanging, curtain, as fitted for αὖλαι halls of the great.

Αὖλαξ, Αὐλὼν, a furrow.—R. αὐλὸς, a pipe. (2) Allied to 'Αλοξ.

Αὐλὴ, a porch, hall, or open airy court before a dwelling;—also a dwelling, countryhouse, palace.—'R. ἄω, ἄημι, to blow:' Dnn. Where the wind blows. (2) 'Hebr. αēl, a tent:' Wr.

Αὐλίζομαι, to stable, sleep, encamp in an

Αὖλις, a dwelling, station, tent, resting-place.—'R. αὐλὴ:' Dnn. 'A stable, but in the open air, and so exposed to the winds,' Valck. i.e. from †ἄω, αὖω. (2) Allied to 'Ιαύω, to sleep. So 'Αεσα is I slept.

Αὐλὸς, a pipe to blow upon; a pipe, tube, trench, reed, vein, &c.—R. †ἄω, αὖω, to blow, as Αὐλὴ. (2) 'Hebr. hul, a pipe:' Wr.

Αὐλὼν, like Αὖλαξ and Αὐλός.

Αὔξω, -άνω: See 'Αέξω.

Αὖος, Αὐαλέος, dry.—R. αὖω.

Αὔρα, fresh air, breeze. 'The air of morning, or that coming from water:' Dnn.—R. †ἄω, to breathe, as in 'Ασθμα.

Αὔριον, to-morrow.—R. αὔρα, the air of morning; whence 'Αγχ-αυρος is near the dawn of morning; and hence Αὔριον is the morrow, as in Shakspeare: 'By the second hour in the *morning* Desire the Earl to see me.' Indeed Todd says that Morrow seems to have originally meant Morning. Compare 'Εσλος. (2) R. αὔρον, gold. The golden hour, as Aurora from Aurum, Hora.

Αὖρον, *aurum*, gold.—Allied to Αὐγή.

Αὖσιος, Doric of Τηὖσιος, Ταὖσιος.

Αὐσταλέος, Αὐστηρὸς, dry, rough,—soiled by dry dust: see Αὐχμός.—R. αὖω, αὖσται.

Αὐτὰρ, on the contrary, but, but then, moreover, &c.: for Αὖτε ἄρ.

Αὖτε, much the same as Αὖ; τε added.

'Αὐτὴ, bawling, shout of war.—R. αὖω.

Αὐτίκα, on the very spot, at the very moment, directly, as In-loco, Illicò:—as a direct example, for instance.—R. αὐτός. So ἠνΙΚΑ.

'Αὐτμὴ, like 'Ατμός.—R. αὖω = ἄω, to breathe.

Αὐτοέντης: See Αὐθέντης.

Αὐτοκέδδαλος, said of things made or done off-hand

20

and in a hurry.—R. αὐτὸς, whence Αὖτως, just as it is, and Αὐτίκα directly: κάπτω, κάἔδην, to eat fast. As said of food eaten in a hurry. (2) Similarly Suidas from κάἔος, a measure of corn. (3) From σκάπτω, †κάπτω, (whence Κάπετος,) to scoop out a σκάφος, skiff. Thus Lycophron has Αὐτοκάἔδαλον σκάφος.

Αὖτος, the same person mentioned αὖτε again; that same person, he and no other;—he by himself, alone;—he of himself, spontaneous, as Ipse is used;—just as he is, without change.

Αὖτως, Αὖτως, in the very state or just as one was, without change:—just as it was, nothing done, to no effect, in vain.—R. αὐτὸς or ὁ αὐτός.

Αὐχέω, to declare loud, protest, vaunt.—R. αὖω, αὖκα, to speak loud. As Νέω, ΝήΧω. (2) R. †ἄω, †αὖω, to blow: as Φυσάω is to puff and blow with pride.

Αὐχὴν, the neck;—neck of land.—R. αὐχέω: 'emotions of pride being often indicated by movements of the head and neck:' Dnn. So 'Τψ-αὐχην is 'having a high neck, proud.' So from Τραχηλὸς is Τραχηλιάω, to behave proudly. 'Speak not with a stiff neck:' Psa. 75. 5. (2) R. αὖω: the neck being bony, hard and dry: (Steph., Damm, &c.)

Αὐχμὸς, drought;—squalidness from dry dust, as in Αὐσταλέος and in 'Αζα.

Αὖω, to dry: from †ἄω, to breathe, as in 'Ασθμα; to blow upon. And also to dry up, parch, burn up, set on fire, kindle. So Ardeo from Aridus. Haggai 1. 9.

Αὖω, 'Αὖω, to shout out, call loudly.—R. †ἄω to breathe, blow, blow out, as above. Silius: 'Mināces *Ex-spirat* sonos.' Cicero: 'Verba inflata et quasi anhelata gravius.'

'ΑΦΑΜΙΩΤΑΙ, Cretan slaves:—Q.? (Very rare.)

'Αφαρ, instantly,—continuously,—after that.—R. ἅπτω, ἅφα, to join on with, as Continuò from Con-teneo, 'Εξῆς from 'Εξομαι. 'From ἀφὴ: Ipso tactu:' Mrt. (2) A for ἅμα; †φάω, φημί: No sooner said than done. (3) For ἄν' ἄρ.

'Αφαυρὸς, weak, feeble.—For ἀφαρὸς (as ἀμαΥρὸς,) from α, φέρω, †φαρέω as in φΑρέτρα, ἰσοφΑρίζω: Not bearing up, like 'Α-ταλός. (2) R. ἀφάω, to handle: Soft to the touch. Compare 'Απαλός. (3) R. ἀφαύω, to parch: Withered. (4) R. α, much; ταὖρος, or φαῦλος.

'Αφάω, 'Αφάω, to handle.—R. ἅπτω, ἅφα, ἅπτομαι, to touch.

'Αφελὴς, plain, level, simple.—R. α, φέλος, a stone: Without stones. (2) R. †ἀφελῶ, ἀφαιρῶ. 'Simplicity is *separation* from all heterogeneous mixtures:' Pkh.

'Αφενος, revenue, income.—R. ἀφ', ἔνος, year: the product ὂf a year, as Annōna. Buttm. says, 'the wealth of many years, like Πλοῦτος from πολυ-ετής.' (2) R. ἀφ' ἑνὸς, from one (year). (3) R. α intens., †φέω, φύω, as in Lat. *fetus, femina, fenus.*

'Αφὴ,—fastening,—touching,—sand put over anointed wrestlers to give a hold.—R. ἅπτω, ἄφα.

Ἄφθαι, fiery pustules in the mouth, thrush. — R. Ἄπτω, ἄφθην, to light up.

Ἄφλαστον, the highest part of a ship. — R. α, φλάω, πέφλασται : As not battered by the waves.

Ἀφλοισμός, foam. — Some as Æolic from ἀφρός. But Hemsterh. from φλέω, πέφλοα, to boil or bubble. Compare Φλοῖσβος.

Ἀφνεὸς, Ἀφνειὸς, rich. — R. ἄφενος, (ἄφνος).

Ἀφόρδια, excrement. — For ἀφορίδια from ἀφορίζω, as Excrement from Excerno.

Ἄφνω, suddenly. See in Αἴφνης.

Ἀφροδίτη, Venus. — R. ἀφρός : As sprung from the foam of the sea. This, says Jamieson, is more natural than most of those given by the Greeks, being congruous to the fable. Called also, Ἀφρογένεια. (2) Frae Dan. and Scotch is ‘froth’, say ‘frod.’

Ἀφρὸς, foam. — Like Ἀβρὸς and Ἀπαλὸς from ἅπτω, ἄφα, ἅπτομαι : Soft to the touch. (2) R. α, φέρω, φορά : Easily borne on the wind, carried away.

Ἀφροσύνη, foolishness : ἀ-φρων dat. pl. ἄφροσι, from φρήν.

Ἀφύσσω, to draw from one vessel into another, pour out or upon, heap or load. — Simply from ἀφ’, from, †ἀφύω : somewhat as Ἄπιος from Ἀπό. (2) R. ἀφ’, ὅω viewed as †ἔω, †ἵω, to send   Ewing takes ὅω literally : ‘ I water from, draw forth.’

Ἀφύω, to become white. — From ‘ the remarkably brilliant white color’ (Dnn.) of the ΑΦΥΗ, a species of anchovy.

Ἀχαιὰ, Ceres. — They say from the ἄχος pain she felt at the loss of Proserpine.

Ἀχαΐνας ἄρτος, a kind of large loaf in Athen. 3. where the context, says Steph., seems to refer it to the large size of the stag called as below.

Ἀχαΐνης, Ἀχαιΐνη, ‘ a two-year stag, from its single pointed horns ἀκίδες : compare Ἀκαχμένος pointed :’ Ldd.

ΑΧἂΝΗ, a Persian measure and word. Also a chest, box : Here perhaps from α, χαίνω, κέχᾱνα.

Ἀχάτης, an agate. — Referred by Pliny to Achates, a river of Sicily. (2) Lennep from α, χατέω, to lack : As lacking no color. Thus Woodward states it to be ‘ spotted with different colors, black, brown, red, and sometimes blue.’ (3) Bochart from the Hebr. and Punic echad, spotted.

Ἀχελῶος, a word applied, says Servius, from the antiquity of the river Achelöus to any water.

Ἀχερωΐς, white poplar : ‘ prob. from Ἀχέρων Acheron : for from its pale color it was thought to have been brought from the shades by Hercules :’ Ldd.

Ἀχέρων, a river of Hell. — Not improb. from ἄχος, ἄχεος, ῥέων, ῥῶν : The river of pain.

Ἀχὴν, Ἠχὴν, poor. — For ἀ-εχὴν, from α, ἔχω. Aristoph. has τοὺς οὐκ ἔχοντας. Eurip. τὸ μὴ ἔχειν. ‘ The poor of the people which had nothing :’ Jerem. 39. 10. Ὃς οὐκ ἔχει : Mark 4. 25.

Ἄχθομαι, to be loaded with ἄχθος a weight, heavy laden or weighed down in mind.

Ἄχθος, a weight. — R. ἄγω, ἄχθην. ‘ Onus quod fertur :’ Ov. Compare Ἔχθος.

Ἀχίλλειος, like Achilles : hence applied to things excellent, as Ἀχιλλῆΐς, an excellent kind of barley.

Ἀχλὺς, mist, gloom : —trouble. — From ἄχος, ἄχεος, for Ἀχελὸς : The ‘ dimness of anguish’, ‘ the darkness and sorrow’, in Isaiah : The ‘ day of darkness and of gloominess, of clouds and thick darkness’, in Joel : the ‘ black cloud ἄχεος of pain’, in Homer : the ‘ cloud of lamentation’, in Euripides : the ‘ hanc animo nubem ’ in Ovid, go in this direction.   And thus Dnn. allies Ὀρφανὸς, bereft, to Ὀρφνη. — But some from α intens., χέω, to pour. Homer has κατ’ ὀφθαλμῶν κέχυτ’ ἀχλὺς, ἔχεεν ἀχλὺν, ἀχλὺν κατέχευε.

Ἄχνα, foam, froth, down, dew, chaff, dross. — Some for Λάχνα, as Λείβω, Εἴβω ; Γαῖα, Αἶα. (2) R. †ἄγω, ἄγνῡμι, ἄχα, frango : Something fragile : So Dr. Major. (3) ‘ R. χνόη, χνόαω, χνοῶ, to comb :’ Dnn.   Or κνάω to rub, brush : Easily brushed off. (4) For ἄ-εχνα, from α, ἔχω : Not adhering.   As Ἀργὸς, for Ἀεργός.

Ἄχος, grief, pain. — R. †ἄγω, ἄγνῡμι, ἄχα : As breaking the spirits. ‘ Animo esse fracto et afflicto ’: Cic.   See more in Ἀγαν-ακτέω. (2) R. ἄγω, as in Ἄχθος, burden.   So Ἄχομαι and Ἄχθομαι would be the same. (3) Allied to Ἀκὴ : Pungent grief. (4) ‘ Hebr. ok, to compress :’ Wr. (5) Our ache, Germ. ach.

Ἄχρι, Ἄχρις, ‘ on the surface, like Ἄκρως : just touching, Il. 17. 599 : — even the outermost, utterly, Il. 4. 522.   From ἄκρος :’ Ldd. and Dnn.   Hence ‘ entirely, up to the place or time that.’ (2) As Ἴκταρ from ἵκω, so Ἄχρι from ἄγω, ἄχα, ‘ to go to’, as in its compounds.   So Ἄγε is Come on.   See Μέχρι.

Ἀχυρμιά, a heap of

Ἄχυρον, chaff. — Many for ἀ-έχυρον : Not firm, weak. (2) Like Ἄχνη, anything fragile, from ἄγνῡμι, ἄχα. (3) Allied to Ἀκὴ : Anything pungent and prickly.

Ἀχὼρ, ος, a continuous scab of the head, scald-head. — Allied to Ἄχνα and Ἄχυρον, a scale, flake, &c. Ending like ἰχ-ΩΡ, ἔλ-ΩΡ. (2) From α, much, χόρος, ‘ prop. the circular movement of dancers in a ring’, (Dnn.) (3) ‘ With very small holes like a honey-comb, [and so called in Latin favus,] but smaller, inasmuch as Galen has handed down that it is so called from their not occupying any χῶρον place, but is confined to narrow spaces :’ Gorr. in new Steph. 2460. As Ἄ-τοπος in form, though in a different sense. (4) As Ἄκαρι, a mite, from α, κείρω, κέκορα : too small to cut. (5) R. α, χωρέω, to yield, retire : From its obstinate continuance. (Very rare word.)

Ἄψ, back, again. — ‘ Prob. a form of ἀπό :’ Dnn.   As Παρὰ, Παραὶ, and Πάρος, so Ἀπὸ, Ἀπαὶ, and †Ἄπος, Ἄπς, Ἄψ. (2) If not from ἅπτω, ἄψω, as is Ἀπὸ, which see.   So Ὀπίσω and Ὀψὲ, from ἕπομαι.   Or for ἄψει, dat. of ἄψις.

ΑΨΙΝΘΟΣ, -ΙΟΝ, wormwood. — ‘ Syriac ab shento, pater somni :’ Dahler.

Ἄψις, a joining, binding ;—joinings or meshes of a net ;—the joining the felloes to form a wheel, a wheel, arch, vault.— R. ἅπτω, ἅψω.

†Ἄω or Ἄω, Ἄημι, to breathe, blow, pant, whence (through †ἄσθην) ἄσθμα. Other senses follow, as may be seen in Ἀάσκω, Ἄατος, Ἄεσα, Ἀστήρ, Ἀΰω, Ἀΰω. —A Primitive word.

Ἄωρος, Ὥρος, night,— sleep.— R. α, ὥρα : Unseasonable, as Ἀωρόννκτος 'at an unseasonable hour of the night' in Æschylus, and 'Intempestâ nocte' in Livy for 'midnight.' (2) 'Sleep,' from the sense of 'night': or from α, ὥρα : When there is no care about anything.

Ἀωτέω, to sleep.— R. ἄωτος : To cull the flowers of anything, or the sweets of things, here of sleep, ὕπνον being joined with it in Homer: πάννυχον ὕπνον ἀωτεῖς. (2) From †ἄω, whence ἄεσα, I slept.

Ἄωτον, Ἄωτον, a flower, blossom ;— hence the most choice and exquisite of its kind, so used of the finest wool.— R. †ἄω, ἄημι, to breathe, as Lennep derives Flos from Flo, (though referred by Lidd. to Φλόος): Lucretius : Et nardi florem qui nectar naribus halat. (2) R. ἄ, intens., ὄζω, ὄσται, ἄται, to smell : as σώζω makes not only σωστέον but σωτήρ without the Σ. See Ὀσμή.

B.

Βᾶ, for Βασιλεῦ, as Δᾶ, Μᾶ, for Δῶμα, Μᾶτερ.
Βᾶ, an exclamation: from the sound, as Bah !
Βαβάζω, to cry βά βά, babble, prattle, talk.
Βαβαί, Βαβαιάξ, Παπαί, Παπᾶ, natural sounds of wonder. See on Παπαί.
Βαβράζω, to chirp like grasshoppers.—'An imitative word :' Dnn. (2) R. βαρὺς, †βαράζω, †βαβαράζω, as Βάρυ-φωνέω, to have a rough voice. See Βράζω.
Βάγμα, speech.— R. βάζω, βέβαγμαι.
Βαγὸς, Spartan for Ἀγὸς, a captain, from ἄγω : as Βαῖνος, Βισχὺς Maittaire p. 373.
Βάδην, step by step. Βάδος, a step.— R. †βάω, †βέβαται, βαίνω, as Στάδην. Hesych. explains it κατὰ βῆμα.
Βάζω, to babble, talk, like Βαβάζω, which see. (2) 'Akin to φημί': Dnn.: i. e. to †φάω. So Βρέμω, Fremo.
Βαθμὸς, a going ;—a step, i. e. one pace;—a stair, and a threshold, by which or on which we go, as also Βάθρον, Βατήρ, Βαλὸς are a threshold.— R. †βάω, †ἐβάθην.
Βάθος, depth.— R. †βάω, †ἐβάθην, for κατα-βαίνω, to descend: or to make to go down, sink. Dnn. explains Βαίνω, 'to go up, down, or against.' Thus Dr. Johnson explains Deep, 'descending far.' Allied are Βόθρος, Βυθός. (2) Allied to Βάσις, a foundation, bottom.
Βάθρον, a threshold, as Βαθμός. Also, as Βάσις, a base, pedestal, foundation,—a bench, seat.
Βαίνω, to go: from †βάω, as †Φάω, Φαίνω ; †Μάω, Μαίνω ; †Σάω, Σαίνω.
Βαιὸς, little in size or number.— R. †βάω, whence Βάδην, step by step, gradually (gradus), little by little. (2) R. †βάω, as allied to †πάω, παύω, whence Παῦρος, small. (3) For Ἡβαιὸς, small.
ΒΑΙΣ, ΒΑΙΟΝ, a palm-branch.— Porphyry states it to be an Egyptian word.
Βαίτη, a shepherd's coat of skin.— R. †βάω, †ἐμ-βάω, ἐμβαίνω, to go into, as from ἐν-δύω, to go into, is Ἐνδυτὸν, clothing, Ἐπένδυτον, a cloak, and Lat. induo, to clothe. So Ἐμ-βὰς is a buskin. The compound omitted as in Ἴτυς.

22

Βαιὼν, 'a gudgeon, any fish not much valued : from βαιὸς, small, trifling :' Dnn.
Βάκηλος, Βακέλας, a eunuch in Cybele's service : 'a lewd or stupid man, like Βλάκος. From βλάξ :' Dnn. But how is this ? Better, Lenn. thinks β as in Βαῖνος and Βαγὸς prefixed Æolicè to a word Ἄ-κηλος allied to Κήλεος glowing, burning i. e. with bad desire. Or †βα, as proposed in Βασκαίνω, Βάτραχος.
Βακίζω, to prophecy like Bakis or Bacis, an ancient Bœotian prophet. (Valck. ad Herod.)
Βάκτρον, a staff, stick.—'R. †βάζω, †βάξω, [†βέβακ-ται,] βαίνω :To walk with :' Dnn. Or allied to Βάσις, a base, 'that on which one stands', (Dnn.) See Βέβαιος.
Βακχεῖος, a foot of one short and two long syllables : 'as being most used in the hymns to Bacchus and in the dithyrambs :' Steph. and Ewing.
Βάκχος, Bacchus.—'Another form of Ἴακχος :' Dnn. Yet B is not I. Rather from βάζω, βέβαχα, βαβάζω, to babble : from the confused babblings of the Bacchanals. So called Βρόμιος from Βρέμω. (2) Rudbeck refers it to one Bagge, who proceeded from the North, and subdued the East. Jamieson to bagge or bock a goat or ram : in the Dionysia the goat always appearing.
Βαλανεὺς, a bath-keeper, having the care of the βάλανος pin or peg for fastening the bolt in baths. Βαλανόω is to fasten with a peg.— Reimer from its prob. being customary to heat the baths with βάλανοι acorns, husks of chestnuts, &c. ?
Βάλανος, acorn,— gland,— pessary. 'That which the tree βάλλει puts forth :' Dr. Jones. Allied to Βλαστάνω.—Also a pin or peg shot into a bolt to fasten the door : So Βλῆτρον, a peg : Ἐπι-βλὴς, a bolt : and Obex, Obicis from Ob-jicio.
Βαλάντιον, Βαλλ-, a purse.—'R. βάλλω, to cast in :' Schleusn. (Much in form as Τάλαντον.) Thus, John 12. 6, Judas 'had the bag and bare τὰ βαλλόμενα what was put therein.' Plutarch : Τὸ βαλάντιον, ἐμβληθέντος τοῦ ἀργυρίου, &c.
Βαλβὶς, barrier, bar, starting-place : beginning,

threshold, ladder which is a starting-place to a wall :— plur. gable-end, top of a wall.—All from βάλλω : Where they throw off i.e. the rope or the horses or themselves. So from ἀφ-ἵημι is Ἀφετηρία.

Βάλε : in Ἀβάλε.

ΒΑΛΗΝ, ΒΑΛΛΗΝ, the *Persian* King. ' Prop. a lord. In the Syriac, *Baal, Bel* is Lord :' Baxt.

Βαλιὸς, swift. — R. βάλλω, βαλῶ : With a fling or plunge, as Ῥίμφα from Ῥίπτω.

Βαλιὸς, spotted.—As above : 'One color being thrown on [or by the side of] another :' Ormst. We say ' SHOT silk ' from SHOOT.

Βαλλίζω, to throw the legs about, briskly dance.— — R. βάλλω, as Βαπτίζω. (2) Our *ball*, Ital. *ballo*, Span. *bayle*.

Βάλλω, to throw, cast. — R. †βάω, as Ϝάω, Ϝάλλω : To make to go forward, προ-βιβάζω. (2) ' Hebr. *beel*, to hurry :' Wr. (3) Thiersch compares our *Ball*.

Βαλὸς, Βηλὸς, a threshold.—R. †βάω as in Βαθμός.

Βάμμα, Dor. for Βέμμα.

Βαμβαίνω, Βαμβαλίζω, Βαμβακύζω, to stammer, chatter with the teeth. — N as μaΝθάνω. For †Βαβαίνω like Βαβάζω. (2) ' An imitative word :' Dnn. (3) ' Hebr. *beem*, to speak inarticulately :' Wr.

Βανὰ Bœot., Γάνα Sicil., for Γυνή. So Βάλανος and Γάλανος, Glans.

Βάναυσος, a mechanic who heats a furnace :—vulgar, illiberal, base. — 'For βαύν-αυσος, from βαῦνος, αὖος :' Ldd.

Βάξις, like Βάγμα.

Βάπτω, Βαπτίζω, to dip, dye, bathe, drench, *baptize*. —As †Δάω, Δάπτω ; Κνάω, Κνάπτω ; from †βάω, for κατα-βιβάζω, ἐμ-βιβάζω, to make to go down or in, plunge, (properly).

Βάραθρον, Ion. βέρεθρον, a deep pit. — ' R. βάρος : Anything weighed down, depressed, sunk :' E. Valpy. As μέλΑΘΡΟΝ. (2) R. βάθος, depth, of †βάθαθρον : which would be softened to βάραθρον, much as meDi-dies into meRidies, aDbiter into aRbiter ; for Δ and Θ are interchanged often, as Θεὸς, Deus ; murTHer, mur-Der ; burTHen, burDen ; BeTHlehem, BeDlam. Thus : †βάθαθρον, †βάδαθρον, βάραθρον. Vice versâ was caDu-ceum from καΡύκειον. So Dnn. from βαθύς. (3) ' Hebr. *bor*, a pit :' Mrt. ' Hebr. *beruth*, a pit :' Wr.

ΒΑΡΑΚΕΣ, explained Μᾶζαι by Athenæus 3. 115, and used only by him.—Q. ?

Βάρβαρος, foreign, outlandish. — Strabo thinks it an imitative word to express the sound of one who speaks harshly, βαρ βαρ. So Lenn. and Forcell. (2) From βαρὺς, †βαρβαρὺς, as Δάπτω, Δαρδάπτω : for Βαρύφωνος is one who has a rough voice. (3) Chald. *bara*, abroad ; or Arab. *barbar*, to murmur. ' Irish *barba* or *beorb*. Russ. *varvar* :' Wbst.

Βάρβιτος, -τον, a lyre. — Written also βάρΜιτον, whence Pollux derives it from βαρύ-μιτον, from its heavy strings. ' *Graviorem* edit sonum :' Forcell.

ΒᾶΡΙΣ, an Egyptian canoe : ' from *Baris*, a city of E-gypt where it was used :' Blomf. Βάρβαροι βάριδες, Eurip.

23

Βάρος, weight.—Allied to Βάθος, depth, and both from †βάω, κατα-βαίνω, to sink down. (2) Wbst. compares our verb *bear*, Goth. *bairan*, and Gr. φέρω, †φαρέω whence φαρέτρα. As ἄμΦω, amBo ; Βρέμω, Fremo.

Βάσανος, the Lydian touch-stone :—trial by torture. — As ἄμΦω, amBo ; Φίλιππος, Βίλιππος ; for †φάσανος from †φάω, πέφασαι, φαίνω, to manifest, show, and so give proof of. So Φάναξ, an informer. In its form compare Λάσανον. (2) R. †βάω, βιβάζω, ἐκ-βιβάζω, i.e. to force out, extort. (3) ' Hebr. *baham*, probavit :' Mrt. As *Εξ, Sex.

Βασιλεὺς, a King. — R. βάσις, foundation ; λεὺς, λεὼς, the people : On whom the people rest and depend.

Βασιλίσκος, the basilisk, a serpent feigned to have on its head tufts like a crown. And a wren, the King's bird, Lat. *regulus.*—Above.

Βάσις, footstep ; †βάω, βαίνω.—A base, pedestal : ' whereon one steps', Ldd. : ' the foot, or sole of the foot, that on which one stands [walks], or anything is fixed, the ground, foundation, pedestal, *base* :' Dnn. Or what anything goes down upon, κατα-βαίνει.

Βασκαίνω, to use ill words to, slander :—bewitch by invidious praise, spells, an evil eye.— ' R. †βάσκω, βά-ζω, to utter, speak :' Dnn. (2) ' The Cretans for βου- seem to have said βα-, as Βασκαρίσαι, Βασπρα-χηλίσαι are put down by the Gramm. for Σκαρίσαι, Τραχηλίσαι : so Βασκαίνω for Καίνω :' Lenn. (3) ' Φάσκω αἰνὰ, to speak horrible things, [B as ἄμΦω, amBo] : or φάεσι καίνω, to kill with the eyes :' Greg. Compare Θεόφατος from Θεός.

ΒΑΣΣΑΡΑ, a fox. — ' Of *Thracian* origin :' Ldd. Βασσάρια, little foxes, are attributed by Hesych. to the *Libyans*. (A rare word.)

Βασσάρα, ' the dress of Thracian Bacchanals, prob. as made of the skins of βασσάραι foxes : also perhaps a Bacchanal ; hence an impudent courtesan :' Ldd.

Βασσαρεὺς, ' Bacchus, whose priests were clothed with foxes' skins :' Forcell. — Above. (2) ' Hebr. *batzar*, gathered the vintage :' Bochart.

Βάσσων, compar. of Βαθὺς, as Γλυκὺς, Γλύσσων.

Βαστάζω, to carry. — R. †βάω, †βέβασται, βαίνω : to make to go forward, προ-βιβάζω.

Βάταλος, cinædus, à †βάω, βατέω, βατεύω, coëo ut animalia.

Βατάνη, the same as Πατάνη.

Βατεύω, Βατέω, ascendo ut mares : ἀνα-βαίνω. Sic Βάτης, equus admissarius.

Βατήρ, a threshold, as Βαθμός : a staff to go with ;— starting-place to go from : †βάω, βέβαται.

ΒΑΤΙΑΚΗ, some cup : ' a *Chaldaic* word' : Bochart. ' Chald. *batiah*, a pumpkin :' Dahler.

Βατὶς, the prickly roach : — a bird frequenting bram-bles.—From

Βάτος, the bramble : ' prop. that grows spontaneously, from βατὸς [from βαίνω] :' Dnn. Going forth. (2) Some think α lost in ἄ-βατος, inaccessible.

ΒΑΤΟΣ, a Jewish liquid measure, in N. T. Bat Hebr.

Βάτραχος, a frog.— Βα for βου- as in Βασκαίνω (2), and ἰτράχον a. 2. of τρήχω, to be rough. (2) Βα for βοά, (Æol. βοά,) voice, much as Θέσφατος for ΘϵΟϲφατος.

Βατταρίζω, Βαττο-λογέω, to say over and over again, like one Battus, a stuttering king of Cyréné. 'Ovid perh. alludes to him in the answer of that babbling Battus to Mercury : Sub illis Montibus, inquit, erunt, et erant sub montibus illis :' Pkh.— But Liddell : 'Formed no doubt in imitation of the sound.'

Βαυθάω, Βαυθαλίζω, Βαυκαλάω, to lull to sleep.— 'Imitated from the nurse's song :' Ldd. 'Baubo in Mythology was the name of Ceres's nurse :' Dnn. But Βαυκαλάω is rather from βαυκός : To say pretty things to. Some however understand these words ' to mutter ' from

Βαΰζω, 'to cry βαῦ βαῦ, to bark : hence to howl, lament, bark with angry reproaches, cry aloud for :' Ldd. Our bay for bark, and bawl are near. All from the sound.

Βαυκάλιον, Βαυκάλις, a vase with narrow mouth, ' for it βαΰζει makes a muttering sound or hum when liquids are poured into it :' Steph.

Βαυκίδες, delicate shoes for women : from

Βαυκός, affected, disdainful, delicate, luxurious.— R. †βάω, †βέβακα, (ν as in our moUntain,) whence Βάδην ' step by step, slowly, with a steady measured step,' (Dnn.) Thus to Mince is ' to walk nicely by short steps, to act with appearance of delicacy, to affect nicety', (Dr. J.) See Βαυός.†

Βαῦνος, a furnace.— R. αὔω, to kindle : as 'Βέθος, Βαθὺς for Ἔθος, ἀθύς,' (Matthiæ Gr. Gr.). So Βεκὰς for ἑκὰς in Hesych. And Maittaire mentions Βισχὺς for ἰσχύς. (2) Allied to Φαῦσις, splendor : as ἄμφω, amBo.

Βαφή, a dyeing : βάπτω, ἔβαφον.

†ΒΑΩ, †ΒΕΩ, and perhaps †ΒΙΩ (as in βίος, βία, Βινέω, Βιάζω,) to make to go.— Primitive words. 'Βά Hebr. to come :' Mrt. Perh. allied to †ΠΑΩ.

Βδάλλω, to suck, squeeze, and Βδέλλα, a leech.— As βαδίζω, so †βαδίω or †βαδάω, †βδέω, †βδάω, to make to pass out. (Comp. ἐπίΒΔΑ.) Thus Ψάω, Ψάλλω : and ΘύελλΑ. (2) ' Hebr. bedel, to separate :' Wr.

Βδελύσσομαι, to stink, defile oneself ;—to turn from what is offensive, abominate. Βδελυρὸς, abominable. Βδόλος, a stench.— From

Βδέω, to emit a noisome stench.— Prop. to make to pass out, as in Βδάλλω. (2) ' An imitative word expressive of disgust :' Dnn. From the sound ΒΔ.

Βδόλος : in Βδελύσσομαι.

Βδύλλω, as Βδέω :—and to turn away from, abhor, dread ;—to insult by the act expressed in Βδέω.

Βέβαιος, firm.— R. †βάω, βαίνω, i.e. to go on, to go well, stand up firm, whence βεβηκὼς, fixed ; τὸ βεβηκὸς, firmness. And see Βάσις, a base. Βε-, as in

Βέβηλος, common, profane.— In form as σϵγΗΑΟΣ. R. †βάω, †βῆλος, βέβηλοὶ : accessible to all. 'Allowable to tread :' Ldd. See Βηλός.

Βεκκεσέληνος, superannuated, doting, silly.— R. βέκκος, σελήνη : As old as bread and the moon. Or calling on the moon for bread. (2) R. βεκὰς, Hesych. for ἑκὰς, Æol. : As far back as the moon. (3) Hesych. has also Βεκὸς, silly : i. e. βεκὰς far from (his mind) : A moon-struck maniac.

ΒΕΚΚΟΣ, a Phrygian word for bread. A curious account of it is in Herod. 2. 2.— Wr. from Hebr. beg, bread.— Wachter compares our BAKE.

Βελόνη, (like Ἀκόνη,) a sharp point as at the end of a βέλος :— needle,— fish with long sharp snout, as a

~ Βέλος, a dart.— R. βάλλω, †βολέω which shows a form †βέλλω. As Jacio, Jaculum.

Βέλτερος, Βελτίων, better.— R. βέλος, †βελώτερος : who aims his dart or hits more exactly. So Ἀρείων from Ἄρης. (2) Pers. behter, our better.

Βέμβηξ, -ιξ, a whirling, whirling-top, whirlpool.— As θάΜΒος, λαΜΒάνω. For βέβηξ redupl. from βέβηκα, †βεβήκω, to go, to go round, as Ἴτυς for Ἀμφ-ιτυς, and Βλῆτρον for Ἀμφι-βλῆτρον. (2) Allied to Πέμφιξ.

Βένθος, depth, like Βάθος, as Πάθος, Πένθος.

Βερίσχεθος, a booby.—'A fictitious word :' Dind. 'A word formed without analogy :' Casaub. ' Prob. coined by Aristoph. :' Ldd. Βαρὸς, (a ' heavy ' fellow,) might have suggested it. See E in πΕλεμίζω.

Βεῦθος, Βεῦθος, some vest.— As Βεκὰς for Ἑκὰς, (as in Βαῦνος,) so these for Εὖθος and Εὖθος ; †Εὖθος and †Ἔθος ;— from †ἴω, ἄθην, ἔννυμι, to put on, as Εἷμα. See Ἔθος. Τ as in our moUntain, and in ἔΤθω.

Βῆ Βῆ, the sound of sheep bleating, more imitative in Doric, Βᾶ Βά.

Βηλός : in Βάλτς.

Βῆμα, a step, pace : †βάω, βέβημαι. And a step, to go up upon ;— a tribunal, for ἀνά-βημα.

ΒΗΡΤΛΛΟΣ, a beryl.— Boch. from Chald. belur by transp.

Βῆσσα, a sheep-walk, wild walk, glen.— R. †βάω, βήσω.

Βήσσω, to cough. Βὴξ, χὸς, a cough.— As Βῆσσα from †βάω, βήσω, so Βήσσω : To make go out, force out, ' to evacuate the peccant matter', (Dr. J. in Cough,). Compare Βία, Βιάζω, Πιέζω. And see Βδέω.

ΒΗΤΑ, beta. Hebr. baith.

Βία, compulsion, force, violence, power.— From the obs. †βίω = †βάω, to make to go : as in Βείομαι, to go on ; Βινέω, co-eo ; and Plautus has BITO to go, whence ad-BITER, arBIter. And see βίος. So γΕΙνομαι, γΙνομαι. Compare also Πιάζω, Πιέζω, with Βιάζω. (2) From 'Ία, explained Βία by Suidas : from †ἴω to make to go, send : Β prefixed as in Βαῦνος. (3) Even Parkh. brings it from the Hiphil of Hebr. ba, to cause to GO.

Βιάζω, to force. Above.

24

Βιβάζω, to make to go, †βάω.

Βιβάω, to stride : i. e. to move out, gen. with 'long, far', &c. — Above.

ΒΙΒΛΟΣ, ΒΥΒΛΟΣ, the *Egyptian* plant, from which paper was made : — a book. Τὸ Βιβλίον, the BIBLE, 'Book of Books.'

Βιβρώσκω : in †Βρόω.

Βιδιαῖοι, Spartan officers having the care of youth. — 'Connected with ἴδυοι, Fἴδυοι, [from ἰδέω, Video,] witnesses or judges over them :' Böckh. B, as in Baΰνος.

ΒΙΚΟΣ, a pitcher, jar. — Some think it Phenician. (2) Our *pitcher*, Fr. *picher*, Lat. *picarium*. Some add, what is more remote in meaning, our *beaker*, Germ. *becher*, Ital. *bicchiere*.

Βινέω, coëo, ut maritus. — Ut 'Αγινέω, 'Ορίνω. Vox affinis est Βαίνω. Vide in Βία et †Βάω. Sic

Βίος, Βίοτος, life, — provisions. — R. βείομαι, to go on in life, as in Il. χ. 431, 'vivam' (Clarke). In π. 852 βέη is explained by Damm βιώσῃ. So βέομαι o. 194. So πορεύεται Œd. T. 874. And we speak of the Path and the Journey of life, and of going on in life. Plautus has *Bito*, to go. Note γίνομαι. (2) R. βία, natural strength and vitality, Il. δ. 314.

Βιὸς, a bow. — 'Perh. the same as Βίος, provisions ; since the first Greeks, like all rude tribes, lived by the chase :' Ldd. and Dnn. (2) As requiring βίαν force, stretched βίᾳ with force.

Βλαβὴ, hurt : βλάπτω, ἔβλαβον.

Βλαδαρὸς, soft, flaccid, moist, — weak, effeminate, stupid. — See in ΠΛαδαρός.

Βλαισὸς, disabled in speech, stammering ; — in limbs, distorted by the feet being bent outwards. — R. βάλλω, †βλάω (as in ΒΛάπτω,) to strike down, to disable. In form as Γαισός. — From βλάπτω, says Martin : rather, allied to it.

Βλάξ, -ακός, lazy, delicate. — R. μαλακὸς, †μλάξ, βλάξ. See Μέμβλωκα. (2) Allied to ΒΛΑδαρός. See ΠΛαδαρός.

Βλάπτω, to disable, damage, hinder, stop ; — from βάλλω, †βλάω, as in Βλαισὸς, Βλαστέω. In form like 'Ιάπτω, and †Δάω, Δάπτω. Eustath. : ΒΛάπτειν, οἱονεὶ ΒΑΛΛΕΙΝ. — Also to mislead, i. e. throw down and disappoint expectations.

†Βλαστάνω, Βλαστάνω, to bud, blossom. — R. βάλλω, †βλάω, †βέβλασται : To shoot forth, as Προ-βάλλω ἄνθος, Dioscor. Φυλλο-βολέω, to put forth leaves. See Βλάπτω. Dnn. compares Βλύω, which is allied.

Βλασφημέω, to defame, slander, blaspheme. — For βλαψ-φημέω, from βλάπτω, ψω, φήμη, to damage the reputation of.

Βλαῦται, sandals, shoes. — Allied to Πλατὺς, flat. So Latin *Plautus*, *Plotus*, is one with flat feet.

Βλεμεαίνω, 'to exult, vaunt, akin to Βρέμω :' Ldd. 'Same sense as Μενεαίνω. R. βρέμω, not βλέπω, [Βλέμμα], which is not an Homeric word :' Dnn. So κΡίβανος and κΛίβανος.

Βλέννα, mucus from the nose : Βλέννος, a driveller,

25

weak, dastardly, vulg. 'a snotty fool.' — R. †βλέω, βάλλω, to throw out, as †Γάω, †Γέω, Γέννα.

Βλέπω, to look at. — R. †βλέω, βάλλω : To throw or cast the eyes at. As δρέπω, δηπω. Homer has ΒΑΛ' ὄμματα ; Eurip. προ-βαλοῦσ' ὄμματα. So παρα-βληθήσην. Homer has βολαὶ ὀφθαλμῶν. (2) R. βλέω, ὦπα.?

Βλέφαρον, 'the eyelid ; freq. the eye. R. βλέπω :' Dnn. Perf. βέβλεφα : Appertaining to the sight. †βλέω, to throw ; βάλλω, †βαλέω.

ΒΛῆτρον, an iron cramp or ring : for 'Αμφι-βλῆτρον. — Above.

Βληχὴ, *bleating* of sheep, whining of children. — Lennep from the sound, *bleee*. (2) R. †βλέω, βέβληκα, to send out (sounds). See on 'Ιά.

Βληχρὸς, dull, sluggish, weak. — 'R. βλάξ, βλακός :' Dnn. (2) R. †βλέω, βέβληκα : Cast down in spirit, ab-ject, re-miss. 'Exposed to a blow', E. Valpy on Il. 5. 336.

Βλιμάζω, to feel hens to see if they have eggs : prop. to squeeze, Βλίω whence Βλίττω.

Βλιτομάμμας, a silly fool, one who is as flat and insipid as the herb ΒΛΙΤΟΝ *blit* or orache, and like an infant calling for its Μάμμα mother's breast.

Βλίττω, Βλίζω, Βλίω, to squeeze or press out, spec. honey ; whence some derive from μέλι, μελίττω, μλίττω, as in Βλάξ. To irritate, some say : i. e. press close, annoy. (2) 'Allied to Φλίω, Φλίβω, Θλίβω :' Dnn. (3) Compare Βλύω, Φλύω, allied to †Βλέω, to throw out.

Βλοσυρὸς, awful, venerable, noble, terrible, fierce. — Formed like Βλωθρὸς, tall, towering, big, huge, and so inspiring awe or respect.

†Βλόω, Βλώσκω, to arise, come forth, grow, go. — Prop. to shoot up : βάλλω, †βολέω, βλόω, as δορέω, δρόω, δρώσκω :' Matthiæ. (2) R. μόλω, †μλόω, †βλόω. See in Βλάξ.

Βλύω, Βλύζω, to spring up, gush forth, bubble. — Allied to †Βλόω, †Βλέω, and Φλύω.

Βλωθρὸς, 'shooting up, tall-growing', Ldd. — R. †Βλόω.

Βλωμὸς, a mouthful of bread. — Allied to Βλωθρὸς, tall-growing ; †Βλόω, to grow. 'Making the mouth protuberant :' Lenn. So Βλύω is 'to be brim-*ful* :' (Dnn.) agreeing with mouth-*ful*.

Βλώσκω : in †Βλόω.

Βόαξ, Βὼξ, 'a fish, called from the sound it makes : *box* !' Ldd.

Βοάω, to bellow, roar, shout out. — 'Prob. imitative :' Dnn. Of the sound *booo*. (2) R. βοῦς, βοὸς, an ox.

Βοεὺς, thong of an ox-hide. — R. βοῦς, βοός.

Βοηθέω, to assist, defend, repel attack. — R. βοὴ, δέω : To run to a noise or cry. So Βοη-δρομέω. 'Ad *clamorem* hominum millia VI. convenerunt': Cæs. 'Concursu ad *clamorem* facto :' Liv. 'On all sides to his aid was *run* :' Milt.

Βόθρος, Βόθυνος, ditch, trench. — Allied to Βάθος.

Boî, *bah! baugh!* — from the sound.

Βόλϐα, the Latin *Vulva.*

Βολϐίτιον, –διον, a small kind of cuttle-fish, 'called from its smell :' Ldd.: i. e. from

Βόλϐιτον, Βόλιτον, filth, dung. — R. †βολέω: Re-jiculum, Re-fuse. Compare

Βολϐὸs, bulbous root, bulb.—'Akin, or deriv., is Βόλϐα, and Lat. *volvo,* from the folding layers of the onion :' Dnn. Say from ἔολα from ἔλλω, to roll : ἔϜολϜa. (2) R. †βολέω, to shoot out, as in Βλαστάνω. Βολϐὸs, as Βαϐέιs.

†Βολέω : allied to Βάλλω.

Βολὶs, a missile, bolt (sent in), plummet (sent down), a cast, &c.—Above.

Βόλιτον : in Βόλϐιτον.

Βόλομαι, the same as Βούλομαι.

Βομϐαλοϐομϐᾶξ, exclam. of wonder or mockery.—'R. βόμϐοs : Hurly-burly :' Dr. Jones. 'Formed like Βαϐαὶ, Βαϐαιάξ :' Voss.

Βόμϐοs, hum, buzz, murmur. —'Imitation of the sound :' Dnn. (2) Allied to Βέμϐηξ.

Βομϐύλιοs, bumble-bee ;—gnat : Βομϐυλὶs, bubble making a noise : Βόμϐυλοs, vessel with narrow mouth, from its hum when liquids are poured into it.—Above.

Βόμϐυξ, a flute, — the wind-pipe of birds, — a wasp : from Βόμϐοs.—Also a silk-worm, and the silk. Vosse and Gataker think that in this sense the word is Eastern. Certainly its spinning seems to produce no βόμϐοs. It may be allied to Βέμϐηξ, a whirling. Thus there is not only πΕμφιs (a blister) but πΟμφόs.

Βόνασοs, a kind of wild ox.—'Perh. from †βονὸs, βουνὸs, a hill :' Lenn. See Βόλομαι. Or for Βούνασοs. See Βουνόs.

Βορὰ, food.—'R. †βόω, to feed. And Hebr. *barah* is, he ate :' Mrt.

Βόρϐοροs, dung, slime, mire. — Redupl. (compare Βάρϐαροs,) 'from βορὰ, food :' Schleusn.: Food reduced to excrement. So Dr. Jones, and Mrt. who adds : 'Arab. *bar* is dung.'

Βορϐορύζω, to rumble as the intestines.—From the sound as βὸρ, βὸρ, as Κορκορύζω from κὸρ κὸρ, and Καρκαίρω. (2) Mrt. from Βόρϐοροs.

Βορέαs, the North wind. — As Λαῖλαψ, a hurricane, from Λάπτω, ψω, to lick up, so Βορέαs from βορὸs, voracious. So Lucan of the sea : 'Omnia pontus Haurit saxa vorax.' Milton : 'Boreas and Cæcias . . . . rend the woods and seas upturn.' (2) Pkh. from βοᾷ ῥέω : 'It usually flows with violence and noise :' Ewing. (3) 'Russ. *boria,* storm and tempest :' Webst. 'Hebr. *boraach,* rapidity :' Heins.

Βόστρυχοs, tendril or cluster βοτρύων of grapes :—ringlet of hair or in clusters, as Epigr., βότρυν κόμηs. Σ, as λέΣχη, ἔΣχον, Lat. feStūca.

Βοτάνη, herb, fodder. And Βοτὴρ, a shepherd.— R. †βόω, βόσκω.

Βότρυs, a grape. — From ποτὸs, drinkable, as Πλαδαρὸs and Βλαδαρόs, Bibo from Πίω. Compare in

26

meaning Poma from Πότιμα. Ovid speaks of the 'pressos *liquōres*' of the grapes.

Βου–, largely, very.— As a Βοῦs, ox, like our Horse in Horse-laugh, Horse-chestnut. So Bull-finch.

Βούϐαλοs, a buffalo.— R. βοῦs, an ox. Comp. ἀρύΒΑΛΟΣ.

Βουϐὼν, the groin : and a *bubo,* swelling in it. — Dr. Grant by redupl. from Hebr. *bo,* to swell ; yet let us not say with him, from the tumor, but the groin itself. We hear of 'the femoral *arch*': and Groin in building is 'an angular *curve*' (Enc. Br.). But then why not from †βῶν, †βάων, βαίνων i. e. ἀνα-βαίνων, as in Βῆμα, Βωμόs, &c.

Βουκανάω, to blow the Βυκάνη, trumpet. Ο as ϑΟυγάτηρ, σΟυδάριον from Sudarium, εἰλήλΟυϑα.

Βουκολέω, to pasture cattle, — tend, cherish, encourage, beguile, deceive ; –λοῦμαι, to roam about like cattle pasturing.—From

Βουκόλοs, a feeder of cattle :—gad-fly feeding on cattle.— R. βοῦs, κόλον, food. (2) R. βοῦs ; κέλλω, κέκολα, to drive.

Βουκαῖοs, 'a cow-herd, one who ploughs with oxen : from βοῦs :' Dnn.

Βουλή, counsel, design.— For βολὴ, (as our moUntain,) from †βολέω, to cast in the mind. 'Βάλλεο in your mind,' says Homer : 'But now the gods ἐϐάλοντο otherwise': 'Let no one βαλλόμενοs, casting his mind on, the spoils, remain behind.' 'Επ' ἐμεωυτοῦ βαλόμενοs ἔπρηξα, Herod. Ξυνέϐαλον πρὸs ἀλλήλουs, λέγοντεs, Acts 4. 15. (2) 'Slavon. *volia :*' Wbst.

Βούλομαι, Βόλομαι, to wish.— As Βουλὴ, from †βολέω, to cast the mind upon. So 'Επι-βαλλόμενοs is 'Επιθυμῶν, Schol. Il. ζ. 68. So "Ιεμαι is to desire, from "Ιημι. (2) 'Germ. *wollen,* Lat. *volo :*' Wbst.

Βουνόs, a mound, hill.— Usually derived from βαίνω, ἀνα-βαίνω, to go up, as Βῆμα, Βωμὸs, &c. For †βονὸs, (See in Βόνασοs,) the Υ as in βοΥλή. Thus βΟθροs is allied to βΑθοs. Hesych. explains βουνοὶ by Βωμοί. (2) 'Eustath. rejects it as a foreign and barbarous word, from Libya or Africa, and Herodotus says it was a word of the Cyreneans :' Stura. (3) *Ben* in *Ben*lomond, &c.

Βοῦs, βοὸs, an ox, cow ;—ox-hide,—money stamped with an ox.— R. βοῶ : or imitated from the sound, *booοο.*

Βού-τυρὸν, 'cows' cheese as distinguished from goats' or ewes', *butter* :' Dnn. : βοῦs, τυρόs.

†Βόω, Βόσκω, to feed cattle, nourish.—'Lat. *pasco :* both perh. from †Πάω :' Dnn. Thus : †Πάω, †Πόω, †Βόω. Allied too to Βύω, 'to stuff up, fill quite full :' (Dnn.) Compare Μύω and Μότοs. (2) To tend Βόαs oxen and cows.

Βραϐεὺs, umpire at the games ; Βραϐεῖον, reward of victory.— R. βάροs, 'dignity of character, influence or authority': (Dnn.) Then, as 'from Ταράσσω was Τάραϐοs or Τάρϐοs', (Dnn.) so from Βάροs was †Βαραϐεὺs or Βραϐεύs. See the senses of Πρέσϐυs. (2) As 'Ραϐδοῦχος has this sense, some suppose †ῥαⓢⓢεὺς, †ῥαⓢⓢεὺς, (as our pluMBer is pronounced pluMMer,) transp. Βραⓢεὺς, much as Μορφά, 'Forma,' and as Βρέφος Bos derives from Φέρⓢω.

Βράγχια, gills serving for the Βρόγχος. And Βράγχος, hoarseness of the Βρόγχος. This and the above show an alliance to Βρόγχος. Note that Βουβὼν means both the groin and a swelling in it.

Βραδὺς, slow.—'Akin toⓢαρὺς :' Dnn.   Βαρὺς, βραⓢs, βραΔὺs, as proDest, proDit. Or βαρὺς, †βαρΔζω, †βαραδύς. Compare ἀρΑΔΟΣ. Or βαρὺς, βαρΔὺς, bardus, as ἕλΔομαι.

Βράζω, to boil, ferment : and Βράσσω, to shake violently, winnow, throw up, boil.—As ῥόδον, Βρόδον, so ῥάσσω, Βράσσω, to dash violently, burst. Compare Βράχω. (2) As Βιⓢάζω, so βαρὺς, †βαρdζω, βράζω, to treat heavily, push with violence, agitate, like Στυφελίζω. (3) Ldd. compares Germ. brausen, our brew.

ΒΡΑΚΑΙ, breeches worn by the Gauls : 'a word common to the Sarmatians, Saxons, Irish, Dutch, Danish, French :' Wbst.

Βράκη, plur. in Theocr. 28. 11, 'costly female garments', says Dnn.; but my Latin Version makes it braccas, as above. See however on 'Ρῆγος and 'Ράκος.

Βρασμὸς, earthquake : from
Βράσσω : in Βράζω.

Βραχίων, the arm,—shoulder.—'R. βραχύς. Prop. the shorter part from the shoulder to the elbow :' Pkh., Mrt., &c. 'Festus says, because the distance from the shoulder to the hands is shorter than that from the hip to the feet. But it was prop. said of the bone between the joints of the shoulder-blade and the elbow : that bone is short, partic. if compared with that of the thigh which corresponds with it. For, as the hands to the feet, the lacertus to the tibia, the elbow to the knee, so the brachium is to the thigh :' Voss. (2) Tooke from Goth. brak, to break; the arm being broken at the joints. Or say, B is prefixed to ῥάσσω, ἐρΡΑΧΑ, 'to divide, sever :' (Dnn.) allied to ῥήσσω, ῥήγνῡμι, to break. As ῥόδον, Βρόδον. See the next.

Βραχὺς, short.—' R. βράσσω, [βέⓢραχα,] Æol. prefix to ῥάσσω, to tear into small bits, curtail :' Dnn. ' Βράσσω is to burst out violently : Βραχὺs, with a burst, sudden :' Lenn. ' So Repens, sudden, from ῥέπω, vergo:' Voss. (2) Or R. βράχω, to go off in a crash : Sudden, of short duration. So Chald. perach, fregit, is compared.

Βράχω, to crash, rattle, clash, roar.—From the sound, as our BREAK. (2) For ῥάχω from ῥάσσω, ἔρραχα, as ῥόδον, Βρόδον. (3) 'Hebr. brek, to send forth lightning :' Wr.

Βρέγμα, the part above the forehead.—R. βρέχω, βέⓢρεγμαι : As soft and moist in infants, long in hardening.

Βρεκεκεκὲξ, sound to imitate the croaking of frogs. So Κόαξ and Latin Coaxo.

Βρέμω, to rustle or roar, rage.— R. βαρὺς, βαρέω,

27

†Βρέω, then as Τρέω, Τρέμω :—βαρέω being here 'to press down or on heavily, make a heavy noise.' So Βριμάομαι. Thus Βαρύ-κτυπος, &c. (2) From the sound.

Βρένθος, 'some water-bird of a stately bearing : hence a haughty carriage ; Βρενθύομαι, to swagger,' Ldd.:—and, as Steph. thinks, ' the same as Βρέμω, am indignant, threaten.' Then R. βρέμω, ἐⓢρέμηθην, for softness ἐⓢρένθην, as N in βροΝτή.—Or, as Πένθος, Πάθος ; Βένθος, Βάθυς, so Βρένθος, †Βράθος, i. e. †Βάραθος as Μέγαθος, from βαρὺς, 'grave, dignified' (Dnn.).

Βρέτας, an image, thought to be for Βρότας (as γόνυ, gEnu ; tOsta, tEsta ; βΟΛέω, βΕΛος ; our brOther, brEthren,) from βροτός : 'An image of a God in the form of a man :' Casaub. and Heins. Compare 'Ανδρίας from ἀνδρός. We say To render homage to, from homo. (2) ' Celt. brith, painted : whence the Britons :' Dr. Jones.

Βρέφος, an embryo :— new-born babe, babe. — R. †βρέω, (as in Βρέμω,) allied to βρύω whence "Εμ-βρυον, an embryo. So Στέρος, Ψέφος. (2) ' Transp. from φέρⓢος from φέρⓢω, to nourish :' Bos. Much as Μορφά, Forma.

Βρέχω, to wet.— R. †Βαρέω, †Βρέω, (as in Βρέμω,) to weigh down, sink down i.e. in water. See Βάⓢτω. (2) 'B prefixed Æol. to ῥέω, 'to (make to) flow, as ῥόδον, Βρόδον.

Βρήσσω, to spit up with a violent commotion.—Allied to Βράσσω, Βράζω ' to be affected with violent commotion :' Dnn. (2) R. ῥήσσω, to burst : B as above.

Βρι—, for Βριθὺ, heavily.

Βριάω, to make or to be strong and mighty. Βριαρὸς, strong.—' The same origin as Βρίθω :' Dnn.

Βρίζω, to be drowsy, i.e. heavy with sleep.—'Akin to Βρίθω :' Dnn. (2) As full of βορὰ, food : †Βορίζω.

Βρίθω, to be heavy laden, press down,— to be of weight or importance, prevail.—'Akin to Βάρος, Βαρύθω :' Dnn. Βριάω, Βρίζω, Βρίθω, are from †Βαρίω, †Βρίω, as Τείρω, Τερⓢ, †Τερίω, †Τρίω, Τrivi, Τρίⓢω.

Βρίκελος, a tragic mask.—' According to Hesych. for βροτῷ εἴκελος [or ἴκελος] ?' Ldd. Βροτ-ίκελος, Βρίκελος, as Funeralis, Feralis.

Βρίμη, force, violence, rage, menace.—Allied to Βριάω and Βρέμω.

Βριμὼ, Hecaté.— The mighty one : Above.

Βρόγχος, the throat, gullet, windpipe, gulp.—' Βράγχος and Βρόγχος from ῥέγχω, to snore, B for the aspirate,' Dnn., as ῥόδον, Βρόδον. (2) Βρόχθος is the same, and 'Ανα-βρόχω is to swallow ; so all from †Βρόω to devour, which English word is explained (inter alia) to ' swallow up' by Dr. Johnson. Γ is added to Βρόγχος as to λαΓχάνω. (3) Βρόχω, to swallow, from Βρέχω : To wet the throat. We say To wet the whistle.

Βρομίος, Bacchus.— From
Βρόμος, noise : Βρέμω.

Βροντὴ, thunder.—' R. βρέμω :' Dnn. i.e. βέⓢρομται, †βέⓢρονται.

Βροτὸς, a mortal, man. Sallust : ' Multos mortales captos.'—Ellendt for μροτὸς (see in Βλὰξ,) for μορτὸς, from μόρος, Lat. *mors*. (**2**) As Βρόδον for ῥόδον, so for ῥοτὸς, from ῥέω : ' *Fluxus*, cadūcus': Damm. (**3**) R. †Βρόω, βρώσκω, to devour : A food for worms. Compare Θνητὸς, a mortal.—Even actively, as Horace : ' Quicumque terræ munere *vescimur*.'

Βρότος, gore.—' Damm. for ῥοτὸς, from ῥέω, to flow:' Dnn. ' Gore is blood *effused* from the body:' Dr. Johns.

Βροῦκος, -χος, a locust without wings.—R. †Βρόω, βρώσκω, to devour.

Βροχὴ, wet : βρέχω.

Βρόχθος : in Βρόγχος.

Βροχὶς, ' from βρέχω ; an inkhorn:' Ldd. ' A vessel for watering :' Dnn.

Βροχὸς, a noose, partic. one for strangling the Βρόχθος throat. These words then may seem allied. Thus Βουθὼν is not only the groin, but an affection of it : Τυρὸς not only cheese, but the cheese-market : &c. Βροχὸς might perhaps have prim. meant Βρόχθος, which see. (**2**) Valck. from βρέχω, βέβροχα : ' Lorum *maceratum*', well soaked.

†Βρόχω : See in Βρόγχος.

†Βρόω, Βρώσκω, to eat.— R. βορά, †Βορέω, †Βρόω : To take food. (**2**) Allied to Βρύκω, Βρύχω.

Βρῦ, Βρῦν, words imitative of the sound of infants asking for drink.

Βρυάζω, to burst forth, as Βρύω : And to burst into joy, to be jolly.

Βρυγμὸς, gnashing of teeth : from

Βρύκω, to bite, eat,—bite or gnash the teeth.—Dnn. and others ally it to Βρύχω, to gnash with the teeth. (**2**) Mrt. from βορά, food : †Βορύκω, βρύκω, to take food. Or allied to †Βρόω, Βρώσκω.

Βρύλλω, to call for βρῦ. As Γρῦ, Γρύλλος.

Βρὺξ, βρυχὸς, the depths of the sea ; from βρύχω.

Βρύον, mossy sea-weed.—The participle of βρύω : Germinating.

Βρύτεα, refuse of olives after bruising.— R. βρύω, to spring out, burst. (**2**) R. βρύττω, to gnash with the teeth, like Βρύκω, Βρύχω, and so suppose to bruise. (**3**) As ῥόδον, Βρόδον, from ῥύω, ῥέω, to flow, ῥυτόν.

Βρύτον, a kind of beer.—Derived like Βρύτεα. (**2**) Allied to our *BREW*, and *BRUISE*.

Βρυχετὸς, chattering of teeth, ague : βρύχω.

Βρύχιος, ' from the depths βρυχὸς of the sea : —deep in sound :' Ldd. See Βρὺξ.

Βρύχω, ' to roar loudly, howl,—chafe, gnash with the teeth :—perh. imitation of the sound :' Dnn. and Pkh. Like our *BREAK*, and Gr. ΒΡΑΧΩ. Dnn. elsewhere allies it to ῥύζω, to snarl : B as Βρόδον. (**2**) R. βρύω, to bubble up. Said of the sea. (**3**) R. βαρὺς, as in Βαρύ-κτυπος, &c. As Βαρῦκω, so †Βαρύκω, Βρύκω and Βρύχω.

Βρύω, to teem, swell, burst forth, overflow, be full of. —' Allied to Βλύω, Φλύω, *Fluo* :' Ldd. (**2**) Βαρὺς, βαρῦθω, through †Βαρύω, Βρύω : To be heavily laden. See Βρίθω. (**3**) ' Hebr. *bur*, a well :' Wr.

Βρῶμα, food ;—a feeding ulcer.—R. †Βρόω.

28

Βρωμάομαι, ' to bray like an ass calling for food : hence they say from βρῶμα, but R. from βρέμω, βρόμος :' Dnn.

Βρῶμος, a stink.—Jones from βρῶμα, ' the food of carnivorous birds', carrion, ' that which has been eaten', (Dnn.) (**2**) But, as it is prop. said ' of beasts at rut', (Ldd.) and ' rut' is (says Roquefort) the French ruit, Lat. rugītus, and (says Serenius) from Su. Goth. ryta, Lat. rugīre, so βρῶμος from βρωμάομαι, rugio. (**3**) R. βαρὺ, ὄζω, ὄσμαι, ὄμαι (see in Ἄ-ωτος **2**.) : Lat. grave-olentia.

Βρώσκω : in †Βρόω.

Βύας, Βύζα, an owl : From its sound βὺ βὺ, whence Lat. *bubo*. So Βύζω to hoot.

Βύβλος : in Βίβλος.

Βυθὸς, depth ; Æol. of Βάθος, and allied to Βόθρος.

Βυκάνη, a trumpet.— R. βύω, βέβῦκα : As filling the *bucca* mouth.

Βύκτης, a wind filling the sail, blustering.—As above : βέβυκται.

Βύνη, ' malt preparing for beer ; from βύω to swell :' Dnn.: prop. to stuff full, swell out.—And the sea, from its swelling waves. ' Fluctibusque *tumentes* :' Virg.

Βύρσα, the raw hide, skin,—purse.—As Θύρσος from δύω, (Dnn.) so Βύρσα from βύω, ' to cover', (Dnn.): The cover of the animal. (**2**) ' Hebr. *PRS*, to sever i. e. from the body:' Pkh. (**3**) Our *purse*, Fr. *bourse*, Ital. *borsa*, Germ. *börse*, &c.

Βύσμα, a plug : βύω.

Βυσσὸς, depth, bottom.—Allied to Βυθὸς, Βάθος, Βόθρος. (**2**) R. βύω, to stuff down.

ΒΥΣΣΟΣ, fine flax.—' Hebr. *botz* :' Mrt.

Βύσταξ : the same as Μύσταξ.

ΒΥΩ, ΜΥΩ, (as Βύσταξ and Μύσταξ,) †ΠΤΩ, (whence Πυκάζω, Πυκνὸς,) Βύζω, Βυνέω, to cram, stuff full, cover.—All Primitives, perhaps from the sound Μυ and the cognate Βυ, Πυ, uttered with *closed* lips. So of Μύω say Damm and Passow.

Βῶλος, a clod, lump.—' R. very prob. βάλλω:' Dnn.: i. e. †βολέω: I suppose as in Xenophon: 'Ως βάλω γε ταύτῃ τῇ βώλῳ ἀνελάν.— Or as a casting up. ' *Cast* her up as *heaps* :' Jer. 50. 26. (**2**) R. †Βάω, †Βάολος, βῶλος, (as †Χάω, Χάζω, †Χάορος, Χῶρος,) for ἀνα-βάω, as in Βῆμα, Βωμός. A slight rising.

Βῶμαξ, Βωμο-λόχος, one who frequents βωμοὺς altars where sacrifices are offered, to steal some, or get some by begging or by low buffoonery ;—a parasite. ' Heus tu ! qui fana ventris causâ circumis :' Plaut.

Βωμὸς, ' a raised place whereon to place a thing, a stand, as Βάσις, Βαθμός : mostly, an altar ;—a funeral barrow :' Ldd. †Βάω, †Βαομὸς, βωμὸς, i. e. ἀνα-βάω : An ascent, Ἀνά-βασις. So Βῆμα. (**2**) ' Hebr. *bamah*, high :' Mrt. As in Ezek. 20. 29.

Βὸξ : in Βόαξ.

Βῶς, *bos*, Æol. of Βοῦς.

Βωστρέω, to shout out. — R. βοάω, βοαστρέω, as †Ἐλάω, Ἐλαστρέω ; Καλέω, Καλιστρέω.

Βώτωρ, a herdsman.— R. βῶς, or †βόω, †βέβωται, βόσκω.

Γ.

Γα, Doric for Γε.

Γαγάτης, (gagat, gaat,) jet.—From the Lycian river Gages. (Strab. xvi.).

Γαγγαλίζω, to excite laughing by *tickling*.—'R. †γάω, †χάω, [as Γαμψὸς and Καμψός,]': Dnn. Allied to Σχάζω, to scarify; Χαράσσω, to indent: Σκάπτω, to dig, as Fodico from Fodio. Now, as Πύκτης, Πυκταλίζω, so from †γάω, redupl. †γαγγάω, is γαγγαλίζω. (2) Allied to Καγχαλάω.

Γαγγάλιον, Γάγγλιον, a tumor under the skin, on or near tendons or sinews.—Redupl. as Γαγγαλίζω, Γάγγραινα, from †γάω, whence γαυσὸς bent, †γάμπτω, γαμψότης, a bend, curvature. See in Γαμψός.

Γαγγάμη, a small round net.—'The Etym. M. from γάω, [γέγαμαι,] capio :' Mrt. Thus : Γάω, †γαγγάω, γαγγάμη. See on Γαστήρ.—Or even from its χάσματα cavities or meshes. (2) Jones from Arab. *gama*, to collect. (3) Dnn. from the ancient form of Γ, *gamma*.

Γάγγραινα, a gangrene.—Redupl. of †γράω, γραίνω, to eat, consume. 'Their word will *eat as* a canker :' 2 Tim. 2. 17.

ΓΑΖΑ, treasury, treasure :—sum of money.—'Jerome says that Γάζα is Persian, and Curtius that the Persians called the royal treasure *gaza* :' Pkh. (2) R. γάω, to hold, contain, as Μάζα, Φύζα, Χθιζά.

Γαῖα, Γέα, Γῆ, earth, land.—R. †γάω, γέγαα, to generate, produce. Or †γάω, capio, to hold, contain. See Χῶρος. (2) 'Hebr. *gia*, a valley :' Wr.

Γαισὸς, a javelin.—R. γάω, capio : Taken or held in the hand. As Ἔγχος from ἔχω. In form, like Βλαισός.

Γαίω, to exult, rejoice in, to be proud of. — Allied to Γάνος gaiety, Γηθέω to rejoice, Χαίρω to rejoice, and from γάω, the same as †χάω, χαίνω, 'to stand open', (Dnn.) opposed to the contraction of the countenance in sorrow. Thus Horace : '*Explicuit vino contracta* 'seria mentis.' Terence : '*Exporge* frontem.' And '*porrecta* frons' is explained by Forcellini 'joyful.' Moreover, Χαίνω, to open the mouth wide (in laughter) may be noticed : See in Καγχάζω. (2) 'Hebr. *gaah*, to be proud :' Mrt. (3) Our *gay*, 'Celt. *gae*. And Icel. *gae* is joy :' Todd.

Γάλα, ακτος, milk.—Tzetzes on Lycophron explains Γάνος by Γάλα, and Γάνος is 'splendor, brilliancy', (Dnn.) and Γανάω 'to shine'. These words then are allied, and also Καλὸς, beautiful, and Ἀ-γάλλω, from which Thiersch deduces Γάλα. Compare Γαλερὸς and Γαλήνη. †Γάω, Γάλα, as †Χάω, Χαλάω. (2) 'Hebr. *gul*, sucking :' Mrt.

Γαλερὸς, cheerful, serene.—Allied to

Γαλήνη, sereneness, serenity, calmness. — Like Εἰρήνη : and allied to Γάνος, brightness, beauty, through

29

Γάλα which see, and to Καλὸς, beautiful : When the sky is bright and fair. All compare Γελάω; to laugh : and see Ἀ-γάλλω. (2) Our *gala*, 'Span. finery, Ital. mirth', (Todd,) seems allied.

ΓΑΛΛΟΙ, eunuch-priests of Cybele. — 'From the Phrygian river *Gallos* :' Ldd.

ΓΑΛΟΩΣ, Γάλως, a husband's sister. — Thought to be from Hebr. *gala*, a relative. (2) R. γάω, i.e. συγ-γενής. Or γάλα, i.e. ὁμο-γάλακτος, 'nursed with the same milk, of the same family', (Dnn.). ?

Γαμβρὸς, son-in-law, brother-in-law, father-in-law.—R. γάμος, †γαμερὸς, γαμρός. B, as in μεσημβρία, nomBre.

ΓΑΜΜΑ, gamma. Hebr. *gimel*.

Γάμος, marriage.—R. †γάω, †γέγαμαι, γέγαα, to generate. So Matrimony from Mater, Matris. (2) R. †γάω, γαίω, to exult, rejoice. (3) Thiersch compares 'Germ. brÄuti-GAM, betrothed to the bride.' (4) 'Hebr. *gamo*, to unite :' Wr.

Γαμφαὶ, the talons, jaws. And

Γαμψὸς, bent.—Allied to Καμψὸς, bent, Κάμπτω, to bend, turn, and Γνάμπτω. And all allied to Γαυσὸς, bent ; Καμάρα, an arch ; to Χάσμα a cavity ; to Κυέω, Κύαρ, 'words implying hollowness and roundness,' (Dnn.); Γύαλον, a hollow ; Γυρὸς, round, curved. In short, they proceed from γάω, †γάω, capio : hollows or curves holding and containing. (2) Allied to Γέμω, to be laden, i.e. bend down with weight. (3) 'Hebr. *caph*, curvo :' Mrt.

Γάνος, brightness, beauty, gaiety, delight, exultation. —R.†γάω, γαίω, which see.

Γὰρ, for, because, so, then.— For γε ἄρ, as Γοῦν is γε οὖν.

Γαργαίρω, to be full, abound.—As ψάω, ψαίρω, so γάω, †γαίρω, γαργαίρω, like Μαρμαίρω : γάω, capio, to hold, contain, being allied to †γέω, γέμω, to be full. We say, It holds a good deal, It's very capacious. (2) From *Gargara*, the top of Mount Ida, 'abounding with such fertility towards Mysia, that, if we denote an infinite number, we liken it to the productions of *Gargara* :' Macrob. 'Ipsa suas mirantur *Gargara* messes :' Virg. — But the reverse seems true.

Γαργαλίζω, the same as Γαγγαλίζω. Here Γαρ- like Δαρ- in Δαρδάπτω. So κυρκανάω.

Γαργαρεών, the uvula, gullet, throat. — Like Γαργαίρω, from the *capaciousness* of the throat, as Λάρυγξ from †λάω, λαβῶ. (2) Lenn. from the sound γαρ γαρ made by the throat, as in Γαργαρίζω. (3) 'Hebr. *gargerah*, the throat :' Mrt.

Γαργαρίζω, to gargle.—'Imitation of the sound': Dnn., i.e. γαρ γαρ.

Γάρον, a pickle made from a fish called ΓΑΡΟΣ.

Γαστήρ, the paunch, belly.—' R. γέγασται, from †γά-ζω, χάζω, to contain :' Valck. See Γάω.

Γαυλὸς, a milk-pail, butter-churn, bucket, bee-hive, 'a Phenician trading-vessel with a capacious round hold, from its form :' Dnn.— R. γδλα, milk. (2) R. γάω to take, hold, as being Capacious. See Γαστήρ. In form like Αὐλός.'

Γαῦρος, exulting, proud.—Allied to Γαίω.

Γαυσάπης, a shaggy woollen cloth.—Dnn. allies this to Γαυσὸς, Γαμψός: Tortuous, and so rugged.

Γαυσὸς, bent, crooked.—'Allied to Γαμψός :' Dnn. Whish see.

ΓΑΩ, †ΓΕΩ, †ΓΥΩ, and †ΚΑΩ, ΚΥΩ, and †ΧΑΩ, Χαίνω, ΧΕΩ, &c., to stand open or hollow,—and so to receive, to hold. Primitive words. Valck..says : 'Γάω will not be found in the Lexicons : but it is thrice noticed by the Etym. M., and explained λαμβάνω, δέχομαι. When Χ was introduced, they began to write it Χάω.'

Γάω, from the above meanings, easily took that of generating or begetting. Thus its likeness Κύω is ' prop. to contain, receive, have within, hence to conceive, be pregnant :' Dnn. Or γάω is even to open, as above : So ' aperīre partūs,' Hor., ' to open the womb :' O. T.

Γε, Γᾶ Dor., Γῖ Att., strongly affirms, assuredly, certainly. 'Εγω-γε, I assuredly, I for my part, I at least.— Dunbar : ' Γε is from †γέω, †κέω, [κεῖμαι,] to lay down, and is emphatical.' As Positively from Pono, Positum. (2) From †γάω, †γέω, γέγαα, γείνομαι, γίνομαι, to be : answering to 'Οντως from part. ὄντος : Really, in fact.

Γέα, the same as Γαῖα.

Γέγειος, earth-born, as Γη-γενής.—R. γέα, †γέω, γείνομαι. But Dnn. from γέα redupl.

Γέγωνα, to speak loud or audibly.—Steph. for γέγνωα, from †γνόω, γιγνώσκω : I make a person know my mind. (2) Αν †φάω, φωνέω, so †γάω, †γωνέω, γέγωνα, in the sense of †χάω, χαίνω, to open the mouth wide, as Soph., χανεῖν δεινὰ ῥήματα. Hor.: ' Quid dignum tanto feret hic promissor hiatu?' (3) Γοᾶ, †γωνέω. (4) Ldd. supposes a root ΓΟ, Engl. HO. But ?

ΓΕΕΝΝΑ, Hell.—A Hebrew word, ' the valley of Hinnom.'

Γείνομαι, Γίνομαι, to be born, to be, to become, to be done, &c.—R. †γέω, γάω, †γείνω, γενέω,' to generate. See the second Γάω.

Γεῖσον, Γεῖσσον, eaves, coping, margin, lip.—For χεῖσον, (much as Γαμψὸς and Καμψὸς,) from χέω, χείω, to let fall, pour : as Eaves are explained ' the part of the roof from which rain-water drops :' Todd. (2) R.† γέω, (as in Γέμω,) γάω, capio, excipio : as received into the roof. Thus Δοκὸς from δέχομαι is explained by Pkh. ' a beam received at its ends into another piece of timber.' (3) 'A Carian word :' Ruhnk.

Γείτων, a neighbour.—R. γέα, γεῖτων : Of the same land, country, city (in Tragedy). So Vicus, Vicīnus. So Populāris is one who lives in the same district. ' Tribūlis noster,' Ter. ' Thy neighbour's LAND-mark :' O. T. (2) ' Hebr. cheten, near relation :' Wr.
30

Γελασῖνοι, the front teeth, made visible by laughing ; —dimples in laughing.—From

Γελάω, to be gay and cheerful, laugh.—Allied to Γαλερὸς and Γαλήνη, which see. So ΒΑΛΛΩ, ΒΕλος ; πΑΛΛω, πΕλεμίζω ; βϐΑΛΛω, βϐΕΛΛα. (2) R. ἔλη, brightness, as Γέθεν for ἔθεν. (3) ' Chald. gelah, to shine : Mrt. ' Hebr. gel, to exult for joy :' Wr.

Γέλγεα, small wares, frippery, sweetmeats.—R. γέλγω, which means to tinge or color, allied to Γελάω to be gay, 'Αγάλλω to adorn, Γαλερὸς, &c. (2) R. ἔλη, †Γέλη, brightness, as above.

Γέμω, to be filled or full.—R. †γέω, γάω, as Τρέω, Τρέμω : to receive, hold : to be capacious, hold much. See Γαργαίρω. (2) ' Hebr. gem, to be full :' Wr.

Γενεά, Γέννα, Γένος, race, generation.—See in Γείνομαι. (2) Chald. genais. Sanskr. janu.

Γενειάς, the beard on the γένυ chin. See on 'Ανθερεών.

Γενναῖος, of good γέννα birth, noble. As Generis, Generosus. See Γενεά.

Γεννάω, †Γενέω, to beget : in Γείνομαι.

Γέντα, entrails.—R. γέντερα. 'Εντὸς, within, ἔντερα : the Γ Æolic :' Dnn. Somewhat as ἔθεν, Γέθεν.

Γέντο, he took.—As ἦΝθον Dor. for ἦλθον, so ἔλετο, ἔλτο, ἔΝτο, and Γέντο, as ἔθεν, Γέθεν. (2) R. γάω, †γέω, to take.

Γένυ, Γένυς, Γένειον, ' the upper jaw, but usu. the chin,— also the cheek :' Ldd. ' The beard,—an edge, —the edge of an axe, and so on :' Dnn.—R. †γένω : as generating the beard.—Or as curved, like Γόνυ, the knee, which see. The meaning of the axe Steph. thus explains : ' Doubtless, because, as the jaw-bone breaks to pieces by chewing, so the axe by splitting.' (2) Wbst. compares ' chin, Sax. cinne, Germ. kinn, and the Persian.'

Γεράνιον, geranium, crane's bill, from ΓΕΡΑΝΟΣ, a crane.

Γεραίρω, to honor.—From

Γέρας, gift of honor or reward.—As put in the χερὶ hand, much as Γῆρυς and Κῆρυξ.—Or, as Χεὶρ, χερὸς, the hand, is ' from χέω, χέω, χάω, to contain,' (Dnn.), and as Κέρας, so Γέρας from †γέω, γάω, to take, receive. (2) R. γέρων. As Πρεσϐεῖα from Πρέσϐυς. But the reverse seems true.

Γεργύρα, the same as Γοργύρα.

Γερουσία, a senate, as consisting of elderly men. R. γέρων, as from a fem. γέρουσα, i. e. βουλή : or after ἐξΟΥΣΙΑ, ἐκΟΥΣΙΑ. So Senex, Senātus.

ΓΕΡΡΟΝ, any wicker instrument, shield, basket, shed. —Dnn. anything carried in the χερὶ band, as Habēna from Habeo, to hold. Compare Γέρας. (2) ' Hebr. gor, to sojourn. As a shed :' Wr. ?

Γέρων, an old man.—R. γέρας : to old men being given embassies, magistracies, &c. Compare Senātus from Senex, Πρεσϐεῖα from Πρέσϐυς. (2) For γε-ορῶν ; γέα, ὁράω ; As bent to the earth and looking at that, and not the sky. So Silicernium, an old man, from

Silices, cerno. (3) Thiersch compares Germ. *gar*, 'what is at an end.'

Γεύω, to make to taste.—R. †γέω, γάω, to take ; here act. to make to take. So Ῥέω, fut. ῥεύσω from †ῥεύω.

Γέφυρα, a bridge.—'Damm from γέα, φέρω: as giving a passage from bank to bank:' Dnn.—Much better from γέα, ἁφή, as joining bank to bank ; †γεάφυρα, like Ἀγκῦρα.—Or, as ψάω, ψαφαρὸς, so γάω, †γάω, to receive, γέφῦρα. See Γεύω, Γέμω. (2) 'Hebr. *Kepher*, to cover: a covered pass:' Wright.

Γεφυρίζω, to jest at.—' There was a Γέφυρα bridge between Athens and Eleusis, which as the people passed in procession, they had an old custom of abusing whom they chose:' Hesych.

Γῆ : in Γέα.

Γήδιον, a little farm.— R. γῆ, after the model of Βοΐδιον : as in ΤυΔΕΙΔΗΣ, &c. : from εἴδομαι, to be like : ' Like father, like son.'

Γηθέω, to be glad, rejoice.— R. †γάω, †ἐγήθην, γαίω. Γῆρας, old age.—Allied to Γέρων.

Γήρειον, ' the feathery substance on seeds, when they reach maturity:' Dnn.—Above.

Γῆρυς, the voice.—Wright properly refers Χῆρος to ' obs. χάω', i. e. χαερός. Now, judging from Κῆρυξ, a herald, Γῆρυς is the same as †κῆρυς or †χῆρυς, allied to that χῆρος, and is from †χάω, χαίνω, 'to speak or utter', Dnn. i.e. open the mouth, χανῶ future producing Lat. *cano*. Compare too Γαμψὸς and Καμψός. (2) ' Hebr. *garon*, the throat : Mrt.

Γίγαρτον, a grape-stone.— Redupl. (as Γιγνώσκω, Μιμνήσκω,) for †γάρτον, allied to Χάρτος from χαράσσω, whence also Κάρχαρος, rough, sharp, cutting. Much as Γαμψὸς and Καμψὸς, Γῆρυς and Κῆρυξ.

Γίγας, a giant.— For γείγας, from γέα, γεγαὼς, or †γὰς like βάς: answering to γη-γενῆς, earth-born.— Some by redupl. from γῆ. ?

Γίγγλυμος, a hinge,—a joint of the body.— From the *gingling* or *jingling* sound, as Lenn. suggests. (2) Allied by redupl. to Γλοιὸς, slippery, i. e. oiled, greased, or as flexible, voluble. (3) R. γλύφω, γέγλυμμαι.

ΓΙΓΓΡΑΣ, a *Phenician* flute of a sad sound.— Mrt. says it is prop. said of geese, from the eastern *gagur* a goose. Curiously *Gingrio* Lat. is to cackle as a goose.

Γίγνομαι, Γίνομαι: in Γείνομαι. †Γένω, †γιγγένω, γίγνω, *gigno*. So †Πέτω, †Πιπέτω, Πίπτω.

Γιγνώσκω, Γινώσκω, †Γνόω, γνάω, to perceive, notice, understand, know.—Redupl. from γνώσκω, (as Μιμνήσκω,) from νοέω, νοῶ, νώσκω, as Φάω, Φώσκω. Then γνώσκω, and γνῶμι, as Γνόφος, Γδοῦπος.

Γίνομαι, for Γίγνομαι or Γείνομαι.

Γλάγος, milk.— R. γάλα, and †γάλαγος, †γάλαξ, g. γάλακτος.

Γλαμάω, Γλήμη, ' Att. [' Doric,' Dnn.] for Λημάω, Λήμη :' Ldd. So Γνόφος, Γδοῦπος.

Γλαρὶς, a sculptor's chisel.—Allied to Γλάφω.

Γλαυκὸς, sky-blue, pale-blue, gray.— ' At first prob.

31

gleaming, glancing. glaring, silvery, without any notion of color :' Ldd. From γλαύσσω. (2) R. γάλα, as Γλάγος. Milk-colored.

Γλαὺξ, -αυκὸς, an owl. — 'From its glaring eyes, as in Γλαυκός :' Ldd.

Γλαύσσω, to shine, glitter, glare : — to see, like Αὐγάζομαι.— R. †γλάω for γελάω or †γαλάω, whence Γαλαρὸς, Γαλήνη, Ἀ-γάλλω. See Γελάω, Γαλήνη. And Γλήνη. (2) Knight from λάω, Ἧλάω, to see. (3) Our *glance, gleam, gleen.*

Γλάφω, Γλύφω, to scrape, hollow, grave, carve.— ' A corruption of Γράφω :' Ewing. So perh. ἄλδω, ἄρδω. (2) To smooth, polish, by chiselling, thus allied to Γλαύσσω, to shine. See Γλαρίς. (3) 'Chald. *gelaph*, to engrave :' Mrt. ' Hebr. *gleb*, to shave :' Wr.

Γλεῦκος, Γλεῦξις, Γλύξις, sweet new wine.—Allied to Γλυκύς. See in Δεύτερος.

Γλέφαρον, Dor. of Βλέφαρον. As Βάλανος, Γάλανος.

Γλήνη, pupil of the eye ; and a little girl, as seen in the Γλήνη, like Κόρη. Γλῆνος, the eye, — a star, — an ornament. All from †γλάω, γλαύσσω.—Also a honeycomb, and the shallow socket of a bone for receiving another : here allied to Γλάφω, to hollow.

Γλία, Γλοιά, glue. From its shiny color. Moxon says that ' the driest and the most *transparent* glue is the best.' Thus allied to †Γλάω, Γλαύσσω, Γλήνη, Γλαυκός. (2) Many refer to Κόλλα, (Κλά,) glue. As Γαμψὸς, Καμψός ? (3) ' Russ. *klei*, Irish *gliu*, *glydh*, Lat. *gluten* :' Wbst.

Γλιχρὸς, sticky, clammy, like Γλία, glue : — tenacious, greedy, stingy, quibbling.

Γλίχομαι, to long for, desire.— From, or allied to, Γλία and Γλισχρὸς for Λιχρός, (as Ἔσχον,) : To stick to, to be greedy of.

Γλοιά : in Γλία.

Γλοιάζω, ' to wink, cast a side glance in derision : γελοιάζω :' Schneid. — Rather, R. γλοιὸς, cunning.

Γλοιὸς, anything sticky as Γλοιά, glue : as gum, oillees : adj. clammy, slippery, cunning.

Γλουτὸς, the rump, buttocks.— Lenn. and Damm from γλοιὸς, slippery, i. e. smooth, polished. So Martial has 'Assiduo *lubricus* imbre lapis', so we may say, 'Assiduâ *lubrica* sede nates.' Greg. thus : ' *Sordida* pars corporis, à γλοιὸς *sordes*.'

Γλυκὺς, sweet.—Allied to Γλοιός : from the viscousness of sweets and sweet-meats. And to Γλισχρὸς, sticky. (2) Allied to Γλίχομαι: Desirable or ' likable.' (3) ' Hebr. *CHLK*, smooth, bland, agreeable :' Pkh.

Γλυφὶς, cleft, notch in the end of an arrow fitting on the string, and the arrow ; — pen-knife.— From Γλύφω : in Γλάφω.

Γλῶσσα, Γλῶττα, the tongue, — language, — hard word in another dialect,— ' a thing shaped like a tongue, mouth-piece of a flute, tongue of leather, flute :' Ldd.— Allied to Γλοιὸς, slippery, i. e. rolling about, 'volūbilis.' Aristoph. has Γλωσσο-στροφῶ. And allied to

Γλῶχες, beards of corn, and

Γλωχὶν, 'any projecting point:—the end of the strap of the yoke, point of an arrow, the world's end. Allied to Γλῶσσα:' Ldd. Γλωσσάριον is explained by Grove 'the tip or point.' As then the Γλῶσσα is pointed, so Γλῶχες and Γλωχίν. (2) Lenn. allies it to Γλαύσσω, from the shining of an arrow-point : 'Cuspis polita.'

Γναθὸς, Γναθμὸς, the jaw, mouth.— 'R. κνάω, [ἐκνάθην':' Dnn.: To grate, γνάπτω to mangle. As Γαμψὸς, Καμψός. (2) Allied to †γνάω, γνάμπτω to bend. Homer: Γναμπτῆσι γένυσι.

Γνάμπτω, the same as †Γάμπτω (whence Γαμφαὶ, Γαμψὸς,) and Κάμπτω. N arbitrarily as T in πΤόλεμος, πΤόλις.

Γνάπτω, the same as Κνάπτω.

Γνήσιος, legitimately born, genuine.— R. †γενέω, or γεννάω, as Genuine from Gigno, Genui.

Γνίφων, the same as Κνισός.

Γνόφος, the same as Κνέφας.

Γνύθος, 'a pit, hole: allied to Γνάθος, the jaw:' Ldd.

Γνὺξ, on the knees : γόνυ, γόνυξ, as anc. †γυναίξ : i.e. γόνυξι.

Γνώμη, the mind, the judgment, &c.—From Γνῶμι ; in Γιγνώσκω.

Γνώμων, one that knows or examines to know ; a judge, interpreter ;—index of a sun-dial by which we know the time ; rule or guide of life,— a carpenter's square.— R. γνῶμι.

Γνωρίζω, to make to know.— R. †γνόω, †γνωρὸς, γνῶμι.

Γοάω, to groan.— Steph. and Lenn. from the sound. (2) Liddell allies our Go and the Greek Βῶ, so Γοάω and Βοάω may be allied. Thiersch says : 'Root ΓΟΑ connected with ΒΟΑ.' So Γλέφαρον, Βλέφαρον: Γάλανος, Βάλανος. (2) 'Hebr. goee, to low. Prob. both imitations of the sound :' Wr.

Γογγύζω, to grumble, mutter.— 'R. γοῶ. Or an imitative word :' Dnn. 'From the sound :' Pkh. (2) Γρύζω, †γογγρύζω, softly γογγύζω.

Γογγύλος, round.—Redupl. of †γύλος, allied to Γυρὸς, round. See Γυλίος. (2) 'Akin to Κόγχος, Κόγχυλος :' Dnn.

Γόης, a howler, from γοάω. A wizard, 'magical incantations being uttered in plaintive wailings :' Dnn. So Seneca : 'Ululatu barbarico magicos cantūs occinebat.' Soph. Aj. 578. Isaiah : 'Wizards who peep and mutter :' but æspec, 29. 4.

Γόμος, a freight : R. γέμω.

Γόμφιος, a grinder-tooth : i.e. a sort of peg, from Γόμφος, a wedge, nail, peg, &c.— 'The ancients derived it from κάμπτω, κέκαμφα, to bend :' Damm. From the curvature of the nail's head. O, as Λαγχάνω, λέλογχα ; Βάλλω, Βολή. (2) For †γόφος, as λαΜβάνω, λάΜψομαι : from κόπτω, κέκοφα, as Γαμψὸς, Καμψὸς ; Γῆρυς, Κήρυξ. As knocked and beaten into wood, into a wall, &c.

Γονεὺς, parent ; Γόνος, offspring, &c.— R. †γενέω, γέγονα.

32

Γόνυ, genu, the knee ; — joint of grasses.—Allied to Γένυ, the jaw-bone ; Γωνία an angle : Κενὸς, &c. Γάω, to take, receive, (as a curve,) could produce Γόνυ, as †Γάω, to generate, produced Γονή. (2) 'Sanskr. janu, Sax. cneow, Germ. knie. As the Saxon means generation, it prob. belongs to γενέω, and is a shoot or protuberance :' Wbst. (3) 'Hebr. keno, to bring low:' Wr.

Γοργιάζω, to speak like the Sophist Gorgias.

Γοργὸς, quick, prompt, fierce, wild, spirited. — As Γοῖνος, Γόρτυξ, Γέντα, so Γοργὸς for Γοργὸς, ὀργὸς from ἔοργα, to do : Working, prompt to act.

Γοργύρη, a dungeon. —'Prob. allied to Κάρκαρον, Lat. carcer :' Ldd. (2) As in Γοργὸς, from ἔργω, ἔοργα, ἔοργα, εἴργω, to shut up. See above. (3) For γεογγύρα : from γέα, ὀρύσσω, ὥρυγα : A place dug in the ground. In form as Ἄγκῦρα. (4) 'Hebr. geree, to cut stones :' Wr.

Γοργὼ, the monster Gorgo, from Γοργός.

Γοῦν : for γε οὖν, as γὰρ is γ' ἄρ.

Γουνὸς, fertile field, corn-land.—Allied to Γονεὺς, &c. As our moUntain.

Γραῖα, an old woman : γεραιά.

Γράμμα, Γράμμη, &c.: from γράφω, γέγραμμαι.

Γράπις, skin thrown off by reptiles : called by Hesych. the γῆρας old age or old skin : i.e. allied to γεραιὸς, γρφὸς. Compare the second sense of Γραῦς. (2) Mrt. from γράφω : from its furrowed or wrinkled state.

ΓΡΑΣΟΣ, 'the grease and filth in a sheep's fleece ;— odor of buck-goats ;— and of the arm-pit :' Dnn.— Mrt. allies it to γραῦς, (γράθς,) scum. (2) Our grease, Fr. graisse, Ital. grasso.

ΓΡΑΣΣΟΣ, shout of soldiers in beginning the fight. (In Plut. Apophth.)—Q. fro mράσσω, to dash down ? Γ as in Γδοῦπος, Γνόφος.

Γράστις, grass.—R. γράω, γέγρασται, to eat.

Γραῦς, an old woman : γραῖα. And Γραῦς, Γρῆῦς, scum in a pot, 'wrinkled like an old woman's skin', (Steph. 2981.). Γραῖα is also so used.

Γράφω, to scratch, grave, engrave, grave with a stylus or pencil, write, paint.— 'Γράω and Χαράσσω are allied, and Γλάφω :' Dnn. †Χαράω, †χράω, γράω, γράφω. See Χαράσσω. (2) Our grave, with affinities in Saxon, Irish, Welsh, Germ., Dan., Dutch, French. Some add the Hebrew and Chaldee : 'Charath, sculpo:' Mrt. 'Hebr. chreb, chisel :' Wr. See Γλάφω.

Γράω, to eat.—Allied to Γράφω and Χαράσσω, which see. (2) Γ added to †ράω, ῥαίω. See Γρῖτος.

Γρηγορέω, for Ἐγρηγορέω.

Γρῖπος, 'a fisherman's net or basket. From ῥὶψ, ῥιπὸς, osier, as made of such materials :' Dnn. As Γρῖνος is Æol. for ῥινὸς, (Eustath.). (2) Ewing compares our Gripe, which has numerous affinities.

Γρῖφος, the same as Γρῖπος. Also, a riddle or captious question, meant to take one in, as a net.

Γρόμφος, a sow.— 'From the sound, like the Scottish grumphie :' Ldd. So Mrs. Grumph. (2) Allied to Γρόσφος, which see.

Γρόνθος, a clenched fist :—projecting part of a step, —and used like Χελώνιον from the same curved form. —For †Κρόνθος. R. †κρόω, κροαίνω, κρούω, to knock, strike, as Knuckle from Knock. Thus the Fist is 'the hand clenched to give a blow:' Dr. J.— Γ as Γαμψὸς and Καμψός, Γῆρυς and Κῆρυξ.

Γρόνθων, 'the first lessons in flute-playing, the position of the lips and fingers': Dnn. 'Fingering the flute': Ldd. — Perhaps, as the word Γρόνθος, from κρούω: The flute being gently struck with the fingers, as Lucretius says of it 'Digitis pulsata canentium.' (2) For χρόνθων, from χρόνος: Lessons to keep time.

Γρόσφος, a javelin, or its point.—For γρόφος, (as βόΣτρυχος, διΣκος,) from γράφω, 'to scratch, to wound': (Dnn.) Ο as πΟρδαλις, βρΟχέας, βΟλος from βΑλλω, λέλΟγχα, and Lat. dOmo from δΑμῶ.

Γρούνος, a form of Γρῦνος. See Ο in βΟυκάνη.

Γρῦ or Γρύ, 'evidently imitative : a grunt, — the smallest thing, a jot, tittle :' Dnn. As our Grunt, Latin Grumnio.

Γρύζω, to grunt : Γρύλλος, a pig.—Above.

Γρυμαία, a pouch, wallet, sack,—prob. as containing Γρυτή. 'Some think that Γρυμαία, as it was derived from Γρυτή, retains also its signification:' Steph. For Γρυμαία is thought to mean also the same as Γρυτή. Perhaps †γρυΜὴ or †γρυΜὸς was used in the sense of Γρυτή, and thence Γρυμαία. Note, that Τυρός is not only 'cheese', but 'the cheese-market.' And so in other words. (Γρυτίμη, Γρυμή, Γρυμαία.)

Γρυμέα, 'a little fish', Ldd. — Prob. as not worth a γρῦ.

Γρῦνὸς, Γροῦνος, a dry stump.— Suidas : 'Γρυνοί, κορμοὶ Δρύϊνοι, oak logs, by change of Δ into Γ.' And so Hesych. Vice versâ is Δᾶ for Γᾶ, Dulcis from ΓΛυκὸς, †Γυλκύς:—But the Etym. M. for γερυνὸς, γέρων, old.

Γρυπὸς, curved, aquiline.— R. γρὶψ, υπὸς, as Ferus from Fera, &c.

Γρυτή, frippery, old clothes done up: only worth a γρῦ.

Γρὺψ, υπὸς, a griffin with a crooked beak.—As Αἰθὸς, Αἰθοψ, so γυρὸς, †γῦροψ, transp. †γρύοψ, γρὶψ. Much as 'δρατὸς for δαρτός,' (Ldd.) ἔδρακον and δράκων from ἔδαρκον; &c. (2) Lenn. from γρὰω, to gnaw, eat.

Γρῶνος, 'eaten out,—deep ; Γράνη, a grot,—kneading-trough : from †γράω, γρῶ:' Ldd. †Γράωνος, as †Φαων, Φωνή.

Γύα, 'a piece of arable ground, a measure of land, a sown-field, a plain ; met. the womb :' Dnn.—As γΥτὴ, so γΥα from †γάω, Γέα, Γῆ. (2) R. κύω, 'to contain, to conceive:' Dnn. (3) Ewing makes it a limb of ground : see Γυῖον. (4) 'Hebr. gia, a valley:' Wr.

Γύαια, cables fastening ships to γύα land.

Γύαλαι, drinking-cups : from

Γύαλον, 'a hollow, cavity,— middle or swell of a cuirass,—a valley,—a plain, prob. surrounded with hills. —Akin to Κοῖλος, hollow:' Dnn. Indeed from †γύω, allied to γάω to contain, and to κύω to contain, and

33

†χάω, χαίνω, to be hollow. See Γύλιος, Γυρὸς, &c.— In the sense of 'plain', prob. from γύα. (2) ' Hebr. kelo, hollow:' Wr.

Γύης, 'the curved piece of wood in a plough, to which the share was fitted:' Ldd.—Allied to Γύαλον. Or even to †γύω, γάω, to take, receive. (2) Dr. Jones 'as the γυῖον limb of a plough.'

Γυῖον, a limb, espec. said of the lower limbs, feet, knees.—I. e. γυῖον. From †γύω, (see Γύαλον, Γύλιος,) γάω, as in Γαστήρ: Each limb holding to or on another, taking it on, taking it up, just as Δέχομαι is to succeed to, come next, 'Εκ-δοχὴ a succession. Somewhat similarly our word Limb H. Tooke derives from Sax. limpian, to belong to.

Γυιὸς, maimed in the γυῖα limbs. We say, To wing a bird.

Γύλιος, a knapsack.—'From, or akin to, Γαῦλος :' Dnn. And to Γύαλον. All from γάω, †γύω, to hold, contain.

Γυμνὸς, naked, bare.—As σεμνὸς is σεσεμμένος, for †γεγυμένος from †γύω allied to Γύαλον, and to γάω, †χάω 'to stand open' (Dnn.). 'With open head and feet all hare:' Gower.

Γυνὴ, -αικὸς, a woman, wife.—'R. perhaps γόνος, γένω, γίνομαι :' Dnn. And thus all say. As ὀνΤμα, ἄγΤρις, ἀπο-πΤδαρίζω. (2) Allied to Κύω, to conceive, be pregnant.

Γύννις, Γώννις, an effeminate man.—Passow: 'From γιννὸς, a young mule : not γυνή, as the υ is long.' Yet γύΝΝΙΣ (two Ν) points to υ as short in itself.

Γύργαθος, a basket. —'R. γῦρος :' Dnn. Or γυρός. Γ, as the Β in βόλΒιτον.—αθος as ψαμΑΘΟΣ.

Γύρινος, a tadpole, as γυρὸς round.

Γῦρις, the finest meal.—'From the γυρὸς circular motion of the mill:' Gail. Thus Ἄλευρον is 'wheaten flour, also fine flour,' (Dnn.) from ἀλέω, to grind.

Γυρὸς, round, curved, bent, crooked. Γῦρος, a circle, &c.—Allied to Κύκλος, a circle, and from †γύω, γάω, κύω, &c., to hold, contain. So Γύαλον, a hollow. †Γύω, †γυαρὸς or †γυερὸς, γυρός. (2) 'Hebr. gur, to stoop:' Wr.

Γὶψ, γυπὸς, a vulture.—'Akin to, or from, Κύπτω : from the usually crouching attitude it observes:' Dnn. (2) ' R. †γύω, †γύπτω, γάω, to take:' Lenn.

Γύψος, chalk, gypsum.— R. γῆ, δψω, [δψα] : 'Limestone prepared for plaster by fire:' Dnn. Τ as in γΤνὴ, ἄγΤρις, ὀνΤμα. (2) 'Chald. GPS, to plaster:' Wbst.

Γωλεὸν, a cavern, den.—'Akin to Γαῦλος. R. κοῖλος;' Dnn. Rather, as Ψάω, Ψαλὴ, so γάω, γωλεόν : allied to †γύω, γύαλον.

Γωνία, Γῶνος, a corner, angle.—As Γράω, Γρῶνος, so γάω, γῶνος : γάω, to hold, contain : allied to Γυρός, curved ; Κάμπτω, to bend, &c. Dnn. compares Γόνυ, a knee. Add Κενός.

Γωρῦτος, a quiver.—'Akin to Χωρέω, to contain:' Dnn.

F

Δ.

Δᾶ : Æolic for Γᾶ. So children say Dood-bye, &c.
Δα-, much.—For δασύ, thick. (2) For δίά. (3)
'Heb. dai, sufficientia :' Mrt.

Δαγὸς, a waxen image.—'A Thessalian word :' Dnn.
—Perh. orig. a melting, dissolving thing, for τάγὸς from
τέτᾶγα (see τάΓηνον,) the regular perf. mid. of τήκω, ξω.
As Men are called Θνητοὶ, Dying persons. Thus in the
O. T., 'My heart is like wax, it is melted :' 'As wax
melteth, so the wicked person' &c. 'The hills melted
like wax.' (Only in Theocr. 2. 110.)

Δάειρα, Proserpine.—'The knowing one,' say Ldd.
and Dnn.: from †δάω, to learn. (2) Tzetzes from
δαΐς : The torch-bearer, as being the same as Hecaté
shining by night.

Δάζομαι, the same as Δαίω. Δάημι, Δαίω, to know.
See in †Δάω. Mrt. proposes Hebr. deah, knowledge.

Δαὴρ, a husband's brother.—'Whom the wife δέδαε
becomes acquainted with on her marriage :' Damm. Or
who becomes acquainted with the wife.

Δαὶ, 'for Δάεε, Δάει, tell me, I pray thee. Πῶς δαί ;
how, pray ? how then ?' Ewing.

Δαιδάλλω, to work cunningly, use curious arts.— As
Ψάω, Ψάλλω, so †δάω, to learn, †δάλλω, δαιδάλλω, like
ΜΑΙμάω : To be learned.

Δαΐζω, to slay.—R. δαίω, to divide, cleave.

Δαίμων, Δαήμων, knowing.— R. δαίω, δάημι, to
learn.

Δαίμων, a god, deity, chance, destiny.—'Some make
it prim. knowing, [above]. but prob. from δαίω, to divide
or distribute destinies :' Ldd.

Δαίνυμι, as Δαίω, to divide, assign a share, espec. at
meals : Δαίνυμαι, to be assigned a meal, to dine.

Δάϊος, knowing, cunning, δαήμων. See Δάημι.

Δάϊος, miserable : i. e. one who has known and experienced ill.—Above. Virgil : 'Haud ignāra mali' &c.

Δάϊος, Δήϊος, burning, consuming, hostile.—R. δαίω,
to burn.

Δαίρω, Δέρω, to flay, skin, cudgel.—R. δαίω, †δέω,
to divide, mangle, &c. So Ψάω, Ψαίρω.

Δαΐς, a torch.—R. δαίω, to burn.

Δαΐς, battle, war.—Allied to Δάϊος, burning, consuming, and hostile. 'The war ἀμφι-δεδήει burnt round
the city,' Hom. And 'The circling press of battle δε-
δήει about thee.'

Δαίς, Δαίτη, a feast.—R. †δαίω, δαίνυμι, to dispense
i. e. viands. (2) R. †δάω, δάπτω, to mangle.

Δαιτρὸς, a divider, carver, who portions out.—R.
δαίω, to divide.

Δαίω, from obsolete †ΔΑΩ. Ormston well unites the
meanings : '1. to divide, part, distribute. 2. to give a
banquet, i.e. distribute viands. 3. to kindle, burn,
glow, for fire resolves and separates what it consumes.'

34

4. to teach, i. e. to dispense knowledge. 5. to know,
i.e. to acquire what is thus dispensed.'

Δάκνω, †Δάκω, †Δήκω, to bite.—R. †δάω, δέδακα,
δαίω, to divide. (2) 'Hebr. dekes, to break :' Wr.

Δάκος, a serpent of dangerous bite.—Above.

Δάκρυ, a tear.—R. †δάκω, δάκνω, to bite: 'Being of
a briny, biting taste :' Pkh. A biting or bitter tear.
'Lucretius speaks of salt tears, others of bitter tears.
Matt. 26. 75 : He wept πικρῶς bitterly :' Becm. Some
explain it as arising ' ex præmorsā animā.'

Δάκτυλος, a finger.—Considered as soft for δέκτυλος
(as τρΕπω, τέτρΑμμαι ; μΕγας, mAgnus,) from δέκω the
same as δείκω, δέδεκται, to point at, as Persius ' Digito
monstrarier, Hic est.' Isaiah 58. 9 : 'The putting
forth of the finger.' And so from Δεικετὸς Pkh. derives
Digitus.— Or from δέχομαι : As receiving or taking up
things. (2) R. δαΐζω, δαΐξω, δεδδίκται, δέδακται, (as
'Αΐσσω, "Δσσω,) a thing divided, a division of the hand.

Δάκτυλος, a dactyl : consisting, as the finger, of one
long and two shorter joints.—Above.

Δάκτυλος, a 'date, in its shape resembling a finger,
' oblongā gracilitate', Forcell.

Δαλὸς, 'a burnt-out torch,—and so an old man ;—
faggot, beacon-light :' Ldd.—R. †δάω, δαίω, to burn.

Δάμαλις, a heifer.—R. δαμάω : Fit to be subdued to
the yoke.

Δάμαρ, a wife.—Tamed to the marriage yoke, from
Δαμάω, Δάμνημι, agrees with δαΐζω in the sense 'to
slay', from †δάω, †δέδαμαι, δαίω.—Also, to tame, subdue, bring under the yoke, whence Damm rightly allies
it to †Δάω, Διδάσκω, to teach, i. e. make tractable and
obedient. 'He learned obedience', Hebr. 5. 8. (2) Our
tame, Sax. tamian, &c. 'Hebr. demec, to level :' Wr.

Δανάκη, freight-money to Charon, from δάνος, a gift.
As 'Ερι8ΑΚΗ. But the Etym. M. from δανὸς, dry, i. e.
a dried-corpse or skeleton (σκελετὸν) money.—Also
a small Persian coin.

Δάνος, a gift, Δανείζω, to give on loan.—R. †δάω,
δαίω, to divide, i. e. distribute, disperse. 'He hath dispersed, he hath given to the poor :' Psa. 112. 9. Allied
to †Δόω, Δίδωμι. Danam, i. e. dabo, is in Plautus.

Δανὸς, burnt, dried up.—R. †δάω, to burn.

Δάξ, with the teeth.—Allied to †δάκω, ξω, to bite.
So Λάξ, Πύξ.

Δανάπη, 'expense, prodigality. R. δάπτω :' Dnn. So
all say. See Δαψιλής.

Δάπεδον, floor, ground, plain.—'R. δᾶ for γᾶ, πέδον :'
Dnn. (2) Δα-, very ; πέδον : Very flat, level, πεδινόν.
(3) See Δάπος.

Δάπις, a carpet, footcloth or footstool.—'Akin to Δάπεδον :' Dnn.— Prob. from

†Δάπος, floor, ground, as in 'Αλλο-δαπὸς, &c.— R.

δᾶ, for γᾶ. See δάΠΕΔΟΝ. In form as ΤρΙΠΟΣ. (2) The same as †Τάπος, whence Ταπεινὸς, and as Δάπις and Τάπις, Τάπης : all from †τάω, τείνω, to stretch out. Compare Τόπος. (3) Corrupted from ἔδαφος, ᾽δάφος. Δάπτω, to rend, mangle, devour.—R. †δάω, δαίω, to divide, as Κνάω, Κνάπτω.

Δαρδάπτω, 'the same as Δάπτω, as Μαρμαίρω :' Ldd. And taken from it, for in the latter the P is accounted for from the following P.

ΔΑΡΕΙΚΟΣ, a Daric, a coin struck in the reign of a Darius.

Δαρθάνω, to sleep.—R. δέρω, ἐδάρθην, to flay a skin, then to lie on it, as from Δέρμα, a skin, is Dormio. Or there was a word †Δάρος or †Δαρή, a skin, as Δέρας : then †δάρθω, δαρθάνω. So Οἰκέω is to dwell in an Οἶκος. Homer : ἐν κώεσιν οἰῶν Ἔδραθεν. Virgil : 'Cæsarum ovium ... Pellibus incubuit stratis, somnosque petivit'.

Δάρος, Att. and Dor. of δηρός.

Δασμὸς, division, distribution, spoil, reward, share of taxes to pay.—R. †δάω, δάζομαι.

Δασπλῆς, -ῆτος, terrific. ΔαΣπλῆτος, like βόΣτρυχος, λέΣχη, for Δα-πλῆτος, allied to 'Α-πλησΤΟΣ : Filled full, then (like ᾽Αδινὸς,) excessive, vehement, oppressive, (2) R. δφσὶ, πλῆτος as in Τειχεσι-πλῆτης : Advancing with torches, frightening. Or δα—: Advancing powerfully, coming on, towering. (3) R. δα, πλήσσω : Striking with awe. But this would be ΔασπλήΞ.

Δάσος, a thicket.—From

Δασὺς, rough, shaggy, bushy, thick.—As Τραχὺς rough from †τράω, τιτράω, to transpierce : so Δασὺς (like Δασμὸς) from †δάω, to divide, δαΐζω, 'to cleave, pierce :' (Dnn.) Piercing to the hand, rugged.—Lennep as divided into numerous particles or eminences, opposed to level or smooth. Compare Κραναὸς, Κραυρός. (2) Allied to Λάσιος, as Δάκρυμα, Lacryma. (3) As Δά-πεδον, so Δα-σὺς, from δα, σὺς : Bristly, hairy like a hog.

Δατέομαι, to divide :—†δάω, †δέδαται, δάζομαι.

Δατισμὸς, tautology.—From one Datis, who said "Ηδομαι καὶ τέρπομαι καὶ χαίρομαι : whence Δάτιδος μέλος in Aristoph.

Δαῦλος, 'rough, hairy, the same as and akin to Δασὺς, and metaph. close, secret :' Dnn.—But better as usu. derived (like Δά-σκιος,) from δα, ὕλη, shrubs, brushwood.—Δαῦλος is also the same as Δαλός.

Δαύω, to burn, as †Δάω, Δαίω.—Also, to sleep : from δα, ὐaω to sleep, as ῎Αεσα, ᾽Ιαύω. (Very rare : in Sappho.)

Δάφνη, a laurel.—' R. δάπτω, δέδαφα : for prophets used to eat laurel as they prophesied, whence the Pythian priestess was called Δαφνη-φάγος :' Lenn. So ' Lauram momordit', Juv. ' Sacras innoxia laurûs Vescar', Tibull.

Δαψιλὴς, 'profuse, sumptuous, abundant. R. δάπτω, ψω :' Dnn. Compare Δαπάνη.

†ΔΑΩ, †ΔΕΩ, ΔΙΩ, †ΔΟΩ, ΔΥΩ, all Primitives,

and allied : signifying to 'penetrate' and 'divide'. Hence Δάζομαι, Δαίω, Δαίρω, Δέρω, Δατέομαι, Δίδωμι, &c. Dunbar explains Δύω 'to penetrate, to go through' : Donnegan, ' to penetrate into.'

Δὲ, but :—sometimes 'and' :—sometimes as Δή.—Ormston says : ' R. δέω, to bind; connect. It is frequently connective.' So Pkh. also. But in the first sense, rather from †δέω, †δάω, to divide : (See δΕρω :) allied to Διὰ and Di- in Di-versely, &c. ' A word of distinction :' Greg. And so Lennep. (2) See in Μέν. (3) Mrt. from δέω, deficio.

Δέατο, he seemed : read by Wolfe in Od. 6. 242, for the old Δόατο, which for δοάσσατο, from δοιάζομαι, to choose between δοιὼ two suppositions. Buttm. refers both to δίδαα, to search out, so judge : He was judged of thought. But how can this possibly be ? Thiersch well keeps to the old Δόατο.

Δεδίσκομαι, Δειδ-, to welcome. As γΙνομαι is allied to γΕΙνομαι and γΕνέω, so δεδίσκομαι to †δείκω, †δέκω, δήκομαι and δέχομαι, to receive. Sometimes to give in welcome as a cup, present.

Δεδίσσομαι, Δεδίσκομαι, to frighten : and Δειδίσσομαι, which is also to be frightened, to fear. So Δέδια, to fear : Δείδω, to fear : Δέος, fear. Also, Δίω, ' to drive, scare, frighten, put to flight, repel : also to be driven away, flee, be afraid :' Dnn. And Διώκω, to drive, impel, expel, pursue, follow.—All these are allied, and mean to go Διὰ through, or cause to go Διὰ through any space, 'per-sequor', pursue, follow, drive on, drive off, scare away. But δΕος, δΕίδω, more immediately from the obsolete †ΔΕΩ, to penetrate through, as Δύω. See on †ΔΑΩ.

Δέελος, Δῆλος, manifest, clear.—Buttm. for ἴδηλος, from ἴδέω, to see. Then δέελος has η resolved into εε, as vēmens into vEhEmens. (2) Damm from †δέω, δεθήει, δαίω, to burn : Bright, conspicuous. (3) Mrt. from δαίω, to know. ' Known and read of all men :' N. T.

Δεέω, to want : in Δέω.

Δέημα, entreaty. Above.

Δεῖ, it is binding, necessary, fitting.—R. δέω, to bind. So Δέον, 'what is binding, needful :' Ldd.

Δείδω, to fear : Δείμα, fear : in Δεδίσσομαι.

Δείκελον, -ηλον, Δίκηλον, a representation. — R. †δείκω, ' to represent by painting' (Dnn.). ' She SHOWS a body rather than a life :' Shaksp.

†Δείκω, Δείκνυμι, to point out, indicate, show.—As Δαῖδα and Tæda, ἀΔμὴν and ἀΤμὴν, Δάτις and Τάτης, buildeD and builT, so Δείκω is allied to Τείνω, to stretch out (the hand), as Τεταγὼν, touching, is referred to Τάω, Τείνω. From the same root is Δέχομαι, to take, receive, and Δεικανόομαι to welcome. Compare Δέω, Δέομαι. (2) ' Hebr. dak, to observe :' Mrt.

Δείλη, 'akin to εἵλη, the time when the day is hottest, just after noon ;—gen. the whole afternoon ;—then the latter part of it, just before evening :' Ldd. But whence the Δ ? Dnn. knows nothing of the first meanings, makes it the latter part of the day, and adds :

35

Some say, towards the morning and evening twilight.' This justifies Lennep's derivation from δειλός, 'cowardly, weak', (Dnn.) then weak in light, dull, faint. Or from δίω, to fail: δεελή, δειλή. Or δέω, ὕλη: a failing of light.

Δεῖνα,' some certain person or thing, that one cannot or wishes not to name:' Dnn.—'The Chald. den, he', Mrt. 'Hebr. denee,' Wr.— Yet perh. allied to †Δείκω, through Τείνω, to stretch out (the hand) towards. 'Digito monstrarior, Hic est :' Pers.

Δεινός, terrible: R. δέος. But Δειλός, fearing, timid, weak, faint. (2) Wr. mentions Hebr. dehel, to affright.

Δεῖπνον, the morning, afternoon or evening meal, victuals.—'Akin to or from Δάπτω, Δαίω :' Dnn. That is, through obsol. †δέω, †δάω. Compare Δέλεαρ, Δέλος, and Δαὶς, and Latin Dapes.

Δειράς, Δειρή : the same as Δέρη.

Δείρω, ten.—'R. †δέκω, δέχομαι : from the TEN fingers, to grasp, hold :' Dnn. 'As containing all the units :' Pkh.

Δεκάζω, to bribe.— Steph. from †δέκω, δέχομαι : To bribe by causing one to hope to receive from me. So Δωρο-δοκέω. (2) R. δέκα : 'To bribe by giving a tenth part :' Dr. Jones. 'R. δέκα, like Lat. decuriare, said of bribing the Roman tribes : Ernest. Clav. Cic. :' Dnn. But Forcell. understands this otherwise.

Δέλεαρ, Δέλετρον, Δέλος, a bait, lure.— As Ψάω, Ψέλιον, so 'R. δαίω, to feast :' Mrt. Through †δέω allied to Δεῖπνον, food. So

Δέλετρον is also a lantern, and, as Δαλὸς, may be from †δέω, δαίω, δέθω, to kindle, burn. Ldd. and Dnn. understand it as 'prob. used in catching fish by night.' See above.

Δέλτος, a tablet, prop. in the form of the Delta Δ, this called from Hebr. daleth. (2) 'Or Δέλτος from Hebr. deleth, column of writing :' Wr.

Δέλφαξ, ὁ, ἡ, a hog, sow.—' Prob. from δελφύς :' Dnn. 'As having a large δελφύς :' Lenn. 'Prop. said of the female :' Greg. 'From its fruitful δελφύς :' Mrt. Perhaps Δελφὺς meant, like Νηδὺς, the paunch as well as the womb.

Δελφὶν, a dolphin. Lenn. from Δέλφαξ, as like it : δελφακίν. Plural, heavy masses of lead let fall from ships. We say a Pig of lead, and Sow metal, though Dr. J. says he knows not why. (2) Common to the Armoric, Irish, Welsh, &c. Webster from Welsh dolf, a curve, winding.

Δελφὺς, Δελφύα, the womb.—The Æol. is Βελφὺς, that is, Ἑλφὺς (B as in Βαῦνος,) from ἕλω, capio, concipio : or from ἕλλω, ἐλίσσω, ἐλύω, to envelope, cover up. Much in form as ΒαΦΟΣ. (2) Δελφύα for δελφύα (as Θεὸς, Deus ; burTHen, burDen,) from ϑῆλυς φυὴ, fœminea natūra. So κΕδνὸς from κΗδος.

Δέμας, frame, body, form of the body, as we use the Build. (Κατὰ) δέμας, in the form or likeness of.— R. δέμω. So Δομή. (2) 'Chald. dema, to be like :' Mrt.

Δέμνια, pl., bed, couch.— Prop. a frame, as above.

(2) R. δέω, δέδεμαι, δεδεμένα : 'Tied together from timbers :' Damm. As ΚρηΔΕΜΝΟΝ.

Δέμω, to construct, build.— R. δέω, δέδεμαι, to bind together.

Δενδαλὶς, Δανδ., a cake of toasted barley.—' R. τένδω, to eat up greedily :' Mrt. Δ as in †Δείκω.

Δενδίλλω, to move the eyes quickly. glance at.— R. †δενδέω, δονέω, δινέω, to stir, ἴλλος, the eye. For δενίλλω ; Δ repeated, as B in βάλΒιτον ; or Δ as τενΔ, tenDo. (2) Δίω, †δίλλω, †δεδίλλω, δενΔίλλω, as ΙΝδάλλομαι : To chase or pursue (with the eye). Compare Βλέπω from †Βλέω.

Δένδρον, a tree.— Δέρω, to peel, †δεδέρω, †δέδρον, δένδρον, as ΙΝδάλλομαι, ταΝρο, μαΝθάνω. So Δόρυ is 'a trunk of a tree, a tree': (Dnn.)

Δέννος, a reviling.—' Perh. Ion. from δεινός :' Dnn. 'To speak δεινὰ dreadful words :' Soph.

Δεξαμενὴ, a tank : A. l. m. of δέχομαι. And 'matter, as susceptible of all manner of forms :' Dnn.

Δεξιὰ, Δεξιτερὰ, the right hand by which we take, welcome, or point.— R. δέχομαι, ξομαι. See †Δείκω.

Δέομαι, to want, ask : in Δέω.

Δέος, fear : in Δεδίσσομαι.

Δέπας, a goblet. — Hesych. for δέκας, (as λόΚος, luPus,) from δέκομαι to pledge. Δεικανόωντο δέπασσιν, Hom.

Δέρας, -ος, -μα, a hide : δέρω.

Δερὰς, Δειρὰς, Δειρὴ, a ridge of hills.— R. δέρη, from rising up as a neck above the parts below. So Λόφος has both senses, 'and compare Collis and Collum, and Jugum :' Ldd.

Δέρη, Δείρη, the neck.—'R. δέρω, to flay : as it was by the neck that operation usu. commenced : Damm :' Dnn. So Λόφος from λέπω, λέλοφα. Compare Τραχηλίζω from τράχηλος, and Σφαγὴ is the throat from σφάζω. Damm says too : 'The neck among the ancients was quite uncovered,' and Δέρω is 'to uncover, expose': (Dnn.)

Δέρκομαι, to look on or at.— R. δέρω, δέδερκα : To uncover or expose for myself (See the last part above), i.e. to open to my view, and examine. (2) Δέρκω, for †δρέκω, ἔδρακον, whence Δράκων. And †δρέκω for †τρέκω, from τορέω, τρέω, to pierce. See Ἀ-τρεκὴς and Τορός. We speak of a piercing eye. (3) 'Δι- -ορέω, to see through, contr. to δρέω :' Damm. Then †δρέκω, &c.

Δέρρις, 'a hide; pl. cloak of skins or leather or hair-cloth.— R. δέρω :' Dnn. So δέρας.

Δέρτρον, the caul, i. e. a skin.— As above.

Δέρω, to skin, flay, strip, bare, stripe.— R. †δέω, †δάω, to divide, δαίρω, to flay. 'Akin is Τείρω, Tero :' Dnn.

Δεσμὸς, bond.— R. δέω, δέδεσμαι, to bind.

Δεσπόζω, to be master or lord of.—' R. prob. δεσμὸς, δέω, to bind :' Dnn. Δέω, †δέπω, as βλέΠω, ὀρέΠω, then †δέσπω, as ἕΣπω, λέΣχη. In form like ἁρμΟΖΩ. Or for δεσΜόζω as corPus, carPentum. (2) For δεπόζω, δεψόζω from δεψέω to soften, tame, subdue.

Δέσποινα, a mistress : Above.

Δετή, 'sticks bound together, a fagot :' Ldd.—R. δέω, δέδεται.

Δεῦκος, sweetness : Ἀ-δευκής, bitter, unpleasant.—R. δέχομαι, accipio : What is acceptable, pleasant. Τ, as δοῦρος, &c.

Δευόμαι, as Δέομαι, Δέω.

Δεῦρο, Δευρί, hither. And plural Δεῦτε, i.e. δεῦρ' ἴτε, says Buttm. As γλεῦκος and γλυκύς, (and see in Δεύτερος,) so δεῦρο from δέω, δῦμι, to come or go in. Δεῦτε might thus be from Δῦμι.

Δεύτατος, last.—And

Δεύτερος, second.—R. δεύομαι, δέδευται, to fail. To come off second best. (2) 'Comparative of Δύο, as γλεῦκος from γλυκύς :' Ldd. This is not so well for Δεύτατος.

Δεύω, to wet, moisten, knead.—The same as Δύω, 'to go under water', (Dnn.) used actively. (2) From obs. †δέω, to divide, allied to Διά through, and Διαίνω to wet. Compare then Δέφω as Γράφω. (3) Our old verb, dew, be-dew, Germ. thau.

Δέφω, to moisten, soften, knead.—'Another form of Δεύω :' Dnn. Thus, δεΤω, δέΓω, δέΘω. (2) From obs. †δέω as in Δεύω. See γράφω.

Δέχομαι, to take, receive, hail, welcome.—See in †Δείκω.

Δεψέω, the same as Δέφω, δέψω.

Δέω, to bind.—Allied to †Τέω, Τείνω, Ταίνω, whence Ταινία, a band, like Διά-δημα. (2) Strangely, it might even be the same as †δάω, δαίω, to divide. Thus in Homer ἥλοισι πεπαρμένον, pierced with nails, is translated by Clarke 'CON-FIXUM,' fixed tight.

Δέω, Δέομαι, to want, need, beg, ask.—Dr. Jones takes it 'to be bound with necessity or want :' making δέω, to bind, passive. This would agree with Δεῖ, it is binding, necessary : for in Norfolk they say, 'You don't want to do this', i.e. are not bound. (2) The same as †Τέω, Τείνω, to stretch out i.e. the hand, to ask from want ;—as Τεταγών, touching, from †Τάω. Compare †Δείκω. So Δάπις and Τάπης ; Δαῖδα, Τεδα.

Δή, for Δάε, 'learn', as To wit is 'to know', and Scilicet is Scire licet, and Videlicet is Vidēre licet : You may know well, be assured, be sure, for certain, indeed, in fact, exactly so, that is to say, forsooth. So Δαί. (2) For 'Ηδη. ?

Δῆγμα, a bite.—R. †δήκω, †δάκνω, δάκνω, δέδηγμαι.

Δηθά, Δην, for a long time, Δηθύνω, to delay, Δηρός, long, too long.—All allied to Δέω, to bind together, as Continual from Con-tenee : and Connectedly. ΔΗΘΑ as ἡλιΘΑ.—Some compare Δή and 'Ηδη, but with no sense.

Δήϊος, same as third Δάϊος.

Δηλέομαι, to lay waste, spoil.—Allied to Δήϊος from †δάω, δαίω, to burn : †δάω, †δάελος, burning, †δῆλος, δηλέομαι : much as Ζέω, Ζῆλος, Ζηλόω.—Or allied to Δαίω, Δαΐζω. (2) 'Hebr. delee, to exhaust :' Wr.

Δήλομαι, to wish. —'Prob. for Θέλομαι :' Wr. As Θεός, Deus ; burTHen, burDen. Ewing : 'R. δηλή,

will, Dor. from δέλω.' Or Δηλή from δηλῶ to signify by words. Then Δήλομαι. (2) Allied to Δέομαι. ?

Δῆλος : in Δέελος.

Δημήτηρ, Ceres.—' Prob. δῆ for γῆ, μήτηρ :' Dnn. Mother Earth. See Δᾶ. (2) For Δηὰ μήτηρ.

Δημεύω, to confiscate.—R. δῆμος : Make public property.

Δημοκόπος, a demagogue.—R. δῆμος, κόπτω a babbler, orator.

Δημάομαι, to banter, jest, i.e. speak in a common vulgar manner, δημωδῶς.

Δῆμος, a people.—'Prob. from δέμω :' Dnn.—Rather from δέω, δέδημαι, (as in Διά-δημα), to bind together. Populus, says Cicero, is a company 'utilitatis consensu sociatus.' Ormston : ' Bound together by the same laws, manners and government.'

Δημός, fat, tallow.—' Perh. from δέω, to bind :' Ldd. 'For the flesh and bones are held together by the cellular membrane, the seat of the fat': Lenn. (2) Passow thinks from δαίω, to burn. 'As wont to be burnt and lighted :' Mrt.

Δήν : in Δηθα.

Δηνάριον, the Roman Denarius, from decem, deoēni, deni.

Δῆνος, plan, deliberation.—' Akin to Δήω :' Ldd. An endeavour to find some means or expedients. (2) R. δήν : Requiring long investigation. (3) ' Or Hebr. din, judgment :' Mrt.

Δῆρις, battle, strife.—' Akin to, or from δαίω :' Dnn. I.e. to kindle, light up, like Δαΐς which see : †δέερις, δῆρις.

Δηρός, Δαρός, long : in Δῆθα.

Δῆτα, the same as Δή. 'R. δή :' Ldd. Compare ἐνΘΑ, &c.

Δήω, to find.—' Prob. akin to †δάω, δαῆναι, to learn :' Ldd. and Dnn.

Δηὼ, Ceres, 'for Δη-μήτηρ, the goddess who discovered corn:' Ewing. Rather then from δήω, to discover.

Διά, through.—R. †δίω, †δάω, δαίω, to divide. See †ΔΑΔ.

Δια-βόω, 'to thrust through so as to stop up :' Ldd. βόω.

Διάζομαι, 'to put the woof διά through the warp, weave', says Dr. Jones. And Ldd. thus : ' To set the threads in the loom, fix the warp, and so begin.' Mrt. makes διά disjunctive, quoting Julius Pollux : 'This one weaves his web, ὁ δὲ διάζεται, but the other (disjungit) divides it.' Dnn. says : ' Perh. from δίς, twice.' I.e. δι-, Διαίνω, to wet, moisten.—'Akin are Διερός, Δεύω :' Dnn. From †δίω, to divide, penetrate : to go διά through. Allied too to Δύω, to go under, Δύντω. See Δεύω. (2) Mrt. from Διός, gen. of Ζεύς : ' Ab æthere lapso.'

Δίαιτα, mode of life, manner of living, regimen.—Lenn. from †δίω, †δάω, δαίω, δέω, δίδωμι : ' A tribuendo, [distribuendo,] eat quæ victūs rationem præscribit, vitæ institutum.'—Or allied to Δίεμαι, Δίζημαι, Διώκω : for Dnn. explains Διαιτάομαι ' to follow a particular mode of life, to follow a regimen.' Compare Διαίνω, and

Δίαιτα, judgment, arbitration. — Allied to Διώκω, to pursue, prosecute ; Δίζημαι, to seek, search ; Διέμαι. I.e. †δίω, †διάω, δίαιτα. Compare Διαίνω. :

Διάκονος, Διήκονος, a servant, attendant, deacon. — ' Buttm. from obs. διάκω, or διήκω, akin to διώκω.' — R. διὰ κόνις, [κονέω]:' Dnn. But Buttmann's idea was to avoid this last, as A is long. This too opposes the R. διὰ ἀκονδω, to urge, stimulate (oneself). But perhaps διΗκονος was an Ionic form, and the H was changed into a Doric long A. The same difficulty prevails in the word which follows. But see especially the last obs. in Ἐδων. And observe δΑρός.

Διακόσιοι, Διηκόσιοι, 200. — Nearly all from δὶs, ἑκατόν, as Δί-αυλος. And, as πλοῦΤΟΣ, πλούΣΙΟΣ, so ἑκατὸν or †ἐκΟτὸν (as τέττΟρα Maittaire p.412,) made ἑκΰΣΙΟΣ, then δι-ηκόσιος, δι-ἀκόσιος, as in Διάκονος.

Διακωχή, Διοκωχή : in Ἀνακωχή.

Διαμπάξ : in Ἄπαξ.

Διαπρύσιος, ' going through, piercing, thrilling, far-stretching ;—manifest. Prob. formed Æol. from περάω:' Ldd. I.e. †περύω, †πρύω, whence Πρύμνα.

Διάσια, a festival Διὸς of Jove.

Δίασμα, warp, web ; διάζομαι.

Διαττάω, to sift. — R. διὰ, ἔττω, ἄσσω, to make to leap through. (2) Dnn. from σάω, σήθω, to sift : but the two T T ?

Διδάσκω, to teach. — †Δάω, †δάσκω, (as †Βάω, Βάσκω,) διδάσκω. (See †Δάω.) So

Διδράσκω, (as Διδάσκω,) to flee: R. δράω, δρήμι.

Δίδυμος, twin. — Usu. derived by redupl. from δύο. But, as we have ΤΡΙδυμοι, Damm rightly from δὶs, and the verb δύω, i.e. two ἐκ γαστρὸς ΚΑΤΑ-ΔΥΣΕΙ μιᾷ. Compare Δίκελλα.

Δίδωμι, redupl. of †δόω, †δῶμι, to give : allied to †δάω, to divide, i.e. distribute, dispense. ' Ready to distribute :' N. T.

Δίεμαι, to hunt after, press out, speed. — R. †δίω, διάκω, See Δίζημαι.

Διέρῆμα, a funnel, tunnel. See †Ἐρύω 2.

Διερὸs, liquid, juicy, fresh, active ; — liquid, of sounds. ' Akin to Διαίνω, to wet :' Ldd. I.e. from †δίω, δενΰ, δύω.

Δίζημαι, to seek out ;— ask a reason, demand. — R. †δίω, †δίζω, the same as Διώκω, to drive, pursue. See Δίεμαι.

Δίζω, to be in doubt : from δὶs : To be of two minds, as Διστάζω. But, as it means also Δίζημαι, it is usu. referred to it.

Διθύραμβος, Bacchus, and a dithyrambic ode named from him. — Gen. referred to δὶs, θύρα, (as Ἴαμβος, Θρίαμβος,) from his double entrance into life, first from Semelé, then from the thigh of Jupiter. Thus Dryden speaks of the door of life.—It is objected that Δι is long. Rather then from Διὸs, θύρα : for Διθύραμβος.

Δικάζω, to judge. Δίκαιος, just : R. δίκη.

Δίκελλα, a two-teethed mattock. — R. δὶs, κέλλω to drive. (2) R. δίχα, bifariam ; -ελλα, as Θύελλα.

Δίκη, right, justice, law, established custom or man-
38

ner acting as law : — action at law, judgment, &c. (κατὰ) δίκην, after the manner of, like.—Allied to Δίεμαι, Δίζημαι, Διώκω, (through †δίω, †δέδικα, as in Δίκω,) to seek, pursue, as the Greeks say Δίκην διώκω, and Plautus ' Jus meum persequi.' One's right sought or pursued at law : — right thus obtained :—the law and justice thus establishing it. (2) R. δίχα, as between two. Aristotle, ' as dividing a thing into two equal parts.' Thus equality is intended in our Bisect. (3) R. δέκομαι, to receive. The received custom. Changed from †δέκη. (4) ' Chald. deca, to be pure, just :' Mrt.

Δίκηλον, the same as Δείκελον.

Δίκροος, Δίκρὸς, double : from δὶs, κάρα, κρά, the head. ' So Δί-κραιος, Δί-κραιρος, Δί-κρᾶνος :' Dnn.

Δίκτῦνα, Diana, goddess of the chace : from Δίκτυον, a casting-net, hunting-net : from Δίκω, to throw. — 'R. δίω, [δέδικα,] to drive :' Dnn. And Δίεμαι is to press on. (2) ' Chald. decha, propello :' Mrt. ' Hebr. deches, to drive :' Wr.

Δινέω, to whirl : to thresh out, ' as done by cattle going round in a circle :' Dnn. And

Δίνη, a whirling, whirlwind, whirlpool. Δῖνος, dizziness :—a round area, threshing-floor : — large round goblet.—R. †δίω, δίεμαι. ' For the [wind or] water δῖνεται :' Mrt. Αs κίω, κινέω. Above. (2) Our din may be allied,

Δῖξὸς, double, from Δὶs, Δισσὸς, as Τρὶs, Τριξός.

Διόνυσος, Bacchus.—' For, when he was born, he pierced ἔνυξε (νύσσω,) the thigh of Jove Διόs : such is the fable :' Mrt. ' He was taken from Semele's womb, and inserted in Jupiter's thigh, and thence in time came forth :' Lenn. (2) ' From Διόs, his father's name, and Νῦσα, the place of his education in India :' E. Valpy. (3) The Etym. M. explains the Ionic form Δεύνυσος ' king of Νυσα', from the Indian δεῦνος.

Δῖος, divine : from †Δὶs, Διόs.

Διπλᾶξ, Δίπλάσιος, double. — 'R. δὶs, πλάσιος, πλήσιος, equal, as in Παρα-πλήσιον. Others prefer δὶs, πλᾶξ, a flat surface, which seems preferable :' Dnn. Δίπλαξ would make Διπλάσιος, much as Ἀφροδίτη Ἀφροδίσιος.

Διπλόος, double : in Ἁπλόος.

Δὶs, twice. — ' For δυὶs from δύο :' Buttm. Τρὶs from τριοὶ is easier. Δὶs by imitation.

Δὶs, g. Διόs, Jove : ' Cretan Θιόs, Laconic Σιόs ; hence a variety Ζεὺs, also Σδεὺs, Θεόs, Deus :' Dnn. See Θεόs. (2) R. †δίω, διαίνω, to wet, διερὸs, δενΰ, &c. From the moist atmosphere.

Δίσκος, a quoit,—round trencher ;—sun's disk.— R. δίκω, to throw, as λέΣχη. Hesych. has ' δίκον καὶ δίσκον :' (Maitt.)

Δισσὸs, double : R. δὶs, as Τρὶs, Τρισσός.

Διστάζω, to doubt.— R. δὶs, †στάω: To stand between two roads, uncertain which to take.

Διφάσιος, double.— R. δὶs, φάσις, appearance : or φάσις, speech, as Lat. bi-fariam from ' fari': said in two ways. So Τριφάσιος.

Διφάω, to seek, search for, enquire.—'Allied to Δίω, Δίζημι:' Dnn. And to Διώκω. (2) R. διὰ, ὑφάω: To seek for by touching softly.

Διφθέρα, hide, sack, parchment, tent.—Soft for †δε-φθέρα, from δέφω, †δέφθην, to knead leather. (2) R. δὶς, φθείρω, φθερῶ, to taint, i. e. soak. As Bis-cuit is French for Twice-baked.

Δίφρος, chariot-board which could hold two;—chariot;—seat, stool.—R. δι-φόρος, from δὶς, φέρω.

Δίχα, Δίχθα, in two ways.—R. δὶς, as Τρὶς, Τρίχα, Τρίχθα.

Διψάω, to thirst.—'Διψάω and Διφάω are kindred words:' Dnn. Prop. to seek or search for (drink). To Thirst, 'to want to drink:' Dr. J.

Δίω, and

Διώκω: in Δεδίσσομαι.—'Or Hebr. delek, to press upon:' Wr.

Διωλύγιος, extending far and wide, great, vehement: For διωρύγιος, (as κλίβανος κΡίβανος, liLium from λεΙΡιον,) from δι-ορέγω, to stretch out. Υ Æol. as in ὄνΥμα, ἀγΥρις.—Ewing makes it 'Killing, wearing out, from διὰ, ὀλύκω.'

Δμὼς, a slave: R. δαμάω, δμῶ.

Δνοπαλίζω, to swing, fling or wrap about.—'R. δονέω, πάλλω:' Dnn. Two verbs, as is thought in Ψηλαφάω. Lenn. from δίνη, πάλλω. (2) Dr. Jones for δνοφαλίζω from

Δνόφος, the same as Γνόφος, Κνέφας, Νέφος.

Δοδάσσατο: in Δέατο.

Δόγμα, opinion, decree.—R. δοκέω, †δόκω, δέδογμαι.

Δόθρα, the Lat. dodrans, which is ultimately Greek.

ΔΟΘΙΗΝ, a whitlow.—Q. ?

Δοίδυξ, δοίδῦκος, a ladle, pestle.—For δόθυξ, (as μαΙμάω,) redupl. from δύω, to penetrate into, and so divide. 'Quo res tundendo dividas': Lenn. Compare Δοιὰ, Δύο.

Δοιή, doubt between two things; and Δοιάζω, to doubt; from

Δοιώ, two, δύο.

Δοκάζω, -άω, -εύω, like Excipio, Intercipio, to look out for, observe, expect, watch, try to take: from δέκομαι, δέδοκα. So Ἐδέγμην is Expectabam; Ποτι-δεγμένοι Expectantes: Προσ-εδέχετο waited for, Luke 23. 51.

Δοκέω, †δόκω, ξω, to look out for: to observe, expect, think likely, judge, determine:—to be thought to be, to seem to be, appear:—to the much thought of. See above. (2) Δοκέω; to seem, from †δείκω, δείξω, δέδοκα, to show (oneself.).

Δόκιμος, well thought of, esteemed, approved. Δοκιμάζω, to examine and judge if a thing is δόκιμον; to judge well of.—Above.

Δοκὸς, a beam, rafter for roofs.—R. δέκομαι, δέδοκα. 'For it is received in the ends by which it is fastened:' Ewing. 'In building, beams are received at the ends into other pieces of timber:' Pkh. See Ἀμείβοντες.

Δόκος, ambush.—R. δοκάω, to look out for.

Δολιχὸς, long: Δόλιχος, a race-course, &c.—For

39

†Τολιχὸς, allied, it seems, to Ἐρ-δελεχὴς, continuing, lasting. The Δ is here for Τ, as Δάτις, Τάτης, &c. and ἐν-Δελεχὴς and Δολιχὸς are allied to Τέλος, end, i. e. the furthest extent, and Τῆλε, far off. (2) R. δό-λος. Pliny: 'Vallem longo tractu fallacem.'

Δόλος, deceit: the same as Δέλος in Δέλεαρ.

Δόλων, a stiletto, from its Δόλος. 'A small sword hidden in the stick,' Hesych.—This leads us to the meaning, 'a lesser sail in a ship,' as hidden among the larger ones.

Δόμος, a house: δέμω, δέδομα.

Δόναξ, a reed, as shaken by the wind: Luke 7. 24. From

Δονέω, to shake, as Δινέω. Compare φθΙνω, φθΟνος.

Δόξα, opinion:—good opinion, when one is well thought of, glory.—R. δοκέω, †δόκω, ξω.

Δορά, a skin flayed: δέρω.

Δόρξ, δορκὸς, wild-goat, gazelle, 'as endued with the keenest sight', Plin., from δέρκομαι, δέδορκα.

Δόρπον, 'the chief meal of the day, dinner or supper. Prob. by metath. from δρέπω:' Ldd. Δέδορπα, δέδορπα. 'Prim. a plucking of fruit:' Lenn.

Δόρυ, wood, plank, spear-shaft, spear.—R. δέρω, δέ-δορα: Wood peeled.

Δόσις, Δόμα, a gift.—R. †δόω, δίδωμι.

Δοῦλος, bondman, slave.—Δέω, †δέολος, δοῦλος: Bound. (2) 'Akin to δόλος, deceit, the natural vice of slaves:' Dnn. 'The Latins called slaves fures:' Damm.

Δοῦπος, noise.—'Perh. imitative:' Dnn. 'An imitative word:' Ldd. 'Without doubt from the sound [δουπ]:' Lenn. Compare our Tap and perhaps Τύπτω.

Δοχὴ, reception, &c.: δέχομαι.

Δοχμαῖκὸν, a dochmiac foot, marked orig. ∪ – – ∪ –, but much varied.—R. δοχμὸς, transverse, or succeeding one another: ∪ succeeded by –∪, then –.

Δοχμὴ, as much as the hand can hold, a span: And

Δοχμὸς, -ιος, 'oblique, from the side, transverse, bent, crooked:' Dnn.—The last meanings justify Mrt.'s deriv. from δέχομαι, δέδοχμαι: What is bent, being able to take in or inclose, contr. to what is straight. See above.

Δράγμα, a handful.—R. δρὰσσομαι, δέδραγμαι.

Δράκος, the eye: and

Δράκων, a dragon: from its quick sight, from δέρκομαι, ἔδαρκον, ἔδρακον.

Δρὰξ, palm of the hand, grasp.—R. δρὰσσομαι, δέ-δραξαι.

Δραπέτης, a run-away.—R. †δράω, διδράσκω.

Δρὰσσομαι, to grasp, hold fast, drag.—As Τάω, Τάσ-σω, so Δράω, Δράσσω. Now words get certain twists in their application, as the word Drama and Dramatic from this very verb δράω. From δράω is Δραστὴρ a worker; Δραστήριος active, vigorous, violent; Δραστι-κὸς, drastic; hence Δράσσομαι seems to have meant, to work energetically or violently with, use force or violence to, clutch, seize, drag. Ldd. says it means, 'to seize, spec. by the hand.'

Δρατός, flayed.—Δέρω, δέδαρται, δαρτός, δρατός.

Δραχμή, drachma, dram.—R. δράσσομαι, †δέδραχμαι: As much as one can lay one's hand on.

†Δράω, Δρῆμι, Διδράσκω, †Δρέμω, (δρόμος,) to run, to run away.—Allied to Τρέω, Τρέμω, to flee, fear: and Τρέχω, which see.

Δράω, 'to be active, to perform, do:' Dns., who explains Κονέω 'to run rapidly, to haste, to be active or busily employed.' Hence then this δράω from †δράω above. Compare too Σπεύδω and Σπουδάζω. Why in fact do we run at all? To do something δραστικώς.

Δρέπανον, a sickle: from

Δρέπω, to pluck off.—Δέρω, †δρέω, δρέπω, as Βλέπω. See Δρύπτω. (2) 'Chald. teraph, decerpeit:' Mrt. 'Hebr. dereb, to be sharp:' Wr.

Δρίλος, stripped bare, circumcised: then the member thus circumcised: then lustful.—R. δέρω, †δρέω, δρέπω; †δρύω, δρύπτω; †δρίω, δρίλος. Thus also

Δριμύς, sharp, stinging, bitter, shrewd.— R. †δρίω, †δρύω, δρύπτω. 'to tear, scratch', (Dnn.) Above.

Δρίος, a wood, copse. 'Some read Δρυός, from δρῦς:' Dnn. Perhaps dialectic, as στΤνος and stIpes, φρΤγω and frIgo, κλΤοντος and clIentis. So κΙνάρα and κΤνάρα are both used. See the next.

Δροίτη and Δρύτη, a wooden tub: from δρῦς. Thus Δοιὼ and Δύω, two. See βΟυκάνη.

Δρόμος, a race, &c.—R. †δρέμω in the first Δράω.

Δρόσος, dew:—a thing tender and delicate, a newborn animal.—As Δνόφος and Νέφος, so Δρόσος and †'Ρόσος from ῥέω to flow. ἔρρωσαι pf. p., ῥόος a stream. (2) Allied to 'Ιδρώς. As †'Ιξενος, Ξένος.

Δρυμός, Δρυός, an oak-coppice.—R. δρῦς.

Δρύοχοι, 'the props or stays on which is laid the keel of a new ship building:' Ldd.—R. δρῦς, υὸς, ἔχω, ὄχα: The sustainers of the oak-keel.

Δρυπεπὴς, Δρύππα, ripened on the oak or tree.—R. δρῦς, πέπτω, to ripen.

Δρύπτω, to tear, scratch, wound. — Δέρω, †δρέω, †δρύω, δρύπτω: allied to Τείρω, Τερῶ, Τρύω. (2) 'Δόρυ, †δορύπτω:' Damm. (3) 'Hebr. tereph, to tear:' Wr.

Δρῦς, 'the oak:—a tree in general, but esp. a tall, strong tree:—an old person, arida quercus (Horace):' Dnn.— Damm says: 'Δρῦς is prop. a tree in general, for it is from Δόρυ'. But Lennep thinks the Δ is prefixed, for ῥῦς, as in Δνόφος, Δρόσος; and ῥυσὸς, shrivelled, wrinkled, would agree with the bark of the oak, which is 'corticis asperi' (Forcell.), and with the Gnarled or knotty oak of our Poet. So Quercus Voss derives from Κερχαλέος (Κερχέος), hard, dry. Indeed †δρύω, δρύπτω, (which see,) to tear, scratch, would thus agree with δρυός. (2) 'R. δέρω, or Hebr. dor, ætas, from its lasting so long:' Mrt.

Δρύφακτος, balusters about a court of justice. —
40

'For ὀρόφρακτος': Ewing: from δρῦς, φράσσω τέφρακται: an oak-fencing.—Dan. from δρῦς only. ?

Δρῶπαξ, a depilatory plaster. — R. δρέπω, δέδρωπα.

Δύη, woe, pain. — 'A going under, from δύω, δύνω to sink:' Dnn. 'A sinking of the mind:' Ewing. 'As sinking deep into the mind:' Damm: as Homer, 'Οφρα δύη ἄχος κραδίην, κάματός σου γυῖα δέδυκε, and ἐ λύσσα δέδυκεν. Dnn. explains δυάω, 'to precipitate into misfortune.' (2) 'Hebr. duce, to languish:' Wr.

Δύναμαι, to have power, be able. Δύναμις, power. —'Midd. of †δύνημι, δύνω, to undergo, undertake, hence to be able:' Dnn. 'Prop. to have entered, introduced myself; hence the idea of power:' Lenn. Thus from †'Ελεύθω to go and come is 'Ελεύθερος, free to act. And Venia from Venio, 'venia proficiscendi'. Cic.

Δύο, Δοιὼ, Δοιοί, two. — 'R. δύω, δῦμι, [†δάω, δαίω,] to penetrate, go through, separate: evidently connected with Διά, through, [Διακόσιοι, 200,] Δίς, Δίχα:' Dunb. and Lenn. (2) 'Sanak. dwi, Gipsey duj, Hindoo, Chald., Pers. du, Slavon. dwa, Irish, Gaël. da or do, Sax. Goth. twa:' Wbst.

Δύπτω, to dip, duck. — R. δύω to make to go under. As †Βάω, Βάπτω.

Δύρομαι, the same as 'Οδύρομαι, to wail, lament. (2) Observe the formation of Δύη.

Δυσ-, with pain or difficulty. — 'Very prob. from δύη, δύσις, δύω:' Dnn. From δύσι, δύη. As Μόγις is Μόγοις, and 'Εγγὺς is 'Εν γόης. See Δύη.

Δυσηλεγής, 'epith. of death and war, that sends one to an ill bed, from δυσ, λέγω, to lay asleep:— hence hard, painful, uneasy;—and of men, hardhearted whence some from δυσ-, ἀλέγω, to care for:' Ldd.

Δύσκολος, hard to please: R. δυσ, κόλον, difficult about his food.

Δυσμὴ, Δύσις, sun-setting. — R. δύω, δέδυσμαι, to go under.

Δύστηνος, wretched, a wretch: R. δυσ, †στάω, sto: Who has no place for his foot to stand on. So "Αστηνος. (2) Dnn. from δυσ-, στένω. Rather, στενός: cramped, straitened.

Δύσχιμος, 'troublesome, dangerous, fearful. Prob. at once from δυσ-, as Μέλας, Μελάγχιμος:' Ldd., Dnn. Perhaps -χιμος in the latter is allied to Χιτὼν, then in the former was imitative.

Δύω, Δύνω, Δῦμι, Δύσκω, to go into, put on;— to go under. — Prop. to penetrate, divide, allied to †Δάω, Δαίω.

Δώδεκα, 12: δύω, two, δέκα, ten.

Δῶμα, a house, δόμος.

Δωρίζω, to speak or dress in the Dorian fashion.

Δωροκοπέω, 'to assail fidelity by presents: δῶρον, κόπτω:' Dnn.

Δῶρον, a gift: †δόω, †δοερὸν, δίδωμι.

Δῶρον, breadth of the hand, palm. — Vitruv.: 'Because the giving of gifts was called Δῶρον, and this is always done by the palm of the hand.'

Δὼς, Δωτίνη, a gift, δῶρον.

E.

*Ε, ˚Ε, ˚Ε˚Ε, ˚Ε˚Ε, alas !—'From the sound made by repeating this letter:' Lenn.

*Ε, acc. of Οὔ, as Σὲ of Σοῦ.

῎Εᾶ, ῎Εᾶ ῎Εᾶ, sounds of wonder or displeasure. Probably from the sound, like ˚Ε and ˚Α: or from these united.

῎Εα, 'like Εἶα, well then, come on, words of encouragement, like ῎Αγε, Φέρε, ῎Εα δή. Prob. imperat. of 'Εάω:' Dnn. Allow it, permit it, let it be. ῎Εα is, let alone, in Mark 1. 24. Luke 4. 34. (2) As 'neut. pl. ἕα whence ἐάων', (Donn.): Good, answ. to Εὖ, Εὖγε, Euge.

'Εὰν, if. — Hoogev. for εἰ ἄν.—But better as infin. of ἐάω, ἐᾷν, as Δοκεῖν and Εἰπεῖν are said simply: Allow it, grant it, as our If is Gif or Give.

'Εᾶνὸς, fit to be put on. — R. †ἕω, ἕννῑμι, to put on : as ῎Εδω, ῍Εδανός. 'Εᾶνὸν ἔσατο, Hom.

῎Εαρ, ῏Ηρ, the spring. — As 'Εάω is properly 'Εδάω, so ἔαρ is ἔασ from †ἕω, to send forth, shoot forth, as Βάλλω, †Βλάω, Βλαστάνω. So ῎Εδω, ῍ΕΔΑΡ, ΕῙΔΑΡ.

'Εάω, to let go, give up, let be, allow. — R. †ἕω, to let go, as Mitto, Per-mitto, Praeter-mitto. Μετ-ίημι I permit (you to go), in Herod. 'Cetera MITTE loqui:' Hor., for ' omitte.'

'Εάων, 'gen., of good things, as from a neut. pl. ἔα ; [as Hesiod, βλέφάρων κυνανεΑΩΝ ; ἔος being = ἐΰς : Or] ἐὺς, ἐέων, ἐήων, ἐάων :' Dnn.

'Εβδομος, for ῎Επτομος from 'Επτά : Seventh.

῍ΕΒΕΛΟΣ, ῍ΕΒΕΝΟΣ, ebony. — 'From the Arabic and Hebrew :' Mrt.

'Εγγίζω, to come ἐγγύς.

'Εγγυαλίζω, to put ἐν γυάλῳ in the hollow (of the hand), give. So

'Εγγύη, 'a pledge put into one's hand, surety, bail : —a betrothing :' Ldd. — R. ἐν †γύῃ, γυάλῳ, in the hollow (of the hand). Above. And thus

'Εγγὺς, near. — For ἐν †γύῃς, or 'ἐν †γύῃς as ἐν ποδῶν, ἐμποδῶν : and so μεσσηγύς' : Dnn. : At the hands or hand, at hand. Compare Δυσ-: and see above. And so 'Εξ ὑπο-γύον is used.

'Εγείρω, to rouse, stir, or wake up. — 'Prob. akin to 'Αγείρω', Ldd. ῍Αγω, 'Αγείρω : †῎Εγω, 'Εγείρω, to drive on. From this †῎Εγω are 'Επ-είγω and ῎Ογμος. Thus 'Αρύω and 'Ερύω, 'Αλίω and Εἱλύω, Εἰκὼς and Αἰκώς, Æquus.

'Εγκὰς, at the bottom, deeply : and

'Εγκατα, the entrails. — Allied both to κατὰ, down, and †κέω, †κέκαται, κεῖμαι, to lie. Above.

'Εγκοισυρούμαι, to be extravagant like Cœsyra, the wife of Alcmæon.

'Εγκολησάζω, 'eat pædico, ἀ κόλον, [intestinum,] et [†βδάω,] βαίνω. Vel, ut Suidas, κατα-πατέω, i.e.

41

ἐπὶ κόλαις βαίνειν κόλα δὲ ὁ γαστήρ : [κοῖλα? an ἀ κόλον cibus, in ventre positus?]' Brunck. Aut a κωλέα, κωλῆ, quod vide. ' In Eustathius 'Εγκολαθίζω, to swallow down, Κόλαθος or Κόλλαθος being a kind of cake : to this, Casaub. and Kust. assent. Schutz thinks it like Κολετρἀω, said of prize-fighters ;—to beat down, trample upon, met. ruin by calumnies :' Dnn.

'Εγκρὶς, ἶδος, a cake seasoned with oil and honey. — R. ἐγ-κεράω, ἐγκρῶ, to intermix. A medley. (2) R. ἐν κρίνω, to select ; κριθὸν, with choice or judgment. See 'Εμπὶς.

'Εγκώμιον, ' pertaining to festivals of Bacchus, or to feasts in which the praises of victorious champions were sung : a panegyric. R. κῶμος :' Dnn. (2) As sung ἐν κώμαις in the villages.

'Εγρήγορα, to awake, to watch. — ' R. ἐγείρω, ἥγορα, ἐγήγορα, ἐρ Ρήγορα :' Dnn. With some view perh. to ἔγρομαι. We say tReasure from tHesaurus.

'Εγρομαι, 'Εγρήσσω, to be watchful. — R. ἐγείρω, †ἔγρω.

῎Εγχελυς, an eel. — ' The etymol. of Damm from ἐν, ἰλὺς, mud, is probable :' Dnn. But the Χ ? and the Ε ? No : Better Lennep, (like ἐΓχος,) for ἔχελυς from ἔχομαι to adhere : Sticky, glutinous.

'Εγχεσίμωρος, ' fighting with a spear, in close fight. Some say, ἔγχος, μωρός : Furious with the spear. Others prefer μόρυς : Whose choice is the spear. Others take μῶρος for μῶλος : Toiling with a spear. Compare 'Ιόμωρος, ' Ὑλακόμωρος, Σινάμωρος, which countenance the last deriv. :' Dnn.— ' R. †μόω, moveo :' Blomf. See Μότος.

῎Εγχος, a spear, —sword. — As λαΓχάνω, for †ἔχος from ἔχω, to hold in the hand. Homer : ῎Εγχε' ἔχοντες, holding. Compare Habēna from Habeo, to hold.

'Εγὼ, 'Εγὼν, I. — ' R. ἔω, I am : Dnn :' Dnn. I.e. ἐὼν, ἐΓὼν, being, existing : 'I who am here :' Thus σιΓαλόεις : and Γοῖνος was said for Οἶνος. Indeed the Bœotians said 'Ιὼ, 'Ιὼν, without Γ. (2) ' Ik Goth., ic Sax. ich Dutch, ig, eg,' Todd. 'Sanskrit, agam :' Wbst.

'Εδανὸς, pleasant. — As ῎Εδανὸς, eatable, from ῎Εδω ; so for 'Ηδανὸς from ἥδω to please. See κΕδνός.

῎Εδαφος, ground, bottom, foundation, bottom. — R. ἔδος, a seat : as κρότΑΦΟΣ. ' That on which anything rests :' Dnn. So 'Εδεθλον is used.

'Εδέατρος, taster of dishes for the diners : R. ἔδω.

῎Εδνα, bridal presents. — For ἐδανὰ, pleasant, acceptable.

῎Εδος, ῎Εδρα, 'Εδώλιον, a seat, foundation ; —seat for a god, statue. — R. †ἔξω, ἔδον, to seat.

῎Εδω, edo, 'Εδομαι, and ῍Εσθω, 'Εσθίω, to eat. — ῎Εδω and †῎Εθω, ἔΣθω (as ἔΣχον,) are from †ἕω. Thus

G

' Ἐώμεν Il. τ. 402 from obs. ἔημι from †ἔω, to satiate: to which some refer ἔμην, ἔντο in the Homeric ἐδητύος ἐξ ἔρον ἔντο, ('satisfied their desire of food,') better referred to Ἴημι :' Dnn. Indeed all these are allied to the simple †ἔω : to send away, dismiss my wants, to satiate myself, to eat. Even the common sense of †ἔω would apply, as Homer : ἐμοὶ κατὰ λαιμὸν ᾽ΙΕΙΗ Οὐ πόσις οὐδὲ βρῶσις : demittetur, Clarke : but Heyne reads ᾽Ιείη, should go, and quotes Horace, ' Descendet in ventrem meum'. Δ, as in εἴλω, βάλην, ἐλην, ἀλέω, ὕδωρ, Lat. luDo. (2) Our verb eat, Icel. eta, Sax. etan.

Ἔζω, εἶσα, to seat, settle, Ἔζομαι, to sit. — R. †ἔω, Ἴημι, to send (down).

Ἔθειρα, hair, mane, crest. — R. ἔθος : As done after the fashion. ' Comtos de more capillos', Virg. (2) R. ἐθείρω, from the great care taken of the hair. Thus Κομέω and Κόμη, Καρη-κομόωντας, Ἐΰ-πλοκαμῖδες.

Ἐθείρω, to pay attention to. — R. ἔθος, as ἀγΕΙΡΩ, ἱμΕΙΡΩ. Thus Homer's ἐθείρει ἀλωήν, ' de more colit' Clarke : and Heyne explains it ᾽ΕΘΟΣ ἔχει ᾽ργάζεσθαι. (2) as Ἐθέλω and Θέλω, so ἐθείρω and †θείρω, θέρω, whence Θεραπεύω. (3) R. ἔθειρα, which see. ' As Fr. peigner is applied in the sense, Take special care of, Keep in a neat trim state:' Dnn.

Ἐθέλω, Θέλω, to wish, desire. — ' Some derive with probability Θέλω from †ἔλω, Θ for aspirate :' Dnn. So ἅμα, θάμα; Θειλόπεδον, &c. Thus the E in Ἐθέλω came from the Augment: some say for ἐρι-. (2) R. ἔθω, to be wont. Thus Φιλέω is to be wont and to like. Indeed Θέλω is also ' to be wont or accustomed', (Dnn.)—Some say ἐθελ λῶ for λάω, to wish.??

Ἔθνος, tribe, nation. — R. ἔθος : Living under the same laws. (2) R. ἔζω, ἔθην, to settle in a place. Compare Ἐσμός.

Ἔθος, custom, usage. — R. ἔζω, ἔθην, to settle, establish : much as Θέμις and Θεσμὸς from τίθημι. (2) From †ἔω, †ἔθην, εἰμί, to be. As Ἕξις and Habitus are ' mos quo res se habent', so ἔθος ' mos quo res sunt.' The verb †Ἔθω, to be, is in Matthiæ. (3) Ἔω, to put on habits and manners. Curtius has ' Induere mores Persarum.'

Εἰ, if. — For Εἴεν or Εἴη, let it be. (2) For †ἔε imperat. of †ἔω, Ἴημι : Let be, allow it, Per-mitte, Permit.

Εἰ δ᾽ ἄγε, ' But then, come on! same as Εἶα δὴ [δὲ] ἄγε. Or Εἶ (ἐθέλεις):' Dnn.—Or for †ἔε imperat. of †ἔω, εἰμι, to go : εἰ ἄγε agreeing with Βάσκ' ἴθι.

Εἶα, come on! — For Ἔα, which see.

Εἰάζω, ' to shout out Εἶα, as Αἰάζω, Εὐάζω :' Dnn.

Εἰαμένη, ' a low moist pasture, water-meadow. Usu. derived from εἴαται, ἥνται, they sat down, whence some write Εἰαμένη :' Ldd. and Dnn. So Ἥμενος is LOW. The rich are said in Eccles. 10. 6 to ' SIT in LOW place'.—But rather, as Δεξαμενή, a tank, is the particip. of ἐδεξάμην, so Εἰαμένη of εἰάμην from †ἔω, εἶα, ἔζω.

42

Εἴβω, for Λείβω, as Γαῖα, Αἶα.

Εἶδαρ, food : for Ἔδαρ from Ἔδω.

Εἴδομαι, to be seen, to be seen to be, to seem, as Video, Videor :—seem what another is, resemble. And Εἶδος, the look, form. R. εἴδω.

Εἰδύλλιον, ' a small representation or picture, mostly of rural scenes, an idyl : from Εἴδω, to behold :' Dnn. Or Εἴδομαι, to be like, as Εἴδωλον.

Εἴδω, to see; Εἰδέω, to know, ' for what one has seen, one knows :' Ldd. ' That they may SEE and KNOW,' Isai. 41. 20.—As Οὖρος for Ὅρος, so εἴδω for †ἔδω, †ἐδέω, (allied to Ἔδος, a seat,) to set or fix i.e. the eyes upon, as Βλέπω is †Βλέω, to cast (the eyes upon), and Ἐπίσταμαι, to know, is from Ἐφίστημι, to set (the mind) on a thing, or place myself over it. (2) ' Chald. yedu, he knew :' Mrt. ' Hebr. idu, to know :' Wr.

Εἴδωλον, an image. — R. εἴδομαι, to be like.

Εἴεν, let it be: for εἴησαν. So ἠγερθΕΝ.

Εἶθαρ, Ἴθαρ, Ἰθύ, Εὐθύς, straightly, directly. — R. †ἔω, †ἔθην, †ἴω, †ἴθην, to go : So as to go on, not turning to right or left, straight on, right on : Prov. 4. 25, 27. So Ἴκταρ from Ἴκω. Compare ἴθμα a pace. See Ἰθύς.

Εἴθε, I wish that. — ' R. εἰ :' Dnn. and Wr. So Αἴθε. Perhaps aspir. from Εἶτ.

Εἴκατι, Εἴκοσι, 20. — R. ἑκάς, as remote from the simple numbers : just as Ἑκατὸν also is from ἑκάς. ΕΙ, as Ἑκάτι and Εἰκάτι. (2) As δέΚομαι, ἐν-έΚω, ἐΚε-χειρία, so εἴΚοσι from †ἔΚω, ἔχω, to hold, contain: on the principle of Δέκα from Δέκομαι : Pkh. See Δέκα. (3) ' R. εἰκὼς, [αἰκὼς, æquus,] æqualis, like, equal : An even number made up of two tens :' Mrt. Or thus : with two like numbers, ten and ten : εἰκόσι dat. plur. — N.B. No foreign Root seems proposed.

Εἴκελος, Εἰκὼς, like, from εἴδομαι, εἴκα, to be like :— like to happen, likely, probable : — seemly, fit, as Videor, to seem.

Εἰκῆ, too readily, rashly, confusedly, in vain. Εἰκαῖος, rash. — R. εἴκω, to yield : ' Yielding to the impulse of the moment :' Ormst.

Εἴκω, to be like, to seem, to seem fit. — R. εἴδομαι, εἴκα, Videor, to be like. (2) ' Hebr. ec, so as :' Mrt.

Εἴκω, to retire, give way, yield, obey. — R. †ἔω, †εἴκα, εἰμι, to go. See Ἥκω, Ἴκω. (2) ' Hebr. ikee, to yield :' Wr.

Εἰκὼν, likeness : Εἰκὼς, like. — R. εἴκω 1.

Εἰλαπίνη δαίς, a banquet. — ' Usu. derived from (κατ᾽) εἴλας πίνω, to drink in companies: others from λάπτω :' Ldd. But ΕΙ ?

Εἶλαρ, shelter, covering. — R. εἴλω, to shut up. So Εἰλεός.

Εἰλείθυια, Lucina, Diana. — R. εἰλευθυῖα, †ἐλεύθω, to come (to one's assistance). ' Ilithyia, tuēre matres :' Hor. (2) R. ἐλεῶ, to pity. (3) ' Hebr. iled, to procreate :' Wr.

Εἰλεὸς, a den, hole, as Εἶλαρ.

Εἰλεὸς, the iliac passion. — ' R. εἰλέω. As causing the patient to writhe, or as seated in the small guts which become unnaturally convoluted :' Dnn.

Εἰλέω, Εἴλεω : See Εἴλω.

Εἴλη, for Ἕλη.

Εἴλη, Ἴλη, a crowd, troop, band. — R. εἴλω, ἴλλω, to roll, to crowd.

Εἰλινδέομαι, the same as Ἀλινδέω. And Εἰλίσσω as Ἑλίσσω.

Εἰλυὸς, -υθμὸς, as Εἰλεὸς 1.

Εἰλυστάομαι, to wriggle about. And Εἰλυφάω, as Εἰλύω in

Εἴλω, Εἴλλω, Ἕλλᾦ, Ἴλλω, Εἰλέω, Εἰλέω, Εἰλύω, Ἑλίσσω, to roll, twist, wrap, crowd, assemble : — enfold, hem in, shut up : — twist, wind, creep or crawl along. — See in Ἀλέω.

Εἴλωτες, the lowest class of slaves in Sparta. — ' Orig. from Ἕλος Helos, Il. β. 584, and conquered by Sparta. Some from ἑλεῖν, to capture :' Dnn.

Εἶμα, a garment. — R. †ἕω, εἶμαι, to put on.

Εἱμαρμένη, fate : ' R. εἵμαρμαι Att. for μέμαρμαι, μείρομαι :' Dnn.: Allotted : one's lot, μόρος.

Εἰμί, I am. — R. †ἔω, ἐμί, ἔμεναι, to be. See Εἶμι.
(2) ' Pers. am, Goth. im, Sax. eom :' Webst. Our am.

Εἶμι, I go. — R. †ἕω, †εἴω, to go.

Εἶν, Εἰν, Ἐν, Ἐνί, in. — Dunb. from ἔννυμι, prop. to put, place in. (2) From ἐν, particip. of εἷς, being, i. e. being in a place. As In-sum. (3) ' En, in, or yn Sax., Goth., Germ., Swed., Welsh, Lat. Antu Sanskr.': Wbst.

Εἰνάτερες, ' the wives of a husband's brothers, sisters-in-law :' Dnn. — As εἰλΕΙθυια for εἰλΕΤθυια, so Εἰνάτερες (like θυγΑΤΕΡΕΣ,) from ΕΤνις a wife : an extended form of meaning, like Avus, Avunculus. So Eustath. and many take it. (2) Lenn. from ἐνος, old : ' Natu grandiores.' Or say ἔνος, last : Affinities in the last degree, remote. See Ἐννέα.

Εἴνατος, ninth, as Ἔννατος.

Εἰραφιώτης, Bacchus. — ' Acc. to some it means Sewn into Jupiter's thigh : ῥάπτω, ἔῤῥαφα :' Dnn. As Εἴληφα, Εἵμαρμαι.

Εἴργω, Εἴργω, Ἔργω, to shut in, confine ; — shut out, drive off, prevent. — R. †ἕρω, †ἕρκα, or ἐρύω, ἐρύκα, ἕρκα, ' to enclose, guard in,' (Dnn.) So Ἄρω, ' to fit closely, to be closed or shut', (Dnn.), whence Ἀρκέω, to keep off, hinder, prevent.

Εἵρερος, · bondage. — R. εἴρω, to bind, ' as perhaps Servus from Sero, Serui :' Ldd.

Εἰρεσία, a rowing. — R. ἐρέσσω.

Εἰρεσιώνη, a harvest wreath bound round with εἶρος wool, and carried by singers : — their song : — a herald's staff so bound.

Εἴρη, Ἴρη, (as Εἴλη, Ἴλη,) place of assembly : ' prob. from εἴρω to speak :' Ldd. Or εἴρω to shut in. See Ἀπελλαί.

Εἴρην, Ἴρην, (as above,) ' a youth from his 20th year, when he was entitled to speak in the [εἴρη] assembly. Prob. from εἴρω to speak :' Ldd. and Dnn.

43

Εἰρήνη, harmony, peace. — ' R. εἴρω, to join, or ἔρω to speak, converse :' Dnn. Compare Ἁρμονία with ἄρω. In form like σεΛΗΝΗ.

Εἰρμὸς, a train. — ' R. εἴρω, like Sero, Series :' Ldd.

Εἴρος, Ἔρος, Ἔριον, Ἐρέα, wool. — R. εἴρω to weave. Dr. J. defines Wool ' that which is woven into cloth.' — Grove says εἴρω ' to hold together' : Joined close to and in itself. See Ἐπήτριμος.

Εἴρω, to join, bind, string together. — R. †ἔρω (in Dnn.), allied to Ἄρω. So Ἄγω and Ἐγείρω, Ἀλίω and Εἰλύω. The Latin Sero.

Εἴρω, to speak, say : — ask, enquire. — As above : i. e. to join words together : so Plato derives it. See Ἐρέω, Ἔρομαι.

Εἴρων, a dissembler : Εἰρωνεία, irony. — Some say, from εἴρω, to talk : A mere talker. ' Who says more than he means', Dr. Jones. — Or from εἴρω to weave (deceit). Μύθους καὶ μήδε' ὑφαίνων, Hom.

Εἷς, neuter Ἕν, one, as Τυφθείς, Τυφθέν. — Some think the Aspirate adscititious, (as Haud from Οὐδ',) and Εἷς to be Εἷς particip. of εἰμί, to be : An individual being. ' Ens est unum': Mrt. (2) Or Εἷς is participle of Ἵημι, letting go (all others), oneself being left alone. (3) Some say for †Μείς, and Ἕν for †Μέν, answ. to Μία : See in Μέν. But ? (4) ' Heb. his, that which is :' Pkh. (5) Todd compares our ace, Germ. ess, Lat. as, assis.

Εἰς, Ἐς, to, into. — R. †ἕω, †ἴσω, εἶμι, to go (to). So from ἴκω is Ἴκταρ. (2) ' R. †ἕω, ἕσω, to send towards (or to)': Ormat. (3) For ἔως.

Ἐΐσκω, to make like. — Allied to Εἴκω, to be like, as ἔΞχον. Some from

Εἶσος, Ἴσος, alike, equal. — R. εἴδομαι, εἴσομαι, to be like. Compare Εἴκω 1. And Ἴσημι.

Εἶτα, so then, thus then, thereupon, therefore, furthermore : — even thus, nevertheless. — ' R. εἰ :' Dnn. : If it be so. Τα, as Ὅτα Dor. of Ὅτε. (2) Εἶτα short for Ἔπειτα.

Ἐκ, or †Ἐκς, Ἐξ, from. — R. εἴκω, ξω, to go away. (2) ' Chald. ΗΚ, to go :' Pkh.

Ἐκὰς, far ἐκ from. Μακρὰν ἀπ' αὐτῶν Matth. 8. 30. But some from Εἴκω to retire.

Ἕκαστος, each separately from the rest. — R. ἑκάς. So our Sundry from Sunder, Asunder : Sever and Several. ' We are separated one far from another :' Nehem. 4. 19.

Ἑκάτερος, each of two, each by himself. — R. ἕτερος ἑκάς reversed.

Ἑκάτη, Hecaté, Diana : Ἕκατος, Apollo, also Ἑκατηβόλος. So both called for their far-shooting. Ἑκὰς, &c.

Ἕκάτι, Ἕκητι, on account of, from ἑκὼν, willing for any purpose or object. ' I did it on account of him.' — Also, ' by the pleasure, will, favor, or aid of : a dative, from the same origin as ἑκών :' Dnn.

Ἑκατόμβη, hecatomb, when prop. ἑκατὸν βοῦς were slain.

Ἑκατὸν, 100. — R. ἑκὰς, far : Remote from the units.

Ἐκεῖ, there. — Allied to Ἑκὰς, far off. Or, At that

distance ἐκ from this spot. (**2**) 'Chald. *haca*, here': Mrt. ?

Ἐκεῖνος, the man ἐκεῖ there, that.

Ἔκηλος, unmolested, at ease, at leisure, secure, quiet. — As Ἑκὼν is Ἥκων from ἥκω, so Ἔκηλος is Ἥκηλος, able to come and go, just as Ἐλεύθερος from †ἐλεύθω. ΗΛΟΣ as βέβΗΛΟΣ.

Ἐκκλησία, assembly ; ἐκ-καλέω, -κλέω.

Ἑκούσιος, willing ; R. ἑκών, οὖσα.

Ἔκπαγλος, striking with awe.—For Ἔκπλαγος, from ἐκπλήσσω, ἐξέπλαγον.

Ἑκτικὸς, habitual.—R. ἔχω, ἔκται, habeo, habitum.

Ἑκτὸς, sixth : ἓξ, ἕκς, ἑκσ?ος, as δέκαΤΟΣ. So the σ is dropt in Ἑκ-καὶ-δεκα.

Ἑκτὸς, on the outside. — Ἐκ, ἐκτὸς, as Ἐν, Ἐντός.

Ἕκτωρ, an anchor : as holding the ship. See Ἑκτικός.

Ἑκυρὸς, a father-in-law. — Dr. Jones says : 'From Arab. *heжar*. It means a father adopted'.—But, (like βθελΤΡΟΣ) as Ἑκὼν is Ἥκων, so Ἑκυρὸς is of the same origin : ad-ventitious, coming into the family. Compare Νέος, new, from Νέομαι, to come : A stranger, Ad-vena, Ἐπ-ηλυς.

Ἑκὼν, willing.—Prop. ἡκων, as Ἕδνα for Ἥδνα, Ἥδανα: Coming (readily). Lo, I come, I delight to do Thy will. Ps. 40. So Ἱκανὸς from ἱκάνω Dnn. explains 'coming without impediments, ready.' And see Ἐλεύθερος. (**2**) R. εἴκω, to yield. Or, Hebr. YKH to obey. Pkh.

Ἐλάα, Ἐλαία. the olive-tree.—Pkh. says : 'From Hebr. *hel*, to shine.' As well then from ἔλη whence Σέλας, splendor. (**2**) R. †ἐλάω, to push forth (leaves) : Damm. So Homer calls it τανύ-φυλλος, ὑψι-πέτηλος, τηλεθδουσα. (**3**) R. ἔλος. As fond of marshy places: Greg.

Ἔλαιον, oil of Ἐλαία, olive. (**2**) Affinities in Sax., Armor., Welsh, Irish, Germ. &c. Lat. *oleum*, our *oil*.

Ἐλάνη, the same as Ἑλένη.

Ἔλασμα, metal beaten out.—R. †ἐλάω, ἐλαύνω, to beat out.

Ἐλάσσων, less. — R. ἐλαχὺς, as Βαθὺς, Βάσσων.

Ἐλάτη, a fir :—oar or spear made of it :—a boat.— 'Perh. from [ἔλαται,] ἐλαύνω : from its straight growth :' Ldd. 'Like mountain firs, as tall as they :' Hom., who calls it οὐρανο-μήκης. — Some make the oar primary: ΕΛΑΤΗΣΙ Πόντον ΕΛΑΤΝΟΝΤΕΣ, Hom.

Ἐλάτη, shoot of the palm-tree, derived prob. as above. Compare Palma, the palm-tree, and the greater shoot or leader of the vine, and the broad part of an oar.

Ἐλατήρ, a broad flat cake, as ἐλατὸς beaten out. See Ἔλασμα.

Ἐλαύνω, †Ἐλάω, to drive, drive or beat away, beat out. — Εἴλω, Εἰλέω, Ἴλλω, Ἐλαύνω, are kindred words :' Dnn. See ΑΛΕΩ, primitive, to drive.

Ἔλαφος, a deer. — As κρόταΦΟΣ, βθΑΦΟΣ. R. ἐλάω, ἐλαύνω, from its agility, which from Ago, Agilis.

44

Ἐλαφρὸς, nimble, light, as an Ἔλαφος : for ἐλαφηρός.

Ἐλαχὺς, small. — Prop. beaten out, ἐληλαμένος.

'Ἐλαφρὸς, Ἔλαφος, Ἐλαχὺς, all perh. from, or at least akin to †Ελάω :' Dnn.

Ἔλδομαι, to wish for, long for.—Mrt. well from †ἔλω, to take (with the eyes,) as Λάω is to take and to desire. See ἅΛΛω, μέλΛω.

Ἐλεᾶς, some bird, 'perh. as frequenting the ἕλεα marshes :' Dnn.

Ἔλεγος, a lament; elegy.—R. ? alas, λέγω. (**2**) Some from ἀλέγω, ?

Ἐλέγχω, to examine, prove, convict, expose, refute.— As ἐνέγκω, καΐχάνω. For †ἐλάχω, from ἔλη, ἔχω, to hold in the light of the sun, as Εἰλι-κρυνῆς, examined in the sun. (**2**) R. †ἔλω, εἶλον, as Ἀλίσκω, to seize, to take in the act. (**3**) Bp. Blomf. from †ἔλω ἔγχος, to seize a spear as in feudal times to determine a charge against one.

Ἐλειὸς, Ἐλειὸς, Ἐλεὸς, Ἐλιὸς, Ἐλυιὸς, Ἴληος, Ὅλιος, 'a dormouse or squirrel ;—also a hawk :—an animal called in Fr. Loir, the same genus as the Dormouse. 'Perh. from Εἰλεὸς a hole or hiding-place :' Dnn. (**2**) R. εἰλέω : the squirrel from whirling its tail :' Greg. (**3**) 'Allied to Ἑλινύω, (which see,) to be inactive: as the dormouse.

Ἐλελεῦ war-cry, like Ἀλαλά.

Ἐλελίζω, to cry Ἐλελεῦ.

Ἐλελίζω, to whirl, twist, much as Ἑλίσσω redupl.

Ἐλένη, a light, lamp.—R. ἔλη.

Ἐλένη, 'a wicker-basket to carry the sacred utensils: perh. from ἐλεῖν to take :' Ldd. and Dnn.

Ἔλεος, pity.—R. εἰλέω to roll ? A commotion of the bowels: 'bowels of mercies :' N. T. So Ἵλαος is propitious from Ἴλλω or †Ἴλλω. (**2**) 'Chald. *ala*, to lament :' Mrt.

Ἔλεος, -ον, 'a table on which meat is cut up, a kitchen-table :' Dnn.—Damm from ἐλεῖν, δι-ελεῖν, to divide. (**2**) Lenn. from εἴλω, to revolve, as Versatilis, that may be easily turned. Sueton.: 'Cœnationes *tabulis versatilibus*.'

Ἐλεσπὶς, 'low ground, marsh land : from ἔλος, ἔλεος :' Dnn. See ἐλΠΙΣ, θλαΣΠΙΣ.

Ἐλεύθερος, free. — R. †ἐλεύθω, as φοβΕΡΟΣ : Coming and going as he pleases. 'Thou walkedst whither thou wouldest', John 21. 18. See Ἱκανός. So Venia from Venio. †Ἐλεύθω is allied to Ἐλαύνω, to advance.

Ἐλεφαίρω, 'to cheat with empty hopes, (from ἐλέφας,) said of the dreams that come through the ἐλέφαντος ivory gate, Od. 19. 565 : a play of words betw. ἐλέφας and ἐλεφαίρω :' Ldd. (**2**) R. ἐλαφρὸς : To make light of. E as νημΕρτης, πΕλεμίζω, κΕλυφος, grEsatus. So ρ dropt in δρύφ(ρ)ακτος.

Ἐλεφαντίασις, a leprosy, wrinkling up the skin like an ἐλέφαντος elephant's.

ΕΛΕΦΑΣ, an elephant. — 'Hebr. *eleph*, an ox :' Mrt. So the Romans called them 'Lucanos BOVES.'

Ἕλη, Εἵλη, the heat of the sun. — Much as †Σάω, Σάλος and Ζάλη; Χέω, Χέλυς; †Τέω, Τέλος; so †ἕω, ἕλη, the emission (from the sun), as ἡλίου Βολή. See Ἕλος. (2) 'R. εἱλέω: As caused by the *revolving* sun:' Ewing. (3) 'Hebr. *hel*, to shine:' Mrt.

Ἑλικὴ, a winding, twisting; — 'a willow, from its flexibility, also Ἕλιξ;— the Great Bear, as seeming to revolve through the Pole:' Dnn. — R. ἑλίσσω.

Ἑλικὼν, thread hanging from a distaff, and winding round the spindle as it turns. — Above.

Ἑλικὸς, tendril, — vine. 'What is wound round or curled :' Dnn. — R. †ἑλίω, ἑλίσσω.

Ἑλινύω, to take rest, keep holiday, stand still, be idle. — 'Prob. from dogs, &c. rolling themselves up in sleep : ἑλίσσω:' Dnn. (2) 'Hebr. *len*, to rest:' Wr. ?

Ἕλιξ, anything twisted or twisting, armlet, earring, — eddy, whirlwind, — tendril, — curl of hair ;— feeler of the polypus;— bowels, from their convolutions ;— a spiral line; — vault. — From

Ἑλίσσω, ζω, to twist, roll, &c. — Allied to Εἱλέω, Εἴλω.

Ἑλίχρυσος, 'a creeping plant with yellow flower or fruit :' Ldd. — R. †ἑλίω, ἑλίσσω, χρυσός.

Ἕλκος, a wound, — running sore, ulcer. — R. ἕλκω; A wound made by a spear dragging the flesh with it and tearing it, like Διa-σπάω. — But Pkh. : 'As the sore seems to *attract* the morbid juices to the affected part.' Schleusn.: 'Quòd vitiosos *attrahat* humores.'

Ἕλκω, to draw, drag. — R. †ἕλω, †ἕλκα, to seize. (2) R. †ἑλάω †ἕλακα, †ἕλκα, ἑλαύνω, to urge forward, drive. Thus †ὁλέω, ὀλέκω. (3) 'Hebr. *hilleck*, to make to go :' Mrt.

Ἑλλεδανοί, band for binding corn-sheaves. Ἑλλάς, Εἱλάς, a bond.—R. ἕλλω, 'to roll up. So ῥιγΕΔΑΝΟΙ.

Ἕλλεψα, 'the same as †ἕλλυρα, ἄλλυντα:' Steph.

Ἕλλος, Ἑλλοψ, οπος, dumb. Plutarch explains τοὺς ἰχθῦς ἕλλοπας by ἔχοντ-ς τὴν Ὄπα Ἑλλομένην καὶ κατ-ειργομένην, having the voice strained and shut up. Ἕλλοψ is also a fish in general, 'mutis piscibus', Hor. — and a particular sort. — 'Some render Ἑλλὸς, swift, from †ἑλάω, ἑλαίνω:' Dnn.

Ἑλλὸς, Ἑλλὸς, a fawn. — As just above, from †ἑλάω, ἑλαίνω, to drive: from their agility, (ago, agilis,) as Ἔλαφ-ς. 'Like the *bounding*, roe:' Pope. (2) 'Hebr. *ayal*, a stag:' Mrt.

Ἕλλω : in Εἴλω. Ἕλλετε is 'come on', and has the sense of Ἑλαύνετε, drive on. So Ἄγε.

Ἕλμινς, a worm. — R. ἕλλω, ἕλμαι, to roll or twist about. See Εὐλή.

Ἕλος, a marsh. — As †Τέω, Τέλος; †Σάω, Σάλος; Χέω, Χέλυς ; so †Ἕω, Ἕλος, (See Ἕλη,): As *emitting* vapors or exhalations. Justin speaks of the '*paludium gravia nebula.* (2) R. ἕλη, heat of the sun, perh. heat generally, just as Ἀλέα is used of both : From the tepid nature of marshes.

Ἑλπὶς, hope or fear. Ἕλπομαι, to hope,— to think.

Like Ἕλδομαι to wish, from †ἕλω, to seize with the mind. Π, as μέλΠω, θάλΠω, σάλΠιγξ, πόρΠη, ἑλεσΠΙΣ, ΣλάσΠΙΣ.

Ἕλῡμα, the stock or handle of the plough as turning it round: — a cover or case, as wrapping or enfolding. — R. ἐλύω.

Ἕλυμος, a case, sheath, quiver : — flute-case, and flute. — Above.

Ἕλῡτρον, a cover, case, as Ἕλυμος : — sheath, shell, cistern, reservoir.

Ἑλύω, Ἑλύω, to roll, wrap, coil : in Εἴλω.

†Ἕλω, to take, seize. —Prop. to hem in, and so take. See ΕΙλω, ΆΛΕΩ, and '. ἀλίσκομαι.

Ἕλωρ, capture, booty. — Above.

Ἐμβὰς, Ἐμβάδιον, a shoe. — R. ἐν, βάς : Into which we get, or in which we go.

Ἐμέω, to vomit. — R. †ἕω, ἕμαι : whence Ἐν-εμα: To throw up, cast the stomach.

Ἐμμαπέως, forthwith. — 'Some from ἅμ' ἕπει, No sooner said than done : — better from ἐν, μαπέειν, to seize : Clutching at, and so hastily :' Ldd. So Rapio, Rapidly, Raptim.

Ἐμμαπέω, to put the fingers down the throat to cause sickness. — 'From μαπέω, allied to μάσσω, to handle, work with the hand :' Dnn. — Allied to Ματεύω, to search, explore.

ΕΜΟΥ, ΜΟΥ, ΕΜΟΙ, ΜΟΙ, ΕΜΕ, ΜΕ, of me, to me, me. —'*ME* Armor., Sax., Sanskrit : *MO* Gaelic. The Hindoos use *ME* in the Nom., as in Celtic *MI* :' What.

Ἐμπάζομαι, to busy oneself about. —As πίΜπλημι, τύΜπανον, ἀΜπλακέω. For †ἐπάζομαι from ἕπω, to be occupied in. See Ὀπάζω. (2) R. ἐν, πᾶς. As the Horatian 'Sam totus in illis.' (3) R. †πάω, *pasco, pavi*, to tend sheep. Compare Παιών. (4) Allied to Ἕμπαιος.

Ἕμπαιος, experienced in. — R. ἐν, παίω : Well beaten or drubbed or stricken in, as Ἐν-τριβὴς, and Τρίβων. We say, Well-stricken in age. (2) 'From, or akin to Ἐμπάζομαι :' Dnn.

Ἕμπας, Ἕμπα, Ἕμπης, i.e. ἐν πᾶσι, in all respects, entirely : — every thing viewed together, taking in every thing, on the whole :— for all that, all the same for that, nevertheless. 'And for *ALL* there were so many', John 21. 11. 'For *all* this,' Isa. 5. 25.

Ἐμπέραμος, the same as Ἐμπείραμος from Πείρα.

Ἐμπὶς, ἴδος, a mosquito.— R. ἐμ-πίνω : Drinking in the blood. As Δι-κλὶς, ἴδος, from κλίνω.

Ἕμπλην, near to; from ἐν, πελάω, †πλάω, to draw near. Also for Πλήν.

Ἐμποδὼν, ἐν in the way ποδῶν of the feet, so as to be an im-pediment.

Ἕμπουσα, a hob-goblin, that went on ONE FOOT as an ass's, the other being of brass. — For ἕν-πουσα, from ἐν, πούς: as ἐΜποδών. (2) For ἕπουσα, as ἑπομένη, following, pursuing. So τύΜπανον. Ἕπομαι is 'to cling, stick to a thing so as to follow its motions': (Ldd.)

(3) 'All call her 'Εμπουσα', says Demosthenes, ' διὰ τὸ πάντα ποιεῖν καὶ πάσχειν, from her wonderful activity and constant change of form': i.e. from ἐμ-ποιοῦσα. But rather in the sense of ἐμ-ποιῶ, ' to excite in, as terror, Polyb. xi. 12. 5 :' (Dnn.)

'Εμφερὴς, like : φέρων bearing ἐν in himself a resemblance to another. So 'Εμφέρω is ' to resemble any one' (Dnn.) ' Qui te tantùm ore re-ferret :' Virg.

'Εν, in : in Εἰν.

"Εν, one thing.—Neuter of Εἷς, as τυφθείς, τυφθέν. (2) Some for Μὲν, which see. (3) ' Sax. an, Germ. ein, Swed. en, Icel. einn, Welsh yn, Armor. unan, Irish aon :' Wbst.

'Εναίρω, to kill.—R. ἐν, αἴρω, to take, as (Inter-emo,) Inter-imo, Inter-ficio, Inter-neco. (2) Buttm. curiously as sending one to the ἔνΕροι infernal regions. ??

"Εναρα, spoils taken from the slain.—R. ἐν.αἴρω, ἐν-αρῶ, to take : see 'Ενέπω. Some from ἐναίρω to slay.

'Εναργὴς, conspicuous.—' Some from ἐν, ἔργῳ. Better, ἐν, ἀργὸς or ἀργής :' Dnn.

'Ενατὸς, ninth.—R. ἐνέα.

'Ενδελέχεια, ' continuance, persistence, duration. The Etymology not to be confounded with ἐν-τελέχεια :' Dnn. Yet very prob. it is the same word, though used in a different sense ; ἐνΔελέχεια being put for ἐνΤελέχεια, as menTior, menTax makes menDax.—R. ἐν, τέλος, ἔχω : A holding on to the end : ' He that en-dureth unto the end', N.T. 'Εν in compounds, says Dnn., denotes ' approach [TO] :' and again, 'Εν is Dor. and Æol. for 'Εϲ, whence the Latin In, TO, governs an accus.

"Ενδον, 'Ενδοῖ. within.—R. ἐν, much as 'Εντός.

'Ενδινα, entrails.—' R. ἔνδον, like 'Εντερα :' Ldd. Rather from ἐν-δινέω, ' to move or roll about' (Ldd.).

'Ενδιος, in the open air, ' sub Jove frigido', from Διΐς, Διὸς, Jove. Also, in mid-day. Διὸς ἐν φάει, Eurip. For Jupiter was the author of light and father of day, called (Dies-pater,) Diespiter. Macrob. says ' Cretenses diem Δία vocant.' (2) The Punic dia, day, Welsh diau, Armor. di, Hind. diu, Gipsey diwes. So Canin., Wachter, Webst.

'Ενδυκέως, ' zealously, heartily, earnestly. Prob. from ἐν, δύω, δέδυκα : piercingly, in the depth of the heart :' Ldd.

'Ενδὺω, induo, to put on : ἐν, δύω.

'Ενία, 'Εννέα, nine.—From ἔνος, belonging to the last year or moon, and indeed ' last' as said in "Ενος. ' Appertaining to the last unit', Lenn. We find ἐΝΝυς as well as ἔΝοs for ' yearly.' (2) Dnn. from νέος, be-cause he finds Novus, Novem, and the Teutonic Neu is New and Nine. But the Ε ? and he is obliged to say that this connection is difficult to explain. In fact ' No-vus' is νέος, νέϜος : and, as δέκΑ, decΕΜ, so ἐνέΑ, eneΕΜ ; and as ΝΕος is ΝΟΥus, so eΝΟΥem is eΝΟΥem, Novem.

"Ενεκα, "Ενεκεν, on account of, with respect to.—As he Aspirate seems uncalled for in 'Ηγέομαι, "Ιστωρ,

46

Haud, &c. so ἔνεκα for ἕνεκα from ἐνέκω, (which see,) ἐνέχομαι, ' to be under the influence of or subject to :' (Dnn.)—'Εχω indeed may here mean what Fero, La-tum, do in ' with re-ference to', ' in re-lation to.' Com-pare oportet, it im-ports, it is im-portant, from porto.

'Ενέκω, 'another form of ἐνέγΧω :' Dnn., and so for ἐν-έχω, as δέΚομαι : To hold in (the hand), bear.

'Ενεός, 'Εννεός, 'dumb, silent, dull, silly.—Some from α, νέος. But it differs from "Ανεως merely in form :' Dnn. Ε, as "Ερσην.

'Ενέπω, to tell : ἐν, ἕπω, prop. to tell among.— Buttm. as lengthening of ἕπω. But the Ν. ?

'Ενερθε, Νέρθε, from below.—For 'Ενέροθε from "Ενεροι.

"Ενεροι, inhabitants of the infernal regions.—R. ἐν, †ἔρα whence ἔραζε, the earth. (2) Simply ἐν, as φο-ΒΕΡΟΙ.

'Ενεσία, suggestion.—R. ἐν, †ἕω, ἕσαι : As sent into the mind. So

'Ενετὴ, a clasp.—R. ἐν, ἕται, from ἕω : Sent in, inserted.

"Ενη, "Ενη : See "Ενος 2.

'Ενὴ, ' in Aristoph. Ach. 610 ' once', from ἐν : writ-ten in the Schol. ἔνη, of the former year, formerly. Brunck has "ΕΝ "Η ΟΥΚ, once or never :' Dnn.

'Ενηὴς, kind.—R. ἐν, ἰὺς, ἐῆος, good.

'Ενήλατα, ' the four posts of a bedstead ;—the two upright sides of a ladder ;—linchpins of a wheel.— R. ἐν, ἐλαύνω, [ἤλαται,] :' Dnn. Driven in.

†'Ενήνοθε : See 'Ανενήνοθε.

'Ενθα, here.—' R. ἐν, in :' Ldd.

'Ενθεν, thence.—As "Ενθα. Θεν as in οὐρανόΘΕΝ.

'Ενί : in Εἰν.

'Ενιαυτὸς, a year.—R. ἐνί, αὐτός : Returning in or into itself. ' In se sua per vestigia volvitur annus :' Virg. (2) R. †ἔνος, a year. ?

'Ενικὸς, single.—R. ἐν, as Μανικός.

'Ενιοι, some : i. e. ἔνι οἱ, ἐνί-εισιν οἱ, there are those who. So

'Ενιότε, sometimes, ἔνι ὅτε. Above.

'Ενίπτω, to address, announce, like 'Ενέπω, and to address with rebuke, to chide :—Also to attack, said of actions.—R. ἐνέπω, much as †πέτω, †πιπέτω, πίπτω. But 'Ιπτω, to oppress, may seem to apply in some senses.

'Ενίσπω, to tell, relate, speak.—R. ἐν, ἕπω, as 'Εχω, 'Ισχω.

'Ενίσσω, ' same as 'Ενίπτω, differing only in form, to assail with reproaches :' Dnn. 'Ενίπτω, ἐνίττω, ἐνισσω.

'Εννέα : in 'Ενία.

"Εννος, "Εννος, yearly. See "Ενος.

'Εννύμι, to put on.—R. †ἕω, as Σέω, Σβέννύμι.

'Εννυὸς or 'Ενυὸς, Νυὸς, a daughter-in-law.—R. ἐν, νεύμαι or †νεύομαι, the same as νέομαι : As coming into the family. So Νέος, new, is from νέομαι : A new comer.

†Ἔνος or †Ἔνος, a year, *annus*, found in the Grammarians.—Like Ἔτος, from †ἔω, εἶμι, to go : much as †Μάω, Μένος ; †Γάω, Γένος. ' *Eunt* anni :' Ov. — Or †ἔω, mitto, prætermitto : Passed by. See the next.

Ἔνος or Ἔνος, ' of a year, a year old, belonging to the last year :— ἔνη καὶ νέα, the old and new moon, the last day of the lunar moon :— ἔναι ἀρχαί, the magistrates of last year :' Dnn. Prop. ' gone ', ' past '; ' last ', from †ἔω, to go, or †ἔω : see deriv. of Ἔνος, above. Some compare Ἄνω, to finish, and αὐθΕντης. So *Plenus* annus, and Πλειών, a year.—But αὔριον καὶ ἔνη, tomorrow and the day after : deduced by Ldd. from εἷς, ἑνός, i. e. *ONE* day more. (2) ' Hebr. *senee*, to change :' Wr.

Ἔνοσις, a shaking.—Many suppose a form ἐνόθω, from ἐν, †ὤθω, ὤσω, to push.

Ἐνταῦθα, Ἐνθαῦτα, in this place, to this place.—The last word points to ἔνθα, αὐτό : in that very place. (2) R. ἐν, ταὐτὸ, with ϑα as ἔνΘΑ : for Ἐνταντόθα.

Ἔντεα, ' arms, armour :—utensils, outfit, furniture, tackling.—Buttm. from ἔννυμι, [ἔνται,] :' Dnn. Or εἷς, gen. ἐντός.

Ἐντελέχεια, ' the absoluteness, actual being of a thing, that by which a thing actually is. Prob. from ἐν τέλει ἔχειν, to be complete or absolute, on the analogy of νουν-έχεια :' Ldd. Therefore rather the *acc.* τέλος : The having perfection in (it).

Ἔντερα, Dnn. the entrails : ἐντός.

Ἐντεῦθεν, Ἐνθεῦτεν, thence. — Like Ἐνθαῦτα. The E like νεὼς, Αεὼς, νημΕρτής.

Ἐντὸς, within : ἐν, as Ἐκ, Ἐκτός.

Ἐντύω, Ἐντύνω, to furnish, provide, prepare. — ' R. ἔντεα :' Dnn. So Σκευάζω from Σκεῦος.

Ἐνυάλιος, Mars, the brother of Ἐνυώ.

Ἐνυδρὶς, an otter, living ἐν in the ὕδωρ water.

Ἐνυὼ, Bellona. — Eustath. from ἔνω, i. e. φένω, (φόνος,) to kill : as Λείβω, Εἴβω. (2) Allied to Ἀνύω to despatch. See αὐθΕντης.

Ἐνώπια, ' the walls at the sides or entrance of a portico or hall (Damm,) or those first seen on entering : ἐν, ὠπί :' Dnn.

Ἔξ, from : in Ἐκ.

*Ἔξ, six. — The Hebr. *shesh* or (softly) *ses* is proposed. — Sanskr. *shashta* ; and affinities are stated in the Saxon, Gothic, German, Danish, &c. — Yet Ἔξ may well be allied to Ἑξῆς, next after, as Ἡ ἑξῆς, the next day. Espec. as in some languages the numbers go to 5 only, and then 5 and 1, 5 and 2, &c.

Ἐξάντης, ' from ἄντα, as Κατ-άντης, Προσ-άντης : Not exposed, hence unharmed, sound, whole :— free from :' Ldd. ' From ἐξ ἐναντίας, in a different state from what he was before :' Herm. — ' For Ἐξανύτης, from ἐξανύω : Perfect :' Dr. Jones.

Ἐξαπίνης, suddenly, ' Ion. for Ἐξαίφνης :' Dnn. i. e. for ἐξαφίνης. But perhaps from ἅπτω, as mentioned in Αἴφνης.

Ἐξαπλάσιος, -πλήσιος, sixfold. — See in Διπλάσιος.

Ἔξαστις, ' rough edge left by tearing linen : also Ἐξεστις. Prob. from †ἐξέδζομαι, as Δίασμα from Διάζομαι :' Ldd. and Dnn. — Ἔξεστις from ἐξ, ἐστάω, as in Εὐ-εστὼ, would agree with Damm's explanation, ' the ends of threads *standing out of* cloth.'

Ἑξῆς, Ἑξείης, one after another, in a row, next :— immediately. — R. ἔχομαι, ἔξομαι, to hold on.

Ἔξις, habit of body or mind. — R. ἔχω, ἔξω, as Habit from Habeo.

Ἐξίτηλος, gone off, vanished. — R. ἐξ, εἶμι, ἵται, to go.

Ἐξούλης δίκη, an action of ejectment. — R. ἐξ, ἔλλω, ἔολα, to roll one out of. ' *Evolvas* istos ex prædâ :' Liv.

Ἐξουσία, power. — R. ἐξ, ὢν οὖσα : as Ἔξεστι, it is in our power. So Παρ-ουσία.

Ἔξοχα : in Ὄχα.

Ἔξω, out : ἐξ, as Ἐς, Ἔσω.

Ἐόργη, a pounder, pestle, spoon. — R. ἔργω, ἔοργα : Working well, kneeding. So Ὀργάζω.

Ἑορτὴ, a festival. — R. ὄρω, ἔορται, (See above,) : Excitatio : A day or occasion of *excitement* and concourse. Aspirate, as in Ὀρμάω and *Hortor*. (2) R. εἴρω, ἔερται, †ἔορται, to join together, to assemble. So Ἑερμένος, joined.

Ἑὸς, his : R. ἐ, as Τέ, Τεός.

Ἔπαλξις, a bulwark. — R. ἐπ', ἀλέκω, whence ἀλάλκω, ἔω, to ward off.

Ἐπασσότερος, one crowding on another. — R. ἐπ', ἀν, †συντὸς as in Θεόσ-συτος. (2) R. ἐπ', ἄσσον, very near.

Ἐπαυράω : in Ἀπαυράω.

Ἐπεὶ, Ἐπειδὴ, Ἐπεάν, &c., thereupon, consequently *upon* that, because :— close *upon* the time that, from or after the time that. — Allied to Ἐπί.

Ἐπείγω, to drive on, press on, press hard on. — Allied to Ἐπ-άγω, as Ἀγείρω to Ἐγείρω, and Ὄγμος to Ἄγω through a verb †Ἔγω. (2) R. ἔπομαι : To make to follow. In form much as τμηΓΩ. (3) Buttm. compares πιέζω. See Ἐθέλω.

Ἐπείσιον, Ἐπίσειον, crinis tegens pudenda. — Grove benè explicat ἐπ-εισ-ιὸν, ' going over into.' Vide Ἐπηγκενίδες, et vocem Ἀορτὴ ut explicatam suprà à Dnn.

Ἔπειτα, thereupon, thereafter, therefore, then. — R. ἐπ' εἶτα. (2) R. ἐπεὶ, and τα as in Ὅτα.

Ἐπενήνοθε : in Ἀπενήνοθε.

Ἐπέτης, an attendant : ἔπομαι.

Ἐπέτοσσε, ' same as Ἐπ-έτυχε, fell in with or met. So Τόσσας, happening to be, like Τυχών. Allied perh. to Τόξον :' Ldd. ' †Τόω, [†τόσω,] is, like †τάω, †τέω, τείνω, to extend to, to reach :' Heyne. — Pauw thought it for †ἐπέθοσσε, from θοός : Ran up to.

Ἐπηγκενίδες, ' the long planks nailed along the upright ribs of the ship : prob. from ἐνεγκεῖν :' Ldd. and Dnn. ' Stretching along over :' Grove. Corrupted from Ἐπ-ηνεγκίδες. See Ἐκπλαγος.

'Επηετανὸς, yearly.—R. ἐπ', ἔτος: Year upon year. The E doubled.

'Επηλυς, a stranger.—R. ἐπ', †ἐλεύθω, ἤλυται, προσ-ήλυτος. Ad-vena.

'Επηρεάζω, to threaten. And

'Επήρεια, a curse: ἐπì, ἀρειά.

'Επητής, 'able and willing to converse, and so rational, kind, gentle :' Ldd.—R. †ἔπω: as Affabilis, Affable: and Ἤπιος.

'Επήτριμος, 'from ἐπì, ἤτριον. Orig. woven on or to, thick, close, thronged :' Ldd. (2) R. ἐπì, τρία : Threefold. H, as in ἐπΗετανός.

'Επì, upon, over, near upon, close upon, dependently upon, upon condition of :—in addition to, i. e. one thing on another.—From †ἔπω as allied to †ἅπω, Lat. apo, (Forcell.) ἅπτω, Lat. apto. So 'Αγείρω, 'Εγείρω ; 'Αρω, Εἴρω ; 'Αγω, 'Ογμος ; &c.

'Επίβδαι, 'Επιβάδαι, the day after a festival.—R. ἐπì, †βάω, βάδην.

'Επιζαρέω, a dialect of 'Επι-βαρέω, as Ζέλλω of Βάλλω. (2) R. σαίρω. To sweep over.

'Επιζάφελος, sharp, vehement.—R. ἐπì, ζα, φέλος, a stone, rock. So 'Α-φελής. (2) R. ἐπì, †ζάφελος allied to Ζάλη and Ζάψ, like Ψάω, Ψαφαρός. (3) 'Hebr. sibel, a torrent :' Wr.

'Επίηρανος, suiting, aiding ;—warding off.—As

'Επίηρος, pleasant. — R. ἐπì, ἄρω, ἦρεν, ἤραρεν, to suit. (2) R. ἐπì, ἐράω, to love.

'Επικάρσιος, from ἐπί-καρ, on the head, head-foremost.

'Επικουρέω, to help, as an

'Επίκουρος, helper in war, from κούρος ; as κούροι 'Αχαιῶν is rendered by Damm 'soldiers', for it is youths who go to war. See 'Οπλότεροι.

'Επινάστιος, sojourning in a country, as "Επ-οικος.—R. ἐπì, ναίω, †νάω, νένασται.

'Επίνειον, sea-port.—R. ἐπì, ναῦς, g. νεώς.

'Επίνεψις, cloudiness.—R. †νέφω, ψω, νέφος.

'Επίξηνον, a chopping-block.—R. ξαίνω, ἔξηνα, to pluck, cut, strike', (Ewing).

'Επίπλοα, "Επιπλα, 'prop. things pertaining to the rigging and equipment of vessels ;—household furniture, moveables :' Dnn.—R. ἐπì, πλόος, πλοῦς, a sailing. (2) For 'Επιπόλαια, things ἐπιπολῆς on the surface, opposed to fixed, i. e. moveable.

'Επίπλοον, the caul, 'membrane which covers and hangs over the fore part of the intestines :' Dan.—R. ἐπì, πέλω, to be, or πολέω, †πλόω.

'Επιπολῆς, on the surface, on the top.—R. ἐπì, on, πέλω, πέπολα, to be.

'Επίσειον: in 'Επείσιον.

'Επίσταμαι, 'to place myself over a thing, understand, know : Ion. for 'Εφ-ίσταμαι, from 'Εφ-ίστημι :' Ewing. We say to Under-stand. (2) R. ἐπ', ἴσημι, whence "Ιστωρ, Knowing.

'Επιστήμη, knowledge.—Above.

'Επιστοβέω, to insult, mock.—R. στείβω, ἔστοβα : To trample upon.

48

'Επιτάρροθος, gen. thought the same as 'Επίρροθος, which from ῥόθος. 'Επì τὰ for 'Επì τάδε. But Lycophron has τάρροθος ; this then, with Ewing, from ταρρὸς, ταρσὸς, the sole of the foot, or simply the foot ; θέω, θῶ, to run : Running on the foot, i. e. to bear help. Compare Βοηθὸς from βοη-θέω.

'Επιτηδὲς, 'from ἐπì τάδε, [or ἐπì τῇδε, for this purpose,] for special purposes, purposely. 'Επιτήδειος, made for the purpose, fit, suitable ; Οἱ ἐπιτήδειοι, serviceable, friendly, as Necessarii : Ldd. (2) R. †τάω, †τήδην, (as παρα-βλήδην,) τείνω, tendo, intendo, attendo, as we say intentionally. Or attentively, as 'Επιτηδεύω is to practise assiduously, study.—Above.

'ΕΠΙΤΥΡΟΝ, a confection of olives : in some way allied, one would think, to πιτυρὶς ἐλαία, a kind of small olive. Τυρὸς seems inapplicable.—(Very rare.)

'Επιφθύζω, to spit upon.—R. ἐπì, πτύω ; πτ becoming φθ, somewhat as δουρ́ιληπτα, δουρίληφθ'.

"Επομαι, to follow 'Επì upon : and allied to "Απτομαι to touch.

'Εποποῖ, a cry to mimic that of the

"Εποψ, οπος, υρυπα, the hoopoe or whoop.—Varro from its sound pu pu. See above.

"Επος, saying, word : ἔπω.

'Επτὰ, seven. 'Hebr. seba :' Mrt. 'So the Chald., Syr., Ethiopic. Sapta Sanskr., haft Pers., hapte Zend. In Chald. and Syriac sebah is to fill or satisfy :' Wbst. (2) As a consecutive number, from ἕπομαι, ἕπεται, to follow. Or, as "Εκτωρ from "Ε.ω, Οἶκτος from Οἴζω, so "Επτὰ from the perf. pass. See "Εξ.

†"Επω, to speak, relate.—Allied to †"ΑΠΩ, Lat. apo, apio, (Forcell.) ἅπτω, to join : To join words together, as Sermo from Sero, to join. Compare 'Ερέω 1. E and A, as 'Εγείρω, 'Αγείρω ; Εἴρω and "Αρω. Gellius says that "Επω belongs to the aspirated "Επω. (2) R. †ἔω, †ἔπω, (as †Βλέω, Βλέπω,): To send forth (sounds).

"Επω, to be engaged 'Επì upon or about. Allied to "Επομαι, to follow, pursue ; and "Απτομαι, to 'engage in,' (Ldd.).

†'Ερα, the earth, ground, whence 'Εράζε, on or to the ground.—Mrt. from Chald. ara, the earth. (2) To ear (Isa. 30. 24,) is to plough, Goth. arian, Sax. erian. And Tooke makes Earth 'that which one eareth or plougheth.' †'Ερα may be allied to these and to 'Αρόω, 'Αρω, aro: to plough. Thus 'Αρύω and 'Ερύω, 'Αγείρω and 'Εγείρω. (3) Hemsterh. thinks it means 'desert land :' allied to 'Ερδω 2, and 'Ερημος.

"Ερανος, a club feast where each contributed his share :—a club of subscribers.—' Some from ἐρᾰω, to pour out : more prob. from ἐρδω to love :' Dnn. So ἠρΑΝΟΣ, κοὶρΑΝΟΣ, οὐρΑΝΟΣ. (2) 'For εἴρανος from εἴρω to join together :' Greg. So

'Ερᾰω, to love. 'Ε ος, 'Ερως, love.—R. εἴρω, †ἔρω, ἄρω, to join, connect. 'Amor est nexus animorum :' Greg.

'Ερᾰω, 'Εξερᾰω, to throw or pour out, empty : whence Δι-ἐρ ἄμα, a funnel.—Allied to 'Ερύω, to draw. Thus

'Αφύσσω is. 'to *draw* from one vessel to another, to *pour out*,' Dnn. who justly allies 'Ερἀω to 'Ραίνω, 'Ρέω. (**2**) ' Hebr. *arag*, nudari :' Mrt. ?

"Εργω, 'Εργάζομαι, to work, do.—As we find "Εργα βοῶν, 'Εργάζεσθαι γῆν, Dr. Jones from Chald. *eerk*, the earth. But as well from †ἔρα, the earth, i. e. to do or work the earth, as Dnn. brings 'Αρόω to plough from †ἔρα. Γω, as τμηΓΩ, ἀρήΓΩ. (**2**) Mrt. from Hebr. *arag*, to weave. Say then from εἴρω, †ἔρω, to weave. (**3**) R. ῥέζω by transpos. (**4**) "Εργω, Wέργω, allied to our *Work*, and its affinities in Sax., Goth., Germ., Swed. &c.

"Εργω, the same as Εἴργω.

"Ερδω, to do, perform :—to perform a sacrifice, as Virgil, ' Faciam vitulâ.' "Ερδειν θυσίας Herod.—Allied to "Εργω 1, and 'Ρέζω.

'Ερέα, wool : in Εἶρος.

"Ερεβος, *Erebus*,—darkness.—R. ἐρέφω, †ἔρεβον, to cover, as στρέφω, †ἔστρεβον, στρεβλός. (**2**) R. ἔρα : Subterranean darkness, much as κολοΒΟΣ. (**3**) ' Hebr. *ereb*, the evening :' Mrt.

"Ερεγμα: in 'Ερείκω.

'Ερεείνω, to ask. ἐρέω.

'Ερείδω, ' to affix, infix, fix on, fix in, fix or press firmly on, lean upon, push into, press against, squeeze, resist, attack, to be quick :' Dnn.—As †'Αρύω and 'Ερύω, 'Αγείρω and 'Εγείρω, so 'Ερείδω is allied to 'Αρω, ' to fix ;—to be fixed: ἄψάρε, it is fixed :' (Dnn.). In form as ὄνΕΙΔΟΣ. (**2**) Buttm. allies it to "Εργω 2.

'Ερέθω, 'Ερεθίζω, ' to provoke to anger, always in the Iliad : but elsewhere to move, affect, distress. Akin to "Ερις and 'Ερέσσω :' Dnn. ' Akin to "Ερις :' Ldd. That is, to lead to strife. (**2**) ' Prop. to nip ἔρος, εος, wool' : Blomf. i. e. to *tease*, a word which is used both ways. (**3**) Steph. : ' Εἴρω is in Eustath. *ἐς μάχην συμ-πλέκω*, whence he derives 'Ερέθω'. (**4**) 'Ερέθω prim. to ' move', then to ' draw', and, as 'Lacio', ' Lacesso', to provoke : Allied to 'Ερύω.

'Ερείκω, to split, burst, bruise, grind.—R. ἐρείδω, ἔρεικα, to press against, squeeze. (**2**) Allied to 'Ερύω, to drag, as "Αγω is to drag and to break. 'Ερεγμα, flour, shows a form 'Ερέκω : and see 'Ερέχθω. (**3**) Allied to 'Αράσσω, 'Ράσσω, 'Ρήσσω, ἔρρηκα.

'Ερείπω, to throw down, overturn, demolish.—Allied to 'Ερείδω, to press against, push violently : and to 'Ερείκω. In form as βλέΠΩ, ὄρέΠΩ. (**2**) ' To throw to the †ἔρα ground :' Mrt. (**3**) Allied to 'Ρίπτω. But the latter is from 'Ερείπω.

"Ερεισμα, a prop, support, pillar ;—rock, sunken rock, being a firm foundation.—R. ἐρείδω, ἐρείσμαι, to fix in, and to lean upon. ' A thing fixed :' Dnn. Like "Ερμα.

'Ερεμνὸς, dark.—R. ἐρέφω, ἐρεμμένος, covered. As 'Ερυμνὸς, Σεμνός. (**2**) R. ἔρεβος, ἐρεβεννὸς, †ἐρεβνός.

'Ερέπτομαι, to browze, graze,—devour.—' Akin to 'Ερείπω :' Dnn. Indeed there is ἐρείπτω in ἀν-ηρείψαντο, snatched up and carried off. Allied also to 'Ερύω, to drag, pull.

49

'Ερέπτω, to crown, allied to 'Ερέφω. But others read otherwise : Pind. P. 4. 240.

'Ερέσσω, to impel, excite, impel to frenzy ;—utter with vehemence :—to row a boat.—' Akin to 'Ερέθω, 'Ερεθίζω :' Dnn. And to 'Ερύω to draw.

'Ερεσχελέω, ' to irritate by mockery, to jest. Akin to 'Ερέσσω and 'Ερέθω :' Dnn. and Ldd. As ἔΣχον, ἔΣπον, for ἐρεχελέω, an extended form of ἔρεκα perf. (**2**) Transp. from †ἐρελεσχέω : ἐράω, λέσχη, to like idle talk. (**3**) R. †ἔρα, ἐρύω, †χέλος, χελῦνη, χεῖλος: To draw out the lip. ' I will make a lip at the physician :' Shaksp.

'Ερέτης, a rower. 'Ερετμὸς, an oar.—R. ἐρέσσω, to row.

'Ερεύγομαι, 'Ερυγγάνω, to belch out, roar, vomit. — Allied to 'Ερἀω, 'Εξ-ερἀω, to throw out, (as Ewing explains 'Ερεύγομαι,) vomit, und 'Ερύω, 'Εξ-ερύω, to draw out. Γ, as in ψέΓω, ἀρήΓω.

'Ερεύθω, to redden: 'Ερυθρὸς, red. — R. ἐρύω. We say, It *drew* blood or color into his face. Thus ' Rubores alicui *elicere*, to put to the blush :' Forcell., ἐρυθαίνειν. And so in general. ' Ovid, nigrum colorem *trahere* :' Id. ' Colorem ducere, is *trahere* : Virgil, Duceret apricis in collibus uva colorem :' Id. In form as ἀερέΘΩ, βεβρώΘΩ. (**2**) Germ. *roth*, red.

'Ερευνάω, to search out, seek, trace. — R. ἐρέω, ἔρομαι, to ask, seek. Much as †'Ελάω, 'Ελαύνω. (**2**) Allied to 'Ερύω, to draw (out).

'Ερέφω, to cover, — to crown. — Allied to 'Ερύω, to draw (over), to veil : Lat. ob-duco. In form as στέΦΩ. (**2**) ' R. †ἔρα : To heap earth over :' Mrt.

'Ερέχθω, to break : allied to 'Ερείκω, ἐρείχθην, 'Ερεγμα. Also to distress, torture, allied by Dnn. to 'Ερέσσω, but perh. the same verb still, i. e. ' to *break* thó spirit of'. Compare 'Αγανακτέω.

'Ερέω, to speak, say, tell. — R. 'ἔρω, for εἴρω, to join together, whence ἔερτο, ἐερμένος :' (Dnn.) To join words together, as Sermo from Sero, to join.

'Ερέω, to ask, enquire, seek or search for. — R. ἐρέω above : to speak, and so to ask. ' 'Ερεείνω', says Dnn., ' to ask ; ἐρεείνομαι, to say'. (**2**) Allied to 'Ερύω, 'Εξ-ερύω, to draw out, search out.

"Ερημος, empty, desert. — R. ἐρἀω, ἐρἀμαι, (Ion. †ἔρημαι,) ἐξ-ερἀω, to draw out, empty out. (**2**) ' R. ἔρα, waste land :' Hemst. ? (**3**) ' Heb. *orem*, to be naked :' Wr.

'Ερητύω, to keep back, restrain. — ' Allied to 'Ερύω, 'Ερύκω and 'Ερωέω :' Dnn. and Ldd.

'Ερι-, very, greatly. — Buttm. from εὐρὺς, wide. (**2**) Better for ἔριδι with ' contention, eagerness, zeal,' (Dnn.) Our transl. ' to speak unto you the Gospel with much *contention* (ἀγῶνι) 1 Thess. 2. 2, applies well. (**3**) R. ἔρω, ἄρω, to join together, and so increase. Compare 'Αρι-.

'Ερίγδουπος, very resounding. — R. ἐρι-, δοῦπος. Γ prefix as in Γνόφος, and Κ in Κτύπος.

"Εργμα, as "Ερεγμα in 'Ερείκω. And 'Ερικὶς, coarsely ground barley, from ἐρείκω.

H

Ἐριδαίνω, Ἐρίζω, to quarrel : ἔρις, δος.

Ἐριθάκη, bee-bread from flour and honey.—Bees might be called ἐρίθοι as laborers. ' The little busy bee.' In form as δανΑΚΗ.

Ἔριθος, ' a daily labourer, mower,—a wool-spinner, hence some from ἔριονwool : others better from ἐρέσσω:' Dnn., i.e. to row: as ῾Υπ-ηρέτης is gen. a servant, minister. (2) A tiller of the †ἔρα ground.

Ἐρινὺς, Ἐρινννὺς, a Fury who punished criminals. — R. ἔρις, acc. ἔριν, ' passion, anger : ἔρις Διὸς, the wrath of Jove :' (Dnn.) So Ἐρινύω, Ἐριννύω, is to revenge, avenge. (2) R. ἐρι-, ἀνύω, to accomplish, dispatch.

Ἔριον, wool: in Εἶρος.

Ἐριούνης, most useful. — R. ἐρι-, ὄνημι, to help.

Ἐρίπνη, ' a steep crag. — R. ἐρείπω, [ἤριπον,]; not ἐρι-, πνέω, [where the wind blows vehemently,]': Dnn. Broken, as Rumpo, Rupes ; Cleave, Cliff.

Ἔρις, ἔριδος, ' fight, battle, contest, rivalry ;—incitement, eagerness, zeal, passion, anger :' Dnn. —R. ἐρείδω, ἔριδον, ' to resist vigorously, attack,—to do anything in a rapid and vehement manner' (Dnn.) (2) R. ἔρω, to join (in fight), Lat. con-sero manûs. (3) ' Hebr. heres, to burn:' Wr. See Δἶς.

Ἔριφος, a kid. — R. ἐρείπω, ἔρειφα, (ἔριφα,) to throw down. Lat. Petulcus, butting, from Peto, to assault. So I in ἔριῖμα.

Ἐριώλη, ' a hurricane, from ἐρι-, ἄω [to breathe, †ἀλλη.] But in A. Vesp. 1148 a play on the word, equiv. to ἐρίων ἀπώλεια:' Dnn. Indeed the word itself may be from ἐρι-, †ἀλέω, ὑλλύμι.

Ἕρκος, a fence, enclosure. — R. ἔργω or ἔργω, ἔρκα, to enclose, εἴργω.

Ἕρμα, ' which keeps firm and steady, prop, support, defence ;—a foundation, resting-point, sunk-rock, sepulchral mound, — ballast, a stone the crane is said to carry as ballast, met. a burden ;— the stone as a starting point in a race-course : — that infixes, causes pain. For ἄρισμα from ἐρείδω, [or ἔρεισμα]:' Dnn.

Ἕρμα, a necklace, chain of pearls. — R. ἔρω or ἔρω, εἴρω, to join.

Ἑρμαῖ, stone statues of Ἑρμῆς.

Ἕρμαιον, unexpected gain. For Ἑρμῆς presided over gain. So Mercurius from Mercis. And Hor. Sat. 2. 3. 24, 25, 26.

Ἑρματίζω, to ballast : ἕρμα.

Ἑρμηνεὺς, messenger, interpreter. For Ἑρμῆς was the messenger and ' Interpres Divûm', Virg.

Ἑρμῆς, Mercury. — ' With wonderful consent Pharnutus, Porphyry, &c. derive from ἐρῶ, ἔρμαι, to speak : As interpreter of the gods :' Scheid. See above : and Acts 14. 12. (2) R. εἴρω, to weave i.e. deceit, as the god of gain. (3) Hebr. aram, cunning.

Ἑρμὶν, a bed-post. — R. ἔρμα, a prop.

Ἔρνος, a young tree, scion, offspring. — Allied to Ἔρχομαι and ΕΡπω, as progressing and growing. (2) R. ἐαρινὸς, ἠρινὸς, vernal : †ἠρνός. E, as Ἔδνα.

50

Ἔρνος is neuter, but so is Ἔθνος. (3) From a word ἔροινος = ἐροθεις, fresh. (4) R. ἐρι-, νέος. ?

Ἐρξείης, ' the translation of Darīus, from ἔργω, ξω, to work : The doer. Or ἔργω, to shut in, &c. : Coercitor :' Ldd.

Ἔρομαι, to love, ἐράω.

Ἔρομαι, to ask, ἐρέω.

Ἔρος, wool: in Εἶρος.

ΕΡΠΙΣ, wine. ' An Egyptian word:' Dnn. (2) Ewing ' from ἕρπω: A creeping vine, wine.'

Ἕρπυλλον, creeping thyme, from

Ἕρπω, Ἑρπύζω, to creep, — go forward, go. — Allied to ΕΡχομαι, ending as ἐλΠΩ, μέλΠΩ: but nearer in sense allied to ἐρύω, to draw (myself on), as we say, to With-draw : To draw on, drawl on, creep on.

ΕΡΡΑΟΣ, Ἕρῥωὸς, aries, ' a ram, a male animal, Lycoph. 1316, or wild boar, ? R. ἄῤῥην :' Dnn. ? (2) ' Hebr. arī or erī, a fighting animal :' Becm.

Ἔρῤω, ' to go about sorrowfully, move with pain, come under an evil omen, go to ruin or perdition. Ἔρῤε, begone, away with thee. Ῥέω and Lat. ruo are allied :' Dnn.— Rather, allied to Ἔρχομαι and ΕΡπω, meaning orig. to go, Lat. eo, then per-eo, to perish, inter-eo, to die. Thus Ἴτω in Eur. Med. 697 is ' Abi (in malam rem)'. (2) ' For φθέρῥω, as Εὐρὰξ is Πλευρὰξ:' Damm. (3) ' Germ. irren, Thüring erren, to go astray, err :' Thiersch.

Ἔρση, Ἔρση, dew,—hence a young tender animal.— As Ἔρσην and Ἄρσην, so ἔρση from ἄρδω, ἄρσω, to irrigate. (2) Transp. for ῥέση, (as RApio and ΑΡπάζω,) from ῥέω, to flow.

Ἔρσις, Ἔρσις, wreath, as Ἕρμα.

Ἐρυγγάνω : in Ἐρεύγομαι.

Ἐρυγμηλὸς, bellowing. Above.

Ἐρυθρὸς, red. — R. ἐρεύθω.

Ἐρύκω, to draw back, ἐρύω.

Ἔρυμα, fence, fort. — R. ἐρύω, to draw off, ward off, draw from danger. As

Ἐρυμνὸς, secured, safe, strong.— For ἐρυμένος from Ἐρύω. See above. As Σεμνός.

Ἐρυσίβη, mildew, rust. — R. ἐρεύθω, ἐρεύσω, to make red. So ἐρΥθρός.

Ἐρύω, to draw, drag, pull,—Allied to Ἀρύω. So Ἀγείρω and Ἐγείρω.

Ἔρφος, a skin, hide.— R. ἐρέφω, to cover.

Ἔρχατος, a fence, like Ἕρκος.

Ἔρχομαι, to come or go.— As ἔρΧατος and ἕρΚος, and νήΧω, so ἔρχομαι from ἐρύω, ἔρυκα, ἔρΚα, (or †ἔρω, ἔρκα,) to draw oneself on, as we say to With-draw. ' He drew near to the city:' N.T. So Ἄγε, ῾Υπ-άγω, and οἴΧΟΜΑΙ. (2) ' Hebr. arach, to journey :' Mrt.

Ἐρῶ, to say, ask, seek : in Ἐρέω.

Ἐρω, to join : in Εἴρω.

Ἐρωέω, to cause to go back, repel, withhold, abandon : to go away, retire, — allied to Ἐρύω, Ἐρύκω. Also, from the same Root, to go out fast, gush out, as blood. Dnn. says from ῥέω, to flow. But ῥέω itself is from †ἐρέω, ἐρόω, to draw on. 'Akin to 'Ρώομαι :' Ldd.

'Ερωή, cessation, respite, retreat : from ἐρωέω to withhold, retire. — Also, impetuous course, impulse, a throw, impetuosity : See the latter part of 'Ερωέω.

"Ερως, love. — R. ἐράω, ἐρῶ.

'Ερωτάω, to ask, enquire. — R. ἐρέω, ἐρῶ.

'Ες, ἰο, iuto: in Eἰs.

'Εσθέω, to clothe. 'Εσθής, clothes, 'perh. for ἐσθῆς from ἕσθην, a. 1. p. of ἕννῡμι :' Dnn.

'Εσθλὸς, good, brave, noble, excellent, &c. — 'From an old form ἐθλὸς, [as Ισθμός,] akin to Germ. edel: Herm. and Boëckh :' Dnn. 'Εθλὸς is from ἐθέλω, ἔθλω, to be willing, ready. Homer: Ἐθέλοντα μάχεσθαι, and "Εθελεν προμάχεσθαι ἁπάντων. Thucyd.: Νομίσατε εἶναι τὸ καλῶς πολεμεῖν τὸ 'ΕΘΕΛΕΙΝ. Xen.: Οὓς ἑώρα 'ΕΘΕΛΟΝΤΑΣ κινδυνεύειν. Eurip. joins ἐσθλὸς καὶ πρόθυμος. But note also Γῇ ἐθέλουσα, Xen. ' Volentia rura', Virg. See Θέλεμος. — Or even thus: to be wished, and so good, as Optimus is Optatissimus.

"Εσθω, 'Εσθίω, to eat. R. ἔδομαι, ἐδέσθην, †ἔσθην.

'Εσία, 'Εσσία, 'a dialectic variety for οὐσία :' Dnn. From εἶς, εἶσα prop. particip. of εἰμί.

"Εσις, impulse, desire. — R. ἔω, ἔσω, to cast, ἵεμαι, to throw my mind on, desire.

"Εσκον, I was. — R. ἔω, †ἔσκω, as Βάω, Βάσκω.

'Εσμὸς, a swarm of bees : — multitude. — R. †ἔω, ἔσμαι, to send out. ' Favis emissa juventus,' Virg. — Or ἕζω, ἕσμαι, to settle. ' In-sidentia examina', Flor.

'Εσπέρα, evening. — R. ἔσπομαι, to follow : What follows the morning. (2) From

"Εσπερος, evening : the evening star. — R. ἑσπέρα. (2) R. ἔσπομαι, as setting after the sun.

'Εσπομαι, the same as "Επομαι. So

"Εσπον, a. 2. of ἔπω, as Ἔχον.

'Εσσὴν, 'a priest at Ephesus, as Lat. rex sacrificulus: according to Etym. M. the king (queen) bee, as akin to ἐσμός :' Ldd. From †ἔω, †ἔσω : The sender out ; or The settler. Or ἔσσαι pass. See 'Εσμός. (2) 'Chald. hasin, potens :' Dahler.

'Εσσην, Ionic for "Ησσων.

"Εστε, until, up to. — ' For ἐς ὅτε, up to when. The Doric form ἔστε has been restored, yet it is not put for ἕως τε :' Ldd. (2) "Εσ-τε, and (that) up to. 'Ες χρόνον, says Ormst.

'Εστί, he is. — As ἐΣμὲν and ἔΣχον, so here the Σ is put in. 'Εμί, Εἰμὶ, properly produced †ἐτὶ, as Τίθητι, Φατὶ, 'Ισᾱτι. (2) ' Sanskr. asti, Pers. est, hist, Germ. ist', &c.: Webst.

'Εστία, 'Εστίη, a hearth; — the home, the family: — the altar of the household gods, as the Latin phrase ' Pro aris et focis.' Also Vesta, the goddess of the domestic hearth. — 'R. prob. Ιζω, ἕζομαι:' Dnn., i. e. ἕζω, ἔσται. So also Hemst., who calls it 'sedes stabilis et certa', and says this was the cause why it meant a house and habitation. — Others from sitting at the

51

hearth, as Cicero ' Sedere ad focum.' (2) Dr. Jones makes it 'a place to eat at, from ἔσθω', or ἔδομαι, ἔδεσται, ἔσται. It belongs, says Lennep, ' ad familiarem victum.' See 'Εστιάω. (3) ' Chald. eschta, fire:' Mrt.

'Εστιάω, to entertain at one's ἑστία. '

"Εστωρ, a peg, or nail, as driven in: from †ἔω, ἔσται: Immissus. So 'Εμ-βάλλω, "Εμ-βολον.

'Εσχάρα, 'a hearth, fireplace on the ground, a place where a fire burns in or out-doors, an altar, prop. the hollow part on which the fire burns: — any contrivance for containing live coals, chafing-dish, portable furniture: — a scar, formed by a burn: scab of a sore:' Dnn. — Simply from ἔσχον, ἔχω, to hold. As μυσΑΡΑ. (2) ' Hebr. esch, fire:' Mrt.

"Εσχατος, extreme, last. — R. ἔσχον: Most holding back, and so last.

"Εσω, within. — R. ἐς, as ἔξω.

†'Ετάζω, 'Εξ-ετάζω, to examine whether a thing is ἐτὸν true.

"Εταρος, 'Εταῖρος, a companion. — ' Prob. from ἔθος, custom: or ἔτης, a friend: and akin to "Ετερος a second :' Dnn. In form as μυσΑΡΟΣ. (2) Damm brings ἑταῖρος by anagram from αἱρετὸς, chosen. ?

'Ετεὸς, true, ἐτὸς.

"Ετερος, one of two, the other, other, distinct, different. — Dnn. says that "Ετερος is akin to "Ετερο-; indeed these may be the same, as μέγΑθος and μέγΕθος. Now "Ετερος is 'a fellow, mate', (Ldd.) agreeing with "Ετερος: Thus Χειρὶ φέρειν ἑτέρῃ, 'to carry in one of the hands', (Ldd.), that which is the fellow of the other. We say, I have lost the fellow to this glove. — Even "Ετης, a companion, could produce "Ετερος: in form like φοΒΕΡΟΣ. (2) Wbst. from 'Hebr. and Chald. yeter, left, remaining'. In this way it might be from †ἐτὸς, ἀνετὸς, left alone. (3) Our other, Germ. oder.

"Ετης, a friend, companion. — R. ἐτὸς, true. Verus amicus. (2) R. ἔτος: One of the same years or age. (3) R. ἔθος, custom.

'Ετήτυμος, redupl. of "Ετυμος.

"Ετι, as yet, still, even now: from †ἔω, ἔται, εἰμί: As said of what has remained and is now, exists to this time. And Οὐκ-έτι, no further, no more, no longer : i. e. it does not still exist. "Ετι μᾶλλον, still or yet more. Also moreover, furthermore. See 'Ετὸς 1. (2) Hebr. edi, up to, unto. (3) Our yet, Sax. get, Welsh etto.

"Ετνος, thick soup of pulse. — As ἀΤμὴν for ἀΔμὴν, so for ἔΔνος, ἔδανὸς from ἔδω: An eating. Though the gender differs. But see "Εθνος.

'Ετοῖμος, prepared, ready; as κυδΟΙΜΟΣ: from †ἔω, ἔται, ἔζω: Set in order, or set on the table. Homer: ἑτοῖμα προκείμενα. Luke 9. 8: τὰ παρα-τιθέμενα. ' Ready to be sent', says Damm. — Also ' of facts and occurrences, real, actual, done, past: — true, actual, certain,' Ldd. who thinks 'Ετοῖμος akin to "Ετυμος.

"Ετος, a year. — R. †ἔω, ἔται, εἶμι, to go on: Always going on. ' Eunt anni', Ov. As λυκά-ΒΑΣ. (2) ' Eth, time, Heb. :' Mrt.

'Ετός, 'Ετεός, "Ετυμος, true.—R. †έω, έται, εἰμί : That which is, which is the case. 'That it was even so', Acts 12. 15. 'Saying that these things were so', 24. 9. So Τὸ ἐὸν, the truth: 'Οντως, truly.

'Ετός, rashly, in vain. As 'Ιτης is 'hasty, rash', from εἰμι, ἴται, so 'Ετὸς from †έω, έται, is hastily, rushly. Or †έω, έται: Cast forth, rejected, useless.— But Dnn. takes 'Ετὸς to be ' truly ? indeed ? in fact ? ironically, Arist. Pl. 404.'

"Ετυμος, true : in 'Ετὸς 1.

'Ετώσιοι, fruitless.—See the last 'Ετός.

Εὖ, well : neut. of 'Εῢς, good.

Εὐ—, readily, too readily.—For Εὐθύ.

Εὖα, Εὐὰν, Εὐοῖ, 'a term expressive of joy or encouragement at the festivals of Bacchus, the same as Εἶα:— an imitation of the bleating of a goat:' Dnn. ' Εα, Εἶα, Εὖα, are kindred words :' Id.

Εὐαγής, 'guiltless, pure;— bright, clear, conspicuous. Like 'Αγνὸς, "Αγιος:' Ldd. In Pers. 472 Blomf. Also, easily moved, from ἄγω: also, easily broken, R. ἄγω, ἄγνῦμι, to break.

Εὔαδον, i.e. ἔΓαδον, from ἀδέω, ἀνδάνω.

Εὐάζω, to cry Εὖα.

Εὔγμα, prayer, &c.: εὔχομαι, εὔγμαι.

Εὐδείελος, clear, &c.: εὖ, δέελος.

Εὐδία, fine weather.—R. εὖ, Διὸς, as in ' Sub Jove frigido', Hor. See in 'Ενδιος.

Εὐδίαιος, the hole by which a ship's sink is emptied ; orifice of a clyster pipe ; the fundament.— Prob. from εὐ-, readily, διὰ through.

Εὕδω, to sleep.— For †ἕ῾ω, (much as ΕΥαδε,) from ἕζω, ἕδο῾, 'to seat or place,' (Dnn.) : To place myself down. ' Volucres somno positæ,' Virg. So to Re-pose. (2) ' Allied to "Αεσα, to sleep:' Ldd.

Εὐεστὼ, prosperity ; i.e. well-being : εὖ, †έω, εἰμι, ἐστί. Or, a good state of things: ἐστάω, ἐστῶ.

Εὐθενέω, Εὐθηνέω, to be well off, prosper.— For εὐσθενέω, from σθένος. (2) ' Perh. best derived like τιΘΗΝΗ, a nurse, from θηλὴ:' Ldd. I. e. from θάω.

Εὐθύνω, to make εὐθὺ straight or right ;—set accounts straight, examine, adjust ;— guide straight, direct, govern.

Εὐθὺς, straight ;—straightly, quickly.—In Εἶθαρ.

Εὔϊος, Bacchus.— From the cry Εὖα. (2) ' From Εὖ υἱὲ, Well done, my son: words addressed by Jupiter to him from his valor in the battle with the Giants :' Forcell.

Εὔκηλος, for "Εκηλος: as "Ορος, Οὖρος.

Εὔκολος, opposite of Δύσκολος.

Εὐλάκα, a ploughshare.—Ldd. allies it to Αὔλακα acc., a furrow. (2) R. †ἐλάω, ἔλακα, to drive on. As ΕΥκηλος. Ζεύγεα δινεύοντες ἐλάστρεον, Hom. (3) ' Suid. has Εὐλάχα, as from λαχαίνω:' Dnn.

Εὐλὴ, a worm.—' Some from Αὐλὸς, from the shape: better from Εἰλέω, Εἴλω, ['Ελύω,] to roll, from its movements:' Dnn. Αἰόλαι εὐλαί, Hom. So 'Ελμινς.

Εὔληρα, reins, Dor. Αὔληρα.—'R. prob. εἴλω,

52

εἰλέω, [ἐλύω,]:' Dnn. As twisted thongs : or from turning the horses round, Lat. ' flectere equos.' (2) As ΕΥκηλος, for ἔληρα, from †ἔλω, to take in the hand. As Habēna from Habeo. Homer: 'Ιππων ἦνι' ΕΛΕΙΝ.

Εὐμάρα, a hide, skin.—R. εὖ, μάω, μάσσω, as in 'Αμφι-μάομαι: Well kneaded. See Μάσθλη.

Εὐμαρής, easy. — Εὐ- readily, μάρη, the hand. As Εὐ-χερής.

Εὐμᾶρις, a kind of shoe or buskin.—R. εὐμάρα, a hide. (2) Antipater has A short ; whence some from εὔμαρής, easy (for the foot). But it is said to have a thick sole.

Εὐμενίδες, the Furies. — R. εὖ, μένος, mens : kindly disposed. A name to propitiate them, as Parcæ from Parco, Εὐώνυμος, 'Αριστερός.

Εὐνὴ, a bed ;—anchor for ships.— R. εὔδω, †εὔδανὴ, εὐνή : To sleep on.

Εὖνις, a wife.—Above.

Εὖνις, bereft.—As ΕΥκηλος, from εἶς, ἐνός : Left alone, as 'alone' is 'all-one.'

Εὐοῖ : in Εὖα.

Εὐράξ, sideways.—' R. εὐρύς: As we say, Broadside on :' Ldd. So some derive Lātus from Πλάτος. (2) Damm for πλευράξ from πλευρά, a side. As Γαῖα, Αἶα, &c.

Εὔριπος, the Eurīpus, the strait between Boeotia and Euboea :—canal, conduit. ' Remarkable for an irregular ebb and flow : hence variable, inconstant.— Prob. from εὐ-, easily ; [ῥιπὴ,] ῥιπίζω:' Dnn.

Εὑρίσκω, †Εὑρέω, 'to find out after a search, discover, find. Prob. from ἐρῶ to search for :' Dnn. Or allied to 'Ερύω, 'Εξ-ερύω, to draw out.

Εὐροκλύδων, a levanter wind.— The readings Acts 27. 14 vary ; the most prob. is Εὐρακύλων, as in Lat. Vulg. euro-aquilo :' Ldd. (2) ' Εὔρου κλύδων, an eastern [or east wind] tempest :' Ew.

Εὖρος, S.E. wind.—Buttm. from ἠὼς, ἔως, the East, as Ζέφυρος from Ζόφος. ' Vires capit Eurus ab ortu :' Ov. ' Εοος Eurus :' Stat. Corrupted from ἔω, ἔωρος. — Becm. from ἔως, ῥέω, ῥῶ. ? (2) R. εὐρώς.

Εὐρὺς, wide.—' Prob. drawn out, from †ἔρω, ἐρύω, to draw :' Lenn. So Wachter brings Lang, our Long, from Lengan, to draw. So 'Ηνεκὴς from ἐνέκω.

Εὐρὼς, mouldiness.—Schneid. from Εὖρος, the S.E. wind, as bringing moisture. The S. wind is thus called Νότος from Νοτὶς moisture. (2) As Εὐρὺς, from †ἔρω, ἐρύω, traho, contraho: Contracted by time or damp.

'Εῢς, 'Εὺς, good.—As 'Ετὸς, true, from †έω, εἰμὶ, to be : That which is in truth, genuine, real, as Good coin, Good friends, &c. (2) Lenn. compares εὐθὺς, 'upright, just, frank,' (Dnn.).

Εὖτε, ' like "Οτε, when. Prob. for Οὗτε gen. of "Οστε, as Quum from Qui :' Dnn.—As it means also ' just as, as', Εὖτε is better for "Ετε, (as "Εκηλος, ΕΥκηλος,) that is, *ἥτε (ὥρα and ὀδῷ). See in 'Εώρα.

Εὐφραίνω, to gladden : Εὔφρων, cheerful.— R. εὖ, φρὴν, φρενὸς, the mind.

Εὐφρόνη, the night.—Above. 'The kindly, or acc. to others The refreshing :' Ldd. Or the time of reflection, φρονέω. Ἐν νυκτὶ βουλή, says the Proverb. So Homer says it does not become the counsellor to sleep all night. 'Favorable to meditation. If it means Well meaning or gentle, then it is a euphemism, as night was associated with terror :' Dnn. As Εὐμενίδες, &c.

Εὔχομαι : 'The common notion is prob. that of loud speaking : for it is clearly akin to Αὐχέω, to declare loud, to vaunt :' Ldd. Thus it means to vow, claim for oneself, affirm confidently. And to pray, i.e. to pray loud. (2) Or from ἔχομαι, i. e. to hold fast for myself, to hold to it, stand by it : as ἔχομαι is ' To stand, Od. ζ. 141 :' (Dnn.) Even 'to pray' may be 'to hold to (the altars)', as 'Ακμάζει βρετέων ἔχεσθαι, Æschyl. ' Talibus orabat dictis arasque tenebat', Virg.

Εὔω, Εὔω, to singe, parch, roast.—'Akin to Αὔω, Αὔω :' Dnn.

Εὐώνυμος, on the left.—R. εὖ, ὄνυμα : Of good name. A form of propitiating, as Εὐμενίδες and Parcæ.

Εὐωχέω, to regale royally.—R. εὖ, ἔχω, ὄχα, whence Ὀχή, food, in Lycophron. Bene habeo, bene tracto.

Ἐφέσια, Diana's festivals at Ephesus. Acts 19. 28.

Ἐφέτης, a commissioner, judge. Ἐφετμή, Ἐφημοσύνη, a commission.—R. ἐφ', †ἕω, ἕται, ἵημι, mitto.

Ἐφθός, boiled, cooked.—R. ἕπω or ἕπω, ἕφθην, as in 'Αμφέπω, to tend, to be occupied with, i.e. as a cook. So from fut. ἕψω is "Εψω, to boil, cook. Βοῦν ἱερεύσαντες μέγαν ἀμφεπον, Hom. And 'Αμφὶ βοὸς ἐπέτην κρέα. – Dnn. allies "Εψω and Εὔω.

Ἐχέτλη, a plough-handle ; Ἐχέτλιον, hold of a ship : R. ἔχω.

Ἐχθές, Χθές, (as "Εκεῖνος, Κεῖνος,) yesterday.— R. ἔχομαι, ἔχθην, to hold on with : As holding on with (this day). So τῇ ἐχομένη Luke 13. 33 is 'the next day.'

Ἔχθος, hatred.— R. ἔχω, ἔχθην, (as "Αγω, "Αχθην, "Αχθος) : Held firm in the mind as a grudge : compare Κότος. 'In imâ mente repostum', Virgil. (2) Aspirated from ἐκτὸς, without : ' Bad feeling to strangers.' (3) Some identify "Αχθος.

Ἐχινέες, 'a kind of mouse with rough bristling hair :' Ldd. From

Ἐχῖνος, a hedge-hog, sea urchin : —its shell as used as a jar :—also ' part of the bit of a bridle, which made it severe ;—the true stomach of ruminating animals, prob. from its rough coat. Perh. akin to 'Ακή :' Ldd. That is, †ἀκῖνος, Pointed. — Or allied to 'Εχυρὸς, 'secure, fortified', (Dnn.)

Ἔχις, Ἔχιδνα, a viper. — As Ldd. allies Ἐχῖνος to 'Ακή, so Lenn. allies Ἔχις to 'Ακίς, a sting. Χ, in 'Ακαχμένος, pointed. (2) 'R. ἔχομαι, to adhere to, ['make fast to', Ldd.] As in Acts 28. 3 a viper wound itself on Paul's hand.— Or Hebr. ΗΚΗ, belonging to a verb To smite': Pkh. (3) One gen. is ἔχιος : so some from ἔχω, ἰὸς poison. ?

Ἐχυρὸς, secure, &c. : R. ἔχω, to hold.

Ἔχω, to hold, keep, have.—As the obsolete Ἔγω (like "Αγω) is established by Ἐγείρω, Ἐπ-είγω and Ὄγμος, then from its perf. †ἔχα could be ἔχω, prim. to take, carry, and so hold in the hand. The fut. ἕξω may suppose an aspir. ἔχω, yet compare "Αγω and 'Ηγέομαι, Ὄρω and 'Ορμάω, Εὔω and Εὔω, 'Αρω and 'Αρμονία, "Ηκα and "Ηκιστος, &c. (2) R. †ἕω, ἕκα, ἵημι, to send on, carry, hold. (3) ' Compare Germ. hec-ke with the notion of hold :' Thiersch.

Ἐψέω, "Εψω, to boil, cook : in 'Εφθός.

Ἐψία, a game played with small stones ;—gen. play, pastime.—'R. ψιὰ, ψειὰ, the same as Ψῆφος :' Dnn. and Wr. But the 'Ε ? — Rather from ἕπω, ἕψω, to be occupied about, busy about, here about sports and games. See the next.

Ἐψιάομαι, 'to play at the 'Εψία ;—gen. to amuse oneself. In Apoll. 1. 459 the Schol. explains it ἀκολουθεῖν, and derives it from ἕπομαι, ἴψομαι :' Dnn. (2) 'To roast a man, taunt at a feast, rail at : ἐψέω :' Ewing. ?

†Ἔω, Εἰμί, I am.—Allied to †'Αω, to breathe : hence to breathe ' the breath of life', to exist. See the senses of Ζάω. Ε, as 'Ερύω, 'Αρύω ; 'Εγείρω, 'Αγείρω ; Εἰλύω, 'Αλίω ; &c. (2) ' Hebr. σἠγεΛ, I shall be :' Mrt.

†Ἔω, Εἶμι, I go.—Allied to †'Εω, I am, just as Γίνομαι, to be, is also 'to come to, arrive, come or go', (Dnn.) and Παραγίνομαι, ' to be present, to arrive or be at hand, come up', (Dnn.) So Παρεγίνοντο John 3. 23. Existence is motion : Gen. i. 20, 21.

†Ἔω, "Ιημι, to send.—The aspirate seems to give to "Εω ' to go' the sense ' to make to go.'

†Ἔω, "Εζω, to seat, settle, place, put : i.e. to make to go, or send, downwards. Above.

†Ἔω, 'Εννῦμι, to clothe : i.e. to make one to go into his clothes, like Δύω, 'Εν-δύω, Induo. Or to ' put ' one's clothes on. Above.

Ἔωλος, kept till the ἕω morning or morrow, as ' He will be here in the morning :'— stale, obsolete.

Ἐώρα, a thing suspended, a noose.— R. ἀείρω, ἤορα, ἕωρα, whence Μετ-έωρος.

Ἔως, 'Ηὼς, the morning. — ' Prob. from †ἕω, [†ἤον,] to shine :' Ldd. So Εὔω is allied to Αὔω. (2) R. †ἕω, ἵημι, to emit (rays). As ἡλίου βολή.

Ἕως, Εἴως, up to such a time or place, as long as, whilst, for a time, as far as :—with a view to, in order that, like 'Ως.—Ἕως answers to Τέως, for Τεοῖς, as 'Ως is Οἷς. Now Τεοῖσι is the article Τοῖς in Herod., as ἀπὸ τέω in Lucian is ἀπὸ τοῦ, &c. (Maittaire, Dialect. p. 104.) Then Τέως is Τοῖς i.e. τούτοις χρόνοις, in or for such times as. To this should answer Οἷς or 'Ως, which seems lengthened to "Εως to correspond with Τέως, as Τηνίκα, 'Ηνίκα ; Τότε, "Οτε ; &c. Maittaire says : ' E is added, poët. as ἐοῖ, ἐὲ, ἐὸς, ἐῆ, ἐὸν, ἔεις for εἷς, one, ἔης article Il. π. 208.

Z.

Za-, very.—Æol. for διά, (as in Δια-φανής,) pronounced dja, or za. Our solDIer is called solJer.

Ζάγκλον, a sickle.—R. ζα-, ἀγκύλον, bent.

Ζαγρεύς, Bacchus. 'They understand the Bacchus below, i.e. Pluto, the hunter and taker of the souls of the dead:' Steph. R. ζα, ὀγρεύς, a hunter. 'Avári Ditis', Seneca.

Ζαής, very blowing.—R. ζα, †ἄω :·or R. ζάω, which see. Ζακυνθίδες, seemingly a corruption of Ζακυνθίδες. A, as Νίτρον, Λίτρον.

Ζάκορος, 'a priest, servant : some make it as Νεώ-κορος, a servant of the temple, from ζα-, κορέω to brush. Buttm. from ζα, κόρος, a servant :' Dnn. So Ζά-κοτος.

Ζακυνθίδες, gourds of the isle of Ζάκυνθος, Zacynthus.

Ζάλη, surge, spray.—'Akin 9s Ζάλος, salum :' Ldd. (2) R. ζάω, ' to blow,' (Dnn.) See Ζάω. (3) R. ζα, ἄω to blow. (4) 'R. ζέω; ἅλς, ἁλός.

Ζάψ, ζαπὸς, the same as Ζάλη.—R. ζάω, to blow, †ζάπτω, as †Δάω, Δαίω, Δάπτω : Βλάπτω, &c.

Ζάω, 'prim. to breathe, to live; — to blow, Æ. Ag. 793. Some object with reason to ζα-, ἄω, ἄημι, that A in ζάω is short.—The same origin as ζέω. Damm :' Dnn. 'From ζέω, to be warm :' Pkh. From the heat of the animal blood.

Ζεά, Ζειά, rye, spelt. 'Perhaps from ζέω, ferveo', Mrt. And not without reason, as Frumentum is Fervimentum. See especially the next. But ZEA is also one of the twelve furrows in a horse's palate : (Very rare.) Q.?

Ζείδωρος, 'the bestower of Ζειά, or corn in general, and so of food. Some say, of life, from ζάω, but better as above:' Dnn. Δῶρον.

Ζειρά, 'a Thracian and Arabian garment falling to the feet : a tunic with a girdle, and hanging over the trowsers': Dnn.—From the Hebrew word signifying 'cinxit', says Becman; yet εἴρω or ἔρω, †σέρω, Lat. sero, (whence Ζειρά, a rope,) to join together, and so to gird, will do as well. Compare Ζάλη and Ζάλος.

Ζέλλω, 'in the Arcadian dialect for Βέλλω or Βάλλω, to throw :' Dnn. See ἐπιΖαρέω. So

Ζέρεθρον, for Βέρεθρον, Βάραθρον. Above.

Ζευγίτης, 'a third-class citizen, as possessing a Ζεῦγος :' Bœckh. See Ζεύγνῡμι.

Ζεύγνῡμι, †Ζεύγω, to join. Ζεῦγος, a pair. Ζυγὸν, a yoke, which, says Plato, the ancients called Δυογόν: i.e. from δύο, ἄγω; O as Ὄγμος allied to Ἄγω: Carrying two together. Much as Δια- became Ζα-. Or rather the foundation was †Δυάγω, †Ζύγω. Z for Δ, in Ζορκὰς, Ζήτρειον, ἀρίΖηλος. (2) †ΖΥΓΩ as τμ ἡ ΓΩ : R. σύω to sew i.e. join together. Euphonic for Σύγω. Thus Ζάλη is 'akin to Σάλος', Ldd. (3) Allied to †Ζόω, Ζώννυμι, to bind with a girdle. †Ζεύγω as

54

τμ ἡ ΓΩ. (4) Corrupted from Ξυν-άγω, †Ξυάγω, †Ξύγω. Z, as Ζότισσα. (5) 'Chald., Syr. and Arab. zug, join : Sanskr. yuga, Slav., Russ. igo, Sax. geoc, Germ. joch, Dutch juk. And Ethiop. zog, a pair:' Wbst.

Ζεὺς, Jupiter. — ' Δὶς, genitive Διός : Cretan dialect, Θιὸς, Lacon. Σιός : hence a variety Ζεὺς, also [Ζεὺς,] Ζδεὺς, Θεὸς, Deus :' Dnn. (2) 'From ζέω. Athenagoras says : The one God, according to the Stoics, is Zeus, so called from that which warms matter:' Ewing. (3) Mrt. from ζάω. Damm from δέος reverence, or δεύω to water the earth. — Wr. from Hebr. tsuee, to command.

Ζέφυρος, the W. wind.—Buttm. from ζόφος, from sun-set taking place in the West. As vOster, vEster. (2) As ὄντμα, for ζύφορος, i.e. ζεσι-φόρος, bringing heat, as Schrevel. explains Ζέσις. ΖΕΦΤΡΙΗ πνείουσα τὰ μὲν φύει, ἄλλα δὲ ΠΕΣΣΕΙ, Hom.

Ζέω, to bubble up, boil, to be glowing hot. — A word imitative of the simmering sound made by a repetition of the letter Z. ' An imitative word:' Greg. 'From the sound:' Wr.

Ζῆλος, emulation, zeal.—R. Ζέω, †Ζέελος, as Δέελος, Δῆλος.

Ζημία, a loss, damage, fine, punishment. — R. ζέω, ἔζημαι : What one is hot after, ardent for: senses appearing in Ζῆλος and Ζητέω. See especially Luke 15. 8 : 'What woman, having ten pieces of silver, &c.' (2) Ζήτημα, a search, i.e. for a thing lost;— shortened to ζῆμα, thence ζημία. (3) 'Hebr. TSM, to be empty:' Pkh.

Ζήν, Ζὰν, Jupiter, 'poët. for Ζεὺς:' Dnn. Apparently it has to do with Ζὼν, the living one: or Ζῆν, to live. (2) From Ζεὸν the reg. acc. of Ζεὺς.

ΖΗΤΑ, zeta. Hebr. sadeh.

Ζητέω, ' to strive to obtain, search for, seek out :' Dnn. — R. ζέω, ἔζημαι : much as Flugito for †Flagrito is to seek ' cum multâ flagrantiâ,' with much ardor. (2) R. ζα-, αἰτέω. (3) ' Hebr. tsada, to seek :' Mrt.

Ζήτρειον, place for chained slaves. — Harsh, (as Ζορκὰς for Δορκὰς,) for Δήτρειον, from δέω, δέδηται, (as Διά-δῆμα,) to bind. (2) R. ζα-, τρέω, tremo.

ΖΙΖΑΝΙΑ, tares. — Pkh. brings it from the Syriac.

Ζόη, for Ζωή, life. — Also the skin on boiled milk : R. ζέω, ἔζοα.

Ζορκὰς, the same as Δορκὰς, then †Ζδορκὰς as Σμικρός.

Ζόφος, darkness ;— the dark West where the sun sets. — R. ζέω, ἔζοα : Hot vapor. See the second sense of Ζόη. In form as Ψόφος. (2) Contracted from ζα-, γνόφος, darkness. (3) 'Hebr. TZPH, to overspread :' Pkh. 'Hebr. zepha, pitch :' Wr.

†Ζόω, Ζώννῡμι, to gird.—Properly, as allied to Ζέω,

prim. to make hot or warm, to buckle or gird on for purposes of heat or warmth. Ezek. 44. 18: 'They shall not gird themselves with anything that causeth *sweat :*' where Poole says, 'They had a girdle of fine-twined linen to gird the coat fast, yet so as not to make them *sweat* or smell offensively.' O as iu ζῶμός. (**2**) 'Akin to Ζεύγνῦμι :' Dnn. (**3**) 'Hebr. *ZNH*, to gird round :' Pkh. But the simple Ζόω has no N, Ζώσω, Ζῶμα, &c.

Ζύγαστρον, 'a chest, of boards strongly fastened together: ζεύγνῦμι, [ἔζυγον,] :' Ldd.

Ζυγὸν, a yoke joining horses: — bench for rowers, joining the two sides ; — beam joining two scales ; — transverse piece joining the ends of a lyre.—R. †ζεύγω, ζεύγνῦμι.

Ζύγωθρον, cross-bar of a door. Ζυγωθρίζω, to balance or weigh by a ζυγὸν beam joining two scales.— Above.

Ζύθος, ale. — 'Perh. from ζέω :' Dnn. 'Doubtless from †ζύω, ζέω, ferveo :' Lenn. Fermented liquor. So Ζύμη, leaven, yeast. — 'R. ζέω :' Dnn. From †ζύω

as above. So Fervimentum, Fermentum, Fermenta-tion.

Ζωγρέω, to take alive, ζῶον ἀγρέω. And to restore life : ζωὴ, ἔγρω, ἐγείρω, to raise, or even ἀγείρω, re-colligo animum.

Ζωὴ, life.—R. ζάω, ζῶ.

Ζῶμα, as Ζώνη.

Ζωμὸς, 'broth, soup : — a fat greasy fellow : — met. bloodshed. Prob. from ζέω, [ἔζοα,] :' Ldd. As boiling, hot.

Ζώνη, Ζωστὴρ, a girdle, *zone :* †ζόω. As Ζῶμα. (**2**) 'Chald. *zonar :*' Dahler.

Ζῶον, a living being, animal : — an animal done from life, an image.—R. ζάω, ζῶ.

Ζώπισσα, pitch scraped from old ships, and mixed with salt water.—Dnn. from ζωὸς, πίσσα. Rather, soft for ξέπισσα, from ξέω, ἔξοα, to scrape, and πίσσα.

Ζωρὸς, 'pure, sheer. Prob. for ζωερὸς from ζωός :' Ldd. As Vivus, Vividus.— Or from ζέω, ἔζοα, as said of ardent spirits. But

Ζωρὸς, in Empedocles, is 'mixed:' short, it would seem, in his strange way, for ἀ-ζωρος. Above.

H.

῞Η—, ἠ—, either ... or ... It is the subj. ῇ of εἰμί : 'Be it this, be it that.'

῍Η, than. — Thus, 'He asked whether I liked a good man better OR a bad man', i.e. 'whether I liked a good man better THAN a bad man'. — Above.

῏Η, truly, certainly. — Contr. from ἐὰ neut. pl. of ἐὸς, (in ᾿Εάων,) the same as ἐὺς, good, neut. εὖ, well, rightly. (**2**) 'From †ἔω, to be', says Martin. Indeed ἴὸς also is from †ἔω, to be.

῏Η, whether? That is, Is it TRULY so? Above.— Or, whether is it so OR not? See the first ῞Η.

῍Η, he said: for φῆ, as Γαῖα, Αῖα.

῍Η, an exclam. of grief, or of reprimand, or of addressing, holla! — For ῎Εα, which see.

῟Η, where. — Dat. sing. of ῝Ος: Quâ.

᾿Ηβαιὸς, small, little. — Usually thought the same as βαιὸς, with ἠ for ἀ, euphon, as in ῾Ηλύγη, and (with some) in ῾Ηθεῖος. (**2**) R. ἥβη, youth. As γεραΙΟΣ.

῞Ηβη, youth. — This, like ᾿Αβρὸς and ᾿Απαλὸς, tender, delicate, from ἅπτω, ἅπτομαι, †ἥβον (as ἔ-βλαβον,) to touch : Easy to the touch, tender. 'The tender age'. — Or, as Ζα-φλεγὴς, 'one who is in vigor-ous health and spirits', Il. 21. 465, is from φλέγω, to burn; and ῾Ηΐθεος, a youth, is from αἴθω, to burn; so ῞Ηβη from ἅπτω, to glow : 'Fervens juventâ,' glowing with the fire of youth. (**2**) 'Hebr. *eb*, vigor:' Mrt. 'Hebr. *ab*, to be verdant:' Wr.

᾿Ηγάθεος, very divine. — R. ἄγαν, Θεός. (**2**) Akin to ἀγαθός.

᾿Ηγέομαι, ῾Ηγηλάζω, to lead, conduct; — and, as

Duco and ῎Αγω, to think. — R. ἄγω, [ἦγον,]: Ldd. and Dnn. See ῾Ηδομαι. ῎Αγει ... σωφρόνως ἡγου-μένη, Theb. 642. (**2**) 'Hebr. *eegee*, to bring:' Wr.

᾿Ηγερέθομαι, to assemble. — R. ἀγείρω, ἤγερον.

᾿Ηδὲ, answering to ᾿Ημέν: i.e. ἤ μὲν, ἤ δέ. Many say, ἤ μέν, ἤ δέ.

῎Ηδη, now, — even now, already ; — but now, pre-sently. — For ᾖδε (τῇ ὥρα or ἡμέρᾳ), in this hour or day. Much as ῟Ωδε is ᾧδε τρόπῳ. (**2**) For ᾖ δὴ, 'eâ scilicet (horâ).' (**3**) Some say ἤ δή.?? (**4**) 'Hebr. *atta*, now :' Mrt.

῞Ηδομαι, to be pleased. ῾Ηδονὴ, pleasure. ῾Ηδὺς, pleasing, pleasant, sweet. — R. †ἁδέω, ἁνδάνω to please. (**2**) 'Hebr. *hedee*, to rejoice:' Wr.

῾Ηδος, pleasure, profit causing it. — Above.

῏Ηδος, 'vinegar: prob. as imparting a flavor, a seasoning: some asp. it, ῞Ηδος:' Dnn.—Above.

῾Ηέ, or : ἤ redupl. So

῾Ηέλιος, lengthened from ῞Ηλιος.

᾿Ηερέθομαι, to be hovering, unsteady. — R. ἀείρω, ἤερον : am raised up, suspended.

῾Ηθὰς, accustomed: R. ἦθος.

῾Ηθεῖος, honored, revered. — As Βαιὸς, ῾Ηβαιὸς, so Θεῖος, ῾Ηθεῖος : Godlike. (**2**) R. ἡθὰς, accustomed, familiar, well-known and tried : or of good ἦθος manners and character.

῾Ηθέω, ῎Ηθω, ῎Ηθω, to pass through a strainer, ῾Ηθμὸς, a sieve.— R. †ἔω, ἤθην, ἵημι, to send (through), as †Πλέω, Πλήθω. Scribonius : 'Oleum *transmissum* per colum'. (**2**) R. †ἔω, to go through. Pliny : 'Aqua per colum *transiens.*'

. Ηθος, custom, manners, character:— accustomed abode. — The same as Ἐθος.

Ἠῖα, 'provisions for a journey, food;— chaff, husks, or pods of pulse. R. ἔω, εἴω, to go:' Dnn. As Via, Viatica. In the sense of 'chaff', Damm from 'easily *going* away and dispersing by the wind'.

Ἠῖθεος, Ἠῖθεος, a young man. — Explained in Ηθη.

Ἠῖόεις, 'for Ἠῖονόεις, from ἠῖὼν, ἠῖόνος: Furnished with steep banks, as being a mountain stream. Also, said of a plain on a river's banks:' Dnn.

Ηῖος, the same as Ἰῆιος.

Ἠῖὼν, a shore, beach. — Like Ἠῖα, from ἔω, εἴω, to go: 'Against which the waves go:' Damm. But 'the most ancient form is Ἠῖον, the bed of a [running] torrent or river:' Schneid.

Ηκα, gently, softly, slightly. — Allied by Ldd. to Ἀκᾶ, Ἀκέων, Ἀκήν.

Ηκαλος, gentle: ἦκα.

Ηκιστος, very gentle, weak, feeble, little. — R. ἦκα. The Aspir., as Ηγον, Ηγέομαι.

Ηκω, to be come, have arrived, proceed. — R. †ἔω, ἦκα: To send myself on. So †Ἰω, Ἰκω. And Ἀγε, come on, and our with-*draw*. (2) 'Hebr *eek*, to go, come:' Wr.

Ἠλαίνω, Ἠλάσκω, -άζω, to wander.— R. ἀλάομαι, ἀλαίνω.

Ἠλακάτη, a distaff:—reed, mast, arrow.;—upper extreinity of a mast:—windlass for drawing in heavy fishing-nets. Ἠλάκατα, thread spun from the distaff. Ldd. and Dnn. take it as allied to, or from, ἠλάσκω, to roam about. (2) As Ἀγω, Κατ-άγω, is to draw out, spin, Ἀγμα, Κάτ-αγμα, a ball of spun wool: so this from †ἔλάω, ἤλακα, to drive, draw. 'The distaff is driven round in spinning:' Greg. 'Threads are drawn from the distaff:' Mrt.

Ηλεκτρον, -ος, 'a mixed metal;—amber, as like it in color: so perh. in A. Eq. 529, as an ornament of the screws of a lyre. R. ἠλέκτωρ, from its color:' Dnn.

Ἠλέκτωρ, the sun.—'R. ἥλιος:' Dnn. (2) Eustath. from α, λέκτρον: as never reposing.

Ἠλεὸς, Ηλὸς, Ἠλέματος, Ἠλίθιος, wandering in mind, silly;—wandering from the mark, ineffectual. — R. ἄλη, a wandering; ἅλιος, ineffectual. (2) 'Hebr. *eel*, to be mad:' Wr.

Ἠλιάζω, to warm in the ἥλιος, sun. Also, to judge causes in the

Ἠλιαία, a court where the judges sat in the open air, in the ἥλιος sun. (2) Ldd. from ἀλής, crowded. See Ηλιθα.

Ἠλίβατος, steep, high: — deep, as Altus. —'The readiest deriv. is ἥλιος, †βάω, βαίνω: Traversed only by the sun:' Ldd. (2) Buttm. for Ἠλιτό-βατος, as Ἠλιτό-μηνος: Missing the step.

Ηλιθα, in vain, from ἠλὸς, ineffectual. — Also abundantly, from ἀλής, crowded: ἅλις, enough.

Ἠλικία, age, stature, manhood.—From

Ἠλίκος, as great as, how great. — Lennep: 'R.

56

†ἀλίω, †ἥλιτο, ἀλίσκω, *cupio: Capax:* Of such a *capacity* or content.' Shaksp. has 'Things base and vile, holding no *quantity*.' Then of such a capacity as another. — Jamieson allies -λίκος, to our *LIKE*. Ηι, quā, 'as.' But see the obss. on Ἀλίγκιος.

Ηλιξ, ἥλικος, 'in the flower or prime of life, of age :— of the same age, a fellow:—later, like, [as Ἀλίγκιος,] :' Ldd. Comparing Ἠλίκος above, we have these meanings: 1. as great as can be, 2. 3. as great or large as another.

Ἠλιοκάνθαρος, 'the dung-beetle: prop. sun-beetle, for it was the Egyptian hieroglyphic for the sun:' Ldd.

Ηλιος, the sun. — R. ἔλη, heat or light of the sun.

ΗλΙΨ, ἥλιπος, a Dorian shoe.— Some say α, intens., λίπα : as made of leather well oiled. ?

Ηλος: in Ηλεός.

Ηλος, a nail, peg, stud. — R. †ἔω, ἴηνι, †ἔελος, as Δέελος, Δῆλος: Sent in, driven in. As Ἐν-ετή from ἔται.

Ἠλύγη, Ηλυξ, duskiness. — Dnn. from α, not, λύκη, light. Others from α, intens., λύγη duskiness, but ν in Λύγη is long.

Ἠλύσιον, 'Elysium, the abode of the departed. — R. ἥλυσις, ἔλευσις, ἐλεύσομαι:' Dnn. To which souls depart or retire. (2) 'R. ἀλύω, to rejoice: Or α, λύω, as the departed are indissoluble in frame : Or α positive, as loosed from the burden of the flesh:' Damm.

Ηλυσις, a coming: As above.

Ημα, 'what is sent or thrown, a dart: from [†ἔω, ἧμαι,] ἵημι:' Ldd.

Ἠμαθόεις, sandy : ἄμαθος.

Ημαι, to sit. — R. †ἔω : To send oneself down, ἧμαι pf. pass. ; or, with Buttm., like δίζΗΜΑΙ.

Ημαρ, the day : 'poët. for Ἡμέρα :' Dnn. (2) As Ἧτορ from ἔάω, †ἧται, to breathe, so Η.αρ from †άω, †ἧμαι, to shine. Compare Ἡώς.' (3) 'Hebr. *yom*, the day :' Mrt.

Ἠμβροτον: in Ἀβροτάζω.

ΗΜΕΙΣ, we. — 'From ἐμὲ, *me*:' Mrt. But this explains nothing.

Ἠμεκτέω, Περι-ημέκτέω, to be pained at, indignant at. — R. ἐμέω, ἥμεκα, as 'I will spue thee out of my mouth' Rev. 3. 16. (2) 'To be wounded (in spirit): αἷμα, αἱμάσσω, ἥμακται :' Dnn. As νημερτής.

Ἡμέρα, the day. — Fem. of ἥμερος, gentle, mild. 'For ἡμέρα ὥρα or φάσις, mild hour or light, in opp. to the gloomy night:' Valck. 'The mild shining or mild state of the air:' Damm. 'The placid time:' Lenn. Used, in opp. to a boisterous day, as Æquor is the level water opp. to the boisterous. (2) Compare Ημαρ.

Ἡμερίς, a cultivated vine: from

Ημερος, tame, reclaimed, gentle. — R. ἧμαι, to sit: Sitting quiet. As ἧσαι, ἥσυχος. Compare Luke 8. 35, 'sitting . . . and in his right mind'. (2) Transp. from †ἥρεμος, as in ἠρέμα.

Ημι, the same as Φημί.

Ημι-, half : for Ἡμισυ.

Ἡμίνα, half a Ἑκτεὺς or Sextarius.—Above.

'Ημίονος, half-ass, mule. — R. ἡμι-, ὄνος.

Ἥμισυς, half. — ' Coray proposes μέσος, middle, as Medius, Dimidius:' Dnn. 'H-, much as 'A in 'Απλόος. (2) Damm from ἄμα, ἴσος: An equal, corresponding with another equal. (3) 'A for ἄμα as at end of 'Αμαξα; ΜΙΣ- as in ΜΙΣτύλλω, to divide.

'Ημιτύβιον, a strong linen towel. — R. ἡμι-, as Lat. semi-cinctium, a napkin. The latter part is obscure. Is the word from ἥμισυ, for ἡμιΣύβιον, as Σὺ, Τὺ : Σεῦτλον, Τεῦτλον ; Σήμερον, Τήμερον. The termination somewhat as ΚισσύBION. (2) Jablonski from Copt. toubo, clean, as a priest's garment. Then ἡμιτύβιον, an adulterated sort.

'Ημὸς, our: R. ἡμεῖς.

Ἦμος . . . , Τῆμος . . : When . . . , then . . . . —From ᾗ, τῇ, i.e. ἡμέρᾳ, or ὥρᾳ, though the meaning of the affix μος does not appear, any more than ικα in 'ΗΝίκα, ΤΗΝίκα. (2) ' R. ἦμαρ:' Mrt. ?

'Ημύω, to bow down, droop, drop. —Like Ἧμα,Ἥμων, from †έω, ἵημι, ἧμαι : Mitto, Re-mitto, Sub-mitto me. (2) Ldd. and Dnn. from μύω, as Hom.: Μύσαν ὅσσε ὑπὸ βλεφάροισι, were closed, or, we may construe, drooped.

Ἥμων, a darter: R. ἧμα.

Ἥν, if : ἐάν.

Ἥν, Ἡνί, Ἡνίδε, lo ! — For 'Ενίδε, from ἐν-είδω, inspicio.

Ἡνεκὴς, Δι-ηνεκὴς, extended, wide, long.—R. ἐνέκω: Brought or carried forward, pro-ductus. ' Borne or bearing to an object, as Latus from Fero :' Schneid. ' Latus' for ' di-lātus.' So ποδ-ΗΝΕΚΗΣ, carried or reaching down to the feet.

'Ηνία, Ἥνιον, bridle, reins : — a shoe-string. R. ἐνόω, ἐνῶ, to bring into one, unite : prop. applicable to a pair of horses, &c. Thus Homer : ἵππΩΝ ἧνι' ἔχοντα, ἵππΩΝ ἧνι' ἐλεῖν. (2) R. ἀνὰ, ἄναξ, ἀνάσσω: By which we have the UPPER hand of. Aspir. as in 'Ηγέομαι.

'Ηνίκα . . , Τηνίκα, when . . . then . . . —R. ἦν, τὴν, i.e. ὥραν or ἡμέραν, at what hour or day, at that hour or day. So αὐτΙΚΑ.

Ἧνις, of a year old : ἔνος.

'Ηνορέα, manliness. — R. ἀνὴρ, ἀνέρος, adj. †ἄνωρ, †ἄνορος.

Ἡνοψ, ἤνοπος, glittering, of brass. — R. ἐν, ὶψ, ὼψ : In which one can see eneself, or the countenance appears. (2) R. ἀν-, not, ὼψ : Too dazzling for the eye to see.

'Ηνυστρον, the fourth or completing stomach of ruminating animals.—R. ἀνύω, ἤνυσται.

'Ηπανία, ' indigence : from σπανία:' Dnn. Thus : σπανία, †πανία, †ἁ-πανία, ἡπανία, as 'Ημύω many for μύω. (2) Better from α, not, πάομαι, to possess.

Ἧ́ΠΑΡ, ἥπατος, the liver. — R. ἥπιος, soft. See 'ΗΠΕΡοπεύω. Aspir. as in 'Ηγέομαι. ?

'Ηπατος, ' a fish, perh. from its [hepatic] color:' Ldd. Above.

'Ηπεδανὸς, ' weak, weakly ; — unsound, halting. —

Schneid. from ἥπιος:' Ldd. As οὐτιΔΑΝΟΣ. (2) R. α, †πὲς, †πεδὸς, whence Πέδη, Πέδιλον : Disabled in the feet, halting. Thus 'A-πους is lame. (3) R. α, πέδον : Infirm on the ground: opp. to 'Εμ-πεδος.

'Ηπειρος, the main-land, continent : i.e. ἄ-πειρος ; ἀ-πείρονα γαῖαν, Hom. Unbounded.

'Ηπεροπεύω, to cheat, cajole. — R. ἥπιος, †ἤπερος, (as μογΕΡΟΣ,), ὄψ, the voice : To say soothing things to. (2) R. α, πέρας ; ἤπειρος. To make unbounded promises to : — or unfulfilled, 'Απέραντα. (3) R. ἠπύω : To SAY and do not. (4) For ἡμεροπεύω.

'Ηπήσασθαι, ' to repair, mend, ameliorate. 'Ηπητὴς, a botcher. Allied to 'Ηπιος mild:' Dnn.: To make mild and tame. (2) R. ἅπτω, apio and the old apo, to join, and so patch.

'Ηπίαλος, a shivering fever. 'Ηπιάλης, the night-mare. — R. ἐπ-ιάλλω, ἐπ-ιαλῶ, to assail, much as Epilepsy from 'Επί-ληψις : And thus 'Επιάλης is the night-mare. (2) Or R. ἐπὶ, ἄλλομαι, to jump upon. And 'Εφιάλτης, where is the Aspirate, points to 'Αλλομαι.

'Ηπιος, mild, gentle, kind. — R. ἔπω : Easy to speak to, af-fabilis, affable. So 'Επητής. Or as Παραμυθητικὸς, consolatory. (2) R. ἕπομαι: Following, submissive. (3) Allied to 'Απαλός.

'Ηπύω, to call out to, ἔπω.

Ἦρ, spring, ἔαρ.

'Ηρα, things pleasant. — R. ἄρω, ἤρον: Suitable, as 'Αρμενα, 'Επί-ηρα', Ldd.

'Ηρα, Juno. — Ldd., Dnn. and Lenn. compare Lat. hēra, mistress: — allied to hĕrus, prob. from †ἕρα, lord of the land, as ' Terrarum dominos', Hor., and much as Domus, Dominus. The same ally 'Ηρα also to 'Ηρως, a hero, and 'Αρης, Mars, whence 'Αρείων and 'Αριστος. (2) ' From ἐράω : [Lovely.] Or ἀὴρ, ἀέρος,' the air :' Mrt. Indeed 'Ηρα is also ' the air'. ' A poëtic name of air :' Ewing. — Compare 'Ηρανος. (3) ' Hebr. ееreе, to conceive:' Wr.

'Ηρανος, ' friend, guardian, ruler. From †ἤρα, things pleasant:' Ldd. Doing things pleasing, gratifying. So 'Επι-ήρανος is pleasing.— Or R. ἄρω, to suit, ἤραρε ; whence 'Αρήγω, to help. (2) R. ἐράω, to love.

'Ηρεμα, softly, gently : — by degrees. — Ldd. allies it to'Ερημος, lonely. (2) Better from ἀρέσκω, †ἀρέω, placeo, whence Placidē, Placidly. (3) Transp. from 'Ημερα.

'Ηρι, in the early morning ; — in the early part θέρους of summer. — ' Akin to 'Ηὼs, the morning : a dative adverbial:' Dnn. But how to get it? — Steph. says: 'Ηρ, the morning, either because 'Ηρ the morning has a certain likeness to 'Ηρ the spring, as noon to summer: or, as 'Ορθρον from 'Ορθοῦσθαι, so from Αἴρω, ('Ηρον,) is 'Ηρ, as raising men from their beds to their work.' — Perhaps 'Αέρι might not only mean Air from †ἄω to blow, but Morning from †ἄω to shine: or indeed it might have meant the Fresh air of morning,

just as Αὔρα did from †ἄω to blow. See on Ἠώς.
(2) 'Sax. *aer*, the morning: whence *early*:' Todd.
(3) 'Hebr. *aor*, light:' Mrt.

Ἡρικαπαῖος, or -κεκ., 'epith. of a god, prob. Bacchus or Priāpus. Usu. derived from ἤρι, κῆπος:' Ldd. Or from ἤρανος κήπου, guardian of gardens, as Priāpus.

Ἡρίον, a mound, barrow, tomb. — 'R. †ἔρα, earth. Prop. a funereal earthen mound:' Dnn. (2) For a *Ἥρως*. (3) R. ῥίον, peak, promontory. H, as Ἠβαιός.

ΗΡΩΣ, 'orig. any free-man, respectable by birth or skill : the Germ. *herr*, sir : — then *hero*, one above the race of common men, — object of worship:' Ldd. 'Irish *earr*, noble, grand, a champion: Germ. *herr*. Dutch *heer*, lord:' Wbst. 'Chald. *hor*, noble:' Mrt. 'Heb. *her*, a noble person:' Wr. 'Damm with the old Gramm. refer ἥρως to Ἄρης, Ἀρετή, &c. He cites also Lat. *herus*, lord:' Dnn. But Ἥρως and *Herus* may flow from ἔρα, as 'land-lord,' much as Domus, Dominus. '*Terrarum dominos*', Hor.

Ἧσις, pleasure : R. ἥδομαι, ἥσομαι.

Ἧσσα, defeat: i.e. inferiority in battle: from Ἡσσάω, to subdue, for ἡσσονάω from ἥσσων, ἥσσονος. So to Worst. (2) R. †ἔω, ἥσω, mitto, sub-mitto. Submission.

Ἥσσων, feebler, weaker, inferior, less. — As Βαθύς, Βάσσων, so ἧκα, ἥσσων, then ἥσσων, as superl. ἥκιστος.

Ἥσυχος, still, quiet. — R. ἧμαι, ἧσαι: Sitting still. See Ἥμερος. (2) R. †ἔω, ἥσω, as in Ἧσσα. 'Submissive': see Ἧσσα. (3) R. ἥδομαι, ἥσομαι, to be pleased : as Placeo, Placidus.

Ἦτα, *eta* : formed after Zeta and Theta.

Ἦτορ, the heart. 'Strictly the breath', Ldd., from †ἄω, ἦται, to breathe. 'So Homer, Ἐνὶ φρεσὶ θυμὸς ΑΗΤΟ:' Dnn.

Ἤτριον, the warp. Ἤτρια, a thin fine cloth. — As Βαιός, Ἠβαιός, so Damm for †τρίον from τρία : a triple thread, as Di-mity from δὶς, μίτος, two threads.

Ἦτρον, 'from ἦτορ [as being contiguous to it :] The part of the body below the navel, the abdomen :— Met. of a pot, — the pith of a reed:' Ldd. and Dnn. (2) R. †ἔω, ἦται, ἴημι: Into which the food is sent. Or ἔω, to go. '*Descendit* in *ventrem*:' Hor.

Ἧὕτε, the same as Εὕτε.

Ἥφαιστος, Vulcan, the god of fire as used in art and working in metal. — R. ἄπτω, ἧφα, to kindle, burn. (2) R. ἁφάω, to handle. 'Fabrilia tractans'. As Ψάω, Ψαυστός.

Ἠχή, Ἦχος, a sound. Ἠχώ, echo. — R. ἄγνυμι, ἧχα, frango: A re-fracted sound. Hesiod: Περὶ δ' ἴγνυτο ἠχώ. Virg.: '*Fractæ* ad littora voces.' So Fragor from Frango.

Ἠώς, the dawn. ἕως. — R. †ἄω, to shine. — Some say R. †ἄω to breathe, from the morning breezes. See Αὔρα.

Θ.

Θαάσσω, for Θάσσω.

Θαέομαι, Doric of Θεάομαι.

Θαιρὸς, hinge of a door. — As we have not only Αἴρω but Αἰρέω and καθαίρω, and not only Ἄρω but Ἁρμονία and Ἁρμόζω, we may suppose Θ to take the place of an Aspirate (as in Θάμα, Θάλασσα, Θειλόπεδον,) in Αἴρω or †Αἴρω to raise, suspend, Ἀρτάω: The Hanger. So Hinge is from Hang. (2) 'Allied to Θέω, Θύω, Θόρω, and ΤΑχύς: 'ἃ motu versatili,' Lenn. Or to ΤΑΡάσσω, 'to put in movement,' (Dnn.) (3) Dnn. and Damm from Θύρα. ? ?

Θᾶκος, a seat. — R. Θάσσω.

Θάλαμος, 'a chamber in the inner part of a house, — a *bridal* chamber, and so marriage; — any sleeping-room; — store-room; — the *female* apartment in the innermost part of the house, — the lower and inner part of a ship where the Θαλαμῖται rowers sat, — the inner chapel in Egyptian temples. R. Θάλπω, to warm, cherish, comfort:' Dnn. — The '*female* apartment' leads some justly to bring it from Θῆλυς, a female: Or, as 'the *bridal* chamber' from Θαλία, festive joy. And thus the *female* or the *bridal* chamber is the first sense. In form as πλόκαΜΟΣ. (2) Jabl. makes it Egyptian.

58

Θάλασσα, the sea. 'Prob. [for ἅλασσα, ending as μέλισσα,] from ἅλς, ἁλὸς, so that Θ is for the Aspirate, as Ἅμα, Θάμα. Or for Σ, [Σάλος, †Σάλασσα,]:' Ldd. Θ, as also in Θειλόπεδον. Possibly the Θ from τὸ ἅλας, †Θάλας. (2) R. Θάλλω, Θαλῶ, 'vireo', whence 'viridis': as we say sea-*green*.

Θάλεια, 'blooming, luxuriant, rich, goodly. The muse *Thalia*, the blooming one. One of the Graces, patroness of festive meetings:' Ldd. So Θαλερὸς, blooming: Θαλία, bloom of life, good cheer, feast. And

Θάλλος, Θάλος, a young shoot or branch. — From Θάλλω, to bloom, flourish. — 'Perh. a form of ἄλλω, ἄλλομαι, [to spring up,] for the aspirate [as Θάλασσα]:' Dnn. (2) Rather, as Ψάω, Ψάλλω, so Θάω, to nourish, Θάλλω. See Θηλή, Θῆλυς. (3) 'Hebr. *tal*, dew:' Mrt.

Θάλπω, to warm, heat, cherish, nourish. — 'Allied to Θάλλω:' Ldd. and Dnn. As μέλος, μέλπω, and ἴλΠω. So Θαλύω is to heat. Some account for Π from πῶ, ποιῶ : To make to warm.? See Θάω.

Θαλύσια, offering of first-fruits after harvest. — R. Θαλύω, Θάλπω, to warm, burn.

Θάμα, together, close, frequently. — For Ἅμα, as Θάλασσα, Θειλόπεδον.

Θάμϐος, amazement. — R. Θήπω, ἔθαπον, †ἔθαϐον, as λαΜϐάνω. Hesych. has Θῆϐοs. So κλάω, κλαΜϐόs.

Θαμίζω, to come Θάμα often to a place.

Θάμνος, thicket, bush. — R. Θάμα, close.

Θάνατος, death; from †Θανέω, †Θνέω, Θνήσκω, to die.—'To lie or be dead', says Dnn. Hence aspir. from †τανέω, ταίνω: To be stretched out. ' Moribundus extendi :' Curtius. Κεῖτο ταθεἰς, Hom. (2) ' R. Θείνω, ἔθανον : To be killed:' Dnn. (3) 'Hebr. teena, dust, clay :' Wr.

Θάομαι, to wonder at : — later, to survey. — For Θεάομαι, to gaze.

Θάπτω, 'to burn the dead: and, as the ashes were gen. inurned and put under ground, to bury:' Ldd. — For ἅπτω, to burn, as Ἅμα, Θάμα. (2) R. Θέω, Θάω, Θάσσω, to put or rest in the ground.

Θαργηλιών, ' an Athenian month, middle of May and June: some say April. — Prob. from Θέρω, as ΘΑρσος, to warm. Some from Θέρω, γῆ ?' Dnn. Some add ἥλιος: When Θέρει γῆν ἥλιος.

Θάρσος, Θάῤῥος, Θράσος, boldness, courage; — over-boldness, rashness, impudence. — R. Θέρω, τέθαρσαι, whence Θερμὸς, hot, ardent, rash, as Ναύταισι θερμοῖς, Soph. ' Periculosa et calida consilia', Cic.

Θασία, pickle from the isle of Thasos.

Θάσσω, †Θάω, to sit down. Θᾶκος, a seat. — Allied by Valck. to †Θέω, τίθημι: To place or set myself down. So Θέσσασθαι, and so from †Θέω Buttm. deduces Θοάζω, to sit. (2) Aspir. from †τάω, τάσσω, to SET in order.

Θάτερον, compar. of Ταχὺς, or †Θακὺς, as Βαθὺs, Βάσσων.

Θάτερον is τὸ ἕτερον, very curiously formed on the model of pl. Θάτερα, i. e. τὰ ἕτερα.

Θαῦμα, a wonder. — R. Θάομαι. Compare Τραῦμα. (2) ' Hebr. thaumah, to wonder:' Mrt., &c.

Θάψος, Θαψία, ' Thapsus, an island; — a town in Africa ; — a town in Scythia : — a herb used for dyeing yellow brought from some of those places :' Grove.

Θάω, to give suck, nourish, warm. — Aspir. from †τάω, τείνω, tendo : To stretch out the hand to give. ' Θάω, to stretch forth and give something to be enjoyed:' Dalz. ' To give milk [or the breast] to be sucked or milked:' Damm. — Or thus: ' Tendo, to tend, am intent on, give attention to,' &c.

Θεά, a Goddess. — R. Θεός.

Θέα, a sight. — From

Θεάομαι, to view, to gaze on with amazement or ad-miration. — Aspir. from †τεάομαι, from †τέω, τείνω, tendo : To look attentively or intently on, just as 'A-τενίζω. (2) R. Θέω, to run i. e. to view an object. (3) 'Hebr. theah, to wonder at :' Mrt.

Θεάρδς, ' Dor. for Θεωρός:' Dnn. So Πρᾶτος for Πρῶτος.

Θέατρον, a theatre for seeing public spectacles. — R. Θεάομαι.

Θειλόπεδον, a sunny place for drying fruits on: — a

hurdle for it. — Aspir. for Εἰλόπεδον, (as Θάμα,) from εἴλη, πέδον.

Θείνω, to smite, strike. — Aspir. from Τείνω, to stretch out, so lay flat. (2) R. Θέω: To make to run, hit, goad on. Much in form as 'Ορίνω. (3) ' Hebr. taghn, he stabbed:' Pkh.

Θειάζω, to inspire as the Θεοί.

Θεῖον, sulphur. — R. Θεῖος. ' A divine fumigation:' Dnn. ' The divine fire, lightning:' Dr. Jones. ' The divine thing:' Pkh. Θεῖον πυρὸς Alcest. 5. ' Flamma Jovis:' Virg. ' Brimstone was thought to have a purifying and averting power:' Ldd. 'Cuperent lustrari, si qua darentur Sulphura:' Juv.

Θεῖος, divine. — From Θεός.

Θεῖος, an uncle. — Contr. from 'Ηθεῖος, a term of respect and regard.

Θελγίν, Τελχίν, Τελξίν, ' an enchanter ; — also, an envious and wicked man. R. Θέλγω:' Dnn. ' Nescio quis teneros oculos mihi fascinat agnos,' Virg.

Θέλγω, to charm, enchant, soothe, flatter. — As Θει-λόπεδον, Θάμα. &c., from ἕλκω, to attract, for †Θέλκω, Θέλγω. (2) Where Θέλω I choose, ἄγω I lead.?

Θέλημος, ' epith. of the Nilo, producing freely, as γῆ ἐθέλουσα, Xen. 'Volentia rura', Virg. For Θέλημος:' Dnn.

Θέλυμνα, transp. for †Θέμυλνα, Θεμέλια, foundations. Θέλω: in 'Εθέλω.

Θέμα, anything laid down, proposition, theme. And Θέμεθλον, Θεμέλιον, a foundation. — R. †Θέω, τέθε-μαι: On which a building is laid. Θεμέλιον τέθεικα 1 Cor. 3. 10.

Θεμερὸς, grave, serious. — R. as above: Com-positus, com-posed, settled. Composito vultu. (3) R. Θέμις : Opp. to ex-lex, disorderly.

Θέμις, Θεσμὸς, a law laid down: a tax, im-post.—R. †Θέω, τέθεμαι, τέθεσμαι, τίθημι. So Θεσμο-θέτης, a lawgiver. 'Ponere mores', Virg. ' To lay down the law.'

Θεμόω, to order, enjoin, compel.—R. Θέμις ; Hesych. Θεμός. To lay down the law.

Θέναρ, the palm of the hand, sole of the foot. — R. Θείνω, Θενῶ : the part of the hand with which we strike. 'Os palmâ pulsat:' Petron. ' Planâ faciem contundere palmâ:' Juv.

Θεὸς, GOD. — R. †Θέω, τίθημι: Who placed in order the universe. So Herod.: Κόσμῳ ΘΕΝΤΕΣ τὰ πάντα πρήγματα. Xen.: Ἥπερ οἱ ΘΕΟΙ ΔΙ-ΕΘΕΣΑΝ. (2) R. Θεάομαι: Who inspects all things. (3) Some, as Plato, from Θέω, to run: from the course of the heavenly bodies which were regarded as Gods. (4) See in Ζεύς. (5) The Egyptian Theus. (6) 'Welsh duw, Irish dia, Armor. doue, Gypsey dewe, Sanskr. deva:' Wbst.

Θεραπεύω, to tend, attend to, take care of, heal, cure. — R. Θέρω, as Θέρων ἕλκος, Nicander: prop. applying warm fomentations to.

Θεράπων, an attendant. — Above: for Θεραπεύων.

Θερμὸς, hot: in Θέρω. Is Θέρμυς allied? viz. ' a

lupine ; the flavor bitter, but made palatable by steeping in water : — they also furnish a *fermented* drink in Egypt :' Dnn. ' *Tepens* lupinus' is found in Martial.

Θέρω, to warm, heat : θέρος, heat, summer, harvest : Θερίζω, to gather in the harvest : Θερμὸς, hot. — Aspirated from τείρω, τερῶ, to rub, and so rub dry, dry, whence Τέρσω to dry up, to parch.

Θέσκελος, godlike. — R. θεὸς, ἴκελος, like. So Θέσπις.

Θεσμός : in Θέμις.

Θέσπις, Θεσπέσιος, that can only be spoken by a God, vast, immense, &c. : spoken by a God, prophetic. — R. θεὸς, ἔσπον, to speak. So Θέσκελος.

Θεσσαλίζω, to act or speak as a *Thessalian.*

Θέσσασθαι, ' to pray for, seek by prayer : perh. from †θέω, τίθημι, [to place myself down,] to sit as a suppliant :' Ldd. and Dnn. See Θάσσω. (2) R. †τέω, τείνω, to stretch out i.e. my hands in prayer. See 'Ορέγομαι.

Θέτης, one who puts down a security : θετὸς, one put for another, spurious. — R. †θέω, τίθημι.

Θεύμορος, the same as Θεό-μορος, as Θευφορία is Θεο-φορία.

†θέω, Τίθημι, to place, lay, put. — For †έω, (as Θάλασσα, Θάμα, Θειλόπεδον,) ἵημι, to send down. (2) Aspir. for †τέω, †τάω, τείνω, τάσσω, ' to place or put in order' (Dnn.).

Θέω, θεύσω, to run; Θύω, to rush. — Aspir. for †τέω, τείνω, tendo, *intendo* cursum. Compare Ταχύς. (2) As Θειλόπεδον, Θάμα, &c., for †έω, ἵημι : To send myself on. (3) ' Allied to Ξεύω :' Dnn.

Θεωρὸς, ' a spectator, as of shows : — a deputy sent to assist at a festival or consult an oracle [or the Gods] : a magistrate attending to sacred rites. Some in the latter sense from θεὸς, ὥρα, or θεὸς, ὁράω : in the former θεάομαι :' Dnn. So Θεωρέω, to behold, view, consider; also go as deputy, &c.' (2) ' Or Hebr. *thoor*, to explore :' Wr.

Θηβάνας, ' the N.E. wind :' Ldd. ' The wind blowing from the quarter of *Thebes* to Athens :' Dnn.

Θηγάνη, a whetstone. From

Θήγω, to sharpen, whet. — As †Τμέω, Τμήγω, so †τέω, †τήγω, aspir. θήγω ; †τέω, whence τείνω, tendo, *intendo*, to give *intensitiveness* to the point. Thus Forcell. explains *Intentus*, by ' acer ', and adds, ' Quia quæ *intenduntur*, majorem vim habent.' (2) Mrt. for †θοήγω, from θοὸς, keen, ἄγω, ἦγον : To bring to a sharp point. ?

Θήκη, case, box : τίθημι, ἔθηκα.

Θηλέω, to bloom : θάλλω, ἔθηλα.

Θηλὴ, a woman's breast. — R. θάω, to suckle : †θαελὴ, θηλή. So, θηλάζω, to suckle.

Θῆλυς, a woman, as distinguished for the θηλή. ' Also, partaking of the fruitfulness, delicacy, &c. of the female sex, as life-giving, tender, soft :' Ldd.

Θημών, a heap. — ' R. τίθημι, as Θῶμος a heap :' Ldd. Put up together, laid up.

50

Θὴν, ' akin to Δή :' Ldd. ' Formed from it :' Dnn., Damm and Dr. Jones. As Θεὸς, Deus ; Θὴρ, Deer. (2) As ἰθΗΝ Doric for ἰθΕΙΝ, and πΛΗΝ for πΛΕΙΝ, so θΗΝ for †θΕΙΝ from †θέω, θήσω, τίθημι : To lay it down, i.e. *positively* which from Pono, *Positum.*

Θήπω, τέθηπα, to be or stand amazed. — R. †θάω, θάομαι, θαῦμα, &c. As βλεΠω, σήΠω.

Θὴρ, Æ. φὴρ, a wild beast. Θήρα, a hunt. — ' R. θέω, to run : From its celerity :' Lenn. and Mrt. Θῶ, θὴρ, as αἴθω, αἴθΗΡ. (2) ' Our *deer,* Germ. *thier,* Dutch *dier,* Dan. *dyr,* Polish *zwiers* : prim. roving :' Wbst.

Θηρίκλεια, drinking cups, ' called after *Thericles,* a celebrated Corinthian manufacturer :' Dnn.

Θὴς, θητὸς, ' a serf, bound to till land for his lord :— a freeman who hires himself to a master ;— hired labourer. — Buttm. from τίθημι, θήσω, like our Settler, from Set or Sit ;' Ldd. — Or, as θεὶς, *placing* out his services on hire, ' qui opus *locatum* facit.' Thus ' ex-positus' is put out for sale. So Θῆσσα, ' a poor girl who was obliged to go out for sale, [θεῖσα,] :' Ldd.

Θησαυρὸς, a treasure. — R. τίθημι, θήσω, to put down. Some add αὔρον, *aurum.* (2) ' Hebr. *thazer* :' Wr.

ΘΗΤΑ, *theta.* Hebr. *teth.*

Θιαγὼν, a sacrificial cake. And

Θίασος, a band marching in honor of a god. — Prob. from θεὸς, θεῖος, θειάζω :' Ldd.

ΘΙΒΗ or ΘΗΒΗ, a chest, ark, basket. ' It might be from [†θέω,] †θέω, to place, [as θὶς.] But it is the Hebr. *thebah* :' Mrt. (Very rare.)

Θιβρὸς, hot, ' Dor. for Θερμὸς :' Ldd. Allied to Τέφρα, ashes, and Τύφω to burn. Aspir. for †Τιφρὸς, then Β as ἀμΒω, amBo. I, as ΛΕχριος, ΛΙκριφὶς ; πΛΕκω, plIco ; ΛΕπος, lIber ; &c.

†Θίγω, Θιγγάνω, to touch. — Aspir. from †τίγω, allied to Τεταγὼν, touching. Compare τΙω, allied to †τάω, †τέω, τείνω. (2) Like Θάμα and Θειλόπεδον : from ἵκω : To come up to a thing, and so touch it. †Θίκω, θίγω. See Θήγω.

Θὶς, θῖν, θινὸς, a heap, sand-heap, beach, shore. —As 'Ρὶς, 'Ρὶν, from ῥέω, ῥῶ, so θὶς, θὶν, from †θέω, θῶ, τίθημι, agreeing with Θημὼν, and Θωμὸς : Com-positus, put together. (2) R. θείνω, to beat : Beaten by the waves. (3) ' Hebr. *teen,* mud :' Wr.

Θλάσπις, ' a sort of large cress, the seeds of which were θλασσὰ bruised or crushed, and used like mustard :' Ldd. So ἰλεΣΠΙΣ.

Θλάω, Φλάω, to crush, bruise. —' Allied to Θραύω, †Τράω, Τιτράω :' Dnn. The Λ and Ρ, as in κΛίβανος, κΡίβανος : λείΡιον, liLium. (2) ' Hebr. *thlo,* to split :' Wr.

Θλίβω, Φλίβω, like Θλάω, Φλάω, to squeeze, pinch, gall. Compare Τρίβω.

Θνήσκω, to die : in †Θανέω.

Θνητὸς, a mortal. —Above.

Θοάζω, to move θοῶς fast.

Θοάζω, to sit :—in Θάσσω. So Θώκος.

Θοίνη, a meal, feast.—Allied to Θοάζω, to sit : A sitting down to table. So Θῶκος, Θόωκος, is a sitting, assembly. So Θῶσθαι is to feast, and Θόσσω. (2) R. Θείνω, τέθονα : 'A slaying of the fatted calf.' (3) Dnn. allies it to Θάω, to nourish, Τιθὴ, Τιθήνη : Wbst. to Δαίνυμαι.

Θολία, a parasol, like a

Θόλος, dome, cupola, round chamber.— R. Θέω, τέθοα, to run (round), as Ἴτυς is Ἀμφ-ιτυς. So Περί-δρομος is a circular gallery. Ἡ λεπτότατος ΘΕΕ χαλκός, Il. υ. 275. In form as Ψόλος. (2) 'R. prob. ὅλος :' Dnn. As Θάμα, &c. · (3) 'Hebr. thalah, to suspend :' Mrt.

Θόλος, mud, dirt.— R. †Θέω, τέθοα, τίθημι : A deposit of mud. (2) 'The Attic is 'Ολός', says Dnn. So that Θολός (like Θάμα) may be for 'Ολός, allied to 'Εόλητο, 'Αλεὶς, collected, 'Ελλω, &c.

Θοός, quick.— R. Θέω, τέθοα, to run.

Θορὴ, Θορός, id quod emittit mas Θορών.

Θόρυβος, uproar, noise.—Allied tυ Θοῦρος, impetuous. (2) R. τορός, loud, audible. (3) Ldd. and Dnn. ally Τύρβη, Turba, but these are from Θόρυβος.

†Θόρω, Θόρνυμαι, †Θρόσω, Θρώσκω, to spring, bound. Allied to Θοός, swift : or Θέω, †Θόω, Θόρω, as †Δέω, Δέρω. (2) As Θάμα, from †Θρω, ὁρμάω, to rush.

Θοῦρος, impetuous.—Above.

Θώκος, the same as Θῶκος.

Θρανέω, to stretch on the tanner's Θρᾶνος form or board, to tan.

Θρᾶνος, a bench, form.— R. Θράω. So Θρῆνυς and Θρόνος. (2) 'Hebr. thren, to seat high :' Wr.

Θρανόω, to break in pieces ; R. †Θράω, Θραΰω. Some explain it to unbench a ship, from Θρᾶνος, much as we say To Wing a bird.

Θρασκιας, 'The Thracian or N.W. wind :' Dnn.

Θράσος : in Θάρσος.

Θράσσω, to trouble, disquiet.— R. ταράσσω, †τράσσω.

Θραῦλος, Θραῦρος, broken ; from

Θραύω, to break, bruise, weaken.—Allied to †Τραύω, Τραῦμα, which see.

Θράω, to make to sit.—'R. Θάω, Θάσσω, to sit : whence [†Θαίρω,] †Θάρω, Θράω :' Valck. Much as ψάω, φαίρω : δόρω : δέρω.

Θρέμμα, a nurseling.— R. τρέφω, τέθρεμμαι.

Θρέομαι, to cry aloud, shriek out. 'R. †Θρέω, aspir. from τρέω, to tremble through fear:' Dnn. (2) Allied to Θραύω, as 'Ρήγνυμι φωνὴν, 'Rumpere vocem :' and Κλαίω from Κλάω. To break out into tears and lamentations.

Θρεττανελὸ, 'formed to imitate the sound of the harp :' Dnn.

Θρέττε : 'Τὸ Θρέττε in Aristoph. is τὸ Θρασό, [Θρατύ,] : prob. a barbarism :' Ldd.

Θρῆνος, lamentation.— R. Θρέομαι.

Θρῆνυς, the same as Θρᾶνος.

Θρῆσκος, superstitious, — religious. — R. Θρέομαι :

61

'From the noises made in the ancient superstitious rites :' Hemst. Allied to Θρόος. (2) Dnn. from †Θρέω, τρέω, to tremble (with religious awe). (3) From Θρῆκες : 'The Thracians being much addicted to superstitious rites :' (Dnn.) See Θραικίας.

Θριαὶ, 'Parnassian nymphs, who invented a kind of soothsaying by pebbles drawn from an urn : they were said to be three, [τρεῖς, τρία,] whence some derive the name :— the pebbles and lots, and divinations :' Ldd. (2) The pebbles first : then. as †Τρίω, Τρίβω, Θρίψω, so †Θρίω, Θράω, Θρύπτω, to break, like Κλῆρος from κλάω, Ψῆφος from Ψάω.

Θρίαμβος, a triumphal procession, and hymn, gen. to Bacchus.—As Ἴαμβος,— for Θρίαβος, aspir. from τριάζω, to conquer, †τριάπτω, much as 'Ιάλλω, 'Ιάπτω. (2) From victors being anciently crowned Θρίοις with fig-leaves.

Θριγκὸς, -χὸς, coping, eaves. — From Θρὶξ, τριχὸς, (Γ as Ἴγχος, λαΐχάνω,) : The coping overhanging the wall as the hair the head. Compare Lat. coma, the leaf on trees as the hair on the head.

Θρίζω : for Θερίζω.

Θρῖναξ : the same as Τρῖναξ.

Θρὶξ, τριχὸς, hair, bristle, &c.— R. Θρίζω, ξω : 'A thing cropped, sheared or reaped :' Dr. Jones. Thus Eurip. has ἀπ-έθρισεν τρίχας. So Cæsaries from Cædo, Cæsum. Θρίζω Æol.

Θρῖοι, reefs or little ropes on the lower part of the sail, used to take it up and make it smaller.—Prob. contr. from Τέρθριοι, ropes from the end of a sailyard.

Θρῖον, a fig-leaf : ' prob. from the τρία three lobes of the fig-leaf :' Ldd. and Dnn.

Θρῖον, 'a kind of stuffing or forced-meat, called from its being wrapped in fig-leaves :' Ldd.—Above.

Θρίσσα, 'a fish, elsewhere Τριχίας, and so from Θρὶξ, τριχός :' Ldd. So Τριχὶς is 'a kind of anchovy full of small hair-like bones :' Ldd.

Θρίψ, ιπὸς, a wood-worm.— R. τρίβω, Θρίψω, to wear away.

Θροέω, to cry loudly,— to utter, say : from Θρέομαι. Also to terrify or disturb by Θρόοι noisy sounds or idle words.

Θρόμβος, a clot, as of blood.— As Στρέφω, Στρόμβος, so Θρόμβος from Τρέφω, τέτροφα, †τέθροβα, to coagulate, whence Τροφαλὶς, cheese. — Others from τέθρομμαι, τέθρομμαι.

Θρόνα, paints, colors ;—drugs ;—figure-work, embroidery.—Allied to Θρόνος, from †Θρόω, Θράω, to sit : Color sitting on the surface of things. 'Pallor in ore SEDET', Ov. 'Pale horror SAT on each Arcadian face :' Dryd. So Ldd. says of Χροιὰ, 'the surface as the SEAT of color.' (2) R. †Θρόω, Θρώσκω : as rising out above the surface, 'eminentia in telâ aut veste :' Damm.

Θρόνος, a seat, throne.— R. †Θρόω, Θράω, to sit. See Θρῆνυς, Θρᾶνος. (2) 'Hebr. thren, to seat high :' Wr.

Θρόος, outcry, loud noise, murmur.— R. Θρέομαι, τέθροα.

Θρυαλλίς, the wick of a candle. — R. θρύον.

Θρυγανάω : in Τρυγονάω.

Θρυλλίζω, 'to break in pieces : akin to Θραύω, Θρύπτω :' Ldd.

Θρῦλος, 'like Θρόος and Θόρυβος :' Ldd.

Θρύον, a rush. — As easily breaking and very brittle, from θράω, θραύω, †θρύω, θρύπτω. Thus in the O. T.: To bow down his head like a bulrush. So Rushlike is 'weak, impotent', Todd.

Θρύπτω, to break, bruise, weaken. — Allied to θράω, θραύω, through †θρύω. (2) Valck. from θόρυβος, †θρόνπτω. (3) 'Hebr. treph, to tear in pieces :' Wr.

Θρώσκω : in θόρω.

Θρωσμὸς, a mound, eminence. — Above : 'Springing from the plain :' Ldd. Rising ground. 'From which one may leap;' Constantine.

Θυάζω, to rave or sacrifice like the Θυάδες Bacchanals. See Θυιάς.

Θυαυία, coarse mockery and quarrelling. — R. θύω, to rage. (2) R. θυάζω, above.

Θυάω, de suibus subantibus. — R. θύω, ruo (in venerem) : Hor. Od. 2. 5. 3, 4. (2) Pro συνάζω, à σῦς, συός : unde Subo.

Θυγάτηρ, (as Εἰνάτηρ,) a daughter. — As loveTH, loveS ; θεός, Σιὸς ; &c. so Θυγάτηρ or Ζυγάτηρ, from †συ-γάω, (as Ξυ-σκάω,) †συ-γέγαται : i. e. σύγγονος, co-gnata, born to parents along with sons. (2) 'We find Daughter used with little variation not only by the Goths, Saxons, Almans, Cimbrians, Danes and Dutch, but by the Persians :' Pkh. 'Goth. dawthar, Germ. tochter :' Dnn. 'Dugida, Sansk. :' Wr.

Θυεία, Θυΐς, a mortar. — R. θύω, from the rapid movement of the pestle. See Θύσανος. (2) As pounding θύος incense.

Θύελλα, a storm, hurricane. — R. Θύω : 'A mighty rushing wind': N. T. So Homer has 'the wind θύων rushing with a tempest.' As †Ἄω, Ἄελλα. Some add ἕλλω, to whirl.

Θυεστὴς, the pestle of the θυεία.

Θυηλὴ, Θύημα, Θύον, a sacrifice, or sacrificial cake : θύω.

Θυΐα, θυΐα, a kind of cedar or lemon tree. — R. θύω, to burn as incense : from the sweet odor of its wood in burning, Od. 5. 59.:' Pkh.

Θυιὰς, Θυὰς, a Bacchante. — R. θύω, to rage : or to sacrifice.

Θυλακὶς, a species of poppy, having an oblong capsule or

Θύλακος, a bag, pouch, pod, wide trowsers. — Aspir. from τύλη, a cushion, pillow, &c., τύλος, a protuberance. (2) As Θήρ, Φήρ, conversely for φύλακος from φυλάσσω, to guard, as φυλακή. (3) R. θύος : 'An incense bag :' Lenn.

Θυμάλωψ, 'a half-burned brand. — For θυμμάλωψ from τύφω, [τέθυμμαι,] like Μώλωψ, Ὑδρωψ :' Dnn.

Θύμβρα, the herb summer-savory, often put for Θύμος thyme, and prob. allied : for †θυμέρα, †θύμρα, B as in μεσημβρία.

62

, altar for sacrifice :—any high place, pulpit in the orchestra, and the whole stage ; — a domestic altar, and the whole house. — R. θύω, τέθυμαι, to sacrifice.

Θυμιάω, to burn θύος incense : to produce thereby vapor or smoke, θυμίαμα. — R. θύω, θῦμα.

Θύμον, Θύμος, thyme. — 'R. θύω, to burn incense :' Mrt.

Θυμὸς, passion, emotion, violence, desire :—the mind affected by such. — R. θύω, 'to move impetuously' : Dnn.

Θύννος, the thunny or tunny fish. — R. θύω, θύνω : 'From the rapidity of its movements' : Dnn. 'From its quick darting motion :' Ldd. (2) 'Hebr. theneen :' Wr.

Θύον, the wood of the Θυΐα.

Θύος, incense. — R. θύω 2.

Θύρα, a door. — TH and D are constantly interchanged, as θεὸς, Deus ; murTHer, murDer ; Θυγάτηρ, Daughter ; Θύρα, Door, &c. and see Θὴν and ἀνΔράχλη. Θύρα then for †θύρα from θύω, θύνω, to enter in, as Homer, Δῦνε δόμον, Δῦνε σπέος, &c. That is, A door by which we enter. Δύω, †θύρα, as Αθω, Αθρᾶ, and Λύω, Λύρα. (2) Lenn. from θύω. Certainly Virgil has, 'Manè ruunt portis', 'Quà data porta, ruunt.' Yet a door is not made to rush out by, but to go out by. (3) 'Germ. thur, Sax. dora, dur, Dan. dor, Dutch deur, Welsh dor, Basque dorrea, Russ. duer, Pers. dar, Sanskr. dura, Armen. turs :' Wbst. who adduces also the Chald., Syr., Arab., Polish, Bohem., Carinthian. Allied perh. to our thorough, through.

Θυραῖος, out of doors : θύρα.

Θυρεὸς, an oblong shield, in the form of a Θύρα ; — a stone put against a Θύρα.

Θύρσος, a light shaft wreathed with ivy and vineleaves, borne by the Bacchanals. Thus are used also Θυσία and Θύσθλα, justifying the deriv. of Θύρσος from θύω, (as Βύω, Βύρσα,) 'in reference to its use in Bacchanalian rites. This far more prob. than from obs. †τύρω, to swell, rise up, whence Τύρσις, Turgeo, Turio :' Dnn. (2) 'Hebr. thurza, branch of the pine :' Dr. Jones.

Θύσανος, fringe, tassel. — 'R. θύω, θύσω, θύσσω, to move rapidly :' Dnn.

Θυσία, a sacrifice ; Θύσθλα, sacrifices, and the same as Θύρσοι ; Θύσκη, a censer. — All from θύω.

Θύω, to rush, to be impetuous. — Allied to θέω, θεύσομαι, to run. (2) For σύω, σεύω, σεύομαι. (3) R. ἰθύω, 'to press right on', (Ldd.)

Θύω, 'to burn perfumes or incense in honor of the Gods ; — to burn in the fire of a sacrifice, to sacrifice, celebrate by a solemn sacrifice and feast :' Dnn. The terms 'burnt offerings,' 'burnt sacrifices of fatlings', &c. are common in the Scriptures. 'After flowers [for incense] victims came to be offered,' says Hemst. But 'to burn' will include both perfumes and animals. — Dnn. says, 'The transition to the sense of impetuous movement from the rushing of flame seems natural :'

much more so is the converse, and so this Θύω is no other than the former: i.e. to make (flame or smoke) to rush out. And so Ormston, 'from the *rapid issuing* of smoke from the censer.' See Θύω above. (2) From εΰω, to burn, as Θάμα, &c.

Θυώνη, Semelé; Θυωνεὺς, Bacchus. — 'Plainly from Θύω:' Ldd.

Θωὴ, an impost, fine. — R. †Θέω, Θῶ, τίθημι, pono, impono, to im-pose an im-post. Θωὴν ἐπι-Θήσομεν, Hom.

Θῶκος, a seat, Θᾶκος.

Θῶμος, a heap. — R. †Θέω, Θῶ, to put (together), as Θημών.

Θῶμιγξ, a cord, whip. — Akin to Θῶμος: String put together, 'in orbem *positus*', Damm.

Θωπεύω, to flatter: Θώψ, Θωπὸς, a flatterer. — R. Θῶ, Θωα, to make up a face. 'Frame my face to all occasions:' Shaksp. 'Com-posito vultu', Tac. 'Ficto vultu:' Cic. Σὺν-Θέτους λόγους, Æschyl.: a made up speech.—Also we say to Im-pose upon, from 'pono': so that Θώψ and Θωπεύω may be (like Μάλων, &c.) from Θῶ only. (2) 'To affect admiration, from Θάομαι, Θῶμαι, to wonder:' Dnn. So Θήπω, to admire.

Θώραξ, the breast: — breast-work: — breast-plate. — As Δρέπω, Δρώπαξ, so Θόρω, Θώραξ. From the pulsations and vibrations of the heart, or breast, which is much the same. Pliny says: '*Pectus præcordiis et vitalibus* natura circumdedit.' And Pectus is constantly taken for 'cor et animus' (Forc.) So Mrt.: 'à corde Θορούντι.'

Θώραξ, a drinking-cup: Θωρήσσω, ξω, to drink sheer wine, to be intoxicated. 'Reimer says it prop. means, To fortify oneself by, as sailors say, To acquire Dutch courage:' Dnn. 'A cup, by which, as by a Θώραξ breast-plate, one drinker was armed against another:' Steph., quoting Aristoph. Ach. 1135, 6.

Θὼς, Θωὸς, a jackal or lynx. — 'Prob. from Θέω, Θῶ, to run, Θωὸς, quick:' Dnn. As Pliny: '*Thoes*, luporum genus *velox* saltu.' (2) R. Θωύσσω.

Θώσσω, to feast jovially: in Θοίνη. (2) Contr. from Θωρήσσω in Θώραξ 2.

Θωΰσσω, to shout out, yell, bark, buzz. — 'I.e. to set dogs on Θῶας wolves:' Bp. Blomf. (2) R. Θοὸς, sharp: To speak to in a sharp tone. Thus Homer has Ὀξέα κεκληγόντες, Crying out sharply.

Θώψ: in Θωπεύω.

I.

Ἰὰ, a sound, voice, cry. — As Ἰὸς, a javelin, from †Ἰω, †Ἰέω, to send, send forth, so Ἰὰ also. Hom.: "ΟΠΑ μεγάλην ἐκ στήθεος "ΙΕΙ: ΙΕΙΞΑΙ "ΟΠΑ κάλλιμον. Æschyl.: "ΙΕΤΕ δύσθροον ΑΤΔΑΝ, Κακο-μέλετον 'ΙΑΝ ΠΕΜΨΩ. Even in Herod.: Βάρβαρον γλῶσσαν 'ΙΕΝΤΕΣ. Livy: 'Si vocem supplicem *mittere* licet.' Hor.: 'Nescit *vox missa* reverti.' (2) R. Ἴω, to go out. Τὸ σὸν φώνημ' ΙΟΝ: Soph.

Ἴα, one. — 'For μία:' Dnn. As Γαῖα, Αἶα.

Ἰάζω, to imitate the Ἰάδας Ionians.

Ἰαιβοΐ: in Αἰβοῖ.

Ἰαίνω, to heat, melt, warm, soften, cherish, cheer: and for Ἰάομαι, to heal. —Allied (like 'Ιάλλω, 'Ιάπτω, Ἰάομαι,) to 'Ιέω, 'Ιημι, 'Εάω, Ἀν-ίημι, (in form as χλιΑΙΝΩ,) mitto, re-mitto, to let go, loose, relax. Thus Forcell. explains 'Ceris re-*missis*', by 'solutis, mollitis, liquefactis.' Virgil: 'Eademque calor *liquefacta remittit.*' (2) For Διαίνω: or Χλιαίνω. As Αἶα, Εἴδω.

Ἴακχος, Bacchus. — R. Ἰαχὴ, vociferation.

Ἰάλεμος, Ἰήλ-, a wail, lament: adj. miserable. — 'Prob. from Ἰὴ, ἰαῦ:' Ldd. Much as κυδΑΛΙΜΟΣ. So from Ἰὴ is Ἰήιος, plaintive. (2) R. ἰὰ, a cry. (3) R. Ἰάλλω, ἰαλῶ, to send forth.

Ἰάλλω, to send forth, throw, cast, assail. — 'R. Ἴημι:' Dnn. I.e. from 'Ιέω, †Ἰάω as 'Εάω, Ἰάλλω as Ψάω, Ψάλλω.

Ἴαμβος, an *iambic* foot; *iambic* verses assaulting and

defaming the character, whence '*criminosis iambis*' Hor., from Ἰάπτω, Ἰαβον. Μ as ΛαΜβάνω.

Ἰαμένη, late form of Εἰαμένη. (2) R. †Ἰάω, Ἰαίνω.

Ἴανθος, the same as "Ιον, a violet: Ewing from Ἴον, ἄνθος. See "Ιονθος.

Ἰάομαι, to heal, and Ἰαίνω, to warm, is so used, and both of the same origin, as Θέρω, and Θεραπεύω to apply warm fomentations to. See Ἰαίνω.

Ἰαπαπαιάξ: in Ἀππαπαί.

Ἰάπτω, the same as 'Ιάλλω, and similarly formed. Compare Βάπτω, Δάπτω. Also, to send oneself on, run, fly.

Ἰάπυξ, υγος, the N.W. or W.N.W. — From Ἰαπυγία in Italy.

Ἰὰς, άδος, Ionian, Ἰωνία.

ΙΑΣΠΙΣ, the jasper stone. — 'Hebr. *jaspé*:' Mrt.

Ἰατρὸς, a physician: Ἰάομαι.

Ἰατταταί, Ἰατταταιάξ, alas, woe to me! —Fanciful imitations like Ἰαππαπαιάξ.

Ἰαῦ, ah! 'cry of grief: like Ἰού. Also, of joy, as Ἰά. Also an exclam. in answer to a call, as HO:' Dnn. Imitative words.

Ἰαυοῖ, much the same as Ἰαῦ.

Ἰαύω, to sleep, pass the night: — give rest to. — 'In some words [as ἸΕΰ(ω] I is prefixed, as Αὔω, Ἰαύω:' Dnn. This I seems contr. from Ἴφι, powerfully. Αὔω compare with "Αεσα, Ἀωτέω.

'Iαχὴ, a cry, shout. 'Iάχω, to shout, resound. —
'R. ἰὰ, a voice, sound:' Dnn.

'Iδάη, "Iδη, the same as Θίδη, as Λείβω, Εἴβω.

'Iδύζω, 'Iδυκινέω, to sound the Βυκάνη, trumpet.
See I in 'Iαύω.

"Iγδη, a mortar. — The Etym. M. says, for Μίγδη,
from μίγνῦμι, μίξω, μίγδην, to mix. As Μία, "Iα:
Λείβω, Εἴβω.

'Iγνύα, 'Iγνὺς, the ham. — 'R. γόνυ:' Dnn. With I,
as in 'Iαύω, 'Iδύζω : Γνὺ, 'Iγνύ.   Γνὺξ is used.

"IΔA, mount Ida near Troy: —any wooded mountain
or forest: — timber.

'Iδανικὸς, ideal. — R. Iδέα, †Iδεανικός.

'Iδανὸς, fair Iδεῖν to see, as Eδανός.

'Iδὲ, 'Iδὲ, 'Epic for ἠδὲ, and :' Dnn. Plato says the
most ancient persons said 'Iμέρα and 'Eμέρα for 'Hμέρα.
So the Cretans said 'Iν for 'Eν, Lat. in.—Perhaps 'Iδὲ
and 'Iδὲ are 'Iν-δὲ and 'Iν-δὲ, and to that (be added).
See 'IN, 'IN.'

'Iδέα, the outward look or appearance : — the kind or
species represented by individual appearances, as Species
from Specio: — the leading idea.—From

†Iδέω, video, εἴδω, εἰδέω.

'Iδιος, special, as this from Specio: Peculiar, individual, personal, one's own. — See 'Iδέα.

'Iδιώτης, a private individual: — hence retired, in-
experienced, ill-informed, ignorant. — R. Iδιος.

'Iδμων, "Iδρις, knowing, skilled. — R. εἰδέω, εἶδον,
Iδον,

'Iδνόομαι, to crook or double oneself up. — Dr. Jones
' from δινέω by transp.' Better, δινόω to twist round,
†δνόω, as Γνύξ.   I prefix, as in 'Iαύω, 'Iγνύα.   And
some say for 'Iνδνόομαι, from Iνες, δινόω: to twist the
nerves ; or Iνίον, δινόω, to twist the nape. — But, as Δ
in Δνόφος, for 'Iνδομαι from Iνες simply, as we say To
wing a bird, To bark a tree.

'Iδος, 'Iδρὼς, sweat ; — violent heat. — 'Akin to
"Iδος, "Iδωρ from δω :' Dnn.   And †Iω and δω are the
same, ' e-mitto.'   And †Iω can be ' to go forth.'   Compare 'Iκμάς.

'Iδρις : in 'Iδμων.

'Iδρύω, to seat, settle, set firm, found, fix. — R. Ιζω,
Iδον, as 'Eζω, "Eδον, "Eδρα, a seat.

'Iδρὼς : in 'Iδος.

'Iέραξ, 'Iρηξ, a hawk, falcon. — ' Some from Iερὸς, as
its flight was observed spec. in divination :' Dnn.
' Accipiter SACER ales', Virg.   So Od. o. 524–8.

'Iερεὺς, a priest. — From

'Iερὸς, consecrated, sacred.—R. Iέω, (like φοβΕΡΟΣ,)
as 'Aν-ιέω, 'Aφ-ιέω, to let go, set at liberty, like "Aφ-
-ετος, set at liberty.   Animals consecrated to deities
received some peculiar mark, and were suffered to wander
at large.   So 'Aν-ετος and 'Aν-ειμένος.   ' Aut aris
servare sacros:' Virg.   (2) ' Hebr. ira, to fear or
reverence:' Dr. Jones.

'Iεῦ, ' ironical exclam., whew!   Lat. hui !' Ldd.

'Iέω, "Iημι: See †'Eω.

"Iζω, 'Iζάνω, to seat, settle. — R. †Iω, to set down, as
†'Eω, "Eζω.

'Iὴ, ' an exclam. of joy, as Lat., Io triumphe.   And
of grief, but rarely :' Dnn.—'An imitative word :' Lenn.
(2) Blomf. supposes these are Egyptian words borrowed
with their theology by the Greeks. ?

'Iήιος, wailing, mournful ; from Iὴ, exclam. of grief.
Or even R. Iὴ Ion. of ἰὰ, a sound or cry.

'Iήιος, epith. of Apollo: 'invoked with the cry 'Iὴ
Παιὼν, [Io Pæan !], not from Iάομαι, as The healer :'
Ldd.   Yet Ovid says of him : ' Opiferque per orbem
Dicor.'   (2) R. Iὼ, to shoot.   'Iὴ Iὴ Παιήον, "IEI βέλος,
Callim.

†'Iημι, to go : †Iω, †έω, εἶμι.

'Iημι, to send: R. Iέω, as †Τιθέω, †Τίθημι.   See †'Eω.
And "Iεμαι, to send my mind to an object, to desire.

'Iθμα, a pace, step.—R. †Iω, Iθην, εἶμι, to go.   Comp.
'Iσθμός.

"Iθρις, a eunuch. — Steph. from Is, strength, Σρίζω,
to cut : Whose power is cut off.   Lat. ex-sectus. — Or
the I a prefix, as in 'Iγνύα, 'Iδύζω.   Eurip. ἀπέΘPIΣεν.

'Iθύνω, to make straight or direct : to direct. —
From

'Iθὺς, straight, straightly : See in Εἴθαρ.

'Iθὺς, impulse, purpose. — For Iθὺς, from †Iω, †Iθην,
Iέω, to send on.   See 'Iθμα.

'Iκανὸς, from Iκάνω, Iκανῶ, or from Iκω, (as σφεδΑ-
ΝΟΣ,) venio, to come, as we say, Be-coming, Come-ly,
Con-venient from Venio, i. e. agreeable to one's wants, as
' Give me food con-venient for me', i.e. enough : So we
speak of the con-veniences of life.   Thus a fitting time
is 'Iκνούμενον, a suitable time or hour 'Iκνουμένα.
' Reaching to what is desired :' Ormst. ' Coming without
impediments, prepared :' Damm.   Better, Coming up to
the mark.

"Iκελος, like, εἴκελος.

'Iκέτης, suppliant. — R. Iκω, to come up to a person
i. e. to beg, like 'Iκτηρ, 'Aφ-ικτωρ.   'Iκέτης ικνούμαι,
Soph.   'Iκάνομαι, I come, says Soph., to your knees.

'Iκμὰς, vapor, moisture. — R. Iκω, Iκμαι, (whence
"Iκμενος,): As coming forth, oozing out of the body or
ground.   'Iκμὰς Iδη, Hom., went out: and Kνίσση
οὐρανὸν IKEN.—' As going through the body :' Greg.

"Iκμενος, a favorable (breeze), i.e. ικόμενος, Iκμενος,
(as "Oρμενος,) coming after a ship, as Sequundus, Se-
cundus.   (2) ' R. ικμὰς, moisture.   The old Grammarians unanimously prefer this, citing Homer, 'Aνεμοι
'ΥΓΡΟΝ ἀέντες, mild moist breezes, opp. to dry stormy
winds :' Dnn.

'Iκνέομαι, the same as "Iκω.   Also to supplicate, as in
'Iκέτης.   As

"Iκρια, ' the partial decks : — cross-timbers of the
decks : — platfórm, scaffold,' Ldd. : senses all agreeing
with the idea of a passage, pathway, from Iκω.   The
termin. as ψαλτPIA, τέρθPIA, ὀρθPIA.   See 'Iκταρ,
"Iκμενος.   Also, ' the roofs of the women's apartments :
some interpret a beam, a pile, stake, cross, &c. placed

upright:—a tower, Strab.:' Dnn. Here the Etymol. M. explains it διὰ τὸ "HKEIN [rather "IKEIN] εἰς ὕψος, from their rising in the air: Hesych. says, τὰ 'ΟΡΘΑ ξύλα. Thus Βωμὸs is 'an elevation or raised spot, from †βάω, βαίνω' (Dnn.). And see Θρωσμός.

"Ικταρ, near, close: — near in time, quickly. — R. ἴκω, ἴκται, to come to, or come together. . ' Prop. said of weapons aimed at a mark:' Dnn. In the sense of ʻquickly' compare Εἶθαρ, 'Ιθὺs, from †ἔω, †ἴω to go on, straightly.

"Ικτεροs, the jaundice:— ' a yellow bird, from the color:' Dnn. — R. ἴκω, ἴκται, (as "Ικτιν, "Ικταρ,) ' to fall upon, attack, as old age, death or fate:' (Dnn.), whence Lat. ico, to strike. So here this disease, much as the Epilepsy from 'Επί-ληψις. (2) ʻ Subitò adveniens', says Lenn., from ἴκταρ.

"Ικτιδέη, a weasel's skin. — R. ἰκτὶs, ἴδos in "Ικτιν, 'Ικτῖνos, the kite. 'Ικτῖνos, a kind of wolf. 'Ικτὶs, a weasel or ferret. — All from ἴκω, ἴκται, to come down upon, attack, — or (like "Ιτης from †ἴω,) adventurous, audacious. See in "Ικτεροs.

"Ικω, to go or come : in "Ηκω.

"Ιλαοs, "Ιλεωs, soothed, made propitious, kindly ;— cheerful. ' Allied [like "Ιλλω and 'Ελύω, to roll,] to "Ελεοs, commotion, pity:' Lenn. See "Ελεοs. So 'Ιλάομαι, to soothe, appease, — atone for. (2) Hebr. hel, to shine: Having the face bright.

'Ιλεὸs, 'Ιλυὸs, the same as Εἰλεόs.

"Ιλη, the same as Εἴλη.

"Ιλιγξ, a whirlpool : " 'Ιλιγγοs, dizziness ; the coil of a serpent. — R. ἴλλω.

'Ιλλὰs, coiled or twisted string or osier: ἴλλω. — And a gregarious kind of thrush, allied to "Ιλη, a company.

"Ιλλοs, the eye, from its rolling about:— also, goggle-eyed : 'Ιλλίζω, to wink. — From

"Ιλλω, to roll, twist, fold : in Εἴλω.

'Ιλὺs, ύοs, mud, slime. — ' Prob. from εἰλύω, ἴλλω :' Ldd. As Lat. volutābrum, in which animals ' volvunt se', roll or wallow. — Or εἰλύω, to envelope. Αἵματι καὶ κονίησιν 'Εκ κεφάλης 'ΕΙΛΥΤ' ἐs πόδαs: Hom.

"Ιμα, 'Ιμονία, a well-rope. And

'Ιμὰs, άντοs, a rope, thong, cord. — Schneid. makes it prim., like "Ιμα, a well-rope, from †ἴω, ἵμαι, ἵημι, to send down, let fall. Or a thong or whip by which we send on : for it means also 'the thong or lash of a whip' (Ldd.).

'Ιμάτιον, a garment. — Like Εἷμα, εἵματοs, from †ἔω, †ἴω.

'Ιμάω, to pull up with an ἵμα rope : — draw up by suction.

'Ιμείρω, to desire. "Ιμεροs, desire. — Allied to "Ιεμαι, to desire, in 'Ιημι.

"IN, "IN, to him, to himself : MIN, NIN, him. "Ιν and "Ον may seem allied. Some make a nominative "I. — Allied to our HIM, ancient Lat. IM acc. of IS. The Celtic NYN is ' our, your, their.'

"Ινα, in the way or place or time that ;—to the end
65

that, in order that : —in or to the place that, where. — As ἐγωνΑ is found as well as ἐγώ, ἐγὼν, so ἵνΑ as ἰν above : To that point, time, end, &c. Thus μιν is ' him, it', &c.

'Ινδάλλομαι, to appear like, seem. — For 'Ιδάλλομαι, (as ἀΝδάνω,) allied to Εἴδομαι, to be like. I, as "Ικελοs and Εἴκελοs.

'ΙΝΔΙΚΟΝ, Indian pepper : — dark-blue dye, indigo.

'Ινέω, 'Ινάω, to make empty, void. — As "Ηθω, to strain through, from †ἔω, to send through, so †ἴω, †ἰνέω or ἰνέω, like "Αγω, 'Αγινέω; "Ικω, 'Ικνέω, 'Ικνέομαι. (2) ' The oriental in, not :' Mrt. I. e. to an-nul, an-nihilate.

'Ινίον, the ἶνεs sinews between the occiput and back, the nape.

"Ινιs, a son, daughter. — R. ἴs ἰνὸs, strength, as Virgil : ' Nate, meæ vires, mea magna potentia.' Or ἴs, the muscle, fibre. Dr. Jones adds ' vein, blood.'

"Ιννos, "Υννos, Γίννos, Γῖνos, Γινὸs, the foal of a mule and a mare : — a dwarfed horse or mule, jennet. — Allied to "Ινιs, a son. "Υννos is allied by Greg. to Τἴόs. Γ a prefix, as in Γοῖνos, &c. (2) R. γίνομαι, to be born.

"Ιξ, ' prob. a form of "Ιψ :' Dnn. and Ldd.

"Ιξαλοs, bounding, wanton. — R. ἴκω, ἴξω, to go forward. So "Ιτης from †ἴω, εἶμι is bold, adventurous, and Αἴξ from αἴσσω, ξω. (2) R. ἰξὸs, lumbus, sedes cupidinis. ' Cùm carmina lumbum Intrant': Pers.

'Ιξία, 'Ιξὸs, the same as, and perh. contracted from Κριξὸs, 'which is Dor. for Κρισσὸs, Κιρσόs :' Ldd. Thus Damm brings Εὐρὲξ from Πλευρὲξ.

'Ιξεύω, to catch birds with 'Ιξὸs, birdlime:— the misletoe producing it. — ' Prob. from ἴσχω, ἔχω :' Dnn. ' From ἴχω, ἴξω, ἔχομαι, to hold to :' Lenn. From its glutinous nature.

'Ιξὸs, the waist, loins. — ' Prob. akin to 'Ισχὺς, ['Ιχσὺs,] strength, like 'Ισχίον. Cic. : Latera et vires :' Ldd. and Dnn. Vice versâ, ἰξὸs, ϝιξὸs, ViSCus.

"Ιονθos, the root of the hair: a pustule on the face at puberty. — ' Akin to ἀνθέω.?' Ldd. ' Prob. from ἀνθέω:?' Dnn. ' From ἄνθos:' Mrt. ' From ἴον, a violet, ἀνθέω: as dark-colored': Dr. Jones. As ' purpureæ genæ', Ov. See "Ιανθos. — Or R. ἴον only.

'Ιὸs, a dart, arrow:—from ἰῶ, to shoot, as 'Ιὸν ἧκε, Hom. Others from †ἴω, to go forward. — Also poison, ' from ἵημι : as ejected from the fangs of serpents:' Pkh. And rust of copper, as poisonous. — Honey, ' as emitted from the bee:' Dnn.

"Ιos, "Ια, "Ιον, one: but the masc. is found in the dative only, ἴῳ. — Properly, it seems, only the fem. should be used, as contr. from μία : then ἴῳ was used from it. As the neut. pl. Θάτερα, (τὰ ἔτερα,) produced the sing. Θάτεροs. (2) For Οἶos.

'Ιότηs, impulse, inclination, will, design. — R. †ἴω, to send (one's thoughts to) : ἴεμαι, to desire. As ἐχυ-ρΟΤΗΣ. (2) Schneid. from ἴs. ?

K

Ioὺ, cry of woe: — and of joy. Like 'Iή, 'Iώ.

"Iουλος, down on the cheek, from οὖλος, downy, I prefix as in 'Iαύω. Also wool, as Οὖλος, woolly. And, like down, the male flower of plants. And a sheaf, as Οὖλος. So a hymn to Ceres, who is hence called 'Iουλώ.

'Iὸφ, an exclamation of abhorrence: pronounced perh. yoff. Imitative word.

"Iπτη, a woodpecker. — R. ἴπτω, ἴπον, to injure (the tree). ' Called also "Iππα, Πιπώ : ' Ldd.

'Iπνὸς, a furnace, stove, kitchen, hearth. — R. πνῶ, to blow, with I prefix as in 'Iαύω, 'Iεῦζω, 'Iουλος: From the blast of the fire. Of the two bellows in the brazier's furnace, the oracle in Herod. says: "Eνθ' ἄνεμοι ΠΝΕΙΟΥΣΙ δύο. (2) The Goth. aufn, Icel. ofn, our oven.

'Iπνὸς, a close-stool, night-chair. From ἰπῶ, to press upon, i.e. press tight or close. Thus our Press is used for ' a kind of case or frame for clothes and other uses:' (Dr. J.) And this too may lead the way to 'a lantern', i.e. ' a close case or frame' for securing a candle.

'Iπos, a pressing weight; — a fuller's press; — a mouse-trap as pressing upon and squeezing the mouse. And 'Iπόω, to press upon, weigh down, oppress. — 'Iπόω from ἴπτω, ἴπον, ' prop. to press, oppress,' (Dnn.) Or, if 'Iπτω is taken in its common sense, to hurt, ' lædo', then as the comp. ' collido,' ' illīdo.' (2) From obs. †πόω, †πίω, πιέζω, to press hard, squeeze: with I prefix, as in 'Iαύω. See Ποῦs, and Πῶμα a lid.

'Iππακαl. ' Ρυππακαl was an exclam. of rowers inciting each other. Here, as horses are rowing, it is jocosely 'Iππακαl:' Brunck, Ar. Eq. 602.

'Iππο-, great, as we say Horse-chestnut, Horse-radish, from

"Iππος, a horse, mare. — I give in to the deriv. from ἵπταμαι ποῦς, to fly with the feet, (as we say, The horse took to flight:) ; or from ἱπῶ ποῦς, to press firm the ground with the feet: for ἵππους as ὠκύ-πους: the Latins say Soni-PES. By constant use ἵπ-ΠΟΥΣ would easily become ἵππΟΣ, as dăbam contrary to amābam, and as in fact 'τρίΠΟΣ poët. for τρίΠΟΥΣ :' Dnn.—Parkh. says : ' Either from the Hebrew, or from ἵπτασθαι ποσί.' So Ewing. (2) Goth. hoppe, a horse; Icel. hoppa, a mare: our hobby.

'Iπταμαι, to fly. — R. πέταμαι, πτάμαι, with I as in 'Iαύω. (2) R. ἰάπτω, ' to run, to fly, to soar,' (Dnn.)

'Iπτω, to afflict, hurt. — For 'Iάπτω, to assail, distress. (2) R. †πέτω, †πτῶ, (whence †πιπέτω, πίπτω,) to fall (upon): I prefix as in 'Iπταμαι. So Ico from "Iκω, to come down upon.

'Iρaξ, 'Iρηξ: in 'Iέραξ. So 'Iρὸς for 'Iερός.

'Iρις, the rainbow: — halo: — iris of the eye: ' the goddess Iris, the messenger of the Gods; from εἴρω to announce, tell, according to the old gramm. and Damm:' Dnn. who says too that "Iρις is ' the rainbow appearing as a sign or announcement Il. λ. 27:' as also that "Iρω is ' an Ionic form for Eἴρω.' (2) ' Or Hebr. aur, light:' Wr.

66

"Is, ἱνὸς, a sinew, tendon, fibre ; — strength. — As 'Pls, 'Pινὸς from ῥέω; Θὶs, Θωὸς from †Θέω, τίθημι, so 'Is, ἱνὸς, from †ἕω, εἶμι : As going through the body, per-vading it. (2) ' Hebr. isch, vir': Mrt.

'Iσάλη, the same as 'Iξάλη, a goatskin. See "Iξαλος.

'Iσειον, temple of Isis.

"Iσημι, to know. — R. εἴδω, εἴσω, whence †εἴσημι, ἴσημι, as Eἴκελος, "Iκελος: "Eἴσος,"Iσος. So "Iδμεν, "Iσκω. (2) Germ. wissen, to know ; weise, our wise ; the Saxon, &c.

'Iσθμὸς, a narrow pass, isthmus; — a pass. — For 'Iθμὸς, (as ἔχον,) allied to "Iθμα.

'Iσικον, 'Iσίκιον, the Latin Insicium, from In-seco : a sausage.

'Iσκω, to liken, as Eἴσκω ; — think like; — think likely, conjecture, say as being likely.

'Iσμα, a seat. — R. ἵζω, ἵσμαι.

'Iσos : in "Eἴσος.

'Iσσα, ' an exclam. of spiteful triumph over another's distress. From the sound, like Σίττα:' Ldd. Perh. from the sound ισσσσ: HISS. (2) R. ἥσσα, a defeat, discomfiture.

†'Iστάω, †'Eστάω, †Στάω, to place, put, put firm or fast, cause to stand up, raise. — ' to place in a balance, poise, weigh', (Dnn.) Neut. and midd. to stand. — From ἕσται and ἱσται, pass. of †ἕω and †ἵω, ἵημι, ' to put, place:' (Ldd.)

'Iστία, Ionic of 'Eστία.

'Iστίον, a sail: 'from ἱστός: any web, cloth or sheet': Ldd. Or R. †ἱστῶ: As fixed to the mast. So

'Iστὸς, a mast; from †ἱστῶ, to make to stand up. 'Iστὸν στήσαντο, Hom. — Also, beam of the loom which stood upright: the warp which was fixed to the beam, — and the web: so Στήμων, and Stamen. Also, the shin-bone, long like a mast.

'Iστορία, acquired knowledge, history. — From 'Iστωρ, 'Iστωρ Ion., ορ, knowing, skilled, — judge, umpire. — Allied to 'Eπ-ίσταμαι, to know. So "Iστε is, ye know, "Iσατε.

'Iσχαλέος, 'Iσχνὸs, dried up, thin, meagre. — ' R. ἴσχω:' Dnn. ' Held in, contracted:' Damm. Shrivelled.

'Iσχὰs, dried fig, as 'Iσχαλέα. — Also, an anchor, as detaining the ship: ἴσχω.

'Iσχίον, the hip. — ' Prob. from ἰσχὺς, strength: akin to 'Iξύs:' Ldd. and Dnn. On 1 Kings 12. 10 Poole says ' His LOINS in which is the principal seat of STRENGTH.'

'Iσχύs, strength. — R. ἴσχω, to hold, as 'Eχυρὸs, firm, from ἔχω. (2) ' Hebr. aschasch, to be strong :' Mrt.

'Iσχω, to hold, hold in, check, stop. — R. ἔχω, much as "Eπω,"Eσπω; and "Eσχον.

"Iσωs, perhaps. — R. ἴσος, like, likely. And

'Iταλὸs, a bull-calf.

'Iταμὸs, 'Iτης, venturous, bold, impetuous. — R. †ἴω, ἴται, εἶμι : Going anywhere and everywhere. So 'Iτὸs, which can be gone through.

'Iτέα, a willow: — wicker-shield. — As above: ' From

the rapidity of the growth of the willow:' Dnn., Mrt., and Ewing. (**2**) Ldd. allies Ἰτέα, the shield, to Ἴτυς. Ἴτης : in Ἰταμός.

ΙΤΡΙΑ, ων, cakes made of sesamé and honey. Q.?— Wright makes it also 'the lower part of the belly', which seems to point to Ἦτρον.

Ἴτυς, edge or rim, as of a wheel or shield. — For Ἄμφ-ιτυς, ambitus, formed as Ἴτης. Περί-δρομον κύτος Æ. Theb. 491.

Ἴϋγξ, the wry-neck, famous for its shrill sound: And, as it was much used in magical love-rites, so a charm or love-wheel.—From

Ἰΰζω, ' to cry out, shout; — to howl, shriek, yell : from an interject. sound like Ἰή, Ἰού, Ἰώ:' Ldd.

Ἰΰκτης, a piper : ἰϋζω, ἴϋκται.

Ἴφθιμος, strong.— R. Ἴφι. Θ as in χθαμαλός, and Τ in πτόλεμος.

Ἴφι, strongly : i.e. with strength, from Ἴς, Ἰνὸς, then † Ἰνιφι, as Βίηφι.

Ἴφυον, some pot-herb.—As Ἰαύω, I prefix to φύον, springing up, as Olus from Oleo, to grow. So δένδρα πεφυκότα.

Ἰχθὺς, a fish.— R. †Ἴχω, Ἴχθην, Ἴσχω, ἔχομαι : From its viscous, glutinous nature. Compare Ἰξὸς, birdlime.

(**2**) ' R. Ἴκω, Ἴχθην : From its swift motion :' Pkh.

Ἰχνεύμων, the Egyptian rat, famous for tracing out the eggs of crocodiles. — From

Ἴχνος, a footstep. — R. Ἴκω, Ἴχα : Made by going forward, as Βαθμὸς, Ἴθμα.

Ἰχώρ, the blood of the Gods.—' R. Ἴκω, Ἴχα : Coming or oozing out, so as to mean any liquor :' Bp. Burgess. As Ἕλωρ.

Ἴψ, ἰπὸς, as Θρίψ, Θριπὸς, a vine-fretter.— R. Ἴπτω, Ἴψω, to hurt.

Ἰὰ, sound of grief, and of joy. As Ἰή, Ἰού.

Ἰωγή, shelter from blasts.—According to Κυματωγὴ from κύματος and ἀγὴ, Ἰωγὴ is from ἰωὴ and ἀγή : A breaking of the sound (of the wind).

Ἰωὴ, ' from ἰὰ, ἰώ : any loud sound :' Ldd.

Ἰωκὴ, the battle ἰωὴ din. (**2**) For Διωκὴ, from διώκω. As raised at the pursuit of an enemy. Much as Γαῖα, Αἶα. See Ἰωχμός.

Ἰωρὸς, the same as Οὖρος, †Ὦρος. I. as Ἰαύω.

Ἰῶτα, a jot : from I the smallest letter. The name of the letter, like most others, is Hebrew, Arabic or Phenician : Jod or Yod.

Ἰωχμὸς, pursuit : for Διωχμὸς from διώκω. As perhaps Ἰωκή.

Κ.

Κάβαισος, gluttonous. —' From κάβος :' Ldd. and Dnn. (**2**) R. κάπτω, to gulp down. B as in ἐκάλυβον.

Καβάλλης, caballus, a nag, hackney. — As the verb Κάπετον for κατεπέτον, so Καβάλλης for καταβάλλης, from βάλλω : On which baggage is thrown : ' Ab injiciendis oneribus', Becm. Called Dossuarii (Dorsuarii,) and Clitellarii. (**2**) ' Russ. kobila, a mare :' Wbst.

ΚΑΒΕΙΡΟΙ, gods worshipped in Lemnos, Samothrace, &c. — Scaliger from Phœnic. kabir, powerful.

Κάβηξ, form of Καύηξ, Κάφηξ.

ΚΑΒΟΣ, a corn-measure. —' Prob. the Hebr. kab, if not a variety of Κάδος :' Dnn. (**2**) Allied to Lat. cavus, through χάω, χαίνω, χάσμα. See Κάβηξ.

Κάγκανος, fit for burning, dry. — Redupl. from †κάνος from †κάω, καίω, to burn. ' So Δαυὸς from δαίω :' Dnn.

Καγχάζω, Καχάζω, Καγχαλάω, to laugh loud. — ' From the radical forms †γάω, †χάω, whence Γαίω, Χαίρω, Χαίνω [to open the mouth wide,] :' Dnn. (**2**) Lenn. from the sound, as our Cackle, Giggle.

Κάγχρυς : in Κάχρυς.

Κάδος, a cask, urn, vote-box. —' R. χανδάνω, [ἔχαδον,] :' Dnn. As holding, containing. So Κεκαδὼν, &c. (**2**) ' Hebr. cad, waterpot :' Dahler.

†Κάζομαι, κέκασμαι, κέκαδμαι Dor., ' to overcome, surpass, excel, to be eminent or distinguished or adorned with : — to be capable of. — Matthiæ and others consider Κάζω like Χάζω To compel to make way : Others

67

consider it as Καίνυμαι, (the same as Κάζομαι,) which perh. from καίνω to slay, i. e. to overpower, beat down :' Dnn. (**2**) Allied to Γαίω, to exult in or be proud of, or Γάνος, brilliancy, brightness. (**3**) Κέκασμαι, allied to Κόσμος. (**4**) Herm. allies κέκαδμαι, &c. to Κῆδος : To bestow care upon.

Καθαίρω, to purge, cleanse. — Buttm., Lenn., Pkh. from κατ᾽, αἴρω, or αἱρέω, to take κατὰ downwards. See on Θαιρός. (**2**) ' Hebr. katar, to fumigate :' Mrt.

Καθαρὸς, pure. — Above.

Καὶ, and, also, even (as Et in Latin,) even though, although.—Allied to Καίω, Κείω, Κεάζω, (and see Καίνω,) to sever, split : Splitting a sentence into sundry particulars, distributing an action between two or more. (**2**) ' Hebr. coh, so, as Eng. al-so :' Mrt. (**3**) ' Sanskr. ka at the end of words :' Dr. Jones.

Καιάδας, Κεάδας, a gulf in the earth, or underground cavern for criminals. — Allied to Καῖαρ, a cavity, Χάος, Χαίνω, Χάσμα, Κεάζω. See the next word. (**2**) ' The Pers. kade :' Dahl.

Καιετάεις, ' epith. of Sparta, as abounding in hollows, and so akin to Καῖαρ, a cavity [in Καιάδας,] : Others from ΚΑΕΤΟΣ said to be the same as Καλάμινθος, calaminth, found on the Eurōtas :' Dnn.

Καικίας, N.E. wind. — ' As blowing from some river Caicus :' Blomf.: ' From Caicus, a river of Mysia :' Mrt. (**2**) Lenn. from καίω, to burn, i. e. to nip, as

Lat. *uro.* ' *Uri* se in montibus patiuntur :' Cic. Κέ-καυκα, prop. κέκαικα.

Καινὸς, new.—Allied to Κάζομαι 'to be adorned or decorated with', (Dnn.) Καλὸς, fair, beautiful, Γάνος, brightness, splendor. Compare the comm. 'to take the shine out of anything'.

Καίνυμαι : in Κάζομαι.

Καίνω, to slay.—Allied to Χαίνω, i.e. to make a χάσμα opening or hollow ; and to Σχάζω to cut open. (2) 'R. †κέω, κείω, κεάζω, to cleave, cut : Or R. †κέω, κείμαι, to make to lie down, throw down prostrate :' Mrt. So Χαίνω, Βαίνω, Φαίνω, Μαίνω, Οἰδαίνω.

Καίριος, critical, vital, fatal : from

Καιρὸς, the nick of time, extreme point, fit proper time, opportunity, occasion ;—due measure or proportion.— ' Perh. allied to Κάρα, as we say, The head and front, the chief thing :' Ldd. We say, The tip or top of expectation. So 'Ακμὴ, the highest point, is the critical moment.

Καῖρος, 'the row of slips or thrums in the loom to which the threads of the warp are attached, Lat. licia :' Ldd., 'the woof crossing the warp :' Dnn.—Mrt. from ' κείρω, ἔκαρον, tondeo, abscindo : whence the Lat. car-men textorium'. Thus Scalig. and Forcell. derive the verb Caro from κείρω, i.e. to break or card wool for spinning. (2) Lenn. from Καιρός : as the sum and substance of weaving. (3) Allied to Κάρσιος, 'Επι-κάρσιος, oblique, i.e side-ways, cross-wise.

Καίω, καύσω, καήσομαι, to burn.—Allied to Κείω, which means, just as Δαίω, to Divide and to Burn : ' Fire most powerfully separates and resolves things :' Damm. ' *Dividit ignibus :*' Hor. (2) Mrt. : ' Hebr. *kavah,* to burn.' Wr. makes it *kooee.*

Κακίζω, to reproach as κακόν.

Κακκάβη, pot or pan.—' Redupl. for †κάβη (as Κάγχανος,) from κάβος :' Becm.

Κακκάβη, a partridge.—Nearly all say, from the sound. In Norfolk *cobback* or *comback* is said of the guinea-fowl. ' In the Sanskrit *Kukubha* of the pheasant :' Wilson.

Κακκάω, Κακκῶ, *caco,* as also the Engl. word. ' From the sound of infants wishing so to do :' Lenn.—If not from χέζω, κέχεκα.

Κακκείοντες, wishing to sleep : i. e. κατ-κείοντες, from Κείω, so used, allied to Κεῖμαι.

Κακὸς, cowardly, dastard, timid,—then (as conv. of 'Αρείων, 'Αρέτη, Virtus, &c.) vile, bad, wretched, &c.— ' R. χάζω, [κέχακα,] to give way in battle :' Pkh. ' For χακός :' Greg. And so κεκάδοντο. (2) Allied to †κέω, κεῖμαι : Lying idle, inactive.

Κάκτος, the cactus.—Contr. by use from †ἄκακτος, i. e. ἀκαχμένος, from ἀκάζω, to sharpen, point. (2) Allied to Κεάζω, Κείρω, Κεντέω. See κΑίω, κΑίνω. (3) ' R. καίω. Urit seu pungit :' Greg.

ΚΑΛΑΒΙΣ, a Laconian dance : and Καλαβίδια, a festival celebrated therewith in honor of Diana.—Q. ?

Καλάβροψ, the same as Καλαῦροψ.

Κάλαθος, a basket.—As made of κάλον, wood. Like ψάμΑΘΟΣ. Κά, as in κάλιά.

68

ΚΑΛΑΪΣ, a precious stone paler than sapphire.—Q. ?

Καλαμὶς, as Κάλαμος, a reed, stick, pen, ' curling-iron, hollow and shaped like a reed : hair-pin :' Ldd.

Καλαμῖτις, a grasshopper, as living among the καλά-μους corn-stalks.

Κάλαμος, a reed, pipe, pole, shaft, &c.—Like ὁρχΑ-ΜΟΣ, from κᾶλον, ' wood, espec. dried wood', (Dnn.) I. e. anything dried or parched : exactly as Κάρφος from Κάρφω. Compare Κηλεὸς and Caleo. Κά, as in Κάλιά. (2) Lenn. from †καὼ, †χάω, χαίνω, to be hollow.

Καλαυρῖτις, dross of silver.—' In Dioscor. 5. 102,— perh. as concocted in *Calauria* or *Calabria,* [B, as in κάΒηξ,] for other sorts he calls from the countries, Attic, Campanian, Sicilian :' Steph.

Καλαῦροψ, οπος, a shepherd's crook, sometimes thrown to drive back the cattle.—As 'Ρόπαλον is 'a club thicker at one end, from ῥέπω', (Ldd.) καλαύροπος (gen.) may be from κᾶλον wood (A short in Κάλία,) and ῥέπω to incline, ῥοπὴ inclination downwards : or, with Ewing, from καυλὸς a handle, shaft, and ῥέπω. In the latter the Υ changes its place, in the former it is added, as in μοΥπος, &c.

Καλέω, to call.—Dnn. compares Κέλομαι, to call out to, Κέλλω. So Κέκλομαι. ' I order you to come. As Αὐτός σε καλεῖ, He urges you to come to him :' Damm. As Latin Accio, to call, from Cic. So Ainsw. explains Appello, ' ad me *pello.*' (2) Wbst. notices our *call,* Swed. *kalla,* Welsh *galw.* (3) ' Chald. *kal,* the voice :' Mrt.

Κάλιά, a cabin, cot, barn, nest.—All from κάλον, wood, ' notwithstanding the ἄ :' Ldd.

Καλινδέω, the same as Κυλινδέω.

Καλιστρέω, the same as Καλέω. As Βωστρέω.

Κάλλαια, a cock's gills.—' Prob. from their change-ful hues, like the Κάλαΐς, shifting between blue and green :' Ldd. (2) As Κάλλεα, so used : as being ornaments, or ornamental appendages. R. καλός.

Καλλάΐνος, purple. — Voss from the color of Κάλλαΐα, a cock's gills. (2) Others from the stone called Κάλαΐς of a greenish blue.

Κᾶλον, ' wood, esp. dried wood for fuel. Prob., as Δαλὸς from δαίω, so Κᾶλον from καίω :' Dnn. ' The combustible :' Ldd. (2) ' Hebr. *kala,* he burnt :' Mrt.

Καλὸς, fine, beautiful, fair.—Allied to Κάζομαι, 'to be adorned or decorated,' (Dnn.) And to Γάνος, brilliancy, 'Αγάλλω, to adorn. (2) ' Hebr. and Chald. *kal,* to finish, adorn :' Mrt.

ΚΑΛΠΗ, the trot of a horse : — a mare.—Budæus allies it with *gallop.*

Κάλπη, Κάλπις, ' for Καλύπη, a covering of skin, bucket, [a cinerary] urn :' Ewing. See Κάλυξ, Καλύπτω.

Καλύβη, a hut. — R. καλύπτω, ἐκάλυβον.

Κάλυξ, a husk, shell, cup or *calyx* of a flower : ' Κά-λυκες, women's ornaments, perh. ear-rings shaped like a flower-cup or bud,' Ldd.: ' like a rose-bud', Dnn.— Allied to

Καλύπτω, to cover, hide, &c. — In form as Κορύπτω.

As Καλυπτὸs is 'wrapped or folded round a thing,' (Ldd.) Καλύπτω may be from κάλως or κάλος a rope: i. e. to put a rope round, wrap round with a rope, gen. 'to cover with something rolled round', as Dr. J. explains the second meaning of Wrap. Somewhat as our verb To Cloak. And see spec. on Κόμβος. (2) R. καλόs. Like καλλύνω, to gloss or cover over a deformity, gen. to cover over. (3) As Κάλως and Χαλάω seem allied, so Καλύπτω, i. e. to let fall anything upon another and shroud it. Compare Χάζω and ΚεΚαδών. (4) Hebr. kala, Chald. kela, he shut.

Καλχαίνω, 'to make purple, from κάλχη: — to make dark and troublous like a stormy sea: — met. to turn over in one's mind, like Volvo, Volūto, to search out: — to be in doubt or trouble:' Ldd. ·

ΚΑΛΧΗ and ΧΑΛΚΗ, the purple limpet; — dye; — herb of purple color. 'Akin to Lat. cochlea:' Ldd. Transp. from †καχλὴ, allied to Κόχλος, a shell-fish yielding a purple dye. A as 'Αστρακὸs and 'Οστρακὸs, ignArus and ignOro. And see the last part of Κάχληξ. Yet? (2) Steph. says: 'Κάλχη is not badly interpreted purple, but I understand it of a fish, which Hesych. says is called also ΚΑΛΤΚΑ.' Whence perhaps ΚΑΛΧΗ. Well then from †καλύσσω, (whence Κάλυξ, υκος,) to cover, conceal: said of a shell-fish. Κάλυξ is a husk, shell.

Κάλως, Κάλοs, a cable. — R. χαλάω, χαλῶ, to let down or loose a rope. So κάλων κατ-εῖναι, to let down a rope: Lat. laxare rudentes. See specially Χαλινόs. K, as κεΚαδὼν ' s. 2. of Χάζομαι', (Dnn.)

Κάμαξ, 'a prop for vines, handle of a spear, pole, palisade:' Dnn. — Contr. from †καλάμαξ from κάλαμος, 'an angler's rod, an arrow:' (Dnn.). (2) Metaph. from κάμνω, καμῶ: Labouring to support the vines. See a metaph. use of κάμνω in 'A-κμων. (3) R. γάω, †χάω, to take, hold, (as in Γαστὴρ, Χάζω,) applying to the handle of the spear. Thus Έχω, Έγχος. Hesych. has a verb Καμάσσω, to shake. (4) As ΚΑΜΙνος, a furnace, from κάω, καίω : ' Præ-usta sudes'.

Καμάρα, an arch, vaulted room, covered waggon, a bed with a tester. Allied to Κάμπτω, to bend. Festus: 'Camara et camari boves a curvatione.' (2) 'R. κάμνω, καμῶ: As labouring under the weight:' Mrt. See Κάμαξ 2. (3) R. γάω, γέγαμαι, to hold, receive, χάζω, &c.

ΚΑΜΗΛΟΣ, a camel. — 'Hebr. gemel:' Wr.

Κάμινος, an oven, furnace, fire. — Nearly all from καίω, to burn. (2) Webst. notices Russ. and Germ. kamín, and affinities in Chald. and Arab. : — Pkh. the Hebr. ΚΜΗ to be warm.

Καμμύω, for κατα-μύω.

Κάμνω, καμῶ, to be weary and fatigued with labor, to toil, work out, to be weak from illness. — Καμῶ, allied to Γέμω, to be laden and overwhelmed, and to Κάμπτω, to bend down through weariness. Od. ε. 453.

Κάμπτω: in Γαμψόs.

Κάμψα, Κάψα, capsa, a basket, coffer: — capsule.
69

— 'R. †κάπω, κάψω, capio, [κάπτω in Hesych., allied to Χάζω, Χανδάνω, and Γάω,] to contain. Or κάμπτω, ψω, [as Καμπύλος, bent, curved,]:' Schneid.

Κάναβος, 'a piece of cane, [reed, or rod,] round which a worker in wax or clay moulded his materials; — a model; — skeleton: hence Κανάβινος, meagre, puny. — R. κάννα:' Dr. Jones and Dnn. Or R. κάνη. As κολοΒΟΣ.

Κάνανθρον, the seat of a body of a cane- or wicker-carriage, and the carriage. — R. κάνη.

Κανδάσσω, to make a sharp gurgling sound with water: Καναχέω, Καναχίζω, to plash like water, to clash, ring. — 'Imitative of the sound:' Dnn. (2) 'R. κάνη: from the rustling sound of reeds shaken by the wind:' Dr. Jones. (3) Mrt. from κενός: As sounding hollow.

Κάνασυρον, a cane- or wicker-basket, canistrum. — R. κάνη.

ΚΑΝΔΑΥΛΟΣ, ΚΑΝΔΥΛΟΣ, a Lydian dish. — Jablonski says in honor of Candaules. As our Sandwich.

ΚΑΝΔΤΣ, a Medish upper-garment with sleeves, and a Medish word.

Κανέον, Κάνης, a basket; — cane-mat. — R. κάνη. (2) Our can, and Germ., Dutch, Corn., &c., referred by Wbst. to Welsh cannu, to contain.

Κάνη, Κάννα, a cane or reed, reed-mat, reed-fence. Allied to Κενὴ, empty, void: Χαίνω, Χανῶ, to be hollow; Χάζω, Χανδάνω, to contain. In form compare γέΝΝΑ. (2) 'Hebr., Chald., Syr., Arab. kaneh : found also in the Armoric, Welsh, &c.:' Wbst. See Κανέον.

Κάνθαρος, a drinking-cup; — a small canoe. Formed as Κανθός : or Χανῶ to be hollow: Χανδάνω to contain. Dnn. says 'prob. from the shape of the beetle called Κάνθαρος.' Just as well however may be the converse. — Also 'a mark or knot like a beetle, on the tongue of the god Apis:' Ldd. — And 'a woman's ornament, prob. a gem like the scarabæi (beetles) so common among the ancient Egyptians:' Ldd.

Κανθήλιον, pack-saddle for a Κανθών.

Κανθὸs, orb of the eye, and the corner: — felly of a wheel. — For Καμπτός, says Becman: Bent, curved. Better, ἐκάμφθην, καμφθόs, (as 'Αχθος,) καμπὸs, κανθός. (2) Formed like Κάνθαρος. Allied to Κενός.

Κανθὼν, a large sumpter-ass; — stupid fellow. — As carrying κάνεα, baskets. See μάλΘΩΝ. (2) R. κάμνω, καμῶ, to toil and labor. For †Κάμθων.

Κάννα : in Κάνη.

Κάνναβις, hemp, flax, tow. — Ldd., Mrt., and Steph. from κάννα: Wbst. 'from the root of κάννα, cane.' (2) Irish, canaib.

Κανὼν, a rod like a Κάνη, rule, measure, plummet, handle of a spear, distaff: — rule of action, canon.

Κατάνη, a Thessalian carriage. — R. · κάπτω in Hesych. and Etym. M., to take, contain, capio, from †κάω, †χάω, χανδάνω.

. Κάπετος, for Σκάπετος.

Κάπη, a manger, stall. — R. κάπτω, to devour, a. 2. ἔκαπον. R. κάπω, Dnn.

Κάπηλος, a salesman, retailer, huckster; — innkeeper; — adulterator of goods. — Hesych. explains it, ' one who buys πρὸς τὴν κάπην,' and rightly so, says Steph.: i. e. for the stall or crib, or, as Pkh. says, for fodder, food, Καππτὸν being fodder for cattle, and Schrevel. says: ' Κάπη, the manger: the food which is put in the manger.' Pkh. makes the first sense 'selling victuals and drink, then making gain of anything, adulterating as vintners do.'—Dnn. says : ' R. prob. (κάπη,) κάπτω'. Κάπτω is ' to eat up hastily, snap at, bolt:' so Κάπηλος may be metaph. one who snatches up little gains. (2) ' Sax. ceap, business, trade: Dutch koop, a bargain, cheap, purchase; Germ. kaufen, Swed. kapa, Russ. kupayu, Lat. caupo, Engl. cheap, chap-man:' Wbst. — Note βέθΗΛΟΣ.

Καπίθη, a measure of corn. — From κάπτω, says Dnn.: i.e. in the sense of capio, to hold, — mentioned in Hesych. and Etym. M. See Καπάνη.

Καπνὸς, vapor, smoke. — R. †κάω 1.

ΚΑΠΠΑ, kappa. Hebr. caph or koph.

Καπράω, to be lustful as a Κάπρος. So Sus, Subo.

Κάπρος, a wild-boar. — 'R. κάπω, to breathe with a noise : or κάπτω, to devour with a noise:' Damm.

Κάπτω, to eat quick, swallow or gulp down. — R. †κάπω, to snap, to bite. (2) R. Χαίνω, Χανδάνω, Χανδὸν, ' with the mouth open, voraciously:' (Dnn.)

Καπυρὸς, 'dried, parched:— ardent, met. eloquent (with στόμα,) as we say glowing: — clear-sounding, sonorous, some say witty. — The old Gramm. for Κατάπυρος, but pref. with Schneid. from κάπω, as Ἀδος from ἄω, ἄημι:' Dnn.

†Κάπω, †Καπύω, †Καφέω, to breathe out hard, pant, gasp. — R. χάω, χαίνω : ' To open the mouth to take in air, take breath, breathe hard :' Damm. (2) Goth. hafyan, Dutch heffen, our heave.

†Κάπω, Κάπτω, to snap, bite. — R. †χάω, χαίνω, to open the mouth wide, as in Χανδόν; or †χάω, χανδάνω, κάπτω (Hesych.), capio, to take.

Κὰρ, Κάρα, Κάρη, the head. — From its curved form, allied to Κέρας, Κόρυς, Χορὸς, Κορωνὸς, Γῦρος, &c. See κΑμπτω in γΑμψός. (2) As shaved, from κείρω, ἔκαρον. Thus also

Κὰρ, the hair of the head: see the last part of the last. ' Thus I esteem him ἐν καρὸς αἴση but as a hair. Some say as a Carian mercenary : — or as death, from †κὰρ, κὴρ, as in Homer, He hated him like κηρὶ μελαίνῃ. But the A ought thus to be long :' Dnn.

Κάρᾱνον, Κάρηνον, the head or top, as Κάρα, Κὰρ. Κάρᾱνος, a prince. Καρανόω, to bring to a head, finish.

Κάρβᾱνος, barbarian. — From Κὰρ, a Carian; βάζω, to speak. Hesych. : Καρβάζει, Καρικῶς λαλεῖ καὶ βαρβαρικῶς.

Καρβάτιναι, shoes of undressed leather. — ' Called from the Κᾶρες Carians,' says Pollux. And possibly a

70

word †Βατίνη, a shoe, from †βάω, βέβαται, βαίνω, as Ἐμ-βὰς a shoe.

Κάρδαμον, the herb nose-smart, i. e. καρά-δαμον, κάρα, δαμῶν, head-subduing. So Nasturtium is Nasi-tortium, Nose-twisting.

Καρδία, the heart, &c. — For κραδία, as Κάρτος for Κράτος. (2) R. κέαρ. (3) ' Dutch hart, Sanskr. herda:' Wbst. ' Hebr. hered, to palpitate:' Wr.

Κάρδοπος, a kneading-trough, bin. — Soft for κάρδοφος, i.e. καρπο-δόφος, (See Ἀδηφόρος,) from κάρπα, δέφω, δέδοφα: In which things are worked powerfully with the hand. Much as Ἰφι-γένεια, Ἰφι-άνασσα. (2) R. κείρω, κέκαρται, κάρδην : as prim. a vessel for mincing things. (3) 'R. κερδω, δέφω:' Mrt. Two verbs, as in Ψηλαφάω. ?

Κάρη, Κάρηνον: the same as Κὰρ.

Καρίνη, a Carian woman employed as a weeper at a funeral.

Κάρὶς, a shrimp, prawn. — Ewing from κάρα: i.e all-head. Though the quantities differ.

Καρκαίρω, to ring or quake. — Mrt. and Lenn. from the sound, Καρ Καρ, like Κορκορυγή. (2) Ewing from κάρχαρος : To make a harsh noise.

Κάρκαρον : in Γοργύρη.

Καρκίνος, a crab : — ' from likeness of shape to its claws, 1. a pair of tongs, 2. a bone forming part of the skull, 3. a kind of shoe, 4. a kind of bandage:' Ldd. — Allied to Κάρχαρος. So Salmas. from its roughness.

Κάρνεια, festival of Apollo Carneus. — 'Perhaps from Carnus the son of Jupiter and Europa :' Hesych.

Κάρνον, Κάρνυξ, ' the Gallic trumpet, Lat. cornu': Ldd. Allied to Κέρας, as μΕνω, mAneo.

Κάρος, heaviness of the κάρα head.

Καρπαία, a Thessalian mimic dance.—Perhaps allied to Καρπάλιμος which see. The Latins said ' carpere gyrum.' (2) ' Prob. after gathering the καρποὺς fruits ;' Ewing.

Καρπάλιμος, ' tearing, rapid, swift: from ἁρπάζω : compare Lat. carpo:' Ldd. ' For ἁρπάλιμος:' Dnn., Mrt. Ewing, &c. And Hemsterh. allies it to carpo. As Rapio, Rapidus. Κ prefix as perh. in Καυχάομαι and Κέλευθος, and as Γ in Γέντο for Ἕντο. See Ἀρπη.

Κάρπασα, sails made from ΚΑΡΠΑΣΟΣ, the Spanish flax.

Καρπὶς, the same as Κάρφος.

Καρπὸς, fruit. — ' Prob. allied to Κάρφω : what is dry and ripe:' Ldd. ' As Frux, Fructus from Φρύγω :' Dnn. (2) Becm. allies it to carpo : Plucked fruit. See in Καρπάλιμος. (3) ' Hebr. garap, he plucked :' Becm.

Καρπὸς, the wrist. Ewing says: ' The wrist or hand attached to the wrist as a fruit καρπὸς to its stem.' Observe the metaph. meaning of Coma, hair. (2) ' Allied to Lat. carpo, to gather, grasp;' Dnn. See in Καρπάλιμος. (3) Damm from κάρφω, as above : ' From its hardness and dryness.'

Καρρέζω, for κατ-ρέζω, to do down with the hand, stroke with the hand.

Κάῤῥων, stronger. — As Βαθὺς, Βάσσων, so Κρατὺς, Κράσσων, Κάρσων, Κάῤῥων.

Κάρσιος: See Ἐπι-κάρσιος.

Κάρσις, a shearing. — R. κείρω, κέκαρσαι.

Κάρτα, strongly. — R. κάρτος.

Κάρταλος, -λλος, a small basket, narrow at the bottom. —' R. καρτός: Made of cut twigs :' Mrt. and Ewing. See Κάρσις. — (Very rare.)

Κάρτος, for Κράτος.

Καρυάτιδες, 'prop. the female inhabitants of Caryæ in Laconia : in Architecture female figures as pillars :' Dnn. and Ldd.

Καρυατίζω, to play at Καρύαι nuts: which may be from κάρα, as the nut is in form like the head: though Ewing makes it from the hard shell. Curiously from Testa, a shell, is the French Tête, the head.

ΚΑΡΤΚΗ, a Lydian sauce prepared with blood and other ingredients, a minced meat, (says Ewing,): so perhaps from κείρω, ἔκαρον, whence Κέρμα 'a minute portion cut from any thing', (Dnn.) : the ending like Lat. lactŭCA, cadŭCA ; so σαμβῡΚΗ, and acc. κῆρῠΚΑ, δοῐδῠΚΑ.

Καρύκινος, blood-red, from the καρύκη.

Κάρφος, a dry stick or twig, straw, chip, &c.: the rod with which the Prætor enfranchised. — From

Κάρφω, to dry up, parch, wither. — Allied to †χάρσω, κάρχαρος 'rough, prickly, esp. parched with thirst, Virgil's siti asper,' (Ldd.) — ΦΩ, as δέΦΩ, στέΦΩ, and as ΠΩ in μέλΠΩ, θάλΠΩ. Allied too to Σκάριφος, Σκαριφῶ. (2) 'Chald. and Hebr. charab, am dried up:' Mrt.

Κάρχαρος, Καρχάλεος, rough, sharp, rugged, dry. — 'Redupl. from †Χάρος, allied to Χαράσσω, to sharpen, grave:' Ldd. (2) Allied to Κέρχω, make dry or rough. (3) 'Hebr. gar, to cut with a saw:' Dr. Jones.

ΚΑΡΧΗΣΙΟΝ, the mast head, main-top, — shrouds, — bandages;— stand or post of the crane : — drinking-cup 'shaped like the ancient round top or cross trees on a mast': Grove. — 'Damm [and Mrt.] from κὰρ, the head, but ?' Dnn. Now Nonius says it is 'the highest part of the mast, in which are foramina holes through which the ropes are passed.' Perh. then from κὰρ, and †χάω 'to stand open', (Dnn.)

Κάρωσις, lethargy stupor.

Κασάλβη, Κασαύρα, a harlot. 'Allied to Κάσσα :' Dnn.

ΚΑΣΑΣ, 'a cushion, housing, skin serving as saddle. — They derive from κασσύω, [κασύω,] κάσσύμα : skins being prob. first used to sit on on horseback :' Dnn. (2) 'Heb. casa, to cover:' Dr. Jones. So our word case Wbst. takes for a bag of skin.

Κάσις, brother or sister. — As Κῆρυξ and Γῆρυς, so Κάσις and †Γάσις from †γάω, γείνομαι, i.e. σύγ-κασις, as σύγγονος, συγγενής: co-gnātus : or as Genuīnus from Gigno, Genni. Homer favors both: Τρεῖς δὲ ΚΑΣΙ-ΓΝΗΤΟΥΣ, τούς μοι μία ΓΕΙΝΑΤΟ μήτηρ.

Κάσσα, a harlot. — Mrt. from κάζομαι, κέκασσαι,

71

κέκασται, as decorating or adorning herself. (2) R. †κάω, καίω, to burn i.e. with lust: πυροῦσθαι 1 Cor. 7. 9. (3) 'Perh. from Κάσας:' Dnn.

ΚΑΣΣΙΑ, cassia. — 'The Hebr. ketzio :' Wr.

Κασσίτερος, tin, pewter. — 'For κανσίτερος, from καίω, καύσω: a sort of comparative : Easier for melting i.e. than brass or silver:' Damm. (2) 'R. κάσσα : from its meretricious appearance of silver :' Ewing.

ΚΑΣΣΥΤΩ, to stitch, sew together. — For κατα-σύω, σύω preserved in Lat. suo, to sew. Goth. siuyan, Dan. syer, Sax. suyian. — Lenn. from 'σύω, σεύω, moveo: κατα-σύω, moveo juxtà, jungo, conjungo.' But those verbs express rapidity. ? Q. soft from ξύω 'to work finely or delicately', (Ldd.)?

Κάστανον, a chestnut, the nut of Castana in Thessaly or Pontus.

Καστόρειος, a song at the horse or chariot races, called from Castor. So

Καστορίδες, famous Spartan hounds, 'said to be first reared by Castor :' Ldd.

Κάστωρ, a beaver. — 'R. κάζομαι, κέκασται ; The adorner, as building its cell with an order and neatness observed by naturalists:' Lenn.

Κασωρὶς, as Κάσσα, Κασαύρα.

Κατὰ, down, down against, down through, down in;— against, through, by, by such a way, according to, in accordance with: or towards, agreeably to. — R. κέιται, (κάται,) κείμαι, to be placed or lie down. See ἐγΚΑΤΑ. (2) Ormston from κεάζω, κέατω : The motion in cleaving being downward. (3) Dunb. allies it, as 'through', to 'Goth. gata, Belg. gatte, Dan. gade, our gate, a way, passage.' But Κάτω establishes the prim. meaning 'down.' Aristoph.: ΚΑΤ-ώρυξέ με ΚΑΤΑ τῆς γῆς ΚΑΤΩ. (4) 'Hebr. chat, subjection :' Wr.

Κατα-, back. As we go UP, and return DOWN. Or as we say, 'It has been so all DOWN from the Conquest.' — And 'thoroughly', as κατὰ is 'through.'

Καταῖτυξ, a low helmet or skull-cap. — R. καταὶ, κατὰ, †τὐξ as in Ἀν-τυξ: A low wrought frame.

Κατακωχή : in Ἀνακωχή.

Καταπέλτης, a catapult, engine for throwing darts.— All from πάλλω, πέπαλται. As νημΕρτής.

ΚΑΤΗΛΙΨ, Ιφος, 'the upper story of a house ; — a stair-case or ladder;— others say the roof. Though the form refers us to ἥλιψ, ιπος, a shoe, this deriv. is hard to explain:' Ldd. ? And the Φ ? (2) As κατ-ηφὴς, κατΗθολή, so from κατὰ, down, λείπω, ἔλιπον: 'Leaving the parts below.' But the Φ ? For the sound ?

Κατηφὴς, with downcast eyes. — Κατὰ, down, φάη eyes, φάος. So κατΗθολέω.

Κατουλὰς, dark (night). — R. εἴλω, ἔολα, †οῖλα, to shut up, envelope. So Ἐξ-ούλης.

Καὖαξ, Καὖηξ, Κάθηξ, Κηῦξ, Κηξ, Καῦης, a sea-mew, from its sound cau, cau.

Καῦκα, Καυκὶς, Καυκάλιον, certain cups: by some thought corrupt readings for Βαυκάλιον, &c. So Καυκὶς, a shoe, is now read Βαυκὶς.

Καυλὸς, a stalk, stem, shank, spear-handle :—cabbage-stalk.—Damm from κᾶλον [or κάλον, see κάλίά,] wood, as the spear-handle. (2) R. καίω, καύσω, to burn : as Κάρφος from Κάρφω.

Καῦμα, -σις, heat : καίω, καύσω.

ΚΑΤΝΑΚΗΣ, a *Persian* fur garment: written also Γαυνάκη. Wbst. compares our *gown*.

Καῦνος, a lot.—Allied to Καυκαλός, dry, from καίω, καύσω, for 'the earliest substances used in casting lots were small *dry* branches :' Damm. (2) R. κάνη, a reed. (3) Some say from the *Caunians* in Caria who much used them.

Καῦνος, bad, only 'a dialectic variety of Κακός :' Dnn. Perh. it is allied to Χαῦνος, 'soft, indolent, effeminate.' Hesych. has Καῦνος, bad. (Only once met with.)

Καυσία, a broad-brimmed hat to keep off the καῦσις of the sun. In Καῦμα.

Καυχάομαι, to boast.—'A kindred form of Αὐχέω, Εὔχομαι :' Dnn. Κ, prefix, as in Καρπάλιμος, and as Γ in Γοῖνος for οἶνος. (2) Better, as redupl. of †χάω, χαίνω, χαῦνος, puffed up.

Καφέω : in Κάπω.

Καφόρη, Σκαφόρη, a fox. — For κατα-φόρη (as Κα-βάλλης,) from φωράω to steal.—Alberti from σκάπτω, φωράω : See Ψηλαφάω. Better from σκάπτω, ἔσκαφα, (only), to dig, i.e. burrow.

Καχλάζω : in Καγχάζω.

Καχλάζω, Καχλαίνω, Κιχλίζω, to bubble or splash as the waves.— Redupl. 'from χλάζω': Ldd. and Dnn. (2) Some make it imitative, as our *Giggle.* Accius : 'Unda, excita saxis, crepitu clangente *cachinnat*,' i.e. *giggles.*

Κάχληξ, a pebble, gravel, shingle on the shore or in rivers : i.e. against which the water καχλάζει splashes. (2) R. κλάω, to break, by redupl. (3) Allied to Κόχλαξ.

Κάχρυς, Κάγχρυς, parched barley.— From κάγκω, to parch, allied to καίω, κέκαυκα, to burn. This word was also used for *catkins* and *capsules.* Will the learned Botanists explain this ?

Κάψα : in Κάμψα.

Κάω, 'Attic for Καίω', Dnn.

Κε, Κεν, giving a potential sense, like Ἄν.— Dunb. for †κέε, R. †κέω, κεῖμαι: Lay down, sup-pose. Or †κέειν, †κεῖν. (2) 'Akin to Γε :' Dnn. and Lenn. ??

Κεδδας : in Καιάδας.

Κεάζω, Κείω, to split, sever,— beat.— R. †κέω, κεάδας, κείρω, κεντέω, κεστός, †κάω, καίαρ, †χάω, χαίνω, χάσμα, σχάζω : To make an opening or hollow.

Κέαρ, Κῆρ, the heart.—' R. καίω :' Mrt. 'As the fountain of vital heat :' Damm. Nearer from κείω ═ καίω, whence κειάμενος, κείαντες.

Κεβλή, i. e. κεφλή, κεφαλή. As ἔμφω, amBo.

Κεγχρὶς, a serpent, from its spots, as Lucan : ' *Cenchris variatam* pingitur alvum.' For ΚΕΓΧΡΟΣ was millet, and so anything in small grains, spawn of fish, small beads, &c.

72

Κεγχρώματα, a beading round the rim of a shield.— Above.

Κεδάζω, Κεδαίω, †Σκεδάω, Σκεδάννυμι, Κίδνημι, Σκίδνημι, ' to scatter, burst in pieces : R. κεάζω, to cleave [sever,] :' Dnn. Thus : †κέω, κείω, †κέδην, as βάΔην, ἀν-έΔην, ὕΔωρ, and ἀν-ήλυΔος. Thiersch compares Σχίζω, ἐσχιδόν. (2) As jacIo, to throw, and jacEo, to lie : so †κέω and κεῖμαι : To throw about. (3) Our *shed*, Sax. *scedan*, to pour out. Mrt. brings Chald. *scheda* to pour or dart out.

Κέδματα, chronic affections of the joints.— For κήδματα, as κΕδνός : R. κῆδος, pain, κήδω. So

Κεδνός, careful, discreet :— cared for, valued, dear. — R. Κῆδος, care, †κηδνός. See on 'Εδνός and above.

Κέδρος, cedar tree : — oil of it :— anything made of it.—' R. κεάζω [i.e. †κέω, κέΔην as βάΔην ; See Κείω,] as being easy to split, εὔ-κέαστος, as Homer calls it :— or the Hebr. KDR to smell, as odoriferous :' Dr. Jones. ' R. †κέω, κείω, to burn : as from it is burnt a famous pitch or resin :' Greg. Hence Κηδεις is odorous.

Κεῖθι, there : ἐκεῖθι.

Κεῖμαι, Κέομαι, to lie down :— in †Κέω 3.

Κειμήλιον, a treasure.—R. κεῖμαι : As lying by with care. Κειμήλια κεῖται, Il. λ. 131.

Κεῖνος : for 'Εκεῖνος.

Κειρία, 'slip or roller of linen for swathing the dead : gen. deduced from κὴρ, death, [called also Κηρία,] but, as Κειρίαι are also slips of cloth, linen or fringe, rather R. κείρω, to cut off :' Pkh. ' As Κόπτω, Κόμματα, [secments,] segments :' Fuller.

Κείρω, to cut off, cut down, clip, diminish.— R. κείω, κεάζω, to sever. So †Φθίω, Φθείρω ; 'Ιμείρω. (2) ' Hebr. *keree*, to cut :' Wr.

' Κείω, to burn, Καίω.

Κείω, to sever : in †Κέω, as Κεάζω.

Κείω : in Κακκείοντες.

Κεκαδὼν, having bereaved.—R. χάζω, ἔχαδον, to bereave.

Κέκασμαι : in Κάζομαι.

Κέκλομαι, to call to.—R. κέλομαι, †κεκέλομαι, καλέω.

Κεκρύφαλος, a woman's head-dress of net to cover and bind the hair :—' the second stomach of ruminating animals, from its net-like structure, Fr. le bonnet :— the pouch or belly of a hunting-net ;—part of the head-stall of a bridle :' Ldd.—R. κρύπτω, κέκρυφα. In form, as φύσΑΛΟΣ.

Κελαδέω, to shout out, sing ; from

Κέλαδος, 'from κέλλω, κελῶ : an exciting with a loud noise or clear voice :' Damm. As of hunters or warriors urging on, a shout, shouting out, murmur, roar.

Κελαινὸς, black.—' R. †κελός, [κήλεος, burning, or say burnt.] from κέω, to burn, κείω :' Mrt.

Κελαρύζω, the same as Κελαδέω.

Κελέβη, a drinking-cup, a basin for sacrifices. Dr. Jones makes it 'a round *wooden* bowl :' then as E in κΕλαινὸς, κΕδνὸς, from κῆλον, wood, and so Dnn. brings κΕλέοντες from κῆλον. B, as from Κισσὸς, ivy, is Κισσύβιον, a goblet. BH, as· in ἐρυσῖBH. (2) Dnn. says curiously, ' R. λέθης.' What of KE ? From χέω, to pour out, as κεΚάδοντο from Χάζω ? Damm from Χέω, λείβω, λοιβὴ a libation. ?

Κελέοντες, ' the beams in the upright loom, between which the web was stretched ﹕ others read κΑλέοντες, from κᾶλον, [wood, as in κᾱλίά,]﹕' Ldd. ' R. κῆλον, wood ﹔' Dnn. (2) 'The drivers, from κέλλω, κελῶ [i. e. κελέω, κελέοντες,]﹕ Pedes e quibus stamina deducuntur ﹕' Berkel.

Κελεὸς, 'a very swift bird', says Suid.﹕ R. κέλης, celer.

Κελευθὸς, a road, way, path.—Buttm. from †ἐλεύθω, to go : K prefix, as in Καρπάλιμος, Καυχάομαι. (2) But nearly all from κέλλω, κελῶ, to go, as Iter from Itum : whence also

Κελεύω, to urge, enjoin, beg, order, command, call to, as Καλέω.—R. κέλλω, κελῶ, to drive.

Κέλης, fast sailer or racer : from

Κέλλω, to drive, urge, thrust, thrust a ship on shore, land : — go forwards. Κέλομαι, to call out to.—For κιλλω from κίω to move, cio, cieo, κινέω. E, as κρίνω, †κΙρνω, cErno ; Ἵππος, †Ἵκκος, Equus. (2) From a form †κέω = κίω, as justified by κΕομαι, κΕῖμαι, and Lat. cEveo. Then ΚΕΛλω, as ΚΙλλω. (3) Dnn. from Ἕλλω﹕ K prefix, as in Καρπάλιμος, Κέλευθος, &c. (4) ' Hebr. kelee, to be swift﹕' Wr.

Κέλυφος, husk, rind, pod. — Allied to Καλύπτω, κεκάλυφα, to cover. So τΕλαμὼν, βΕρεθρον.

Κέλωρ, a son. One whom the father †κάλει, κέλεται bids or commands. Ewing understands it as 'One·who is commanded by an oracle, a delegate.' (Very rare.)

Κεμὰς, a fawn. — ' R. [κεῖμαι, κέομαι,] κοιμᾶσθαι, as still lying in the cave ﹕' Mrt. Compare

Κέμμα, the bed of a wild animal.—' R. κεῖμαι ﹕' Dnn. Above.

Κίνδυλα, as Σχίνδυλα.

Κενέβρία, carrion.—Damm as transp. for Νεκρέβια, R. νεκρὸs a corpse. ' Κενέβρίus the same as Θνησείδιος ﹕' Dnn.

Κενεὼν, hollow between the ribs and hip. And

Κενὸς, empty.—Allied to Χάνος, a cavity, Χαῦνος, ' prop. lax, gaping', (Dnn.). Χειὰ, a hole, Κοῖλος, hollow. So Κακὸς and Χάζω. Κενὸς as Γένος, Μένος. (2) ' Hebr. kaneh, hollowness, emptiness, and a cane ﹕' Pkh. ' Hebr. kenee, to contain : ' Wr.

Κενταύριον, centaury.—'From the Centaur Chiron': Dnn.

Κένταυρος, a Centaur. ' Prob. from κεντῶ, ταῦρος : from bull-fights, or as being mounted horsemen ﹕' Ldd. Or from κεντῶ only, as ΔησΑΤΡΟΣ.

Κεντέω, and inf. κένσαι, to prick, pierce, sting, goad. — R. †κέω, κείω, κεάζω, to cleave, split, κεστὸς, pricked. Allied to Καίνυμαι, Καίνω,†Κένω,†κέκενται. See Κενός. So †Φένω, †Γένω.

Κέντρον, puncture, central point.—Above.

Κέντρων, a culprit pricked with a goad or spike : — patchwork sewn together by the prick of a needle : a joint composition. — Above.

ΚΕΠΦΟΣ, a sea-bird, remarkably light and easily caught: — a silly person easily duped. — Ewing and Mrt. from κοῦφος, light, †κόφος, †κόπφος, and E as βρΟτὸς, βρΕτας; γΟνυ, gEnu ; vOster, vEster; tOsta, tEsta. But ?

Κεραία, like Κέρας, a horn: — 'anything like one, growing or projecting like one, and so a yard-arm, projecting beam of a crane ; — antennæ of the crab; — branching stake of wood; — little projection or mark at the top of any thing, mark or sign in writing, a tittle, abbreviation; — the leg, point of a pair of compasses; — a bow﹕' Ldd.

Κεραΐζω, to butt or strike with the κέρας horn, overthrow, lay waste. (2) R. κείρω, κερῶ, to cut off.

Κεραΐς, a worm that preys on a κέρας horn.

Κεράμβιξ, horned or stag-beetle. — R. κέρας. Κεράβιξ, κερᾱβιξ; κεράβιξ (as κάβηξ,) κεράΜθιξ, as λαΜθάνω.

Κέραμος, potter's earth, vase, tile, brick, &c. — ' Perh. from κεράω, to mix: for well-tempered earth is desirable for making earthen-ware﹕' Greg. ' Earth well kneaded and prepared for making earthen-ware﹕' Lenn. (2) Dnn. and Mrt. from ἔρα, earth. K prefix as in Καρπάλιμος, Καυχάομαι, Κέλευθος. (3) Some from †κέω, κείω, to burn, and ἔρα earth. (4) Rossi notices Coptic heromi, furnace-earth. ' Hebr. gerem, to pulverize﹕' Wr.

Κέραμος, 'dungeon, in Il. 5. 387, χαλκέῳ ἐν κεράμῳ. Perh. allied to Χήραμος﹕' Ldd. ' A chamber of brick, [See Κέραμος above,] still retaining the name when of brass, [as in Homer just quoted,] as a candle-STICK of brass; HORN-book, &c. ﹔' Grogan. So Mile-STONES are said, even of iron or wood. — Ewing says : ' Place of confinement where they were obliged to work in clay.'

Κέρας, a horn: ' anything of horn, drinking-horn; horn guard or pipe at the end of a fishing-book; — arm of a river ; — wing of an army ; — sail-yard ; — any projection, as a mountain-peak, &c. ﹕' Ldd. — In form like Γέρας, Τέρας, Πέρας ; and allied to Χορὸς, Κόραξ, Κορωνὸς, Γῦρος, Κυρτὸς, &c. (2) Lenn. allies it to Κάρα, the top. (3) ' Hebr. keren, a horn﹕' Pkh.

Κερασβόλος, hard, intractable. — R. κέρας, †βολέω. From the silly notion that such corn as struck against the horns of oxen in sowing, produced hard fruit. ' Quod tetigerit cornu, non est coctibile﹕' Plin.

Κέρασος, a cherry-tree. — From Cerasus in Pontus.

Κερατέα, ' the carob-tree : τὸ Κεράτιον, the fruit of the tree, which is corniculated. R. κέρας﹕' Dnn. and Schleusn.

Κερατίας, a cuckold, from the expression To make κέρατα horns for, give horns to. ' That the husbands of false women wear horns, is an old saying, and common in other countries also﹕' Todd.

Κεραυνὸς, thunderbolt, lightning which strikes the earth. — R. κείρω, κερῶ: from its cutting down and destroying. Some add αἴω, to shine or to burn: but -αυνὸς much as Θησ-αυρος. (2) ' Chald. keran, to shine:' Mrt.

Κεράω, Κεράννὑμι, to mix, — pour out. — R. κείρω, κερῶ, ' to take from, diminish', (Dnn.). (2) ' R. κέρας: To pour prop. into cups of horn, of which the ancient cups were made. Later, to mix:' Pkh. ' To pour into cups having the figure of horns: and, because they used to temper wine, it came to mean mix:' Damm.

Κέρδος, gain: — craft in getting it. — R. κείρω, κέκερται, κέρδην. ' From the little clippings of money, as in Κέρμα; anciently gained by trading. So in Hebr. a piece of money broken or cut off, is used of gain:' Pkh. See Κέρμα.

Κερδὼ, a fox. — R. κέρδος, craft.

Κερκὶς, ' a staff or rod with which the web was struck to make it thick and close: — later, in the horiz. loom, the weaver's stay or comb : but comm. the shuttle containing the spindle;—any taper rod, reed, quill, skewer, peg, pin, small bone of the shin: — a kind of poplar, the trembling aspen, from the rustling of its leaves [as the shuttle from the noise]. — Prob. from κέρκω, rarer form of κρέκω, to strike, beat : ' Ldd. So all.

Κερκὸς, a tail. — ' R. κρέκω [as Κερκὶς :], to strike, beat :' Mrt. Thus Virgil of the dolphins : ' Æquora verrunt caudis.' And our More: ' The lion will strike such a blow with his tail that will break the back of his encounterer.' Waller : ' And men and boats his active tail confounds.' Dryden speaks of the lion as ' Roused by the lash of its own stubborn tail.'

Κέρκουρος, a light vessel. — ' Κέρκος and Οὐρὰ are both a tail : hence called as very long, and ending both ways in a tail :' Forcell. (2) The Schol. Aristoph. from the island Κέρκυρα, Corcyra.

Κέρμα, ' a minute portion cut from anything, hence a small coin :' Dnn. ' For in the rude state of ancient money small pieces were often clipped off from larger to make weight:' Ewing. — R. κείρω, κέκερμαι.

Κερματιστὴς, a money-changer: Above.

Κέρνος, a large dish of earthen-ware : perh. contr. from Κεράμινος. (2) As it contained various fruits, Greg. from κεράω, κιρνάω. It is called a Κρατὴρ by the Schol. on Nicander.

Κερουτιάω, to toss the horns, hold the head high. — R. κέρας. ' Lift not up your horn on high :' O. T.

Κέρτομος, sarcastic, reviling. — For κεάρ-τομος or κῆρ-τομος, cutting the heart. So κΕδνός. (2) R. κείρω, κέκερται. As ἔδδΟΜΟΣ.

Κέρχνη, ' a kind of hawk, called from its hoarse noise, said to be the kestrel :' Ldd. — From

Κέρχω, to make rough, dry, hoarse. — ' Kindred words are Κάρφαρος, Καρχαλέος, all apparently formed to express a shrill sound. R. κρέκω:' Dnn.

Κεσκίον, refuse of flax, ' quod detrahitur e lino :' Steph. — R. ξέω, to scrape off, i.e. σκέω, †σκεσκέω, †κεσκέω: as σκύλλω, ΚΟσκυλμάτια. (Very rare.)

Κέσκομαι, to lie down. — R. κέομαι, κεῖμαι, as Βάω, Βάσκω.

74

Κεστὸς, pricked, embroidered: in Κεντέω.

Κέστρα, a hammer with a sharp head, javelin, awl. Κέστρον, a graving tool, stylus. — R. κεστὸς, allied to Κεντέω, Κεάζω, Κείρω.

Κεστρεὺς, ' a mullet, from κέστρα, from its shape. Called also the Faster, as believed to be empty whenever caught : hence it means a starveling :' Ldd.

Κεύθω, to hide, conceal. — As ἐλΕΥΘΩ. R. †κέω, κέομαι, κεῖμαι : To put down, put by, put away : pono, re-pono, se-pono. (2) ' Akin to Κύω, Κυέω :' Dnn.

Κεφαλὴ, the head. — As Κάπετος for Σκάπετος, Κεφαλὴ is allied to ΣΚέπασμα, a covering, case, integument, from σκέπω, ἔσκεφα. See Κῆπος. In form as χθαμΑΛΗ. (2) Damm for κυφαλὴ from κύπτω, κέκυφα, from its convexity : as Κύβη. We have pejēro from jūro. But ?

Κεφαλὶς, head or chapter of a book, principal part, &c. — Above. As Caput, Chapter.

†Κέω, Κείω, to burn, allied to Καίω.

†Κέω, to cut: in Κεάζω.

†ΚΕΩ, ΚΙΩ, (as Ψάω, Ψέω, Ψίω,) ΧΕΩ, ΧΥΩ, seem Primitives, and to be allied, and to imply movement. Thus Κίω, Κινέω, Cio, Cieo, are to move, move forward: †Κέω, Κέλλω, to move or drive on : Κέομαι, Κεῖμαι, Κέσκω, to move or place oneself down, to lie down: Χέω, Χύω, to throw or pour down. — Dnn. refers Κίω [See Καρπάλιμος,] to †Ἴω, Εἶμι : and Κέω might thus be referred to †Ἕω, Εἶμι, and Χέω to †ἕω, ἵημι, to send: but it seems safer to take them as Primitives. Ewing considers Κίω as transp. from Ἵκω, i.e. make to go.

Κῆγχος, Κῆχος, ' the same meaning as παῖ γῆς, Hesych. From κῆ for πῆ, ἄγχος [i. e. ἀγχοῦ or ἄγχι :' Dnn.

Κῆδος, concern, anxiety, sorrow, prop. in bereavement, as allied to †Καδέω, Κεκάδοντο, Χάζω, Ἔχαδον, ' to make one quit, bereave :' (Dnn.) So mourning for the dead, a funeral, burial : — any object of care or concern, as a relationship or connexion in life. (2) R. †κέω, κείω, καίω : Ardent glowing affection and interest. Or as Δαίω, to light up, is used for ' to be loud, as wailing:' (Dnn.). And Damm from burning the dead. (3) R. κήδω.

Κήδω, to injure, distress, annoy. — Prop. to bereave, as in Κῆδος. (2) R. κάω, καίω, to burn, consume.

Κηθὶς, voting-box. dice-box. — ' R. †χάω, [ἐχήθην,] χαδεῖν :' Ldd., to hold, contain. (2) ' Others prefer χέω :' Dnn. : to pour in (dice). (3) Lenn. compares Κεύθω.

Κηκὰς, ' said to be an Ion. word from κακὸς, mischievous : Κηκάζω, to insult :' Ldd.

Κηκὶς, juice, fat: — a gall-nut, ' produced by the sap oozing from punctures made by insects :' Ldd. From

Κηκίω, to ooze, gush forth. — Redupl. of Κίω, to go (forth or out.)

Κηλεὸς, burning, blazing. — R. †κάω, καίω, †καελὸς, κηλός.

Κηλέω, to charm, beguile, coax. — ' Ἕκηλος, †ἐκη-

λέω:' Buttm. : To make calm. As Ἐκεῖνος, Κεῖνος.
(2) Lengthened from καλός, (as κΗκάς:) : To say
pretty things to, as Αἰκάλλω. And allied to †Κάζω,
Κάζομαι, to embellish. (3) R. καλέω, παρα-καλέω, to
soothe. (4) ' R. χαλάω, to unbend :' Dnn. (5)
' Chald. kal, the voice :' Mrt.

Κήλη, Attic Κάλη, ' a tumor, esp. of a rupture. R.
χαλάω, to slacken :' Dnn. (2) ' R. κηλεός: An inflam-
mation :' Ewing. (3) ' Hard as κᾶλον wood:' Mrt.
Compare Durus from Δοῦρυ.

Κηλίς, spot, stain, blemish. — ' Very prob. from
[κάω, καελίς,] καίω, to burn : The effect of fire :' Dnn.
As a burn or brand. See Κῆλον.

Κῆλον, Κᾶλον, ' dry wood fit for burning : — hence
(the earliest weapons being of wood hardened by fire,)
arrow, weapon : — sun-beam :' Dnn. — Above.

Κηλὸς, dry: in Κηλεός.

Κήλων, a stallion, gen. he-ass : — lascivious. —
Allied to Κηλεός : Ardens (cupidine).

Κήλων,' Κηλώνειον, a swipe, machine for drawing
water. — As Ὄνος, an ass, is used also for a windlass,
crane or pulley, so Κήλων, an ass, for Κήλων a swipe.

Κηλωστά, a brothel. — From Κήλων 1.

Κημὸς, ' a muzzle for a horse : — also a net or basket
of reeds through which the Ψῆφοι were dropt into the
urn : — a basket containing them, — a fishing-basket ;
— head-dress, bond :' Dnn. — Some of these senses agree
with Κηθίς, an urn or dice-box, which seems allied. —
Others agree with Ewing's deriv. ' from κάμπτω,
[κέκαμμαι,], to curve : a kind of fetter or chain, bit or
bridle.' — Varin. from κάπτω, to eat, as Virgil: ' Fræna
ferox sonipes spumantia mandit.' But this is only in-
cidental.

Κῆνσος: the Lat. census, ultim. from Κένσαι.

Κήξ: in Καῦαξ.

Κῆπος, a garden, orchard. — As Κάπετος for ΣΚάπετος, so Κῆπος from σκέπω, to protect, σκέπη a shel-
tered place. Perh. allied to our word keep. Wbst.
explains Garden ' land enclosed for the protection of
fruits.' So Pkh. from Hebr. ΚΡΗ, to cover, protect.
(2) Mrt. from κάπω, from the exhalations. Cic. speaks
of the odors ' qui afflantur e floribus.' Hesych. calls
it περι-πνεύμενος καὶ εὔ-ήνεμος τόπος.

Κῆπος, a fashion of cutting the hair: perh. from the
care and dressing of a garden, as Κόμη, hair, from Κομέω
to attend to. Hesych. calls it καλλωπισμὸς τριχῶν. —
Also, as Hortus, for τὰ αἰδοῖα γυναικεῖα.

Κῆρ, the heart: in Κέαρ.

Κὴρ, fate, death, doom, disease. — Allied by Lenn.
to Κάρ, Καιρὸς, whence εἰς καιρὸν τυπείς, mortally
wounded, καίριος, mortal, deadly. (2) R. †κέω, κείω,
to cut : from the Fate cutting the threads of life. In
form as Θέω, Θὴρ ; Αἴθω, Αἴθὴρ. (3) R. κείρω, to
destroy: as Κηραίνω. (4) Damm from κερδώ : Fate
mixing the cup of bliss or woe. But Κὴρ is always
used of woe.

Κηραίνω, to injure, destroy. See in Κήρ. — ' Some

75

derive it in sense To be anxious, from κῆρ, the heart :' Dnn.

Κηρίον, honey-comb ; — the scald-head, as Latin
Favus. — From

Κηρὸς, bees' wax, wax. — ' R. κεράω: A thing mixed:
the alloy of honey:' Dr. Jones. (2) R. †κάω, καίω :
Fit for burning, whence Κηροὶ wax-tapers.

Κῆρυξ, a herald. Κηρύσσω, ξω, to herald. R. γῆρυς,
the voice. So all. — Also, a kind of shellfish: ' its
shell being used by criers and heralds:' Dnn.: ' with a
wreathed shell which might be used as a trumpet.
Also, a prickly instrument of torture': Ldd. (2) Hebr.
kerez, to proclaim:' Wr.

Κῆτος, a whale. — Not improb. Lenn. from χάζω,
κέχασται, χανδάνω, †χάω, †κέχηται, from its vast capacity : Capax. Compare the formation of Χῆτις.

Κητώεσσα Λακεδαίμων, large as a Κῆτος, whale.
Others make Κῆτος the same as Καῖαρ, a depth, gulf :
full of hollows, says Buttm., applying it to the country.
See Κῆτος above.

Κηΰξ in Καῦαξ.

Κηφὴν, a drone-bee: ' metaph. of old birds with the
pen-feathers gone :' Ldd. — R. κάπτω, κέκαφα, κέκηφα,
to devour : Eating, but not working. ' Fruges consu-
mere natus,' Hor. ' Immunisque sedens aliena ad pabula
fucus:' Virg. See Τενθρήνη.

Κηώδης, smelling as of burnt incense. — R. καίω, a
1. κῆα, to burn, and ὄζω, ὄδα, odor. Passow compares
Flagro and Fragro. So

Κηώεις, fragrant. — Above.

Κιάθω: the same as Κίω.

Κιβδάω, ' to look of a pale yellow, like gold alloyed
with base metal: to have the jaundice :' Dnn. From

Κίβδηλος, base, spurious, adulterated. — For κίδηλος,
as ' ἁλιβδύω for ἀλιδύω', (Dnn.) from κίς, κιὸς, a worm,
†δηλέω, δηλέομαι, to injure: Worm-eaten, and so rotten,
worthless, base, &c. Thus opposed to Ἀ-κιος. (2)
From ΚΙΒΔΗΣ, clay, in Hesych.; hence is assumed a
sense dross, which Κιβδηλίς bears. (3) Constantine
from Χῖοι, †δηλέω: said of corn damaged by the Chians.
Eustath. from Χῖοι, δηλόω: such coin of the Chians
as the Athenians repudiated being marked by a Χ. (4)
' Chald. kidba, (kibda), a lie:' Mrt.

Κίβισις, and Ætolian Κίβα, pouch, wallet, knapsack.
— R. κίω, to go, i. e. for a journey, much as Via, Viatica,
and Ἐφ-όδιος. B, as in βόλβιτον, κλωβός. (2) As
carrying cibum food, obsol. in Gr., but which might
have existed, from the κίω above, (like Κίβα,) to go, as
Viatica. See Festus below in Κιβωτός. (3) Whiter
mentions the elements C, B ; C, P, in ' cepan, capio,
kίβισις, kepen, our keep, coop.' (4) ' Hebr. kebitzee,
collection:' Wr.

Κιβώριον, a cup, ' from the material or the shape of
the Κιβώριον or seed-vessel of the Egyptian bean:'
Ldd. But this last prob. from Κίβα, a bag, above. See
ΚΙΒΩΤός.

Κιβωτὸς, a box, chest, in which, says Festus, we put
cibum food. See in Κίβισις. Ldd. indeed allies Κιβω-

τὸς and Κίεισις. (2) Some from κίω, βετέω, as feeding on a journey.

Κιγκλίζω, to wag the tail ;— to change continually. — R. κίγκλος.

Κιγκλὶς, ' a folding-door, railed fence, inclosure with folding doors, place of sitting of the Athenian senate :' Dnn. Hence Κιγκλίδες, quibbles at the bar, logical quibbles. — For κικλὶς, (as Κίγκλος,) redupl. for κλὶς allied to Δι-κλὶς and to Κλισιάδες, ' folding-doors or large gates :' (Dnn.)

Κίγκλος, a kind of wagtail. — For κίκλος, (as λαιΓχάνω,) from κίω, κέκικα, cio, cieo, κινέω, to move, as Lat. moticilla from motum.

ΚΙΔΑΡΙΣ, a Persian turban. ' Cidarim Persæ regium capitis vocabant insigne :' Curt. — It means also an Arcadian dance: perh. from κίω, †κίδην, cio, κινέω. As βάδην, στάδην.

Κίδνημι : in Κεδάζω.

Κιθάρα, a guitar. — Usually thought a foreign word, but so contradictorily that it seems rather from κίω, ἐκίθην, cio, κινέω, to move. (As ψαφΑΡΑ.) Ovid : ' Cithæram cum voce movēre :' ' Fila sonantia movit.' See Κίγκλος, Κίσσα, Κισσός. Wr. says it is the Hebr. ketheroos.

Κιθὼν, Ion. for Χιτών.

Κίκιννος, a curled lock. — Redupl. from †κίννος (as Κικλήσκω,) from κίω, ' elegantly going across the head : — Or moved (round), twisted :' Damm : Κίω here as Lat. cio, and Κινέω, to move. See both Κίκυς and Κίγκλος.

Κικκαβαῦ, imitated from the sound of screeching owls. Κικκάβη, a screech-owl.

Κικλήσκω, i. e. καλέω, †κλέω, †κλήσκω, as Μιμνήσκω.

Κικυμὶς, an imitative word like Κακκάβη.

Κίκυς, ' lit. power of motion, prob., from κίω: strength, vigor : according to some, as Κηκὶς, juice, blood, spurting out, also from κίω :' Dnn.

Κιλικίζω, to play the Cilician.

Κιλίκιον, ' a coarse cloth, strictly of Cilician goats' hair :' Ldd. ' Commonly manufactured in Cilicia :' Dnn.

Κιλλίβας, an ass-mounter, as we say a Horse, frame to put a shield on. — As Λυκά-βας. From

Κίλλος, an ass. — ' R. κίλλω, quasso :' Mrt. As Persius : ' Nec manus auriculas [asini] imitata est mobilis', and Jerome : ' Aut manu auriculas agitari asini.' Moving its long ears, as the wag-tail Κίλλ-ουρος does its οὐρὰ tail.

Κίλλω, ' a form akin to Κέλλω and ῎Ιλλω :' Dnn.

KIMBEPIKON, a kind of garment. ' From the place', says Suidas. ' So called as made by the Cimbri ; says Dr. Brasse. As Cambric from Cambray, Worsted from that place in Norfolk.

ΚΙΜΒΙΞ, -ηξ, niggardly. — ' Suid. states that these are the same as Βέμβιξ, -ηξ, a wasp or bee :' Steph. As then Σφηκόω is to constrict and tighten in, from σφὴξ,

76

σφηκὸς, a wasp as narrow in the middle, so Κίμβιξ can be tight, pinching, screwing. And B and K ? Yet perhaps liQUor or liKor from λὴψ, λιβός. For K and Π are often interchanged. ?

Κιμωλία, fuller's earth. ' Cretosaque rura Cimōli :' Ov.

Κινάβρα, Κιναύρα, ' smell of the he-goat, a rank smell :' Dnn. — Supposed by some to be put for κινάβρα, κυνο-βόρα, dog's-meat : as κινάρα and κΎνάρα, plsimus and pUsillus, (Forcell.). — But, as it should thus be rather κυνΟβρα, better with Damm : ' Notat gravem odōrem salacium animalium, à κινέω quod idem ac βινέω.' Sic in Fabulâ Otwayanâ : ' How the old fellow stunk, when the fit was on him !' Vide Κίναιδος. Ι brevis est, ut in Κινάθισμα.

Κίναδος, a fox :—a cunning knavish fellow. — The latter seems the prim. sense, from κυνέω, as Livy ' movēre ac molīri', and as the expression Πάντα λίθον κινεῖς. Stirring everything, bustling, active. Somewhat similarly the Lat. Versūtus from Verto. Ldd. makes it a ' shifty' fellow. Ι short as in

Κινάθισμα, a rustling motion. — R. κινέω. So Κινάτετον.

Κίναιδος, catamīta :— ' à κινέω=βινέω :' Dnn. Alludit fortasse vox ad αἰδὼν=τὰ αἰδοῖα.

Κυνάρα, Κυνάρα, the κυνὸς dog thorn, garden thorn, called also Κυνόσ-βατος : a kind of artichoke. For the I see on ὁρίος.

Κίνδαξ, the same as Σκίναξ.

Κίνδυνος, risk, hazard, danger. — ' Prob. from κινῶ : prim. of throwing the dice :' Ldd. — Or, (as ἰΝδάλλομαι and ἀΝδάνω,) for κίδυνος from κίω, to go, †κίδην as Βάδην, Σταδην. I. e. in which we go up to anything, as ῎Ιτης, ' going', is Venturous which from Venio, and as from Per-eo some derive Periculum.

Κινέω, to move. — R. κίω, cio, cieo. As Δίω, Διίέω.

Κίνναβος, the same as Κάνναβος.

KINNAMΩMON, cinnamon. ' From the Phœnicians :' Ldd.

KINTPA, an Asiatic instrument with ten strings. — ' Chald. kinnara, a harp; kinah, lamentation :' Mrt.

Κινυρός, plaintive, like the tone of the Κινύρα. Κινύρομαι, to bemoan.

Κινώπετον, ' a deadly beast, espec. a serpent : said to come, notwithstanding the ῐ, from κινῶ, to move, as ῾Ερπετὸν from ἕρπω :' Ldd. A moving thing. Compare the termin. in ὁραΠΕΤΗΣ. The ῐ as in Κινάθισμα.

Κίξης, Κιξάλης, Κιξάλλης, a highway robber. — ' Prob. derived from κιχεῖν,' Ldd. : i. e. to come upon, or up to. †κίχω, †κίξω.

Κιόκρανον : ' = κιονό-κρανον,' Ldd. As Idolo-latry, Idolatry.

Κιρκαία, thought to be nightshade, from Circé, the enchantress in the Odyssey.

Κίρκος, Κρίκος, a circle, ring ;— a hawk or falcon flying in a circle : ' Ducensque per aëra gyros Milvus', Ov. Allied by many to Γῦρος, a circle, Κυρτὸς, curved,

Κέρας, a horn, &c. (2) Κρίκος from κρίζω, to creak, i. e. as a wheel turning on an axle-tree : That wheels round with noise. (3) 'Welsh cyrc, from cwr, a circle, limit :' Wbst.

Κιρκόω, to bind with rings : Above.

Κιρνάω, the same as Κεράω, like Πετάω, Πιτνάω, Πίτνημι.

Κιῤῥὸς, tawny, yellowish.—Prob. from the color of the Κιρσὸς. (2) Κηρὸς, wax, †κηρερὸς, †κηῤῥὸς, κιῤῥὸς.

Κιρσὸς, Κρισσὸς, Κριξὸς, a varicose vein, dilated blood-vessel.—Salmas. allies it to Σκίῤῥος or Σκίρος, (as Μάραγδος, Σμάραγδος,) scirrus or schirrhus, a hard knotty, tumor. (2) Like Κίρκος, allied to Κυρτὸς and Γυρὸς curved, Κέρας a horn, Χορὸς, &c.

Κὶς, κιὸς, an insect in corn or wood, corn weevil.— Allied to Σχίζω, to rend, Κείω, to sever, Κεάζω, Κείρω.

Κίσηρις, pumice-stone.—R. κὶς : As seeming worm-eaten.

Κίσσα, Κίττα, the jay or magpie ; and, like Pica, any eccentric appetite.—Menage from κίω, κίσω, cio, cieo, κινέω, to move, like Κίγχλος the wagtail : 'From its frequent motion of the tail and body.' So

Κισσὸς, the ivy.—Menage deduces this, like Κίσσα, from κίω, κίσω, as going about trees : (See Ἴτυς :) 'Thus Persius calls it Sequax, and Virgil Errans.'

Κισσύβιον, a cup, properly as made of ivy-wood.— Above. A cup has the epithet Κίσσινος applied to it by Euripides.

Κίστη, a wicker-basket, hamper.—R. κίω. to go, κέκισται. For the purposes of journeying. (2) Allied to Κύστη, Κύστις, from κύω, 'prop. to contain', (Dnn.). As μ'Υστίλη, μΙστύλη ; κΎνάρα, κΙνάρα. (3) Some ally our chest, 'a word found in Sax., Germ., Dan., Swed., Welsh and Irish :' Wbst.

ΚΙΤΡΕΑ, 'lemon or citron tree. Hebr. keter, to smell :' Wr.

Κιχάνω, Κίχημι, †Κιχέω, to come up to, reach, meet, light on, find.—R. κίω, κέκικα, to go, go to. So In-venio, to find.

Κίχλη : in Κιχλίζω.

Κιχλίζω, to titter, giggle, but others make it to eat κίχλαι, thrushes, to live luxuriously :' Ldd. 'Fare well, revel, make merry, laugh heartily :' thus Grove brings the senses together. Κιχλίζω can be however an imitative word, like our Giggle, Cackle. Κίχλη, a thrush, is classed by Menage with Κίγκλος and Κίσσα, which see.

Κίω, to move, go : See in †ΚΕΩ.

Κίων, 'a pillar :—gravestone :' Ldd.—As Βῆμα is ἀνά-βημα, a raised place, so Κίων for ἀνα-κίων, going up: 'a column rising on high', Lenn. 'Κίει in altum :' Mrt. So Celsus, high, from Cello, Excello, and Ex-celsus.

Κλαγγή, 'clang, ciangor, a loud and shrill cry or sound. R. κλάζω, γξω : or both formed to imitate the sound :' Dnn. 'Clang, Germ., Swed., Dan.:' Wbst. (2) Damm from κλάω to break ;—Hemst. from κα-λέω to call out to.

77

Κλαδαρὸς, easily broken.—R. κλάω, †κλάδην, as Βάδην.

Κλαδάω, Κλαδάσσω, to shake. — I suppose from κλάδοι branches shaking by the wind. See Δόναξ.

Κλαδεύω, to break off young κλάδους.

Κλάδος, 'from κλάω : a young slip or shoot such as is broken off for grafting ; a young branch :' Ldd. Κλάδοι ἐξ-εκλάσθησαν, Rom. 11. 19. Πτόρθον κλάσε, Hom. So Κλῆμα, Κλών.

Κλάζω, γξω, to make a shrill cry, scream, shout, chaunt.—The same as Κράζω, which see. So κλίβανος, κρίβανος. From its own sound, say many ; but this would be more applicable to Κλαγγή, which however is from κλάζω.— Others from καλέω, to call out to, or κλάω, to break (out).

Κλάζω, to shut : R. κλαῒς, a key : κληΐζω.

Κλαίω, κλάω, f. κλαύσομαι, to weep : i.e. κλάω break forth into crying or into tears, as the voice is broken and interrupted with sobbings. 'Dat gemitum, rumpitque has imo pectore voces,' Virg. And : 'Suo rumpebat pectore questus.' The Greeks said ῥῆξαι δάκρυα, ῥῆξαι φωνήν. So with us To burst into tears.

Κλαμβὸς, mutilated. — R. κλάω, †κλαβός : M as λαΜθάνω. So Θάμβος.

Κλὰξ, a key.—R. κλάζω, ξω.

Κλαύμα, Κλαυθμὸς, a weeping : κλαίω.

Κλάω, to break.—Allied to Κόλος, broken ; Κολάπτω, to strike, beat, through †κολάω, κλάω. Some ally it to Θλάω : but ?

Κλάω, to weep : in Κλαίω.

Κλέηδην, by stealth : κλέπτω. As ἙΠΤὰ, ἕΒΔομος.

Κλεὶς, Κληῒς, Κλαῖς, a key, bolt : —collar-bone, clavicle, as this from Clavis : 'as if from locking the neck and breast together', Ldd. And a bench for rowers, 'for the benches are placed before the aperture which receives the oars, and so are called from the resemblance which rowing bears to the action of a key in locking or unlocking :' E. Valpy.— From

Κλείω, to shut.—As Ἔμβολον is a peg, bolt, from βάλλω, so κέλλω, κιλῶ, †κλεῶ, κλείω, to drive (in), and so shut. (2) As shutting in is for privacy, it may be allied to Καλύπτω, (κλύπτω,) and Κλέπτω. (3) 'Hebr. kela, he shut :' Mrt.

Κλείω, to make famous : Κλεινὸς, renowned. — R. κλέω.

Κλέμμα, fraud, theft : κλέπτω, κέκλεμμαι.

Κλέος, glory : κλέω.

Κλέπτω, 'to do anything by stealth or privately, conceal, deceive, steal. Akin to Καλύπτω, [Κλύπτω,] :' Dnn. (2) 'Chald. keleph, covering :' Pkh.

Κλέτας, 'prob. ═ κλιτύς :' Ldd.

Κλέω, to call, καλέω.—Also, as Κλείω, to make famous, celebrate : prop. to call out the name of, proclaim it. Thus Nominatus is explained Celebratus by Forcell. We say, He has a great name.

Κληδὼν, report, fame, κλέος, κλέω.

Κλῆθρον, Κλεῖθρον, Κλᾶθρον, a bolt, bar : κλείω.

Κλῆμα : in Κλάδος.

Κληρικὸς, pertaining to the Clergy.— R. κλῆρος. From St. Matthias being chosen by lot, Acts i. 26. Or as having public allotments of lands. Or (as the tribe of Levi) being the lot or inheritance of the Lord.

Κλῆρος, a lot.—' Perh. from κλάω, [κλαερὸς,] ; for twigs, potsherds, or other κλάσματα were used for it :' Ldd.

Κλίβανος : for Κρίβανος. As λείριον, liLium.

Κλίμα, inclination ;—' the supposed slope of the earth from the equator towards the pole, hence, a region, zone, clime; climate :' Ldd.— R. κλίνω.

Κλιμακτὴρ, a climacteric, a step or stop in human life every 7th year.— From

Κλίμαξ, ακος, a ladder, staircase, ' from κλίνω, from its leaning aslant,' Ldd. Also a climax in rhetoric :— ' a wrestler's trick, Soph. Tr. 521, variously explained : —part of a chariot, i. e. blocks of wood placed above the axle, and narrowing like steps :' Ldd.—And

Κλίνη, Κλιντὴρ, Κλισμὸς, a bed on which we recline. —From

Κλίνω, to bend, turn, turn aside, &c.—'Ο-κλαδὸν is on bent knees, from κλάω, to break, (See fully in Ἀγκή,) so Κλίνω to bend is from κλάω :— as from Τάω is Τίνω; from Ψάω is Ψίνομαι ; from Ἄγω is Ἀγινέω ; so Φθίνω, Βινέω, &c. (2) As Νεύω, to incline, from Νέω, to go (down), so κέλλω, κελῶ, †κλέω, †κλίω, κλίνω, to urge or press (down). (3) ' Sax. hlinian, Germ. lehnen, to lean :' Wbst.

Κλισία, couch for reclining on ;—chamber, tent, hut, for reclining in.— R. κλίνω, κέκλισαι.

Κλισιάδες, folding-doors. Dindorf reads always Κλεισιάδες from κλείω, σω, to shut. Yet so δι-ΚΛΕΣ. Others from κλίνω, as Κλισία : Inclining one to the other.

Κλίτος, like Κλίμα.

Κλίτος, Κλίτὺς, slope, de-clivity, clivus.— R. κλίνω, κέκλιται.

Κλοιὸς, collar for a dog,—pillory.— R. κλείω, κέκλοια, to shut in.

Κλονέω, to throw into κλόνος confusion.

Κλόνος, press of battle, throng of men or spears, battle-rout, a rumbling noise.—Jones compares clan. — But, as Θράω, Θρόνος, so Κλάω, Κλόνος, as said of things broken, broken ranks, &c. So Frango, Fragor. And see Ἠχή. (3) R. κλίνω, to rout an army.

Κλοπὴ, theft : κλέπτω, κέκλοπα.

Κλοποπεύω, to spin out time by false pretences. — Soft for κλοσοπεύω, (as for softness δέδοικα for δέδοιδα,) from κλοπή, ὁψ ὀπὸς : Steal away the time by words. Or transp. for Κλοποτεύω, simply from κλοπή. (2) As the reverse of ὄντμα for ὄντομα, for κλυτοπεύω, from κλυτός : To use splendid, fine words.

Κλύδων, a wave : Κλυσμὸς, surge.— R. κλύζω, ἔκλυδον, κέκλυσμαι.

Κλύζω, to dash, wash.—' A word obviously formed in imitation of the sound :' Dnn. ' From the sound :' Lenn. (2) R. κλύω, to make an audible noise. (3) R. κέλλω, κελῶ, †κλέω, †κλύω, to drive (against).

Κλύω, to hear, listen to. Κλυτὸς, famous.—' Κλέω, Κλύω, are akin : Κλέω, to render famous [or as Καλέω, to call to] : Κλύω, to hear such report :' Dnn. As from Αὐδὴ, the voice, is Audio to hear a voice. Or say, To learn by report. Damm says : ' To be called, from καλέω, κλέω : then to hear.'

Κλωβὸς, a bird-cage.— R. κλείω, κέκλοια, †κλοιβὸς, κλωβὸς, to shut in : as Κλοιός. Note κολοΒΟΣ. (2) ' Hebr. kleb, wicker basket :' Wr.

Κλώζω, κέκλωχα, from the sound, as Glocio, to cluck, clack, as said of hens and daws. And ' to expel from the theatre by a sound made in striking the palate when pronouncing ΚΛ :' Scap.

Κλώθω, Κλώσκω, to spin, wind yarn. — As Βεβρόθω, ᾽Ρόθων, Ψώθιον. To spin is ' to draw out into threads', (Dr. J.), and Κατ-άγω is ' to draw out, to spin', (Dnn.) ; so κλώθω, from κέλλω, κελῶ, †κλέω, †κλῶ, to drive (out into threads). (2) Our word cloth is observable.

Κλῶμαξ, or Κρῶμαξ, ' heap of stones, rocky place :' Ldd.—R. κλάω, κλῶ, to break : as Rumpo, Rupes, and ᾽Ρηγμίν.

Κλὼν, as Κλάδος and Κλῆμα, from κλάω, κλῶ. A branch.

Κλωψὸς, for Κλοιός.

Κλωστὴρ, thread, — spindle.— R. κλώθω, κέκλωσται.

Κλὼψ, a thief : κλέπτω, κέκλοπα.

Κμητὸς, wrought.— R. κάμνω, †καμέω, †κμέω, to labor at.

Κνάμπτω, ☰ γνάμπτω.

Κνάπτω, to scratch, scrape, as Κνάω, to tease, card or comb wool, mangle, &c. Hence Κναφεὺς, a fuller, and Κνάφος, the teasel.

Κνάφαλλον, wool clipped off by fullers in dressing cloth, used for stuffing pillows.— Above.

Κνάω, Κναίω, Κνῆμι, Κνήθω, Κνόω, Κνίζω, Κναδάλλω, Χναύω, to scrape, grate, scratch, tickle.—' Κένσαι,' says Dnn., ' is aor. 1. infin. of †κένω the same as κεντέω.' From this obsolete †Κένω was †Κενάω, Κνάω ; †Κενίω, †Κνίω, Κνίζω ; †Κενόω, Κνόω. (2) ' Our gnaw, Sax. gnagan, Swed. gnaga, Welsh cnoi ; with Irish cnagh consumption :' Wbst. (3) ' Hebr. ΚΝΑ, to eat into, corrode :' Pkh.

Κνέφας, darkness.— Allied to Νέφος, as Γ in Γνόφος, Κ in Κνύπος. So Κμέλεθρον is Pamphylian for Μέλαθρον. (2) ' Hebr. gnaph, darkness :' Dr. Jones : ' gneph,' says Wright.

Κνήθω : in Κνάω.

Κνῆκος, the bastard-saffron, ' agreeing with the thistle in most of its characters,' (Johns.) and prob. therefore from κνάω, ἔκνηκα, to scratch, whence Κνάφος, ' the teasel used to card cloth, and a carding comb,' Ldd.

Κνηκὸς, pale yellow, the color of the dye of the above: said ' of the goat and the wolf ; hence the goat is called Κνάκων :' Ldd.—Above.

Κνήμη, ' the part of the leg between the knee and.

ankle,—the leg,—spoke of a wheel, &c.:' Ldd.—'R. κνάω, ἔκνημαι. Prop., what is hard, and easy to scrape: thence applied to the hard bone of the tibia:' Hemsterh.

Κνημίς, a boot for the Κνήμη.

Κνημὸς, part of a mountain rising from its foot, as the Κνήμη from the foot. 'So Ποὺς (pes) and Πρό-πους are used of the lowest parts of a mountain:' Ldd. Compare Λόφος, Δείρη.

Κνίδη, a nettle: R. κνίζω, ἔκνῖδα, to tickle, chafe. So Κνήφη is the itch, from κνάω.

Κνίζω : in Κνάω.

Κνιπὸς, Κνιφὸς, Σκνιφὸς, stingy. — R. κνίζω, to scrape : Scraping, as a Scrap in Norfolk. (2) ' Compare our Nip, Snip :' Ldd.

Κνῖσα, Κνίσσα, pungent smell or steam from fat or flesh burning.— R. κνίζω, σω, to make to itch.

Κνίψ, ἰπὸς, an emmet which gnaws figs.—Allied to Κνίζω, Κνάω.

Κνόη, Ionic of Χνόη.

Κνόη, Κνόος, Κνοῦς, grating noise of an axle-tree ;—creaking noise of shoes.— R. κνάω or †κνέω, †ἔκνοα, to grate.

Κνῦ, a mote. ' Thus Οὐδὲ κνῦ, not a jot. As Γρῦ from γρύζω, so Κνῦ from κνύζω. Some say, not so much as a nail could scrape off :' Dnn. See the Next.

Κνύζα, the itch ; from κνύζω, κνύω, κνάω, to scratch.

Κνυζάομαι, to whine, whimper, yelp. Ldd. from Κνῦ like Γρῦ, and Κνύζω like Γρύζω, to grunt. Dnn. allies it to Γάνυμαι, †Γνύμαι, formed as Γνύξ. (2) R. κνύω, κνάω : I. e. to cry out in a grating manner.

Κνυζόω, to disfigure ; prop. as Κνάω, Κνύω, to scratch, claw.—Ldd. ' from κνύος, the itch, scurvy ; and so to make scabby.' Or from

Κνύω, to scratch, Κνάω.

Κνώδαλον, any wild dangerous animal.—'As Σκάνδαλον. For κινώδαλον from κινῶ : from its power of motion :' Bochart. So Ldd.: ' Like Κινώπετον.'—But perh. from κνάω, κνῶ, ' to scratch, tear, rend, hack,' Grove : as Δάκος from δάκνω. So Κνώψ is used by Nicander.

Κνώδαξ, iron pin or pivot.—'Allied to Κνώδων :' Salm.

Κνώδοντες, two projecting teeth on the blade of a hunting spear ; sing. point of a sword.— R. κνῶ, to graze ; ὀδόντες, teeth. Or κενὸς : κενόδους is found : Having a hollow space between the teeth.

Κνώσσω, to nod, slumber,—to sleep soundly, to snore, say Hesych. and Eust. Hence Damm from κνάω, κνῶ : To send out a grating unpleasant sound in sleep.

Κνώψ : in Κνώδαλον.

Κοάλεμος, a blockhead. — 'Usu. deriv. from κοῶ, ἀλέος = ἠλέος,' Ldd. Missing of perception. Above. And so Dnn. See Κοάω.

Κοὰξ κοὰξ, comic imitation of the croaking of frogs.

Κοάω, Κοέω, to have perception, understanding.—Allied by Dnn. to Ἀκούω, ἤκοα, ἀκήκοα, to hear, apprehend, understand. Thus Γρηγορέω for Ἐγρηγορέω.

Κόβαλος, 'one who lives by flattery, jesting or knavery:'

79

Dnn.: ' an impudent rogue : Κόβαλοι, a set of mischievous goblins :' Ldd.— R. κόπις, an idle talker : †κόπαλος. (2) For Κόβαλος, (as κάβηξ,) from κοάω : A knowing one. (3) ' Hebr. kobal, to receive :' Dr. Jones. A parasite.

Κόγχη, a shell-fish, muscle, cockle,—anything hollow, concave or convex, as the hollow of the ear, of the eye, the knee-pan ; boss of a shield, case round a document-seal.—Allied to Γογγύλος, round ; Κοῖλος, hollow ; Χαίνω, to be hollow ; Κύω, to contain, &c. (2) Lenn. thinks Κ a prefix as in Καρπάλιμος, and derives from ἔχομαι, ὄχα, †ὔχη, †ὄγχη, (as λαγχάνω), from its adhering to rocks.

Κόγχος, boss of a shield,—upper part of the skull,—a bean boiled in the shell or pod, which appears u kind of shell, as opposed to bruised beans.—Above.

Κογχύλιον, cockle or muscle yielding a purple dye ;—the dye.— R. κόγχη.

Κοδράντης, the Lat. quadrans, quadrantis.

Κοέω : in Κοάω.

Κόθορνος, a buskin : i. e. ' a kind of half boot, coming to the mid-leg', (Dr. J.) : other boots coming up to the thigh or hip. Hence Κόθορνος means ' cut short, curtailed', as explained in Κόθουρος. The termin. much as hybERNUS.

Κόθουρος, ' a drone-bee, wanting a tail or sting :' Dnn. —Euphon. for Κότουρος, (as perh. in αὐθέντης 2.) from κόττω, κόπτω, to mutilate, οὐρά, the tail : agreeing with Κόλ-ουρος, curtailed of its tail. Eustath. explains Κοθὼ by Βλάβη. (2) Tzetzes explains it as κεύθων hiding its sting in its οὐρὰ tail : from perf. mid. κέκουθα, as εἰλήλΟΥθα. And κΟΥθουρος is found in Suidas.

Κοΐ κοΐ, sounds imitative of the squeaking of young pigs.

Κοικύλλω, to look staring like a booby.—Dnn. from κοΐ, and κύλα (as Γύαλα) the hollows of the eyes : With eyes as stupid as a pig's.—But perh. only redupl. from κύλα, as Ποιπνύω, Μαιμάω. (2) R. κυλίω to roll.

Κοιλία, the hollow of the belly, belly, &c.—any hollow.—From

Κοῖλος, hollow.—'Allied is Γύαλον : compare Κύλλος and Κύω :' Dnn. ' For Κόϊλος from the prim. †κάος, for which they said also κάος, a cavity, Lat. cavus :' Hemsterh. So Καιάδας, Καῖαρ, Χαίνω, Χάος, &c. (2) ' Hebr. khal, to perforate :' Mrt. ' Hebr. kelo, hollow :' Wr. Some compare our Coil.

Κοιμάω, Κοιμίζω, to cause to rest, put to sleep.—Allied to Κεῖμαι : through †κείω, †κέκοιμαι, †κέκοιται, whence Κοίτη.

Κοινὸς, common.—For κοινὸς from †κέω, κεῖμαι, †κέκοα, κοιμάω : Laid down amidst or between : ' in medio positus', proposed or exposed to all. Πᾶσι προ-κείμενος, says well Varin. (2) Dnn. allies it to Ξυνὸς, i. e. σκυνός. ?

Κοινόω, to defile, i. e. make κοινὸν, ' common or unclean' Acts 10. 28.

Κοινωνὸς, a partner.— R. κοινός, as Ἰωνός.

Κοῖος, Ionic of Ποῖος.

Κοίρανος, a chief, prince.— For †κόρανος (as κοικύλλω) allied to Κάρανος and Κύριος. So Κόρυς is the top of the head, and Κορυφή. The Cossacks say Hetman for Headman. In form like ούρΑΝΟΣ.

Κοίτη, a place to lie down in, bed, couch. And a place to lay things in, chest, coffer.—Allied to Κεῖμαι and Κοιμάω : through κείω, †κέκοιται. (2) Sax. cot, our cot, sheep-cot.

Κόκκος, a kernel, berry,— pill,— grain of mustard-seed and corn, also of the ilex famous for a worm in the grains which contained juice dyeing Κόκκινον scarlet.— Allied to Κόγχη, boss of a shield, &c., Γογγύλος, round, &c. (2) 'Hebr. kang, a circle :' Pkh.

Κόκκυ, ' cry or call to a person, explained Quick, make haste :— strictly, the cry of a cuckoo:' Ldd. Compare Κοκκύξ, a cuckoo, from the sound of the bird. 'Armoric coucoug, Germ. kuckuck, Welsh, cog', &c.r Wbst. 'In anatomy, the bone joined to the extremity of the os sacrum ; called, as some think, from its resemblance to the beak of a cuckoo :' Todd. Also, ' an early fig that ripens when the cuckoo is first heard :—a term of reproach for a libertine :' Dnn., from the cuckoo sucking the eggs of other birds, and laying her own in their place.

Κοκύαι, forefathers.—Hesych. has Κούκα· πάππον, grand-papa. And Κούκα seems nothing but the Ionic of Πόππα or Πάππα, papa. So 'Ω ποποῖ was O gods ! (i.e. fathers,) in the language of the Dryopes.

Κολαβρίζω, to insult, ill-treat, i. e. buffet, beat, allied to Κολαφίζω.— Also, to dance in armor, and the dance is Κόλαβρος : perh. from beating the ground. Hesych. however has Κόλα, armour, but whence this ΚΟΛΑ ?

Κολάζω, to clip, mutilate, prune, punish. Κόλασις, punishment.—R. κόλος.

Κόλαξ, a parasite, flatterer.— R. κόλον, food, as Parasite from παρά, σῖτος corn. Living at another's table. (2) 'Hebr. chelek, to smooth or flatter :' Wr.

Κολάπτω, ' to strike upon, hollow by striking,—peck, cut with the beak :' Dnn.— Like Κολάζω, allied to Κόλος battered. (2) 'Hebr. keleph, to impel :' Wr.

Κόλαφος, a blow on the face, a cuff, an affront.— R. κολάπτω, κεκόλαφα.

Κολεὸς, a sheath.— ' Prob. akin to Κοῖλος :' Ldd.

Κολερώ, short-wooled.— R. κόλος.

Κολετράω, to trample on, beat, as Κολαβρίζω.

Κόλλα, glue, is allied by Lenn. and Damm to Κέλλω, which (inter alia) means to thrust hard on, fix fast in. As Galen explains ἐγ-κέλοπη in Hippocr. by ἐν--ερείση, ἐν-ΣΤΗΡΙΣΗΤΑΙ. (Steph. 4841.) Actively, to fix fast, would well agree with Κόλλα. (2) Allied to Γλοιὰ, (†Κλοιὰ,) glue. (3) In French colle. (4) ' Hebr. cal, complecti :' Mrt.

Κολλαβίζω, allied to Κολαφίζω : To play a game in which one gives a box on the ear.

Κόλλαβος, ' the same as Κόλλοψ : And a kind of cake or roll, named from its shape,' Ldd. So

Κόλλιξ, ' a roll of coarse bread :' Ldd. As Κόλλα-

Βος above. Some derive it from κόλον food, as also Κόλλαβος.—So Κολλύρα.

Κολλοπόω, to glue together ; from κόλλα, glue ; or κόλλοψ.

Κόλλοψ, the CALLOUS or thick skin or the upper part of the neck of oxen, ' of which Κόλλα glue was made :' Dnn. I.e. from producing the Κόλλα, as Μέλισσα, a bee, is by Ldd. derived from its producing Μέλι, honey. But some ally Κόλλοψ to Κολάπτω, As anything beaten hard and tough.— Also, the peg or screw of a lyre tightening the strings; for Κολλάω is to join fast together. And ' a machine for turning a wheel, analogous to the use of the foregoing:' Dnn.— Also, a youth who has become CALLOUS and hardened in vice.

Κολλυβιστής, a moneychanger, like Κερματιστής.— From

Κόλλυβος, a small piece of money, ' allied to Κολοβὸς, clipt, as Κέρμα to κείρω,' Riem. See Κέρμα.

Κολλύρα, ' prob. much the same as Κόλλιξ :' Ldd.

Κολλύριον, salve for the eye in the form of Κολλύραι round cakes.

Κολόβιον, under-garment with its sleeves curtailed, from

Κολοβός, mutilated, κόλος.

Κολοιὸς, jackdaw. — R. κόλον, food: As voracious. (2) Buttm. allies it to Καλέω, Κέλομαι. As clamorous : ' ut clamosus:' Greg. Allied to Κολοσυρτός.

Κόλον, food : i.e. battered corn; from κόλος.

Κόλον, 'the intestine. — Kust. takes it to mean the chopped maw and intestines of meat puddings and sausage eaten; but Dindorf prefers the sense of beat until the intestines protrude:' Dnn. From Κόλος. (2) Some for Κῶλον so used: as the member, i. e. the largest division of the intestinal canal.

Κόλος, battered, clipt, mutilated.—R. κέλλω, κέκολα, to drive, thrust, as in the first sense of Drive in Dr. J., ' to produce motion in anything by violence, as, The hammer drives the nail:' Driven hard, beaten, &c. So Per-cello (from κέλλω) is explained by Forcell., ' ferio, percutio', to strike, beat.

ΚΟΛΟΣΣΗΝΟΣ, ' of wool : Colossian-dyed. What this meant is unknown :' Ldd. ' So called from the city of Κολοσσαὶ in Phrygia :' Dnn.

Κολοσσός, a gigantic brazen statue, the Colossus of Rhodes. — As Νέος, Νεοσσὸς, so Κόλος, Κολοσσός : Κόλος being understood as prim. hammered out, beaten out (from brass). ' Allied to Κολάπτω, tundo:' Lenn. (2) R. κέλλω, κέκολα, cello, celsus, ex-cello, ex-celsus, high. Or in the sense of ex-cello, ante-cello, as Έκπαγλος, surpassing, from ἐκ-πλήσσω. See on Κολωνός.

Κολοσυρτὸς, noisy crowd, noise. — ' From κέλλω, [to call to, κέκολα, like Κέλαδος,] according to Döderlin. But prob. akin to Κολφὸς, brawling, wrangling, allied to Κολοιὸς, a jackdaw :' Ldd.—Σύρω, σέσυρται is added by Ewing: ' Sweeping with a noise.'

Κολούω, to make κόλον, to mutilate.

Κολοφών, completion, finish, pinnacle, summit. — Strabo: 'For the people of *Colophon* were so superior in their cavalry, that, wherever that was present, they put an end to the fight and gained the victory.' But the Schol. on Plato: 'For, when the votes of the 12 Ionian cities were equal, the *Colophonians* gave the casting-vote.'

Κόλπος, any hollow, the bosom, lap, bay, creek. — 'Akin to Κοῖλος:' Dnn. And to Κολεός. (2) Dr. Jones as transp. for κλόπος from κλέπτω, = καλύπτω: 'A thing which *hides*, such as the doubling of a garment, fold; a place *concealed* by folds, a bosom', &c.

Κόλυθροι, testiculi. — R. κολεοί, sheaths.

Κολυμβάω, to dive, swim.—For κολνεάω, (as λαΜΕάνω,) allied to Κολάπτω, to beat (the water with the hands.) (2) R. κολοεός (or †κολνεός, as ὄνΥμα,) from the body appearing mutilated in swimming.

Κολχικὸν, meadow-saffron. — From *Colchis* in Asia, near Pontus.

Κολωνὸς, a hill. — In form as κοινΩΝΟΣ. It seems formed from κέλλω, κέκολα, but from the sense which the Latins preserve in *celsus, ex-celsus,* from *cello.* See on Κολοσσὸς 2. The compound omitted, as Ὄχα is for Ἕξ-οχα, eminently. So Ἴτυς, &c. Driving up.

Κολῳὸς, brawling, wrangling, as of so many κολοιοὶ jackdaws.

Κομάω, to let the κόμη hair grow long; — and, as long hair was accounted a great ornament, it meant to plume oneself, give oneself airs. See on Κόμη.

Κόμβος, 'a scarf or band used as a girdle, and, like that used now by the Orientals, serving for a pocket:' Dnn. Perhaps contr. from Κόσυμβος.—'Fischer shows that Κόμβωμα and Ἐγ-κόμβωμα are' said not only of knots and bands of knots, but of vests drawn tight by such: and mean generally to put on an elegant [i.e. κομψὸν] vest, or one over others. Hence 1 St. Pet. 5. 5, 'Ἐγκομβώσασθε be clothed with humility:' Schleusn. Hence it may be allied to Κομψὸς, Κομμὸς, Κομέω. 'Made for the sake of ornament, from κομῶ,' says Greg.

Κομέω, to attend to, take care of, nourish. — From †κέω, pono, whence Κεῖμαι, Κοιμάω, †κέκομαι, whence this Κομέω, and Κόσμος: Pono, dis-pono, to dispose, set in order. (2) R. κόμη; but rather the reverse.

Κόμη, the hair. — R. κομέω: the hair being deemed worthy of peculiar care. 'Comta et curiosiùs culta:' Schleusn. So Festus explains *Coma* 'capillus aliquâ cum curâ compositus.' The Greeks were called Καρη-κομόωντες. (2) 'Hebr. *kom,* to arise': Wr.

Κομήτης, hairy; — a comet, with a hairy tail :— &c. — Above.

Κομιδῆ, Κομιδῇ, with care, carefully; — thoroughly, altogether, quite. — R. κομίζω, ἐκόμιδον.

Κομίζω, like Κομέω, to take care of, provide for, supply. — Also 'to carry away; attention to, care or security being implied:' Dnn. So Ldd.: 'To take up and carry away, in order to keep or save it, — as a corpse, to save it from the enemy, — carry to a place of safety.' (2) For †Γομίζω; to carry a Γόμος, freight.

81

Κόμμα, the stamp or impression of a coin;—the coin; a short division of a period, &c. — R. κόπτω, κέκομμαι.

Κόμμι, gum. — Greg. says not badly : 'The dried tear of certain trees: is it as flowing from the κόμμα incision of the tree ?' See on Μέλι. (2) 'Sax. *goma,* D. *gom,* Russ. *kamed:*' What.

Κομμὸς, a striking; — lamentation attended with beating the body, as Latin Planctus from Plango. — R. κόπτω, κέκομμαι.

Κομμὸς, an ornament. — R. κομῶ, to attend to.

Κόμπος, stamping of feet, ringing of metal, any din or noise ; — noisy high-sounding words, vaunting. — As τύΜπανον, for κόπος from κόπτω to stamp. Thus Ὑπέρ-κοπος and Ὑπέρ-κομπος are both found for a 'superjactator.'

Κομψὸς, 'from κομέω : well-dressed, attired, decked; *comtus:* — elegant, pretty, refined, affected:' Ldd.

Κόναβος, a ringing, clashing, din. — 'Imitated from the sound; perh. akin to Κόμπος:' Ldd. Or to Κανωχὸς, noisy. Κοναβίζω is much the same as Καναχίζω.

Κόνδαξ, Κόνταξ, was a game played with a peg or pin, from κυντὸς, which, like Palus, was so used : (Steph. 279 p. Not.) The peg was called also Κύνδαλος.

ΚΟΝΔΥ, 'a drinking-cup, a kind of measure. A word foreign to Greek, probably Persian :' Dnn. *Gondola* is allied by Nugent. (Very rare.)

Κονδύλη, a lump produced by a blow or fall. — From Κόνδυλος, a knuckle; — knob: — a blow with the fist, a cuff.— The same word produced Γόνυ a knee and Κόνδυλος, just as Γαμψὸς and Καμψὸς were both said. Dr. Johnson explains the Knuckle as the Knee joint of a calf: and Liddell allies 'Γόνυ, Genu, Knee, Knuckle.' Κόνδυλος in form like Σφόνδυλος.

Κονέω, to raise the κόνις dust, haste, wait on with despatch.

Κόνις, Κονία, 'ashes, dust, *cinis,* lye for washing. Prob. the R. καίω, to burn, κάω :' Dnn. As †Γάω, Γόνος; †Τάω, Τόνος. Burnt ashes: others say, dust from anything burnt. (2) R. †κέω, κείω, to cut. 'Dust being earth reduced to the smallest particles:' Greg. See Deut. 9. 21.

Κόνις, *ἰδος,* a nit. — Allied to Γόνος, offspring, as Γῆρυς, Κῆρυξ.

Κοννέω, to know, from κοέω. Compare κόΝΝος, ῥωΝΝύω, σάΝΝat. Found in Æ. Suppl. 175. 'The reading is dubious. Some read Κοέω:' Dnn. (2) *Connan* Sax. 'They con to heaven the high way,' says Spenser. So *ken, cunning, can,* &c.

Κόννος, the beard. — The same as Γόνος: What is produced: And Γένειον. So Γῆρυς, Κῆρυξ. See Κόνις 2.

Κόνος, Κόννος, an ear-ring. — 'Allied to Κῶνος, a *cone:* Anything narrowing into a sharp point :' Toup.

Κόντος, a barge-pole, pole, pike-handle. — Damm, Lenn., Mrt., Ewing, &c. all join in deriv. from κεντέω, κέντρον, a goad, κένσαι; to prick, i.e. from †Κένω,

M

·Κέκυνται: To stick the ground with. Or to drive on a boat with, for Κεντέω is also 'to drive on' (Dnn.). (2) ' In Norfolk called a *quant;*' Maltby.

Κόπάζω, am tired by laboring, — rest after labor: R. κόπος.

Κόπανον, an instrument for braying, pestle. — R. κόπτω, κοπῶ.

. Κοπετὸς, wailing, from κόπτω, as Κόπος and Κομμός.

Κοπιᾶται, *copiâtœ* (in Constantin. and Julian.), men who had the charge of carrying out the dead at night. From

Κοπιάω the same as Κοπάζω.

Κοπὶς, a dagger, sword, knife, sting. — 'R. κόπτω:' Dnn.

Κοπὶς, 'a festival at Sparta in which the share of each was *carved* for him: hence Κοπίζω, to share in such a feast;' Ewing. — R. κόπτω, whence Κοπὶ a knife.

Κόπις, a babbler, wrangler, orator. — R. κόπτω, 'cædo sermones' in Terence, to *chop* logic. — Or κόπτω, to stamp money, &c., is here to make a great noise: as in Κόμπος, 'din, and high-sounding words.'—Hence Δημο- -κόπος, a demagogue. — Some compare Κόπτω in sense with Τρίβω, and Κόπις with Τρίβων, 'Εν-τριβὴς, 'one who is well practised.'

Κόπος, a blow, R. κόπτω to beat: — grief, from beating the body in grief, as Κοπετὸς, Κομμός: — also toil, fatigue, Dnn. explaining this by Ἵππος κόπτει τὸν ἀναβάτην, 'fatigues the rider by jolting', i. e. by bumping, causing blows and wounds, and so Κοπόω is to *fatigue*. Or, says Dnn., ' from the sense in Hom. Il. ν. 60, of urging on and so *fatiguing* a horse by *blows*.' Damm from the enormous labor of anciently *beating* out corn with stones: 'Fruges . . parant . . frangere saxo', Virg.— Then Κόπος is weariness from toil, and Κοπάζω.

Κοππατίας, a horse marked with the Κoppa, the *Koph* of the Phœnicians, the inverted P, or our q. Κόππα in the alphabet stood, like our Q, between π and ρ: hence, as π' was 80, κόππα was used for 90.

Κόπρος, dung, dirt, — cattle-stall. — Damm makes it orig. shreds, minute cuttings, riff-raff, from κόπτω, to cut. Κυλινδόμενος κατὰ κόπρον is explained κατὰ Κόνιν, (Heyne and Steph. on Il. χ. 414.) Like Τίλαι from τίλλω: Excrement from Εκ-cerno, Ex-cernimentum. So

. Κόπτη, chives, threads or filaments in flowers. — Prop. cuttings, splittings. See in Κόπρος.

Κοπτὴ σησαμὶς, a cake of pounded sesamé; and Κοπτὴ alone. 'Coptam, quam tibi misit, edat;' Martial. — From

. Κόπτω, to beat, batter, stamp; — cut, chop. — For Κυλάπτω. (2) Allied to Κόγχη, Κοῖλος, &c.: To hollow out. (3) Wbst. compares our *chop*, Fr. *couper*, G. and Du. *kappen:* Pers. and Chald. *kafa*, a blow.

Κοράλιον, -άλλ-, *coral.*—' R. κόρος, ἁλός: Sprout of the sea:' Becm. and Lenn.

Κόραξ, a raven, crow: ' anything hooked or pointed like its beak, as an engine for grappling ships, hooked

82

handle of a door, instrument of torture,' Ldd. Comp. the senses of Corvus and Κορώνη.—Τὸ κόραξ Dnn. allies Κοράνη, Κορωνὶς, *Curvus*, from the shape of the bill. Thus also Κέρας, Χορὸς, Γῦρος, &c. (2) R. κείρω, κέκορα, ' to eat up, devour', (Dnn.) so δημὸν κείροντες Il. φ. 204, Damm explains ἀ-πλήστως ἐσθίοντες. An Ἅρπαξ. (3) R. κορέω, to glut. (4) Lenn. from the sound: κορ κορ. (5) Our *crow*, &c.— 'Hebr. *korang*, to rend:' Wr.

Κόρδαξ, a kind of wanton dance ; danced, Brunck thinks, to a rope or cord. — Perh. from κρότος, noise by stamping: κρόταξ,†κόρταξ, κόρδαξ, as menTior, menTax, menDax. Compare Δόρπον.

Κορδύλη, a club, cudgel, — bump, tumor. ' As Κορύνη:' Mrt. With a big Κόρυς or Κορυφὴ top. Some from κείρω, κέκορται: A club cut off, as Κορμός. But κορδύλη is also a head-dress, evidently allied to Κόρυς and Κάρα.

Κορεύω, stuprare κόρην.

†Κορέω, Κορέννυμι, to satisfy, satiate. — Prop. to carry to a Κόρυς, Κὰρ, head, like Κορύσσω, Κορυφόω, and Καρανόω. (2) R. κείρω, κέκορα, to devour, whence better the subst. κόρος, satiety, and then κορέω.

Κορέω, to sweep, clean, take care of. — I.e. to clean with a Κόρος broom. (2) R. κείρω, κέκορα, to cut off: as Cōlo, (κολάζω,) is ' to clip, pæne, trim, dress, take care of': Forcell.

Κόρη, Κούρη, a little girl. — R. κόρος, as Puer, Puella: Some however from κορέω, to sweep the house, or to take care of it. — Also, the pupil of the eye, as Pupa, Pupilla, Pupil: images of beholders being seen in the eye like little girls. — Also, the drachma, as bearing the image of the Virgin Minerva. (Steph. p. 294.) — Also a long sleeve reaching to the hands: perh. allied to Κορυφὴ ' the finish' (Dnn.) i.e. a finish to the vest : — or to Κορύσσω ' to equip, array.' But ?

Κόρη, Proserpine, the κόρη daughter of Ceres. 'The two are often mentioned together, as Μητρὶ (Matri) καὶ τῇ Κούρῃ:' Ldd.

Κορθύω, as Κορύσσω, to raise up. And Κόρθυς, a heap.

Κορίζομαι, ' to act like a Κόρη maiden, fondle:' Dnn. ' To caress a κόρον or κόρην' : Schrevel.

Κόρις, a bug. — R. κείρω, κέκορα, ' to eat to satiety,' (Damm on Il. λ. 559). Or κορέω to glut. ' R. κείρω, scindo:' Mrt.

Κορκορυγὴ, a rumbling, grumbling of the bowels:— From the sound κὸρ κὸρ, as from βὸρ βὸρ was Βορ-βορυγὴ.

Κορμὸς, trunk of a tree.— R. κείρω, κέκορμαι: Lopped off.

Κόρνωψ, a locust or gnat.—Formed prob. like Κόρις. (Used only once.)

Κόρος, Κοῦρος, a lad, boy. ' Usu. referred to κείρω, [κέκορα]: strictly one who is just beginning to shave:' Ldd. We say commonly ' a young shaver.' — Κόρος is also a shoot, sprout, scion, and this may be the original sense:

As cut or lopped off, like Κορμός: and Κλάω, Κλάδος.
— Also, à broom of κόρων young twigs. — Also the
Hebrew word for a dry measure in the O. T. and N. T.

Κόρση, Κόρρη, 'the side of the fore-head, plur. the
temples: R. κάρα:' Ldd. And the hair on the temples,
in which sense it is thought allied to

Κόρσης, one who cuts his hair and keeps it short. —
R. κείρω, κέκορσαι.

Κορύβας, αντος, a priest of Cybelé. — 'R. κορύπτω,
ἐκόρυβον, to strike with the horns, toss the head, as
they did when beating their timbrels and dancing:'
Forcell. (2) R. κόρυς, a helmet, βάς, as Λυκάβας:
Going helmeted or armed. (3) As affected in the κόρυς,
head, prop. crown of the head: frenzied. (4) Servius
from Κόρυνον, a mountain in Cyprus, bearing brass.

Κόρυδος, Κόρυς, the crested lark: its tuft resembling
the crest of a κόρυς helmet.

Κόρυζα, a cold in the κόρυς head, running of the
nose: — drivelling, stupidity, as Βλέννα.

Κόρυμβος, like Κόρυς, head, top, peak, high curved
stern of a ship, cluster of fruit and flowers on the top of
the stalks.

Κορύνη, 'a stick with a knob at the end, club, mace:
— knot in trees from which the shoot springs, a bud,
shoot, flower-stalk. R. κόρυς:' Dnn.

Κορύπτω, to butt with the κόρυς head.

Κόρυς, the crown of the head, — a helmet with a
horse-hair crest — crested lark. — 'It belongs to the
original κάρα, the head:' Dnn. Or curved like a Κέρας
horn. So Κορωνός, curved. (2) R. κείρω, κέκορα, to
shear the head.

Κορύσσω, to raise to a κόρυς head, make to rise up
and swell, of a wave; — raise the head threateningly, of
a bull. — Also, to furnish with a κόρυς helmet; gen. to
arm, equip, furnish.

Κορυφή, head, top, principal point: like Κόρυς.

Κορυφόω, to bring to a head, accomplish. — Above.

Κορώνεως, epith. of a fig, of a raven-gray color, from
Κορώνη, a sea-crow;— a kind of crow, perh. the daw.
' Anything hooked or curved like a crow's bill ; esp. the
handle on a door by which it was shut; later also, like
Κόραξ, a knocker;—the tip of a bow, on which the bow-
string was hooked; gen. the end, tip;— the curved stern
of a ship;— tip of the plough-beam:' Ldd. ' The acute
process of certain bones, from a fancied resemblance to
the crow's beak:' Dnn. — R. κορωνός, curved or bent.
(2) ' Crown, Irish corvin, Wel. coron, Armor. curun:'
Wbst. ' Hebr. keren, horn:' Wr.

Κορωνιάω, to arch the neck, be proud.—And

Κορωνίς, 'a wreath or garland, corôna;— curved line
or stroke with the pen at the end of a book, chapter, &c.
— the end, completion, — the topmost member of a
building, our cornice:' Ldd. ' The lower circle of the
javelin, which used to be fitted to the string to keep it
from missing its aim:' Hemst. — R. κορώνη.

Κορωνός, curved, bent. — Allied to Γύρος, Κέρας,
Χορός, Κυρτός.

83

Κόσκινον, a sieve. — For †κόκινον (as Ἔχον), redupl.
from κίω, cio, κινέω, †κοκίω, to move about. See Κίσσα,
Κισσός. Redupl. as in Κοχυδέω. And

Κοσκυλμάτια, parings of leather. — For †σκοσκυλ-
μάτια redupl. from σκύλλω, to skin or rend. — Some
add κώς, a skin.

Κόσμος, order, arrangement ; — beautiful order, deco-
ration, elegance; — the world, as well ordered and
arranged, as Mundus adj. and subst. Hervey says:
' The Greeks, those refined judges of things, called the
World by Beauty.' — R. †κέω, †κέκοσμαι, to place,
κεῖμαι. So Κομέω. (2) R. κάζω, κέκασμαι, κέκασται.
(3) ' Hebr. KSM, to trim :' Pkh. ' Arab. KSM, to
distribute:' Jones.

Κόσσος, a box on the ear. — R. κόπτω, κόττω,
†κόσσω, to strike.

Κόσσος, Ion. of Πόσσος.

Κόσυμβος, the edge, border, fringe, fastening of a
tunic when tucked up. — 'R. κόρυμβος or κώμβος':
Dnn. But how? Rather, as Κομέω from †κέκομαι, so
Κόσυμβος (in form like κόρΥΜΒΟΣ,) from †κέκοσαι
perf. p. of †κέω, κεῖμαι, jaceo, ad-jaceo, to lie near or
upon. See κεῖτος from †κέκοΤαι. And see Κόσμος.
Compounds are often omitted as in Ἴτυς, Βῆμα.

Κότος, grudge, rancor; allied by Ldd. to Χόλος, anger,
i.e. through χάομαι, or †χόομαι, †κέχοται : — but
rather from †κέω, †κέκοται, κεῖμαι, as lying deeply
rooted in the mind, 'in imâ mente repostus,' Virg.
' Anger resteth in the bosom of fools:' Eccles. 7. 9.
Espec. as in 'Αλλό-κοτος, &c. κότος seems to mean
inherent disposition.

Κόττα, the head. — 'Akin to Κόρση, Κόρρη, Κόρρα:'
Ldd. Κόρσα, †κόσσα, κόττα.

Κότταβος, a game played by flinging from a cup the
remains of liquor into a basin on the floor, and trying to
produce the most sound. — R. κόπτω, †κόττω, to knock.

Κοττάνη, a fishing instrument: perh. to catch the
Κόττοι. (Only in Ælian, N. A. 12. 43.)

Κόττος, a fish, the bull's head or chub: R. κόττα,
head.

Κοτύλη, a hollow vessel, cup, measure. — 'Derived
from, or akin to Κότττα or Κοῖλος :' Dnn. And Κόγχη,
Κολεός. (2) Mrt. from †κέω, †κέκοται, κεῖμαι : In
which things are placed.

Κοτυληδόν, like Κοτύλη, hollow of a cup, — socket
of the hip-joint, — ' plur. the hollows forming suckers
on the feelers of the polypus:' Dnn.

ΚΟΤΤΣ, a goddess of debauchery, and Κοτυτώ. —
Perh. from κοίτη, ' sexual intercourse' (Dnn.). (Very
rare.)

Κουρά, a shaving: from κείρω, κέκορα. And Κουρεύς,
a barber.

Κουρεῶτις ἡμέρα, the third day of the festival 'Απα-
τούρια, on which the sons of citizens were introduced, 3
or 4 years old, and registered. — ' Some from κοῦρος, a
boy; — others from κουρά, as the child's hair is said to
have been cut on that day:' Ldd.

Κούρητες, 'armed κοῦροι youths:' Dnn.

ΚΟΤΡΗΤΕΣ, 'Curētes, inhabiting Pleuron in Ætolia Il. 9. 529: — a Cretan tribe, devoted, like the Corybantes, to the worship of Cybele:' Dnn.

Κοῦρος, a boy, Κόρος.

Κοῦφος, light. — For †κόφος from κόπτω, κέκοφα, to beat or hammer out: Beaten out thin and light, κεκομμένος, 'ἐληλαμένος. Compare Ἐλαχύς. So Κωφὸς from κόπτω is 'invalidus, inefficax:' Steph. (2) Lenn. allies it to Κοῖλος, hollow, i.e. empty. In form as Ψόφ ɩς. (3) Wr. from Hebr. koophá, hollow.

Κόφινος, a basket, hamper, measure. — 'R. κοῦφος, from its lightness: or R. κόπτω, κέκοφα, as made of cuttings or twigs of trees:' Pkh. and Ewing. (2) Wbst. compares our coffin, and coffer, Irish kofra, Welsh cofawr, from cof, a hollow trunk. 'Hebr. KPH, cavitas:' Bos.

Κόχλαξ, 'the same sense as Κάχληξ, a pebble, esp. on the sea-shore:' Dnn. Perhaps though of distinct origin, and (like ΚΟχυδέω) redupl. from κλάω, to break.

Κοχλίας, cochlea, snail with a spiral shell; — a spiral stair; — screw. And

Κόχλος, shell-fish with a spiral shell; — also a cockle. — 'R. κόχλω, to turn, twine or twist round:' Schrevel. 'And this perh. from [or allied to] Κύκλος, a circle:' Greg. So Wbst. compares Wel. cocos, Ir. coccia, 'prob. from the same root as Sp. cocar, to wrinkle, twist, Engl. cockle, to shrink or pucker, Ir. coachaim, to fold.' (2) 'From the Κόχος juice in it:' Mrt.: Κόχος meaning 'abundans humor.' See the Next. (3) With K prefix, as in Καρπάλιμος, 'from ἔχομαι, ὄχα, to stick (to the rocks):' Lenn.

Κοχύω, Κοχυδέω, 'to flow down profusely or with noise. R. χύω [redupl.]:' Dnn.

Κοχώνη, the joining of the haunch with the buttocks. — Dnn. allies it to Κόκκυξ; better Lenn. redupl. for χάνη, for χαόνη from †χάω, χάζω, 'capio, excipio,' to take on. So Dnn. himself understands it in the sense of 'a drunken woman' 'for Χώνη,' a 'funnel', met. one that pours down her throat.

Κράβατος, Κράββ., grabātus, a couch, pallet-bed. — 'R. κρὰ, the head, βάω, [βάσις, a base or support,]: On which the head rests' Lenn. 'A bed to rest on:' Forcell. Simply a bed without conveniences.

Κραδάω, -αίνω, to shake, brandish. — Some from the palpitations of the κραδία heart: others reverse this. (2) Some from κράδη, 'the twig at the end of a branch': others with Ldd. reverse this. (3) 'Welsh cryd, a rocking, Ir. creathan, to shake, Heb. KRD, to tremble, and our cradle:' Wbst.

Κράδη, 'from κραδῶ: The quivering twig at the end of a branch, esp. of fig-trees; — a fig-tree: — a blight in fig-trees:' Ldd. — Others reverse this, and ally Κράδη to Κλάδος a branch, as κΡύπτω for †κλύπτω.

Κραδία, the heart. — R. κραδῶω, to shake, from its palpitations. (2) For καρδία. (3) R. κάρα, κρά.: as the head or fountain of vitality.

84

Κράδος, disease in figs, &c.: κράδη.'

Κράζω, to croak, scream, screech, cry, bawl. — 'An imitative word like Κρώζω:' Dnn. From the sound κρὰ κρά.

Κραίνω, Κραιαίνω, like Καρανόω, to bring to a †κρά, κάρα head, fulfil, accomplish. — Also, to be at the head, reign over: — to 'come to a particular end, result in. (2) R. κρέω, (κρέων, ruling,) κραίνω, as 'Ρέω, 'Ραίνω.

Κραιπάλη, a swimming of the head after excess, head-ache. — Like Κρή-δεμνον: from κάρα, †κρά, with the head: πάλλω, παλῶ, to shake, palpitate.

Κραιπνὸς, rapid. I.e. headlong, from κάρα, κρά, with the head. Compare Κύμβαχος. (2) For κραπνὸς, transp. for †καρπνὸς, = καρπάλιμος. Transp. as Δέρκομαι, Δράκων.

Κραῖρα, a horn. — R. κέρας, a horn, κέραος, †κρᾶος, †κράϊ.

Κρᾶμα, Κρᾶσις, a mixture; — crasis. — R. κερδάω, κράω.

Κράμβος, dry, parched, shrivelled: — dry-sounding, clear, loud. Allied to Κρανὸς and Κραῦρος. 'R. κάρα, †κρά, [as κλαμβός]: not level, but split into many tops and surfaces:' Lenn. So Damm: 'Having many heads and rising places, rough.' See Κρανός. — And so Κράμβη, cabbage, is referred by some to κρά, 'capitata.' Indeed a species of the Brassica is called 'capitata.' (2) R. κέρας. Hard as a horn. See Κραυρός.

Κρανὸς, rugged, rocky, hard. — 'R. κράνον:' Dnn. Full of peaks and crags. See above. (2) R. κέρας, a horn.

Κράνιον, Κρᾶνον, the skull of the κάρα, †κρά, head.

Κρανον, Κράνεια, the corneil-tree. — In Latin Cornus from Cornu, whence Turton from κέρας, †κράς, a horn. 'From the hardness of its wood; allied to Κραναός:' Dnn.

Κρανος, helmet for the head, formed as Κράνιον.

Κραντῆρες, the wisdom-teeth: as completing the set. — R. κραίνω, κέκρανται.

Κρὰς, κράτὸς, as Κάρα, †κάρᾶτος, κάρητος, head, top, peak.

Κράσπεδον, edge, border, rim, bank. — The old deriv. was for κρεμάσπεδον, R. κρεμάω, πέδον: Hanging to the ground. Σ, as ἔΣχον. (2) Dr. Jones: 'The κράς head or end of a garment towards the πέδον ground.' (3) Döderl. allies it to Κρηπὶς, Dor. κραπὶς, ῖδος, a bank. Σ as ἔΣχον. (4) Dnn. and Wr. from ἄκρος, πέδον. But the Α before Σ ?

Κράστις, like Γράστις.

Κρατευταὶ, supporters, the frame on which a spit turns. — From

Κρατέω, to have κράτος power over.

Κρατήρ, a vessel in which wine and water or spices are mixed. — R. κερδάω, κεκέραται, κέκρᾶται.

Κράτος, dominion, power, authority, might, strength. — 'Akin to κράς, the head, summit:' Dnn. Headship. 'R. κρέω, κρέων': Mrt. 'R. κραίνω or κρέω: or κάρα, κρά, the head:' Greg. Κραίνω supposes †κράω, as Βαίνω, †Βάω: then κράτος, as †Στάω, Στατός. (2)

Ewing from κέρας, †κρὰς. Cruden: 'The Scripture mentions the *horn* as the symbol of *strength*.'

Κραυγή, vociferation. — R. κράζω, κραγῶ. So Κραυγὸς, a wood-pecker. — Above. From its shrill cry.

Κραυρὸς, dry, hard. — Jones makes it 'horny' from κέρας, which could make †κεραρὸς, as Γέρας, Γεραρός: then †κραρὸς, κραυρός. (2) R. κάρα, †κρὰ, as in Κράμβος and Κραναός.

Κρέας, flesh, piece of meat. — Heyne from γράω, to eat, as Γῆρυς, Κῆρυξ. (2) R. κείρω, κερῶ, †κρεῶ. Thus Homer: Γῦπε ῆπαρ 'ΕΚΕΙΡΟΝ, 'depascebantur' (Damni). And Δημὸν κείροντες. — Or, as a *piece* of meat, from κείρω, to cut or clip off. So (3) 'Hebr. *KRH*, to cut:' Pkh.

Κρείων, meat-tray, dresser. — R. κρέας.

Κρείσσων, κρέσσων, == κράσσων from κρατύς, strong, as Βαθὺς, Βάσσων. Or at once as a compar. from κρέων as follows.

Κρείων, Κρέων, ruling, ruler. — 'R. prob. κρὰς, the head, κραίνω:' Dnn. Rather, from obs. †κρέω, †κράω, κραίνω: all from κάρα, †κρά.

Κρεκάδια, curtains. — 'R. κρέκω:' Ldd. So all. From the web being well struck. Κρέκω, says Brunck, is not only said of the beating of string-instruments, but of the beating and thickening of the web.

Κρέκω, to knock, strike with the shuttle or plectrum. — Schneid. allies it to Κρούω, Κροαίνω, Κροτέω. (2) Dr. Jones from the harsh sound, and compares our *creak;* Wbst. the Welsh *crecian*, to crash, Russ. *crik*, a cry.

Κρέμαθρα, a basket hung up to keep provisions in. — From

Κρεμάω, Κρεμάννῦμι, to hang up. — Hemsterh. from κρέω, †κέκρεμαι, κρείω, (See Κρείων,) to be at the head: i. e. actively, to make a thing to be at the head of or *above* another. Thus Suspendere ædificium is '*in altum* SUPER arcus exstruere', (Forcell.). Pliny: 'Allium SUPER prunas suspendere.' (2) R. ἄκρος, high, †ἀκρεμὴς, (as 'Αρτεμὴς,) allied to 'Ακρέμων.

Κρέμβαλον, castanet. — As τύΜπανον, — for κρέβαλον, from Æol. †κρέπω, crepo, whence *crepitaculum*, == κρέμβαλον. See in Κρηπίς.

Κρὲξ, g. κρεκὸς, the bird rail, or some such. — From the sound. Wbst. compares our *crake.* 'Its cry is very singular, *crek crek*:' Enc. Brit.

Κρήγυος, 'good, useful or agreeable:' Ldd.—Brought by Arnold on Il. α. 106 from κῆρ, γαίω, †γαύω, [whence Γαῦρος,] for †κήργυος. (2) Rather from κῆρ, χύω, as in Homer 'ΕΧΘΗ οἱ θυμὸς, 'His mind overflowed with joy', (Ldd.): †κρήχυος, κρήγυος. (3) Some ally it to ΧΡΗστὸς, ΧΡΗσιμος.

Κρήδεμνον, head-band. — R. κάρη == κάρα, δέω δεδεμένον.

Κρήμνημι, == κρεμάω.

Κρημνὸς, hanging cliff, crag, precipice: 'pendula rupes,' Claud. 'saxis suspensa rupes,' Virg. — R. κρήμνημι, to hang.

85

Κρήνη, a fountain. — R. κάρη, κρὴ, 'caput aquæ,' Hor. Ewing from κάρηνον.

Κρηπὶς, ῖδος, a foundation, basement, — 'walled edge of a river, a quay, which resembles the basement of an altar,' &c.: Ldd.—As the shore is called 'Ρηγμὶν from ῥήγνῦμι, 'as on it the sea breaks with loud noise', (Dnn.) so Κρηπὶς, 'the bank of a river', (Dnn.) from †κρέπω, *crepo*, (See in Κρέμβαλον,) Æol. of κρέπω, (as λύΚος, †λύΠος, luPus,) to strike, knock. So Κροκὴ, a beach, is from κρέκω. (2) Lenn. from †κράω, κραίνω, κράτος, from its strength in supporting. (3) Allied to Σκηρίπτω, †σκρήπτω, to lean upon. As Κάπετος for Σκάπετος.

Κρηπὶς, ῖδος, crepida, a soldier's boot or shoe, — a soldier.—*Solea*, 'a sort of open shoe, Σανδάλιον, 'Υπόδημα, Κρηπὶς,' (Forcell.) is from *Solum*, which, though meaning the Sole of the foot, meant prim. like Κρηπὶς a foundation. Thus this Κρηπὶς and the preceding seem allied.

Κρησέρα, a sieve: Lat. *cribrum*, which, says Forcellini, is 'from *cerno*, *CREvi*, for *CREbrum* :' rather *CREvibrum*, *CREibrum*. And whence this *CREvi* ? From the same root as ΚΡΗνέρα, i.e. κείρω, κερῶ, †κρέω, †κρήσω, †κερίω, †κρίω, κρίνω, 'to separate', (Dnn.) whence through †κίρνω is *cerno*, *ex-cerno*, to SIFT. Thus Martin is right at last, who says: 'Κρησέρα from κρίνω.' Compare Τρίβω from Τείρω.

Κρησφύγετον, an asylum. — From Κρὴς, ητὸς, φυγή : A refuge *from* Minos the *Cretan*. Schrevel. says: 'An asylum *belonging to* Minos the *Cretan*'. Dnn. says: 'An asylum *for* the *Cretan*.—Others from κρῆς for κρὰς.' A flying for one's head or life.

Κρητίζω, to deceive as a *Cretan*. Tit. 1. 12.

Κρητικὸν, a Cretan vest.

Κρητικὸν μέλος, Κρητικὸς ῥυθμὸς or ποὺς, 'the Cretan rhythm or foot, the invention of which is referred to the *Cretans* :' Steph. The *Cretan* foot or *Cretic* is — ᴗ —.

Κρῖ, Κρῖθή, barley.—Pkh. says from Eustathius : 'From κρίνω, to separate : for the grains of this corn grow *separate* from each other in the ears.' 'The holm is more jointed and *divided* than in wheat:' Greg. But better for this reason : 'Barley is the most difficult of all the species of corn to save in a precarious harvest: and usually requires more labor in threshing and dressing, partic. in *separating* the awns from the grain, for which a hummelling-machine is sometimes added to the threshing-mill:' Enc. Brit. (2) Buttm. allies it to Κρύος, 'Οκρυόεις, as Hordeum from Horridum, Hordum, from the beards on the ears. And so 'Ακοστὴ from 'Ακή.———N.B. The absence of deriv. from foreign sources in this word is remarkable.

Κρίβανος, pot or pan to bake bread in.—R. κρῖ, †βάνος, βαῦνος, oven. See ΒΑΝαυσος.

Κρίζω, ξω, Κρίκω, to creak, screech, squeak. —'Akin to Κράζω, Κρώζω.' Ldd.

Κριθή : in Κρῖ.

Κυδώνιον μῆλον, a quince, from *Cydon* in Crete: Germ. *quidden* or *quiddens*, abbrev. to *quince*.

Κνέω, the same as Κύω.

Κυζικηνὸς, a gold coin from *Cyzicus* in the Propontis, a *cyzicene*.

Κυθέρεια, Venus, ' *Cytherēa* Venus,' Hor. ' From the city Κύθηρα *Cythēra* in Crete, or the island on the S. of Laconia:' Ldd.

Κύθρα, == χύτρα.

Κυκάω, to stir up and mix, confound. — R. κύω, κέκυκα : To make to swell up. Hemsterh. supposes an old word †κύκος 'flour kneaded and swelling with leaven : R. κύω.' (2) R. χύω, κέχυκα, fundo, confundo.

Κυκάω, a mixed drink : Above.

Κυκλαμὶς ,-μῖνος, *cyclamen*, sow-bread.— 'R. κυκλὰς, as having a round root:' Dnn. For it is ' a bulbous plant', (Ldd.)

Κυκλικὸς, one who goes round and round the old paths, writing about the old fables and stories, 'scriptor *cyclicus*:' — a strolling circulator of his poems. — From

Κύκλος, a circle, round, ring, orb, ball, — circular movement. — R. κύω, κέκυκα, to swell up. A tumid figure, as Κύμα. (2) R. κυλίω, κεκύλικα, †κέκυκλα, to roll.

Κύκνος, *cygnus*, a swan : from κύω, κέκυκα. ' *Tumens superbiâ*,' says Phædrus of the daw, which is as true of the swan. — Also, ' Some ship, from the figure-head, or from the curve of the prow, like a swan's neck:' Ldd.

Κύλα, the κοῖλα hollow parts under the eyes. — Dnn. from κοῖλος. See on Κύαθος. So

Κύλιξ, *calix*, a goblet. — 'R. κοῖλος:' Dnn. See on Κύλα, Κύαθος, and Γύλιος, Γύαλον, and

Κυλίω, Κυλίνδω, Κυλινδέω, to roll, roll round. — 'R. κύω: the notion of it is from the ROUNDNESS of anything swelling:' Lenn. To roll ROUND as a Κύκλος circle. Allied to Κύλα, as convex and concave are both round. See in Κύαθος, Κύαμος. Dnn. compares Κυλλὸς. Add Κύπτω. (2) ' Heb. *gal*, to roll:' Mrt.

Κυλλήνιος, Mercury, from mount *Cyllēne* in Arcadia. ' *Cyllenia proles*,' Virg.

Κυλλὸς, crooked, halt, lame. — Grove allies it to Κόλος, mutilated : Ldd. to Κοῖλος, hollow : Χωλὸς, lame, may be added. Dnn. compares also Κυλίω, to roll. Add Κύπτω.

Κῦμα, ' from κύω : anything swollen, hence a wave ; — foetus in the womb; — young sprout of a cabbage :' Ldd.

Κυμαίνω, to swell, rise in waves. — Above.

Κύμβαλον, a *cymbal*, musical instrument like a hollow basin. — R. κύμβος.

Κύμβαχος, head-foremost. — R. κύβη, a head; †κύβαχος, κύμβαχος, as λαΜβάνω. Allied to Κυβιστάω.

Κύμβη, a boat ; — cup, *cymba*. — R. κύμβος.

Κύμβη, ' perhaps a tumbler-pigeon : allied to Κύμβαχος:' Ldd.

Κύμβος, any hollow, a hollow vessel.— As λαΜβάνω,

for κύΒος allied to κύβη, from κύω, as in Κύαθος. (2) Our *combe*, as Brockley *Combe* and *Combe* Lodge in Somerset.

ΚΤΜΙΝΟΝ, *cumin*. — ' Hebr. *kemen*:' Wr.

Κυνάγχη, the quinsy. R. κύων, κυνὸς, ἄγχω: A suffocation of the throat where the patient throws open his mouth like a mad dog. — Also, a dog's collar.

Κυνὰς, dog's meat, — dog-briar: plur. dog-days. — Above.

Κυνέη, dog's skin, — cap, helmet, as made of it, much as Galea from Γαλέη, and Ἰκτιδέη. — Above.

Κυνέω, to kiss;— venerate, as in Psalm 2, ' Kiss the Son lest He be angry.' — R. κυνὸς, of a dog, from its kissing and fawning. The aor. 1 is κύσσα, κύσα, i. e. ἐκύνησα, †κύνσα, κύσσα. (2) To venerate, the first sense : — R. †κύω, κύπτω, to bend forward. (3) R. †γύω, (see Γυλὸς, Γύαλον,) allied to γάω, to take, i. e. to take with the mouth or lips, as Λάω, 'to see' is 'to *take* with the eyes:' and vice versâ Labium, a lip, is from †λαβῶ, i. e. by which we *take*. Γ and Κ as Γῆρυς, Κῆρυξ. (4) ' *Kiss*, Sax. *cyssan*, Su. Goth. *kyssa*, Wel. *cusan*: *Kuss* in some parts of the N. of England : Gr. κύω, κύσσω:' Todd. The fact that there is no present κύσσω, but only aor. 1 κύσσα, seems to establish the priority of the Greek word.

Κύνικοι, the Cynic philosophers, snappish or filthy as (κύνες) dogs.

Κυνόσαργες, a gymnasium at Athens. — Ewing says, from κυνὸς, ἀργός: The white dog.

Κύντερος, more dog-like, impudent, shameless. — Formed from κύων, κυνός: == †κυνώτερος. ' Ain' verò, *canis l*' Terence.

Κύος, Κύημα, the fetus. — R. κύω.

ΚΤΠΑΣΣΙΣ, ' a short man's frock or tunic:' Ldd. — Q. ?

Κύπελλον, ' a *cup*, goblet, bowl. Prop. dimin. of Κύπη: compare Κύββα, Κύβος, Σκύφος:' Dnn. (2) Our *cup*, Sax. *cop*, Du. *kopp*, Span. *copa*, Ir. *capa*: and Wbst. adds the Chald. and Arab. ' Hebr. *kooph*, hollow:' Wr.

Κύπη, ' the same sense as Γύπη, a hollow, a kind of boat:' Dnn. — R. κύω, as Κύβη, &c. See obss. in Κύαθος.

Κύπρις, Venus, ' the *Cyprian* queen,' Pope. ' *Diva potens Cypri*,' Hor. Called Κυπρο-γένεια in Pindar, *Cyprus-born*.

Κύπρος, a corn-measure. — Allied to Κύπη; and to Lat. *cupa*, a cask.

Κυπτάζω, to keep stooping, pry into. — From

Κύπτω, to bend down, stoop.— R. κύω, †γύω whence Γυρὸς, bent, and allied to †Κάω, Καμάρα, Κάμπτω; †Γάω, Γαυσὸς, Γαμφός : to Κυλίω, Κυρτός. Indeed a cavity is a *bend*, and this is seen in various words beginning with ΚΤ—. (2) ' Hebr. *kephee*, to bend:' Wr.

Κυρβαίη, epith. of pottage, ' a doubtful word : otherwise read Γυραίη from γῦρις, Τυρβαίη from τύρβη *turba*, &c.:' Ldd.

Κυρβασία, cónical cap or helmet.—Allied by Dnn. to Κύρβεις, triangular tablets in a pyramidical form and turning on a pivot, having the earliest laws written on the three sides; derived by Heyne from κῦρος, authority, validity. Dnn. with the old Gramm. allies it to Κόρυμβος, Κορυφή, Κόρυς. Κύρβεις are also any other tablets or pillars. 'Κύρβις, a petty-fogging lawyer, i.e. a walking statute-box, Lat. leguleius (from Leges):' Ldd.

Κυρέω, Κύρω, to light upon in the καιρὸς nick of time, hit or chance upon; chance to be, am by chance. — Allied to Καιρὸς, the nick of time, through Κάρα, Κόρυς, Κὰρ, †Κὸρ, Æol. †Κύρ, as γῑνὴ, βῑθὸς, ἀπο- -Ῡδαρίζω. Dnn. allies both Κυρέω and Κύριος to Κόρυς, Κάρα, Κὰρ. Thus Κυρέω would mean 'to be head or master over', as in Κύρμα. (2) Allied to Κυρίσσω, to butt, i.e. to strike (upon). (3) ' Hebr. karah, contingo:' Mrt.

Κυρηβάζω, Κυρίσσω, Κυρίζω, 'to butt with the horns like goats; gen. to strike,' Ldd. — Allied to Κέρας, †βάω, βαίνω. Or rather (like Κῦρος,) to Κόρυς the head: = †κορη-βάζω, to go with the head forward. Υ, as γῑνὴ, ὀνῩμα. And so Dnn. Comp. ὀκρίΒΑΣ, λυκάΒΑΣ.

Κυρηβία, explained by Hesych. 'shells of beans;' gen. husks, chaff, bran. — Perh., (like Κυρηβάζω,) allied to Κόρυς the top; i.e. the mere surface and outside, the coats. B, as κολοΒὸς, κενέΒρἴα, ἐρυσίΒη.

Κύριος, having κῦρος power, — a lord; — valid, decisive, fixed, of things, times, &c.

Κυρίσσω: in Κυρηβάζω.

Κυρκανάω, for Κυκανάω, Κυκάω. So δαΡΒάπτω.

Κύρμα, booty. — R. κύρω : What one lights upon.

Κῦρος, 'supreme power, authority; —validity, security. Akin to Κάρα head, Κόρυς, the head :' Ldd. (2) Κ κύρω, to light on, attain.

Κυρόω, to give κῦρος validity to.

Κυρσάνιος, ' Lacon. for a boy? prob. from κόρος, as Νέος, Νεάνίας :' Ldd. The Υ, as ὀνῩμα, ἄγῩρις. And perh. there was †κόρρος, †κόρσος.

Κυρτεὺς, a fisherman.— From

Κύρτη, Κύρτος, a fishing-basket; Κυρτία, wickerwork :—From the bending and interlacing of the twigs: ' Retia TORTA,' Tibull.—From

Κυρτὸς, curved, bent, arched.—As Γυρόω is 'to render round, to bend', (Dnn.) so γυρωτὸς, †γυρτὸς, κυρτός. Or there was a word †γύρω (as Σύρω, Πτύρω,) †γέγυρται.

Κύρω: in Κυρέω.

Κύσθος, Κύσος, any hollow, like Κύαρ : and from κύω, ἐκύσθην. See Κῦμα.—Also, foramen muliebre.— So Κύστις, the bladder;—bag, pouch.—R. κύω, κέκυσται. See in Κύαθος and Κύσθος.

Κυτμὶς, a kind of plaster.—For the κύτος, Lat. cutis, skin, σκύτος. Festus : ' Cutis is Greek, for they call it Κύτος.' Dnn.: ' From Κύτος is the Latin cutis :' See Κύτος. (Only in Lucian.)

Κύτος, ' from κύω, to hold, contain,—a hollow, as of a shield, hold of a ship;—any vase, urn, vessel,—cavity of the body, trunk :—hence any outer covering, the skin, cutis :' Ldd.

Κύτταρος, like Κύτος, a hollow, cup, vault, cell of a honey-comb.

Κύφελλον, ' akin to Κύπελλον, a cup : pl. hollows of the ears ;—clouds of empty mist ;' Ldd. ' Cavity or empty space,' Dnn. Like Χάος Chaos and Χάσμα a Chasm..

Κυφὸς, bent, bowed.—R. κύπτω, κέκυφα, to bend. So Κῦφος, a hump, bench.

Κύφων, a crooked piece of wood, the bent yoke of a plough :—a heavy log fixed to criminals' necks, keeping the head stooping forward.—Above.

Κυψέλη, a hollow vessel, chest, box, bee-hive. Also, orifice of the ear, as Κύφελλον, being hollow ;—and wax in the ear.—R. ' κύπη, γύπη :' Dnn., who allies κύπη with κύπτω, κύψω. So Mrt. from κυφός. 'A vessel made of bent and woven twigs :' Greg.

Κύψελος, ' the sand-martin, that nestles in holes in banks.—R. κυψέλη :' Dnn.

†Κύω, to kiss : in Κυνέω.

Κύω, Κυέω, 'strictly to hold, contain', Ldd. Allied to †Κάω, Χάζω, †Γάω, Γαστήρ, †Γύω, Γύαλον. See ΓΑΩ.—Also, to hold or carry in the womb, conceive, or be pregnant.

Κύων, g. κυνὸς, canis, a dog : sea-dog ;—dog-star ;— the worst throw at dice, as ' Damnosi subsiluere canes,' Propert., and ' Damnosa canicula' in Persius : — the frænum præputii, ' called 'also Κυνο-δεσμιον, Canīnum vinculum :' Steph. Perhaps from dogs' chains : see spec. on Σκύλαξ 2.: also the membrum virīle itself. And Κύνες are explained by Ldd. the fetlock-joints of horses : by Steph., the bones between the hoof and the ' sura' of horses. Called also Κυνή-ποδες, dogs' feet. Whence Κυνο-βάμονος ἵππου is a horse going on too short pasterns.—And whence is Κύων? Schleusner says : 'Without doubt from κύω, to carry in the womb, for it is a prolific animal.' The Bearer. Improp. for Κύουσα. But so Σκύμνος too according to Schneider. And Ldd. says of 'ΑηδΩΝ : 'Prob. at first a SONGSTRESS, from ἀείδω, but early, a Nightingale.'—Leun. from κύω, to swell (with rage). Thus the R is called the dog's letter, as imitative of its snarl. Snarling, snappish. ' Beware of dogs', says St. Paul metaph.—Some say The Kisser or Fawner, from †κύω, κύσσα, κυνέω : while others reverse this and bring Κυνέω from κυνός.

Κῶας, Κῶς, a soft fleece, skin.—R. †κέω, †κῶ, κεῖμαι, (as in Κῶμα, Κοιμάω,) to lie on. From the habit of lying on skins. ' Effultus tergo stratisque jacebat Velleribus,' Virg. Hence the phrase, ' Quiescere in propriâ pelle.' 'Εν κώεσιν οἰῶν 'Εδραθεν, Hom.: He slept on skins of sheep.—Or †κέω, to place or put, viz. over other things. Hom.: ἐπ-εθάλετο μέγα κῶας, δίφρον καὶ κῶας ἐπ' αὐτῶν, κατ-εστόρεσεν βοέην αὐτὰρ ὕπερθεν. (2) 'Hemsterh. from ὄϊς, Fόϊς : the F represented by Κ:' Dnn.?

Κώδεια, Κώδη, the head, as Κόττα ;—spec. a poppy-head. Also, the broad part of an hour-glass.—'R. κόττα :' Ldd.; then †κόδδα.

Κώδιον, a little κῶς.

Κώδων.—ΚΩδων and ΚΩθων (in form as 'Ρώθων,) seem both allied to ΚΟῖλος hollow (just as Dnn. allies ΚΩμη to ΚΟῖτη,): the one being convex, the other concave,—just as Κῦμα a wave and Κύαθος a cup are both referred by Liddell to κύω. Κώδων is a bell and a trumpet, Κώθων is a goblet. Κώδων may also be allied to Κώδη the head ; and Κώθων to Κοτύλη a cup.

Κωδωνίζω, to try horses by bells to see if they will stand the battle-din, and soldiers by striking a bell which they were to answer :—also to try the purity of a coin by the sound.—Above.

Κώθων : in Κώδων.

Κωκύω, to lament.—'R. κόχος, a full stream :' Mrt.: To pour forth a *flood* of tears. '*Rivers* of water run down mine eyes :' O.T. Both words allied to χύω, to pour : by redupl. (2) Lenn. from the sound.

Κωλέα, Κωλῆ, the hind-quarter, ham. All derive it from κῶλον, a limb, but used specially of the extremities. Thus 'Hands and κῶλα legs :' 'The fore κῶλα legs.' So Ldd.: 'Κῶλον, gen. of the extremities.'—Κωλῆ is also τὸ αἰδοῖον, perh. as the extremity. Or allied to Κῶλον, membrum (virile). Τὸ κῶλον.

Κάλην, 'the hollow or bend of the knee,' Ldd.—From κῶλον, the hinder-part, as in Κωλέα. (2) Allied to Κοῖλον, hollow.

ΚΩΛΙΑΣ, '*Colias,* a prom. of Attica, with a temple of Venus, invoked by courtesans ;—a feast of Ceres ;—potters' clay of high repute, dug at the same place :' Ldd. And Κωλῶτις is Venus in Lycophron.—Perhaps allied to Κωλῆ, τὸ αἰδοῖον. But ?

Κῶλον, a limb or member of the body ;—of a sentence, marked by a *colon, semi-colon.* Also 'one limb or half of the course in racing,' Ldd. Other meanings see in Κωλέα.—As Μέλος a limb is allied to Μέρος a part, division, so Κῶλον is Κόλον, docked, mutilated. Similarly Dnn. from κολούω to curtail.

Κόλον : the same as Κόλον 2.

Κωλύω, to impede, prevent.—Prop. to disable the κῶλα legs, much as Im-pedio and 'Εμ-ποδίζω. (2) R. κόλος, mutilated. Dnn. allies with it Κολούω, Κολάζω.

Κῶμα, a deep sound sleep.—R. †κέω, †κῶ, κεῖμαι, κοιμάω to make to rest.

Κώμη, a small open town or village,—a quarter of a city.—'Allied to Κεῖμαι, Κοιμάω, Κοίτη :' Dnn. 'In ancient Greece, when all were husbandmen, that place was called κώμη to which men retired in the evening to sleep :' Valck. 'Errabat sylvis, rursusque ad limina notâ Ipse domum serâ quamvis se in nocte ferebat :' Virg. (2) From the same root as Κοινὸς, common : which see.

Κῶμος, 'a band of revellers, who after a feast go through the streets singing and dancing ; — revelry, banquet ;—a band, even of mourners.—R. κώμη : as in Bacchanalian processions they went from village to vil-

lage :' Dnn. (2) 'Prop. a deep sleep, κῶμα, with which men lie oppressed when heavy with wine.' Valck.—'From the lying down on couches at feasts :' Damm. I.e. from κεῖμαι, κοιμάω.

Κώμυς, ὕθος, a bundle, truss ; — marsh where reeds grow thick with tangled roots :—a lark, with its tuft on its head.—Lenn. from κομίζω, to carry,—or allied to it. (2) As Γῆρυς, Κῆρυξ, so Κώμυς from γόμος, a freight. (3) As Θωμὸς, Θημών, a heap, from †θεώ, θῶ, τίθημι, to put (together), so Κώμυς from †κέω, κεῖμαι, &c., to lay (together).

Κωμῳδὸς, a comedian.—Some say, as going from κώμη village to village, singing ᾠδὰς songs. 'The village song', says Bentley of Κωμῳδία. (2) Hemst. from κῶμος.

Κωνάω, to daub with κῶνος pitch :—to turn round as a κῶνος top.

Κώνειον, hemlock.—As ἀρΩγὸς from ἀρήγω, ἀνΩγω from ἀνάσσω, so κΩνειον from καίνω, κανῶ, to kill. (2) R. κωνάω, to turn round (the brain with vertigo).

Κῶνος, a cone, pine-cone, cone of a helmet,—a spinning top, from its *conical* form ;—pitch from the pine, but Dnn. from the earthen furnaces in Sweden and W. Bothnia for preparing pitch being *conical.*—Κῶνος from †κένω, κένσαι, κεντέω, †κέκονα : from ending in a *sharp* point. (2) 'Hebr. ken, conus, lancea :' Becm.

Κωνωπεῖον, a gnat-gauze in beds, *canopy.*—From Κώνωψ, ὦπος, a gnat.—Bp. Blomf. says : 'R. κῶνος, ὤψ : for, they say, it has a conical nose. A pretty idea, and perhaps true.' (2) With Κῶνος, from †κένω, †κέκονα, κένσαι, to prick : -ωψ being a termination.

Κῷος or Κῶος, 'the highest throw with the pastern-bone, counting six,—opposed to Χῖος, counting one : hence the proverb 'Κῶος against Χῖον,' and also probably 'Not Κῶος but Χῖος :' Ldd.—'From Κὼς, the isle of Cos :' Dnn.

Κώπη, handle of an oar, of a sword, of an olive-mill, of a torch.—Damm says : 'R. κόπτω, κέκοπα : For we lay hold of it in cutting with a sword or in striking the water with an oar.' (2) 'As Λαβὴ from λαμβάνω, so Κώπη from †κάπτω, κάπω, capio :' Dnn. Lat. capulus. Ω, as ἄλασσω, ἄνωγα.

Κώρυκος, a leathern sack : allied to Γωρυτός. 'R. χωρέω, to contain ·' Dnn.

Κῶς : in Κῶας.

Κωτίλλω, to chat, prate, prattle, talk down, talk over, cheat.—From κοτύλη, a goblet : To chat ἐπὶ κοτύλαις over one's cups. Somewhat as Isa. 24. 9 : 'They shall not *drink wine with a song.*' (2) Passow from κόπτω, κόττω : to tease and bother with idle talk. (3) Lenn. from κῶς : from companions lying on the same extended hide :—chatting : better if the gen. was κωτός. (4) Our *quoth.*

Κωφὸς, battered or blunted in body or mind, deaf, dumb, silly.—R. Κόπτω, κέκοφα. So Obtuse from Obtundo. Æschylus has φρενῶν κεκομμένος, frenzy-struck.

Κωχεύω, 'mostly used in 'Ανα-κωχεύω', (Dnn.) to hold back. See 'Ανακωχή.

Λ.

Λα-, Λαι-, very. — R. λάκκος, as in Λακκό-πρωκτος. The I in Λαι- seems introduced as in λαιθαργος, αἰόλος, αἰθύσσω, &c. (2) 'Some from λάω, †λάβω, capio:' Dnn., à capacitate. (3) R. λαῦρος or λάβρος, mighty, powerful.

Λᾶας, Λᾶς, a stone. — R. †λάω, λάζομαι, to take: One that you can take in your hands, as opp. to a large bit of rock. As Χερμάδιον.

Λαβδακίζω, to mispronounce the Λ, called Λάβδα as well as Λάμβδα.

†Λαβέω, to take: R. λάω, λαύω and λάϝω, †λάβω. See Λάω.

Λαβή, a handle by which we take, &c. — Above.

Λάβραξ, a sea-wolf. — And

Λαβρεύομαι, to talk boisterously and boastfully. — From

Λάβρος, furious, boisterous. — R. †λαβῶ: As Rapio, Rapidus. — Also, greedy, voracious, either as above: or from λά-βορος from λα, βορά, food.

Λαβύρινθος, a labyrinth, esp. the Cretan one; — a maze, net : — sea-snail, as coiled up. — The first sense may be a 'net,' and so may well justify Lennep's deriv. from †λαβῶ: 'Aptus ad capiendum.' Then the other senses. Much in form like Ἀσάμινθος. (2) Jablonski makes it an Egyptian word.

Λάγανον, 'a kind of cake baked in oil', Dnn. — From λα, γάνος, deliciæ, anything causing delight. Thus Κρηναῖον γάνος, 'the fountain delight, viz. a grateful draught,' (Dnn.)

Λαγαρός, 'slack, lank, sunken, thin, flaccid, hollow. Akin to Λακαρός:' Ldd. and Dnn. But Γ and Π? — Rather, lank and sunken like a Λαγὸς, hare. (3) From λαγάν, says Ewing. (4) R. λήγω, ξω, †έλαγον, to leave off, stop, i.e. to be slack: allied to Λαγγάζω, to remiss. (5) Allied to our lag.

Λαγγάζω, &c. to be remiss, loiter, tarry. — See above. (2) Some compare longus: to be long about a thing. And to lag.

Λάγδην, == λάξ. See Λακτίζω.

Λᾱγέτης, i.e. λαοῦ ἡγέτης, leader of the people.

Λάγηνος, Λαγ̄ῑνος, lagēna, a bottle, flagon. — R. †λάω, λάζομαι, †λέλακα, to take, hold. Compare Λάκκος, Λάκος. So Ldd. derives Λαγὼν from †λάω. (2) Greg. from λα, γάω, †γύω, capio, (whence Γαστήρ, Γυλιὸς, &c.): 'Valde capax.' Forcell. explains Lagēna 'vas fictile CAPAX.' And see Λεκάνη. (3) Todd mentions Hebr. lag, and our flagon, French flacon.

Λαγκία, the Lat. lancea.

Λάγνος, Λάγνης, lewd, lustful. — R. λα-, γυνή: λά--γυνος: Valdè mulierosus. — (2) 'R. λα, γόνος: Or better R. λαγνὸς, a hare:' Dnn.

Λαγὸς, Λαγὼς, Λαγωὸς, a hare : — a bird, rough-

91

footed like a hare. — Not badly Mrt. derives λαγωὸς, for λαϝωὸς, from λα, οὖας, from its large ears. As Γοῦνος for Οὖνος. (2) 'Λα, γάω, †γενέω: Fœcundus, multi--parus:' Greg. Whence Dnn. derives Λάγνος from Λαγώς.

Λαγχάνω, (as Μανθάνω,) †Λαχέω, †Λήχω, †Λέγχω, λέλογχα, to get hold of by lot or fate; — obtain as one's share; — fall to one's lot. — R. †λάω, †λέλακα, †λαβῶ, to take (out a lot,) to take (by lot). (2) Wacht. notices Germ. gluck, good fortune, our luck, Swed. lycka. 'Hebr. lachah, he received:' Mrt.

Λαγὼν, the λαγαρὸς loose and boneless cavity below the ribs, — any hollow. — Ldd. from †λάω, to hold. (2) R. λαγαρὸς, †λαγαρὰν, Λαγών.

Λαγωὸς, Λαγώς: in Λάγος.

Λάζομαι, to take: λάω.

Λάζω, to be injurious to, insult. — Contr. from Λακτίζω. See Λαχμός (2) Allied to Λάζυμαι. 'Αἱ νόσοι Λάζονται, corripiunt et invadunt:' Steph.

ΛΑΘΑΡΓΟΣ, a shred of leather. — Q. ? (Only in Nicand. Θ. 422.)

†Λαθέω, Λανθάνω, †Λήθω, to escape or elude the notice of, — cause others not to know or to remember, make to forget. — R. λάω, †ἐλάθην, λάζομαι, †λαβῶ, capio, de-cipio i.e. de-capio, take in, deceive. (2) 'Hebr. lat, clam:' Mrt.

Λάθρα, -η, by stealth, without the knowledge of. — Above.

Λαι-: See in Λα-.

Λαία, stones used as weights in the upright loom. — R. λᾶας.

Λᾱῖγξ, a small λᾶας stone.

Λαιδρός, bold, impudent. — I.e. †λα-ιδρός: λα, ἰδέω video: Looking much at. Opposed in sense to Αἰδώς i.e. ἀ-ιδώς. (2) R. λαι-, δρῶ: Active, quick, ready, &c.

Λαίθαργος, Λήθαργος, Λάθαργος, 'forgetting, — said of dogs, cunning, [i.e. evading, shuffling, as in †Λαθέω, 'biting secretly', Ldd.]: Subst. the lethargy. R. λήθη': Dnn. — In the sense of cunning, Wright says 'secretly mischievous', adding ἀργός, quick. See λῑτΑΡΓΟΣ.

Λαικάζω, to be a prostitute, or associate with such. — R. λαὸς, λαϊκός: Make oneself public. So Λαϊκόω is to make common. (2) R. λαι, †κάζω, κέκασται, to adorn, set out.

Λαῖλαψ, απος, a hurricane. — Redupl. †λάπτω, λάψω, whence ἀ-λαπάζω to consume. (2) 'R. λαι-, λάπτω:' Valck.

Λαῖμα, 'in Aristoph. Αv. 1563, seemingly a play on the words Λῆμα, Αἷμα, and Λαιμός:' Ldd. and Dnn.

Λαιμάσσω, to swallow greedily, from

Λαιμὸς, the throat. — 'Perh. akin to Λάμος, abyss,

gulf: whence Λαμυρὸs, full of abysses, hence gluttonous; and Λαμία, *Lamia*, a monster said to feed on man's flesh:' Ldd. (2) R. λάω, λέλαμαι, to take. 'Allied to λαύω:' Lenn. (3) ' Hebr. *leem*, to eat:' Wr.

Λαῖνα, the same as Χλαῖνα, as ἀράχνη became ' aranea', and compare Φεῦ, Heu. See Λιαρόs.

Λαῖον, Doric for Λήϊον.

Λαιὸs, the left. — On the same principle as 'Αριστερὸs, left, from ἄριστος, best, so Λαιὸs for Λαϊὸs (as Λέϊτος, Λεῖτος,) from λάω, λιλΑΙομαι, to wish: Desirable, good, as from Λῶ to 'wish' is Λωῖων, 'better.' See Λαρόs.

Λαισήϊον, ' a shield covered with raw hides: from λάσιος. Others from λαιόs: The left-hand armor:' Ldd.

Λαίσπαις, for λαί-παις, λα-παῖς. Σ, as in λάΣταυρος, δίΣκος, μιΣγόω, λέΣχη.

Λαῖτμα, the deep sea. — R. λα-, †ῗω ῗται: i. e. the great passage. Compare 'Ισθμόs. See the next.

Λαῖφος, ' a shabby tattered garment; then gen. cloth, esp. sailcloth:' Ldd. — I see not why we should reject λα, †ῗπτω †ῗφα, †ῖπτομαι, to hurt, harm: Much injured, according to the meaning of the word. ''Αμφὶ δέ λαῖφος Ἕσσω, I will put on you such a garment as seeing you wear a man shall hate:' Hom. See Λαῖτμα. (2) Dnn. allies it to Λεῖος, Λῆδος.

Λαιψηρὸs, swift. — R. λα, αἰψηρόs. (2) ' R. λαι–, ψαίρω, to brush:' Ldd.

Λακερὸs, tattered: R. λακίs. Talkative: R. λακέω.

Λάκέω, Λακάζω, Λάσκω, Ληκέω, to crash, rattle, ring; — crack, break with a λακὶς crack or crash, — scream, howl, speak loud. — Dnn. well compares 'Ράκος (a rag) and Λακίs, ' one liquid letter being exchanged for another', as λεῖβιον, ἔρις, 'Pls, Lis. 'Ράκος he also allies to 'Ρήγνῡμι to break, 'Ράσσω, ἔρραγον, 'Ρηγή, 'Ρήγμα. Hence then Λακέω, is †'Ρακέω, to break, burst, rend, &c. (2) ' Chald. *leka*, frangi:' Mrt.

Λακίs, a burst or rent with a crack, — as 'Ράκος, rags, tatters. —See in Λακέω.

Λάκκος, Λάκος, a pit, hollow, pit, tank, *lacus*. — 'R. λακεῖν, to burst, break asunder': Dnn. So Mrt. from Λακίζω, Λακίs. (2) R. λάω, λέλακα, λάζομαι, 'capio, comprehendo', as a 'hollow.' (3) So ' Hebr. *lekee*, to hold:' Wr.

Λακτίζω, to kick with the heel or foot. Allied are Λάγδην and Λάξ, with the heel. Voss from λήγω, ξω, λήγω, ξω, to ' leave off, end', (Ldd.) Λάξ, i. e. Where the foot ends. (2) Steph. brings all from Λάζω, to insult.

Λαλαγέω, as follows.

Λαλέω, Λαλαγέω, to chatter, prattle, talk, speak. ' Lat. *lallo*, our *lull*, *lullaby*:' Ldd. From the sound λὰλ λὰλ. Germ. *lallen*, ' corruptè et impeditè loqui ut pueri:' Wacht.

Λάλλαι, babbling pebbles of the brook. — Above.

Λάμβα, ═ λαμία.

92

Λαμβάνω: for †λαβέω, as †Μαθέω, Μανθάνω; †Λαχέω, Λαγχάνω. Herod. has λάμψομαι.

ΛΑΜΒΔΑ, the letter L: ' Hebr. *lamed*.'

Λαμία, a voracious monster, and a shark : — in Λαιμόs. See also

Λάμος, an abyss, gulph. — 'R. λάω, [λέλαμαι,] λαμβάνω, to receive, contain:' Dnn. Much as Ψάω, Ψάμμος.

Λαμπάδιον, ' bandage of lint for wounds, as made of *lamp*-wick; — called also Λύχνωμα and Ἐλ-λυχνιωτὸs μοτόs:' Steph. — From

Λαμπὰs, άδος, a lamp: R. λάμπω. — ' A warlike engine, perh. for throwing combustibles:' Dnn.

Λάμπη: the same as Λάπη.

Λαμπήνη, a covered chariot. — ' Prob. from ἀπήνη, λ prefixed:' Ldd. And M in λαμβάνω. (2) Some make it a showy, brilliant, royal carriage, from λάμπω. See Λαμπουρίs.

Λαμπουρίs, a fox. So Λάμπ-ουρε κύων, Theoc. having a white or brilliant tail: λάμπω, οὐρά.

Λάμπω, to cause to shine. — For †λάπω, (as in †λαβῶ, λάΜψομαι,) allied by Lenn. to Λέπω, Λύω, &c. to disclose, reveal, Λύκη, Λύχνος. (2) R. λάω, to see: To make to be seen, to disclose by shining. Λάμπω as Πέμπω. (3) R. λα, φάω, φῶ, φαίνω, to shine. M as in λαΜπήνη. (4) 'Chald, *lamprd*, a torch:' Dahle.

Λαμυρὸs, 'full of abysses, hence gluttonous : — [audacious,] bold, wanton, coquettish, piquant, arch. R. λάμος:' Ldd. and Dnn. (2) R. λαιμὸs, the throat : Mrt.

Λανθάνω: in †Λαθέω.

Λάξ: in Λακτίζω.

Λαξεύω, to cut or polish stone. — R. λᾶs, ξέω.

Λάξις, as Λάχεσις, what is allotted. — R. †λάχω, †λέξω, λαγχάνω. Herod. has λάξομαι. Or Λάχεσις, Λάχεσις, Λάξις.

Λαὸs, a people, the people. — R. λάω, λάζομαι, (See Λέγω,) prehendo, comprehendo, colligo, to collect : A collection of men. (2) ' See Pind. Ol. 9. 66 for a fanciful deriv. from λᾶαs a stone, founded on the tradition of Deucalion:' Dnn.

Λαπάζω, 'Α-λαπάζω, to empty, plunder; — empty the bowels. — R. λάπτω, to lap up. ' Now shall this company *lick up* all that are round about us, as the ox *licketh up* the grass:' Numb. 22. 4. (2) Dnn. from Λάω, to take up.

Λάπαθος, a pit, pitfall. — R. λαπάζω to empty out, make a vacuum.

Λαπάρα, 'the loins, the abdomen, i. e. the soft part of the body:' Dnn. From

Λαπαρὸs, the same as Λαγαρὸs, slack, loose. — R. λαπάζω, to evacuate.

Λάπη, phlegm, — any filth, damp, &c. — Allied to Λαπάζω, to evacuate.

Λαπίζω, to vaunt.—Dnn. and Ldd. say with Eustath., from the Λαπίθαι, *Lapithæ*, who were bullies and boasters. Or allied to Λαπάζω to empty: Make empty boasts. Mrt. from λα, ἕπω. ?

Λάπτω, 'prop. to *lap* as dogs, drink greedily. R. λάω:' Dnn.: to take, as †Λάω, Λάπτω.

Λαρινὸς, 'fed [deliciously] luxuriously, fattened. R. λαρός:' Dnn. As χαλΙΝΟΣ, ἐχΙΝΟΣ.

Λάριξ, the larch-tree. — ' R. λαρός: from the sweetness of its odor:' Forcell.

Λαρὶς, Λάρος, a gull; perh. allied to Λάρυγξ, the throat.— ' Akin to Λάβρος,' Dnn.— R. λάω, λάζομαι, to take.

Λαρίσαιος, 'a kind of kettle, invented or made at *Larissa*. So Τάναγρα a kettle, and the town Tanagra:' Ldd.

Λάρκος, a wicker-basket.— As †Μάω, Μάργος, and Λάω, Largus, so nearly λάω, λάρκος: as taking, containing things, or that which you take in your hand, like Φορμὸς from Φέρω. So λαιθΑΡΓΟΣ. (2) R. λάριξ, ικος: As prim. made of larch.

Λάρναξ, a coffer, urn, — a kind of vehicle, — vessel, ship.— Allied to Λάρκος. (2) As made of Λάριξ larch.

Λαρὸς, grateful, agreeable, delicious, sweet. — Hemsterh. from λάω, to wish: Desirable. See Λπίων. (2) R. λα, ἄρω, apto, ἥραρεν, he suited, &c.

Λάρυγξ, the *larynx*, swallow, gullet. — Passow from λάω, to take. Or λαύω, to enjoy.

Λᾶς, for Λᾶας.

Λάσανον, chamber-pot, nightstool. Also 'a stand for a pot, grid-iron:' Ldd. — Simply from λάω, λέλασαι, to take, contain. So Βάσανος. (2) Mrt. from λάσιος, rough. Note the senses of Εχῖνος.

Λάσθη, insult. — R. λάζω, to insult; or, as that seems to make λάξω, R. λάζομαι, ' corripio et invado', (Steph.). (2) R. λάσκω, to yell. (3) ' Hebr. *latz*. to mock :' Mrt.

Λάσιος, 'rough, hairy, shaggy, woolly: bushy: only diff. from Δασὺς, (δασέος,) in dialect, Λ and Δ being often exchanged:' Ldd. As Δάκρυμα, Lacryma. (2) R. λάω, λέλασαι: easy to take, lay hold of : opp. to smooth.

Λάσκω: in Λακέω.

Λάσταυρος, 'lewd, lit. hairy like a bull: λάσιος ταῦρος:' Dnn.—Or λα, ταῦρος. Σ, as in λαῖλαπς, βόστρυχος.

Λάταξ, the liquor which fell from the cup in the play of Κότταβος, — and its noise.—' Akin to *latex*, *laticis*:' Ldd. ' Perh. from the sound:' Lenn. ' The learned Grammarians derived it from λα, and ταξ, τὲξ, imitative sound of water falling:' Scheid.

Λάτρις, a hired servant, slave. — Ruhnk. from λάω, λέλαται, to take, receive (wages). Lenn. as taken in war. (2) ' R. λα, τρέω, *tremo*: Mal. 1. 6. Eph. 6. 5: Be obedient to your masters with fear and *trembling*:' Pkh.

Λάτρον, pay, hire. — Above.

Λατύσσω, to clap, strike. — Dnn. from Λάταξ, liquor thrown into a basin with a splash.

Λαυκανίη, the same as Λαιμὸς, the throat. — Dnn. from λάω, †λαύω, †λέλαυκα, to take, or to enjoy.

Λαύρα, a street, quarter of a town, alley ; — ravine, —

— drain, sewer; — cloister. — Steph. says : ' It may seem to be put for a broad way, from λαύρος': λαύρος taken as ' capax' from λάω, ' capio.' (2) Hesych. from λαὺς, (λαερά): Frequented by the people, as Λεώ-βατος, Λεω-φόρος.

Λαῦρος, the same as Λάβρος.

†Λαύω, Ἀπο-λαύω, to receive good or evil from :— R. λάω, †λαύω, λαβῶ, λαμβάνω, to take. As Ψάω, Ψαύω.

Λάφυρα, spoils taken in war. — R. λαφύσσω: As emptying and exhausting cities. And allied to Λαπάζω, ἀλαπάζω.

Λαφύσσω, to swallow greedily.—R. λάπτω, λέλαφα, to *lap* up. (2) Λα, ἀφύσσω.

Λαφρία, for λαφύρία (above): said of Minerva and Diana. ' The forager,' Ldd. ' Gatherer of booty:' Dnn.

Λαχαίνω, to dig. — Dnn. from λακὶς, a rent, fissure. Valck. from λα, †χάω, χαίνω, χάσμα, an opening.

Λάχανον, garden herbs in dug ground, opp. to wild. R. λαχαίνω, λαχανῶ. Valck. says, as dug out of the ground.

Λάχεια, 'epith. of an island: for Ελαχεῖα from ἐλαχὺς: little, small, low ; some even read Ελάχεια. Some from λαχαίνω: good soil, easily dug, opp. to rocky:' Ldd.

Λαχμὸς, = λακτισμὸς from λακτίζω. From λάζω.

Λαχμὸς, destiny, λάχος.

Λάχνη, wool, down; — leafage.—' Akin to Ἄχνη': Dnn. With λα prefix. (2) ' R. λα, χνοῦς:' Scap.

Λάχος, lot, portion: λαγχάνω, †λαχέω.

ΛΑΩ, Λάζομαι, †Λαβέω, Λαμβάνω, &c., †ΛΕΩ, whence Λεία, to lay hold of, take: — to take with the eyes, to see, as Ὄμμασιν λαβὼν, Soph., ' *Capies* oculis', Virg. — to take with the mind, wish, (Compare †Ελα, Ελδομαι,): — to take with the palate, to enjoy. — Primitive words, unless from †ἐλάω, to take, then †ἐλάω, λάω. Or even from †ἐλάω, ἐλαίνω, as in Λε-ηλατέω. to drive off and take booty. Some refer λάω, to *see*, to †γλάω, γλαύσσω, γλήνη.

Λέα, Λεία, 'a stone used by weavers as a weight, any weight. R. λᾶας, [λεᾶς,] :' Dnn.

Λέαινα, a lioness: λέων.

Λεαίνω, Λειαίνω, Λειόω, to make λεῖον smooth.

Λεβηρὶς, a skin or slough; = λεπηρὶς from λέπω.

Λέβης, a caldron, boiler, basin, pan, urn. — R. λείβω, to pour libations : into which liquid is poured. Thus Servius explains *lebes* ' a vessel into which water *falls* while we are washing our hands.'

Λέγαι, 'lewd women: akin to Λέχος, [Λέγομαι] :' Ldd.

Λεγεὼν, the Lat. *legio*, from *lego*, λέγω.

Λέγνη, hem, edge. — For λήγνη, ληγάνη, from λήγω, to leave off. So Εδνα for Ηδνα, κεδνὸς for κηδνός.

Λέγω, 'to gather, collect: gather *words*, speak: gather *ideas*, infer, think: gather *facts*, recollect, affirm: [gather numbers, compute, calculate:] Λέγομαι, to gather myself together so as to be at rest, lie down:' Dr. Jones.— From †λέω, (as Ψέω, Ψέγω,) whence Λεία, allied to Λάω, Λάζομαι, ' prehendo, comprehendo', to take up one after another. Curiously Λέγω came to mean in Latin Lego, to collect *words*, to READ. · Festus derives *Lectus* (Λέκτρον,) from 'gathering' leaves to lie on. Here then is another account of Λέγομαι above. (2) Ldd. makes Λέγω the same as our *lay*, *lecgan* Sax., *leggen* Dutch, *lagjan* Goth., to place: ' 1. To *lay* asleep; 2. to *lay* in order, arrange, gather, pick out; 3. to reckon among, count; 4. to account, tell.' (3) 'Hebr. *leek*, to collect, summon:' Wr.

Λεία, Λητη, Λητς, booty: Λητζομαι, to plunder.— Damm for ἕλεια from †ἕλω, to take. Or for ἕλεια allied to †ελάω, ελαύνω, ἤλαται, to drive; whence Λε-ηλατέω, to drive away booty: for Λει-ηλατέω. (2) R. †λέω, †λάω, to take.

Λειαίνω: in Λεαίνω.

Λείβω, to pour, pour forth, *libo*, make a *libation* ;— trickle, moisten. — Allied to Λύω, to untie, let go free, as Dr. J. defines Pour ' to *LET* some liquid out of a vessel.' R. †λέω, λύω, as στΕΙΒΩ, ἀμΕΙΒΩ. For †λΕω compare λΕίπω, λΕπω.

Λειμαξ, Λειμών, where water trickles through, i. e. a moist or low grassy place, meadow ;— and like Κῆπος and Hortus for τὰ αἰδοῖα γυναικεῖα.—R. λείβω, λέ-λειμμαι, †λείμμαξ. ' So a fountain λείβεται, when it flows gently:' Hemst.

Λείμαξ, a shell-less snail: from its slow-flowing or oozing moisture. See just above.

Λείμμα, a remnant: λείπω, λέλειμμαι.

Λεῖος, smooth. — Plato notices in his Cratylus the slippery smooth nature of the letter Λ, and hence deduces Λεῖος, Λιπαρός, &c. Rather however ' rubbed smooth.' See the obsol. †λέω, †λίω. And Λισσός, Λιμήν, Λίμνη. (2) ' Hebr. *lehee*, smoothness:' Wr.

Λείπω, to leave. — Allied through †λέω to Λήγω to cease, and through †λίω to Λιάζομαι, to separate from, remove, and to Λύω. So Λέπω, prop. to separate and sever the outside of a tree. (2) Sax. *lafan*, Icel. *leifa*, to *leave*.

Λείριον, a lily. — R. λειρός, pale.

Λειρός, thin, wan, thin in color, pale. — 'R. λεῖος:' Mrt. Well, for λεῖος is ' rubbed smooth,' (Dnn.) ' rubbed thin.'

Λεῖτος, Λεῖτος, of or for the λεὼς people, common.

Λειχήν, tree-moss, moss-like plant, *lichen*. Also, a *lichen-like* eruption on the skin, scurvy, &c.—Mrt. from λείχω. Exactly as Persius: 'Quorum imagines *lambunt Hedera* sequaces.' (2) Allied to Λεῖος, smooth. ' The surface is sometimes quite *smooth*: sometimes provided with hairs &c.'. Enc. Brit.

Λείχω and Λίζω, to lick.— From the obsol. †λέω, (See Λεία,) †λίω, λάω, to take up, λάπτω, to lap up. So στΕΙΧΩ, κΙΧΩ, νΗΧΩ. (2) Our *lick*, *leoken* Dutch, *liccian* Sax. ' Chald. *lechac*:' Mrt. ' Hebr. *lehek*:' Wr.

Λείψανον, remnant: λείπω, ψω.

Λεκάνη, Λέκος, a dish, pot, pan. — Allied to Lat. *lagena* by Liddell, who notices the Doric Λακάνη. So Λάγηνος is a bottle : which see. And Λάκκος, Λάκος. (2) The Doric form Mrt. from λα, χαίνω, χανῶ, to lie open. (3) Perhaps, as ἕΠομαι, ἕΚομαι, †theQUor, seQUor: ἵΠΠος, ἵΚΚος, eQUus: so λέΚος is allied to λέΠις, a bark, shell. So Ποῖος, Κοῖος. And

Λέκιθος, pease-soup. Also, the yolk .of an egg: as thought by Suidas to be like *shelled* pease or pulse in color. — Perh. λέκιθος is †λέπιθος, (K and Π as above,) i. e. *shelled* pease. (2) R. λέκος above. We say, Pot luck.

Λέκτρον, a couch.—R. λέγομαι, λέλεκται, to lie down. See in Λέγω.

Λελίημαι, to strive eagerly: λελιημένος, zealous, eager. — ' Prob. for λελίλημαι, λελιλημένος, from λιλαίομαι, to long for:' Ldd. ' Adopted by Buttm.:' Dnn.

Λέμβος, a skiff. Also ' a ship's cock-boat ; and met. a parasite': Ldd. — R. λέπω, as Τύμβος from τύφω, Θάμβος from θάπω or θήπω. Like Λεπτὸς, it means slender ; and has the sense of Λεπτόδομος, built or constructed lightly ; or of Λεπτηκής, thin at the point.

Λέμφος, mucus: allied by Ldd. to Λάμπη.

Λέντιον, the Lat. *linteum*, from *linum*, Λίνον.

Λέπαδνον, ' a broad leathern thong, fastening the yoke under the neck, and passing between the fore-legs to join the girth,' Ldd. — ' From λεπάζω, decortico,' Bp. Blomf.: Peeled hide. Formed like 'Αλαπαδνόν.

Λέπας, ' from λέπω: a bare rock;—also a limpet, from its clinging to the rock:' Ldd.

Λεπαστή, a drinking-cup, shaped like a limpet-shell. —Above.

Λεπὶς, scale, rind: Λέπρα, *leprosy* or scaly skin. —And Λεπτὸς, peeled, husked ;— hence fine, light, thin, slight, refined. —R. λέπω, λέλεπται.

Λέπω, to strip off the skin, husk, pod, rind :— to thresh soundly.— From †λέω, λύω, to loosen: allied to Λήγω, Λείπω, Λιάζομαι. So †βλάω, βλέΠΩ. And δρέΠΩ.

Λεσβιάζω, to imitate the *Lesbians*.

Λεσπὶς, the same as 'Ελεσπίς.

Λέσχη, as ἔσχον, from λέγω, λέλεχα, for λέχη : a resort for talking and gossiping ;—talk, conversation, deliberation. (2) Lenn. allies it to Λέχος. Thus Cubiculum is ' a part of the house in which we both *pass the day* and sleep the night:' Forcell. (3) 'Chald. *lischan*, lingua:' Mrt. ' Or Hebr. *lischcah*, conclave:' Dahler.

Λευγάλεος, ' in sad plight, wretched, —sad, gloomy, dismal, mournful ; allied to *lugeo*, (*lugubris*) :' Ldd. and Dnn. And to Gr. λύζω, λέλυγα, to sob, λύγδην. Compare πΕυκάλιμος.

Λευκανίη, Ion. of Λαυκανία.

Λεύκη, the white poplar; white leprosy.—From

Λευκὸς, bright, clear, white. — Damm : ' R. λύκος,

the sun'. E as in λΕυγάλεος, πΕυκάλιμος. So allied to *lux*, *lucis*. (**2**) R. λεύσσω, †λέλευκα, to see: Clear to the view. To this and to Γλαυκὸς Dnn. allies it.

Λευρὸς, smooth, level.—' Ion. for Λεῖος:' Dnn. ' From λεῖος:' Ldd.

Λεὺς, Dor. of Λᾶας, stone.

Λεύσσω, to look or gaze on.—Allied to Λάω to see, i.e. to TAKE with the eyes: through †λέω, whence Λεία, &c. In form as πράΣΣΩ. Mrt. adds ὄσσε, with the eyes. ?

Λεύω, to stone.—R. λεύς.

Λέχος, a bed, &c. *lectus*.—R. λέγομαι, act. λέλεχα. So Λέκτρον from λέλεκται.

Λέχριος, slanting.—R. λέγομαι, to lie down, as Λέχος: So Tecta cubantia, in Lucretius, are explained ' which hang sideways.' Damm : ' One who bends himself seems as if he meant to lie on the ground.' Compare Cumbo with Κύπτω.

Λεχὰ, a woman in λέχος child-bed.

†ΛΕΩ, Lat. †*leo*, *levi*, †ΛΙΩ, whence Λισσὸς, †ΛΟΩ, as in Λοέω, ΛΤΩ, Primitive words, prim. to rub, scrape, —scrape off, undo, loosen,— rub away in smoothing or polishing, smooth.— Possibly allied to Λάω, to take (off the surface).—Plato deduces the sense of *smooth* from the *liquid* nature of the letter Λ.

Λέων, *leo*, a *lion*.—The seizer, from λάω, λάζομαι, †λέω, whence Λεία. So Κρέων, the ruler.— Or, The seer : from λάω, †λέω, λεύσσω, to see. ' A very sharp-sighted beast, say Bochart and Manetho:' Pkh.

Λεὼς, the same as Λαός.

Λέως, entirely, wholly.— Herm. from λεῖος: 'smoothly: much like the vulgarism Slick away:' Ldd.

Λεωργὸς, audacious.—R. λέως, entirely, ἔργω ἔοργα to do : Who does entirely what he pleases. The use of Λιτουργὸς in this sense gives much support to this deriv. (**2**) R. λα, ἔοργα.

Λήγω, to cause to cease, to give over.—' Obviously another form of Λέγω', says Dnn. i.e. of Λέγομαι, to lie down, Λέχος, &c. (**2**) Rather allied to Λαγαρός, Λείπω, Λιάζομαι, Λύω, through †λάω or λέω, as †τμέω, τμΗΓω. See †ΛΕΩ. (**3**) Allied to our *lag*.

Λήδανον, the gum collected on the leaves of the shrub ΛΗΔΟΣ. Some say *laudanum*: Mrs. Loudon denies it.

Λῆδος, Ληδάριον, Ληδίον, Ληΐδιον, a light thin summer dress.— Damm from λεῖος, †λῆος, smooth. So 'Ρεῖα, 'Ρηΐδιος. See the end of Ἄΐς 2.

Λήθη, forgetfulness, from λήθω, to escape the notice of (myself) :— in †Λαθέω.

Ληΐζομαι, to plunder.— R. λεία, ληῒη, ληῒς, booty.

Λήϊον, a corn-field, corn standing on the land, or a field with its crop. Also Doric Λαῖον, which means besides a *sickle*, and so seems allied to Λεία, plunder. The sense of corn-field and corn agrees well with the senses of ' Ληῒς, for Λεία, booty in general, slaves, cattle, *acquisition, property :*' (Dnn.)

Λήϊτον, a town-hall. — R. λεὼς, people : Λεῖτον.
95

Ληκέω : in λακέω.

Ληκέω, = λαικάζω.

Ληκυθίζω, to anoint with salves or cosmetics kept in a Λήκυθος.

Λήκυθος, oil-bottle, flask, bottle ;— big-sounding words, as Ampullæ.— Allied to Λέκος, Λεκάνη, pot, pan.

Λῆμα, wish, will, disposition :— high-mindedness.— — R. †Λάω, λῶ, †Λέλημαι, to wish.

Λήμη, blearedness, sore-eyes.— I. e. an affection of the sight, from λάω, λέλημαι, to see. So Frenzy from φρενός : Nervousness, where the Nerves are affected : Βουβὼν, both the groin and an affection of it : Valetūdo, bad health. (**2**) ' The forms Γλήμη, Γλάμη, are quoted : Lat. *gramia* :' Ldd. ΓλήΝη is the eye, †γλάω, γλαύσσω, to see.

Λῆμμα, anything received or taken, &c. R. λαμ₁ βάνω, †λήβω, λέλημμαι. Also, an assumption, taking for granted, a *lemma* spec. in Mathematical books.

Λημνίσκος, woollen fillet, ribbon.—As ὅΜβριμος, πίΜπλημι, for ληνίσκος from λῆνος.

Ληναῖος, Bacchus. — R. Ληνὸς, the wine-press.

Λῆνος, D. λᾶνος, *lana*, wool. — The Etymol. M.: ' Λεαίνω, λεανῶ, to make soft, λεανὸς, λῆνος'. So Ψηνός. (**2**) ' Arab. *lan*, to be soft ;' Mrt.

Ληνὸς, D. λᾶνὸς, ' like Lacus, anything shaped like a tub, trough, kneading-trough, wine-fat, socket for the mast, coffin :' Ldd. —'R. †λάω, λαμβάνω, to contain :' Dnn. As Ψάω, Ψηνός. (**2**) 'Ληνὸς, the vat, where the grapes are trodden : perh. from λεαίνω, to bruise :' Schrev.

Λῆξις, cessation : λήγω, ξω. And the casting of lots : †Λήχω, ξω, λαγχάνω.

Λῆρος, silly trifling talk, pompous nonsense.— Mrt. from λα, ῥέω, to speak. Or λα, ἐρῶ. (**2**) Better, as contr. from λακερὸς, talking : †λακερὸς, λῆρος.

Λῆρος, ' a golden ornament in the female head-dress:' Dnn.— Perh. from λῆρος, trifling, frivolous nonsense : Above. Note our sense of Trifle at the table.

Λησμοσύνη, Λῆστις, forgetfulness, λήθη.— R. †λήθω, λέλησμαι, λανθάνω.

Λῃστὴς, Λῃϊστὴς, a robber.—R. λ ηΐζομαι, λελήϊσται.

Λῃτῶον, a temple of ΛΗΤΩ, *Latōna*.

Λι-, for Λίαν.

Λιάζομαι. The prim. meaning of †Λιάζω, says Heyne, is to *loosen*, disjoin : Λιάζομαι, to move myself from a place, to go or come. Hence, 'Α-Λίαστος, very much moved, disturbed.—†Λιάζω, to *loosen*, allied through †λίω and †λέω to Λύω, Λείπω, Λείβω. See Λισσὸς, Λίγδος, &c.

Λίαν, very.— Prop. vehemently, allied to λε-λιημένος ' vehement', (Dnn.) Like Ἄγαν, Πέραν.

Λιαρὸς := χλιαρός.

Λίβανος, the frankincense-tree.— Dnn. from λείβω, λιβῶ, to drop, shed. ' It is well-known that the ancients used frankincense in their libations and sacrifices :' Lenn. (**2**) Bp. Butler: ' The best frankincense being white, Arab. *liban*, *libanos* became the Greek for it, and *olibanum* among the modern merchants.'

Λιβάς, a dropping, trickling.— R. λείβω, λιβῶ.

Λίβος, the Lat. *libum*.

Λιβρὸς, dripping, wet;— hence, looking dreary, gloomy. — R. λιβάς.

Λιβυρνίς, a *Liburnian* ship.

Λίγα, for Λιγέα, as 'Ωκα for 'Ωκέα.

Λίγγω, to twang. 'We Romans,' says Quintilian, ' are not permitted to make words *like the sound* : who would tolerate our forming anything similar to that deservedly-celebrated expression of Homer, Λίγξε βιός, The bow twanged ?' (2) Dnn. from Λιγύς.

Λιγδην, superficially ; prop. just licking or grazing. — R. λείχω or λίζω, λέλεικται or λέλικται.

Λίγδος, a mortar. .Διάζω shows a verb †λίω = λύω, to loosen, whence as †Μίγω, so †Λίγω, and Λίγδος as Μίγδα. ' Perh. from λειῶ, tero :' Mrt. See Λίσγος.— Also, a crucible for melting metals, from the same sense of loosening and dissolving.

Λιγνὺς, soot, smut, smoke, a smoky fire.—' A smoky blaze', says Wr. Whence from λίζω or λείχω, as we say a *Lambent* flame : ' playing about,' (Dr. J.). The flame, says Horace, ' properabat *lambere* tectum'. (2) *Dissolved* coal, from the same root as Λίγδος.

ΛΙΓΎΡΙΟΝ, the *ligure* stone. ' A sort of amber which the alders are said to throw out at the Po which flows from a spring on the boundaries of the *Ligures* Vagienni :' Steph. (2) See Ldd. below in Λυγκούριον.— (Very rare.)

Λιγὺς, Λιγυρὸς, shrill, high-sounding, full-sounding, clear.— ' R. λίγγω :' Mrt. (2) ' Some from λίζω, to lick, graze, which, however, occurs only in the later writers :' Dnn.

Λίζω, ξω, ' the same sense as Λείχω, ξω; both kindred forms :' Dnn.

Λίθος, a stone ;— blocks of stone used for rostra.— Allied to Λισσὸς, smooth: Λειῶ, to smoothe: †Λίω, †λ-λίθην. A smooth pebble on the shore. ' He chose him five *smooth stones* λίθους λείους out of the brook :' 1 Sam. 17. See also Λιμήν, Λιμήν.

Λικμὸς, Λίκνον, a wicker fan for throwing corn against the wind to winnow it.— Allied to Λίγδην ' superficially,' through λέλιχμαι, (as Λίκτης from λέλικται is one that ' licks,')— the process being superficial, dispersing the lighter particles, but retaining the substance.

Λίκνον, also ' a fan-shaped basket, and a cradle prob. of wicker-work,' Ldd. Above.

Λικριφὶς, obliquely.— Allied to Λέχριος. For λεκρι-φὶς : ending as ἀμφΙΣ. I, as τΕγγω, tIngo : sEmi--caput, sEm-caput, sEnciput, sInciput. (2) Dnn. notes Lat. *liquus*, *ob-liquus* : and refers Λικριφὶς and these last to λίζω.

Λιλαίομαι, to desire.— R. λάω, to wish, †λιλάω, as ΜΙμνήσκω.

Λίμβος, a late word for Λίχνος. Allied to Λίζω, λεί-χω, through a form †Λίπτω.

96

Λιμήν, ένος, a harbor, and Λίμνη, a lake or pool, are both allied to Λειῶ, to make smooth. Λιμήν, says Valck., is where the waves of the sea are smoothed and quiet. And Λίμνη i.e. λεισυμένη or †λελιμένη is water smooth and quiet. From a form †λίω, whence Λισσὸς, smooth. See †ΛΕΩ. (2) Some deduce Λίμνη from λείβω, λε-λειμμένη, to pour forth water, as Stagnum, says Ldd., from στάζω.

Λίμνη : in Λιμήν.

Λιμὸς, hunger, famine.— The old form is said to be λειμὸς, which from λείπω, λέλειμμαι, deficio : Deficiency or defect of food. The Latins say Fame defectus. (2) R. λίπτομαι, λέλιμμαι, to long for (food).

Λιμπάνω : form of λείπω, λιπῶ, as λαΜβάνω.

Λινευτὴς, a hunter *using* nets.— From

Λίνον, *linum*, the plant producing flax ; hence anything made of flax, angler's *line*, thread, cord, *linen*, linen cloth, sail, net, string of a lyre.— ' The Etym. M. from λείον, smooth : and perhaps truly :' Schneid. So Mrt. from λείον. Flax, says Dr. J., is ' the fibrous plant of which the *finest* thread is made.'

Λίνος, the song of *Linus*, son of Apollo.

Λίπαρὴς, ' persisting, persevering in ;— earnest in begging or praying ;— Λιπαρῶς ἔχειν, to be in earnest, long earnestly. Prob. allied to Λίπτομαι, Λίσσομαι, am eager for, long for :' Ldd. Far better than Schneider and Passow, who ally it to Λιπαρός : ' From the viscidity of unctuous substances.' The quantity opposes.

Λιπαρὸς, oily, shining, sleek, fat, plentiful.— R. λίπος.

Λιπερνὴς, ' desolate, outcast : for λιπο-φερνὴς, from λείπω, φερνή :' Ldd. So Λιφερνέω. (2) ' R. λείπο-μαι, to be deficient ; ἔρανος, benevolence, alms :' Grove. (3) R. λιπῶ, †ἔρα : Fugitive from the ground or land.

Λίπος, Λίπας, grease, fat, lard, oil.— ' Ἀλείφω and Λίπος, are prob. akin :' Ldd. And Λείος, smooth, and Λισσὸς, smooth, and Λίμνη, Λιμήν, prop. a smooth lake, a smooth harbor.

Λίπτομαι, to be eager for: the same as Λίσσομαι, Λίτπομαι, to supplicate.

Λιρὸς, bold, impudent.— Mrt. for λι-ορὸς, from λίαν ὁρῶ : Looking too much at. So Meletius explains it ' ἐν-ορῶν ἀ-τενὲς ' (intently). See Λαιδρὸς, and the contrast in Αἰδὼς. (2) R. λίαν, or λι-, only: for †λιερός. See Μαλερός. (Rare.)

ΛΙΣ, a lion.— Some say, for λέων: but how ? Better Bochart, &c. from Chald. *lés*.

Λὶς for Λισσὴ, smooth. And to this is allied the Homeric dat. λῖτὶ and plur. λῖτα, 'plain smooth linen cloth or stuffs,' Ldd. : ' fine linen, prop. a smooth tissue,' Dnn.

Λίσγος, spade, mattock. — ' Strictly, a tool for levelling, from Λισσός. Akin to *ligo*, *ōnis* : and to Λί-στρον :' Ldd.

Λίσπαι, ' dice cut in the middle and [as in Λίσπος,] *worn* by use,' Ruhnk. They were in pairs, and fitted each other exactly by the indenture ; and, on friends separating, one was kept by each to prove afterwards the reality of the bond. But rather, as made level at first, than worn by use. — From

Λίσπος, Λίσφος, smooth, polished, worn fine or thin: like Λισσός.

Λισσάνιος, as Ὦ λισσάνιε, O bone! I. e. O my fine fellow! Λισσός signifying smooth, and Λίσπος smooth, fine.

Λίσσομαι, to ask, beseech. — Mrt. for Λίπτομαι through Λάω, to wish, and †Λίπτω as Νίπτω. (2) As Ἐκεῖνος, Κεῖνος, and Ἱκτιδέη, Κτιδέη, so for ἐλίσσομαι, to roll myself (before a person) ' Advolvor, in the manner of one supplicating or adoring: Livy, Omnium genibus se advolvens. Velleius, Genibus ejus advolutus est. Curtius, Advoluta est pedibus ejus. Propertius, Bacche tuis advolvimur aris ': Forcell. (2) Schneid. from λι- for λίαν, vehemently. ?

. Λισσός, smooth. — All compare Λεῖος: i.e. from obs. †λίω, λέλισσαι, to make smooth. See Λιμήν, Λίμνη.

Λίσσωμα of the hair, i.e. the crown from which the hair sets different ways. — R. λισσός, smooth, bare: The bare part.

Λίστρον, tool for levelling or scraping, shovel, hoe. — Allied to Λισσός, and Λίσγος, ligo, ὄνις.

Λῖτα: in Λίς.

Λίταργος, hastening; Λιταργίζω; and Ἀπο-λιταργίζω, 'to slip off. Perhaps from λι-, and ἀργός:' Ldd. But the T ? — Since the Anthol. P. 6 332 has Λῖτα short, so Λίταργος from †Λῖτός = λιτός, prop. ' smooth,' and ἀργός. As To slip off, is from Sax. ' slipe,' slippery; and To slide away, is prop. to pass along smoothly; (Todd.) and To glide, is to move swiftly and smoothly along, (Id.)

Λίτομαι, = λίσσομαι. So Λιτή prayer, Λιτανεία, &c.

Λιτός, plain, simple: properly ' smooth, even, as Λεῖος, Λισσός:' Ldd. ' As Λίτομαι is a form for Λίσσομαι :' Dnn.

Λιτουργός, a wicked doer. — This is strictly to be compared with the observ. of Liddell on Λεώς, and with Λεωργός: noting also Λίταργος above.

Λίτρα, a pound weight. — ' Perh. from Λιτός, small, slender, as denoting a smaller kind of weight:' Pkh. Thus Salmas. observes of Λίτρον, that ' it was said of minute silver money, not of heavy copper money.'

Λίτρον : for Νίτρον.

Λιφερνέω, = λιπερνέω.

Λίχανος, licking: λείχω. Ὁ λίχανος, the forefinger with which dishes are tasted. Λιχάνη χορδή, the chord struck with the fore-finger.

Λιχμάζω, to lick. — R. λείχω.

Λίχνος, dainty so as to lick his fingers or dishes, lickerish, greedy ;—greedy after, curious, eager. — R. λείχω.

Λίψ, the S. W. wind. — R. λείβω, ψω: ' because it brought wet :' Ldd. ' Leuco-notus Libs,' Auson.: ' notus' being from νοτίς, moisture.

Λίψ, the same as Λιβάς. Also a cliff, i.e. from which water flows. Or short for Αἰγίλιψ. — And a longing, from λίπτω, ἴψω.

97

Λοβός, skin, hull, pod. — R. λέπω, λέλοπα, λοπός. Any fleshy protuberant part like a pod: as a lobe of the lungs or ears. Λοβοί, kidney-beans, as eaten pod and all.

Λογάδες, the eyes: i.e. the speakers. — R. λέγω, λέλογα.

Λογὰς, picked, chosen : — unhewn, said of stones, ' taken just as they were picked :' Ldd.

Λογγάσια, stones with holes in them through which cables were passed to moor vessels. — From λογγάζω = λαγγάζω, to slacken, and so rest. Allied to Λαγαρός.

Λογεῖον, a pulpit, &c. — R. λέγω : Place for speaking.

Λογίζομαι, to reckon, judge. — See Λόγος 2.

Λόγιμος, of good account, well judged or thought of. — Above.

Λόγιον, oracular answers — From

Λόγος, word said, report, fable, as this from Fari. — R. λέγω, λέλογα.

Λόγος, counting, i. e. collecting numbers ; here Λέγω is lego, colligo : — (and as æligo, to select,) judgment, reasoning, as in logic : proportion, as in homo-logous sides.

Λόγχη, a spear-head :— spear, lance. — For λόχη, (as λαΐχάνω,) from λείχω, λέλοιχα, to lick, says Dr. Jones, as thinking that it prim. and properly meant the tip of the tongue. Compare Γλῶσσα with Γλωχίν. O, as στΕΙχω, στΟχος. (2) The words Λογχός, Λοιμὸς, Λαιδορέω, show an obsol. word †λόω, to be injurious. (See Λοιγός.) Then from †λέλοκα may be †λόχη, λόγχη : the head of the spear being the injurious part. (3) Ormst. from λαγχάνω, λέλογχα : ' As allotting the life or death of the soldier.' Too figuratively. (4) Some ally it to Lat. longa : As meaning the whole spear.

Λόγχη, a lot : λαγχάνω, λέλογχα.

Λοέω, Λόω, Λούω, to wash. — ' Allied to Λύω, to loose the dirt : As Homer uses λύματα for filth washed off :' Pkh. ' Akin to Λῦμα, Λύω : from it Lat. di-luo, e-luo :' Dnn.

Λοιβή, libation : λείβω, λέλοιβα.

Λοιγός, destruction, ruin. — ' If any one attends to the analogy, he will see that Λοιγὸς and Λοιμὸς have a common origin : from the prim. †λέω, †λείω, †λοίω, to destroy :' Hemsterh. This †λοίω or †λόω is allied to Λύω, to loosen, as is seen in Λοέω. (2) ' Akin to Λυγρός :' Dnn. ?

Λοιδορέω, to hurt a character, defame, revile. — As Blaspheme is from βλασ-φημῶ = βλαψ-φημῶ, to injure the character, so ΛΟΙδορῶ is allied to ΛΟΙγὸς, ruin, as Blomf. truly allies it.

Λοιμὸς, plague, pestilence. — Allied to Λοιγός. (2) ' Hebr. leem, to eat :' Wr.

Λοιπὸς, left, remaining. — R. λείπω, λέλοιπα.

Λοῖσθος, the last. — Ldd. thinks from λοιπὸς, λοίπιστος, †λοῖστος. (2) As Λοιγὸς, Λοιμὸς, Λοιδορέω, — from the obs. †λοίω, †ἐλοίσθην : Hurt, disabled, lagging, as in an army, or as in a race, as in Virg. Æn. 327, &c. Thus Blomf. derives it.

O

Λόκκη, a cloak, and Λόκμη.—Prob. Æol. for λόπκη, as in λέκιθος, from λέπω. Λόπος is a hide. (Only in an Epigram.)

Λοξίας, Apollo.—R. λοξός: From the oblique course of the Sun through the Zodiac, or its oblique rays. Some from the tortuous answers of his oracle. (2) Ldd. from λέγω, λέξω, as the interpreter of Jupiter.

Λοξός, oblique, distorted.—Allied to Λέχριος, (which see,) through λέγομαι, λέλεχα, λέλεξαι. (2) 'Hebr. *lez*, to turn aside:' Wr.

Λοξώ, Diana, sister of Λοξίας.

Λοπάς, a flat dish or plate: i.e. 'λεπτή thin as λοπός bark:' Steph.—Also, a coffin: I suppose one of flat thin boards. We say The *shell* of a coffin. From Λοπός, rind, peel, shell, bark, husk;—hide, leather. —R. λέπω, λέλοπα, to peel, &c.

Λορδός, bent forwards or inwards.—As Κυρτός is allied ultimately to Κύω, and Μαργός to †Μάω, and Largus to †Λάω, so Λορδός from the obsol. word †λόω, †λοίω, to hurt, as seen in Λοιγός, Λοιμός, Λοιδορέω. Generally, injured. (2) 'Lord,' says Todd, 'is a ludicrous title given by the vulgar to a hump-backed person.'

Λούω: in Λοέω. Λουτρόν, a bath.

Λοφνίς, for †λεπνίς, a torch made of the λοπός bark of the vine.

Λόφος, the neck,—ridge of a hill, as Δειρά;—crest of a helmet,—tuft on birds' heads.—'As Δείρη from δέρω, so Λόφος, Λόφος, Λόφος, from λέπω:' Dnn. See altogether in Δέρη. (2) Our *loft*.

Λόχιος, appertaining to child-birth. Allied to Λέχος, a bed.. So Λοχεύω, to bring forth;—attend in childbirth.

Λόχμη, a thicket, bush, 'from λόχος, as serving for the lair of wild-beasts,' Ldd.: i.e. allied to Λέχος, a bed. Or λόχος is a place of *lying* in ambush.

Λόχος, ambush, lying in wait, from λέγομαι, λέλοχα, to lie, λέχος, a bed. The men in ambush;—any regular armed band,—body or company.

Λύα, Λύη, a dissolving,—hence faction, riot.—R. λύω.

Λυαῖος, *Lyæus*, Bacchus.—R. λύω: Deliverer from care.

Λύγδην, (as Μίγδην,) with sobs; Λυγμός, a sob; Λύγξ, violent sobbing, hiccup.—R. λύζω, λέλυγμαι, &c.

Λύγδος, a dazzling white stone, white marble.—Allied to Λύκη, and *Lux, lucis, Lucidus*. 'R. λευκός, white:' Greg. We have Λύγδη, ἡ λεύκη, the WHITE poplar, in Hesych.

Λύγη, gloom, darkness.—Allied to Λυγρός, doleful, melancholy, sad, from λύζω, λέλυγα, to sob. (2) Dnn. allies Λύγη (Λύξ) and Νύξ, 'N and Λ being freq. interchanged.' So Νίτρον and Λίτρον.

Λυγίζω, 'to bend, twist. From ΛΤΓΟΣ, a willowtwig:' Dnn. Λύγος was also the willow-like tree, the agnus-castus used for wreaths. Perh. from λύω, as being loose and flexible.

Λυγκούριον, Λεγκούριον, Λιγγούριον, 'a kind of gem, reddish amber, or as others the hyacinth. Some from

98

λυγκός οὐρά [urine], from the vulgar belief that it was *lynxes'* water petrified:' Ldd., who identifies it with Λιγύριον, the *ligure* stone.

Λύγξ: in Λύγδην.

Λύγος: in Λυγίζω.

Λυγρός, sad, gloomy, dismal, as *lugubris*:— R. λύζω, λέλυγα or ἔλυγον. Also, causing gloom and wretchedness, baneful, hurtful, as Λευγαλέος.

Λυδίζω, to imitate the *Lydians*.

Λύζω, to sob:—to hiccup.—R. λύω, as Μύω, Μύζω: To have the voice loosed and broken into sobs, much as Κλαίω from Κλάω, and 'Ρῆξαι as is stated in Κλαίω. We say, To be *dis-solved* in tears. (2) Lennep says, 'Undoubtedly from the sound.' (3) R. ὁλολύζω.

Λύθρον, *lutum*, filth, defilement;—gore: also as Λῦμα, filth, dirt, 'removed by washing; prob. from Λοόω, *luo* (*diluo*):' Ldd. and Dnn. Or λύω, ἐλύθην, to loose, do away with.

Λυκάβας, αντος, a year.—R. λύκη, βάς: The periodic course of the Sun.

Λύκαια, ων, festival of *Lycæan* Jupiter, called from Mount *Lycæus* in Arcadia.

Λύκειον, the *Lycëum*, gymnasium at Athens, named after the neighbouring temple of

Λύκειος, Apollo, 'as the killer of λύκοι, wolves: or as the *Lycian* god: or from λύκη, the light. Æschylus: Λύκει' ἄναξ, λύκειος γενοῦ, *Lycæan* lord, be a very wolf to the enemy:' Ldd.

Λύκη, *lux, lucis*, light.—'As λευκή, white:' Schrev. (2) 'The sun is called λύκος from λύω, λέλυκα, to loosen, unbind, open:' Lenn. It is a λυαῖος: 'Solvit crassitiem aëria,' says Mrt. (3) Sanskr. *loch*, to shine.

Λύκιον, 'a *Lycian* kind of thorn;—a liquor from it as a medicine:' Ldd. and Dnn.

Λυκόποδες, tyrants' body-guards, 'perh. because they wore wolf-skin boots:' Ldd.—R. λύκος, πόδες.

Λύκος, Æol. †λύπος, *lupus*, a wolf;—spikes on horses' bits jagged like a wolf's teeth, Lat. *lupáta*; 'a hook or knocker on a door;—hook of a well-rope;—nickname of Κίναιδοι:' Ldd.—'From λεύσσω [λέλευκα,] to gaze upon, or from λύκη, light:' Ewing. Pliny says that a wolf's eyes Splendere et *lucem* jaculari.—Wr. from λευκός. 'From its white color, whence Theocr. calls it πολιὸν λύκαν:' Scheid.

Λυκόφως, twilight.—'R. λύκος: Wolf-light, when the wolf prowls, like Owl-light, Bat-light:' Ldd. (2) For λυγόφως, R. Λύγη darkness, φῶς light.

Λῦμα, *lutum*, filth, as in Λύθρον:—moral defilement, disgrace:—also as

Λύμη, ruin, destruction, allied to Λοιμός, and Lat. *lues*. Hemst. says 'as λύουσα (dissolving,) destroying.' Also, injury done to another by outrage and insult. Defilement, as Λῦμα.

Λύπη, pain, grief.— R. λύω, solvo. Plato calls it the διά-λυσις of the body, and Cicero the '*Solutio* totius hominis.' 'My limbs λύεται λύπη,' Eurip.

Λυπρός, painful.—Above.

Λύρα, *lyra*, a *lyre* or harp. — R. λύω, as Αύω, Αύρά. That is, λυκαῖος, 'delivering from care,' (Dnn.) as Bacchus was called for that reason. In 1 Sam. 16. 23 David took a harp and played, and Saul was 'refreshed.' — Mythology derived it from the same λύω, the honor of the invention being given over by Mercury to Apollo as a λύτρον compensation for stealing his cows. See Hor. Od. 1. 10. 6.

Λυσι-ᾠδὸς, (ἀοιδὸς,) 'one who played women's characters in male attire: from *Lysis* who wrote songs for such :' Ldd.

Λύσσα, frenzy, madness. — R. λύω, λύσω: Solutio, dissolutio animi, lit. *loosening* of the mind, as Λύπη of the body and mind. (2) R. ἀλύω, ἀλύσσω, am frantic.

Λύται, *Lytæ*, law-students ready to be examined and λύειν solve questions. So

Λύτης, a deliverer; Λύτρον, ransom paid for deliverance. — R. λύω.

Λύχνος, a flambeau, *lychnus*. — R. λύκη, light.

Λύω, to *loose*, *loosen*, release, dissolve : — to pay a debt, *luo*, as Solvo is used. Also, to pay cost, to be worth while, to be of use or profit: so Λύει τέλη, it pays toll, it pays one, it profits. — See in †ΛΕΩ.

Λῶ, I wish, for Λάω.

Λώβη, outrage, ill-treatment, maiming. — From the obsol. †Λάω, λοίω, to injure, as in Λοιγὸς, Λοιμὸς, Λοιδορῶ. Comp. κλωΒΟΣ, κολοΒΟΣ. (2) 'Chald. *laab*, to mock :' Mrt.

Λωγάνιον, dewlap hanging from the neck of oxen. — Perh. from λέγομαι, λέλογα, to lie down : Recumbent on the ground. Our word says it *laps* the *dew*. 'Their heads are hung With ears that sweep away the morning dew, ... Dew-lapp'd :' Shaksp. (Only in Lucian.)

Λωίων, Λῴων, more to be desired, better. — R. λῶ, to wish. As Optimus is Optatissimus.

Λῶμα, a hem, fringe. — R. λάω, λῶμα, as Κλάω, Κλῶμαξ: Which you lay hold of by. Or which takes up and holds the vest, 'to keep the threads from spreading :' (Dr. J.)

ΛΩΟΣ, a Macedonian month. — Q. ? (Very rare.)

Λώπη, a skin, husk, shell, like Λοπός : — hence a covering, mantle, robe.

ΛΩΡΟΝ, the Latin *lorum*.

Λῶτος, a pipe made of the ΛΩΤΟΣ *lotus* plant, which Athenæus makes an *Egyptian* word.

Λωφάω, to take rest, or cause to do so : 'prop. of oxen, when their yokes are taken from their λόφοι necks :' Steph.

M.

Μᾶ, mother, for Μᾶτερ.

Μὰ, 'by,' in oaths, as Μὰ Δί', By Jove. — 'Μὰ and Μὰν,' says Liddell, 'are near akin.' And Μὰν is a form of Μήν, verily. So that Μὰ Δί' is properly 'Verily (by) Jove.' So Νυν and Νυ, Σφιν and Σφι. So our AN becomes A before a consonant. (2) Dnn. makes it 'A particle of *denial* formed from μή.' (3) 'Chald. *ma*, certè :' Mrt.

ΜΑΓΑΔΙΣ, a harp with 20 strings ; — also a Lydian flute. And ΜΑΓΑΣ, άδος, the bridge of a lute, 'whence', says Steph., 'is Μάγαδις.' But these seem foreign words.

Μάγγανον, 'a means of deception, a charm or drug ; — [any clever machine, as a hunting-net,] a machine for throwing missive weapons, — the axis of a ball in a spinning wheel, by which a powerful effect is produced. Most prob. from μάγος, a magician :' Dnn. So Mrt. Also, a bolt, which may be from μάσσω, μαγῶ, whence ἐν-εμάξατο in Nicander, 'he pushed or forced in.'

Μαγδαλιὰ, a crumb used for wiping the hands at table. — R. μάσσω, μέμακται, μάγδην.

Μαγεία, the theology of the *Magians* : — the *magic* art. — R. μάγος.

Μάγειρος, 'a cook : from μάσσω, [μαγῶ,] for [kneading flour and] baking bread was the chief business of the ancient cook : — a butcher, for in early times the cook was butcher also :' Ldd.

99

Μαγὶς, a kneading-trough ; — cake kneaded. — R. μάσσω, μαγῶ.

Μάγνης, a *Magnesian* : — a *magnet*, 'first found near the city of *Magnesia* :' Dnn.

ΜΑΓΟΣ, a Persian priest and philosopher : — a magician. — Thought by all a *Persian* word. 'They write it *magusch* :' Mrt.

Μαδάω, Μυδάω, *madeo*, to be moist, and putrid through moisture ; — to fall off or melt away ; — lose the hair. — The peculiarity here (as in μΑσταξ, μΥσταξ,) is that both μΑδάω and μΥδάω are found. Which is the original ? Μύδος is damp, and Lennep refers it to M prefix (as in many words,) and Ύδάω. See in Μαυλιστὴς, Μερμὶς, &c. (2) 'Hebr. *met*, to be dissolved :' Wr. (3) Allied to our *mud*, *mod* Su. Goth., *moder* Germ. Μαδίζω, to pull out the hair : i.e. make it fall off. — Above.

Μᾶζα, Μᾶζα, a cake of barley-meal. — 'R. †μάζω or μάσσω, to knead : for farína subacta :' Hemsterh. (2) 'Hebr. *mezes*, to press :' Wr. 'Hebr. *mazzah*, a fermented mass :' Dahle.

Μαζὸς, the teat, dug : — a wet-nurse. — 'Akin to μάσσω, μασάομαι :' Dnn. (2) 'R. μάω, to seek for ardently. The Etym. M. well explains it τὸ τοῖς βρέφεσι (ζητούμενον :' Valck. (3) R. μᾶ, mother. (4) 'Hebr. *mezes*, to squeeze :' Wr.

ΜΑΘΑΛΛΙΔΕΣ, cups or measures :—occurring only in Athen. 487.—Q.?

†Μαθέω, Μανθάνω, to learn. — ' R. μάω, [ἐμάθην,] to seek, or desire to know :' Dnn.

Μαῖα, like Μᾶ, ma, mother, nurse, midwife, grandmother :—title of respect. (2) Some from μάω, to be eager, anxious.

Μαίανδρος, ' a winding way. From a river in Asia, the Mæander, remarkably winding, Il. 2. 169.:' Dnn.

Μαιμάκτης, Jupiter ' the Boisterous, in whose honor the Mæmacteria were kept at Athens in the first winter month :' Ldd. From μαῖμαξ, violent, μαιμάσσω, = μαιμάω.

Μαιμάω, to rage :—violently long for.—Redupl. of †μάω, †μαμάω.

Μαίνω, to drive to fury, make mad.— R. μάω, as †Βάω, Βαίνω.

Μαίομαι, like †Μάω, to seek after.

Μαῖρα, the dog-star, ' strictly, the Sparkler, from (†μαίρω,) μαρμαίρω,' Ldd.

ΜΑΙΣΩΝ, a native cook at Athens, opposed to a foreign one :—and ' the comic mask of a cook, sailor,' &c.: Ldd. — Q.? (Very rare.)

Μαιωτιστί, in the Scythian fashion.—From the people adjacent to the Lacus Mæotis.

Μάκαρ, blessed, happy. — Formed like Μακρὸς, which see: and meaning ' Advanced ' or ' got on ' well, as in εὖ βεβηκὼς, ἥκων δυνάμεως, &c.: Getting on in the world. (2) Aristotle from χαίρω, χαρῶ: then MA for μάλα. See on Μαυλιστής. (3) ' Chald. mejakkar, precious, honored :' Mrt.

Μακαρίτης, 'of blessed memory. — Above.

Μάκελλα, Μακέλη, a mattock, spade. —' From κέλλω, cello, to drive: if with two prongs, δί-ΚΕΛΛΑ :' Ldd. The MA- Portus derives from MIA, one. For μά-κελλα, opposed to δι- i. e. δὶς in δί-κελλα.

ΜΑΚΕΛΛΟΝ, ' the shambles: the Lat. macellum Grecised :' Schrev.

Μακιστήρ, long and tedious. And Μάκιστος, very long, from Μᾶκος, length, allied to Μακρός.

Μακκοάω, am silly. —' Said to be from Macco, a stupid woman. Cf. maccus foolish in Apuleius:' Ldd. So Ἀκκίζομαι from one Acco.—Or M as in Μέρμις.

Μακρὸς, Μακεδνὸς, long, large. — If we compare Μάκαρ and Μέγας, we may be led to refer Μακρὸς to †μάω, †μέμακα, (as in Αὐτό-ματος like Αὐτό-μολος,) to move on, go on : Advanced, got on, grown long or large, as in the expressions προ-βαίη μεῖζον, εὖ ἥκω τοῦ βίου, &c. See †ΜΑΩ.

Μάκτρα, kneading-trough ; — hence bathing-tub. — R. μάσσω, μέμακται.

Μακὼν, moaning : μηκάομαι.

Μάλα, very, much.—For Μεγάλα, greatly, as Si-vultis Sultis, Volis Vis, Renideo Rideo, Funeralis Feralis. (2) R. μάω, to be vehement. (3) ' Hebr. mela, to fill :' Wr.

Μαλακὸς, soft, mild: from μαλάσσω. As Φιλάσσω,
100

Φυλακή. (2) Dnn. makes Μάλακὸς, Μλᾰκς, Μλᾰξ, the same as Βλᾰξ: thence Μαλάσσω. But the first A in μΑλακός ? (3) 'R. μαλὸς or μαλλὸς, wool:' Hemsterh.

Μαλάσσω, to soften.—As ἀλλΑΣΣΩ. R. μάλα, much: To do or work a thing much, work it well. Thus Δεψέω is ' to soften by working in the hands,' (Dnn.). Compare Ldd. below in Μαλερός. (2) See Μαλακός.

Μαλάχη, the mallow. — R. μαλάσσω, μεμάλαχα. From its softening the bowels, as Ewing ' from its emollient properties.' — ' From its soft downy leaves,' Ldd.

Μαλερὸς, ' from μάλα: vehement, fierce, furious, devouring, fiery, glowing:' Ldd. (2) Schneid. from μαλὸς, white, i. e. clear, bright, burning, &c.

Μάλη, the arm-pit.—For Μασχάλη. (2) R. μαλὸς, soft: from the softness of the flesh there.

Μάλθα, ' mixture of pitch and wax for calking ships: the soft wax laid over writing-tables. Akin to Μαλθακή:' Ldd.

Μαλθακὸς, soft, Μαλακός.

Μάλθων, a weakling, as Μαλακίων.

Μάλιον, a lock of hair, as Μαλλός.

ΜΑΛΙΣ, Μαλίη, a disease in horses, the Malanders, Lat. malandria in Vegetius, ' from mal (Lat. malè) andare Ital., to go ill:' (Todd.) (Very rare.)

Μάλκη, numbness from cold. — Lenn. says, Perhaps for Μαλάκη, much as Φυλακή. I. e. a languor of the circulation. R. μαλακός.

Μαλλὸς, fleece, wool,— lock of hair. — Ldd. allies it to Μαλακὸς, soft. Or from ἀμαλὸς, tender. Greg. from μῆλον, μᾶλον, a sheep.

Μαλὸς, white: but others say soft, woolly, and write Μαλλός: or connect Μαλὸς with Ἀμαλὸς: and some contract it from Μαλακὸς, says Dnn. All the senses agree with the color and the feel of Μαλλὸς, wool, and of Μᾶλον, a sheep. ' Lucida ovis', Ov. In Il. 22. 310, is read both ἄρνα μαλὴν and ἄρν' ἀμαλήν.

ΜΑΜΕΡΤΟΣ, the Oscan Mamers for Μάνορς, Mars. And Μάμερσα, Minerva. Barbarous words in Lycophron.

Μάμμα, a child's inarticulate sound of mama:— mother; mother's breast; grandmother. — ' This word is said to be found in all languages, and is therefore supposed the first syllables that a child pronounces:' Dr. J.

Μαμμάκυθος, a booby ; prop. one who (κεύθει) hides himself in his mother's lap, tied to his mother's apronstrings. — Above.

Μαμμᾶν αἰτεῖν, to cry for food, as infants for the μάμμα breast.

Μὰν, = μήν.

Μανδάκη, hide, skin.— For μαδάκη, (as N in μαΝδάκης, μάΝδαλος,) allied to Μάσσω, to squeeze, press. ΑΚΗ: see on ἈθυρΤΑΚΗ. (Very rare.) So

Μανδάκης, a band to tie trusses of hay.—As ἀΝδάνω, for μαδάκης, from μάομαι, †μάδην, (as Βδδην,) ἐπι--μάομαι, to grasp. So

Μάνδαλος, a bolt.—As ἀΝδάνω, for μάδαλος, from μάομαι, †μάδην, (as above,) ἐπι-μάομαι, to grasp, and so to hold tight. So'Εν-εμάξατο in Nicander, pushed or forced in.

Μανδαλωτὸς, with the μάνδαλος bolt shot out: applied to a lascivious kiss protrusâ linguâ.

Μάνδρα, stable, stall, pen, monastery. — Lennep compares Lat. *Mando*, to eat. Both are allied to Μασδομαι, to bite, and Μάσσω; and these two last are referred by Dnn. to μάω. Then †μάδρα, μάνδρα, as ἀΝδάνω.

ΜΑΝΔΤΑΣ, a military cloak or *mantle.* — Allied by Ldd. to Κάνδυ. ' Akin to Κάνθη: both *Persian.*' Dnn. But Μ and Κ ?

ΜΑΝΗΣ, ' a proper name, *Manes* ; a common name for slaves:' Dnn. Thus *Manes* was the well-known name of the servant of Diogenes. Also a little image, placed in water in the game Κότταβος. — Q. if connected with our word *Man ?*

Μανθάνω: in †Μαθέω.

Μανία, frenzy, mania. — R. μαίνω.

ΜΑΝΙΑΚΗΣ, a bracelet or necklace (see Μάννος,) worn by the *Celtæ,* says Polybius. — Chald. *menicha.*

ΜΑΝΝΑ, a sweet gum of *Arabia,* ' a kind of aerial honey which falls on certain trees,' Salmas. Also a grain or crumb of frankincense, as Pliny: ' Thuris *manna* una.' ' For the Hebrew *manna* was like grains of coriander;' Steph.

Μαννάριον, ' = μαμμάριον, *mama:*' Ldd.

Μάννος, Μάννος, a necklace. — Prob. allied to Μανιάκης : and, some say, to Lat. *monile.*

Μανὸς, rare, spare, thinly scattered, in small quantity, loose. — Dnn. derives Μόλωψ from Μάω, Σμάω, (as Μῶδιξ and Σμῶδιξ.). From this Μάω, which Ldd. makes the origin of Σμάω, is Μᾶνός: i.e. rubbed, rubbed thin, rubbed off, as Ψηνὸς, Ψανὸς, a bald head, from Ψάω.

Μαντίλη, ' the Lat. *matula:*' Ldd.

Μάντις, a diviner, soothsayer. — R. μαίνω, μέμανται : From the furious extravagances of the pagan seers. Æn. 6. 46, 77.

Μάομαι, to touch, handle: seek after. See Μάω.

Μαπέω, to seize: allied to †μάω, μάομαι, to handle. †Μάω, †μάπτω, as †Δάω, Δάπτω.

Μάραγδος, Σμάραγδος, an emerald, ' of a green and transparent color', (Dnn.) whence well derived by Mrt. from μαίρω, μαρῶ, μαρμαίρω, to shine: μαραυγέω.

Μάραγνα, Μάραινα, Σμάραγνα, a whip. — As held in the μάρη hand. Much as Habēna from Habeo. (2) R. σμαραγέω: A resounding scourge.

Μαραίνω, ' to parch, wither, consume, extinguish as fire. — Prob. akin to Μαίρω, Μαρμαίρω : by a transition of shining to heat:' Dnn. So Αὔω is to cause to shine, to parch, to set on fire.

Μαράσσω, through ἐμάραγον, = σμαραγέω.

Μαραυγέω, to dazzle the eyes. — R. μαίρω, μαρμαίρω, to shine, αὐγαὶ the eyes. (2) R. μαραίνω to wither, and αὐγαί

Μάργαρον, a pearl, and Μαργαρίτης. — Mrt. from μαίρω, μαρῶ: better from μαραυγέω, contr. to †μαργέω. (2) Lenn. from ἀργὸς, white: Μ prefixed, as in Μέρμις.

Μαργέλλια, ' a kind of palm-tree: the fruit compared to μαργέλλια, pearls:' Dnn.: from μάργαρα, pearls.

101

Μάργος, mad, furious. — R. μάω, μέμαα, μαίνω : through a form †μαίρω, †μέμαρκα, just as *Largus* seems to have come from λάω, ' capio', ' capax.' Thus -αργος in Λήθαργος is thought to be a termination. (2) Some for ἀργὸς, rapid, swift: Μ prefixed as in Μαυλιστής, &c.

Μάρη, the hand. — R. μάω, μάομαι, to handle. Much as Αὔω, Αὔρα. (2) R. μείρω, μαρῶ: As divided into fingers.

Μαρίλη, Σμαρίλη, embers of charcoal. R. μαίρω, μαρῶ, to shine: as Favilla from φάfος, light. Hence 'Ω Μαρίλδη, Oh Mr. Collier, in Aristoph.

ΜΑΡΙΣ, a liquid measure. — Q. ? (Rare.)

Μαρμαίρω, to flash, sparkle, shine. — Reduplic. of μαίρω, which from μάω, (like Ψάω, Ψαίρω,) to move about, as in Μάσσω and Αὐτό-ματος; just as Μίς̄ω ' to move to and fro with a quick motion', is also ' to sparkle, glitter', (Riddle). See Μάσσω. (2) ' Hebr. *mareeh,* visus:' Mrt.?

Μάρμαρος, a rock, ' always with some notion of brightness or whiteness ;—later, *marmor,* marble:' Ldd. Above.

Μαρμαρυγὴ, a flashing: μαρμαίρω.

Μάρναμαι, to fight, i. e. join μάρας hands, ' consero manûs.'

Μάρπτω, to grasp with the μάρη hand. (2) Some compare 'ΑΡΠάζω. Μ, as in Μαυλιστής.

Μάρσυπος, -ιπος, -ιππος, a bag, purse, *marsupium.* — Perhaps, (as βλαΣφημέω for βλαΨφημέω, so) for μάρΨυπος, R. μάρπτω, ψω, ' to grasp, hold', (Ldd.) In form, much as κισσΤΒίον.

Μάρτυρ, a witness. — ' R. μείρω, μέμαρται, divido, discerno, dirimo:' Valck. I. e., a settler of disputes, decider of controversies.

Μασδομαι, Μασσ-, to chew; — ' to bite the tongue, as angry persons do:' Schneid. — Allied to Μάσσω, to press, knead. Dnn.

Μάσθλη, -ης, ' a hide well beaten and thumped:' Brunck. Allied to Μάσσω, to squeeze, knead. Hence one well-stricken in villany, well-practised in guilt, as 'Εν-τριβὴς, 'Εμ-παιος.

Μασθὸς, Μαστός: = μαζός.

Μάσμα, enquiry. — R. μάομαι, μέμασμαι.

Μάσσω, to work or squeeze with the hand; — knead into a cake; — wipe or smear over; — choose by feeling. — ' From †μάω; prop. to handle', Ldd. As †Τάω, Τάσσω, so †Μάω, Μάσσω: †μάω being, as in Σμάω, to move to and fro, rub, and in 'Επι-μάομαι, to grasp. (2) Our *mash.* (3) ' Hebr. *mezes,* to squeeze:' Wr.

Μάσσων, longer, more. — As Βαθὺς, Βάσσων; so Μακρὸς, Μάσσων.

Μαστάζω, to chew, as Μασδομαι.

Μάσταξ, that with which one *masticates,* the mouth : —a mouthful to *masticate:*—' a locust, from its greediness:' Ldd.: ' All-mouth', Dnn. Also the upper lip, as Μύσταξ, and the *moustache.* Ewing says: ' The jaws, lips, mouth, the hair on the upper lip:' Thus it fell to the last meaning. — Above.

Μασταρύζω, ' to mumble, like one with his mouth full; so Μαστιχάω:' Ldd. See Μάσταξ.

Μαστεύω, to long for, search, seek.—R. μάω, μάομαι, μέμασται, the same.

Μάστιξ, -ίγος, a whip.—R. μάω, μέμασται, to touch, as Horace: 'Flagello *Tange* Chloen.' So 'Επι-μαίομαι in Homer: Μάστίγι θοῶς ἐπεμαίετο Ἵππους. Or even to excite, goad, as Μαίνω. (2) R. μα for μάλα, στίζω, to prick: μαστίζω, μάστιξ.

Μαστιχάω, to chew, *masticate*, Μαστάζω, and to gnash the teeth.

Μαστίχη, gum mastic. — 'Chewing this gum formerly, as now, prevailed in Greece: R. μάσσομαι, μάσταξ:' Dnn.

Μαστὸς, the breast, as Μαζός. 'Met. any round object, — hill, — round piece of wool fastened to the end of nets:' Ldd.

Μαστροπὸς, -ωπὸς, a pander, pimp.—Like Μαστώρ and Μαστήρ, (See Μαστεύω,) a seeker out (of objects). Or Μήστωρ. (2) Mrt. for ματροπὸς as βόΣτρυχος: Having ματρὸς ὄπα, a mother's voice is soothing. ?

Μασχάλη, an arm-pit. — As ἀγκΑΛΗ, χθαμΑΛΗ. And, as Φάσγανον for Σφάγανον, so Μασχάλη for †Σμαχάλη from Σμάω, to rub, allied to 'Επι-μάομαι to touch and Μάσσω 'to touch', (Ldd.) What the arm is constantly touching and rubbing against. As Axis is that about which the world turns; and Axilla, an arm-pit, is an Axis or pivot. In form, compare Ψάω, Ψακὰς, Ψάκαλον. — Or Μασχάλη is for †Μαχάλη, (as βόΣτρυχος,) from †μάω, ἐπι-μάομαι, to touch. (2) R. μα for μάλα, (as has been thought in ΜΑκαρ and ΜΑστίζω,) and χάω, χαίνω, prim. to be hollow. See 'hollow' in the next Paragraph. (3) Ldd. and Dnn. from Μάλη, but surely the reverse must be true.

Μασχάλη, from the above, is 'the hollow under a fresh shoot, like Pliny's *ala, axilla:* hence the young shoot itself esp. of young palm-twigs;—a bay, gulf:' Ldd.

Μασχαλίζω, 'to put under the Μασχάλαι arm-pits: — hence to mutilate a corpse, as murderers formerly fancied, that, by cutting off the extremities and placing them under the arm-pits, they would avert vengeance:' Ldd.

Μάταιος, rash, foolish, useless; Ματάω, to be in vain or fruitless, spec. to loiter and lose time;— Μάτη, Ματία, fruitless attempt;— error, folly, fault. —From Μάταν, Μάτην, rashly, at random, to no purpose, in vain. — Ldd. compares Ital. *matto,* our *mad;* Fr. *mat,* to ruin, as in our check-*mate.* — The R. is μάω, μέμαται, μέμαα, to be eager, press eagerly on, μαίνομαι. Ldd. says from μάω, to seek (without finding.)

Ματεύω:= μαστεύω.

Ματρύλη, lena; Ματρυλεῖον, 'like Μαστροπεῖον, a brothel:— and Ματρύλη from the same root as Μαστροπός:' Ldd.

Ματτύα, a rich-flavored dish.—'R. μάσσω, [μάττω,] to pound. Hesych. has Ματτύαι even for jaws:' Mrt.

Μαῦλις, a knife. (Very rare.)—As Schneid. derives Μαυλιστής, so the Schol. Thucyd. derives Μαῦλις, from

102

ὁμοῦ αὐλίζομαι: 'for many knives can lodge in one sheath:' (Steph.) Or, as Μαυλιστής with Passow, simply from αὐλίζομαι. (2) Allied to Αὐλὸς, 'an opening, vein or artery, a stream of blood', (Dnn.)

Μαυλιστής, 'a pander, pimp. From ὁμοῦ αὐλίζομαι, [facio pernoctare cum,] Schneid. Or directly from the latter, M euphonic, says Passow:' Dnn. Or M is perh. for †μα-, μάλα. See Μέρμις.

Μαῦρος, obscure, dark. — For 'Αμαυρός.

Μάχαιρα, 'large knife or dirk, to slaughter animals for sacrifice: used by Machaon the surgeon to cut out an arrow; — gen. a knife; — short sword or dagger, rather an assassin's than a soldier's weapon; — sabre; — razor:' Ldd. However, Dnn. and many moderns, with the old etymologists, bring it from μάχη: A battle-knife, sabre.

Μάχη, battle, fight. — R. μάω, μέμακα, μέμαα, to be eager, press forward. Μέμασαν μάχεσθαι, Hom., Μέμασαν πολεμίζειν, &c. and Μεμαὼς is ardent for the war. (2) 'Passow transp. for αἰκμή, αἰχμή:' Dnn. ? (3) 'Hebr. *macha,* to strike:' Mrt. See

Μάχλος, lustful, wanton, insolent, — luxuriant. — R. μάω, μέμακα, μέμαα, μαίνω: Ardens in Venerem. 'Tribuitur potissimùm mulieribus virum appetentibus. Hēsiod "Εργ. 586:' Scheid.

Μάψ, like Μάταν, rashly, to no purpose. — Formed like Ψάω, Ψῆφος, &c. from μάω: i. e. from †μάπτω, †μάψω, as †Δάω, Δάπτω. Compare Μαπέειν.

†ΜΑΩ as in Μέμαα, Αὐτό-ματος (like Αὐτό-μολος,) 'Επι-μάομαι; †ΜΕΩ as in Latin *Meo, Meāre,* (Bp. Burgess,); †ΜΟΩ as in Latin *Moveo* (Bp. Blomf.,): are Primitive words, prim. to *move:* to move towards, seek for, and then lay hold of, grasp, or to *move* my hand to, to touch: — to *move* about, to *move* to and fro, knead, squeeze: — to *move* with vehemence, to excite vehemently. — †Μάω is probably the same as †Βάω, i. e. to make to go, move. (2) 'Μάω, to seek, from Hebr. *mah,* what ?': Mrt.

Μὲ, me, for Εμέ.

Μεγαίρω, to envy and grudge and refuse. — Prop. to look on a thing as being μέγα great or too great for another person. So Γέρας, Γεραίρω. 'Summa petit *livor:*' Ον.

†Μεγάλος in Μέγας.

Μεγαλύνω, to magnify. — Above.

Μέγαρον, 'a large room, chamber, hall, — a house, esp. a large one, a palace: — sanctuary. Τὰ μέγαρα, underground caves sacred to Ceres and Proserpine:' Ldd. 'A large mansion as that of a chief, a palace. R. μέγας:' Dnn. 'Ες ΜΕΓΑ δῶμα, Hom. 'Domus *ampla',* Virg. The end as βλέφΑΡΟΝ. (2) As exposed to envy, R. μεγαίρω, ἀρῶ. 'Thou shalt not *covet* thy neighbour's *house:*' Exod. xx. (3) 'Hebr. *meger,* subterranean repository:' Wr.

Μέγας, †Μεγάλος, (as Φύσαλος,) great.—If we compare Μάκαρ and Μακρὸς, we may be justified in referring Μέγας to R. †μέω, †μέμεκα, preserved in Lat. *meo, meāre,* to go on, allied to †μάω, whence μακρός: Got on, advanced, as in προ-βαίη μεῖζον, ἧκω δυνάμεως, ἧκω καλῶς χρημάτων. So ἐληλακὼς πρὸς &c. (2) Μεγάλος, μεγάλ-, our *mickle*, ' old Teut. *mikil*, Ioel. *mikel*, Sax. *micel.* A most ancient word, says Serenius:' Todd. Then Μέγας short for Μεγάλος.

Μέδιμνος, a dry measure. —'Allied to *Modius, Modus, Moderor,* through μέδω, μέδομαι:' Hemsterh.

Μέδω, to rule. Μέδομαι, to regulate, direct, provide for, plan or devise.—Nothing but †μήδω, μήδομαι, made short as κεδνὸς, Ἕδνα. (2) Νέμω is ' to distribute, dispense, apportion, regulate, sway, rule', (Dnn.). Thus Μέδω may ' be the same as Μείρω or Μερῶ, to divide: indeed μέΔω may be †μέΡω, as caDuceus is put for caRuceus. See Μείρω.

Μέζεα, genitalia; Sicil. μέσα, media: i. e. from μέσσος, as glaSSier, glaZier; EliSSa, EliZa. ' Quia in medio corpore:' Greg.

Μέζων, Μείζων, greater. — R. μέγας, whence †μέσσων, as Βαθὺς, Βάσσων; and μίζων, as glaSS, glaZier; braSS, braZier. See above.

Μέθη, strong drink; — drunkenness. — R. μεθῦ, μεθ-ίημι, remitto, to relax (in mind): as Λύω, Λυαῖος: Χαλῶ, Χάλις. Οὔτω μεθήσομεν ' remissò agēmus' Il. o. 553. (2) Ldd. compares our *mead,* Germ., *meth.*

Μειαγωγέω, I ἄγω bring the μεῖον lamb which was offered at the Apaturian festival: — if not of a certain weight, it was rejected as μεῖον, too little: i. e. less than was right. Μειαγωγῶ τὴν τραγῳδίαν is ἄγειν to weigh tragedy by μεῖον scruples (i.e. very small weights,) or with minute accuracy. Or by metaphor from the above.

Μειδάω, Μειδιάω, to smile. — Allied to Μείων less. See Μείρομαι. Thus ' To Smile: to CONTRACT the face with pleasure:' Dr. Johnson.

Μείζων: in Μέζων,

Μείλια, soothing things, propitiations. — And

Μειλίσσω, to make mild, appease; — beseech with mild words. — R. μέλι, *mel:* (formed as Εἰλίσσω:) To use honied words to.

Μεῖον: in Μειαγωγέω.

Μεῖραξ, a lad or lass, 'in about the fourteenth year,' Ldd. As Μειρακίζομαι is ' to reach the age of puberty,' Ldd., Μεῖραξ must admit an age somewhat later, and therefore may be for ἱμείραξ from ἱμείρω, to desire: Of the age 'of desire. See in Τρᾶγος. Nicander indeed uses Μείρομαι for Ἱμείρομαι. (2) Some think M added, (as in Μορφνὸς, Μοχλὸς, Μέρμις,) and μεῖραξ is εἴραξ = εἴρην, as now able to speak reasonably or in an assembly.

Μείρομαι, ' to share, partake; passive, to be divided, allotted, allotted or decreed by fate. The old Gramm. suppose Μείρω, to divide:' Dnn. And, as Ἀγείρω and Φθείρω in form, so Μείρω from the obsol. †μείω, †μίω, μικρὸς, μινύθω, *minuo,* whence μείων, *minor,* less.

Μεὶς, Μὴς, Μὴν Μηνὸς, a month. — Allied to Μείων and Μείρω, as meaning a division i.e. of the year. (2) Many refer Μὴν to Μήνη the moon. As Month from Moon.

Μείων, ον, less. Μειόω, to lessen, for †μειονόω. —

Allied to Μία one, Μικρὸς small, Μινύθω, *Minuo, Minor.* ' According to analogy, from μέος not in use:' Dnn., so that it comes near to μείρω to divide. See Μείρομαι.

Μέλαθρον, ' the ceiling or the mainbeam supporting it; gen. a roof, — a house. — Acc. to Etym. M. from μέλας, as Atrium from Ater. Hence some take Αἰθαλόεντος ἀνὰ μεγάροιο μέλαθρον for the smoky venthole:' Ldd. ' Assiduâ postes fuligine nigri:' Virg. And ' Culmina fumant.' ' From the volumes of smoke that rolled in it:' Quayle.

Μέλας, μέλαινα, μέλαν, black. —' A kindred form, or dialectic variety is Κελαινός;' Dnn. (2) Allied to Πελὸς dark, as our Meggy, Peggy; Molly, Polly. (3) Many from μὴ, ἔλη a shining. But derivatives from Μὴ are not to the taste of modern critics.

Μέλδω, to *melt.* — Allied to Μέλος, Μέρος, Μείρω, to divide or separate the parts, part, dissolve. As ἔλΔω, ὄρΔω, ἔλΔομαι. (2) Our *melt* and *smelt,* Sax. *meltan.* (3) ' Hebr. *melet,* to set free:' Wr.

Μελεδαίνω, Μελετάω, to care for. And

Μέλει, it is a care to. — R. μέλω.

Μέλεος, unhappy, i.e. to whom things μέλει are a care. So Μελεδώνη is care, sorrow.

Μέλεος, idle, unprofitable, vain: i.e. relaxed εἰς τὰ μέλη as to the limbs, says Schol. Hom.: and Timæus μέλεσι μάταιος. Ὦ μέλε i e. μέλεε, (as Ἠλεὰ, Ἠλὲ,) is O wretch; O *male!* though some say O bone! i.e. worthy of one's care and thought, from μέλει: yet it is somewhat ironical.

Μελετάω: in Μελεδαίνω.

Μελητίδης, a blockhead, ' in form a patronymic of Μέλητος;' Ldd. (2) Perhaps from †μέλος or μέλεος, useless. See Μέλε in Μέλεος.

Μέλι, *mel,* honey. — Thiersch ' from μέλω: The desired, cared for.' Rather, The attended to, elaborated. But rather the *bee* Μέλισσα is *first* (though see Οἴνη:): The sedulous, The busy, as we say As busy as a bee, and Dr. Watts ' How does the little busy bee Improve each shining hour' &c. Μέλισσα as βασιλΙΣΣΑ: then, much as Ἄλφιτον, Ἄλφι, so †Μελίσσιτον, Μέλι. (2) ' Hebr. *meleng,* sweet:' I'kh.

Μελία, a spear: as made of ΜΕΛΙΑ, ash. Called also μείλινον ἔγχος.

Μελίαι, 'ash-nymphs, as Δρυάδες are oak-nymphs:' Ldd.—Above.

Μελίζω, to tear in pieces μέλος limb by limb. — Also, to sing, warble a μέλος song.

Μελί-λωτος, *melilot,* a clover, the honied *lotus.*

Μέλισσα, a bee: see in μέλι honey: — pure nymph or priestess. ' Hebr. *melez,* intercessor:' Wr.

Μελιτώδης, like honey; ' and a name of Proserpine, like Lat. *Mellita ;'* Ldd.

Μέλλω, to intend to do, to be about it, to be about to do, to be going to do or to be: —⬤from μέλει, it is a care to me, i.e. I think of doing. — But, as things intended to be done, are too often delayed, Μέλλω is to loiter, delay. ' I am always about it, but never do it:' Ormst.

Μέλλω, 'to be about to do, whether one will or not ; and so to be made to do, 1. by divine will, fated to do, 2. by man ; 3. it means 'must,' and 4. ' may or will,' hence ' perhaps ':' Ldd.—Above.

Μέλος, a limb i. e. part of the body, nothing but Μέρος, as γράφω and γλάφω. Μέρη καὶ μέλη, μέλη καὶ μέρη, in Plato. (2) ' Hebr. mel, to cut off :' Wr.

Μέλος, melos, a song.— Dr. Jones: 'R. μέλι, from its sweetness.' So Μελί-γηρυς, Μελι-φθογγος. ' Melody : sweetness of sound :' Dr. Joh. (2) Some from μέλος above : Of proper members and proportions. As Number is 'harmony, proportions calculated by Number,' (Dr. J.) ' Carmen modulatum', says Scheid.

Μέλπω, to sing a μέλος song. So Ἕλπω, Θάλπω, ἕρπω.— Some say μέλος ἕπω.

Μέλω, to be an object of care to ; — to be anxious.— As μέλος and μέρος, so Damm identifies μέλω and μεΡῶ. Indeed Μέλω is in one sense Μερίζω, to distract another's mind,—in another sense Μερίζομαι, to be myself distracted. Compare Μεριμνῶ and Μερ-μηρίζω. (2) As Δ and Λ are allied in Δάκρυμα Lacryma, Ὀδυσσεὺς, ULysses, so μέλω and μέΔομαι, μήΔομαι.

Μέμβλεται, = μέλει : from μέλομαι, μεμέλομαι, μέμλομαι, μέμΒλομαι, as in ΜεσημΒρία, and French nomre, nomBre, numBer. Some for μεμέληται.—So Μέμβλωκα, pf. of μολέω, μλόω, μέμλωκα, μέμΒλωκα, as above.

Μέμνονες, black birds said to have issued from the funeral pile of Memnon. Ov. M. 13. 617 : ' Ab illo Memnonides dictæ.'

Μέμνων, an ass.—R. μένω, redupl. †μεμένω, †μέμνω. ' From its patient nature :' Ldd. and Dnn.

Μέμονα ' is to Μέμαα, as Γέγονα to Γέγαα :' Ldd.

Μέμφομαι, to blame. — Like λαΜΒάνω, for †μέφομαι, allied (through a form †μέπω) to Μαπέειν to seize, Μάομαι to lay hold of : as Re-prehendo, to Re-prehend, blame. Formed like Πέμπω, Πτέμβω.

Μὲν, in truth, indeed.— R. μένω, ' to remain firm or fixed', (Dnn.). An affirmative particle ; particula perseverandi, asseverandi. (2) Many imagine Μὲν to be Ἓν (as fem. Μία,) and connect Δὲ with Δύω : In one case, In the second. But ?

Μενεαίνω, Μενοινάω, to desire earnestly ; — purpose earnestly ; — am furious, angry.— From

Μένος, ardor of mind, spirit, inclination, purpose, allied to μάω, μέμαα, as †Γάω, Γένος. Also, energy of body, vigor, strength : μένος τε καὶ ἀλκή, Hom. (2) Some from μένος : ' Steady purpose, firmness, force.'

Μένω, Μενέω, to remain firm and fixed, to remain. ' Μέμονα', says E. Valpy on Il. 5. 482, ' is .from μένω, promtus sum, prob. the prim. meaning of μένω, and hence the sense of persisting in a will, and also sustineo, maneo.' Μάω, Μένω, as †Φάω, †Φένω ; †Γάω, †Γένω, Γενέω.

Μερίζω, to divide into μέρεα parts.

Μέριμνα, distracting thought, anxiety.—For μεριζομένα, or μεμερισμένα, μεμερμμένα. ' In .curas animus
104

diducitur omnés,' Virg. ' Animum nunc huc, nunc dividit illuc,' Id. ' Tot me impediunt curæ, quæ meum animum divorsim trahunt :' Ter. So

Μέρμερος, anxious, disquieted ;—causing annoyance, peevish. So

Μέρμηρα, care ; Μερμαίρω, Μερμηρίζω, am anxious, form plans.—R. μερίζω, to divide, as Μέριμνα :· redupl. †μερμερίζω, &c. Or μερίς, a division, †μερμερίς, &c. See above.

Μέρμις, ῖθος, a cord.—Ldd. for †ἕρμις from εἴρω, ἕρμαι, to join, as Ἕρμα a chain. M as Μοχλὸς, &c. This M for ἅμ', as N in Νηλεὴς is really AN, Ἀν-ηλεὴς.— Or M for †μα—, μάλα. (2) R. μηρύω, μεμήρυμαι : as Μήρινθος, a cord. But all these are allied.

Μέρος, Μερὶς, a part.—R. μείρω, μερῶ, μείρομαι.

Μέροψ, speaking articulately.—R. μείρω, μερῶ, ὄψ or ὄψ.

Μεσηγὺ, -γὺς, in the midst : See Ἐγγύς.

Μέσος, middle.— Allied to Μείρω to divide, Μείων less, &c. which from obsol. †μέω, 'as †Φθέω, Φθείρω. (2) Dnn. allies it to Μετὰ, in the midst of : 'as Μεταίχμιον for μεΞαίχμιον, μέΤαυλος for μέΞαυλος.' (3) ' Chald. metza, partiri :' Mrt.

Μεστὸς, filled full, full.—' The Gramm. Vett. from ἐστὸς, with M added': Dnn. Ἐστὸς would mean ' satiated,' from †ἕω to satiate. See fully in Ἕδω. M; as in Μέρμις. (2) Allied, through M and B, to Βυστὸς, filled quite full: and †Ξέεστὸς, stifled, ἄ-σβεστος. So Βόω and Μύω are the same.

Μέσφα, up to a point, meanwhile.—' For ἔσφα, M prefixed [See in Μέρμις :] : ἐς and φα, [as φι in Ἀμφί,] :' Lenn. ' Anciently there were terminations φε, φα, φι, φιν:' Id. (2) From the obsol. †μέω, Lat. meo, meáre, to go, as Ἴκταρ from Ἴκω. ' QUO simul MEARIS,' Hor. Ξ, as in Ἔξχον. See Μέχρι.

ΜΕΤΑ, Μετ', Μεθ', together with, amid, among ;— following with, close upon, after. In comp., it is often ' following one after another, succession, transition change', as in Meta-morphose.—' Very slightly varied in form and meaning in all the Gothic dialects : mith, mid, mit, med, mede : The Goth. from the verb signif. to meet. So our mate, Alem. mate, maet, socins : Isl. Su. G. mat, maet; Teut. maed :' Dmb.

Μεταλλάω, ' to enquire after, ask. — Damm from μετ' ἄλλα, [one after another,] approved by Buttm. Hence Μέταλλον, a search for metals, then the place searched, a mine :' Dnn. But Pott makes it ' Ore, combined WITH OTHER substances.'

Μεταμώλιος, Μεταμώνιος, vain, useless.—Thought to be for μετ-ανεμώλιος, -ώνιος. (2) Prop. ' vain μετὰ μῶλον after all the toil :' much as Μόλις,hardly,scarcely, is prop..with Μῶλος trouble. Or, coming μετὰ μῶλον after the battle, as we say ' after the fair'.

ΜΕΤΑΞΑ, raw silk.—' Used by the later Greeks :' Steph.— Can it be from μετ-άγω, ξω : Ậ thing imported or exchanged ?

Μεταξὺ, as Μετὰ, between, among, after. — As διΞ-

Σὸς, διΞὸς, so for μετασσὸ, like περὶ, περισσά. So Μέτασσαι, 'lambs younger than the firstlings, but older than the last-born, and so *middle-born* or summer lambs:' Ldd.—Above.

Μετήορος, like Μετέωρος, raised up.— R. ἀείρω, ήορα.

Μέτρον, a measure; proper measure, moderation; measure in verse, *metre*.—Allied to *Metior*, to *Mete*. ΜΕΤρον is to be compared with ΜΕΔω, ΜΕΔομαι, to regulate, Lat. *medus*, *moderor*, to *moderate*. 'Damm refers it to Μείρω. Compare also Μέσος, with which Μέτριος espec. seems allied:' Dnn. (2) ' Hebr. *mad*, to measure': Mrt.: ' *med*,' Wr.

Μέχρι, -ις, like Ἄχρι, -ις, up to, unto, until.—Allied to Μῆκος, length, and Μακρὸς, long. See Ἄχρι. (2) From the obs. †μέω, †μέμεκα, Lat. *meo*, *meavi*, to go forward. So Ἴκταρ from Ἴκω. See Μέσφα.

Μὴ, not, whether or not, do not—, &c. — Hoogeveen thinks it to be Μάω, imperat. of μάω ' to desire eagerly, ardently, vehemently:' (Dnn.) and says : ' It shows a mind anxious in bewaring, serious in dissuading and prohibiting, ardent in deprecating, vehement in hating, desirous in asking.'—Scheide takes it in the sense of Μάομαι, to ' seek' *whether* a thing is so or not. (2) Dunb. connects it with Μείων, less : ' See that you do *not*.' ?

Μήδεα, pudenda.—Ut Αἰδὼς, Αἰδοῖα, et Pudenda, et Verētrum, sic Μήδεα h Μῆδος, prudentia.

Μηδίζω, to imitate the *Medes*.

Μῆδος, a plan, scheme ; — counsel, prudence, discretion, carefulness : and Μήδομαι, as Μήδομαι, to design, plan, work. — ' R. μάω, [μέμηται, †μήδην as Στάδην, Βάδην,] to seek eagerly:' Mrt. Compare Μῆτις. (2) R. μέδω.

Μηκάομαι, to bleat,— scream, shriek. — From the sound μὴ μὴ, whence Μῆλον a sheep. So from μὺ is Μυκάομαι to low: from βὰ βὰ Lat. balo.

Μηκέτι, no longer.—R. μὴ, ἔτι : the K appears taken from οὐκέτι.

Μῆκος, length.—Allied to Μακρὸς, long.

Μήκων, poppy.— From its μῆκνος, tallness ; exemplified in Tarquin's cutting off the tallest poppies in his garden. Mrt. says ' à capitis μήκει.'

Μηκωνὶς, lettuce : thought to have soporific virtues like the Μήκων.

Μήλη, a surgeon's probe.— R. μάω, μάομαι, ἐπι- -μάομαι, to handle, feel: †μαέλη, μήλη. Or μάω, to search.

Μήλιος λιμὸς, a great famine.— From the siege of *Melos* by the Athenians in the Peloponnesian War.

Μῆλον, the female breast, and a cheek : From the round form of the ΜΗΛΟΝ apple or orange.

Μῆλον, a sheep, from the sound μὴ μὴ, as Μηκάομαι to bleat.

Μὴν, assuredly, indeed :— ' R. μένω:' Mrt. See Μέν. (2) Hebr. *amēn*, verily.

Μὴν, a month. — From μεὶς, μεὶν, a month. (2) R.

μήνη, the moon. As Moon, Month. (2) ' Or from Hebr. *manah*, numeravit :' Schleusn.

Μήνη, the moon. —' From the obs. †μέω, *meo*, *meāre*:' Lenn. (See in †ΜΑΩ.) ' *Meo* is often said of things which (eunt redeuntque) go and return:' Forcell. ' Prop. returning:' Scheid. Μήνη, as Ψέω, Ψηγή. So Σελήνη. (2) Goth. *mena*, Sax. *mona*, Teuton. *maan*. (3) ' Hebr. *manah*, numeravit:' Mrt.

Μήνιγξ, ' a skin or membrane, espec. what envelopes the brain, the pia mater. R. prob. μανός: Schneid.:' Dnn. I.e. thin, fine. ' Pia Mater, a *thin and delicate* membrane', says Dr. J.

Μῆνις, wrath. — R. μαίνω, ἔμηνα, to make to rage. As ' Ira brevis FUROR est.' Or the same as Μένος, fury. (2) R. μένω. ' Ira per-*manens*:' Mrt.

Μηνύω, to inform, show, discover. — Μένος is ' mind, disposition, in Εὐ-μενὴς, Δυσ-μενὴς', (Dnn.) and in Latin is *Mens*, as Γένος is Gens. Hence Μηνύω, to put into another's *mind*, suggest, inform. Whence also (μενάω,) †μνάω, μιμνήσκω, to re-*mind* one of. (2) ' May it not be from μήνη, the moon, formed for signs, Gen. 1. 14: or for the ἀνάδειξιν χρόνων signification or declaration of times, Ecclus. 43. 6?' Pkh. (3) ' Chald. *man*, quid ?' Mrt.

Μήρινθος, a cord, string, line, the same as ΜΕΡμις, and allied to ΜΗΡύομαι, to twine. Comp. our noun Twine.

Μηρὸς, the upper, fleshy part of the thigh. — R. μείρω, μερῶ, to divide: The body there dividing. So nearly all.

Μηρυκίζω, to chew over again, ruminate. — R. †μηρύω, μηρύομαι, to wind round, i. e. to roll over the food already chewed. (2) ' R. ἐρύγω: Μ prefix:' Dnn.

Μηρύομαι, to draw up, furl, as ἱστία μηρύσαντο, Hom. Also to draw close together, wind off, twine. — With Μ prefix, from ἐρύω, to draw: †ἀμ-ερύω, †ἀμηρύομαι. See for Μ in Μαυλιστής.

Μήστωρ, a planner, deviser ;— adviser, leader. — R. μήδομαι, μέμησται.

Μήτηρ, a mother.—R. μάω, μέμηται, to have an impulse after, ardently desire or seek after. ' From her ardent and tender love:' Valck. (2) Our *mother*, and the northern affinities. Sansk. *matara*.

Μῆτις, counsel, wisdom, skill.—' Μήδομαι, Μῆδος are akin to Μῆτις, and all referred to μάω, [μέμηται,] :' Dnn.

Μήτρα, the womb, from μήτηρ, μητρός. Also, the soft pith or heart of oak, &c.

Μητρυιά, a step-mother: R. μήτηρ.

Μηχανὴ, art, contrivance, invention, *machination*: a *machine*. — From

Μῆχος, contrivance; as Μῆδος, art, contrivance;— contrivance against, remedy. — ' Akin to Μῆδος, Μῆτις, Μάω:' Dnn.

Μία, fem., one. — Allied to Μικρὸς, Μικρὸς, Μίος, Μείων less, Μινύθω, Μίνυω, Μιστύλλω: words all having the sense of smallness. See †Μίω. So Merus from Μείρω is ' alone', i. e. ' all-one': and Privus from Πρίω, to cut off.

P

Μιαίνω, to stain, pollute, corrupt. — If to ' corrupt',
' adulterate,' is considered the orig. meaning, Μιαίνω is
allied to Μινύθω, Μίνυω, to di-minish (the strength of),
deteriorate: and to Μείων, less. — Schleusn. notes that
the Schol. on Il. 4. 141 has rightly explained there μιήνη
by its proper meaning χρίσῃ, βάψῃ, plunge: and μίξαι
ἄνδρας κακότητι καὶ ἄλγεσι, in the Odyssey is explained
by Dnn. ' to plunge men in calamity and affliction.'
Μιαίνω and μίγνῦμι then may be allied. See †Μίγω.

Μιαρὸς, foul. — Above.

†Μίγω, ξω, Μίγνῦμι, Μίσγω, to mix. — As Θίγω,
Ψίγω, Τμήγω. From the obs. †μίω, whence μικρὸς,
μείων less, μινύθω, μίνυω, μιστύλλω: i. e. to lessen the
force of, i.e. in mixing water with wine, as often in
Homer. (2) ' Hebr. masach, to mix:' Mrt.

Μίδας, the luckiest throw on the dice, called from
Μίδας, as also 'Ηρακλῆς Hercules, and Lat. jactus
Veneris, the throw of Venus.

Μικκὸς, Μικρὸς, small. —'R. †μίω, †μέμικα, to diminish, μείων less, μειῶ to lessen, μινύθω, μίνυω,
μιστύλλω. (2) ' Hebr. mek, to decay:' Wr.

Μιλιάζω, ' of immense depth, whence the name:' Forcell.
But Dnn. says: ' a caldron like a mile-stone.'

ΜΙΑΤΟΣ, red lead, red earth. — Q. ?.

Μίλφαι, a falling away of the hair of the eyebrows.
—A rare medical word. Perhaps for μέλφαι, (as λίκριφις
and λέχρις, τέγγω and tIngo,) allied to Μέλδω to melt.
So Ἕλλω and Ἴλλω.

Μιμαλὼν, Μιμαλλών, a Bacchante. — ' Prop. women
were so called, as imitating men, from μιμεῖσθαι. Some
say from their imitating Bacchus in wearing horns:'
Steph. In form, much as Βέβηλος, Æol. Βέβᾱλος.
The I in the Latin Poets however is short. (2) Better
then with Madan from ' Mimas, a mountain of Ionia,
sacred to Bacchus.'

Μίμαρκις, a pudding of hare's flesh and the blood. —
Like λΙλαίομαι; — redupl. from μείρω, μέμαρκα, to
divide, cut into μέρεα parts, i.e. mince. (2) R. †μίω,
†μέμιμαι, †μέμισται, whence μιστύλλω, to cut up into
pieces. In form, much as μυλΑΚΡΙΣ. (3) Ldd.
thinks it a foreign word.

Μιμέομαι, to imitate. Μῖμος, an actor, mimic, buf-
foon. — As pictures of nature and of animals reduce the
proportions of what they represent, and imitations are
for the most part shadows and faint expressions of the
originals, μιμέομαι could mean to do things on a small
scale after something else, from the obs. †μίω, †μέμιμαι,
as in many words above and below. Thus Miniature,
(from Minium,) says Dr. J., is representation in a small
compass, less than the reality.

Μιμνήσκω: in †Μνάω.

Μίμνω, for μένω, †μιμένω, as †Πέτω, †Πιπέτω, Πίπτω.
Μιμὼ, an ape, i.e. an imitator: μιμέομαι.

Μιν: in Ἴν.

106

ΜΙΝΔΑΞ, a kind of Persian incense. (Only in
Athen. 691.)

Μίνθος ' is an ill-odored flower, and dung, or the smell
of goats, by antiphrasis from ΜΙΝΘΑ, mint:' Hemst.
See 'Ονθυλεύω.

Μινύθω, μίνυω, to diminish. Μίνυὸς, small. — R.
obsol. †μίω, μικρὸς, μείων, minor less. So

Μίνυνθα, a little. — Above.

Μίνυρὸς, whining, whimpering. — R. μινυὸς, small:
A speaking in a slender, feeble voice. In Μινύθω.

Μινύρομαι, Μινυρίζω, minurio, to sing plaintively—
Above.

Μίσγω: in †Μίγω.

Μισέω, to hate. — R. †μίω, μέμισαι, as in Μινύθω:
I.e. to think or make little of, vili-pendo. So ' to Slight
is from the adjective Slight:' Dr. J. ' Μῖσος is a vice
by which you desire to make others minūtos small:'
Lenn. — And, as allied to Μείρω, to divide, it may be
compared with Temno from Τέμνω, and our verb ' To
cut a person.' (2) Some compare Μῦσος: as μΙτυλος
and μΥτιλος. (3) Mrt. from μὴ ἴσος, not acting fairly?
(4) ' Hebr. mes, to despise:' Wr.

Μισθὸς, wages, pay, hire. — As Mereo, to earn, is
from μέρος a part, portion, — and Μοῖρα is one's due
portion, from μείρομαι to divide, — so Μισθὸς from the
obs. †μίω, †ἐμίσθην, to divide, as in Μιστύλλω. ' Will
appoint him his PORTION:' Luke 12. 46. Compare
Δίδωμι, and Δασμός. (2) ' Hebr. masseth, a gift :' Mrt.

Μιστύλη, -λη, a piece of bread hollowed, and serving as a spoon: from

Μιστύλλω, to cut up, mince: allied to Μίτυλος,
Μύτιλος, mutilus, mutilated, and to Μινυὸς small, Μινύθω, μίνυω, to diminish, Μικρὸς small: so that there
was an old word †μίω, †μέμισται.

Μίσχος, Μίσκος, the footstalk of leaves or fruits,
which unites them to a plant. — M is thought by Lennep,
as in many cases, a prefix; and μίσχος as = ἴσχος from
ἴσχω = ἔχομαι to adhere to. M: see Μέρμις, Μηρύομαι. Dnn. compares Μόσχος.

Μίτος, a thread, string, belt, bolt, chain.—'R. μεῖον,
being thin:' Mrt. Compare Μίτυλος, Μινυὸς, Μιστύλλω. Damm explains it ' lamina tenuis, longa.'

Μίτρα, band, girdle, fillet for the hair, mitre.— ' If
not directly from μίτος, it has the same origin:' Dnn.

Μίτυλος: in Μιστύλλω.

Μίτυς, called by Aristotle, Hist. Anim. (and used by
him only,) ἀπο-κάθαρμα τοῦ κηροῦ: whence prob. formed
like Μίτυλος, Μιστύλλω, Μίτος: I.e. what is divided
off, separated, thrown away.

†Μίω, to diminish, an obs. word, much introduced
above, and allied to †Μάω, Μάομαι, 'Επι-μάομαι, to
touch, handle, — exactly as Ψάω is both ' to touch' and
' to scrape, rub off.' ' Allied to †Μάω, †Μόω, moveo,
movendo detero, minuo:' Lenn. Compare Μείρω,
Μείων, Μικρὸς, Μίτυλος, Μιστύλλω, Μισθὸς, &c.
Μάω, †Μίω, as Ψάω, Ψίω. †Μίω is acknowledged by
E. Valpy on Hom. Il. 1. 465.

MNA, à *mina*. — 'We find *mina* ovis, *mina* mamma, and in Hesych. μίνα are *small* figs [as allied to Μικρά, Μιννά, &c.], but still *MNA* is written in so many letters in the *Hebrew*:' Valck.

Μνάομαι, to. woo, court. — From μένος, in the sense of *mens*: 'To have in the *mind*, desire eagerly, hence to seek after, strive to obtain': Dnn., who however refers μνάω immed. to μάω. Or Μένος here is 'desire', whence μέμωνα, 'to desire ardently, strive after': then †μενδόμαι, μνάομαι.

†Μνάω, †Μνήσκω, Μιμνήσκω, to cause to remember: Μνάομαι, to remember. — I. e. to bring into the μένος, Lat. *mens*, (as Γένος, Gens,) *mind*: 'to put in *mind*,' (Dnn.) (2) R. μένω: 'To cause things to *remain* in the knowledge and memory:' Lenn.

Μνεία, memory; Μνῆμα, a remembrance, memorial, monument. — Above.

Μνηστεύω, as Μνάομαι, ἐμνήστσαι, to woo.

Μνίος, soft. Μνίον, moss. — R. μνίω, to eat: Fit for eating. Thus from †μίω (see Μνίω,) is prob. *mitis*, prim. soft, as ' *Mitia* poma', Virg.

Μνίω, to eat, in Hesych. — Formed from †μίω, just as Dnn. forms Μνάω from Μάω. See †MIΩ: and compare πΝίγω, and σιΝιάζω.

MNOIA, servitude; Μνωῖται, Μνῷται, serfs. But Pollux writes that Μνωῖται were among the Cretans ' middle between the free and the slaves'; so perhaps they had so many Μναῖ *minæ* paid for them. (2) R. μάνης, (μήης,) a common name for Slaves.

Μνόος, Μνοῦς, fine soft down. — ' Akin to, or from Μνίον:' Dnn.

Μογγὸς, with a thick voice, hoarse. — R. μόγος: Where the voice issues with much labor: μογικὸς, (as Μαγικὸς, Λογικὸς,) †μογγικὸς, †μογγός. Compare Μόργος. ΓΓ, as φέΓΓος, φθόΓΓος.

Μόγις and Μόλις, scarcely, hardly; i.e. with great toil. — For Μόγοις, Μόλοις.

Μόγος, Μόθος, Μόλος, Μόχθος, are usually classed together, and mean labor, toil. — Bp. Blomf. says: 'The primitive of Μόγος was, if I mistake not, †μόω, †μοέω, *mo*Veo:' (See on Μολεῖν:) Thus Μόγος is much like †*Movimentum, Momentum*, ' which very often means a force impelling to action, a weight or power by applying which anything becomes easier:' Forcell. Μόγος then could easily mean any 'toil or labor' by applying which anything is done. ' *Moveo*, to design, attempt,' says Forcellini.

Μόδιος, the Lat. *modius*. R. μέδω.

Μόθαξ, Μόθων, said of Helot-boys, brought up as foster-brothers of the young Spartans: and, as thus taking liberties and becoming *troublesome* and impudent, it so meant : As Vernilia was so used from Verna. — R. μόθος = μόλος. For from μόλος is *molestus*, and from Πόνος ' labor' was Πονηρὸς, ' causing trouble, troublesome, depraved,' Dnn.

Μόθος, battle, battle-din. — Explained ' labor' by Hesych., like Μόγος and Μόλος. I.e. the struggle of

107

the battle-field, and the accompanying noise and tumult.

Μοῖρα, a part, portion, lot, destiny. — R. μείρομαι, μέμοιρα, to divide.

Μοῖχος, adulter. — Hemsterhus. et Schultens ' à μέμοιχα pf. τοῦ Μείχω vel Μίχω [unde Ὀμιχέω], mingo, meio.' Nam et Horatius habet ' *meiat*' ipsā coëundi significatione. Et Liddell notat ' Οὐρέω esse, ut Lat. *meio*, τὴν γονὴν emittere.' Hoc quidem et de marito verum: at videatur esse et solum et totum opus adulteri. (2) Ut ὅμ-ηλυς ab ἥλυθον, sic ὅμ-οιχος ab οἴχομαι: Qui co-it cum alterā. Nota M in Μαυλιστὴς, Μέρμις, Μίσχος, &c. In Shakp., K. Lear, 'Let copulation thrive', i.e. μοιχεία, Act 4. Sc. 6. (3) ' Qui facit τὸ Μὴ Ἐοικός: Mrt. ?

Μολγὸς, a hide, —bag, as Βολγὸς, *bulga*.—' Prob. from †μέλγω, ἀμέλγω, = μέργω, ἀμέργω, as Δέρω, Δορά:' Ldd. (2) As a 'bag', R. μολεῖν: To go with on a journey.

Μολεῖν, to come or go.— Bp. Blomf. supposes the obs. †μόω, †μοέω, *mo*Veo, to move oneself : Allied to †μάω as in Αὐτό-ματος like Αὐτό-μολος: and allied to Lat. *meo*, *meāre*. Hence then Μολεῖν. See on Μόγος. (2) R. Βάλλω, βολέω, βολῶ, μολῶ, as Βύρμηξ and Μύρμηξ, Βύω and Μύω. See †Βλέω, Βλώσκω. (3) ' Hebr. *mol*, to go aside :' Wr.

Μόλιβος, Μόλιβδος, Μόλυβδος, lead. Scheide asks: ' An a *mole* et gravitate ?' This well agrees with this mineral, and Dnn. allies *Moles* with Μόγος, Μόλος, Μῶλος.

Μόλις: in Μόγις.

Μολοβρὸς, a greedy beggar. — Usu. thought = †μολοβόρος, μολὼν εἰς βορὰν, going for food. (2) ' Riem. refers it to μώλυς, *mollis*, fat, lazy: connecting it with Μολόβριον, a young pig with its soft tender flesh :' Ldd.

Μόλος, Μῶλος, 'toil, espec. warlike toil, strife. — Akin to Μόγος, Μόθος:' Dnn. (2) R. μέλει, †μέμολε, it is a care. (3) R. μολεῖν: Toil of journeying. (4) As Βδέω, Βδόλος, so μάω, (to be ardent, i.e. for the fight,) μόλος. Compare Μάχη. (5) Our *moil*.

Μολοσσὸς, a dog of *Molossus* in Epirus.

Μολοσσὸς, a foot, consisting of 3 long syllables. From *Molossus*, son of Pyrrhus and Andromache:' Dnn.

Μολπὴ, song. — R. μέλπω, μέμολπα.

Μόλυβδος: in Μόλιβος.

Μολύνω, to spot, stain, pollute. — As Δηθύνω, Βαρύνω. Valck. says: ' I suspect it is prop. to contract dirt from the mud in journeying, from μολεῖν.' (2) Or from laboring, from μόλος. (3) R. μέλας, black. O, as Lat. pOndus from pEndo.

Μομφὴ, blame. — R. μέμφομαι.

Μοναχὸς, solitary : a *monk*. — R. μόνος.

Μονὴ, a mansion. — R. μένω, μέμονα. As *maneo, mansum, mansion*.

Μόνιμος, permanent; — steady. — R. μένω.

Μόνος, alone. — R. μένω, μέμονα, to remain. 'Often said of one left and remaining behind : Matth. 14. 23 : 17. 8. Mark 9. 8. Luk. 24. 12:' Scheide. Μόνος μένει, John 12. 24. 'Here I *remain alone*:' Gray's Letters.

Μόρα, a division of citizens, or of soldiers, regiment. — R. μείρομαι, μέμορα, to divide. 'The whole army was DIVIDED into μόραι regiments:' Rob. Gr. Ant.

Μόργνυμι: == ὁμόργνυμι.

Μόργος, explained by Hesych. 'an enclosure, and a covered part in waggons in which they carry chaff:' whence it is probably from μόρα, a division: 'divided off.' Thus: †μορικὸς, †μορκὸς, μόργος. Thus Μοργὴ in Pollux is a small part or portion. Hence Μοργεύω, to convey straw, &c. in a Μόργος. (Very rare.)

Μορία, == μωρία, folly.

Μορίαι, 'with or without ἐλαῖαι, the sacred olives in the Academy: all olives that grew in the precincts of temples: prob. as parted or propagated μειρόμεναι, μεμορημέναι, from the orig. olive-stock in the Acropolis. Hence Ζεὺς Μόριος, as the guardian of them :' Ldd. — Or, as Τέμενος from Τέμνω, being cut off and separated from common olives.

Μόριον, a small μόρος piece.

Μόρσιμος, Μέρσιμος, allotted, fatal. — R. μείρω, μέμορα, whence Μοῖρα, lot.

Μορμολύττομαι, to scare: and

Μορμορωπὸς, hideous. — From Μορμώ.

Μορμύρω, to rush, roar, *murmuro*, to *murmur*. 'Written also Μυρμύρω. In the same relation to Μύρω, as Πορφύρω to Φύρω: formed in imitation of the sound {μορ μορ}:' Dnn.

Μορμώ, a hag, hob-goblin: — exclam. of fright. — 'R. μόρμος, idle fear. Perh. allied to Μορμύρω, in allus. to frightful *sound*; — or to Μαυρὸς, Μορφνὸς, dark, black, gloomy, in allus. to *appearance*:' Dnn. As Λόγιμος, Μόρσιμος, suppose †μαύριμος, †μαύρμος. Compare the double adjectives Teter, Tetricus; Unus, Unicus. (2) Allied to Μέρμερος, 'causing care and sorrow, trouble, or injury': (Dnn.).

Μόροεις, 'skilfully-wrought: Ernesti from μόρον: Mulberry-colored. Others make it Glistening, shining:' Ldd. — Or, according to its just proportions, from μόρος. — Or for μολόεις from μόλος laber: Elaborated. See μοΡύσσω.

Μόροεις, destined: — from

Μόρος, appointed lot, fate, death, *mors*. — R. μείρομαι, μέμορα.

ΜΟΡΡΙΑ, ΜΟΡΡΙΝΗ, Lat. *murrha*. 'Some make it a natural substance, as agate: others Chinese porcelain, china:' Ldd. 'Prob. from an Eastern dialect. Passow compares Russ. *murawa*, glaring, for earthenware:' Dnn.

Μορτὸς, *mortal*. — R. μόρος.

Μορύσσω, like Μολύνω, to defile: as γλάφω, γράφω.

Μορφὴ, outward form, shape, figure. — We speak of 'the *different* forms of government, of public Worship,' &c. so Μορφὴ may be from μείρω, μέμορα, to divide i. e. distinguish. As τόρΠΗ, &c. (2) Transp. from †φορμὴ, Lat. *furma*; R. φέρω, πέφορα, φορίμη, *bearing* on its

surface certain shapes, Lat. re-*ferens*. So 'Εμ-φαφὴς is 'like.'

Μόρφνος, said of the eagle, but variously explained : 1. 'dusky', from ὀρφνη, with M prefix as in Μέρμις, &c.: — 2. 'graceful', from μορφὴ, form: — 3. 'deadly, killing', for μορο-φόνος.

ΜΟΣΣΥΝ, a wooden house or tower. — 'A *Scythian* word: *maçon* French. Serenius allies our *mason*:' Todd.

ΜΟΣΧΟΣ, musk, '*muschio* Ital., *musc* Fr., from Arab. *moscha*:' Todd.

Μόσχος, 'a tender shoot or *sucker*,—met. an infant, young maiden, young bullock. R. ὄσχος, ὄσχη, M euphonic:' Dnn. See Μέρμις.

Μοτὸς, lint. —'From †μόω, to fill, cram: applied to hollow wounds to fill up the flesh:' Blomf. This †μόω is allied to Μύω and to Βύω to close. So †Πόω and Πῶμα, a lid.

Μουνυχιών, 'the tenth Attic month, in which was a festival of Diana of Μουνυχία, Μουνυχία, one of the havens of Athens:' Dnn. The word apparently is from μόν-ονυξ, μῶνυξ, applied to horses.

Μοῦσα, Μοῖσα, Μῶσα, Μᾶα, 'the *Muse*, the Goddess of Poetry, Music, Song, Dancing, the Drama, &c.: met. *music*, song, eloquence:—a poetess, musician, songstress. — Prob. from obsol. μάω, μῶ, μάομαι, to search, and so invent :' Dnn. and Hemst. 'The ancients thus : Μοῦσαι ἀπὸ τῆς Μασέως, ζητήσεως:' Dnn. (2) 'Hebr. *musar*, eruditie:' Dahler.

Μουσεῖον, temple of the *Muses*. Above. — Also, a *museum*, 'said to be the place at Athens where *Musœus* sang and was buried. Later, the Opus *musivum*, mo*saic*:' Ldd.

Μόχθος, the same as Μόγος, and allied to it by all.

Μοχλεύω, to move heavy weights; Μόχλευσις, a moving by a lever. — From

Μόχλος, a bar, bolt, crow, lever, pole. — As ΜΟτὸς is for stopping up a wound, so ΜΟχλος is for stopping up a door; and both allied to Μύω and Βύω, to stop up. (2) But gen. thought the same as ὀχλεὺς, M prefixed, as in Μέρμις.

Μοψόπιος, Attic: from King Μοψευς.

Μὰ μῦ, Μὺ μῦ, 'formed to represent a sound uttered with closed lips, expressive of discontent, complaint or mockery. Lat. *mutio*, *museo*:' Dnn. The very pronunciation of the M is by closing the lips.

Μύαξ, a sea-muscle: μῦς, μυός.

Μυδάω, to bite or compress the lips in displeasure. — From μῦ.

Μυγμὸς, a *muttering*. — R. μύζω, μέμυγμαι.

Μυδάζομαι, == μυσάττομαι.

Μυδάω, *madeo*, to be moist, wet; damp, clammy, putrid from wet. — See Μαδάω.

Μύδος, *mutus*, dumb. — From μῦ, or μύω, μύζω.

Μύδρος, a mass of red hot iron. — R. μύζω, ἔμυδον, (Plutarch uses μύσας from μύζω) : for Budæus says that Gaza explains μύζω '*mutire* et *STRIDERE*.' A muttering, hissing sound well agrees. So Dnn.

makes μῦ to be a sound of 'mockery', i. e. of *hissing*.
(**2**) 'Ready μυδῶν to fall off and melt:' Lenn.

Μυελὸς, marrow, pith. — Allied to Μυχὸς, 'the innermost part', (Dnn.) 'R. μύω: Inclosed in the innermost part of the flesh and bones:' Damm.

Μυέω, to initiate into the μυστήρια *mysteries* : — instruct. — All from μύω, i. e. to close against the profane, but by consequence to open to the disciples. 'Eustath. from μύω, because the initiated were to shut their mouths, and not discover what they were taught ;'Pkh.

Μύζω, *mutio*, *musso*, to *mutter*, grumble : — to drink with closed lips. — R. μῦ, μυάω, μύω. (**2**) ' Hebr. *mazah*, exprimo:' Dahler.

· **Μῦθος**, 'an announcement in order to guide, direct, advise, warn, enjoin, command, relate : a word, saying, speech, discourse, narrative, tale, fable, proverb, advice. According to the old Gramm. it expresses less the result of the reasoning powers than Λόγος, and is prop. referable to the will, mind, disposition, being formed by transp. from Θυμός: so also Damm:' Dnn. (**2**) Much better from μυέω, ἐμυήθην, to instruct, by contraction, as Πηγνῦτο for Πηγνύοιτο, (Matthiæ G. G. 204. 3.) and see Μύστης: A didactic tale, &c. (**3**) Others from μύω to shut the mouth : prop. a dark mysterious tale, which one must speak of with one's-self rather than with others.

Μυῖα, Μύα, a fly : ' μυῖα χαλκῆ blind-man's buff, Ital. mosca ceca (*musca cæca*):' Dnn. — 'R. μύζω, to murmur:' Schrevel. Nearer, from μῦ. (**2**) R. μεμαυῖα, bold, daring, as called also Κυνό-μυια. ' Homer praises it for its perseverance and boldness, and blames it for its impudence:' Damm.

· **Μυκάομαι**, *mugio*, to low, bellow, bray. — From the sound *moo* of oxen, as Μηκάομαι of sheep.

Μύκης, a mushroom, 'allied to Μῦκος,*mucus*, from its shiny moist nature; — any knobbed round body, like a mushroom, as the cap at the end of a sword's scabbard ; — the snuff of a lamp-wick ; — a fleshy excrescence:' Ldd. ' The pommel of a sword,' says Portus, ' as pommel is from a resemblance to a Pomum.'

Μύκλος, Μύχλος, = μάχλος, lascivious. And an ass, ' as being remarkably lascivious,' Schneid. So μῦδάω and μᾶδάω.

Μῦκος, *mucus*, allied to Μυκτήρ. See Μύξα.

Μυκτήρ, the nostril, nose. R. †Μύσσω, μέμυκται. **Μυκτηρίζω**, to turn up the nose, sneer at: 'Naso suspendere adunco,' Hor. 'Tacito rides naso,' Martial.

Μυλακρὶς, a *mill*-stone ; — cock-roach found in *mills* and bakehouses. — From

Μύλη, *mola*, a *mill* ; — nether *mill*-stone ; — barley coarsely bruised in a *mill*; **⊥** *hard* formation in the womb, false conception, *mola*, a *mole* ; — the knee-pan, ' called also patella or *mola*,' Dr. J. Al μύλαι, the grinders. — R. μύλλω.

Μυλιάω, to grind the teeth. — R. μύλη.

Μυλλὸς, ' prop. compressing or writhing · the mouth : hence contorted, crooked. R. μύλλω:' Dnn.

109

Μύλλω, 'Μοιμύλλω [as Μαμάω] redupl., to squeeze the lips, utter a murmur, mutter in a low voice: — to bruise, grind, and Μύλη, a mill. All from [μῦ,] μύζω, μύω: Schneid..and Passow:' Dnn. Compare Βύω, and †Πύω, Πυκνὸς and Πύλη.

Μύλλω, *molo*, ut Lat. *per-molo*, unde Μυλλὸς = τὰ αἰδοῖα γυναικεῖα: et Μυλλὸς == meretrix. V. supra.

Μῦμαρ, 'Æol. for μῶμαρ, μῶμος,' Ldd. Blame, censure. So ΦΩρ, fUr. Homer has Ἀ-μύμων. (**2**) Hebr. *mum*.

Μυνδὸς, as Μύδος, *mutus*, dumb.

Μύνομαι, to fend off ; Μύναι, pleas and excuses. — 'Buttm. well allies *munio* ;' Ldd. See Ἀμύνω.

Μύξα, *mucus* from the nose: from †μύσσω, ξω, to wipe the nose ; — the nostrils: — a lamp-nozzle.

Μύξα, ων, a kind of plum or damson, so called, says Pliny, ' ob *mucosum* lentorem:' alluding to Μύξα, *mucus*, above. — So

Μυξῖνος, 'a smooth sea-fish, as if Slime-fish, Lat. mugil:' Ldd. — Above.

Μυοπάρων, a pirate vessel. — ' R. μῦς, μυὸς, πάρων:' Dnn. See Πάρων. But μυο- rather from μύω, to be closed. (**2**) 'Bayf compounds it of a vessel made at Myus and of another made in *Paros*:' Steph.

Μυρίνης, Μυρρίνης, 'a sweet wine, Lat. potio *murrhina* or *murrata*: prob. flavored with μύῤῥα or rather with μύρον :' Ldd.

Μυρίος, numberless, immense: Μυρίοι, 10,000: Μυριὰς, άδος, the number of 10,000, whence *myriad*.— Valck. says on Eur. Phœn. 1485: ' Μυρίον εἶμα is elegant, Plurimum sanguinis fluebat. For μυρίον is used properly of *fluids*, ἐπὶ τῶν μυρομένων, but was afterwards applied to any magnitude.' Bp. Blomf. also refers it to Μύρω. So Abundant from Uuda. So Ex-undo, Undanti crnore, Virgil. So Ezek. 43. 2 : 'His voice was like a noise of many waters.' Rev. 14. 2. Isa. 17. 13. ' The *multitudinous* sea:' Shaksp.

Μυρμηκιαί, ' conceits of a harp-player, who runs up and down the notes, in and out and all ways, like a nest of ants:' Ldd. — From

Μύρμηξ, Μύρμος, Βόρμος, Βόρμηξ, an ant. — Wachter and Mrt. from μυρίοι, from their myriads of numbers. Or at once R. μύρω, μέμυρμαι, by metaph., whence Μυρίος, which see. (**2**) †Φύρμηξ seems to have existed, ace. †φύρμηκα, Lat. *formica*: then, like Φόρμιγξ, from φέρω, to carry. ' Magni formica laboris Ore *trahit* quodcumque potest:' Her. (**3**) If Βόρμος is the orig., then from its exertions in carying βορὰ for itself. So some bring Formica from *ferre micas*. See Horace above.

Μύρμηξ, 'a sort of gauntlet with metal studs like warts on it: for Μυρμηκία are warts, Lat. *formicationes*', Ldd.: and these as being like ants' hills, or as stinging like ants. — Above.

Μύρμηξ, a sunken rock in the sea. Allied apparently to the word above, but the reason does not appear. Steph. mentions Μυρμηκίας λίθος, ' having black eminences like warts.' Μύρμηξ is also a strange animal described by Herod., throwing up sand as an ant: 3. 102.

Μύρον, ' any sweet juice distilling from plants, and used for perfumes: derived from μύρω, to trickle, by the Ancients; or, acc. to Athen., from μύῤῥα, myrrh-oil: ' Ldd. ' Certainly allied to myrrh:' Hemst.

Μύῤῥα, ' juice of the Arabian myrtle, myrrha, murrha:' Ldd. ' Myrrh:' Dnn. — R. μύρω to flow. (2) R. μύρον. (3) ' Hebr. mar, to be bitter:' Wr.

Μύῤῥινον, ' myrtus seu pili inferioris partis verĕtri:' Brunck. An quia 'formosae Veneri gratissima myrtus,' Virg.? et ergò ut ' myrtea sylva' ap. eund.? Sic dicitur Μυρόχειλα: et Μύρτων est ' Veneri deditus.' — Compara

ΜΤΡΤΟΣ, Μυρσίνη, Μυῤῥίνη, myrtus; myrtle: —' a fly-flap made of myrtle branch,' Ldd.—The Persian mourd.

Μύρω, to flow or shed copiously, weep copiously. — Short for Μορμύρω. (2) Like Πτύρω, Ξύρω, Δύρομαι: and allied to Μάω, (as in Αὐτό-ματος,) to move on, to Meo, meāre Lat., Moveo Lat. and Μολεῖν. ' Eunt more fluentis aquae:' Ov. So Νέομαι is to go, Νάω is to flow. (3) ' Hebr. mar, a drop:' Mrt.

Μῦς, g. μυὸς, mus, mouse: — muscle-fish: — muscle of the body. — All the senses from μύω, to keep close. ' A mouse, as shutting itself up in hiding-places:' Voss. I.e., in μυχοῖς. (In Persian mush.) So a Muscle shuts itself up. A Muscle of the body, says Celsus, in some way resembles a little mouse.

Μυσαρὸς, a wretch. And

Μυσάττομαι, to abominate. — From

Μύσος, abomination, abominable crime. — R. μύω, μύσω: ' At which we shut our eyes, not daring to look: or our mouths, not daring to speak:' Eustath. ' That stoppeth his ears from hearing of blood, and shutteth his eyes from seeing evil:' Isa. 33. 15. Note In-vIsus, hated. So Μύσις is a closing of the lips and eyes. — Others from μύζω. (2) ' Hebr. mes, to despise:' Wr.

†Μύσσω, (used in compounds,) to make to blow the nose. — R. μύω, μύσω, to close the nostrils:' Schneid. Allied to μΑσσω, μνγώ, muNgo.

Μύσταξ, upper lip; moustache: = μάσταξ.

Μυστήριον, a mystery. — From

Μύστης, initiated in the mysteries. — R. μυέω.

Μυστίλη, Μιστύλη, ' a hollowed bit of bread for sipping gravy with, making a' (Μύστρον) spoon: from μιστύλλω, to cut into bits:' Hemst. So both Μίτυλος and Μύτιλος are mutilated.

Μύστρον, a spoon, as in Μυστίλη. And a measure, = 2 spoonfuls.

Μυτακισμὸς, fondness for the letter Μῦ.

Μύτιλος, mutilus, mutilated. See Μίτυλος.

Μυτίλος, Μιτύλος, the muscle fish, or limpet. — R. from μῦς, μυὸς, the muscle fish. (2) Heindorf says:

' Not from μῦς, but of Latin origin.' Ldd.: ' From Lat, mytilus.' But whence this ?

Μύτις, like Μυκτὴρ, ' the nose of certain marine animals; what lies under their mouth, and through which the stomach stretches.' So Aristotle, who adds that these have no liver, but instead have the Μύτις and upon it the Θόλος.

Μυττωτὸς, Μύσωτος, ' a savory dish made of cheese, honey, garlic, &c. mashed up: — from μύω, μύζω, μύσσω, because its pungent taste made people wince:' Ldd.

Μυχθίζω, ' to breathe strongly through the nose, with the lips closely pressed together, as in anger, sorrow, or contempt: moan, deride. R. μύζω, (ἐμύχθην):' Dnn.

Μυχὸς, the innermost part of a house, cave, bay, &c. — R. μύω, μέμῦκα, to be shut. · As Close and Closet.

Μύω, to be shut : — to shut the eyes and the mouth. —R. μῦ, μνάω, &c. See Βύω.

Μυὼν, muscular part of the body. — R. μῦς, μυὸς, muscle.

Μυοξὸς, Μυοξὸς, a dormouse. — R. μῦς, μυὸς, mus, mouse.

Μυωψ, ' short-sighted, closing the eyelids to see more clearly:' Dnn.— R. μύω, ὠψ, ὠπὸς the eye.

Μυωψ, horse-fly, gad-fly; —a spur, a stimulant. Called by Suid. and Hesych. a μυΐα, musca : = †μνιώψ. Hence Μυωπίζειν τὸν ἵππον, to spur a horse.

Μῶκος, mockery ; Μωκὸς, a mocker. — R. μάω, μῶ, to lay hold of, ' prehendo, re-prehendo', to chide, rate, ἐπι-μάομαι. (2) Our word mock, Fr. mocquer, Welsh moccio.

Μῶλος, toil, like Μόλος, broil, spec. of war. Allied to Μόλος, but Wr. from Hebr. mool, to cut off. — Also, a mocker, like Μωκός. — Also, a pier, but this is a sort of barbarous word of late age, agreeing with Lat. moles. See on Μόλιθος.

Μῶλυς, ' worn out by Μῶλος toil, feeble, sluggish :', Ldd.

Μώλωψ, weal of a stripe or blow: —' A mark left in μῶλος battle:' Schleusn. (2) ' R. μάω, σμάω, as Μῶδιξ, Σμῶδιξ from σμώχω:' Dnn.

Μῶμος, blame, ridicule. Momus, the god of censure and ridicule.—R. μέμφομαι, μίμομμαι, to blame. (2) Allied to Μῶκος. (3) ' Hebr. mum, a spot :' Mrt.

Μῶν, whether. — For Μὴ ὂν, Μὴ οὖν, Whether or not ? (2) Particip. of μάω: Seeking, enquiring.

Μῶνυξ, for Μόν-ωνυξ, having solid hoofs, not cloven-footed. Thus our Ido-latry for Idolo-latry. — R. μόνος, ὀνυξ.

Μώριον, ' a species of mandrake, supposed to have the property of producing madness :' Dnn. — From

Μωρὸς, prim. tasteless, sapless, insipid ; and allied through μάω, †μαορὸς, (as †Χάω, Χῶρος,) to Μάτην, in vain, Μάταιος, ' unprofitable', (Dnn.) Then dull, slow, stupid. (2) R. μὴ, ὁρῶ. ?

110

N.

ΝΑΒΛΑ, Ναῦλα, a musical instrument.—'The Hebr. *nebel :*' Becm. and Mrt.

Νάγμα, a stone-wall: as piled up.— R. νάσσω, νέναγμαι.

Ναέτης, an inhabitant.—R. †νάω, ναίω.

Ναὶ, Νὴ, Ναιχὶ, (as Οὐχὶ,), yes, truly. — Becman says that in 600 places Ναὶ is nothing but 'I pray, I ask you.' I suspect then that Ναὶ is short for "Οναιο, 'ναι', ' may you prosper (as you grant me) !' (**2**) ' Hebr. *ná*, now :' Mrt.

Ναιὰς, ἀδος, Ναΐς, a water-nymph.—'R. ναίω to dwell : or νάω, to flow :' Forcell. 'R. νάω, to flow :' Dnn. Or νάω ' in the sense of *float,* whence Ναῦς :' (Dnn.)

Ναίω, †Νάω, ἐνάσθην, Ναιετάω, to dwell. — Dnn. says : ' In Od. 9. 222, ὁρῷ ναῖον ἄγγεα, (some read νᾶον,) The vessels *were full of* milk. Hence this verb is prim. *to fill,* then *fill* with inhabitants, and occupy, inhabit, as Damm and Passow.' Allied to Νάσσω. Like Νάσσω, Ναίω might mean ' to heap or pile up a building, build, and so make habitable :—make habitable for, cause to dwell', as it is often thus used with an Accus., and ἐνάσθη, he settled or dwelt. (**2**) ' Hebr. *navah,* to dwell :' Mrt.

Νάκη, Νάκος, a goat's skin, sheep's fleece.—'A skin with the wool on : R. νάσσω, νέναχα : Something να-στὸν close and tight :' Schrevel. ' Perh. from νάω to pile up :' Lennep. Κ, as φυλάσσω, φυλακή. (**2**) In Norfolk a *nacker* is a collar- or harness-maker.

Νᾶμα, Νασμὸς, a stream, spring, river.—R. Νάω, to flow.

ΝΑΝΟΣ, Νάννος, a dwarf, *nanus.* — Wr. from Hebr. *neen,* a babe, Becm. from Hebr. *neen,* ' subolescebat.' The old deriv. is at least more to the purpose, from νὴ, or νὲ, ἀνὰ : One ' not' grown ' up' to his proper size, as Νηλεὴς, Νήπιος, &c. But ?

Ναξία λίθος, a whetstone, from *Naxos* in Crete.

Ναὸς, Νηός, a dwelling of the gods, a temple, or its inmost part.—R. †νάω, ναίω, to dwell. ' The house where God is worshipped :' Hesych. Called οἶκος Luke xi. 51. So 'house ' 1 Kings 5. 18. 'The house of GOD' is common.— Or ναίω, †νάω, to build, as Hom. νηὸν ἔνασσαν.

Νάπη, Νάπος, a woody dell.—'R. prob. νάω :' Dnn. 'R νάω, as in a Νάπη much moisture flows:' Greg. So Hederic '& frequentiâ fontium et rivorum.' ' A watery place:' Hesych. Πη, as πόρΠΗ.

ΝΑΡΔΟΣ, spikenard.—'The Hebr. *nerd :*' Wr.

ΝΑΡΘΗΞ, ' the giant-fennel : — the stalks were used as canes, rods, ferules : the dried pith as tinder : a box [made of it] for containing unguents : copy of Homer kept by Alexander in the perfume-box of Darius :' Dnn. —' The Etym. M. from ναρὸς, humid, flowing : Hesych. calls it a reed-plant :' Scheide. It may be so.

111

Νάρκη, numbness, torpor :—the torpēdo fish.—The old deriv. is νὲ, ἀρκώ, to be capable of : A state of incapacity. (**2**) R. νάω, νασσω, †ναίρω, ' to press down firmly', (Dnn.) ναστὸς, ' closely pressed, compact,' like Πηκτὸς, ' compact, curdled, condensed.' Compare in form Λάρκος and Μάργος.

Νάρκισσος, the narcissus, from its *narcotic* properties.—Above.

Νάρὸς, νηρὸς, flowing, liquid.—R. νάω, to flow.

Νασμός : in Νᾶμα.

Νάσσω, ' to press down firmly, heap up, pile. Akin to Νέω, Νήω, to heap, and perhaps Ναίω:' Dnn. See in Ναίω and †Νάω. In form, as Πράσσω, Τάσσω.

Ναστὸς, close-pressed : ὁ ν., a well-kneaded cake.—R. νάσσω.

Ναύκραρος, ' also written Ναύκλαρος, and so the same as Ναύκληρος : the chief of a division of the citizens :— we do not find they had anything to do with the *navy,* till Solon charged each with furnishing 1 ship and 2 horse-men : so that Böckh's deriv. from ναῦς is less prob. than from ναίω :' Ldd. ' Eustath. explains it having κρόραν ἐν νηῖ, the head in the ship : And well, for the Greeks often compare a republic to a ship, and its governors to pilots :' Port.

Ναῦλα : in Νάβλα.

Ναῦλον, passage-money in a ναῦς ship.

Ναῦς, ναυΐς, a ship. — R. νάω, ' fluo, fluito', to float : Floating on the waters. Or R. νέω, to swim, as the gen. is νεώς. (**2**) Sanskr. *nav,* Pers. *nauh.*

Ναυσία, Ναυτία, sickness on board of ναῦς ship, nausea.

Ναύτης, nauta, a sailor: ναῦς.

Ναυτίλος, a seaman, *nauta :* — the *nautilus,* a shell-fish, with a membrane serving it for a sail : The sailor.—Above.

ΝΑΦΘΑ, *naphtha,* ' a bituminous substance in a liquid state :' Dnn. — ' By the Persians still called *Naft :*' Dahler. (**2**) In form as "Αφθαι, ῶν, the thrush. R. νάω, to flow. ?

ΝΑΩ, Νέω, †Νίω in Νίσσομαι, †Νόω in Lat. *Nuo,* Νυστάζω, seem to have meant prim. to *Move,* and to be the same as Μάω, &c., M and N agreeing as Μιν, Νιν ; Μὴ, Νη-, Νε, &c. Mrt. however adduces 'Hebr. *nah,* moveri'; Wr. representing it as 'Hebr. *nuo,* to move.' Hence

1. Νέω, Νέομαι, Νίσσομαι, to go, i.e. to *move* onwards. Also, to return.

2. Νέω, *nó,* to swim, i. e. to *move* in the water. ' Hebr. *nah,* moveri :' Mrt.

3. Νεύω, to bend forwards or down, i.e. *move* the head thitherward. ' Hebr. *nah,* nuto': Mrt.

4. Νάω, to flow, i. e. *move* on.

5. Νάω, to settle a person in a place, i. e. cause him

to *remove* and go there : and Ναίω, to dwell. Ormston says : ' To flow or flock to, people, inhabit.' See also a different method in Ναίω.—' Hebr. *navah*, to dwell :' Mrt.

6. Νέω, to heap, pile, i.e. *moveo* in unum, much as Σύρω, to draw, is also ' to sweep or brush into a heap, collect', (Dnn.).—' Allied to Germ. *nähen*, to sew, i.e. join together :' Thiersch. See No. 7.

7. Νέω, neo, to spin, i.e. ' to roll or wind up thread ': Grove. See No. 6. But Ormston reverses 6 and 7.

8. Νίζω, Νίπτω, to wash : i.e. to *move* the hands about in water, as Χεὶρ χεῖρα νίπτει. I, as in νίσσομαι. And νίφω.

Νέ-, not. See in Νη-.

Νέα, Νεὸς, Νειός, fallow ground.— R. νέος. I.e. renewed.

Νεάνιας, Νεανίσκος, a young man, as Νέος ;— also as Νέος, new, fresh.

Νέατος, Νείατος, last, uttermost. — Prop. the newest, from νέος, as Lat. novissimus.

Νεβρὸς, a fawn : from νέος, νέβος, (as *noVus*,) νε-φρός : A young deer. Somewhat as Juvenis, Juvencus.

Νείαιρα, Νεῖρα, the latter or lower part of the belly : γαστὴρ sometimes added. Like Νέατος, Νείατος, last.

Νεικέω, to quarrel, wrangle : Νεῖκος, contention. — Usually derived from νή-, or νε-, εἴκω : Unyielding conduct : Or Unsuitableness of temper, for 'Α-εικὴς is Unsuitable. Or as 'Α-είκεια, Αἰκία, unseemly conduct. (2) R. νέομαι, νείσσομαι, †νένευκα, ' eo, gradior', i.e. ' co-eo, con-gredior,' to meet in a hostile manner.

Νειόθεν, from the bottom.— R. νέος, whence Νέατος the last.

Νεῖον, Νέον, Νεωστὶ, recently.— R. νέος, fresh. So Novus, Noviper, Nuper.

Νέομαι, Νείομαι, Νείσσομαι, Νίσσομαι, to come or go. See ΝΑΩ 1.

Νέκταρ, nectar, the drink of the gods :—afterwards, food. — ' Usually derived from νε-, not, and †κτάω, κτείνω : and so == ἀμβροσία :' Ldd. As conferring immortality. (2) R. νέον κτέαρ, a new possession of the Gods. ?

Νέκυς, Νεκρὸς, dead ; — a dead body. — Lenn. well from ἠνεκὴς, 'νεκὴς, (as 'Εκεῖνος, Κεῖνος; 'Ενερθε, Νέρθε,) explained by Steph. : ' porrectus et protentus in longitudinem.' Stretched out, laid flat. Homer: Κεῖτο ταθείς. (2) R. νέω, taken as Νεύω, to bend forward, much as Cadāver from Cado, Πέσημα from Πίπτω. Νέκυς, as Ψέω, Ψεκὰς. (3) ' Chald. *necas* is Mactāre, *neca* Percutere :' Mrt.

Νέμεσις, just retribution, vengeance, spite, ill-feeling ; — just remorse. — Nemesis, the goddess of Retribution. And Νεμεσάω, to feel just indignation at. — ' R. νέμω, to distribute, assign :' Dnn.

Νέμος, ' a pasture, from νέμω :— a wooded pasture, glade, nemus :' Ldd.

Νέμω, to distribute, assign, allot :— midd. divide among themselves, possess, have in use ; — dwell in as a possession :— act. to dispense the affairs of a house or

112

state, govern, rule : — to feed, put to pasture ; midd. to devour : i.e. assign to animals their proper pastures.— From νέω, (See ΝΑΩ:) prop. to move, i.e. one from another, or into their proper places, re-moveo, a-moveo, di-moveo, se-moveo. Νέμω (and Νωμάω), also ' to brandish', i.e. to *move* up and down. ' Νωμάω, *MO-VEO*, agito:' Steph. — In form compare Γέμω, Βρέμω, Δέμω.

Νεπρὸς, Νεννὸς, Νεπήλος, foolish, — purblind. — ' R. νε-, not, νοῦς. [As τρίΠΟΥΣ becomes τρίΠΟΣ.] Or Hebr. *neen*, a child :' Mrt. Note our ninny, Span. *nino*, a child.

Νεόγιλος, new-born, as Νεό-γονος. — R. νέος ; —γιλος seems in some manner connected with Γίνομαι.

Νεολαία, a band of youths, the youth of a nation. — R. νέος, young ; λαὸς, people.

Νέομαι, Νείομαι, Νείσσομαι, Νίσσομαι, to come or go. — See in ΝΑΩ 1.

Νέος, νέFος, no Vus, new, fresh ;—young, young man. — R. νέω, νέομαι, to come: Just come, fresh come, νέ-ηλυς. So Ad-vena, a stranger,'from Ad-venio. ' New gods that came newly up :' Deut. 32. 17. 'We Belgians say *een aankomeling* :' Lenn.

Νεοσσὸς, a young animal, esp. young bird, from Νέος. Also Νοσσὸς, Νοττὸς. As Δὶς, Δισσός.

Νεοχμὸς, == νέος.

Νέποδες. ' The seals are called the νέποδες of Amphitritē, explained 1. νε-, νε-, πόδες, pedes, the footless ones, fish ; 2. νέω, to swim, *no :* the swimming or fin-footed; 3. νέποδες == a brood, as if from νέος : Lat. *nepos*, *nepōtis* :' Ldd.

Νέρθε, for 'Ενερθε: Νέρτερος for 'Ενέρτερος.

Νευρά, a string, bow-string. And

Νεῦρον, Νεῦρον, nervus: a sinew, tendon, nerve :— string made of sinew ;— fibre. — Lennep says : ' R. νεύω. Prop. quod facit *vergere*.' Martin : ' R. νεύω: nam est instrumentum *inclinationis*.' Now Dr. Johnson defines Sinew ' the ligament by which the joints are *moved*.' So that evidently *motion* is implied in Νεῦρον. And ΝΑΩ, ΝΕΩ, mean prim. to move. See ΝΑΩ.

Νεύω, †νευο, nuto, to nod,—nod to, beckon ;—bend forward, incline, decline: Νευστάζω, to nod, fall asleep. — R. νέω, νέομαι, to go, i.e. downwards. See in ΝΑΩ 3. (2) ' Hebr. *nah*, nuto:' Mrt.

Νεφέλη, nebula, and Νέφος, cloud, mist :— and a fine bird-net, much as Ovid's Vellera *nebulas* æquantia. ' Theophrast. uses Νεφέλαι of light fleecy clouds:' Ldd. —There was a verb Νέφω, whence 'Επί-νεψις: and (as Στέφω,) ' prob. from νέω, νήω, to heap, accumulate:' Dnn. — Or even νέω, νέομαι, to go (over): That which comes over (supervenit) the sky. (2) The old deriv. was νε-, φάος: No light. (3) ' Chald. *noph*, stillo:' Mrt.

Νεφροὶ, the kidneys. — The Etym. M. from νείφω == νίφω, to wet, ' quòd irrigantur *urinâ*.' ' R. νέω, no, fluo:' Mrt. (2) ' Prob. from φρένες by transp., as ForMa from ΜορΦή:' Dnn.

Νέω: For the various senses see in ΝΑΩ.

Νεώριον, a dock-yard. — R. νεὼς gen. of ναῦς: and perh. ὥρα, attention to.

Νεωστί: in Νεῖον.

Νέωτα, for εἰς ν., next year, i.e. the new year coming. — R. νέος, new; or νέομαι, to come.

Νη-, as Lat. ne-, not, the same as Μὴ, as Μιν, Νιν. (2) Some bring νὴ from ἄνευ, and indeed it sometimes occurs as Νε-. Blomf. rejects Νη-. (3) Sax. ne, not. Νὴ Δία, νὴ μὰ τὸν Δία, yes by Jove. — Allied to Ναί. So Ναὶ and Δή.

Νηγάτεος, new-made. — R. νέος, νέα; †γάω, γέγαα, †γέγαται, γίνομαι. Passow for Νεή-γατος.

Νήδυμος, Homeric epith. of sleep, ' 1. from νὴ, δύω, for ἀν-έκ-δυτος, from which one rises not, as ν-ήγρετος: — 2. Usu. derived from ἡδὺς, sweet, i.e. ἥδυμος, which often occurs, but not in Homer: a very old mistake then for Ἥδυμος; Ν introduced to supply the place of the defunct digamma: otherwise ν is contrary to all analogy, [though it may be like νὴ = ναί, and indeed Ldd. himself says on Νήχυτος: ' Prob. formed on the supp. that νὴ is intensive:' and the same in Νηπεδανός:] — 3. Some even make it Intimus sopor, from νηδὺς, the bowels, stomach:' Ldd. So Jones: ' Vital sleep.'

Νηδὺς, the belly, bowels, womb. — As Νῆσις is the act of heaping, accumulation, so Νηδὺς the part of the body where the food is accumulated. Δ, as ἐπ-ήλυΔος, ὕΔωρ, ὓΔος, μῆΔος, βραΔύς. (2) ' Hebr. nód, uter:' Mrt.

Νηέω, Νηνέω, to pile: νέω.

Νήθω, to spin: R. νέω, ἐνήθην.

Νῆϊς, g. νήϊδος, not knowing: νη. εἰδέω, εἶδον, ἴδον.

Νήκεστος, Νηλεὴς, Νημερτὴς, Νήνεμος: all from νη-, with adjunct from ἀκέομαι ἥκεσται, ἔλεος, ἁμαρτάνω, ἄνεμος. So

Νήπιος, Νηπύτιος, an infant. — R. νη-, ἔπω: as In-fans, not speaking. Νηπύτιος perh. from νη-, ἀπύω.

Νηρίτης, Νηρείτης, sea-snail or periwinkle. — Grove from νέω, to swim: ' As swimming on the water.' Or νηρὸς, wet, liquid: A liquid substance. So Dnn.: ' R. νήριτος, same sense as Νηρός.'

Νήριτος, ' = νήριθμος, countless:' Ldd. I.e. νη-, ἀριθμος. But ΘΜ? Better from νη-, ἔρις, or ἐρίζω, ἥριται: So Ἀδήριτος, not to be disputed. Incontestably great. Or νη-, ἐρῶ, to speak, like Ἄ-σπετος, Unspeak-ably great.

Νηρὸς, as Ναρὸς, flowing, wet: νάω.

Νῆσος, an island. — ' R. νέω, to swim:' Dnn. Or to float, as in Ναῦς. ' To νέω (to swim,) Dionysius seems to allude in his Perieg. 7. 8: 'Ἧτε ΝΗΧΟΜΕΝΟΝ κικλήσκεται οὔνομα ΝΗΣΟΣ. So Insula is In-salo:' Pkh. (2) R. νάω, ναίω, to dwell. Dr. Jones calls it ' a place inhabited by men.' Opposed to a desert island.

Νῆσσα, a duck. — 'R. νέω, (†νήσσω,) to swim:' Ldd. Anacr.: 'Ἴδε πῶς νῆσσα κολυμβᾷ. Or, to float. (2) Lenn. for νήεσσα, like a ship.

Νῆστις, Ἄνηστις, fasting, starving. — For νή-εστις, from ἔδω, ἔδεσται (whence Ἐδεστὸς, eatable,) contr. †ἔσται. So In-edia.
113

Νῆστις, the Intestinum jejunum, from its being al-ways found empty. Above. — And used by Empedocles for the element of air and water: Q. as empty and light, as Horace, ' Per VACUUM æthera.' Homer has: ' May you become water and earth,' i.e. may you die, Il. 7. 99. But Ldd. ' prob. from a Sicilian goddess so called.'

Νήτη, the νεάτη lowest chord in the lyre.

Νήφω, ' am sober, esp. drink no wine:' Ldd. — R. νη, ἀφὴ or perf. ἧφα, ἄπτομαι: Not to touch. See Νῆστις.

Νήχω, as Νέω, †νένηκα, to swim.

ΝΙΓΛΑΡΟΣ, a pipe or flute to regulate rowers. — Q.?

Νίζω, Νίπτω, to wash: — see Νίπτω, and in ΝΑΩ 8.

Νίκη, victory. — As Φρίσσω, Φρίκη, so †Νίσσω, Νίκη. †Νίσσω is active of 'νίσσομαι, fut. νίσομαι, to go away, return', (Ldd.). i.e. to make to retire, and so to turn back. ' By the way that he came, by the same shall he return,' 2 Kings 19. 33. So Τρέπω is used, Τρο-παῖον, &c. (2) The old Gramm. deriv. was νε- or νη-, εἴκω or †ἴκω as in Ἴκελος: Where the party does not yield. (3) 'Hebr. nekee, to smite:' Wr. As well ally it to Neco from Νέκυς. But I ?

Νιν, the same as Μιν.

Νίπτω, to wash, and Νίζω. — 'Allied to νάω, to flow, νέω, to swim, νέφω, νίφω:' Lenn. ' R. νείφω or νέφω, to wet:' Pkh. and Ewing. ' R. νέω, to swim:' Mrt. Or allied at once to Νάω, prim. to move, which see. As in Χείρ χεῖρα νίπτει. See ΝΑΩ.

Νίσσομαι: in Νέομαι.

Νίτρον, nitre, but explained natron or potasse, and, when mixed with oil, used for soap. — ' R. νίζω, [νένι-ται,] νίπτω:' Dnn. ' That by which you can νίπτειν:' Lenn. (2) 'Hebr. neter, to dissolve or cleanse:' Wr.

Νίφω, to snow. — Allied to Νίζω, to wash, and Νίπτω. (2) 'Hebr. noph, stillo:' Mrt.

Νίψ, νιφὸς, snow. — Above.

Νοέω, to observe, perceive, have thought, think, understand, purpose. — R. νόος.

Νόθος, illegitimate, spurious. — R. νέομαι, †ἐνόθην: Adventitious. 'Advena pellex,' Ov. See Νοστέω. (2) R. νὴ, ἔθω, ἔσθα: Against the established custom.? (3) R. ὀνοτὸς, 'νοτὸς, contemptible: Or a. 1 ὀνόθην.

Νομεὺς, a shepherd. R. νέμω, νένομα, to feed cattle. — A dealer out, distributor: R. νέμω, to distribute. — Νομέες, ' the ribs of a ship, which are the basis of the whole,' Ldd.: i.e. directors. Or as equally distributed, as Homer's νῆας ἔισας.

Νομίζω, to observe or practise as a νόμον law or custom. Νομίζω θεοὺς, to believe in the gods as recognized by the state; — own, acknowledge, hold to be right, — gen. to think.

Νόμισμα, usage, custom; — the common current coin of a state, — established weight or measure. — Above.

Νόμος, usage, law. — R. νέμω: Assigning to each his own : or an assigned, allotted state of things.

Νόμος, a musical note, strain. 'According to a pre-scribed form, as the Lydian measure, the highest; the Dorian, the lowest:' Dnn. — Above.

Q

Νόμος, allotment of land, division, district: νέμω.

Νομὸς, a pasture; from νέμω, to feed. And Νομὴ, devouring violence.

Νόος, Νοῦς, the mind. thought, purpose, &c. — 'As Πλέω, Πλόος, so Νέω, Νόος. Νέω is prop. glomero: Νόος is that which glomerat, which coagit, cogit, cogitat:' Valck. So Lenn. 'from νέω, necto, cogo, cogito.' Thus Necto, says Voss, is prop. to join together by SPINNING. Then to connect, connect ideas.

Νόσος, a disease, disorder, &c.—Few words have given etymologists more trouble than this. They say, from νὴ, not, σόος, sound: but the O ? — Or from the Hebr. nos, to flee: but this is beside the mark.—I imagine that, as Νίτρον and Λίτρον, Νὺξ and Λύγη, (Dnn.), Νύμφα and Lympha, Nanciscor and Λαγχάνω, so Νόσος and †Λόσος were the same, and that †Λόσος belonged to that numerous class Λοιγὸς, Λοιμὸς, Λοιδορῶ, Λορδὸς, &c. and meant ' a hurt', &c. Compare on similar principles Λάσιος and Δασύς.

Νοσσός: in Νεοσσός.

Νοστέω, to go or come home, return. — R. νέομαι, †νένοσται. So κΟρμὸς.

Νόσφι, Νόσφιν, aloof, apart, away, far from:—except. — R. νόστος, νόστοφι, νόσφι: By a going away, by retiring from, as μάχης ἒκ νοστήσαντες, having retired from the battle. So 'Υπο-νόστησις is explained by Steph., 'by which anything goes back, and betakes itself or sinks away (clanculùm) by stealth.' Thus in full, Νόσφιν ἀπ' ἄλλων in Homer, and 'Απο-νόσφι.

Νοσφίζομαι, to separate from.—Above.

Νότις, moisture.—R. νέομαι, νένοται, to go, i.e. issue forth. As 'Ικμὰς from "Ικω. (2) Allied to Νάω, to flow. ' R. νέω, no, fluo.— Chald. neda, aspersit :' Mrt.

Νότος, notus, the S. wind. — R. νότις, moisture. ' This wind gen. brought rain in Greece :' Dnn. ' Humidus Auster,' Virg. ' Udo Noto,' Hor.

Νοῦμμος, nummus, a coin, Νόμισμα.—'R. νόμος:' Dnn.

Νυ : the same as Νυν.

Νυκτερὶς, a bat, flying νυκτὸς by night.

Νύμφη, a bride, allied to the Latin Nubo, Nubes, Νέφος, Νεφέλη, &c. from her veiling her face : — any married woman,— even a marriageable maiden : — a Nymph. 'The Muses are called Nymphs : hence all raptured persons were called Νυμφό-ληπτοι, caught by the Muses:' Ldd. Also a baby, chrysalis or pupa of moths, young bee or wasp, &c.; opening rosebud : — water, Lat. lympha, ' prob. from the water-nymphs :' Ldd. Αἱ νύμφαι, the nymphæ in the female body.' The word †Νέφω (whence Νεφέλη) is established by 'Επί-νεψις. Then †νένοφα, Γνόφος, and a verb †Νύφω, Nubo, as βΥθὸς, γΥνὴ, ῥΥμβος, Æolicè.

Νύμφιος, a bridegroom.—Above.

Νῦν, now. —' It seems contr. from νέὺν, [Æol. of] νέον, which often means now in Homer, as in Il. γ. 394.' Scheide. So Brunck. translates Νέον in Œd. T. 155. Thus ΕΥντα for 'ΕΟντα. (2) R. νέον, part. of νέω, to go : The time passing. (3) ' Hebr. ná, now :' Mrt. ?

Νυν, then, as in Come on then : or now, as Now it came to pass,— and seems to Hermann to be the same as Νῦν :—without its emphasis.

Νὺξ, νυκτὸς, night, nox. Νύχιος, nightly.— Dnn. allies it to Λύγη, darkness, N and Λ being freq. interchanged as Νίτρον, Λίτρον. See on Νόσος. (2) Allied to Κατά-νυξις drowsiness, Νυστάζω to droop the head in sleep : The time of thus doing. (3) Allied to ΝUbo, ΝΥμφη, γΝΟφος, Νέφος, &c.

Νυὸς, nurus, a daughter-in-law, bride.— Contr. from 'Εννυὸς or 'Ενυὸς, which see.

Νύσσα, a starting-post, turning-post in a race-course. — R. νύσσω: Where the horses are spurred. St. Gregory : ' Spur your horses about the νύσσα.'

Νύσσω, ξω, to goad, prick, pierce, spur.—As Νυστάζω, to nod drowsily, is prop. to go (downward), so Νύσσω is to make to go (onwards), make to move on. See the obs. on ΝΑΩ. (2) ' Hebr. naschach, to bite :' Mrt. ?

Νυστάζω, = νευστάζω, νεύω, nuto, to nod.

Νύχιος. by night : Νύχα, by night ; so that there was Νὺξ, †νυχὸς as well as νυκτός.

Νάγαλα, ων, says Jones, ' a cake or sweet-cake : from νέον γάλα, = νεόγαλα : Made prob. of fresh milk.' So 'Αφρό-γαλα was frothed milk or whipped cream.

Νωθὴς, ΝΩθὴς, sluggish, and ΝΩκαρ, sloth, seem allied : for, (amid many conjectures) Νώκαρ may be from νη, ὠκὺς, swift : ὠκὺς being itself from ὠθῶ ὥσω ὦκα to push, as ' ὠθεῖν to push matters on, hurry,' Ldd. And Νωθὴς from νὴ, ὠθῶ. (2) Dnn. says : 'Νώκαρ, from νη-, σκαίρω': But Ω ? Yet so Mrt. derives Νωθὴς, νωθὸς, 'from νη-, ϑέω, to run.'

ΝΩΙ, Νὼ, nos, we two.—The Hebr. nú, as in Emma-NU-el, GOD with us.

Νώκαρ : in Νωθής.

Νωλεμὲς, unceasingly, continually.— From νη, εΙλω ἔολα to turn, roll : Steadily, firmly : 'firmè,' Steph. on Ap. Rh. 2. 605. (2) R. νη-, †όλέω, ὅλλῦμι, to destroy : Indestructibly, for ever. As Νώνυμος. (3) ' R. νη-, λείπω, [λέλειμμαι,] :' Dnn. But Ω and the other M ? Compare ἀρτΕΜΕΣ.

Νῶμα, for Νόημα from νοέω.

Νωμάω, to distribute, allot : R. νέμω, νένομα. So Στρωφάω, Τρωπάω. And, like Εΐμω, to direct, guide, manage, ply, sway,—move or revolve in the mind, observe ;—move oneself.

Νέροψ, οπος, gleaming.— From νὴ, ὁρῶ, ὁρόω, to see : ' Too bright to look at :' Ldd. (2) From ἐν, ὁρῶ, ὅπα, the eye or face. For ἐνόροψ : In which one sees one's face. As Έκεῖνος, Κεῖνος.

Νῶτος, -ον, the back.—Damm from νῶ, νέω, to heap (burdens). We comm. say, The back is equal to the burden. (2) ' R. νεύω, [or allied,] to incline :' Mrt.

Νωχελὴς, sluggish. —' Usu. deriv. from νη, ὀκέλλω = κέλλω, to drive : [One whom you cannot drive.] Passow and Dœderlein from νη, ὠκὺς, swift :' Ldd.—Or R. νη, ὀχέω : of a horse that won't carry you.

Ξ.

Ξαίνω, to scratch, like Ξέω, to scrape ;—then to card, comb, full, clean ;— treat one as a fuller does cloth, beat, strike, scourge. Ξάσμα, carded wool, supposes a word †ξάω = ξέω. So †Βάω, Βαίνω.

Ξανθός, gold- or pale-yellow.—As 'Εκεῖνος, Κεῖνος ; ῞Ενερθε, Νέρθε, — for ῞Εξανθος, from 'Εξ-ανθέω, in the medical sense ' to lose its blossoms, to fade,' (Dnn.) and so it agrees with Flavus, which some deduce from Flacceo, Flaccīvus : — Of the color of faded autumn leaves. Or from the sense of ' efflorescence ' in 'Εξ-άνθησις, and ' to break out into eruptions ' in 'Εξ-ανθέω. (2) As Ξουθὸς is somewhat like Ξανθὸς, both may be thought allied to Ξέω, Ξαίνω, ἐξάνθην, to rub, polish, i. e. make bright.

Ξένος, Ξεῖνος, strange, foreign ;—stranger, foreigner, guest. Also the host as stranger to the guest. — For ῞ξενος, (as Κτιδέη for 'Ικτιδέη,) from ἵκω, ἵξω, to come. So ῎Επ-ηλυς and Ad-vena.

Ξερὸς, = ξηρός.

Ξέστης, a measure, the Lat. sextarius : — transp. from σέξτης.

Ξέω seems formed from the harsh sound made by the letter ξ repeatedly pronounced : ξξξξ : — a letter called by Cicero ' vastior litera.' Ξέω then meant to scrape, plane, carve, polish, smooth.

Ξηρὸς, dry.—R. ξέω : As said of timber easy to be scraped. (2) Our sere.

Ξίφος, a sword.—' Accord. to Et. M. from ξύω : [to polish, smooth] :' Ldd. Allied to Ξέω. And there was an obsolete Ξίω, as there were Ψέω, Ψίω.

Ξόανον, any carved work,— statue,— musical instrument.— R. ξέω, ἔξοα.

Ξουθὸς, ' of a color between ξανθὸς and fiery-red, brown-yellow, tawny : — but in some places, as ξουθὰ λαλῶν, it is said of sound, as thin, fine, delicate : — prob. from ξέω, (ἔξοα) :' Ldd. In the last sense, smoothed, polished, as in Ξίφος. And the color perhaps from smoothing and polishing.

Ξυήλη, a tool for scraping wood, plane, or rasp : — also a Spartan ' falchion, a kind of Ξιφίδιον,' Steph. — And

Ξύλον, ' prob. from ξέω, ξύω : wood cut and ready for use, firewood, timber, piece of wood, — cudgel, — heavy collar of wood, — pole, cross, — bench, table ; — measure of length :' Ldd. ' Ξύλον means rasum :' Valck.

Ξύλοχος, woody country.— R. ξύλον ; and ἔχω, ὄχα, to have.

Ξὺν, the same as Σὺν, ' together with.'

Ξυνὸς, common ξὺν with, in common. So 'Αντίος, Περισσός.

Ξυράω, Ξύρω, to shave ; Ξυρὸν, a razor.— R. ξύω, to scrape.

Ξυστὶς, a robe of state, i. e. made fine, finely worked. — R. ξύω. A garment, says Homer, which Minerva ἔξυσ' ἀσκήσασα.

Ξυστὸν, the polished shaft of a spear ;—a spear, dart ; — chisel.— R. ξύω. ' Rasilis hasta :' Sil. ' Rasæque hastilia virgæ :' Virg.

Ξυστὸς, xystus, a covered gallery for wrestlers and walkers : called from the floor being made particularly smooth and level.—And

Ξύστρα, a curry-comb ; Ξυστήρ, graving-tool ; Ξυστρὶς, scraped or graved fluting of pillars, &c.— From

Ξύω, like Ξέω, to scrape, plane, polish ;— scrape off.

Ο.

'Ο, 'Η, ΤΟ, ' the ' : and ΟΣ, ῞Η, ῞Ο, ' who, which,' &c.— Primitive words. ' Hebr. hu, this, or há :' Mrt. ῟Ο and our Who seem allied : 'Ον, Whom : &c.

Ο-, like Α-, is ' together ' or ' intensely.' And, as Α- for ῞Αμα, so Ο- for 'Ομοῦ, together.

῟Ο δ ὂ, exclam. in Aristoph. : from the sound, as it would seem.

'Οà, as Οὐà, Οὐαί, oh ! ah ! — From the sound. (2) ' Vai, Hebr. :' Mrt. ' Oi, Hoi, Hebr. ι' Schleusn. (3) Our woe.

'Οα, a sheepskin : from ὅïs, o Vis.

῟Οαρ, g. ὄαρος, a mate, consort, wife.— From O prefix, ἄρω, to join. As 'Ομ-αρτέω.

'Οαρίζω, to converse familiarly with ; ῟Οαρος, converse. — Above.

'Οβδη, sight : for †ὕπτη from †ὕπτομαι, as ἔπτομος into ἐβΔομος.

'Οβελὸς, a spit in the form of a βέλος, dart, Ο prefixed : 'Οβελίσκος, a small spit ;—an obelisk ; — a mark of censure.

'Οβολὸς, a small coin : thought to be = ὀβελὸς, as being stamped with a spit. But Dnn. : ' In form like a spit.' Some think that ' copper nails ὀβελοὶ were used as money :' Ldd.

῎Οβρια, 'Οβρίκαλα, the young of wild animals.— Many make ὄβρια = ἔμβρυα, embryos and also things newly born. For †Βρίω seems allied to βρύω through βαρύς. Compare Βριάω, Βρίθω. (2) ' Perh. allied to ῞Οβριμα [and Βριαρὰ] from βριάω :' Mrt. and Wr. As said of young fierce animals, wolves, lions, &c.

Ὄβριμος, strong, mighty. — Allied to Βρίμη, might, violence : and 'Οβρἰμώ, Hecaté. (**2**) ' Hebr. *aber*, strong:' Wr.

Ὄβρῦζον, metal purified.—The O is prefix. ' Βρύω and Βρύζω are the same, just as Βλύω and Βλύζω. The Greeks explain Βρύειν by ἀνα-βλύειν, ἀνα-πηδᾶν, of things which cast out a foam in bubbling :' Salmas. So that Βρύζω also may mean ἀνα-βλύω. The P and Λ are often interchanged.

Ὄγδοος, eighth. — R. ὀκτώ, ὕκτοος, ὕγδοος, as Ἷ-ΛιΚΤαι, ἐλΓΔην.

Ὄγκα Πάλλας, Pallas or Minerva worshipped at *Onca*, a village near Thebes.

'Ογκάομαι, to bray. From the sound ONK. (**2**) Dr. Jones from ὕγκος : ' To *swell* oneself with sound.'

Ὄγκος, *uncus*, a bend, curve, hook, barb ; — angle ; — anything swelling out, as a tumor ; — a lofty head-dress ; —swelling spirit, arrogance, high dignity ;—heap, mass, bulk. 'Ογκωδέστερος is ' more swelling out or rounded ;'—but, as used by Ælian of an ass, is explained by Ldd. ' of a louder note, from ὀγκάομαι.'—As Ὄγμος is allied to Ἄγω, so Ὄγκος to Ἄγκος, 'Αγκή, 'Αγκύλος, &c. See the next.

Ὄγμος, a furrow, row, line, orbit.—Just what would be meant by †ἄγμος, ductus, from ἄγω ἄγμαι, duco. So both 'Αγείρω and 'Εγείρω are found : so Ἄκρις and Ὄκρις, Ἄμα and Ὁμοῦ. The Schol. Nicand. p. 48 identifies ' 'Αγμὸς, ὕγμος '. See above. Ὄγμον ἄγειν is in Theocr.

'Οδάξω, to bite, sting : o, δάκνω, †δάξω. So 'Οδα-κτάζω to bite : from perf. pass. †δέδακται.

'Οδελὸς, form of 'Οβελός.

'Οδί, Attic for ὅδε, ὁ δέ.

'Οδμή, a smell, odor. — R. ὄζω, ᾦδον, ὅδον. 'Οδμὴ ὀδώδει Od. ε. 59. So 'Οδωδή.

'Οδὸς, a way, path, road. And 'Οδὸς, Οὐδὸς, a threshold. Ldd. calls ἡ ὀδὸς and ὁ ὀδὸς ' Kindred words'. And Damm calls the latter ' a *way* into a house or chamber.' They seem to come from ἔται and ἔται, pf. pass. of †ἔω, †ἔω, ἵημι, εἷμι: By which we send ourselves forward, By which we go. The O, as in κορ-μὸς, φÓρτος, νÓστος: and Δ, as in βαδίζω, ὕδωρ, στάδην, στάδιος, ἀν-έδην, &c. Compare in sense Κέλλω and Κέλευθος.—They may be otherwise compared with Ἕδος, a base, foundation. (**2**) ' Chald. *ada*, to pass:' Mrt.

'Οδοὺς, g. ὀδόντος, a tooth.—R. ἔδω, ὕδα: With which we eat. ' *Edens, edentis*.' (**2**) *Danta* Sanskr., *dentis* Lat.

'Οδόω, to show ὁδὸν the way.

'Οδύνη, pain, grief.—R. ἔδω, ὅδα, ἔδο. ' *Curas edūces*,' Hor. ' *Si quid est (edit)* animum :' ' Te tantus *edat* dolor,' Virg. So Homer: θυμὸν ἔδοντες, θυμὸν κατ-έδων, ἔδεαι κραδίην. (**2**) R. o, and δύη, anguish. (**3**) R. δύνω. 'Οξεῖαι 'ΟΔΤΝΑΙ ΔΤΝΟΝ μένος, Hom.

'Οδύρομαι, to be afflicted, grieve, deplore.—' Allied to 'Οδύνη, grief, 'Ωδίν, 'Ωδίνω:' Dnn. See Δύη and Δύρομαι. (**2**) For †ὀδυνύρομαι, as 'Ολοφύρομαι.

116

†'Οδύσσομαι, fut. ὀδύσομαι, to be grieved at, angry. — ' Allied to 'Οδύρομαι to grieve, 'Οδύνη, 'Ωδίν :' Dnn. 'Οδωδὴ, odor : in 'Οδμή.

'Οζαινα, an *ozæna*, fetid polypus; — a strong-smelling sea-polypus. — R. ὄζω.

Ὄζος, bough, branch : —scion : Ὄσδος, Ὄσδος in Sappho. — As Ὄ-τλος from τλάω, τλῶ, so Ὄ-ζος from ζάω, ζῶ : a *living* branch, opp. to a dead one.

Ὄζω, to have a smell or smack, to yield odor. — As †Ἄω, Ἄζω; †Ἔω, Ἔζω; so †Ὄω, Ὄζω, †Οἴω, οἴσω: Simply, to *carry* with it (a smell). (**2**) As Ἄωτος to breathe, supposes a form from ἄω †άόω, hence a form †άόζω, ὕζω. (**3**) ' Hebr. *hozi*, it made to go out ;' Mrt.

Ὄθεν, whence: 'Οθι, where: from ὃς, as Οὐρανόθεν, Οὐρανόθι.

'Οθνεῖος, alien, foreign.—Many from ἔθνος : From another nation. Much as we say a Gentile. O, as pEndo, pOndus; Ἔλαιον, Oleum. (**2**) R. νόθος, νόθειος, ὀθνεῖος. As Φάσγανον for Σφάγανον.

'Οθόμαι, to have a care or concern for. — Hemsterh. takes Ὄθω as = ὠθῶ, to impel: ' To be *moved* on account of anything.' So Damm explains 'Οθη, care, ' Res quæ me *movet*.' (**2**) R. ἔθω, ὅθα : To have an *habitual* care or concern for, to be constantly thoughtful of.

'Οθόνη, fine linen, linen veils, cloths, sails. — From o, θείνω, τέθονα : Beaten fine, as 'Ελπλαμένος from ἐλαύνω. ' Mostly, *fine* linen:' Dnn. (**2**) ' Chald. *atuna*, funis, linteum :' Mrt. ' Hebr. *aten*, to spin :' Wr.

Οθρῖξ, with like hair: o, θρίξ.

Οἰ, oh! — ' From the sound:' Lenn. (**2**) ' Hebr. *hoi*:' Mrt.

Οἱ, to him: dat. of ὁ or ὃ, like οἵκΟΙ whence οἵκωι, οἵκῳ. So

Οἷ, whither. — Dat. of ὃς: ᾧι, ᾧ. So Quδ is used for Whither. So Εδ and Illδ; and our Where for Whither.

Οἴαξ, ἀκος, Οἰήϊον, the handle of a rudder, the helm. ' R. *οἴω*, fero :' Mrt. and Wr. As the means of bearing on or guiding a ship on its way. The Etym. M. says, δι' οὗ τὸ ΠΗΔΑΛΙΟΝ ΦΕΡΕΤΑΙ. Οἴηκες are the rings through which the reins are passed : ' the reins,' says Eustath., ' which οἰακίζουσι pilot the mules.'

ΟΙΒΟΣ, meat from the back of an ox's neck, the best part. — Only in Lucian 2. 324. — Q. ?

Οἴγω, ξω, Οἴγνύμι, to open. — R. †οἴω, †οἶκα, (as τμῆΓΩ,) to carry up, lift the latch, as also 'Αν-οίγω. (**2**) As 'Ογμος is found, and allied to Ἄγω, so Οἴγω, to Ἄγω, to carry up.

Οἰδέω, Οἰδάνω, to swell or make to swell. — Scheide well from †οἴω, οἴσω, 'tollo, attollo: οἶδος, quod attollit se:' Which carries itself up. Δ, as in ὕνειλος, ἐρείλω, σκεύδω, βαδίζω, ὕδωρ.

Οἴδνων,a fungus-ball. — Above.

'Οϊζὺς, affliction. — From

Οἰζω, to cry οἰ oh! — wail. . So Ὄ Ω, Ὄζω.

Οἴη, a village. — ' Prob. from οἶος, (οἴα,)' Ldd. By itself. (**2**) R. †οἴω, like Οἶκος which see.

Οἰήϊον : in Οἴαξ.

Οἴημα, self-opinion.— R. οἴομαι, οἴημαι.

Οἰκέω, to dwell in an οἶκος; Οἰκεῖος, belonging to one's house or family, private, one's own, as Private property; Οἰκειόω, to make or claim as my own; Οἰκίζω, to establish a household or colony; &c. — From

Οἶκος, a house.— R. †οἴω, οἴσω, οἶκα : Whither one *betakes* oneself, a retreat, spec. after the day's labors. ' *Domum* se nocte *ferebat*:' Virg. ' Vespertinus pete tectum:' Hor. ' It is', says Bp. Horne in a Sermon, ' like a warm and comfortable house, into which a man *retreats*, where he finds good provision', &c. And thus Valck. and others from εἴκω, ἔοικα, to retire. Οἶκος is also used for a dining-room.

Οἶκτος, a wailing :— pity, commiseration, as this from Miser. —R. οἴζω, οἴκται.

Οἶμα, impetuosity, attack.— R. †οἴω, †οἶμαι : Which carries one on. So Οἰμάω, to pounce upon.

Οἴμαι : in Οἴομαι.

Οἴμη, Οἶμος, a way, road, tract, course.— R. †οἴω, οἶμαι: ' Quà te DUCIT via,' Virg. 'Η ὁδὸς φέρει εἰς ἱρόν, Herod. We say, That roads *leads* to such a place. So Ἄγυια.

Οἴμη, Οἶμος, a song ; explained by Ldd., 'the path or course of a tale, the course or strain of song.' Above. Some say, as sung in the οἴμαις streets. Dnn. compares Οἶτος.

Οἰμώζω, to cry Οἴ μοι, oh me! bewail.

Οἶνη, Wine, οἶνος. Also, the vine, producing the οἶνος, as many derive Μέλισσα from Μέλι.

Οἴνη, the ace on dice. Allied to Οἴα, alone. Lat. *una*.

ΟΙΝΟΣ, wine.— Although the sense of 'impetuosity' in Οἶμα and Οἴστρος, and the expression of Horace, ' Quò me, *Bacche*, *rapis?*', might point to †οἴω, to carry away, yet all derive from abroad : Hebr. *YYN*, Aram. *jena*, Teuton. *wein*, Sax. *vin*, Dutch *vinn*, Lat. *vinum*, our *wine*. So the Goth., Welsh, Cimbric.

Οἴομαι, Οἶμαι, Οἴω, to think, from the obsol. οἴω, 'duco', as 'duco' is used and Gr. ἄγω and ἡγέομαι. Ἐν γνώμᾳ τόδ' ἐδάσασεν, Æ. Prom. 913.

Οἶος, such as. — From οἶ = φ, quo (modo), i.e. tali modo quo, in such way as.

Οἶος εἰμί, Οἶός τε εἰμί, lit. I am such as to do, i.e. I can do.

Οἶος, alone.—From o, ἴος, one: All-one, whence ' alone.' ' And I am all alone.' (2) R. οἴ, alas! expressive of desolation. Αὐτὴ πρὸς αὑτὴν πατέρ' ἀπ-οιμώξη φίλον, Eur. Med.

Ὄϊς, ὄϊος, oVis, a sheep.— From †οἴω, οἴσω, to bear, carry, i.e. wool. In Latin lani-*GER*, from *gero*. So Dr. J. defines Sheep 'the animal that *bears* wool.' Ovid: ' Molle *gerit* tergo lucida vellus *ovis*.' And, ' Vellera *fertis*, oves.'

Οἰσπη, Οἰσπώτη, Οἰσύπη, 'sheep-dung, espec. the dirt which collects about the hinder part of (οἶς) a sheep. Prob. from ὄϊς, οἶς, though said also of a goat :' Ldd.

Οἰστὸς, borne. — R. †οἴω, οἶσται.

117

Οἰστὸς, an arrow : i.e. carried forward, when shot from the bow. — Above. So

Οἴστρος, violent impulse, fury, desire. As carrying forward. Above. Also the gad-fly as driving cattle on and making them furious, *æstrus*.

Οἶσον, any plaited work, rope. From ΟΙΣΟΣ, ΟΙΣΤΑ, an *OSIER*, Eng. and French. — Mrt. says, ' Οἶσον, a rope, from οἴω, fero.' Then Οἰσύα would be The rope-tree. ?

Οἰσύπος: in Οἴσπη.

Οἶτος, lot, doom.—R. †οἴω, οἶται : Borne or endured. ' Totque *tuli* casus,' Virg. So Fors, Fortuna, from φέρω, πέφορται. (2) R. οἴ, alas!

Οἴφω, Οἰφέω, to come together in marriage, &c.— Οἴφω seems allied to †Οἴχω, Οἴχομαι, from †οἴω, οἴσω: Eo, co-eo, to come together. Φ as in διφάω, δέφω, γράφω, ξίφος, ψῆφος. (2) Greg. allies it to 'Οπυίω. (3) Note our *Wife*, as Οἶνον, Wine.

Οἴχομαι, †Οἴχέομαι, Οἰχνέω, to go, go away,—perish. — Οἴχομαι as Ἔρχομαι. R. †οἴω, οἶκα : Carry myself on, as Ἄγε, Age, Ἵπ-άγω, Περι-ῆγεν, and our With-draw. Χ, as νήΧω, στενάΧω, αὐΧέω.

†ΟΙΩ, οἴσω, and †ΟΩ in ἭΩμος, &c., to bear, carry. — A Primitive, perhaps through †Ὄω allied to †Ἔω, †Ἴω, to send (on).

Οἰωνός, solitary bird of prey, as Sola cornix, Virg.: from οἶος, alone. As Ἴωνος, Κοινωνός.

Ὄκα, Πόκα. Doric of Ὅτε, Πότε.

Ὀκέλλω, the same as Κέλλω.

Ὀκλαδίας, a camp-stool, admitting of its sinking with us, or simply as bent. — From

Ὀκλάζω, to crouch down on bended knees, sink, — slacken.—R. κλάω, to break: o as Ὀκέλλω. The knees seem broken under us. Indeed Κλάω is explained to ' bend' in Ἀνα-κλάω, Περι-κλάω.

Ὄκνος, reluctance, slowness, sloth. — R. ἔχω, ὀχα, ὄχνος: By which we hold back. Homer: Ἴσχει ὄκνος. Κ, as δέΚα, δέΚομαι, φυλαΚή. (2) ' Hebr. *ogen*, to be detained :' Wr.

Ὄκος, Ὄκκος, oculus, the eye.—Æol. of †ὄΠος, from ὀψ, ὀπός: as ἵππος, Æ. Ἴκκος, equus.

Ὀκριάομαι, am exasperated, as this from Asper.— R. ὄκρις, as

Ὀκρίβας, pulpit, scaffold. As Ὄκρις = ἄκρις, so †Ὄκρος = ἄκρος, and βὰς, as Λυκάβας. Going to, or by which we go to, a height. Also, a buskin, high shoe, *OCREA*.

Ὀκριόεις : in Ὄκρις.

Ὀκρυόεις, = κρυόεις, with o prefix, from κρυός: Cold, chilling : — making one cold, horrible.

Ὄκρις, ' like Ἄκρις, Ἄκρα, a point, prominence, roughness. And Ὀκριόεις, rugged :' Ldd.

Ὀκτὼ, octo, eight.— Pkh. says that Mrt. ingeniously derives it from ὄχα δύω, ' eminently two', because 2 × 2 × 2 = 8. Well: though more simply from ἔκται, (as in Ἑκτικὸς, Πλεον-εκτέω,) and †ὄκται, (as O in Ὄχμα, Ὄχθη, Ὀψὲ, Ὀπτάω, κορμὸς, φὄρτος,) from ἔχομαι, to be next to: Next to the number 7.

Οκχος, = ὄχος, as 'Οκχή = ὀχή.

'Ολαὶ, Οὐλαὶ, ' coarse barley, sprinkled with salt on the head of the victim before the sacrifice. — Usu. considered = ὄλαι, the whole unground barley-corns. But Buttm. from ἔλλω, ἔολα, ἀλέω, ἄλευρον, as bread-corn prepared for use by grinding, applied aft. to barley only:' Ldd. (2) ' Hebr. olee, burnt offering:' Wr.

'Ολθος, prosperity, felicity. — ' Prob. akin to †ἄλφω, ἀλφαίνω, to bring in, yield :' Ldd. And Passow allies it to ὀφέλλω, †ὄφλω, †ὄφω. B, as ἄμΦω, amBo. Better from ἔλλω, ἔολα, ὕλΓος, as ὅλα, ὅλΓα, sylVa. A rolling together, accumulation. So 'Αλής, 'Αολλής, collected together, 'Εόλητο, &c. Compare θάμΒΟΣ, κλαμΒΟΣ.

'Ολεθρος, destruction. — R. †ὀλέω.

'Ολέκρᾰνον, = ὠλέκρᾱνον.

'Ολερὺς, = θολερὸς, impure. As Γαῖα, Αἶα. See 'Ολὸς 1.

†'Ολέω, 'Ολλύμι, 'Ολλύω, 'Ολέκω, to make to perish, destroy. — R. †ἕλω, †ὅλα, to take, and (like Αἱρέω,) to take away, destroy. — Or from ἔλλω, εἵλω, ἔολα, to roll, i. e. to roll down, precipitate. ' Multi fortunis pro-volvebantur': Tac. ' Armenta virosque In-volvens secum ': Virg. ' Volvo, prosterno : Virgil, Semineces volvit multos:' Forcell. Τὸ κοινὸν κυλίνδεται, Aristoph. Eccles. We say, He in-volved many in ruin. Steph. explains 'Ελλερα ' ὄλυρα, ὄλλυντα'. See 'Εξ-ούλης. (2) From o, and the obs. †λέω, †leo, levi, whence de-leo, to destroy. So Λεαίνω is 'to destroy', (Ldd.)

'Ολίγος, little, few. — ' Perh. from o, λίγος, from †λίω whence Λιτὸς, thin:' Lenn. So Λισσὸς, is rubbed smooth: and see Λῖθος, Λίσγος.

'Ολίζων, less. — R. ὀλίγος, as Μέγας, Μεῖζων.

'Ολισθος, penis coriaceus. — Forsan, ut 'Ολμος, cylindrus : ad quam vocem vide Ldd. infra. Et quòd est ' volubilis ', ' lubricus', affinis sit voci 'ΟΛΙΣθος, et 'ΟΛΙΣθέω. ΒΟΣ, ut ὁλΒΟΣ.

†'Ολισθέω, -άνω, to slip ; — slip or glide along. — Like 'Ολισθος and 'Ολμος, from εἵλω, ἔολα, ὅλα, to roll. — But Ldd. makes both 'Ολισθέω, and 'Ολισθος slipperiness, smoothness, allied to ΛΙΣοὺς, smooth : o prefix, as 'Οκέλλω.

'Ολκαία, a tail. — R. ἕλκω, ὅλκα: ' because it is trailed along :' Ldd.

'Ολκὰς, a towed ship, ship of burden. — As above.

'Ολκεῖον, the under part of a ship on which it is drawn along ; — a large bowl or basin for washing cups, capable of being drawn along. — Above.

'Ολκὸς, ' a machine for hauling ships, — shed into which ships are drawn up, — strap or rein, [as drawing on,] — furrow, track, made by trailing along :' Ldd. — Above.

'Ολιξ, a drinking-bowl. — Perh. allied to 'Ολμος, ' any bowl-shaped body', (Ldd.) Only in Athen. 494, and a rather doubtful word. — Note Olla Lat.

'Ολλῦμι : in †'Ολέω.

'Ολμος, ' a round smooth stone ; — the human trunk,

118

without head, arms, or legs, — any cylindrical or bowl-shaped body, as a mortar, kneading-trough, the hollow seat on which the Pythia prophesied, a drinking-vessel, the mouth-piece of a flute : — No doubt from εἵλω, to roll:' Ldd. I. e. ἔολα, ὅλα, or εἵλω, ἔολα, ὅλα, whence †'Ολμος, 'Ολμος.

'Ολολυγὼν, ' an unknown animal, named from its note: thought to be a small owl, or the thrush, or the tree-frog :' Ldd. From

'Ολολύζω, to speak with a loud cry or noise. — ' Formed from the sound': Ldd. As Ululo. (2) R. λύζω, †λυλύζω, ὁλολύζω. (3) ' Hebr. helil, ululāre :' Mrt.

'Ολολυς, an effeminate dissolute man. Redupl. from †ὀλέω, †ὀλῶ. Perditus. As

'Ολοὸς, destroyed, undone ; — destructive. — R. †ὀλέω, †ὅλοα.

'Ολόπτω, to peel or pluck off, bark. — From o, λέπω, λέλοπα, to peel.

'Ολὸς, = θολός. As Γαῖα, Αἶα.

'Ολὸς, = ὀλοός.

'Ολος, the whole, all, entire. — Allied to 'Αολλής, collected together ; 'Αολλήθην, in a compact body : and to 'Αλεὶς, collected. From εἵλω, ἔολα, to bring together. So Cunctus is Con-junctus. Compare Οὖλος, a sheaf.

'Ολοσχος, ' a leathern sack or purse. R. ὅλος, ὀσχη:' Dnn. So

'Ολοφλυκτὶς, ' as Φλύκταινα, a pustule, blister. R. ὅλος, φλύζω:' Dnn. See above.

'Ολοφυγδὼν, as 'Ολοφλυκτὶς, and allied to Φυσάω, to inflate.

'Ολοφυθνὸς, wailing. — Allied to

'Ολοφύρομαι, to wail, weep, — weep for others, pity. — R. ὀλόπτω, ὅλοφα, to pluck off. The Etym. M. explains it to weep with plucking of the hair. ' Luctus evellens comam': Seneca. 'Αμφι-δρυφέας in Herod. Much as Κόψονται Revel. i. 7. Lat. plango from πλήσσω, πλαγώ. (2) Eustath. from ὅλος, φύρομαι. See 'Ολοφλυκτίς. But note ὀλοφυΔνός.

'Ολπη, 'Ολπις, olearium vas, an oil-flask : — a ewer. — The deriv. of the Gramm. was ἐλαίου ὀπός : As containing the juice of oil. Rather from ἔλαιον only, as πόρΠΗ. Curiously the Latin is OLeum. So pOndus from pEndo. (2) Allied to 'Ολμος, 'Ολλιξ. As πόρΠΗ.

'Ολυμπιὰς, victory at the Olympic games. From 'Ολυμπος, Mount Olympus on the frontier of Thessaly, fabled to be the seat of the gods.

'Ολυνθος, a fig that seldom ripens, destroyed before the time. — Pkh. from ὄλλυμι : or ὀλέω, to destroy. So Ewing : ' R. ὄλλυμαι : an early fig which is apt to fall ; — the first figs which easily fall off by the wind'. ' As a fig-tree βάλλει τοὺς ὀλύνθους αὐτῆς, casteth her untimely figs :' Rev. 6. 13.

'Ολυρα, a kind of corn, distinct from wheat and barley, and perh. a kind of spelt :—compared by Ldd. with 'Αλευρον, flour of wheat and barley.

'Ομᾶ, 'Ομοῦ, much as 'ΑΜΑ, together. See on 'Ογμος.

Ὅμαδος, noise or din of many voices ; — crowd, concourse : — din of battle.— R. ὁμᾶ, together. Or from ὁμὰς, ἀδος.

Ὁμάκοοι, fellow-hearers of the philosophers. — R. ὁμᾶ, ἀκούω ἥκοον, to hear.

Ὁμαλὸς, even, level ; of equal or like degree ; — ordinary, average, i.e. like the great mass. — R. ὁμᾶ, together ; or ὁμὸς, common, joint : — i.e. of one common level or surface. As χθαμΑΛΟΣ.

Ὁμὰς, ἀδος, the whole. — R. ὁμᾶ.

Ὅμβρος, *imber imbris*, a heavy shower, storm.— Allied to Ὀμβριμος, Ὅβριμος, vehement, and perh. transp. from the latter, with the ejection of I : much as Ἐκπλαγος, Ἐκπαγλος. (2) 'For ὄβρος [as λαΜβάνω,] from ο, and the root of Βρύω:' Lenn. I.e. βαρέω, †βρέω, to press weightily on. (3) An old deriv. was ὁμοῦ ῥέω, ῥῶ : ὑμρος, ὑμβρος, as μεσημβρία : Waters flowing in concert. (4) 'Hebr. *ober*, a cloud :' Wr.

Ὅμηρος, 'from ὁμὸς or ὁμοῦ, ἄρω (ἤρον), like Ὁμαρής and Ὁμήρης, joined together, united, a husband :— also a pledge, surety or security for the maintenance of union (or peace), a hostage :' Ldd.

Ὅμιλος, a crowd, throng of soldiers or people. — R. ὁμᾶ, ἴλη a band.

Ὁμίχλη, a mist, fog, smoke: ο, †μίγω, μίξω, μέμιχα: As mixed, confused. 'Turbid state of the air:' Jones. Compare the French *Brouiller* and *Brouillard*. (2) Pott from the root of

Ὁμίχω, -έω, fut. ὁμίξω, as Lat. (*mĭgo*) *mĭNgo*, *minxi*, to make water. — O prefix, and the obsol. μέω, (See ΜΑΩ,) preserved in Lat. *meo*, to pass, as we say To *pass* water, Lat. *meio*. And perh. μειω was an old Greek word, for Μοιχὸς seems to Hemsterhuis to come from 'Μείχω or Μίχω.'

Ὅμμα, the eye. — R. ὄπτομαι, to see, ὄμμαι, ὄμμαι.

Ὅμοιος and Ὁμὸς, like, resembling, equal.— R. ὁμᾶ, ὁμοῦ.

†Ὁμόργω, Ὁμόργνυμι, to wipe, wipe off, press out ; allied to Ἀμέργω, to pluck off, and Ἀμέλγω, to squeeze out.

Ὁμός : in Ὁμοῖος.

Ὁμοῦ : in Ὁμᾶ.

†Ὁμόω, Ὁμνῦμι, Ὁμνύω, to swear, &c.— 'From ὁμοῦ or ὁμὸς : To unite, bind together :' Schneid. That is, so as Ὁμο-λογεῖν to make an agreement by a solemn compact. Budæus quotes Ἐν-ώμοτος ὁμολογία, a sworn agreement. Compare Ὅρκος and Ἕρκος. 'Our ancestors', as Edwards renders it, Lat. Ex. p. 92, 'did not regard any bond for ensuring an *engagement* to be more binding than *an oath*.' Ezek. 17. 13 : 'And hath made a *covenant with* him, and taken an *oath* of him.' Psa. 89. 3 : 'I have made a *covenant with* my chosen, I have *sworn* unto David.' Josh. 9. 15. (2) 'Chald. *omi*, he swore :' Mrt.

Ὁμπνη, and perh. Ὅμπνη, food, esp. corn: Ὅμπναι, cakes of meal and honey laid on altars. Ldd. supposes it = ὅπνη, (as λαΜβάνω,) allied to *ops, opes, opimus*,

119

opiparus, &c. — It is allied also to Ἔπω, Ὅπα, to be busy about, and to cook in Ἀμφ-έπω : whence Ὀπτάω, to bake.

Ὀμπνια, Ceres.—Above.

Ὀμπνιος, nourishing,—hence abundant, large, huge. — R. ὄμπνη.

Ὀμφαλὸς, the navel, — centre, — raised boss or knob in the middle of a shield, *umbo ;* — knob on the horse's yoke to fasten the reins to.—As χθαμΑΛΟΣ, ὀμΑΛΟΣ. And, as Ἅμα, Ὁμᾶ ; Ἀγμὸς, Ὄγμος ; (Schol. Nicand. p. 48,) Ἄγκος, Ὄγκος, so Ὀμφαλὸς and †Ἀμφαλὸς from ἀμφί. (2) For ὀφαλὸς (as ῥίΜφα,) from ο, φάλος, 'a knob, stud, something prominent or projecting,' (Dnn.) (3) 'As the fœtus is nourished through the navel-string, some suppose an affinity to Ὀμπνη, as Schol. Nicand. :' Dnn. Or Ὄμπνη, whence Ὀμπαλος, Ὀμφαλος. (4) 'Hebr. *anbl :'* Wr.

Ὄμφαξ, αγος,' an unripe grape ; — unripe, harsh, morose.—R. ὠμὸς, raw : Schneid. and Pass.': Dnn. Most add properly φάγω to eat : Unripe for eating.

Ὀμφὴ, a voice, esp. a divine voice, oracle, omen ;— melody ; — fame, report. — For ὀφὴ, (as ῥίΜφα,) from ἔπω, †ὄφα, to speak. (2) Mrt. from (τὸ) ὀν, φᾶ, φημί : As foretelling the fact. ? (3) 'Hebr. *anba :'* Wr.

Ὁμῶς, equally, alike.—R. ὁμὸς.

Ὅμως, equally for that, all the same for that, nevertheless. — Above.

Ὄναγρος, a wild ass : ὄνος, ἀγρὸς, ἄγριος. — Also, a machine for hurling stones. 'For the wild asses, when hunted, kick up the stones behind them, and send them against their pursuers :' Ammian.

Ὄναρ, Ὄνειρος, -ραρ, -αρ, a vision in sleep opp. to a waking vision. Dnn. says : 'A dream in opp. to a real appearance, something vain, illusory or transient.' It is well known that Homer says Οὐκ ὄναρ ἀλλ' ὕπαρ : yet *St. Matthew* was far from understanding Ὄναρ as a *false or vain* dream : 2. 12. I give in therefore partly to Becman who says : 'The ancients formed Ὄνειρος on the strength of a *good* omen, for they formed it from ὀνείω ἐρῶν :' i.e. from assisting and advantaging mankind by telling them something. Thus Ὄναρ would be from Ὄνειαρ. But better Ὄναρ simply from †ὀνάω, ὤνησα, †ὀνῶ, to benefit. As Δένω, ΔένAP. Ὄνειαρ is indeed both 'a dream' and 'an advantage'. — We might however well adopt here the *euphemismic* or *propitiatory* sense found in Parcæ, Εὐ-άνυμος, Εὐ-μενίδες, Ἀρίστερος.

†Ὀνάω, Ὄνημι, Ὀνίνημι, †Ὀνέω (whence Ὄνειαρ,) to benefit, gratify, delight : But Ὄνομαι, to vituperate, blame. Thus also Ὄνειδος is both good fame and bad fame, glory and disgrace. These opposite meanings are found also in the Lat. *Honor*, honor, and the old French *Honi*, shame, which are compared by all.— Mrt. deduces Ὄνομαι 'from Arab. *hon*, to despise'. And †Ὀνάω 'from, *ani*, to profit'. (2) But both senses may flow from O prefixed to †νάω, νέω, to heap up : †νάω producing Νάσσω, 'prop. to heap up, akin to Νέω, to heap :' (Dnn.)

Then 1. to heap favors or delights on one, 2. to heap insults and bad names on one. (**3**) Dnn. supposes with Buttm. a verb †˝Ονω, thought by Dnn. to mean 'to make mention of, good or bad:' but who can tell us about this †˝Ονω ? As to ˝Ονομαι above, that may be contr. from †ὀνόομαι, a verb †ὀνόω for ἐνοσάμην being authorised by Buttm.: And †ὀνόω being from ο, νέω, νένοα.

˝Ονειαρ, profit, advantage, succour. 'Ονείατα, refreshments, victuals. — 'R. ὀνέω, ὄνημι:' Dnn. See †˝Ονάω.—A dream: See ˝Οναρ.

˝Ονειδος, good and bad fame, honor and disgrace : in †˝Ονάω. Ει as in ὀνΕΙαρ. Δ as in ὕΔος, ὕΔωρ.

˝Ονειρον: in ˝Οναρ.

'Ονεύω, to lift up with an ˝Ονος windlass.

˝Ονθος, dung.— ' Prob. the same as 'Ονὶς, the dung of an ὄνος ass :' Schneid. (**2**) For ὄθος, as λαΝθάνω; then, (as 'Ο-πλος,) from δέω, δῶ, τίθημι, depono : A deposit.

'Ονθυλεύω, ' to dress with forced meat, — to doctor wine. — Passow from ὄνθος: lit. to stuff with dirt: — comparing Germ. mästen, misten. Compare Πηλός:' Ldd. Bedung — vitiate, adulterate — season. See Μίνθα.

'Ονίνημι: in †˝Ονάω.

'Ονὶς: in ˝Ονθος.

˝Ονομα, a name. — From ο, νέμω, νένομα, to distribute, attribute, assign: What is assigned to us at our birth, That by which we are distinguished. (**2**) Dnn. from †ὄνω, †ὄνομαι, ' to make mention of.' See on †'Ονάω. (**2**) Nam Sanskr. and Pers. ' Hebr. nam, to say:' Wr.

'Ονομάω, to vituperate, blame: in †'Ονάω.

˝Ονος, an ass. — Mrt. from †ὀνάω, †ὀνῶ, ὄνημι, to be a help to. As Jumentum is Juvamentum. Virgil of the dying ox: ' Quid labor aut benefacta JUVANT'? (**2**) From ο, νέω, νῶ, to heap up: On which burdens are piled. up. So Lat. ONUS, a burden of things heaped up.

˝Ονος, 'Ονίσκος, also a kind of codfish, Lat. asellus, of which Ovid: ' Et tam deformi non dignus nomine asellus.' Applied also, like Latin Porcellio from Porcellus, to a woodlouse, and a kind of wingless locust, drawing itself up when touched into a round ball. — ˝Ονοι are two stars in the breast of the sign Cancer. The asses. ? —Above.

˝Ονος, ' from its being a beast of burden, meant a windlass, crane, pulley; — the upper millstone which turned round.—Also a beaker, wine-cup, prob. from its shape:' Ldd. ' A kind of vessel with two long ears': Wr. — Above.

˝Ονος, ' = οὔνη, the ace:' Dnn.

'Οντως, as it is, in truth. — R. ὤν, ὄντὸς, part. of εἰμί.

˝Ονυξ, υχος, a nail, claw, talon, hoof : — the onyx stone ' which has spots like nails when polished,' Dnn.: ' in color resembling the nail of the finger,' Enc.

Br. —˝Ονυξ is from †ὀνύσσω, i.e. Ο, νύσσω, ξω, to prick, pierce.

˝Ονυξ, ' anything like an ὄνυξ claw, the hook of an anchor, an instrument of torture : — the white part at the end of rose-leaves, &c. by which they are attached to the stalk, as it were their nail-mark, Lat. ungues rosarum: — a thickening like a nail on the cornea of the eye; — a part of the liver:' Ldd.

'Ονυχίζω, to examine ὄνυχι with the nail if a work is well done. The Latins say ' Factus ad unguem.'

'Οξὶς, a vinegar-cruet. — And

˝Οξος, vinegar, Fr. vinaigre, vinum-acre. — From

'Οξὺς, ύος, sharp. — R. ο, ξύω, to scrape, scratch. (**2**) Allied to 'Ακὴ, a point, as ˝Ογμος to ˝Αγω.

'Οπάδος, 'Οπηδὸς, 'Οπάων, a companion, attendant. — From

'Οπάζω, to follow. R. ἕπομαι, to follow; ὅπα, †ὀπάζω. Also, to make anything accompany a person, cause him to take it with him, and so present, give.

˝Οπεας, Æol. ὕπεας, an awl: ' to bore holes with,' Todd: i.e. to bore ὀπάς.

'Οπὴ, an opening, aperture, hole. — R. ὄπτομαι, ὄπα, ὅπα: Through which one can see. (**2**) Todd compares ope, open, opening.

˝Οπη, ˝Οποι, ˝Οπου, 'Οποῖος, &c., the same as Πη, Ποι, Παυ, Ποῖος, &c. See ΠΟΣ.

'Οπίας, cheese of milk curdled with ὀπὸς juice partic. of the fig.

'Οπίζομαι, to have ὄπις a care for.

'Οπίζω, to extract ὀπὸς juice.

'Οπικὸς, ' Lat. opicus (in Juvenal, &c.) with a play on ὀπὴ:' Ldd.

†˝Οπιν, in Κάτ-οπιν, ˝Εξ-οπιν, at the back, behind. — R. ἕπομαι, ὅπα, to follow.

˝Οπιον, poppy-juice, opium. — R. ὀπός.

'Οπιπτεύω, 'Οπιπεύω, to look about, stare about, observe, watch. — See in ˝Οπτομαι. (**2**) R. †ὕπτω, †ὕπτομαι, redupl. †ὀποπτεύω, soft ὀπιπτεύω.

˝Οπις, divine vengeance, retribution. R. ἕπομαι, ὅπα, to follow. ' Sequitur ultor Deus,' Hor. Also, reverential regard, respect, awe, as Ob-sequor and Obsequium. (**2**) R. †ὕπτομαι, ὥπα, ἵπα, to look upon (with regard).

'Οπισθε, 'Οπιθε, 'Οπίσω, behind. — Above. 'Οπισθεν ἔπεσθε: Xen.

'Οπίστατος, most behind: = ὀπισότατος, from ὀπίσω behind.

˝Οπλη, a hoof, the peculiar ὅπλον of the horse, &c. Nature, says Anacreon, ˝Οπλας ἔδωκεν ἵπποις.

'Οπλομαι, to provide myself ὅπλα instruments or means of living.

˝Οπλον, a tool, implement, instrument; — of war, armour, weapon, shield; — of a ship, tackle, cordage. — R. ἕπω, ὅπα: By or with which we labor at, instrument for working. Compare ˝Οργανον.

'Οπλότερος, younger; prop. more fit to carry ὅπλα arms. So 'Υπέρ-οπλος confident in arms, &c.

'Οπὸς, juice, gum, fig-juice. — ' From the ὀπὴ opening whence it flows:' Mrt. Thus also Steph.: ' Succus castratione, terebratione, vel alio vulnere effluens.' So Dnn. says of Χυλός: 'That which exudes naturally, or from *incisions* made.' (2) 'R. ἔπω, ἔψω, ὄπα, coquo:' Hederic.

'Οπτάω, to roast, broil, bake: 'Οπτὸς, roasted, &c.: allied to 'Οψον, broiled meat, fish, and to 'Εψω, to boil ; 'Εφθὸς, boiled. — All from ἔπω, ἔψω, ἔπται and ὕπται, ὕψαι, to prepare with fire. O, as in κΟρμὸς, φΟρμός.

'Οπτιλος, the eye. — From
†'Οπτομαι, ὕψομαι, ' to see, see to, look to, take care': Ewing. — In comparing this with 'Οπίζομαι (from ὄπις, reverence, concern,) ' to stand in awe of, respect, follow upon, attend,' (Ewing,) and 'Οπιπτεύω, ' to look at, observe with attention or curiosity', we refer 'Οπτομαι (like 'Οπις, &c.) to ἔπομαι, ὄπα, to follow after i. e. with the eye, regard, look to. (2) As †Δάω, ΔάΠΤω, so οἶω, †δω, †δΠΤω, and †δσσω, δσσομαι, (an older form, says Ldd.) to carry (the eye) to, like †Βλέω, Βλέπω, to cast (the eye) on. Virg.: ' Passim *oculos* per cuncta *ferenti.*' Sil.: 'Circum-ferre *oculos*.' Quintil.: '*Mittamus oculos*.' (3) R. ἔπω, ἔπται and ὕπται, (as φΟρμὸς, 'Οπτάω,) to be busy in (with the eye).

'Οπυίω, 'Οπύω, to· marry, of the man. — ' Allied to 'Επω, ὄπα, necto, connecto, conjungo (matrimonio):' Scheide. And to 'Απτω, to join: and to 'Επομαι, to accompany. (2) R. ἔπω, to join, as Æn. 3. 136: ' CONNUBIIS arvisque novis OPERATA juventus.' (3) Ab ὀπὴ, forāmen (muliebre) ?

'Οπώρα, the end of summer, fruit-time, full age of puberty. — Some from ὀπὸς, ὥρα: The time when the fruits of the earth are full of juice, &c. (2) R. ἔπομαι, ὄπα, to follow: The season at the end of summer. (3) R. ὁ, ὀπος, supplies.

'Οράω, 'Ορέω, ' to see, stand seeing, look at,' Dnn. — ' To look at an object as a fixed ὄρος mark or boundary,' says Lennep, i. e. To take a mark with the eye. As from Templum is Con-templor. (2) R. ὁρω, or ὁρω, (as in 'Ορμάω and Hortor,) to raise or lift up i. e. the eye. ' Attollere *oculos*' is in Ovid and Propertius. So in the Psalms : ' I will lift up mine eyes unto the Heavens.' Compare Βλέπω, to see, from †Βλέω, to cast the eyes on. (3) ' Hebr. *raah*, to see:' Mrt.

'Ορβίκλατον, the Lat. *orbiculātum*.

'Οργάζω, to batter, beat, soften. — R. ἔργω, ἔοργα, ὄργα : To work well. See 'Εόργη.

'Οργανον, an instrument, tool, machine:—instrument of music, organ. — R. ἔργω, ὄργα : By which we work.

'Οργὰς, ᾶδος, 'a fertile spot of land, esp. meadow-land, partially wooded — a rich tract of land sacred to the gods; — adj. teeming, fruitful, of women :' Ldd. — R. ὀργάω, to teem, to be fruitful.

'Οργάω, to feel an ardent tendency to, a desire or passion for; from ὀρέγω, ὀρέγομαι. Hence of trees, to burst with a kind of eagerness, swell and teem with vegetative power, become fruitful. Or stretch out.

121

'Οργεὼν, one who performed sacrifices, — a priest. — R. ἔργω, ἔοργα, to sacrifice. So Facio is to sacrifice.

'Οργὴ, impulse, temperament, temper ; — violent passion, anger. — R. ὀρέγομαι, to desire. Aristotle defines it ὄρεξις μετὰ λύπης. (2) R. ὁρω, ἔορκα: That which excites.

'Οργια, the *orgies* of Bacchus, from the furious transports of the worshippers.—Above. (2) R. ἔργω, ἔοργα, as Lat. facio, to sacrifice.

'Οργίζω, to make angry: ὀργή.

'Οργυια, 'Ορόγυια, the length of the outstretched arm, — measure of length. — R. ὀρέγω, ὄργα, †ὀρογυία.

'Ορέγω, 'Ορέγνυμι, to stretch out in a line ; — hence reach out, offer, give; — reach to, desire to obtain, 'Ορέγομαι ;— reach to, obtain. — In comparing 'ΟΡθὸς, straight, and 'ΟΡμος and 'ΟΡμαθὸς, a row or series, we easily see how 'ΟΡέγω is to make straight or put out in a straight line. Comp. ἀρΗΓΩ, τμΗΓΩ, ψΕΙΩ. (2) Germ. reck-en, to stretch. (3) ' Hebr. *oreg*, to stretch out:' Wr. ' Chald. *areg*, desidero:' Mrt.

'Ορέξις, appetite. — R. ὀρέγομαι, ξομαι, to desire.
'Ορεὺς, a mule for the ὄρος mountain.
'Ορεύω, to watch, guard. — R. ὀρέω, ὁω, to see to.

'Ορεχθέω, to lie panting, heaving, stretching oneself as in the agonies of death ; — of the sea, stretch itself, rolling to the beach. — R. ὀρέγω, ὀρέχθην. Some understood it formerly as = ῥοχθέω.

'Ορθὸς, 'Ορθιος, erect, high, steep; — lifted up, loud, — straight up, upright, — straight on, right. — R. †ὅρω, ὀρθην: orior.

'Ορθοῦμαι, to succeed: i. e. go right on, or direct, regulate things well. — Above.

'Ορθρος, dawn of day. — R. †ὅρω, ὀρθην: orior, ortus solis.

'Οριγνάομαι, = ὀρέγομαι.

'Ορίζω, to divide, limit, bound, define, settle, ordain, decree. — R. ὄρος.

'ΟΡΙΝΔΗΣ, bread made of 'ΟΡῦζα, rice. Perhaps they are allied. ?

'Ορίνω, ὀρνύμι, to raise, rouse, from †ὅρω, orior. As 'Αγω, 'Αγινέω.

'Οριον, = ὄρος.

'Ορκάνη, ' = ἑρκάνη, ἔρκος, enclosure, fence; — net, trap:' Ldd.

'Ορκος, 'Ορκιον, an oath, allied to 'Ερκος: for an 'Ορκος is an 'Ερκος fence or security to engagements. See the next and the last.

'Ορκοῦρος, ' = ἑρκοῦρος : ἔρκος and ὄρκος being orig. synon. :' Ldd.

'Ορμαθὸς, 'Ορμος, a row, chain, string as of beads.— Allied to 'Ερμα, the same, from ἔρω, Sero, to join, Series, pf. ἔρμαι, ὅρμαι. So Εἰρμὸς is a train.

'Ορμαίνω, 'Ορμάω, to excite, set in motion, rouse; — turn over, ponder in the mind. So 'Ορμὴ, excitement, impulse, passion, &c.—R. †ὅρω, ὅρμαι, ὅρω, to rouse, and Lat. *hortor*.

R

'Ορμιά, a fishing-line: allied to 'Ορμαθὸς and "Ορμος, a string, chain.

"Ορμος: in 'Ορμαθός.—Also, a roadstead, anchorage, haven, place of shelter or refuge, ' from ἔρμαι, pf. of εἴρω, to join, as the other "Ορμος: as it is nothing but a place where ships are fastened :' Ldd. ' Moored by cables:' Dnn. So "Ορμος is also a cable. Ο, as φΕρω, φΟρτος.

"Ορμος is also a dance performed in a ring. — See in 'Ορμαθός.

"Ορνις, ιθος, "Ορνεον, a bird ; — spec. a cock or hen. — ' Prob. from †ὄρω, ὀρνῦμι (orior):' Ldd. As rising in the air.

"Ορνῡμι, to excite, stir up, rouse : from †ὄρω: orior, ortus, &c. So 'Ορίνω.

"Οροβος, a chick-pea.—Mrt. perh. rightly from ἐρέπτω, to eat, ἐρεβον, ὀροβα.

'Ορόδαμνος, 'Οραμνος, ramus, a bough. — R. ὄρω, orior, as rising or springing up, growing. Scheide considers -δαμνος a termination. Much as ῥιγεΔΑΝΟΣ. Comp. "ΟΡπηξ. (2) Lenn. seems to suppose it a pompous word, ' subdued on the mountains': ὄρος, δαμνάω.

'Οροθύνω, like 'Ορίνω, "Ορνῦμι.

"Ορομαι, to watch: referred by Ldd. to ὁράω: but perh. is the middle of †ὄρω : To rouse oneself.

"Ορος, εος, a mountain : from †ὄρω, whence orior, to rise.

"Ορος, Οὖρος, a bound. Οὖροι, ' marking stones, bearing inscriptions. And stone slabs set up on mortgaged property :' Ldd.—Lenn. allies it to ὄρος, a mountain: and Scheide to ὄρω or ὄρω, as anything RISING high, as a mountain, &c. Likewise as in 'Ορμάω. (2) R. ὁρῶ. That is, as far as you can see, as ὁ ὁρίζων, the horizon, is the line bounding the view. So Τέλος (from †τελέω, τείνω,) is as far as you can stretch out, the furthest extent. Some say, as visible boundary marks. (3) R. οὐρός, a trench or channel, then a bound generally.

'Ορός, 'Ορρός, serum of blood, whey of milk. — Prob. from ο, ῥέω, ῥῶ, as "Ο-ρΛος from ῥλάω, ῥλῶ: Of a liquid, fluid nature, running matter. (2) ' Separated from the coagulum by an action signified by ὄρω, to raise :' E. Valpy. (3) ' The form Οὐρός is found in Nicander, which may indicate a relation to Οὖρον, urine :' Ldd.

'Ορος, 'Ορρος, ' the end of the os sacrum on which the Οὐρά tail of beasts and birds is set ; — of man, the space between the anus and the Αἰδοῖα ; — gen. the tail, rump. Akin to Οὐρά :' Ldd. Or to "Ορος, a bound.

'Οροúω, to rush, hasten ; gen. to rise, as orior, ὄρομαι.—R. †ὄρω, ὀρίνω :' Ldd.

"Οροφος, reeds used for thatching houses : R. ἐρέφω, ὄροφα. Also a roof.

'Ορπηξ, "Ορπηξ, a sapling, young shoot or tree : — a goad, lance, made of such. —' Usu. deriv. from †ὄρω, for ὀρόπηξ [somewhat as πορΠΗ,] : — acc. to others from ἅρπη, so that the orig. notion would be a point or spike : Lat. urpex, a harrow :' Ldd. ' "ΟΡπηξ and 'ΟΡοδαμνος both from †ὄρω :' Schneid.

'Ορρός : in 'Ορός.

'Ορρωδέω from ὄρρος above and δέος fear: from dropping the tail as dogs : i. e. to fear. But Passow ' from the sound, as Lat. horreo, horridus.' 'Αρρωδέω also is found. So 'Οστακὸς and 'Αστακός. (2) ' Hebr. rod, to tremble :' Wr.

'Ορσόλοπος, ' eager for the fray, tempestuous, of Mars. — Said to be derived from †ὄρω, (ὅρσω,) and λοπὸς, λόφος: Bristling the mane; but prob. only a poetic form from ὄρσω, and so sometimes written 'Ορσόπολος, and 'Ορσοπολεύω, to provoke, assault :' Ldd.—' "Ορσω : to raise the λοπὸς peel or skin with a whip; gen. to afflict, vex, provoke :' Dr. Jones.

'Ορταλὶς, 'Ορτάλιχος, the young of any animal ; chick. — Ldd. allies it to "ΟΡνις, and so to †ὄρω, ὄρται, as springing up in the nest. 'Ορταλίζω, ' to begin to have feathers, to begin to grow and RISE,' Nugent.

'ΟΡΤΑ, the gut, — guts or intestines chopped up into mince as sausages. — Q. as connected with "Ορος the end of the os sacrum ? For the Gut is ' the long pipe reaching from the stomach to the vent', (Dr. J.).

'ΟΡΥΖΑ, oryza, rice. — Q. ?

'Ορυμαγδὸς, loud noise, din, rattling, confused inarticulate sounds.—R. ὀρύομαι in Steph., fremo, as 'Ωρύω. The Γ is inserted for sound, as it is merely a poetic word. (2) R. ὀροúω, to rush.

'Ορυξ, a pickaxe or sharp tool for digging. And an antelope, from its sharp-pointed horns. R. ὀρύσσω, ξω. And so probably 'Ορυξ, a great fish, acc. ὄρυγα, Lat. orca, orc or ork. '

'Ορύσσω, ξω, to dig, dig up. — From ἐρύω, †ὄρνα, to draw (up). (2) Ldd. allies it to 'Αρᾶσσω, to break (the sod). As "Ακρις and "Οκρις, &c.

'Ορφανός, left orphan, bereft : — ὀρφός.

"Ορφνη, darkness. — R. ἐρέφω, ὄροφα, (ὄρφα,) to cover. (2) ' Hebr. oreb, night :' Wr.

'Ορφὸς, bereft, orphan. — ' Akin to 'Ορφνη, darkness, 'Ορφνὸς, black :' Dnn. That is, from ἐρέφω, ὄροφα, to cover. From the gloominess of desolation. See partic. in 'Αχλύς. (2) 'Αν-ερείπομαι was to snatch up and carry off : ἐρέπτω was to feed on. These appear allied : suppose ἐρέπω or ἐρέπτω to snatch away, perf. ἔρεφα, ὄροφα: then ὀρφὸς, ὀρφανός. (3) Scheide allies it to 'ΑΡΠάζω, "ΑΡΠυια, "ΑΡΠη. So "Ακρος and "Οκρις, "Αγω and 'Ογμος, "Αγκος and 'Ογκος, &c.

'Ορχαμος, ' first of an ὄρχος row, file-leader :' Ldd. — Or ἀρχή, †ἄρχαμος, as "Αγω, 'Ογμός : "Ακρος, "Οκρις.

'Ορχὰς, "Ορχις, a kind of olive from its ὄρχις shape.

'Ορχέομαι, to dance : 'Ορχέω, to make to leap. "Ορχηστρα, part of a theatre on which the chorus danced, orchestra. — R. ὄρχος: A row of dancers. (2) The sense of leaping agrees better with the usual deriv. from †ὄρω, ὄρκα, orior. — Or even †ὀρέγω, †ὀρεχα, to stretch out (hands and feet).

'Ορχις, testiculus : — an orchis, from the form of its root, comm. called fool-stones. ' It has a remarkable resemblance to the scrotum of animals :' Enc. Br. —

' Some Etym. from ὀρέγω :' Dnn., i.e. ὀρέγομαι, to desire : perf. act. ὄρεχα. So 'Οργάω, ' tumeo cupidine, special. venereâ :' (Dnn.).

'Ορχος, "Ορχατος, ' a row of trees, place planted with such rows, orchard, Milton's orchat, garden :' Ldd.— —Allied to 'Ορθὸς, straight ; "Ορμος, 'Ορμαθὸς, a row. (2) ' Hebr. to arrange :' Wr.

†'Ωρω, ὄρσω, to stir up, excite, rouse.—Allied to Αἴρω, 'Αείρω, to raise, †'Ερω, 'Ερύω, to draw. (2) ' Chald. aar, to excite :' Mrt. ' Hebr. or, to raise :' Wr.

*Ος, who, which. See in 'Ο.

"Ος, his : short from 'Εός. — R. ἑ. acc., as 'Εμὲ, 'Εμός.

'Οσιος, hallowed and sanctioned by the laws of God or nature, of God or man : — pious to the gods, devout, and so thought to be from σ, and σιὸς Lacon. for θεός : = †σιμό-σιος, god-like, godly. See Σίβυλλα. Σ and Θ, as our loveS, loveTH. 'Ιερὰ καὶ ὅσια is the property of gods and men, sacred and profane. (2) R. †ἔω, ἔσαι, whence 'Εδω, to let be, let alone and free for religious purposes. (See 'Ιερός.) †'Εσιος, 'Οσιος, as 'Ερμα, "Ορμος ; &c.—Wr. from ἄζω, to stand in awe of. As "Ακρος, "Οκρις. (3) ' Syr. chasi, sanctus :' Mrt.

'Οσιόω, to make holy, hallow, purify, consecrate.— Above.

'Οσμὴ, smell, odor, ὀδμή.— R. ὄζω, ὄσμαι, to smell.

'Οσος, "Οσσος, how great, how much or many. — R. ὂς, redupl. into ὂσ-σος, like Lat. quis-quis, quot-quot, &c., and means 'who-soever, what-soever,' &c. As 'Οσσαι νύκτες τε καὶ ἡμέραι εἰσὶ, Whatsoever nights and days there are, i. e. how many soever.

'Οσπριον, pulse, vegetables. — As from τλάω is 'Ο--τλος, so from σπείρω ἔσπαρον to sow is †'Ο-σπάριον, 'Ο-σπριον : Any common sowing or seed.

'Οσσα, a warning or prophetic voice, from ὄσσομαι, to forebode : — any voice, report, rumour, — sound.

'Οσσε, the two eyes, for ὄσσεε, as Μέλεε, Μέλε,—from 'Οσσομαι, ' an older form of †'Οπτομαι, ὄψομαι, as Πέσσω of Πέπτω : To see, look on : — see in spirit, in my mind's eye, presage, forebode :' Ldd. See 'Οπτομαι.

'Οστέον, a bone.—' R. †στάω, ἵστημι :' Dnn., i. e. †στάω, †στάω, to stand firm, with Ο prefix. ' So the Arabians called a bone from its compact and hard nature :' Scheide. Compare "Αστυ, "Αστεος.

'Οστις, whosoever, whatsoever : — i. e. ὂς and τις : Any one who it may be.

'Οστλιγξ, "Αστλιγξ, a curled flame, flash, spark : — a curled tuck of hair, bunch of grapes, tuft of flowers.— For "Οτλιγξ, (as Σ in βόΣτρυχος, δαΣπλὴς, ὀΣφύς), from σ, τέλλω, †τέλλιγξ, τλίγξ, i. e. ἀνα-τέλλω, to spring up. Thus 'Οσταφὶς and 'Αστ. for Σταφὶς. (2) Lenn. from σταλάζω, as we say To drop in curls. For ὀστΑλιγξ is found, but a ' suspecta vox'. (3) Greg. from αὔω, αὔσταιι, αὐσταλέος, burnt, warped. As cAUda, cOda : cAUdex, cOdex.

'Οστρακον, hard shell of snails, muscles, tortoises, eggs; — allied to 'Οστέον, bone, and "Οστρεον, oyster. Also tile or potsherd, earthen vessel, voting-tablet, &c.

123

"Οστρεον, an oyster : —purple from it.— From 'Οστέον, or allied to it. (2) R. σ, στερεὸν, firm.

"ΟΣΤΡΙΜΟΝ, a stable. — Schneider from "Οστρον, 'Οστρεον. But ? — Very rare and out of the way.

'Οστρύα, "Οστρυς, ' a tree with very hard wood, like the horn-beam :' Ldd. — Allied to 'Οστέον, "Οστρεον, 'Οστρακον.

'Οσφραίνομαι, †'Οσφρέομαι, to smell, scent: 'Οσφραίνω, to make to smell. — All say, allied to 'Οζω, 'Οσμή. Perh. †ὀσφρέω = †ὀσμο-φορέω, †ὀσφορέω, to convey an odor. Or even for ὀ-φρέομαι, (as in ὀΣφύς,) simply from φρέω, to carry (an odor) with it.

'Οσφὺς, g. ὀσφύος, as ἔΣχον, for ὀφὺς, ὀφυὸς, from σ, φύω, to produce : Ο, as in "Οτλος. The loin, as Inguen from †Ingeno, Ingenui. So, ' of the fruit τῆς ὀσφύος αὐτοῦ of his loins,' Acts 2. 30. ' He was yet ἐν τῇ ὀσφύϊ in the loins of his father,' Heb. 7. 10. See ὀΣτλιγξ.

'Οσχη, "Οσχος, a sucker, shoot, branch. As ἐΣχον, from ἔχω, ὄχα : Adhering to the trunk. Also the scrotum, corpori adhærens. Dnn. says: ' A branch of vine with grapes ; espec. the scrotum'.

"Οτε, Τότε, 'when,' 'then.'— For ᾦ-τε, τῷ-τε : Quo tempore, eo tempore, χρόνῳ. ' What time as . . . .', Ps. 81. 7.

'Οτι, "Οτ', Lat. uti, ut, that. — ' Orig. the neut. of ὅστις : i. e. διὰ τοῦτο ὅ τι, δι' ὅ τι, hence often written [ὅ τι or] ὅ, τι :' Dnn.

'Οτι, why ; —because.— I. e. δι' ὅ τι, Proptereà quod, Propter quod.

'Οτλος, labor, suffering : σ, †τλάω, τλῶ, to endure : Much enduring.

'Οτοβος, "Οττοβος, loud wild noise, din of battle, rattling of chariots, sound of the flute. — ' From the sound,' say Ldd., Dnn., and Lenn. (2) Or K was dropt. For Κότταβος, the cottabus, or Sicilian game, Passow mentions another form "Οτταβος ' allied to "Οττοβος.'

'Οτοτοῖ, 'Οττοτοῖ, Τοτοῖ, exclam. of pain and grief,— from the sound, as "Οτοβος. (Dnn.)

'Οτοτύζω, to wail, cry ὀτοτοῖ.

'Οτράλεος, 'Οτηρὸς, quick, nimble, ready. — Allied through †τράω, †τρέω, to

'Οτρύνω, to push on, as trudo, stir up, excite. ' Trudo, push, urge, move forward :' Ridd.—' Perh. from τρύω ': Lenn. With σ prefix. As trudo is used above. Τρύω is ' to molest, vex,' Dnn : also ' to bore a hole, perforate' : and 'Οτρύνω is ' to spur, goad', (Ldd.) Compare the Latin Fodio, Fodico.

'Οττεύομαι, = ὄσσομαι, ὄττομαι.

'Οττις, sight : Above.

Οὐ, Οὐκ, Οὐχ, Οὐχὶ, (as Ναὶ Ναιχὶ,) not, no.— Οὐκ is prob. from οὔ γ', οὐγ', as from νῦν γε, νῦγ' is nunC, from ὅ-γε, ὄγ', is hoC. So Εὖ γε. And Οὐ seems nothing but the imperat. of †ὅω, †οἴω, οἴσω, i. e. †ὅε, take it away, like "Απ-αγε, Apage. 'Απο-πέμπομαι ὄψιν, Eur. Hec. 72. Compare 'Αρνέομαι. (2) From ouk, a natural sound of aversion.

Οἶ, where: gen. of ὅς, 'which,' Lat. quà, where. Prop. οὗ (τόπου). The gen. resembles the Lat. gen. in Domî, Militiæ, Humi.

Οὐά, vah, an exclam. of astonishment and horror. — I suppose from the natural sound: Whah! — 'Hebr. aueeh:' Wr.

Οὐαί: in 'Οά.

Οὖας, Οὖς, †'Οας, 'Ως, οὔατος, ὠτὸς, the ear. 'Αμφ--ώης, having two ears or handles. — Many from ἄω, ἀίω, to hear. From ἄω, says Damm, is †ἄος, ὄας, οὖας. The Laconic is Αὖς. (2) From the obsol. †ὄω, †οἴω, to carry: Into which sounds are carried. Plautus: 'Neque id immitto in aures meas:' 'Ne aures immittas tuas.' So 'Nescit vox missa reverti,' i.e. missa in aures.

ΟΥΓΓΙΑ, Οὐγκία, 'Ογκία, uncia, an ounce. 'From the Latin,' says Steph. That is, unica, uncia. 'A Sicilian word,' says Pollux. 'Arab. ukia', Turton. 'Irish unsa', Lluyd. Says Scaliger: 'As from ἑνὸς is Οὐγκία, uncia, so from νέος is Νοὔγκιος, nuncius.' But how is this?

Οὖδας, †Οὖθος, the ground, earth, pavement, floor. — Dnn. compares 'Εδος, 'a seat, basis, foundation.' The †Οὖθος is a 'Εδος. So 'Εδαφος is the ground or pavement. R. ἕζω, ἕδον, ὅδα. So 'Οὖδος, Οὐδός.

Οὐδὸς, a way, ὁδός.

Οὐδὸς, a threshold, ὀδός.

Οὖθαρ, gen. οὔθατος; the udder, breast :—fertility.— For οὖθαρ, (as ὄρος, οἴρος,) ὅθατος, from o, θάω, τέθαται, to suckle: like 'Ο-κέλλω.— AP as ἰθΑΡ. Compare Οὐτάω. (2) Germ. uder, our udder. Sanskr. udar.

Οὐκ: in Οὐ.

Οὖλα, the gums.— As being οὖλα soft.

Οὐλαί: in 'Ολαί.

Οὐλαμὸς, a crowd, troop, band.—R. οὖλος, in a mass. In form, as 'Ορχαμος.

Οὐλὴ, a wound healed, scar: from οὖλος, whole or sound.

Οὖλος, for 'Ολος, whole, as 'Ορος, Οὖρος.

Οὖλος, Οὔλιος, pernicious. — R. †ὀλέω, †ὀλῶ, to destroy: as 'Ολοός.

Οὖλος, curled,—rolled, round, in a mass, thick.—R. εἴλω, ἕολα, ὄλα, to roll.

Οὖλος, woolly, downy, soft. From the senses above. (2) Allied to our wool.

Οὖλος, a sheaf of corn, as rolled or bound round by an 'Ελλεδανὸς band. — Above.

Οὖλος, a song in honor of Ceres who was hence called Οὐλὼ and 'Ιουλὼ, 'the goddess of sheaves,' Ldd.—Above.

Οὖλος, 'of full force, able, substantial ;— said of sound, continuous, incessant:' Ldd. — From the sense of WHOLE: ὅλος.

Οὖλω, I am οὖλος whole or sound.

Οὖν, therefore. — R. ἐὸν, οὖν, it being so. 'Quæ cùm ità sint.'

Οὕνεκα, = οὗ ἕνεκα.

Οὔπιγγος, a hymn to

Οὖπις, 'Οπις, 'Ωπις, Diana : — also a companion of hers. — R. ἔπω, ὄπα: As attending to women in child-

124

birth. (2) From her retributive character, as the same with Nemesis. See 'Οπις.

Οὐρά, a tail. — Lenn. from οὖρος, ὅρος, a limit, end. (2) Schneid. allies it to 'Ορος, 'Ορρος.

Οὐρανὸς, Heaven. — R. οὖρος, a boundary. (2) R. ὁρῶ, to see: As far as we see: or the visible Heavens. (3) R. †ὄρω: Raised up, as Heaven is Heaved. (4) 'Chald. ora, light :' Mrt.

Οὐρίαχος, the οὐρὰ hindmost part, butt-end.

Οὖρον, urina, urine. Οὐρέω, to make water. Οὐρήθρα, urethra. — 'Either from ὀρὸς, whey: or ὀρὸς, ὅῤῥος:' Dnn. Both seem improbable. (2) Οὐρέω may be for 'Ορέω, (as 'Ορος, Οὖρος,) from o, ῥέω, to (make to) flow. See Οὐτάω.

Οὖρος, Οὖρον, the same as 'Ορος, bound.

Οὖρος, a watcher, guard. — R. ὁρῶ, to see, see to. (2) R. ὄρω: An impeller, leader, director.

Οὖρος, a fair wind: from †ὄρω, as exciting, impelling the sails and ship. So Οὐρίζω, to waft on one's way: Οὔριος, said of a good or prosperous voyage. (2) Viger from οὐρὰ, the tail, in a ship the poop, as Fr. le vent en poupe. Virgil: Surgens à puppi ventus.

Οὖρος, a mountain, ὄρος. And a wild-bull, urus, perh. from its mountain life.

Οὐρὸς, a trench or channel for hauling up ships ashore, and launching them again. — R. ἐρύομαι, †ὄρνω, to launch ships. (2) R. ὄρω: By which a ship is impelled into the water.

Οὖς: in Οὖας.

Οὐσία, that by which we are, essence, matter ; — that which is or belongs to us, property. — R. ὢν, οὖσα, being. So Παρ-ουσία.

Οὐτάω, -ημι, -άζω, to hit, wound.—For †ὀτάω, from o, †τάω, †τέω, τενῶ, tendo, to aim a dart, as 'Ορέγω is to aim a blow at. The Υ disappears in 'Ωτειλὴ, a wound. O, as 'Ο-κέλλω.

Οὐτιδανὸς, being οὖ τι nothing, powerless, worthless. As 'Ελλεδανὸς, 'Ργεδανός.

Οὖτος, Αὖτη, Τοῦτο, this: = ὁ αὐτὸς, ἡ αὐτὴ, τὸ αὐτό: 'The same.'

Οὖτω, Οὕτως, in this manner. — Old dat. sing. and plur. of Οὖτος.

Οὐχ: for Οὐκ before Aspirate.

'Οφέλλω, to increase, multiply, augment, —augment the resources of, help, serve: and 'Οφελος, advantage, help, service, kind office. 'Οφελέω, to assist. — Thiersch mentions 'Fελλεῖν' as connected with 'εἰλέω to roll.' Hence ὀ-Fέλλω, ὀφέλλω. Ldd. makes Εἴλλω to 'crowd thickly together:' hence to increase, &c. — This more right than viewing †'Εφ-έλλω an independent verb †'Εφέλλω, †ὀφελλα, as 'Απειλὴ, 'Ηπείλουν, &c. (2) Hemsterh. fancifully speaks of a verb †ὄφειν 'whence ὀφελίω, ὀφέλλω.' Allied to ἅπτω, to join, ἄφα, ἀφάω, &c. O, as 'Αγω and 'Ογμος. We find in Isaiah, 'Woe unto them that join house to house.' Here is the idea of 'adding to, increasing.' (3) 'Germ. voll, full: with O:' Thiersch.

'Οφέλλω, 'Οφείλω, †'Οφλέω, 'Οφλισκάνω, I owe: I ought. Also, I wish that, i.e. how *ought* it to be so!— Perhaps, as above, to increase, multiply (expenses), and so get into debt. — Or thus: Ewing says: 'Χράομαι, I have for my *use*, I borrow, receive for *use*.' And so Χρέος is a debt, Χρήζω, to lend. No wonder then, if to 'Οφελος, *utility*, is allied 'Οφείλω, 'Οφέλλω, to borrow, owe. Or to 'Οφελος, kind service.

'Οφέλλω, to sweep, i.e. 'increase, heap up together,' Ldd. — Above.

'Οφελτρον, a broom. — Above.

'Οφθαλμὸς, an eye. — R. †ὄπτομαι, ὄφθην: By which we see.

'Οφίασις, a bald place on the head, of serpentine form. — From

'Οφις, a serpent, snake. — As Δράκων from δέρκομαι, so 'Οφις from †ὄπτομαι, †ὄφα act.: from its power of sight. Pkh. says: 'A *serpent's eye* was a Proverb among the Greeks and Romans.' (2) Todd compares our *eff*, *eft*, *evet*. 'Hebr. *epha*, a viper :' Dahler.

'Οφις, a serpent-like bracelet; — a creeping plant, 'serpens.' — Above.

'Οφλισκάνω : in 'Οφείλω.

Ὄφρα, with a view to, to the end that, in order that ; up to the point that, until, while. — Mrt. from ὅς. O much as in Ὅτε, for Ὧ (χρόνῳ). Then ΦΡΑ? For φορά neut. pl. adv. Thus Ὄφρα is, *to what* point bearing: Τόφρα, to *that* point bearing. As Quo-*versum*, Quorsum. (2) R. †ὄπτομαι, pf. act. ὄφα, whence 'Οφις: With a VIEW to.

'Οφρὺς, ύος, the eyebrow,—brow of a hill. — 'Sanskr. *bhru*, Pers. *abru*, our *brow*:' Ldd. (2) R. ὄπα, ὦπα, the eye, and †ρύω, ῥύομαι, ἐρύομαι, to guard: The eye-guarder. I.e. ὀπ-ῥύος.

Ὄχα, and 'Εξ-οχα, eminently, by far. — R. ἔχω, ὄχα, ἐξ-έχω, to hold oneself out from or among.

'Οχέα, = ὀχή, a cave.

'Οχετὸς, a conduit, canal, water-pipe: from ὀχέω: as carrying water forward. So 'Οχετ-ηγὸς is conducting water by a canal : from ἄγω which ὀχέω means.

'Οχεὺς, anything for holding or fastening, band, strap, clasp, bolt. — R. ἔχω, ὄχα, as Homer has 'ὀχῆες εἶχον the gates.'

'Οχέω, de equo equam ascendente. Vide 'Οχέω. 'To cause to be covered:' Ewing.

'Οχέω, as 'Εχω, (ὄχα pf. m.) to hold, support, bear, endure, — carry, — let another ride on one.

'Οχὴ, support, sustenance : from ἔχω, to hold, sustain. — Also a cave, like 'Οχεια: which may be called from simply holding, containing. Others compare Χεια.

'Οχθέω, 'prop. to be heavy-laden, bút only used met. to be heavy or big with anger or grief, vexed in spirit, heavy at heart. Prob. from ἄχθος: and is to 'Αχθομαι as Ὄγμος to 'Αγω, &c.:' Ldd. (2) 'From ὄχθη: The mind rising and swelling with passion :' Steph.

Ὄχθη, Ὄχθος, the bank of a river or of a dyke, any rising ground. — R. ἔχω, ἔχθην or ὄχθην, — ἐξ-έχω, to stand out, project: or as κατ-έχω, to keep off, close in.

'Οχλεὺς, a lever, bar, bolt. — R. ἔχω, ὄχα, or ὀχέω, ὀχῶ, to support, lift up (loads). So 'Οχεὺς is a bolt.

'Οχλεύω, 'Οχλίζω, to move with an ὀχλεὺς lever, move a great weight.

Ὄχλος, a throng, crowd, multitude : — tumult. 'Æol. ὄλχος, Cret. πόλχος, *volgus*, *vulgus*, Germ. *volk*, our *folk*:' Ldd. — R. ἔχομαι, ὄχα, to hold together: as Ξυν-εχὴς, closely crowded.

Ὄχμα, as 'Εχμα, a hold, band, and

'Οχμάζω, as 'Εχμάζω, to bear, support; — bind fast, gripe. — R. ἔχω, ὄχα.

Ὄχος, anything which ἔχει holds, as a harbor; or which ὀχεῖ carries, as a ship, a carriage.

'Οχυρὸς, as 'Εχυρὸς, firm, strong, secure. — R. ἔχω, ὄχα, to hold.

Ὄψ, g. ὀπὸς, a voice. — R. ἔπω, ὄπα, to speak.

Ὄψ, g. ὀπὸς, the eye. — R. †ὄπτομαι, ὦπα, †ὄπα, to see.

'Οψὲ, late, at length, late in the day, &c. — R. ἕπομαι, to follow, ἕψαι or ὄψαι, as O in 'Οψον': So as not to keep up, but to follow behind. 'Akin to 'Οπίσω:' Dnn.

'ΟΨΙΑΝΟΣ λίθος, 'a black stone, perh. a kind of agate, *obsidian*, Pliny's Lapis *Obsidianus* or *Obsianus*:' Ldd. Found in Æthiopia, says Pliny, by one *Obsidius*.?

'Οψις, sight. — R. †ὄπτομαι, ὄψομαι.

'Οψον, 'boiled meat, opp. to bread, from ἕψω, (ὄψα,) to boil: — then anything eaten with bread, as a relish, — seasoning, — dainties, — fish, the chief dainty of the Athenians, — the fish-market:' Ldd.

'Οψώνιον, *obsonium*, provisions, esp. supplies for an army, pay in the shape of provisions. — Above.

Π.

†Παγέω, †Πήγω, Πήγνῦμι, to fasten, fix, make fast, firm or stiff: Lat. (*pago*,) pa*Ngo*,(*pagtus*,) pactus, com-pactus, compact : to pack close: so Teuton.*pack*.—From the obs. †παίω, †πέπακα, πάζω, †πίω, πιέζω, to press close, †πύω, πυκνὸς, &c. Compare Πάσσαλος, Παχύς. See †ΠΑΩ.
125

Πάγη, Παγὶς, that fixes or holds fast, a noose, trap, net. — Above. So Πηκτὴ is a net or cage for birds, from πέπηκται. Dnn. says of Πηκτὴ, 'Composed of pieces put together,' i.e. fast, tight. See on Πακτών.

Πάγος, compact or solid ice, hard frost; — salt, —

thick scum, — membrane. — R. †παγέω: so Πάχνη, also from its *compactness.*

Πάγος, a mountain peak, — a hill — 'A firm-set rock: R. πήγνυμι:' Ldd.

Πάγουρος, 'a kind of crab, from †παγῶ, as having a solid coat; or †παγῶ, οὐρὰ, hard-tail, shell-tail:' Ldd. Some call it *pungar.*

Πάγχυ, i. e. πάνχυ, (as πάГκαλον is πάN-καλον,) from πᾶν: altogether, entirely.

†Παθέω, †Πήθω, †Πέσθω, †Πένθω, †Πείθω, Πάσχω, to experience such and such feelings, feel towards another, am affected by anything good or bad, am treated well or ill, suffer ill. Πάθος, feeling, suffering.—' From †πέσθω,' says Matthiæ, 'is πέποσθε for πεπόσθατε, but others for πεπόνησθε, or *indeed from* †πόω'. ' *From* πόω':—indeed we recognize among these verbs not only †πόω, but †πάω,ἐπάθην, †πέπακα, †πέω, †πείω. Thus of Ταλαί-πωρος says Hemsterh. : ' Πῶρος is contr. from Πάορος from †πάω whence †πάθω, †πήθω.' These seem to proceed from †πάω, πάομαι, to *taste,* to have *tastes* or feelings towards, to feel towards or on account of, as Dr. Johnson explains To *taste* ' to feel, have perception of.' So ' Εἴπερ ἐγεύσασθε if you have *tasted* that the Lord is gracious' (N. T.,) '*experti estis*', says Schleusner, who states it to be a common expression, as Γεύεσθαι πόνων, μόχθων: to *taste* of suffering.

Παθικὸs, a *pathic,* i. e. ' passive' from '*patior.*'— Qui *patitur,* non agit.— Above.

Παιὰν, Παιήων, Παιὼν, *Pæan,* the physician of the gods :— a physician, gen. deliverer, savior ;— a *pæan,* choral song to Apollo the healer ;— triumphant song.— ' The Schol. Aristoph. from παίω [rather πάω,] θεραπεύω : good, if such could be proved to be a true sense. Bos assents, and there is some reason for it, for among the ancient Greeks †πάω or †παίω [as Μάω, Μαίομαι,] existed, whence *pasco, pavi,* i. e. *curo,* and so, *sano.*— Much better this than the Gramm. deriv. from the words of Apollo's mother Latona calling out to him to destroy the serpent Python, "Ιε παιὰν, βάλλε παιάν: παίω meaning to strike.— Better than this is the deriv. from παύω, to make to cease i. e. diseases, &c. :' Hemsterh. So Lenn. from ' πάω, curo.' Allied to †Βόω, Βόσκω, and Ποιμήν. See Παῖς.

Παῖγμα, a play, sport. — R. παίζω, πέπαιγμαι.

Παιδεία, the education παιδὸs of a child.

Παίζω, to play as a παῖς child. Zech. 8. 5. We say, Child's-play.

Παίπαλα, places rugged and steep. — R. πάλλω, redupl. παιπάλλω (as Μάω, Μαιμάω,) παιπαλῶ, to shake: Shaking, jolting. So

Παιπαλόεις, craggy, rugged.—Above.

Παιπάλη, redupl. of πάλη.

Παῖς, g. παιδὸs, a boy, girl. — 'R. †πάω, curo:' Lenn. 'R. πάομαι, nutrio:' Mrt. See in Παιάν.

Παιφάσσω, 'to look wildly, stare about, am mad ;— run wildly about, rush, quiver:' So Ldd., who reduplicates it from φάω, †φάσσω, παιφάσσω,— allied to Φάος

126

the eye.—Grove says, from παίω, φάος: To strike with the eye, dart a glance or look quickly.

Παίω, to strike, beat.—' R. πάω,' say well Dnn., Mrt., Lenn. See the obsolete †πάω, to press firm : allied to †Παγέω, Πήγω, and to Μάω, Μάσσω, to squeeze, knead. Some compare †Βάω, Βιβάζω, to make to go on.

Παίω, some consider to mean, to eat, taste, like Πάομαι.

Παιών : in Παιάν. — ΠΑΙΩΝ meant also, the foot called a *Pæon,* ‿◡◡◡, ◡‿◡◡, ◡◡‿◡, or ◡◡◡‿. But whence, Q. ?

Πακτόω, to make fast or close. — R. παγέω, †πάγω, †πέπακται, πήγω, Lat. com-*pactus.*

Πακτὼν, a boat which admitted of being taken to pieces.—'As made of sticks and pieces of wood fastened and *compacted* together:' Salmas.— Above.

Παλάθη, ' a ball, cake : a cluster of dried figs pressed together :' Ewing. — Prob. allied to Πάλλα, a ball. So Παλάσιον.

Πάλαι, formerly, of old, long ago.—Allied to Πάλιν, back.

Παλαιόω, to abrogate as παλαιὸν old, Lat. antiquo.

Παλαιστὴ, the same as Παλάμη, palm of the hand ; — a palm, four fingers' breadth.

Παλάμη, D. πάλαμα, *palma,* the *palm* of the hand : — art, contrivance. — R. πάλλω, παλῶ. By which weapons are brandished and hurled. (2) Jones and Wr. from πάλη : ' The instrument of wrestling.'

Παλαμναῖος, whose πάλαμαι hands are defiled with another's blood ;— also the avenger of such.

Παλάσιον, = παλάθιον, dimin. of παλάθη.

Παλάσσω, to draw πάλους lots.

Παλάσσω, to scatter, besprinkle, moisten ;— stain, defile. — Prop. to throw πάλην fine dust over anything. (2) Ldd. from πάλλω : To sprinkle by shaking or swinging about.

Παλεύω, to decoy, or catch by decoy-birds :— gen. to ensnare. — Some say, prop. to decoy by sprinkling πάλην flour to catch birds.—But Ldd. allies it to Παλαίω, Πάλαισμα 'a bout in wrestling,— a struggle,— a trick or artifice.'

Πάλη, finest meal or flour, as well παλλομένη shaken or sifted.—R. πάλλω, παλῶ.

Πάλη, wrestling, ' from πάλλω, to swing round :' Ldd. So Παλαίω, to wrestle ; Παλαίστρα, *palæstra,* wrestling school.

Παλία, the feast after the wedding-day. — R. πάλι, πάλιν : A repetition, Lat. re-potium.

Πάλιν, Πάλι, back, back again, again, on the contrary.—Valck. from πάλλω, παλῶ, to shake backwards and forwards. Hooger. makes it an accus.: ' retrogrado motu.'

Παλίωξις, a pursuit in turn. — R. πάλι, ἴωξις = ἴωχὸs and thought = δίωξις.

Πάλλα, a *ball* for playing with. — ' R. πάλλω :' Dnn. and Wr.

Παλλάδιον, image of *Pallas* or Minerva.

Παλλάκη, a concubine, as also

Πάλλαξ, ακος, a youth ;—a maiden ; mostly a concubine. — R. πάλλω, as prop. one who can brandish a spear : like 'Οπλότερος. 'From the vigor enjoyed in youth :' Riemer.—'R. πάλη :' Mrt. (2) 'Hebr. pillegesch, pellex :' Dahler.

Παλλὰς, Minerva.— R. πάλλω, as being warlike and brandishing the spear.—But Hemsterh. supposes it properly to mean a maiden unmarried, (see Πάλλαξ,) which was the characteristic of Minerva.

Πάλλω, to shake, toss, brandish, wield, whirl ;—midd. to quiver, leap, bound.—Allied to Βάλλω, to throw, i.e. backwards and forwards. So 'Ρίπτω, to throw; 'Ριπτάζω, to fling to and fro. Allied also to Παίω, to beat.

Πάλμη, a shield,—R. πάλλω, πέπαλμαι.

Παλμὸς. palpitation : Above.

ΠΑΛΜΥΣ, a Lydian word for king.—Very rare.

Πάλος, the lot shaken and thrown from a helmet ; one's lot. — R. πάλλω, παλῶ.

Παλτὸν, a brandished spear. — R. πάλλω, πέπαλται.

Παλύνω, to sprinkle. smear: = παλάσσω.

Πᾶμα, property. — R. πάομαι.

Πάμπαν, altogether.— Πᾶν πᾶν, as Προπρὸ, Lat. quisquis, French 'bon bon,' our 'so so.'

Παμπήδην, entirely. — R. πᾶν, πάομαι, †πήθην, as Βάδην, Στάδην. I.e. the whole property, as Παμπησία : Above.

Παμφαίνω, to shine brightly. — Redupl. from φαίνω, i.e. παφαίνω, παΜφαίνω, as λαΜβάνω : To appear clearly and visibly. (2) R. παν-φαίνω: πᾶν, entirely.

Παμφαλάω, to look around, esp. in fear.— R. πᾶν, φάη the eyes.

Παμφανόων, = παμφαίνων.

Πανδελέτειος, 'devouring the sentiments of Pandeletus, noted for his litigious and slanderous writings :' Brunck.

ΠΑΝΔΟΥΡΑ, a musical instrument with three strings, pandure and bandure which is found in the Catalogue of Charles I.'s collections. 'The pandore and the theorbo strike :' Drayton. — Q. ?

Πανεῖα, festival of Pan : — also panic fears, a panic, from Pan, as Polyæmus tells us. So τὸ Πανικόν.

ΠΑΝΕΜΟΣ, ΠΑΝΗΜΟΣ, one of the Corinthian and Macedonian months. Some make it July. If so, perh. from πᾶν, ἧμαρ : When it's all day, and no night.

Πάνθηρ, a panther.—'Perh. πᾶν, θήρ: altogether ferocious :' Dnn.

Πάννυχος, all night.—R. πᾶν, νὺξ †νυχὸς = νυκτός.

Πανὸς, panis, bread. — R. †πάω, pasco, pavi. See in Παιάν.

Πανὸς, for Φανός.

Παντοῖος, of πάντων all kinds. So 'Αλλοῖος.

Πάνυ, entirely. — R. πᾶν.

Πάξ, hush ! still ! — enough ! So Pax ! in Plautus and Terence. 'Πάζω in Hesych. is Παύω. From the Lacon. πάξαι for παῦσαι comes Πάξ, be quiet, hush :' Dnn.

†Πάομαι, to taste, to eat : — to possess : in †Πάω.

Παπαῖ, exclam. of surprise, as Lat. Papæ in Terence. Also of delight, even of dissatisfaction, and sorrow.— Bp. Blomf. makes it the plur. of πάπας : Ye fathers, ye gods ! Dnn. allies it to Πόποι. Compare Βαβαί.

Παπαιάξ, 'a stronger expr. than Παπαῖ, of distress or vexation, impatience, delight :' Dnn.

·Παππάζω, to call any one πάππας papa.

Πάππας, papa, father, 'mostly voc. πάππα, as 'Αππα, 'Απφὰ, 'Αττα, Τέττα. Formed to imitate the first sounds of children :' Dnn. 'Chald. abba :' Mrt., as in Rom. viii. 15.

Πάππος. 'a grand-father : metaph. the down on the cheek, — the down on the seeds of thistles, &c. :' Dnn. —Above.

Παπταίνω, to look round about carefully or timidly. — For παν-οπταίνω from †ὔπτομαι. Πάντη παπταίνοντι, Hom. 'Passim oculos per cuncta ferenti :' Virg. (2) R. πτάω, πτήσσω, †πταίνω, παπταίνω.

Παπταλάω, = παπταίνω.

ΠΑΠΥΡΟΣ, the Egyptian papyrus, of which paper was made.

ΠΑΡΑ, Πὰρ, Παραὶ, by the side of, alongside of, as in par-allel straight lines :—from the side of, from beside, aside. In things put side by side or compared, some are like ; others unlike and contrary to each other. Hence Παρά is 'contrary to,' as in para-dox, contrary to expectation. So Παρὰ is either on this side, or beyond it. —'Bonar allies it to par, paris. The Fr. parer un cap, to double a cape, is to leave it on one side : to parry a blow, is to turn it aside :' Dunb.

ΠΑΡΑΔΕΙΣΟΣ, a garden, park. Paradise.—'Pers. pardes :' Mrt.

Παρά-κοπος, 'struck falsely, prop. of money, counterfeit, from κόπτω. Metaph. mad :' Ldd. 'Prop. of a harper, beating out of time :' Bp. Blomf. So Παραπαίω is to go mad.

ΠΑΡΑΣΑΓΓΗΣ, a Persian land-measure.

Παράσηρος, white παρά along the side. This word seems now generally read Παρά-σημος from σῆμα.

Παράσιτος, a parasite, flatterer, eating σῖτον food παρὰ beside another, at other persons' tables.

Παρδακὸς, wet.—Voss. and Ldd. for ἀρδακὸς from ἄρδω to water. Say ἐπ-αρδακός. Dnn. παρ-αρδακός. (2) R. πείρω, πέπαρται, to pierce, run through : Penetrated with water, or Permeated. Δ as ἀνα-φανΔόν: And so

Πάρδος, πάρδαλις, a pard, leopard. — I think from πείρω, πέπαρται, to pierce, as being pierced with spots, as to Distinguish (from Stinguo) is from στίζω, ἔστιγον, 'to puncture, mark, spot', (Dnn.). I.e. πεπαρμένος. So Pkh. from Hebr. PRD, to divide, 'from its distinct marks.' See above.

Παρειά, Παρηῒς, Παρήϊον, the cheek. — R. παρά, by the side of : As being by either side of the face.

ΠΑΡΕΙΑΣ, -ώας, a reddish-brown snake.—'Supposed to be called from having inflated παρειὰς cheeks : or from its raising its cheek and face, creeping with its hinder part alone :' Forcell. ? ?

Παρήορος, either ' hanging beside,' from ἀείρω, ἤορα, as Μετέωρος ; or ' joined beside,' from εἴρω, ἔορα, ἤορα, to join : Said of a horse drawing by the side of the regular pair, 'lying along, sprawling, hence helpless : and beside oneself, mad :' Ldd.

Παρθένος, a maiden, virgin. —' R. παρ-θέω, παρα-θεῖναι, to lay up, set apart : alluding to their retired life in the East, and among the ancient Greeks :' Pkh. (2) ' As she παρ-θεῖ runs still by her mother's side :' Mrt. (3) Scheide ἀ πείρω, ἐπάρθην : Penetrabilis, quippe quæ sit ὡραία.

Πάριος, of Parian marble.

Πάρμη, ' the Latin Parma :' Dnn.

Πάροιθε, = πάρος.

Παροιμία, ' a proverb, saw, common saying; from πάρ-οιμος, at the road-side :' Ldd. — R. οἴμη.

Παροιμιακός, a parœmiac, a line completing a system of Anapæsts, as well fitted for a proverbial saying.—Above.

Πάρος, before. — ' Akin to Παρά :' Dnn.

Πάροχος, one who furnished necessaries on the public account to travellers. — B παρ-έχω, πάρ-οχα, hold out, give.

Παῤῥησία, for Παν-ρησία, liberty of speaking everything; — freedom. — R. πᾶν, ῥέω, ῥήσω, to speak. So παΝουδίη, παΣουδίη.

Παρών, a pinnace, light ship.—' The Schol. Aristoph. from the isle of Paros :' Steph.

Παρῴας, Παρῷος : in Παρείας.

Πᾶς, Πᾶσα, Πᾶν, all, every. — As Ἅπαξ is derived by Pott from a, †πάγω, †πάξω, πήγνυμι, ' close and joined together,' (as Παχύς,) so †Πᾶξ, that is †Πᾶγς or Πᾶς. So Cunctus is Con-junctus. Compare Ὅλος. (2) ' Hebr. pasch, a multitude :' Mrt.

Πασπάλη, = παιπάλη. Dnn. from πᾶς, πάλη. Better, πάλη, †παιπάλη, then Σ as in δαΣπλὴς, βόΣτρυχος.

Πάσσαλος, Πάσσαξ, a peg to fix anything on, from †πάσσω, †πήσσω, πήξω, to fix :— a pin or bolt to fix by : — ' from the likeness of the form of a peg, a gag; the fall of a mouse-trap; a wooden peg or pin for boring; a sucker or cutting for planting :' Ldd. Compare †Παγέω, †Πήγω, Παχύς.

Πάσσος οἶνος, the Lat. passum, raisin wine. Pando, pansum, passum, to stretch out, dry.

Πάσσω, to sprinkle, strew, powder ; — sprinkle with embroidery. — Short for Πάλασσω. (2) Ewing says, ' Also Doric for Πήσσω, to fix in.' The sense of ' embroider' seems to agree with this : then to add on in any way. A as πΛάσσαλος.

Πάσσων. Παχὺς, πάσσων, as βαθὺς, βάσσων.

Παστὰς, a porch in front of the house; —a hall next to the porch;—chamber, nuptial chamber.—As having the walls wrought with embroidery, παστὸς, from πάσσω. (2) Passow makes it = παρα-στὰς, ad-stans, adjoining.

Παστὸς, bridal chamber; — chapel or shrine of a god. — Above.

128

ΠΑΣΧΑ, the Hebrew passover. — ' Hebr. pasach, to pass over :' Mrt.

Πάσχω : in †Παθέω.

Πάταγος, a clatter: πατάσσω.

Πατάνη, patina, a hollow dish, platter.—' R. πετάω, to lay open :' Mrt. Transp. πατέω, as in Lat. pateo, patulus. Thus μιστΥλη and μΥστΙλη, μιττΙλος and μΥτΙλος.

Πατάσσω, ' to strike, beat, hit, pat, palpitate, throb:' Grove. To patter, Ewing adds. Beat, batter, Fr. battre, and their northern affinities, are mentioned. Mrt. from πατέω: at least allied to it. And all from †πάω, †πέπαται, †παγέω, †πήγω, †πίω, πιάζω, πιέζω, to press tight. (2) R. †βάω, †βέβαται, βιβάζω: To make to go on.

Πατέομαι, to taste, feed on, eat, Πάομαι.

Πατέω, to tread, tread ·on, walk : Πάτος, a path. — R. †πάω, πιάζω, πιέζω, to press close : — or even †βάω, to go. See Πατάσσω.

Πατήρ, pater, a father. — ' Prop. a nourisher, from †πάω, †πέπαται, pasco, pavi, [see in Παιών,] to feed, nourish': Lenn. Allied to †Βόω, Βόσκω, Ποιμήν, &c. Thus Eurip. in Ion: τὸν βόσκοντα, for father. (2) Our word father. ' The northern languages give fader, vader, fater. Persian pader :' Todd. Pitara Sanskr.

Πάτνη, = φάτνη.

Πάτος, a path. — R. πατέω.

Πάτρα, Πατριὰ, Πατρὶς, &c. fatherland, lineage, &c. as Patria. — R. πατήρ.

Πάτρων, the Lat. patrōnus.

Πάτρως, paternal uncle, patruus.—R. πατήρ, πατρός.

Παῦλα, a resting-point. — And

Παῦρος, small in number or size.—R. παύω: Having stops or intervals, ' few and far between.' (2) See in Φλαῦρος.

Παύω, to make to cease, to stop. — Παύω and Πάζω (in Hesych.) are allied to †Παγέω, †Πήγω, Πάσσαλος, Πατέω, Παχύς, &c. and mean to keep fast or tight, hold back, ' premo, reprimo,' repress. So Premo for Re-primo. ' Vestigia pressit', Virg. ' Dolorem rex pressit,' Curt. — In form as Λαύω, Ψαύω. (2) ' Hebr. peah, a corner, end :' Mrt. ?

Παφλάζω, to bubble, froth: — storm, bluster. — ' R. φλάζω :' Dnn.

Πάχνη, congealed dew, congealed blood. — R. παχὺς, †παχίνη : Compact.

Παχὺς, thick, coarse, fat: i. e. closely packed, compact, from †πάγω, †πέπαχα, †πέπακται, πακτόω, πήγνυμι.

†Πάω : ' Πέπαμαι, to acquire, possess. Compare Πατέομαι: though Passow considers them as different. Hemst. and Valck. assign both of them to †πάω, to feed, fodder, pasture; then πάομαι, to feed, graze, and keep cattle for one's own use: from this, to possess, the earliest sort of property being cattle: — to enjoy possession, to eat: — In aid of this deriv. compare Lat. pasco, [pavi,] :'

Dnn. The sense of *feeding* may be seen in Βύω, ' to stuff up, to fill quite full', (Dnn.). And with this sense of †πάω, to feed, and to taste, must be compared †Βόω, Βόσκω, Βοτάνη, and Πόα, Ποία, Ποιμήν. — In the sense of *eating* †Πάω should be compared rather with Μάσσω through Μάω, and Μασάομαι, to chew. And it is thus allied to the verbs which follow. (2) ' Hebr. *peh*, the mouth :' Mrt.

†ΠΑΩ, †ΠΕΩ, †ΠΙΩ, †ΠΟΩ, †ΠΤΩ, (as Ψάω, Ψέω, Ψίω, Ψόω, Ψύω,) to press close, or press firm : allied to †Μάω, Μάσσω, to Βιάζω, Βύω, Μύω, Πιάζω, Πιέζω, &c. Hence are †Πάγω, Πήγνυμι, Παχὺς, Πατέω, Παύω, Πέζα, Πέδον, Πίνω, Πότος, Ποῦς, Πυκνὸς, Πῶμα (lid), Πύλη, &c. — Compare too Ἰπόω, to press upon.

Πέδα, Æol. for Μετά. Π and M, as our Polly, Molly; Peggy, Meggy. Δ and T, as Δαῖδα, Tæda.

Πεδανὸς, low on the πέδον ground, low, as Humi, Humilis.

Πεδόρσιος, = μετ-άρσιος. — See Πέδα.

Πεδάω, to bind πέδαις with fetters. See the next.

Πέδῑλον, a sandal, and Πέδη, a fetter, — from the old †πὲς, †πεδὸς, *pes, pedis*, a foot, allied to πους, ποδός. So Fetter is Feeter.

Πέδον, Πεδίον, the ground, land, plain. — As trodden by the *pes, pedis*, †πὲς, whence Πέζα, the foot, and Πεζικὸς, ' on foot or by LAND,' Ldd. See Πέδῑλον.

Πέζα, the foot, *pes* :—a fringe or border ;—like Πέδον, used of a country, region ;—and a net, where it is allied perh. to Πέδη or Πεδάω. — See Πέδῑλον.

Πεζὸς, on foot. — Above.

Πεῖαρ : the same as Πῖαρ.

Πείθω, to induce, persuade, make to give credit to or believe. Πείθομαι, to give credit to, believe, trust, obey. — ' From the old †πίω, †πείω :' Lenn. Whence Πιάζω, Πιέζω, to press closely. See †Πάω. So γηθέω, νήθω. See Πεῖσμα. (2) Allied to †Βέω, Βείομαι : To make to go. (3) ' Hebr. *pittah*, to persuade :' Mrt.

Πείκω : the same as Πέκω.

Πεῖνα, hunger. — ' R. πένω :' Dnn. And Πένης, poor.

Πεῖρα, attempt, trial, experiment, Lat. †*perior, ex- -perior*. — ' R. πείρω, to pass, traverse, perform a journey :' Dnn. So *Pirates* are Πειράται. Allied to Περάω, ' to hazard, risk' (Dnn.). So we have ἐμ- -πΕραμος.

Πειρὰ, a point, edge. — R. πείρω, to pierce.

Πεῖραρ, Πέρας, the furthest point, end. ' I.e. as far as you can pass :' Hemst. From πείρω, to pass. So Πεῖραρ is ' that which finishes, and hence a goldsmith's tools are Πείρατα finishers of art. Πείρατα γαίης, the ends of the earth : πείρατα, ends of ropes, knotted ropes :' Ldd.

Πεῖρινς, ' a wicker-basket which held the load of a cart, the body tied on the carriage :' Ldd. : ' a case in which things are conveyed in a chariot :' Dnn. — R. πείρω, to journey : A travelling-case. (2) Some from πείρας : as placed at the extremity of the carriage.

Πείρω, to pierce, pass through : —cut my way, pass through, journey. — From †πίω, †πείω, πιέζω, to press

129

firmly, as said of nails, studs, &c. As †Φθέω, Φθείρω; Ψάω, Ψαίρω, so Πείρω. (2) Allied to †Βέω, Βείομαι, to make to go or pass i. e. through. (3) R. πέρα, or πέρας. (4) Allied to Lat. *PER*, through.

Πεῖσα, persuasion. — R. πείθω, σω.

Πεῖσμα, a rope, cable, fig-stalk. — Valck. thinks that Πείθω meant orig. to bind, (See in Πίθος,) and then to oblige, compel, urge, persuade : and that from πέπεισμαι Πεῖσμα meant a rope to bind with. Ldd. considers it metaphorical : ' That which holds in obedience.' Thus πεῖσμα is also ' persuasion.'

Πείσομαι, fut. of πάσχω, through παθώ, †πείθω. See †Παθώ.

Πέκω, Πείκω, to card wool, — comb ; — to shear, and Πεκτέω, Πεκτῶ, *pecto*, whence *Pecten*, a comb. — Πείκω and Πείρω seem allied ; i. e. πείκω is to pass through, with a comb, scraper, &c. Compare too Πιέζω.

Πέλαγος, the sea, open sea, *pelagus*. — As Τέναγος, Γλάγος. From πελὸς, dark, livid. Thus we find μέλαν ὕδωρ, μέλας πόντος. (2) Hebr. *palach*, disseco. As Horace : ' Quâ medius liquor *Secernit* Europen ab Afro.'

Πελάζω, Πελάθω, Πελάω, to make to come πέλας near.

Πέλανος, a half-liquid mixture of oil, or honey, or clotted blood, — mixture to the gods of meal, honey and oil. Lennep allies this as a cake to Lat. *planus*, plain, flat, level, and the Etymol. M. from πλατὺς : but the E? Yet compare πἘλεθρον. But better from πελὸς, black, dark, as πέλανος is used with the epithets ἐρυθρὸς, αἱματρός. In form like οὐρΑΝΟΣ. Ldd. accounts for Πέλανος being used by Nicander for an 'Οβολὸς : for that ' perhaps the Πέλανοι came to be made up into round cakes when offered.'

Πελαργάω, to admonish. — ' Prob. from the caution of Πελαργοὶ storks, which set a watch, like rooks, to warn the rest of coming danger :' Ldd.

Πελαργὸς, the stork. — All say from πελὸς, ἀργός ; from its having black and white feathers : The black- white. — ' Sometimes for Πελασγὸς (*Pelasgian*, of the *Pelasgic* race) : prob. from the notion that the Πελασγοὶ meant a roving tribe, and so were the same with Πελαργοὶ, storks being birds of passage :' Ldd.

Πέλας, near. — ' The Etym. M. explains Πέλω by προσ-εγγίζω, to come near : hence then let Πέλας be :' Greg. ' Akin to Πέλομαι, Πέλω :' Dnn. Seen better in Πολέομαι, to go about in, dwell in, as Lat. *versor*, con- versor *inter, apud*, i. e. among, by, near.

Πελάτης, a neighbor : R. πέλας. And one who comes near for protection, a client, &c.

Πέλεθος, Σπέλεθος, ' human excrement. R. πηλὸς :' Dnn. Like Μέγεθος. Compare κΕδνὸς, Ἑδνα, πλΕθρον.

Πέλεθρον, used by the Poets for Πλέθρον, and sup- posed to be an extended form. But see Πλέθρον.

Πέλεια, wood-pigeon, ring-dove, from its dusky color, ' black color,' Ldd., ' blueish color,' Dnn. R. πελὸς. ' Said also of the prophetic priestesses, prob. from the prophetic pigeons of Dodona :' Ldd.

S

Πελεκὰν, the wood-pecker, and a water-bird of the *pelican* kind. Jones calls it 'the ΑΞΕ-bird, with a bill capable of scooping trees.' R. πέλεκυς.

Πελεκίνος, 'a water-bird of the *pelican* kind': Ldd.: 'the *pelican* or some species of bittern:' Dnn. Also 'a plant, axe-fitch, axe-wort:' Grove. See above. And 'a species of joiners' work, from the form: Lat. securicula, (r·m secūris,) swallow's-tail:' Steph. — R. πέλεκυς.

Πέλεκυς, a hatchet, axe; Πελεκάω, to hew with it: — derived by some from Hebr. *pileg* or *palach*, to divide. — But Dnn. makes it 'akin to Πελεμίζω, Πολέω, Πάλλω.' Thus Virgil: ' *Quatiens* Tarpeia *secūrim*.' ΠέλΕΚυς in form somewhat as ὀλΕΚω. There is also Πέλυξ, an axe. See Πέλω.

Πελεμίζω, like Πάλλω, Παλῶ, to shake, swing, quake. E as in πΕλτη; κατα-πΕλτης; τΕλαμών; ΒΑΛΛω, ΒΕλος; κΕλυφος; ΒΟΕΛΛΑ. See Πέλω.

Πελιδνὸς, Πελιὸς, ═ πελός.

Πάλλα, a skin, hide. — As Μορφὰ, Forma, so λεπὶς (a skin) became †πελὶς and πέλλα and Lat. *pellis*, much as λοπὸς became φολίς. See Φελλὸς 1.

Πάλλα, Πελλὰς, Πελλὶς, Πελίεη, Πέλις, Πέλιξ, a bowl, basin, cup. Allied to Πέλλα above. So 'Ασκὸς is 'a wine-*skin*, and a *bottle* made of goat's-*skin*': Dnn. Who observes of Πέλλα that it is 'the skin considered as a vessel containing the intestines: Lat. *pellis*.' (2) Our *pail*, Span. *paila*.

Πελλαστὴ, a leathern bandage worn by runners next the foot and ankle. — R. πέλλα, a skin.

Πέλμα, ατος, the sole of the foot : — any extremity. —'R. τέλμα, the end: Ernesti:' Dnn. Thus Πίσσυρες for Τέσσαρες, σΠάδιον for σΤάδιον, λίΤρα into λίΠρα, liBra. (2) For πέλμα, from πέδον, the ground, as Solum and Solea, the sole. Δ, as in Δασέος and Λάσιος ; Δάκρῦμα, Lacryma; ὀδυσσεὺς, uLysses, &c. (3) An old deriv. was from πελόν: the sole being *dingy* from its treading on the ground. (4) As Ταρσὸς is both the palm of the hand and the sole of the foot, Παλάμα, the palm of the hand, might be the sole of the foot, contr. into Πάλμα, Πέλμα; E, as πΕλτη, πΕλεμίζω, grEssus. But the genders vary.?

Πελὸς, Πελλὸς, Πέλιος, Πέλειος, Πελιδνὸς, black, dark, ash-colored, livid. — As λύΚος, luPus, the same as †Κελὸς, Κελαινὸς, Κήλεος. (2) A dialectic variety of Μέλας, black; as Μετὰ, Πέδα; ὀΜΜατα, ὀΙΠΠατα; our Molly, Polly; Meggy, Peggy. (3) R. πελειὰ, a dove, from its color: but the converse is generally supported.

Πέλτη, 'a small light shield; — a shaft, pole. R. πάλλω, [πέπαλται]: Dnn. For Πάλτη, as grAdior, grEssus. See in πΕλεμίζω. Πάλτας πάλλουσι, Eurip.

Πέλω, Πέλομαι, †Πλάμαι, to move or be in motion: Πόλοι, the *poles* on which the world turns. Also, as Lat. Versor from Verto: thus, Age and death ἐπ' ἀνθρώποισι πέλονται, versantur inter homines, attend upon or simply are among men: and so Πέλω, Πέλομαι are often 'to be.' — Allied to Πάλλω, Πελεμίζω, to shake to and
130

fro, change position, as Verto, Verso, Versor, Conversor, Gr. στρωφάομαι. See Πολεύω, Πολέω, &c.

Πέλωρ, a monster, prodigy.—Dnn. says, 'Akin to, or from πέλω, venio, ventito.' The idea is a hobgoblin or monstrous being HAUNTING a person. '*Foul spirits haunt* my resting place:' Fairfax. In form as †ϜΕλω, Ϝελωρ.— Mrt. says: 'R. πέλω, verto, as our Wunder (Wonder) from Wenden (to Wind).' (2) *Pele*, Hebr., is, mirabile.

Πελωρὶς, the giant-muscle.—Above.

Πέμμα, dressed food, esp. pastry, cakes.— R. πέπτω, πέπεμμαι.

Πεμπάζω, to reckon on the πέμπε five fingers, count by fives ; — count.

Πέμπε, five.— R. πέντε, πέντε, πέμπε. As Τέσσαρες and Πίσσυρες.

Πέμπελος, very old. — Dnn. for †πέπελος (as τύΜπανον,) from πέπτω, πεπῶ, to ripen : Fully ripe. (2) Some say : Ready to be conveyed (by Orcus): πέμπω.

Πέμπτος, fifth.— R. πέμπε.

Πεμπτηρα, a street in a camp for market, as Lat. 'quintana.'—Above.

Πέμπω, to send, send forward, convey, accompany as in a procession called (from πέπομπα) πομπὴ, pompa, a splendid show.—As τύΜπανον and πέΜπελος : — for †πέπω, and this from the obs. †πέω, (as δρέΠω, βλίΠω,) allied to †Βέω, Βείομαι, Βιβάζω, to make to go on. Compare λάΜΠΩ, στΕΜΒΩ, μΕΜΦομαι. (2) Or from †πέω, †πίω, πιέζω, Βία, Βιάζω. See Πέδον, Πέζα, &c.

Πέμφιξ, Πεμφὶς, Πομφὸς, Πομφόλυξ, a vapor, ray, pustule, bubble ; — departed soul, a mere breath. — R. πέμπω, πέπεμφα, 'like 'Ανα-πέμπω, to send up,' Ldd. Or 'Εκ-πέμπω : What bodies send up or out. Something emitted. (2) Dnn. compares Βομβὸς, Βομβυλίς.

Πενέστης, a laborer, servant. — R. πένομαι. (2) Ldd. from *Penestia* on the borders of Macedonia : A Thessalian serf.

Πένης, poor.— R. πένομαι.

Πενθερὸς, a father-in-law : brother-in-law : son-in-law. —As Κηδεστὴς from κῆδος, so Πενθερὸς from πένθος : Taking Πένθος as Πάθος, from πάσχω 'to have a feeling for.' (2) Ldd. 'from Sanscr. *bandhu*, relation, *bandh* to join, our *bond*, *bind*.'

Πένθος, suffering, misfortune, grief, sorrow.— Πάθος, Πένθος, as Βάθος, Βένθος.

Πένομαι, and perhaps Πένω, to work for one's daily food, toil ;—am poor and needy;—work at, get ready.— Σπεῖν is mentioned by Ldd., and Περι-σπεῖν, to be busy about. Now, as †Φάω, †Φένω, †Γάω or †Γίω, Γένω, so might be †Σπένω, †Σπένομαι, then Πένομαι, as Στέγω and Τέγος, Tego; Σφιν and Φιν; 'Κάπετος for Σκάπετος', Ldd.

Πέντε, five.- ' Nature, says Goguet, has provided us with an *arithmetic* instrument, our fingers. These were used to assist in mensuration. May we not then derive with Mrt. πέντε from πάντες, as equal to ALL the fingers on either hand ?': Pkh. Thus Σ is lost in Lat. quatuor, i.e. from Æol. κέτορε for κέτορεΣ. E, as grAdior, grEssus; πΑλλω, πΕλτη. (2) R. παύω, πέπαυνται: as they stopped at the fifth finger in counting.

Πέος, penis. —'Compara [antiq. †πès, pes, et] πούς ἡ †πέω:' Lenn. Ut affine sit τῷ †πίω, πιέζω ut πΕζα, &c. Nota com-pressisse Ter. Hec. 5. 3. 30. Mirum est quòd Euripides similiter usurpet ἀπκοῦ τὸν προβχοντα ΠΟΔΑ, Med. 677. Sic et est Ποδεών.

Πεπαίνω, to make mellow or ripe. — R. πέπτω, πεπῶ, whence Πέπων, ripe.

Πεπαρεῖν, to show, manifest : an uncertain word, adopted by Boeckh in Pind. P. 2. 57. If genuine, from πείρω, as πεπαρμένος, pierced, i.e. opened, laid bare. — Boeckh allies pāreo, appāreo.

Πέπειρος, mellow, soft.—Allied to πεπαίνω.

ΠΕΠΕΡΙ, pepper.—'The Persians to this day say biber :' New Steph.

Πέπλος, a cloak, robe ; — sheet, veil, hanging. —'For †πέπελος, from πέλω, verso : [or πολέω, †πέπολος, πέπλος,] i.e. in-volucrum [from in-volvo] :' Lenn. The Et. M. says : περί-πολός τις ὢν, ὁ περὶ τὸν φοροῦντα περι-πελόμενος καὶ εἱλούμενος, rolled round the wearer.

Πέπνυμαι, 'to have breath or soul, [Compare Ἄνεμος, Anima and Animus ; and Spiro and Spirit,] met. am wise, prudent. From πνέω, ἀμπνύω, &c. Πεπνυμένος in later Prose, ζῶν καὶ πεπνυμένος, to live and breathe :' Ldd.

Πέπτω, Πέττω, Πέσσω, to boil, cook, digest, soften : — cherish, cherish in the mind, brood over ; — nurse, heal ; — digest an affront.— Dnn. has ''Εφ-έπω, to follow, to attend to, pursue an occupation.' And again, ''Επέπω, to follow, Ion. for 'Εφ-έπω.' Now this 'Επέπω or 'πέπω is our Πέπτω, for Dnn. says again, ' Πέπειρος, from †πέπω, πέπτω.' In Πέπτω understand πυρί : ' to be busily engaged over the fire,' to cook, boil, &c. Or to boil, as said of the fire Il. σ. 348, πῦρ ἀμφ-ΕΠΕ.

Πεπρωμένη, ἡ, what is fated, πεπερατωμένη. (2) Schneid. from πόρω. ?

Πέπων, as Πέπειρος, ripe, mellow, soft, tender, gentle : —' in a good sense, as a term of endearment ;—in a bad sense, soft, weak.—'Ω πέπονες, Hom., Ye weaklings :' Ldd.

Πέπων, a pompion, pumpkin. — As soft: Above.

Περ, entirely, altogether, thoroughly, throughly. Πάντα ἅ-περ λέγει, All things soever which he says. He went to Cyrus ἥ-περ ἦν, just exactly as he was. Tydīdes faced the enemy αὐτός περ ἐὼν, being quite alone, altogether alone as he was, though entirely alone. 'Ολίγον περ, ever so little, though very little.—'R. πέρω :' Dnn. I.e. πείρω, περῶ. And so Hoogeveen, who explains it 'penetrando', ' penitùs.' (2) 'R. περι-, valde :' Herm.

Πέρα, Πέραν, quite through or over, across, beyond. And

Περαίνω, to bring or carry πέρα through or across, complete, finish ; — extend, reach. — Allied to

Πέρας, the end: in Πεῖραρ.

Περάω, to pass through or across, pass beyond or surpass ; — penetrate, pierce, reach. — R. πείρω, περῶ.

Περάω, †Πράω, Πιπράσκω, Πέρνημι, to sell, to pass or carry goods over the sea for sale, as Περάω above is to pass.

Περγαμηνή, parchment, as made at Pergamos in Asia.

Πέργαμον, ' a citadel, that of Troy.—Akin to Πύργος. From it Βέργη in Thrace, and Πέργη in Pamphylia. The Germ. Philol. note the affinity of the old Teutonic Purg, and the more modern Bergh, whence Burgh, Borough :' Dnn. So Edin-burgh, St. Peter's-burg.

Πέρδω, -ομαι, to break wind. — R. πείρω, περῶ, to pass (out). So μέλλω, ἔρδω, ἔλδομαι.

Πέρθω, Πορθέω, to ravage, destroy.—Buttm. allies it to Πρήθω, †Πἰρθω, to burn. (2) ' The Etym. M. from περι-δέω, [περιθῶ, περθῶ,] from plunderers and besiegers running round a city. — I prefer it from περάω, περῶ, transeo, pervădo :' Greg. Or πείρω, †ἐπέρθην, to pierce through, i. e., penetrate with flame or sword.

Περί, round, round about ; — about, concerning, in regard to.—Bonar well for πέρατι, -αί. In the boundary or limit all round, as the 'Ορίζων horizon or bounding line goes all round us and about us. ' In the utmost limits :' Lenn. And see Πέρα.

Περί, over, beyond, more than others, as Πέρα. So Περι-, very : allied to Περάω, Περῶ, to pass : Surpassingly. Above.

Περι-, negligently. For he who throws his eyes or mind on all things περί about him has an unsteady, unfixed attention.

Περιβάρίς, ' a kind of woman's shoe [partic. of maidservants]. — R. περί, βάρις, a canoe :' Dnn. From its shape, as it seems.

Πέριξ, the same as Περί.

Περιστερά, a dove, pigeon. —'For Περισσοτέρα : as very abundant or producing abundantly :' Bos. ' So quick their increase, that in 4 years 14,760 pigeons may come from a single pair :' Enc. Br.

Περιώσιος, ' prob. Ion. for Περι-ουσιος from περι-ὢν, (περι-οῦσα): immense, vast :' Ldd. Περί, beyond, surpassingly: -ουσιος as in Παρ-ουσία.

Πέρκη, ' a river fish so called from its dusky color, the perch, perca :' Ldd. The Encycl. Brit. speaks of its ' BLACK bands as very conspicuous,' and this was probably the exact cause of the name : from

Πέρκος, Περκνός, dark-colored, dark, dusky: Περκάζω, to turn black as fruit, and met. of young men ' whose beard begins to darken their faces :' Ldd. So Περκνός, a black hawk or eagle. — Mrt. from περι-κάω, to burn round : rather περι-καὴς, (περκῆς,) quite burnt. (2) ' Marked with black spots or streaks', Steph. says ; from πείρω, πέπερκα, to pierce ; — and so spot, like Στίζω. See Πάρδος. (3) Compare Fr. percer, our pierce.

Πέρνα, a ham : in Περόνη.

Πέρνημι: in Περάω 2.

Περόνη, a clasp, buckle, as piercing through, from πείρω, περῶ, to pierce, as Figo, Figibula, Fibula: — a pin for twisting ropes, — linchpin, — the small bone of the arm or leg, (Πέρνα above being therefore allied by Ldd. to Περόνη,): a sea-fish, 'because like a pin in shape;' Ldd.

Πέρπερος, talking absurdly, vain-glorious.—Redupl. of Περὶ whence Περισσὸς, or of Πέρα, over and above. Περὶ περὶ, for animation, as in Fr. bon-bon. (2) Mrt. from περι-φέρομαι, to be hurried away, be led a-stray. (3) Πέρπερος is no doubt allied to Lat. per-peram, rashly, wrongly. Schleusn. derives the Greek word from the Latin. But whence then that?

ΠΕΡΡΑ, a barbarous word for the sun in Lycophron.

ΠΕΡΣΕΑ, the peach tree, Persian apple. — And an Egyptian tree, 'fructu noxio in Perside,' says Pliny.

Περσικὸς, Persian: 'hence al Περσικαὶ, thin shoes or slippers: Περσικὸς ὄρνις, the common cock [others say, the peacock,]: τὸ Περσικὸν, the peach, mālum Persicum: al Περσικαὶ, Persian nuts, walnuts;' Ldd.

Πέρυσι, in the past year. — Ldd. and Dnn. from πέρας, an end. The year last ended. Grove: 'Perhaps from περάω, to pass.'

†Πεσέω, †Πετέω, †Πτέω, †Πέτω, †Πιπέτω, Πίπτω, †Πετόω, †Πτόω, to fall.—'From the sense of hovering over in Πέτομαι, Ἵπταμαι, we may trace its affinity to Πέτω, to fall: the action of birds in expanding the wings in descending from flight is imitated by persons falling, who spread the hands to break the fall;' Dnn. (2) Allied seem Lat. ex-peto, im-peto, to fall or light upon. Virgil's 'Submissi petimus terram' may be added. And so †πέτω may be allied to †βητῶ, (as ἀμφισ--βητῶ,) in Plautus beto, bito, to go towards, and spec. here in a downward sense.

Πέσημα, a fall.—Above.

Πέσκος, a hide, skin, prop. a fleece, = πέκος. As ἔχγον.

Πεσσὸς, Πεττὸς, 'an oval-shaped stone for playing a game like our draughts; — the board on which it was played: οἱ πεσσοὶ, the place, and the game: πεσσὸς, any oval body:—in Strabo, a cubic mass of building to hold the piers of arches;' Ldd.—Πεσσὸς is brought by Eustath. and Hesych. from πεσεῖν, to fall. The lat-ter explains Πεσσοὶς not only by stones for draughts, but by βολίοις, κύβοις, and Eustath. says that the ancients by πεσσοὺς meant τὰ βόλια κυβιστῶν. So we find Πεσσικὸς βόλος, and Πεσσο-ριπτέω. And Ldd. says that Πίπτω is said of the dice, 'to fall in a certain position.'

Πεσσὸς, a pessary; 'called from the shape of the [above] Πεσσός;' Dnn.

Πέσσω: in Πέπτω.

Πέταλον, a leaf; prop. expanded, from

Πέταλυς, expanded, growing up, said of calves, young girls, &c. And Πεταλὶς is a full-grown sow. From

Πέταμαι, Πετάομαι, Ποτάομαι, Πτάομαι, †Πτάμαι, †Πτέομαι, Ἵπταμαι, to fly: prop. to expand (the wings). R. πετάω, to expand.

Πέτασος, a broad-brimmed hat; — broad umbellated leaf. - R. πετάω, to expand.

Πέταυρον, Πέτευρον, a pole, perch for fowls to roost on: from †πέδαυρος, Æol. for μετέωρος, raised. See Πέδα. Also, a stage for rope-dancers, or, as others, a machine from which they darted their bodies. (2) R. πετάω, to stretch out.

Πέταχνον, a broad flat cup. - R. πετάω, πετέτακα, like Pateo, Patera.

Πετάω, Πετάννῦμι, to stretch out, lay open, expand. — As Περί-τασις, so †Περι-τάω, Πετάω. Τάω Herm. and Matthiæ acknowledge. (2) Compare Πείθω to press or urge on, Πεύθω to press out or elicit, †Πείδω or Πετάω to press out at length, 'premo, ex-primo.' (3) R. †πέτω, πίπτω; prim. to make to fall down on the ground, to make to fall flat, (as in Josh. 6. 5,) to cast down at length. So Cadaver is a body fallen and stretched on the ground. (4) 'Chald. petach, to open;' Mrt.

Πέτομαι: in Πέταμαι.

Πέτρα, a rock; Πέτρος, a piece of rock, stone, rock.— As Πέσημα is a falling body, and Πτῶμα and Cadāver are a fallen dead body, so Πέτρος, a falling or fallen piece of rock, from †πέτω, †πιπέτω, πίπτω. (2) Scheide from πέταω: as a cliff spreading wide, stretching out on high; — Virgil: 'Hinc atque hinc vastæ rupes, ge-minique minantur In cœlum scopuli.'— Or R. πέτρομαι, as seeming to hover over the abyss. (3) 'Hebr. BTR, to divide, separate, or be craggy;' Pkh.

†Πέτω: in †Πεσέω.

Πεύθομαι, Πυνθάνομαι, to ask, enquire;—learn by enquiry. — Ernesti and Pott derive Πυνθάνομαι from πύνδαξ, fundus: to search to the bottom, fathom, as Lat. per-contor. But N is clearly foreign to the root, as appears by Πεύθω. Rather then from the obs. †πέω, †πεύω, allied to Πείθω, †Πίω, Πιέζω, premo, i.e. ex-primo, to press out, get out by asking. See on Πετάω. 'Cùm a me premeretur', says Cicero of a boy inter-rogated by him. (2) Mrt. from πόθος.

Πευκάλιμος, 'lengthened form of Πυκινός;' Ldd. Compare ΛΕυγαλέος.

Πευκέδανὸς, Ἔχε-πευκης, Περι-πευκης, 'not bitter, but keen, piercing;' Ldd. For Buttm. thinks the rad. notion of Πεύκη is not that of bitterness, but of sharp-pointedness, from its pointed shape or its spines: as in our pike, peak. Yet Πεύκη and Πικρὸς, (through Πέ-κω, Πείκω,) are prob. allied, just as πΗδάω and πΙδύω are the same. See especially on Πικρός.

Πεύκη, a torch or tablet made of Πεύκη of fir. See above.

Πευστὸς, learnt by enquiry: πεύθομαι.

Πέφνω: = †φόνω, †πεφένω.

†Πέω, obsol.= πιέζω: See †Πάω.

Πη, fem. of †πος, any, some, allied to obs. †πος, gen. του, dat. τῳ. See ΠΟΣ.

Πῇ, which way; ποῖ = πῷ, whither ? — Allied to the above. As Quò ?

Πήγανον, rue. —' Prob. from πήγω, πήγνυμι : From its thick fleshy leaves :' Ldd.

Πηγή, a fountain. — Nearly all from πηδάω, and some add γῆ ; Springing from the earth : but, as παρ-δΑΚΗ, so †πηδΑΚΗ, contr. †πηκὴ, πηγή. Γ as πλάΚα, plāGa. Compare Πῖδαξ. (2) 'Hebr. PG, to pour out :' Pkh.

Πῆγμα, a platform joined together ; — congealed mass ; &c. — From

Πήγνυμι : in Παγέω.

Πηγὸς, from πήγνυμι : firm, solid ; hence strong, powerful, huge. Some add 'white', which was ' prob. from the fact that Πάγος, Παγετὸς, Πηγετὸς, Πηγυλὶς, hoar-frost was white :' Ldd.

·Πηγυλὶς : in Πηγός.

Πηδάλιον, a rudder. — Dnn. from πηδὸν, a 'rudder:' both derived, it seems, from ΠΗΔΟΣ some tree of which, says Etym. M., they were made.

Πηδάω, to leap, bound ; — i. e. to strike the πέδον ground ; — or throw up my †πέδας = πόδας, pedes feet : See Πέδίλον. Horace : ' Ter pede terram,' &c. Ποσ-σὶν ἐπήδα, Hom. : jumped with his feet. Πήδημα πη-δήσας ποδοῖν, Eurip. 'In country footing,' Shaksp. for dancing.

Πηδὸν, the blade of an oar : — oar. The Lat. 'in-surgere remis' might be translated πηδᾷν ἐπὶ πηδοῖς. Indeed Ldd. thinks Πηδὸν may be from πηδάω. — Or the same R. as the sense ' a rudder': See in Πηδάλιον.

Πηκτὴ, like παγὶς, a trap-cage for birds : R. †πήγω, πέπηκται. Also, congealed, curdled milk, cheese : from the same : Com-pacta.

Πηκτὶς, a shepherd's pipe, joined of several reeds : As above. Com-pacta. It was also a harp, introduced from Lydia : perh. as joined of several strings.

Πηλαμὶς, -ίδος, a kind of tunny. 'A species of this fish is at this day called Palymede by the fishermen at Marseilles :' Dnn. and Ldd. — All say, as born and living in Πηλὸς, mud.

Πήληξ, a helmet. — R. πάλλω, ἔπηλα, to vibrate, from the nodding of the plume, as Κορυθάιξ. (2) Dnn. compares it with Πέλις, Πέλξ, and adds : ' It is found written †πέληξ, and may be referred to Πῖλος, a cap.' So πΗδάω = πΙδύω.

Πηλίκος, how great : i. e. ἡλίκος with πός, or πή. So Πηνίκα.

Πηλὸς, potter's earth, clay, mud. 'Also thick or red wine, from its muddy appearance :' Schrevel. — Mrt. from πελὸς, dark-coloured. (2) R. πάλη, fine flour : From the color of clay.

Πῆμα, suffering, misery. — R. †πήθω, πέπημαι, πά-σχω, to suffer. Πήμαθ᾽ ἃ 'πάθες, Eurip.

Πηνέλοψ, a kind of duck. — R. πήνεα, a web: Web-footed. So

Πήνη, Πῆνος, thread, woof ; plur. the web. — R. πέ-νομαι, to labor. So

133

Πηνίκα, at what time: i. e. ἡνίκα with πός or πή. As Πηλίκος.

Πηὸς, Παὸς, a kinsman, esp. by marriage. — 'R. πά-ομαι : Acquired by marriage. The Greeks said γαμ-βρὸν πεπᾶσθαι :' Valck.

Πήρα, a knapsack, ponch for victuals. — 'R. πάομαι, to feed : †παέρα, πήρα :' Valck.

Πηρὸς, disabled in a limb, maimed ;— blind,—stupid. —Allied by Schneid. to ΠΗμα, injury. Thus : †πήθω, †πηθερὸς, πηρός. (2) 'Hebr. poor, to break :' Wr.

Πῆχυς, the fore-arm from the elbow to the wrist, and, as a measure, to the point of the little finger.—Thought by Ldd. and Passow allied to ΠΑΧΥΣ, thick. Compare the senses of Πυγμὴ and Πυκνός. — Mrt. and Ewing from †πήγω. And so Pkh. who says : ' R. †πήγω, to fix : Which in reclining is fixed on some support, as Cubitus from Cumbo.' ' Et oubito remanete PRESSO:' Hor.

Πῆχυς, ' the centre-piece which joined the two horns of an ancient bow, the handle ;—plur. the horns or sides of the lyre, opposite to the bridge ;—in the balance, the beam ; — a cubit-rule ; — an angle:' Ldd. — Above.

Πιάζω, Πιέζω, to press, press hard, squeeze ;— lay hold of ; — oppress, repress. Πιάζω seems much the same as Βιάζω, 'to press hard', (Ldd.). See the obss. on Βία and the second †Πιάω.

Πιαίνω, to make fat. Πῖαρ, fat, tallow. Πίων, Πί-ειρα, fem., fat, plump. Πιμελὴ, fat. — All allied, through the obs. †πίω, to Πιάζω, Πιέζω, to press close. See Πίσσα.

Πῖδαξ, a spring, fountain : R. πιδύω, 'as our Spring is used in both senses :' Ldd.

Πιδύω, to sprout, — to make to gush forth.—Compare with Πηδάω and Πηδύω, to spring. I like that in πλίνθος, πλίνθομαι, Lat. rItus from ῥΗτὸς, formIca from βύρμΗκα.

Πιέζω : in Πιάζω.

Πιθανὸς, persuasive. — R. πείθω.

Πίθηξ, Πίθηκος, an ape. — ' Doubtless,' says Ldd. ' from πείθω, πιθανὸς, as Μιμὼ,' (an ape). I. e. from the middle πείθομαι, to comply with, follow, therefore to imitate, as we say To ape the manners of another. See Πίσυνος.

Πίθος, a cask, tub. — Valck. from πείθω, which, he says, orig. meant ' to bind': i. e. from †πείω, πιέζω, to press close. See Πεῖσμα. And Πίσσα. (2) Ewing from †πίω, πίνω, to drink : ' A large vessel of liquor.'

Πικέριον, butter. — Prob. allied to Πῖαρ, fat, and Πι-μελή. We say, As fat as butter. (Rare.)

Πικρὸς, sharp, pungent, bitter. — It seems allied to Πείρω, to pierce, Πιέζω, to press, Πείκω, to pluck, twitch, &c. Lenn. from the obs. '†πίω, [πέπικα,] figo, pungo'. (2) Allied to French piquer, our piquant. (3) 'R. πεύθη, or Chald. pekar, scindo :' Mrt.

Πιλνάω, Πίλνημι, the same as Πελάω, as †Σκεδάω, Σκίδνημι ; Κερδάω, Κίρνημι.

Πῖλος, wool or hair wrought into felt ; a felt-hat, pi-leus ; — felt-cloth for carpets, mats, tents ; — felt-cuirass.

—' R. πιέζω, for Πίελος:' Greg. Or the obs. †πίω, whence Πιέζω: as Ψίω, Ψιλός.

Πιλόω, to felt Πίλος wool, press close.

Πιμελή, fatness: in Πιαίνω.

Πιμπλάω, Πιμπλέω, Πίμπλημι, redupl. of †πλέω, †pleo, im-pleo, to fill. See Πλέος. So

Πιμπράω, Πίμπρημι, = πρήθω.—Above.

Πίναξ, a board, plank, tablet, table.—Valck. and Hemsterh. suppose an obs. word ΠΙΝΟΣ, pinus: As made of pine. ' Pinea claustra,' Virg. So 'a table of PINE', Longfellow's Standish, I. 16.— Or perhaps πίτυς, pinus, πιτύινος, πιτυίναξ, contr. πίναξ.

Πίννα, a shell-fish of the muscle kind. ' The silky filaments by which it adheres to rocks were used for ornaments :' Dnn. Hence from obs. †πίω, πιέζω, to squeeze, as Βλέννα, Γέννα.

Πίνον, ' a liquor made from barley, beer. R. πίνω :' Dnn. (2) Root as Πίννα.

Πίνος, 'filth, dirt, partic. of grease; prop. the oil on the body of the gymnasts: — met., an antique diction, vigorous and simple, like that of the ancients, possessing a rude but masculine beauty. Allied to Πίων [and Πίαρ]:' Dnn.

Πινύσσω, to make wise: πινυτός, wise. — Allied through Πνύσσω, to Πέπνυμαι to be wise. So I in saIna from Μνᾶ, sIbi from σφί, U in ÆscUlapius from Αἰσκλήπιος.

Πίνω and †Πίω and †Πόω, to drink. — Allied to Πιέζω, to press close : ' Bibe pressis labris,' Lenn. Compare Πῶμα a lid. (2) ' Hebr. pi, the month:' Mrt. and Greg.

Πιπίσκω, to give to drink. — R. †πίω, †πίσκω, πίνω.

Πίπος, a young piping bird. And Πιπώ, a kind of wood-pecker. — ' Perh. from the sound:' Lenn. and Greg. So

Πιπτίζω, πιπίο, to pipe or chirp as a Πίπος.

Πιπράσκω, to sell: = περάω, †πράω, †πράσκω, πι-πράσκω.

Πίπτω : in †Πεσέω.

Πίσον, Πίσος, pisum, a pea. — Mrt. and Greg. well from πτίσσω, 'most prob. orig. πίσσω,' (Dnn.) as πΤόλις.

Πίσος, moist ground, meadow. — R. πιπίσκω, a. 1. ἔπισα to give to drink, here to drink, as in Πίστρα. As imbibing moisture. ' Sat prata biberunt,' Virg.

Πίσσα, Πίττα, pitch, — turpentine; — fir. — From †πίω, †πίσω, πιέζω, to press close: answering to Lat. spissa. (2) ' From πίος, fat: or πίτυς, a pine: or πήσσω, πήγνυμι, to coagulate:' Greg.

Πίστις, trust, belief. — R. πέπεισται, πείθομαι.

Πιστὸς, trusty. Above.

Πίστρα, trough for watering cattle. — R. †πίω, †πέ-πιστσι, πίνω, to drink : allied to πιΠΙΣκω.

Πίσυγγος, a shoe-maker. ' R. πίσσα, pitch ? Perh. we should read Πίσσυγγος with Dind.:' Ldd.

Πίσυνος, trusting in. — R. πείθομαι, as ΠΙΣτις.

Πίσυρες, Æol. of Τέσσαρες.
134

Πίτνω, from †πέτω, †πεσέω, to fall, as Πέτνημι, to stretch out, from πετάω. The same as Πίπτω.

Πίτυλος, beating of the water by oars;—blows given in boxing, — any violent or continued noise or motion. —Ldd. thinks Πίτυλος called from the imitation of the plash of oars: (2) Transp. for Τύπιλος from τύπος, a blow, impression. As Φάσγανον, Ξφάγανον. (3) Dr. Major from πίπτω. Or †πέτω, †πέτυλος, πίτυλος.

Πίτυρα, husks, bran, refuse; — dandriff. — Soft for Πέτυρα from †πέτω, to fall, or Πίπτυρα from πίπτω. ' When the head is rubbed, there ἀπο-πίπτει fall out thin πίτυρα bran, whence the disease πιτυρίασις, scaly eruption:' Hippocr. (2) Allied to Lat. pituita, spit. What is spit out in winnowing: πτύω, †πτύρα, πίτυρα, as I is added in πίνυσσω, mIna. (3) R. πτίσσω, orig. πίσσω, πίττω, as Dnn. thinks.—Comp. ἐγκΤΡΑ.

Πιτυρὶς ἐλαία, 'small olive of the color of πίτυρα:' Ldd.

Πίτυς, the pine-tree. —' R. πίος, [and πιμελὴ,] fat, with which it abounds:' Greg.

Πιφαύσκω, to make manifest, show, declare.—†Φάω, φάσκω, (as Βάω, Βάσκω,) †πιφάσκω, as Διδάσκω: Either as Φημὶ, Φάσκω, for, fari, to speak ; or as Φαίνω, φανῶ, to show.

Πίων: in Πιαίνω.

Πλαγγόνιον, a kind of ointment. — R. πλάσσω, to smear. So

Πλαγγών, wax-doll. — Ldd. and Dnn. from πλάσσω, to form, which should rather make Πλαδόν: but, as in Πλάζω, we may suppose a fut. πλάγξω. So in Πλαγ-γόνιον.—Or as smeared over : Above.

Πλάγιος, oblique, transverse, perverse. — R. πλάζω, πλαγῶ: Wandering out of the straight way. (2) Schneid. from πλάγος or πλάγος, a side: Side-ways. But this out-of-the-way word seems to have the same origin.

Πλαδαρὸς, and Βλαδαρὸς, moist, flaccid, flabby: Πλάδος, moisture. — Prob. all allied to Φλέω and to Βλύω, Φλύω, to gush, teem, overflow: and Φλάζω whence Παφλάζω to froth, foam. See Πλύνω. (2) With ΒΛΑΔαρὸς compare ΒΑΛΞ.

Πλαθθίδα, ' to talk nonsense: perh. from πλατύς, flat, like Des platitudes in French: or an imitative word, as Lat. blatero, Scottish blether:' Ldd.

Πλάζω, Πλανάω, ' to cause to wander, drive forth, to wander, drive about:' Ewing.—R. πάλλω, παλῶ, †πλάω : To move to and fro. Allied to Πέλω, Πελεμίζω, Πολέω: and, if there was †Πολάω, (as there was Ἐμ-πολάω,) then again †πλάω. (2) R. κέλλω, †πέλλω, the Lat. pello, (as λύΚος, luPus; Κοῖος, Ποῖος,) to drive about.

Πλαθάνη, a platter, dish or mould in which bread or cakes were baked. — R. πλάσσω, †επλάθην, to mould. (2) R. πλατὸς, flat : †πλατάνη.

Πλάθω, the same as Πελάω, †Πλάω, to come πέλας near.

Πλαίσιον, an oblong figure or body, — a square. — Thought allied to ΠΛΑτὸς, flat. Grove says, for

Πλάσιον, from πλάσσω, πλάσω, to mould: 'A mould to form bricks, the shape of a brick.'

Πλακερὸς, broad as a Πλάξ, ακὸς, board.

Πλακοῦς, a flat cake, like Πλάξ, πλακός. Acc. πλακοῦντα: Lat. placenta.

Πλανάω: in Πλάζω.

Πλάνος, a deceiver, i.e. leading astray: Above. Or vagabond, liar.

Πλάξ, g. πλακὸς, a flat body, plank, board, table;—leaf;—plate,—flat space, plain, acc. πλάκα, Lat. plăga;—flat cake.— R. πλατὺς, †πλάταξ, (as Πόρπαξ, Δόναξ,) πλάξ. (2) 'R. πλάσσω:' Dnn.

Πλάσσω, to smear, cover over, plaster, for Παλάσσω, to besprinkle, stain. Also, to cast figures i.e. with plaster, give form to, mould. (2) R. πηλὸς, mud: †πηλάσσω, as 'Ανάσσω.

Πλάστιγξ, perh. for Πλάτιγξ, 'from πλατὺς, flat, broad: A dish, scale of a balance, draught-board:' Grove. Also, a splint for keeping broken bones in their place:—a yoke for horses, called from a pair of scales or balance;—'the scale on which the wine was thrown in the cottabus;—from the likeness the shell of an oyster:' Ldd. The scale struck in the cottabus by the wine thrown, was perhaps, like the other sense of Πλάστιγξ, Πλήστιγξ, a whip, allied to Πλήσσω, to strike.

Πλαταγὴ, 'any noise caused by the collision of two flat bodies: from πλατύς:' Ldd. (2) R. πλάτη: as prop. the dashing of water by oars. See Πλαταγίζω.

Πλαταγὼν, a clapper, rattle. And

Πλαταγώνιον, 'petal of the poppy and the anemony: for lovers took omens from it by striking it with the right hand, and its burst with a loud crack was a good omen:' Ldd.— R. πλαταγή.

Πλαταμὼν, a flat stone; flat beach; flat reef of rocks. And

Πλάτανος, platanus, the plane tree. From its broad leaves. R. πλατύς.

Πλατεῖα, a broad street, platea; flat of the hand.— Fem.of πλατύς. 'The broad places thereof', Jerem. 5. 1.

Πλατειάζω, to speak broad or with a brogue.— Above.

Πλάτη, the flat blade of an oar; any flat body.— R. πλατύς.

Πλάτις, Πελάτις, a wife;—concubine.—From πελάω, †πλάω, sc. τῷ ἀνδρί. Thus, 'I produce a son, πλαθεῖο 'Αχιλλέως παιδί,' Eurip. So 'Εμ-πελάτειρα.

Πλατυγίζω, 'to beat the water with the πλατὺ broad end of an oar,—make a plash, sputter, swagger:' Ldd.

Πλατὺς, flat, level, wide, broad;—'salt, brackish, prob. because orig. used of the wide sea:' Ldd.— R. λάζω, to move or roam about,—hence, be at large, expatiate free: Spacious, extensive, ample. 'Spatiosus in latitudine:' Valck. (2) Our flat, plat, plate. 'Flatr, Icel. Flad, Dan. Plat, Fr.:' Todd.

Πλέθρον, Πέλεθρον (poët.) 100 feet; race-course of this length:—10,000 square feet, as a measure.—
135

'R. prob. πλήθω:' Passow. A plenary number. E, as κΕδνός. (2) Πέλεθρον from πέλω, πέπολα, to drive round with the plough, as τρί-πολον Il. 6. 542: στρέψαντες 544-6.

Πλεῖν, 'for Πλέον, more, as Δεῖν for Δέον:' Ldd.

Πλεῖστος, most, greatest. —R. πλείων.

Πλείων: in Πλέων.

Πλειὼν, a year: i.e. 'a full time or period, from πλέος. πλεῖος:' Ldd. 'Si tener PLENO cadit hœdus ANNO,' Hor. 'Centum totos regnabitur annos', Virg. 'Two full years', Jer. 28. 11. And 2 Sam. 14. 28: 27. 7.

Πλέκος, wicker-work; Πλεκτάνη, coil, wreath; Πλεκτὴ, cord, fishing-basket: &c. —From

Πλέκω, plico, plecto, to knit, plait, weave, fold.— R. πολέω, †πλέω, (whence Δι-πλόος,) to turn round, then πλέκω as †'Ολέω, 'Ολέκω. (Thus Blomf. on Matth. Gr. Gr.) 'Plicat cogitque in orbes,' Seneca. 'Quæ plicamus, invertimus et flectimus:' Greg.

Πλέος, plenus, full. †Πλέω, im-pleo, re-pleo, Πλήθω, to fill.— Allied to Πολύς, πολέος, much. (2) Allied to Φλέω, Φλύω, to overflow.

Πλεύμων, pulmo, the lungs. — For Πνεύμων, as Νίτρον, Λίτρον. R. πνέω, to breathe.

Πλευρὰ, a side;—a wife, i.e. one's rib. — R. πολέω, †πλέω, to turn round, (whence the πόλοι poles): As the ribs turn (vertuntur, versantur.) round the body, encircle or gird it. So 'Αμφι-πολέω, 'to stand round, to surround' (Dnn.). (2) R. πολὺς, πολέος, many. There are as many as 24 ribs. (3) R. πολυ-ευρύς.

Πλέω, to fill: in Πλέος.

Πλέω, πλεύσω, to sail.—Dnn. allies it to Πλύω, and to Φλέω, Φλύω, fluo, fluito, to float. So Πλωΐζω is to swim or float, and Πλώς a swimmer. (2) Contr. from Πωλέω, to traffick, 'Εμ-πολάω: To go on the sea for traffick. See the end of the obss. on Πλοῦτος. (3) 'R. πολέω, to turn or drive hither and thither:' Lenn. 'The ships are turned about with a very small helm:' N. T. So Thiersch compares Πολεύω, Πλέω.

Πλέων, Πλείων, more in number, more, greater. — R. πολὺς, πολέος, many, much: †πολείων, πλείων. Or πλέος, πλείων: more full.

Πληγὴ, a stroke: πλήσσω, πέπληγα.

Πλήθω, to fill. Πλῆθος, great number or size. — In Πλέος.

Πληκτίζομαι, to fight, i.e. strike blows, from πλήσσω, πέπληκται, Lat. plecto, to beat.

Πλῆκτρον, an instrument to strike with, a quill, plectrum;— cock's spur;—punting-pole.—Above.

Πλήμη: the same as Πλήμμη.

Πλημμελέω, to commit a fault, err.— As 'Εκ-μελὴς is 'out of tune,' 'absonus,' so Πλημμελὴς is πλὴν (i.e. πλεῖν, πλέον,) beyond or beside the μέλος tune; and the verb is to make an error in singing, and so to trans-gress generally. So

Πλήμμυρὶς, a flowing beyond. R. πλὴν, μύρω, as Πλη" μμελέω. Hence, a flood, flood-tide. (2) R. πλήθω, πέπλησμαι, to fill full. Some would read Πλημυρίς. See Πλήσμη.

Πλήμνη, the nave of a wheel, the hole in which the axle turns.— All derive from πλήθω, for πεπλημένη: The nave as filled up by the axle. (2) Yet it may be for πεπολημένη, turned round in, allied to the Πόλοι, poles.

Πλήν, except,— the same as Πλεῖν, Πλέον, more. Thus, 'There is no other πλὴν ἐγὼ,' more than I, but I, except me. 'Tell me what you wish πλὴν ἑνὸς, except this one thing.' So Πλὴν is but, save, unless, except if, except when, &c.

Πλήρης, plenus, full.— R. πλέος.

Πλησίος, near.— R. πελάω, †πελάω, †πλήσω, to come near.

Πλήσμη, Πλήμη, the flood-tide.— R. πλήθω, πέπλησμαι, to fill.

Πλησμονή, as Πληθώρη, plethora, re-pletion.— Above.

Πλήσσω, to strike, to beat, to stamp. — As Percutio, to strike, from Quatio, so πάλλω, παλῶ, †παλέω, †πλέω. Or πέλω. (2) Dnn. allies it to Πλάσσω. (3) R. κέλλω, †πέλλω, (as Κοῖος, Ποῖος; λύΚος, luPus,) pello, to drive. (4) Allied to †Βλέω, †Βλήσω, 'to strike, beat,' (Dnn.) So Βλαδαρὸς and Πλαδαρός. (5) 'Hebr. palletz, to terrify:' Mrt. ?

Πλίνθος, a brick, tile;— plinth, ingot of metal;— plinth of a column.— Allied to Πλάθανος, a mould. As βάθος, βΕΝθος; πάθος, πΕΝθος, so †πλΕΝθος seems to have been formed, then πλίνθος, as I in the next word πλίσσω and plico. So 'Εν, In. See λικριφίς.

Πλίσσω, ξω, πέπλιχα, 'like PLICO, to fold: midd. to cross one's legs in walking, and hence to stride, step out. Akin to Πλέκω:' Ldd., †πλίκω, Plico. ' To go at a round pace,' adds Dnn., i. e. to trot, amble, which agrees with Virgil's ' Insultare solo, et gressus GLOMERARE superbos,' i. e. says Forcell., 'celeri passu et CONVO-LUTO gradu incedere.' Πλιχθεὶς agrees with Πλεχθεὶς, com-plicatus.—Πολέω, Πλίσσω, as Εἰλέω, 'Ελίσσω.

Πλιχὰς, the inside of the thighs, which is chafed by walking.— R. πλίσσω, πέπλιχα.

Πλοῖον, a ship; Πλόος, sailing.— R. πλέω, πέπλοα.

Πλόκαμος, Πλόκος, a lock or curl of hair;— twisted rope. — And

Πλόκανον, anything twined;— a wicker sieve or fan.— And

Πλοκή, a weaving.— R. πλέκω, πέπλοκα.

Πλόος: in Πλοῖον.

Πλούσιος, wealthy.—R. πλοῦτος above, as 'Αφροδῖτη, 'Αφροδίσιος. (2) R. πολυ-ουσία: Schrevel.

Πλοῦτος, wealth.— Valck. for πολύ-ετος. R. πολὺς, ἔτος: A copious year, Annona. Or the produce of many years. (2) Lenn. from πλέω, πέπλοα, πλήθω, to fill.— Jones from πλέω, to sail: Voyage-money.

Πλούτων, Pluto, 'the god of the nether world: orig. epith. of Hades, because corn, the πλοῦτος wealth of

early times, was sent from beneath as the gift of Hades: hence Pluto was confounded with Plutus:' Ldd.

Πλύνω, to wash, rinse.— Dnn. says: ' Prop. to wet or soak in water.' Then for Παλύνω, ' to wet', (Dnn.)— However he adds: ' From πλύω, another form of πλόω, πλεύω, to flow, to swim.' Allied to Φλύω, Φλέω. Compare Lat. pluo, pluvia.

Πλύνω, to abuse, revile. As Fr. laver la tête à quelqu'un. To Asperse from Ad-spargo is much the same. — Above.

Πλὼς, a swimmer: in Πλέω.

Πνεῦμα, breath, spirit, wind.— R. πνέω.

Πνεύμων: in Πλεύμων.

Πνέω, to breathe, blow. Germ. pfnegen.— Prop. ' to be faint or exhausted from exertion', a sense given by Dnn. to Πονέω: as from Κόπος, labor, is Κοπιάω, ' to be exhausted from fatigue, to cease.' Then to puff, blow. Conversely, to Breathe is ' to take breath, to rest:' Dr. J. And Ποιπνύω from Πνέω is ' prop. to pant for breath, put oneself out of breath by exertion', (Dnn.).

Πνίγω, ξω, to stifle, suffocate. — Schleusn. from πνοιά, †ἄγω ἄγνῦμι, to break the breath: †πνοίγω. (2) Better thus: As Σινιάζω, to sift, from Σείω, so from the obs. †πίω, whence πιέζω, to press close, might be †πινίω, †πνίω, πνίγω, as τέμνω, †τεμέω, †τμάω, τμήΓΩ. Observe too τείρω, τερῶ, †τερίω, †τρίω, τρίβω. (3) As Πνὺξ has gen. πυκνὸς, evincing its relation to adj. πυκνὸς, close: so πυκνὸς might produce †πυκνίζω, †πνίζω or πνίγω: To pack close, compress, as Πυκνόω. (4) ' Hebr. pne, the face:' Mrt. ?

Πνοή, breath: πνέω.

Πνὺξ, g. πυκνὸς and πυκνὸς, the Pnyx where the assemblies of the people were held.—R. πυκνὸς, crowded, packed.

Πόα, Ποία, herb, grass: — allied to ΒΟτάνη, ΒΟσκω, and Pasco. See on †Πάω. And see Ποιμήν. (2) R. †πάω, whence πόσις, to drink: as imbibing moisture. ' Sat prata biberunt.'

Ποδαρὸς, ' of what country or race ? — Valck. from πός, ὁάτος, as meaning Δάπεδον, 'Εδαφος, Τόπος. (2) ' Passow from ποῦ, ἀπὸ, Δ euphon. As like French d'où:' Dnn. Δ, as in proDest, proDit. Or for δὲ, as in Τῇδε. But observe ἀλλο-ΔΑΠΟΣ.

Ποδεών, any extremity, as Πούς, πουδὸς: ' plur., the ragged ends in the skin of animals, where the feet and tail have been; sing., the neck or mouth of a wine-skin, formed by one of these ends, the others being sewn up; — neck of the bladder:' Ldd. And = πέος, which see.

Πόθεν, whence ? As ῞Οθεν.— R. πός.

Πόθος, Ποθή, ardent longing for, deep regret for the loss of.— Allied to Πάσχω, to have feeling for, or Πάθος, suf-fering, Πένθος, ΠέπΟνθα, ΠέπΟσχα, ΠέπΟσθε. Compare βΟθρος, ποΒόρδαλις, βρΟχέας in Sappho; δΑμῶ, dΟmo.

Ποῖ, whither, as Οῖ. — R. πός.

Ποιέω, Ποέω, to do or make: to make verses: Ποίημα, poëma, a poem: Ποιητὴς, poëta, a poet. Spenser: 'Her peerless skill in MAKING well.' Dryden: 'A *poet* is a MAKER.' — Pkh. from ποιός: 'To endue a thing with a *certain* quality. As, *Make* His paths *straight*.' (2) Ποίω short for Πονέω: To labor at. (3) R. ἔπω, to be employed about, ὄπα whence *Opus, Operor*: then ὀποιέω, (as Λοέω,) and ποέω, as 'Δόρομαι for 'Οδύρομαι', (Ldd.) — Or, as Σπεῖν and Περι-σπεῖν are acknowledged by Ldd., then †σπέω, †έσποα, as 'Ρέω, Έρροα: †σποέω, ποέω, as ' Κάπετος for Σκάπετος' (Ldd.). So Στέγω, Τέγος, Tego.

Ποικίλος, many-colored, spotted; of varying turns of mind, changeful, artful; — of varying art, elaborate. The Ποικίλη, *Pœcilé*, a portico at Athens adorned with paintings. Ποικίλλω, to execute skilfully in variegated embroidery. — As Στίζω, to prick, is 'to mark with stripes, to variegate', (Dnn.) so Ποικίλος from πείκω, πέποικα, is striped by lines drawn as in combing or carding. (2) Ποικίλος 'artificially wrought', and Ποικίλλω ' to execute with art and skill', from ποιέω, πεποίηκα, †πέποικα: Wrought, e-laborated, τετυγμένος. (3) Allied to Πύκα, Πυκνὸς, 'clever, skilful :' (Dnn.).? Ποιμήν, a shepherd, as BOτήρ : Ποίμνη, a flock. — See Πόα.

Ποινή, 'a compensation, satisfaction, punishment, *pœna*. Orig. the compensation was a ram given to the relations to be sacrificed. From φόνος, †φένω:' Dnn. So Φοινὸς is bloody.

Ποῖος, of what kind ? As Οἷος. R. πός, ποῖ, πῷ. And Ποιὸς, of some kind: R. πος.

Ποιπνύω, am busy, serve.— R. πνέω, †πνύω, (whence Πέπνῡμαι,) redupl. ποιπνύω as Παιπάλλω : To breathe hard, pant, run about, a sense given by Ldd. to ΠΟΙπνύω and to ΠΟΙφύσσω. Thiersch brings the ΠΟ from πολύ. (2) R. πονέω.

Ποιφύσσω, to *PUFF*, blow. — From φυσάω. See Ποιπνύω. (2) From the sound, as *PUFF*.

Ποκα for Ποτε, as "Οκα for "Οτε.

Πόκος, a fleece. — R. πέκω, πέποκα.

Πόλεμος, fight, war. — As Bellum is Duellam from Duo, so Πόλεμος from Πολὺς, πολέος, many. In form as ἄργΕΜΟΣ, ἄνΕΜΟΣ. (2) In defence of one's πόλις, πόλεως, city. (3) 'For Πολ-όλεμος, from πολὺς, ὀλέω :—Or with Damm from παλάμη, the hand :' Pkh.: much as Pugna from Pugnus. So O in Æol. πΟρθαλις. (4) R. †βολέω, βάλλω, to throw darts. (5) Allied to Πελεμίζω, to brandish (darts or spears).

Πολέω, Πολεύω, to turn round, — turn the soil, plough; — go round or about, range over, frequent, as Lat. Versor, and Gr. Στρωφάομαι. — Dnn. allies Πολέω, Πόλος, Πέλω, Πέλομαι. See in Πέλω.

Πολιὸς, hoary, white. — R. πολέω, to turn, here to turn in color. We say, ' Too much care will *turn* a young man *grey*.' (2) Ewing from παλαιός. ?

Πόλις, a city : i. e. where men πολοῦσι, πωλοῦνται, versantur, con-versantur, dwell or have their conversation together. (2) R. πολὺς, many, in opp. to the scattered and scanty inhabitants of villages.
137

Πολίτης, a citizen. — Above.

Πολίχνη a little Πόλις.

†Πολλός : in Πολύς.

Πολλοστὸς, very little.— As Πεντηκοστὸς, the 50th, is one out of 50; so Πολλοστὸς is one only out of many. Above.

Πόλος, a pivot, hinge, on which anything turns : a *pole* of the earth; — orbit of a star; — earth turned by a plough, &c.—R. πολέω.

ΠΟΛΤΟΣ, porridge, pottage, *pols* or *puls pultis, poultice; (pultimentum,)* *pulmentum.* — Q. if transp. from Πλωτὸς, (Πωλτὸς,) floating: as said of pot-herbs, &c. floating in water. Thus Porridge is from Porrum, a leek.

Πολύθεστος, much-desired. — R. πολὺ, θέσσασθαι, pass. †τέθεσται, to pray for.

Πολύ-πους, the *polypus*, fish with many feet.

Πολὺς, much, many. — As Vastus from *Fάστυ*, i. e. large as a city: — as In-gens from Gens : — as Oppidò, much, from Oppidum, ('Quod vel *oppido* satis,' says Festus,) — and as we say Nation large, so Πολὺς from Πόλις. (2) 'Many', from Πολέω, Πολέομαι as Στρωφάομαι, versor, con-versor. See Πόλις.

Πόλφος, porridge, πάλτος : *pulpa.* Πόλτος perhaps became †Πόλτος, (as σΤάδιον, Æol. σΠάδιον, sPatium ; λΙΤρα, Æ. λΙΠρα, liBra,) then Πόλφος.

Πομπὴ, a conveyance, procession; show, *pompa, pomp.* — R. πέμπω.

Πομφὸς, Πομφόλυξ : = πέμφιξ.

Πονηρὸς, laborious; — laboring under disease of body, ill, — and of mind, bad, depraved, as Wretch compared with Wretched. — From

Πόνος, toil, trouble. — R. πένομαι, πέτονα, to toil.

Πόντος, the sea, *pontus.* — As Τάφος transp. from τρέφω, and Δράπων from δέρπω, so Πόντος for πνότος from πνέω: Blown upon by the winds, Perflatus ventis.

Πόπανον, a baked cake. — R. πέπτω, πέποπα.

Πόπαξ, 'an excl. of surprise and anger. Akin to Πόποι': Ldd. and prob., says Dnn., to Πύπαξ.

Πόποι, 'an excl. of wonder, anger, distress : ὦ πόποι, = ὦ θεοί, πόποι among the Dryopes meaning this [perh. allied to Πάπας, father:]: an excl. of complaint, as Παπαί:' Dnn. (2) 'Rather, from the sound, an echo to the sense, as Παπαί:' E. Valpy.

Ποποί, the cry of the "Εποψ, "Εποπος, *hoopoe.* 'Επωποὶ ποποπὸ ποποὶ ποποί, Aristoph.

Ποππύζω, ' to whistle or chirp with the lips compressed: hence 1. to call to, coax, encourage: 2. applaud, flatter; 3. smack, kiss loud ; 4. make an inarticulate sound on hearing thunder, &c. 5. play ill on the flute:' Ldd. — It seems an imitative word. Thus Dr. J. says of our word *POP*: 'A small smart quick sound. It is formed from the sound.'

Πάρδαλις: = πάρδαλις.

Πορθὴ, crepitus ventris. — R. πέρδω.

Πορθέω, = πέρθω, πέπορθα.

Πορθμὸς, ferry, strait, &c. as Πόρος: Πορθμεύω, to carry or ferry over.

T

Πορίζω, to convey, pass, bring, furnish, supply, get ready. Like Πορεύω in Πόρος.

ΠΟΡΙΣ, Πόρτις, Πόρταξ, a heifer, calf, bullock, stag. — Etym. M. from its ἄρτι εἰς πόρειαν καὶ νομὴν ἔρχεσθαι. ? (2) R. πόροι, resources, revenue. ?

Πόρκης, a ring or hoop round which the iron head of a spear was fastened to the shaft. — R. πείρω, πέπορκα, to pierce (with nails), as Περόνη from πείρω is a clasp. Compare ΠΟΡπη.

Πόρκος, a hog, porcus : whence our pork. (Very rare.) R. πείρω, πέπορκά : from its perforating the ground with its snout. Formed like Πόρκης. (2) From the Πόρκης in its nose.

Πόρκος, a fishing-net. — I.e. pierced and perforated, as Πόρκης.

Πόρνη, a harlot. — R. περνάω, to sell : As selling herself. So some connect Whore with Hire. Ldd. says : 'Because the Greek prostitutes were usu. bought slaves.'

Πόρος, a passage, way through : from πείρω, πέπορα, to pass. Also, a pore, passage of perspiration ; — means or place of passing, a ferry, strait, frith ; — way or means of doing anything ; — ways and means, revenue : &c. So Πορεύω, to make to pass, ferry.

Πόρπαξ, 'the handle of a shield, prob. a ring inside the shield which could be taken out at pleasure ; — part of the head-gear of a horse :' Ldd. — From Πόρπη, 'that part of a clasp in which the Περόνη was fastened, hence gen. a clasp, buckle, brooch. — No doubt from πείρω, to pierce :' Ldd. Πέπορα, πόρπη, as τολύΠΗ, τρύΠΑ, and perhaps ἀγαΠΗ.

Πόρρω, forwards, further on, far off : Lat. porro, furthermore. — R. πρὸς, πρόσω, πόρσω, πόρρω.

Πορσαίνω, Πορσύνω, like Πορίζω, ἴσω, to supply, furnish, get ready ; furnish supplies to, attend to, wait upon, pay our regards to.

Πόρτις : in Πόρις.

Πορφύρα, the purpura, purple dye of the shell-fish ΠΟΡΦΥΡΑ : — a purple dress : — also a maiden, in that out-of-the-way writer Lycophron, perhaps so dressed ? And Πορφυρὶς, a red water-fowl, and a red vest. — See Πορφύρω.

Πορφύρω, to have a purple or dark color, as when the sea is agitated and dark from a storm : — then to be disquieted in one's mind and in doubt. — Comm. deduced from the above : yet the converse may be true, as Πορφύρω sounds as much Greek as Μορμύρω, and may be redupl. from φύρω, 'to put into confusion, embroil, perturb', (Dnn.).

Πόρω, = πορίζω, paro.

ΠΟΣ, ΚΟΣ, ΤΟΣ, some, any : also, who ? what ? Moreover we find Πού and Ὅτου, Πῆ and Ὅπη, &c. Q. ?

ΠΟΣΕΙΔΑΩΝ, Neptune. — 'Herod. seems to think it an African word, and Bochart attempts so to explain it :' Scheide.

Πόσθη, præputium ; — et idem quod πέος. — 'Prob. à πρόσθε :' Dnn. Ut ποτὶ pro πΡοτί. (2) Ab obs. †πόω,

138

†ἐπόσθην, unde Πῶμα, operculum, affine τῷ Μότος, Βύω, Πύλη, &c.

Ποσθία, tuberculum in palpebris : 'forsitan quòd τῷ ἀκρο-ποσθίῳ non absimile est, quod et ipsum ab hordei grano non multùm differt :' Steph. Vide supr.

Πόσθων, cui est magna Πόσθη : unde est verbum comicum pro puerulo.

Πόσις, drink, potus. — R. πίνω, †πόω, †πώσω, to drink.

Πόσις, maritus. — R. †πόω, πόσις, potus, ποτίζω, ut πιπίσκω, bibere facio sc. γύας τῆς γυναικὸς, ut Ἄρσην Mas ab ἄρδω irrigo, Σπείρειν γύας, Ἀρόω ut Soph., τὴν τεκοῦσαν ΗΡΟΣΕΝ, et Ἀροτὴρ parens.

Πόσος, how great ? like Ὅσος. As Οἷος, Ποῖος.

Ποσταῖος, on what day ? — R. πόστος : as Πεμπταῖος, on the fifth day.

Πόστος, what number ? how many or how few ? — Πόσος, Πόσατος, (as Μέσατος,) Πόστος.

Ποταίνιος, newly told of, new, fresh, — unheard of. — R. ποτι, αἶνος, a tale, story. Ποτι, 'towards,' is here 'near to,' 'near in time,' 'just or only now.' So πρὸς in Πρόσ-φατος.

Ποταμὸς, a river. — R. ποτὸς, drinkable, in opp. to sea-water. Æschyl. : εὔ-ποτον ῥέος. And, ἄρδει πεδίον εὐ-μενεῖ πότῳ. 'Potis rivis,' Virg.

Ποτάομαι, to fly, πέταμαι.

Ποταπὸς, 'same sense and R. as Ποδαπὸς :' Dnn.

Πότε, when : R. πός, πῷ τε (χρόνῳ), as Ὅτε is φ̓ τε.

Πότερος, which of the two ? — R. †πός, which, and ἕτερος, one of two : Which one of two ?

Ποτήρ, Ποτήριον, a drinking-cup ; Πότης, a drinker ; Ποτὸν, drink, potus. — R. †πόω, πώσω, πόσις, πίνω.

Ποτὶ, soft for Προτί.

Πότιμος, drinkable, fresh, therefore sweet and pleasant. See Ποτήρ.

Πότμος, what falls to one's lot, or befals us ; — lot, destiny. — R. †πέτω, †πέποτα, πίπτω, to fall : †πότιμος, πότμος. As Casus from Cado.

Πότνα, Πότνια, honorable, revered, lady, mistress, powerful over, as πότνια θηρῶν, like Hor. ' potens Cypri.' — As Πότμος, from †πέτω, πέποτα, to fall : Before whom one falls down.

Ποτνία above is applied to many goddesses : but Πότνιαι is partic. said of Ceres and Proserpine, and Ποτνιάδες of the Furies and the Bacchanals.

Ποτνιάομαι, to cry to the Πότνιαι, invoke, implore. Much as Veneror from Venus, Veneris.

Πού, where ? που, anywhere, anyhow. — Like Οὗ. R. Πός.

Πούς, g. ποδὸς, pes pedis, a foot ; — the lower part, as of a mountain : — 'Πόδες are the two bottom corners of the sail ; and the ropes fastened to them, the sheets :' Ldd. — From obs. †πόω, †πίω, πιέζω, to press firm or close. See †Πιόω in †ΠΑΩ, and Πῶμα, a lid. So from †πέω were †Πὶς, †πεδὸς, Pes, pedis, Πέδιλον, Πέζα, Πέδον, &c. : -δος, as Θέμις, Θέμιδος. (2) 'Chald. pesah, incèdo :' Mrt. (3) Ποδ-, allied to foot, fot Icel , voet

Dutch, &c., called by Serenius ' a very ancient word, seen in all the Scytho-Scand-dialects.' *Pada*, Sanskr.

†Πόω, to press hard : in †ΠΑΩ.

†Πόω, to drink : in Πίνω.

Πρᾶγμα, ατος, a thing done or doing, deed, act, transaction, occupation, business, trade.— R. Πράσσω, πέπραγμαι.

Πραγματεύομαι, am engaged in, busy with, traffic, &c.: Πραγματικὸς, *pragmatic*, conversant in business.—Above.

Πρᾶγος, as Πρᾶγμα, a thing, affair, public affairs, weal.—R. πράσσω, πέπραγα.

Πραιτώριον, the Lat. *prætorium*.

Πράκτωρ, an exactor of debts and fines.— R. πράσσομαι, πέπρακται, to do one out of, extort.

Πράμνειος, *Pramnian* (wine), from Mount *Pramné* in Icaria.

Πρὰν, for Πρώαν, Πρόην. Formerly ; — lately, i. e. a little before. Allied to Πρό and Πρίν.

Πρᾶος, Πραΰς, mild, soft, meek.—For Πέραος, from περάω, ' to penetrate or pierce right through,' Ldd., so opposed to Impenetrable. Greg. from περάω, ' transeo : i. e. εὐ-πρόσιτος, accessible.' (2) 'R. ῥᾶος, easy :' Dnn. But the Π? Elsewhere he refers it to πρό : Inclined to, disposed to. Rather from παρά, †πραλ, Lat. *præ*.

Πραπίδες, the midriff, diaphragm, — heart, mind.— ' Allied to Φράζω, [Φράζομαι, to think,] Φρήν :' Dnn.— Or to Φράσσω, whence Διά-φραγμα. (2) For παρ-απίδις. See 'Απίδας in 'Απάδις. (3) Some from πρᾶος, as Εὔ-φρων from φρὴν shows an affinity between Πρᾶος and Πραπίδες. Mrt. from πράω, transeo, penetro.—In form, compare ἐΛΠΙΣ, ἐΛΠΙΔΕΣ.

Πρασία, a bed in a garden.— ' Perh. from ΠΡΑΣΟΝ, a leek : A bed of leeks :' Ldd. ' So Λαχυνείαι was said. Some from πέρας, an end, border :' Dnn.

Πρᾶσις, a sale. — R. περάω, †πράω, to sell.

Πράσσομαι, to require, exact, extort, i. e. DO one out of.— From

Πράσσω, to do, act. — R. περάω, πράω, as †Τάω, Τάσσω : To go through, accomplish. And Πρήσσω is to accomplish a journey, which Dnn. thinks corroborates the above. (2) R. πέρας, περάσσω, as 'Ανάσσω : To bring to an end. (3) ' Hebr. *brd*, creavit :' Mrt.

Πραΰς : in Πρᾶος.

Πρέμνον, the root or bottom of anything ; bottom of the trunk of a tree. — ' No doubt akin to Πρυμνός :' Ldd. (2) Scheide for πεπρημένον, burnt, from πρήθω. E as ῞Εδνα, &c. Or used for burning.

Πρέπω, am conspicuous or distinguished in look, or voice, or scent, or dress ; — also in conduct and behavior am seemly, fitting, worthy. — ' R. πέρω, πείρω, περάω :' Buttm.: i. e. †πρέω, πρέπω, as βλέΠω, δρέΠω. Buttm. understands the prim. sense of †πέρω ' to break forth, become perceptible.' ' To pierce, prop. to force through :' Dnn. — Or περάω, to pass, and so surpass.

Πρέπω, am like. Thus ' She πρέπει is as conspicu-

ous as a queen to look at,' i. e. she is like a queen. Thus Εἴδομαι, ' to appear,' is also ' to be like,' and Videor, to seem like.— Above.

Πρέσβυς, old, aged ; — a chief, prince, ambassador, as gen. elderly. — For πρέβυς, as λέΣχη : from πρέπω, (as B in ῥέμβω,) to be distinguished among others, just as Γέρων is allied by Dnn. to Γέρας, honor. ' The hoary head is a crown of *glory*,' &c.: O.T. (2) Scheide allies it to Lat. PRIScus through πρὶν, &c. Compare Πέρυσι. (3) Pkh. from †προ-εσ-βῶ, as advanced in years. (4) Bos from παρε-σέβυς, from πόρω, paro, σέβας, as conciliating veneration.

Πρευμενής, of a mild temper. — R. πρηὸς, πραΰς, gentle ; μένος, mens, disposition. For πρηϋμενής.

Πρηγορεών : for Προηγορεών.

Πρήθω, σω, Πίμπρημι, Πρημαίνω, to blow out, swell out, force out : — blow out into a flame, set on fire.—As Δαίω is to burn, from †ὃάω to divide, so Πρήθω from πέρδω, †πράω, to pierce, ' prop. to force through ', (Dnn.) (2) R. πυρὸς, †πυρέω, †πρέω : To set on fire.

Πρηνὴς, *pronus*, headlong, steep. Πρηνὼν, Πρὴν, a prominent part of a mountain. ' R. πρὴν for πρὶν, πρό :' Dnn. ' Πρηὼν, R. πρό :' Ldd. The adverb Πρὴν is rather contr. from Πρώην, before : so Πρὰν is for Πρώην. There is also Πρώων (= Πρηὼν,) which from πρὸ, or πρὸ ὢν, or, as some say, προ-ιὼν.

Πρήσσω : in Πράσσω.

Πρηστὴρ, a fiery whirlwind. R. πρήθω, πέπρησται. Also, a poisonous serpent which inflamed the body. ' Rubor igneus ora Succendit,' says Lucan of it.

Πρίαμαι, to buy. — ' Akin to Περάω, Περνάω :' Dnn. I.e. to pass over to myself. Indeed all derive from περάω : †πράω, †πρίω, πρίημι in Etym. M.

ΠΡΙΑΠΟΣ, *Priäpus*, the god of gardens, worshipped in a licentious manner, and used for Πέος. — Q.?

Πρὶν, before ; — before that. — Allied to Πρὸ, and perh. short for comparat. †πρίον, like ῞Ωκιον, i. e. *prius*.

Πρίστις, ' a large fish, as if Πρῆστις (which some read), the Spouter, from πρήθω : according to Buttm. it never = πρίστης, the saw-fish. — A ship of war, prob. from its shape; and a cup, for the same reason :' Ldd. ' A ship,' as in Virgil: ' Velocem Mnestheus agit acri remige *pristin*:' where Pierius derives it from πρίω, πέπρισται, from cutting the waves.

Πρίω, ' to saw, cut through, divide; — gnash the teeth ; — bind fast; — become inflamed with anger, which may be referred to the sense Gnash. — Buttm. after the Etym. M. establishes an affinity with Πρήθω. Compare also πρίστις and πρΗστις :' Dnn. And allied to Περάω, Πράω, to pass through, then πρίω, as in the allied word πρίαμαι. As τείρω, τερέω, †τερίω, †τρίω, trivi, τρίβω, so πείρω, περέω, †περίω, πρίω.

Πρὸ, before: — for. — As ἀπΑΙ and ἀπΟ, so παρΑΙ, †παρΟ, πρό.

Πρόβατον, a sheep, a goat: even a horse, but espec. the others, and from πρὸ, †βάω, βαίνω, as walking forward as it eats. Yet perh. of cattle going before

139

the shepherd: ' The flock before him stepping to the fold :' Thomson. ' The oxen προ-γένοντο, and the shepherds ἕποντο', Il. σ. 525. Thus in the O. T.: ' I took thee from *following* the sheep.'

Προ-βοσκίς, *proboscis*, an elephant's trunk. — R. βόσκω.

Προ-ηγορεών, a bird's craw. — R. ἀγείρω, ἤγορα: Where first the food is collected.

Προῖξ, Προῖξ, a gift; — dowry. (Κατὰ) προῖκα, by gift, without cost, gratis. — Hemst. from πρὸ, ἵκω ἴξω to go. As Gen. 32. 20 : ' I will appease him with the present that goeth before me.' Shaksp.: ' If money go *before*, all ways lie open.' (2) R. προ-ίσσομαι, ἵξομαι.

Προΐσσομαι, ξομαι, to ask a προῖκα gift. — Referred by Dnn. to Προ-ίσχω, to hold forth the hand. Then transp. προΐχσομαι, προΐσσομαι.

Πρόκα, instantly.—Lenn. from πρὸ, much as αὐτίΚΑ, ἡνίΚΑ. Right forward. (2) For (κατὰ) πρόκα, (as (κατὰ) Προῖκα,) from πρὸξ a fawn. ' Like the bounding roe.'

Πρόλοβος, ' the crop of a bird: equiv. to τὸ προ-λαμβάνειν [or προ-λαβεῖν] τὴν τροφήν. Written also Πρό-βολος:' Dnn. O, as τέττΟρα, marmOris.

Προ-μηθής, fore-thinking : allied to Μῆτις.

Προ-μνηστῖνοι, one by one, one after the other. — R. μένω, to wait: Each waiting for the one before. Buttm. writes Προμενεστῖνοι. Or †μενέω, †μνέω, formed like †μνάω, μνάομαι.

Πρόμος, 'the foremost man, champion: lat. a chief Πρό:' Ldd. So Ξυνὸς, Ἄπιος. Or for Πρόμαχος.

Προνωπής, forward, headlong. — Supposed = προ-ωπής, N added; from ὄψ ὠπὸς the face : With the face forward. But, as N is wanting, better from πρὸ, ἐν-ωπή. Thus

Πυονώπιος, before the walls. — R. πρὸ, ἐνώπια walls.

Πρόξ, προκὸς, a roe-buck, or fawn. — Mrt. for Προ-δὶξ, προ-δίκος, as impetuously rushing forwards. In form as Πράξ.

Προ-πετής, falling forwards. — R. πέτω, †πιπέτω, πίπτω.

Προ-πηλακίζω, to fling πηλὸν mud in one's face, treat with indignity.

Πρό-πολος, as Ἀμφί-πολος, one serving before his master. — R. πολέω.

Προωρεών, = προ-πρηνής, forward, inclined to do. See Πρηών.

Πρὸς, towards, to; — near to, at; — in addition to ;— in regard or respect to; — from towards, from.— For πάρος. (2) For πρὸ ἐς.

Προσελέω, to ill-use, maltreat. ' Dawes from πρὸς, ἕλος: To bemire, like Προ-πηλακίζω. But προσ- is long in this word. Dawes refers it to the digamma, Προσ-Ϝελέω, supported by Ϝelia derived by Dion. Hal. from ἕλος. Porson proposed Προυσελέω, as the Gramm. give Προυσέλλω as an old word: and is followed by Blomf. and Dind. and the Ravenna MS. of Aristoph.:' Ldd.

Προσφηὴς, kindly, well disposed; — inclined to, suit-

140

able to. — R. πρὸς, ἐνηής. (2) R. ἠνία :- Coming readily to the bridle: opp. to Ef-frænis. (3) R. προσ-ενόω.

Πρόσθε, before. — Πρὸς, Πρόσω, Πρόσωθε, Πρόσθε, as Ὀπίσω, Ὄπισθε.

Πρόσ-φαιος, striking upon, sudden, new, recent. — R. παίω, to strike.

Προσ·οσθεν, = πρόσωθεν in Πρόσθε.

Πρόσ-φατος, recently slain. — R. φάτος, as in Ἀρηΐ-φατος: πρὸς, near to, near in time. Compare Ποτ-αίνιος. And see Πρόσφαιος.

Πρόσω, forward.—R. πρός. Ewing from πρό. Dnn. curiously thus : ' R. (πρὸς,) πρό.'

Προταίνιος, recent: like Ποταίνιος, for Ποτὶ is the same as Προτί. But Προταινὶ τῶν ταξέων in Eurip., ' before the ranks :' which Ewing from προ-τείνω: rather τΑίνω, whence τΑινία.

Πρότερος, before.—'R. πρό:' Dnn. As in Ἡμέτερος : Or a comparative : More before. Compare Πρῶτος.

Προτί, as Πρὸς, towards, before. Perhaps προ, τι : ' a little before.'

Πρό-τονοι, ropes extended from the masthead to the bows of a ship, &c. — R. τείνω, τενῶ, tendo, τέτονα.

Προΰνεικος, Προΰνικος, 'from πρὸ, ἐνεγκεῖν, [a. l. ἤνεικα,] bearing burdens, a porter : and like Προ-φερής, [ferens se in,] lustful:' Ldd.

Προ-φήτης, a *prophet.* — R. πρὸ, φημί.

Προ-χάνη, a pretext. — Valck. for Προ-εχάνη, from ἔχω: As held out.

Πρόχνυ, for Πρόγνυ, 'πρὸ, γόνυ : With the knees forward, i. e. kneeling: ἀπ-όλωνται πρόχνυ κακῶς, Hom., may be brought upon their knees, i. e. brought low and perish. Then, from ignorance of the true signif., it was used for, entirely:' Ldd.

ΠΡΥΛΕΕΣ, ' heavy-armed infantry, opp. to those fighting in chariots ; — hence, as infantry are usu. in close masses, crowded. Akin is Πρόλις, a dance by armed men:' Dnn. — Perhaps Æolic for Προιλέες from πρὸ, ἴλη: Before the ranks. Some compare *prœlium* and Sanskr. *pralaya.*

Πρύμνα, the poop or stern of a ship. Allied to Πέρας, the end, whence obs. †περάω, †πεπερυμένος, †πεπρυμνὸς, whence Πρυμνὸς, the hindmost. Comp. διαπρΥσιος, πέρΥσι.

Πρύτανις, a prince, ruler; — president, there being 50 of them: Πρυτανεῖον, the presidents' hall, law-court, and Πρυτανεία, sums deposited in it on commencing a law-suit to defray the costs. — R. πρῶτος, †πρότος, †πρότανις, πρύτανις, as ὄνΟμα, ὄνΥμα. So ἀγΥρις.

Πρώην, from πρὸ or πρωΐ: The day before, — a little before, just now.

Πρωΐ, Πρῶ, from πρό: In the forepart of the day, early.

Πρώϊζος, the day πρὸ before yesterday, used thus : ' Yesterday καὶ πρώϊζα'.

Πρωκτὸς, the rump. — For †Προ-εκτὸς, as Ἀνεκτὸς, from προ-έχω, to be prominent. (2) R. πρό-ακτος, as

Ἔπακτος: Advanced forward. (**3**) R. προ-ίκω, προικτός: Coming forward.

Πρών: in Πρηών.

Πρώξ, ωκὸς, a dew-drop.— R. πρωΐ, at morn; †προικὸς, †πρωκός.

Πρῷρα, or πρώρα, *prora, prow* of a ship.— R. πρό.

Πρῶτος; first: πρὸ, πρότατος, most forward, πρόατος, πρῶτος.

Πταίρω, Πτάρνυμαι, to sneeze. — These and ΠΤύω Lenn. brings well from the sound ΠΤ, as SN in English in SNeeze, SNore, SNort, &c.

Πταίω, to stumble against, fall against: i. e. †πέτω, †πετάω, †πτάω, πταίω, to fall: †πέτω as in Προ-πετής. See †Πετέω. So Πτήσσω, Πτώσσω.

Πτάξ, ακὸς, a hare, i. e. a timid animal; and Πτώξ,—allied to Πτήσσω, ξω, and Πτώσσω, ξω.

Πτελέα, elm.— For †Πεταλέα from πέταλον: i. e. full of leaves. 'Fœcundæ frondibus ulmi:' Virg. — Or from πετάω, †πτάω, to expand: *patula*, says Ldd. So Πέτηλος is out-spread.

Πτερὶς, fern.—R. πτερόν: from its leaves resembling feathers, 'pennata' Plin.

Πτέρνα, a ham, as Πέρνα, *perna*. So ΠΤόλις, ΠΤόλεμος.

Πτέρνα, a heel: Πτερνίζω, to trip up. Πτέρνα is also 'met. the foot or lower part of anything:' Ldd. — Mrt. and Ewing from πατέω †ἕρα, as treading the ground: thus Λιπερνὴς perh. from λιπῶ, †ἕρα. Πατερίνα, πτέρνα. Or it may be simply from πατέω, †πτέω. The Latins from Calx, the heel, formed Calco, to tread.—Note Lat. hybERNA.

Πτερὸν, Πτέρυξ, a wing; — any winged creature, hence omen, fate; — anything like wings or feathers.— As Πετεινὸς, †Πτεινὸς, winged, from πέτομαι, †πτόμαι, or †πτέομαι, to fly.

Πτέρυξ, as Πτερὸν, a wing: 'anything that hangs like a wing, 1. a rudder; 2. the flaps or skirts at the bottom of a coat of armour; 3. the edge of an axe, sword, or knife; 4. the lobe of the ear, lungs; 5. wing of a building :' Ldd.

Πτηνὸς, winged : as Πετεινός.

Πτήσσω, to crouch or cower down through fear: from †πτάω, †πτήσω, πταίω, to fall, fall down. So Πεπτηὼς is, frightened.

Πτίλον, a feather; à wing, as Πτερόν. 'Of feathers some are called Πτίλα, some Πτερά:' Schol. Aristoph. —'Some from πτῶ, ἵπτημι. Prob. from τίλλω:' Dnn.

Πτίλος, a disease in which the eyelashes fall off.— R. †πτόω, †πτῶ, πτῶσις, or †πετέω, †πτέω, πεπτηὼς, falling. Compare Πτίλον from πτῶ, ἵπτημι. — But some from τίλω, as mentioned in Πτίλον. Ἀπὸ τοῦ ΤΕΤΙΛΘΑΙ τὰ βλέφαρα, Etym. M.

Πτισάνη, peeled barley;—decoction from it, a *ptisan*. — From

Πτίσσω, to pound, winnow, grind, peel.— R. †πετέω, †πτέω, πεπτηὼς, to fall: To make to fall off, winnow. (**2**) Dnn. and Lenn. for Πίσσω, as πΤολις, πΤόλεμος.

141

And Lenn. from †πίω, πιέζω, to squeeze, then pound, grind. (**3**) Allied to Πτύω, to spit out.

Πτόα, fear; Πτοέω, to frighten, scare, make to flutter or be excited: — allied to Πτώσσω, to crouch, Πτήσσω. (**2**) R. πέτομαι, †πτόμαι, to fly, and so flutter.

Πτόλεμος, Πτόλις: for Πόλεμος, Πόλις. So χθαμαλὸς, ἰφθῖμος.

Πτόρθος, a young branch, shoot, sucker, sapling. — 'Like Πτερὸν, a wing, from πετάω, †πτάω, †πτέω, †πτείρω, †ἐπτόρθην, to expand:' Hemst. ' *Patulis ramis*,' Cic. ' R. πτάω, ὀρθός :' Mrt. (**2**) ' Akin to Στόρθη, Στόρθυξ :' Dnn. ?

Πτύελος, for Πύελος: as Πτόλεμος.

Πτύρω, the same as Πτοέω, Πτώσσω.

Πτύον, a winnowing-fan.—R. πτύω : As spitting out.

Πτὺξ, υχὸς, a fold, layer, leaf, plate: — the flat plate of a ship's stern. Πτύχες, 'a hilly, or the sides of a hilly country, which, viewed from a distance, appear to be in folds:' Ldd. — From

Πτύσσω, ξω, to fold up, double. — Allied to Πετάω, †Πτάω, to lay one thing over another. So Πτὺξ is a layer. (**2**) Passow allies it to Πυκνὸς, as πΤόλις. And see Πύλη. Compare Πτίσσω.

Πτύω, to spit. — From the sound ΠΤ, as Πταίρω, to sneeze.

Πτῶμα, a fall :—dead body, as Cado, Cadāver.—R. †πέτω, to fall : †πετόω, †πτόω, †πέπτωμαι. So Πτῶσις, a fall.— Above.

Πτώσσω, to crouch, from †πτόω, †πτώσσω, to fall, as Πτήσσω.

Πτωχὸς, a beggar, as crouching and cringing.— Above. So Πτὺξ is crouching.

ΠΤΑΝΟΣ, wheat boiled whole ;— others make it a mixture of boiled barley and pulse ;— and Ldd. explains Πυάνιος 'made of beans,' so that thus Πύανος would = κύαμος. As λύΚος, luPus ; Κοῖος, Ποῖος. Yet Q. ?

Πῦαρ, Πῦος, Πυετία, the first milk after calving that curdles in the second stomach of ruminating animals, and called beestings. — Allied to Πυκνὸς, thick, Πύκα, thickly. Called in Lat. 'coagulum,' i. e. coagulated liquor.

Πυγή, the rump, buttocks. Hence Πύγ-αργος, 'white-rump, esp. of an antelope, and an eagle :' Ldd. — Allied to Πυκνὸς, like

Πυγμὴ, a fist, *pugnus ;* — space from the elbow to the knuckles, (compare Πῆχυς,) whence Πυγμαῖος, a *pigmy*, dwarf, i. e. only so much in height.— Above.

Πυγὼν, the elbow ;— and the distance from the elbow to the first joint of the fingers, as Πυγμή.

Πυδαρίζω, to hop, dance. — The Et. M. makes it = ποδαρίζω, from πόδες : To kick the feet about.— Some read Πυγαρίζω, to kick the πυγή with the feet.

Πύελος, a tub, trough, pail, vat ; — a coffin. — As it means a bathing-tub in Aristoph., Buttm. supposes it soft for πλύελος from πλύω, πλύνω, to wash. Dnn. prefers the old deriv., ' as a vessel in which milk is set to form πῦος cream.'

Πύθιοι, four persons at Sparta who consulted the *Py-thian* or Delphic oracle. — From

Πύθιος, *Pythian* or Delphian, as epith. of Apollo: The *Pythian* Apollo. — From Πύθά, *Pytho*, ' older name of that part of Phocis at the foot of Parnassus, where lay Delphi: — also Delphi itself :' Ldd. But some from Πυθών; and some from πεύθομαι, to enquire of.

Πυθμήν, bottom, base, trunk, abyss. — Allied to Βυ-θός, bottom: †Βυθμήν. And to Πύματος.

Πύθω, to make to rot: as Lat. *puteo.* Allied by all to Πύος, purulent matter. And this Πύος is also the first milk after bringing forth, biestings, the same as Πύαρ. These last are allied to Πύκα, Πυκνὸς *thick*; and so is Πύος, *pus*, purulent matter; as Pliny, when distinguishing Sanguis and Sanies and *Pus*, says : ' *Pus* est CRASSISSIMUM, GLUTINOSIUS et sanguine et sanie.'

Πυθοί : in Πύθιος.

Πυθών, ' the serpent *Python*, slain by Apollo, thence surnamed the *Pythian* :' Ldd. — R. πύθω, ἔπυθον, as having rotted on the spot, and so giving its name to Πυθώ, Delphi. (2) Wr. from Hebr. *pethen*, a serpent.

Πύθων, from Apollo being so called, was applied to any diviners, and even to ventriloquists.—Above.

Πύκα, thickly, closely, — strongly ; — prudently, care-fully. Hence Πυκάζω, to make thick or close, cover up, shut up, &c. And Πυκινὸς, Πυκνὸς, thick.—These are allied to Βύω, to fill quite full ; and to Μύω. See Πύλη. Through obsol. πύω.

Πύκτης, a boxer, *pugil, pugilist* : — allied to Πύγμη, the fist, and Πυκνὸς, close, Lat. *pugnus* : and Πὺξ, with the fist. Above.

Πυκτὶς, a writing-tablet. — Soft for Πτυκτὶς, from πτύσσω, ἔπτυκται, to fold. ' Said of folding tablets, two thin plates of wood, one folding upon another :' Ldd.

Πύλη, a gate, entrance, pass ; — ' entrance into a country through a mountain-pass ; hence Πύλαι, the usu. shorter name for Θερμο-πύλαι, *Thermopylæ*, the pass from Thessaly to Phocis, considered the Gates of Greece : — narrow straits :' Ldd. — Allied to Βύω, to close, and Πύκα, and Μύω. The French say, ' *Fermez* la porte', from *firmus.*

Πυλαγόρας, a deputy sent to the ἀγορὰ Council at Πύλαι *Pylæ.*

Πυλεὼν, a wreath. — ' Prob. from φύλλον, *folium* :' Ldd. — Or allied to Βύω, Πύκα, Πυκάζω to cover.

Πύματος, hindmost. — All say for Πύθματος from Πυθμήν, the bottom. Then for Πυθμενότατος, as Imus from Inferissimus. Compare Βυθός.

Πύνδαξ, *fundus* Lat., the bottom.—' It has a com-mon origin with Πυθμήν:' Dnn. And Βυθός. Thus: βύθαξ or τύθαξ, πύνθαξ, (as μαΝθάνω,) πύνδαξ. As δόνΑΞ.

Πυνθάνομαι : in Πεύθομαι.

Πὺξ : in Πύκτης.

Πυξὶς, a box of ΠΥΞΟΣ *box* wood, *pyxis.*

142

Πύον, *pus*, purulent matter : in Πύθω.

Πύος : in Πύαρ.

Πύπαξ, Πύππαξ, excl. of wonder or admiration, like Πόποι, Παπαῖ, *Papæ.*

Πῦρ, g. πυρὸς, fire. — As γείνω, γέγονα, γΥνή, so πείρω, πέπορα, πΥρὸς, to pierce through, i. e. penetrate as fire, like Δαίω and Καίω, which both mean prim. to divide or cut. Horace has ' *dividit ignibus.*' So some ally it to Πράω, Πρήθω. Compare Υ also in βΥθός, νΥμφη, σμΥρις, κΥθηλις, ὑνΥμα, ἄγΥρις, espec. δια-πρΥσιος, and in a kindred word πρΥμνα. (2) Many ally it to ' *Fire* : a very ancient Scytho-Phrygian word,' says Serenius. ' Sax., Icel. *fyr*, Germ. *fewr* :' Todd.

Πυρά, a funeral pile : Above.

ΠΥΡΑΜΙΣ, ίδος, a *pyramid.*—' The old Gramm. from πῦρ, g. πυρός, from its conical appearance: — most likely an Egyptian word :' Dnn. ' From the Coptic *bour-à-mit*, a cave of the dead :' Volney. ' Hebr. *bar-moot*, pit of death :' Wr.

ΠΥΡΓΟΣ, Βύργος, a tower, turret, rampart ; plur. the city walls with their towers, — oblong square or column of troops like a tower. — Derived by many from πῦρ, like the above, as mounting in the air, like fire : †πύρικος, †πύρκος. Too metaphorical. It is found in the Arabic and Sanskrit, and in nearly all the European dialects : *burgh*, Edin-*burgh*, St. Peters-*burg*, ice-*berg*, &c. See Πέργαμον.

Πύρεθρον, a hot spicy plant, fever-few. —And

Πυρετὸς, fever. — R. πῦρ, πυρός : From its fiery nature. As Febris from Ferveo, Ferbui, †Februi.

Πύρην, ' the stone of stone-fruit ;—hard bone of fishes; —round head of a probe ; — Any GRAIN of salt :' Ldd. —Allied no doubt to Πῦρὸς, 'pl. divers kinds of GRAIN:' (Ldd.)

Πυριάτης, beestings, = πυαρίτης from πύαρ.

Πύρνον, wheaten bread. — R. πυρὸς, πύρινον.

Πῦρὸς, wheat : ' pl. of divers kinds of grain. Usu. derived from πῦρ, from the red-yellow color of wheat :' Ldd. And so Dnn. (2) ' Or Hebr. *bar*, wheat :' Mrt.?

Πυρραλλὶς, ' a red-colored bird, prob. a sort of wood-pigeon ['ignaria,' Steph.] : — a reddish olive :' Ldd. — R. πυρρός.

ΠΥΡΡΙΧΗ, a morris-dance, the *pyrrhic* dance. Pliny says that *Pyrrhus* instituted the dance in Crete: others say that one *Pyrrhichus* did so. But ?

Πυρρίχιος, a *pyrrhic* foot ◡◡: ' much used in the Πυρρίχη, war-song :' Ldd.

Πυρρὸς, Πυρσὸς, flame-colored, of bright gold. — R. πῦρ.

Πυρσὸς, firebrand, torch. — R. πῦρ.

Πύστις, enquiry ; — tidings on enquiry. — R. πυνθά-νομαι, †πεύθω, πέπυσται.

Πυτία, = πυετία and πύαρ.—Also a kind of cake, made with beestings, as it seems. See Πύαρ.

Πυτίζω, to spit, spirt out ;—taste, try: Lat. *pytisso*, *pytisma.*—' A frequentat. of Πτύω :' Dnn. Perf. πέπτυται, πτυτίζω, πυτίζω. So T lost in Πυκτὶς for Πτυκτίς.

Πυτίνη, 'a flask covered with plaited willow-twigs:' Ldd.—R. †πύω, πέπυται, = βύω, to shut up, like Πυκάζω, Ἅμ-πυξ, Πυκνός.

Πώγων, a beard.—As Ἀνθερεὼν from ἄνθος, so from πόα herbage was Ποάγων, Πώγων: somewhat as Σιᾱγών. Perh. through †ποάζω, πέπκακα.

Πωλέομαι, like Lat. 'versor,' to frequent, am conversant' with. See Πέλω. So Πέτομαι, Πωτάομαι.

Πωλέω, to sell: allied to Ἐμ-πολάομαι, Ἐμ-πολὴ, i. e. 'versor inter,' as above,— go about, frequent places, deal in them. Above.

Πῶλος, a foal, colt, young horse, a youth, maiden.— R. πάομαι, †πάω, pasco, pavi, †πάολος, πῶλος, (See Παῖς:) Feeding and doing nothing else. See Κηφήν. (2) 'For πόαλος. R. πόα, ἅλλομαι:' Ewing. Leaping among the grass. ? (3) Dnn. compares pullus, Sax. fola, Germ. fohlen, our foal. So tad-pole.

Πῶμα, a draught,—drinking-cup.— R. πίνω, πώσω, πέπωμαι.

Πῶμα, a cover, lid.— From the obs. †πάω, or †πόω, †πῶ, †πάγω, πήγνυμι, allied to Πιέζω, Πυκάζω to cover,

βόω, to stop up, &c. (2) 'Chald. pům, a mouth:' Mrt.?

Πώμαλα, 'for Πῶς μάλα; how in the world ? hence, not a whit:' Ldd. Or, by a polite mode of speech, for Οὐ πω μάλα: As the French say Merci, (No) I thank you.

Πῶρος, 'tuff-stone, friable and porous , — also = πόρος, a kind of marble like the Parian ;— stalactite in caverns ;— chalk-stone, &c. :' Ldd. —' Very probably from its texture (as porous) from πείρω, πέπορα, to penetrate :' Dnn.

Πωρόω, to turn into πῶρος stone, harden.

Πῶς, how : Πως, in any way.— From πός, dat. pl. ποῖς, quibus modis. So Οἶ is Ὧ, Οἴκοι is Οἴκῳ.

Πῶς, I wish that. — I. e. O that there were some way how ! Above.

Πωτάομαι, the same as Πέτομαι.

Πῶϋ, a flock of sheep.— R. †πάω, †πῶ, pasco, pavi, to feed : as Ποιμήν, a shepherd.— Or πάομαι, †πάομαι, to acquire, possess, as Κτάομαι, Κτῆνος : Cattle being the chief property.

Πῶϋγξ, 'an unknown water bird ;' Ldd.—Allied perhaps to Πῶμα drink, Poto to drink, from †πόω, †πῶ, πώσω. Compare Πῶϋ.

Ρ.

Ῥα, for Ἄρα.

Ῥαβδάσσω, Ἀραβδάσσω, 'to make a noise, esp. by beating time ; Ἀρράβαξ, a dancer, and met. a brawler :' Ldd. So Lat. rabula, is a brawler, wrangler, allied by Todd to our rabble.—' The same origin as Ἀράσσω, Ῥάσσω :' Dnn. More immed. from Ἄραβος.

Ῥάβδος, a rod, wand, stick, spear-shaft, sceptre :— streak, line, seam, vein in metals, sunbeam, &c.—Ldd. compares Ῥαπὶς a rod, and our Rap. Ῥαπὶς, ῥαπίδος, †ῥάπδος.

Ῥαγὰς, a rent, chink. Ῥάγδην, tearingly, violently. —R. ῥάσσω, ἔρραγον.

Ῥάδαμνος, a young shoot or branch. Allied by Ldd. to ῬΑΔινὸς, flexible; pliant. So Ῥαδανίζω, to move to and fro.

Ῥάδινὸς, 'flexible, pliant, nimble, slender, delicate :— met. feeble, soft ;' Dun. Compared by Leun. and Dnn. with Ῥέδιος, easy. A is short, but is so perhaps from the omission of I in Ῥαΐδιος, †Ῥαΐδιος.

Ῥάδιξ, a branch, switch, rod.— Mrt. from ῥάδιος, like Ῥαδινὸς, flexible, and Ῥάδαμνος. (2) 'R. ῥάσσω, as Κλάδος from κλάω :' Dnn. See Ῥαίω.

Ῥάδιος, Ῥηΐδιος, Ῥῄδιος, easy,—easy to make or do: — careless, reckless. — Mrt. well from ῥέα, ῥεία, easily. As μαψΙΔΙΟΣ, so ῥεΙΔΙΟΣ, ῥηΐδιος. We find also Ῥάιος. (2) Sax. raed, our ready.

Ῥάζω, to bark, snarl.— Ldd. compares ΡΑθο and

143

RΛbies. The R was called the dog's letter, Canīna litera, producing Lat. hiRRio, iRRio, iRa, and Ῥάζω. Ῥάθαγος, 'the same sense and R. as Ῥόθος;' Dnn. See the next.

Ῥαθαίνω, Ῥαθαμίζω, Ῥαθάσσω, to besprinkle: Ῥαθάμιγξ, a drop.— R. †ῥάω, †ἐρράθην, ῥαίνω, ῥέω, to make to flow. See Ῥαίνω. —' Ῥαθαμίζω, from ῥαίνω δάμα :' Mrt. ?

Ῥαθαπυγίζω, to give a slap on the πυγὴ buttock.— 'R. ῥάσσω, πυγή;' Ldd. That is, through †ῥάω, ἐρράθην, whence ῥαίω and ἄρρατος.

Ῥαιβός, crooked, bent, bandy-legged.—Eustath. from ἐρραισμένος βάσιν. Reject the latter word: Ῥαίω, Ῥαιβός, as κολοΒΟΣ. (2) 'Akin to, or from 'Ῥέμβω:' Dnn. And Scheide compares Ῥάμφος, (Ῥάφος).

Ῥαΐζω, am ῥάων easier, recovering from sickness, rest from labor.

Ῥαίνω, to sprinkle, wet. Ῥάσσατε, sprinkle, Od. v. 150. And Ἐρράδαται. These verbs show a word ῥάω, allied to ῥέω to make to flow, as Ἔρρει χοάς. Indeed nearly all refer it to ῥέω. Steph. says: ' Χῶ, χαίνω ; Βῶ, βαίνω: Ῥῶ, ῥαίνω.'—Dnn. allies 'Ῥαίνω to Ῥάσσω : but indeed he allies all of these. (2) Allied to our rain: Ῥάϊος, = ῥάδιος.

Ῥαιστήρ, a smasher, hammer.— R. ῥαίω, ἔρραισται. Ῥαίω, to break, smash, shiver, as Ῥάσσω, which like Ῥαίω, is from †ῥάω, as Τάω, Τάσσω. So Ἄρρατος. Τό

this are allied 'Αράσσω, "Αραβος, &c. Some think 'Α-
ράσσω, or 'Ράσσω the original, and formed from the
sound, then softened down to 'Ράω.—But all these seem
to be from ἄρω, (prim. to draw,) †ἔρω, ἐρύω, to draw,
&c.: then, like 'Αγνῦμι from "Αγω, to drag, drag violently, break. As to Λ, observe ἐρΛω to love, which
is from †ἔρω: also Λ in ἐξ-ερΛω, ἐξ-έρΛμα, δι-έρΛμα, a
funnel by which we draw out. (2) Some compare
Βράζω, Βράσσω, Βράχω. (3) 'Chald. rea, to break,
bruise:' Mrt. And 'Ράσσω, or 'Ρήσσω he brings from
Hebr. rats, to break.

'Ράκος, 'Ράγος, 'Ρῆγος, 'a rag, ragged garment, remnant of cloth. R. ῥάσσω, [ἔῤῥαχα,] ῥήσσω:' Dnn.

'Ράκος, Βράκος, a costly female garment.—See Βράκη
and 'Ρῆγος.

'Ραμνουσία, epith. of Nemesis from her famous temple
at Rhamnus, 'Ραμνοῦς, in Attica.

'Ραμφίς, a hook: 'Ραμφή, a hooked knife. — From
'Ράμφος, the crooked beak of birds, a bill: and 'Ραμφὸς,
crooked. — Probably from 'Ρέμβω, ἔῤῥεμφα, to turn
round. (2) Lenn. allies it (for 'ΡΑΦος, as M in ῥίΜφα)
to 'ΑΠΙάζω, transposed 'ΡΑΠΙάζω, RAPio. Then the
adjective is 'crooked as a beak'. Compare 'ΕΡδω and
'ΡΕζω. (3) Mrt. from ῥάω to break, whence "Αῤῥατος.
The adj. in the same way again. Or, if we want an independent sense of 'bending or crooked', then we can compare 'Αγνῦμι to break and Περι-ηγὴς curved; Κλάω to
break and Ο-κλάδον in a bent position.

'Ρανίς, a drop: ῥαίνω.

'Ράξ, ῥαγὸς, 'Ρὼξ, ῥωγὸς, a berry, grape-berry.—
Blomf., Ldd., Dnn., &c. from ῥάσσω, ἔῤῥαγον, ἔῤῥωγα,
to break. 'Ρὼξ, rock, stone, grape-stone:' Ewing.

'Ρακάτη, a shepherd's pipe. — Perh. allied to
'Ρανίς, 'a rod: 'Ρανίζω, to RAP or strike with a
stick, strike, slap:' Ldd. Brought by Mrt. (Compare
ἀΛΠΙΣ,) from ῥαίω or †ῥάω whence 'Α-ῤῥατος, and
'Ράσσω, which last is 'mostly, to divide, sever, rend, force
generally implied', (Dnn.): Rent off. As Κλάδος and
Κλῆμα from Κλάω. 'Ρανίς is also, says Hesych., a
Περόνη i.e. an instrument for piercing, which agrees
with the above. (2) Some compare 'Ρέπω and 'Ρόπαλον.

'Ράπτω, to sew, stitch. — As Hesychius gives the
sense of Περόνη to 'Ρανίς, and Περόνη is a bodkin,
'Ράπτω might be allied to 'Ράσσω, (as Πέπτω to
Πέσσω), could the sense of 'Ράσσω be modified to that
of Πείρω whence Περόνη. — Otherwise, as ἐρΛω in
ἐξ-ερΛω, ἐξ-έρΛμα, δι-έρΛμα, is allied to 'Ερύω and
†'Ερω, to draw, and to "Αρω, to draw together, join, suppose ἀρΛω, ῥάω, ῥάπτω, as †Δάω, Δάπτω. Compare
'Ερύω, 'Ρύω, 'Ρύπτω. And see further for the Λ in 'Ραίω.
(3) 'Hebr. repha, to restore, heal:' Wr.

'Ραριάς, Ceres, to whom was sacred the Rarian plain
near Eleusis, whence the Eleusinian mysteries.

'Ράσσω, ξω, to strike, smite: — shiver, shatter. And
'Αράσσω. — See in 'Ραίω. (2) Dnn. makes it an imi-
tative word. (3) 'Hebr. reza, to dash:' Wr. (4)
Germ. reissen, to burst.

144.

'Ρᾷστος, most easy: superl. of 'Ράων.

'Ραστώνη, easiness of doing anything, or of temper,—
ease, leisure, rest. — Above.

'Ραφίς, a needle, pin. — R. ῥάπτω, ἔῤῥαφα, to sew.

'Ραχία, 'Ρηχίη, from ῥήσσω, ἔῤῥηχα, to break: 'The
sea breaking on the shore, breakers, surf; — flood-tide;
— roar of the breakers, met. a crowd of people; — a
steep shore on which the waves break:' Ldd.

'Ραχία, 'a rugged mountain ridge;—an enclosure,
hedge, fence; — prison:' Ldd. Above. Prop. broken.

'Ραχίζω, 'to cleave through the ῥάχις back-bone, cut
up; — vaunt falsely, brag, probably orig. from vaunts
made as to extraordinary feats in battle:' Dnn.

'Ράχις, 'the back of men or animals, the chine; the
sharp ridge along the back of an animal, and so the
back-bone; — anything ridged like it, the ridge of a
mountain-chain, sharp projection on the middle of the
shoulder-blade, bridge of the nose, mid-rib of a leaf:'
Ldd. Hence the 'Ραχῖτις, the rickets, spinal complaint.
— 'Like 'Ράχος, R. ῥάσσω: from the rugged appearance:' Dnn.

'Ράχος, 'Ρῆχος, 'Ράχη, 'thorn-bush, briar, hedge;—
thorn-stick, gen. a twig, small branch:' Ldd. —Above.

'Ράχος, ' = ῥάκος, a strip, shred: esp. a piece cut
from the ῥάχις chine:' Ldd.

'Ράων: Compare 'Ρᾴδιος.

'Ρέα, 'Ρεῖα, easily, with or at ease. — Mrt. says: ' R.
ῥέζω, as Facilis from Facio.' But the Ζ ?—Rather
from ῥέω, as to be Fluent, to speak with Fluency, from
Fluo, and an easy Flow of words. 'To Flow, to glide
smoothly:' Todd.

'Ρέγκω, 'Ρέγχω, to snore, snort. — Jones from ῥὶν,
the nose. (2) Dnn. from ῥήγνυμι i.e. πνεῦμα, as commonly ῥήγνῦμι φωνήν.

'Ρέγος, 'for 'Ρῆγος:' Dnn.

'ΡΕΔΗ, in Rev. 18. 13, prob. from the Latin rheda,
'a Gallic word', Quintilian says. — Schleusn. would
have better derived it from ῥέα than ῥέω, 'à celeri motu
quo ferri solet.'

'Ρέεθρον, 'Ρεῖθρον, a river, stream.— R. ῥέω.

'Ρέζω, fut. ῥέξω, allied to "Ερξω fut. of †ἔργω, ἔοργα,
to do, make:—to do sacrifice, as Faciam vitulâ, Virg.
' 'Ρέζω and "Ερδω are the same word:' Hemst.

'Ρέθος, a limb, — face, — body. — Allied by Mrt.
(through †'Ρύθος,) to 'Ρυσμὸς, 'Ρυθμὸς, proportion, form,
shape. This seems likely from the identity of 'the root
PE-, PΥ-,' as stated by Ldd. in 'Ρέω, whence he derives
'Ρυθμός. (2) Greg. makes it an ὄργανον, instrument,
'each from ἔργω or ῥέζω.'

'Ρείη, 'Ρέα, Rhea, 'by transp. from "Ερα, the earth;
the very prob. conj. of Passow:' Dnn.

'Ρέμβω, 'to turn round, turn about, roam, wander,
waver. Compare 'Ραιβός. Akin perh. also to 'Ρέπω:'
Dnn. 'Ρέπω, ῥέμβω, as τρέπω, τρόπΒυς. Observe
στέμβω. (2) Allied to 'Ράμφος. (3) Our ramble, Swed.
ramb. 'Hebr. rom, to be violently moved:' Wr.

'Ρέπω, to bend down, incline, verge, sink. — ' R. ῥέω:

Hemst:' Dnn. From the *inclined* course of a stream or river. In form as ΒΛΕΠΩ, δρΕΠΩ. (**2**) Allied to 'Ρύω, 'Ερύω, to draw (down). Compare Νεύω and Νέομαι.

'Ρεῦμα, a flow, flood, stream:— flux, *rheum*, thin watery matter oozing through the glands.— R. ῥέω. So 'Ρευστός.

'Ρέω, to say; for 'Ερέω. (**2**) Some ally it to 'Ρέω, to flow: citing Il. α. 249: ' Speech ῥέεν flowed sweeter than honey from his mouth.' ' So the Lat. *instillare* doctrinam. See Deut. 32.4:' Greg. So *Fluency* of speech.

'Ρέω, to flow: and 'Ρύω, whence 'Ρύαξ, 'Ρυτός: hence from 'Ερύω, ' to draw, to drag along,' (Dnn.), whence ῥυστάζω, to drag, and ῥύω, (Dnn.), ῥύομαι. (**2**) ' Hebo. *reva*, to irrigate:' Mrt.

'Ρήγμα, a fracture: and
'Ρηγμίν, the sea breaking on the beach, breakers:— the sea's edge. — From

'Ρήγνῡμι, to break: allied to 'Ρήσσω and 'Ράσσω; see 'Ραίω.

'Ρῆγος, ' a coverlet, covering for a bed or seat. Passow, through 'Ράκος, from ῥήγνῡμι, in the sense of a *piece* of cloth: countenanced by Βρόκος. But, as brilliancy of color is espec. assigned to it, the usual deriv. from ῥέζω to DYE seems quite as probable:' Dnn. 'Ρέζω, to do, then to do it well with the hand, as 'Οργάζω from ἔργω is to dress leather, macerate, mix. (**2**) Our *rug*.

'Ρηΐδιος, *ready, easy*. — In 'Ράδιος.

'Ρῆμα, a word, saying,— a verb, i.e. the principal word.— R. ῥέω, to say: ἔρρημαι.

'Ρῆμος, only in Athen. III.: a peel to put bread into the oven. ' Thought to be the Lat. *remus*, an oar, from its likeness to which it was called :— esp. as Ματερία and Φοῦρνος, Materia and Furnus, are there used also:' Steph. And *remus* from ἐρετμὸς, 'ρετμὸς, 'ρεμμὸς.

'Ρὴν, a sheep, lamb: = †ἀρήν, g. †ἀρένος, ἀρνός.

'ΡΗΠΑΙ, piles for building on;— only in Diod. S. 2. 309. — Q.?

'Ρήσσω : in 'Ρήγνῡμι.

'Ρητίνη, *resina*, *rosin*.— R. ῥέω: Flowing from trees.

'Ρήτωρ, *rhetor*, *rhetorician*. — R. ῥέω, to speak.

'Ρηχίη, Ion. of 'Ραχία.

'Ρηχὸς, Ion. of 'Ράχος.

'Ρῖγος, shivering or stiffness of the limbs with cold;— dread, horror;—frost, cold, Fρῖγος, *Frigus*. Allied too to *Rigeo*, *Rigor*, *Rigidus*. 'Ρίγιον, more horribly. — See in Φρίσσω, Φρὶξ, Φρίκη. (**2**) ' *Rigo* Hebr., to be stiff:' Wr.

'Ρίζα, a root. — Much as Φύζα is allied to Φεύγω, so 'Ρίζα to 'ρείδω, ἐρείδω, to fix firm, press hard: Fixing itself or the tree firm. So 'Ριζόω is to fix deeply or firmly. (**2**) Damm from †Ἐρα, Ἰζω: ἐρίζα, Establishing itself in the earth. Or, as Χθὲς, Χθιζὰ, simply from †Ἐρα.

'Ρικνὸς, ' stiff with cold or shrivelled, hence withered, bent, crooked. R. ῥῖγος, †ῥιγανὸς, whence we sometimes find 'Ριγνός:' Ldd. and Dnn. (**2**) For †ῥηγνὸς, R. ῥήγω, ῥήγνῡμι: Broken, furrowed. As ῥΗγμα, rΙma.

'Ρίμφα, swiftly, fleetly: i.e. with a fling or plunge: or with the rapidity of a thing flung. — R. ῥίπτω, ἔρρῑμμαι. Or ἔρριφα; M, as χρίΜπτω, θάΜβος.

'Ρὶν, Ρὶς, ῥινὸς, the nose. — As Θὶν, Θὶς, from †Θέω, τίθημι, so 'Ρὶν, Ρὶς from ῥέω, ῥεῖος: From the flowing of the nostrils. So 'Ρώθων: and Nasus from Νᾶσις a flowing.

'Ρίνη, a file, rasp. — Scheid compares the motion to and fro ῥινῶν of the nostrils, and that of the ῥίνη file. And perhaps justly. Compare the metaphors in 'Ρίον and Κνήμη. (**2**) Mrt. from ῥαίω. Somewhat as †Φθέω, Φθίνω, Φθίνα mildew.

'Ρίνη, a shark with a rough skin used like a file for polishing. — Above.

'Ρινὸς, hide, skin: — shield made of it. — Usually allied to the origin of 'Ρὶν, from the *flowing* from it of the humours of perspiration. See †'Ρινὴ in 'Ρινοῦχος. (**2**) Short for 'Ρικνὸς, wrinkled. Somewhat as πΤυκτὶς, πυκτίς. (**3**) Our *rind*.

'Ρινοῦχος, a sewer, rinser. Only found in Strab. 14. — As 'Ρὶν, 'Ρινὸς, the nose, is allied to 'Ρέω to flow, so Coray derives 'Ρινοῦχος from a word †ῥινὴ = ῥοὴ or ῥύσις, a flowing, and ἔχω ὄχα.

'Ρίον, peak of a mountain: headland, foreland. — Nearly all from ῥὶν: ' The nose of a mountain.' Much as Κνήμη and Κνημὸς.

'Ριπὴ, swing or force with which a thing ῥίπτεται is thrown,— the motion, rush, quivering, twinkling, &c. — R. ῥίπτω, ἔρρῑπα.

'Ριπὶς, a bellows or fan, causing a rush or blast of fire or wind. And 'Ριπίζω, to blow up, fan;—blow the fire to boil or roast. — Above.

'Ρῖπος, the same as 'Ρίψ.

'Ρίπτω, to throw, cast, hurl, dash. — Allied to 'Ερείπω, 'ρείπω, and 'Ερίφος. (**2**) ' Compare the kindred forms 'Ρέπω and 'Ρέμβω:' Dnn.

'Ρὶς: in 'Ρὶν.

'ΡΙΣΚΟΣ, *riscus*, a coffer, casket.— Jablonski after Donatus makes it a *Phrygian* word. (Rare.)

'Ρίψ, ῥιπὸς, a reed, rush: mat or hurdle. — As Δόναξ from δονέω, so 'Ρίψ from ῥίπτω, ψω, whence 'Ριπτασμὸς is a tossing oneself to and fro: ' As floating in the wind:' Dr. Jones. ' From its flexibility and lightness:' Schol. Aristoph.

'Ροὰ: a stream: — ῥέω, ἔρροα, to flow.

'Ροὰς, the flowing or falling off of grapes at the time of knitting. — Above.

'Ρόγκος, a snoring. — R. ῥέγκω.

'Ρογμὸς, the same as 'Ρόγκος.

'ΡΟΓΟΣ, a rick, stack, barn. — Very rare. A *Sicilian* word.

'Ροδάνη, spun thread, woof or weft. — All consider it as the fem. of 'Ροδανὸς, slight, slender.

'Ροδανὸς, ' slight, slender, lank, easily moved: compare 'Ραδινός: both from ῥᾴδιος:' Dnn. ' Waving, flickering:' Ldd.

'Ροδιὰς, a kind of cup made at *Rhodes*.

'ΡΟΔΟΝ, the rose, ross.—Perhaps allied to our *red*, which is in 'Welsh *rhud*, High Dutch *rot*,' (Todd.)

'Ρόθος, 'Ροῖζος, 'Ροῖβδος, 'Ρόχθος, a tumultuous, rapid or whizzing noise. — R. ῥέω, ἔῤῥοα: The sound of flowing water. But consider these words, esp. the three last, to be imitative of the sound. — And 'Ρόχθος is deduced by some from ἐρέχθω, ἔροχθα, to belch out. — 'Ρόθος is also 'a mountain path-way, perh. from that of a 'Ρόος current, a course, which 'Ρόθος seems sometimes to mean:' Dnn.

'Ροιβδέω, to suck down with a ῥοῖβδος rushing noise. See in 'Ρόθος.

'Ροῖζος : in 'Ρόθος.

'Ροϊκὸς, flowing, fluid, flabby, soft; — suffering from diarrhœa. — R. ῥέω, ἔῤῥοα.

'Ροικὸς, crooked, bent. — As 'Ρόος is a stream and 'Ροϊκὸς is fluid, from ῥέω, ἔῤῥοα, so 'Ροικὸς Schrevel. understands 'winding like a stream, bent'. Compare 'Ρέπω. (2) R. ἐρείκω, ἔροικα, 'ροῖκα: Broken, bent. See partic. in 'Αγκή. (3) Some compare 'Ραιβός.

'Ρόμβος, a whirling motion; — a whirling thing, a top, wheel;—the *rhombus* or *rhomb*, a four-sided figure, with two opp. angles obtuse and two acute: perh. from the unsteady tottering position of this figure compared with the square. Also a turbot, from its *rhomb*-like form;— surgical bandage of *rhomboidal* form. — R. ῥέμβω.

'Ρόμμα, ' = ῥόφημα from ῥοφέω:' Ldd. : i.e. ῥόφμα, ῥόμμα, as 'Ερετμὸς, 'ρεμμὸς, Remus.

'Ρομφαία, a large sword. — R. ῥέμβω, ἔῤῥομφα, to turn round, turn about. (2) Valck. will have it a *Thracian* word.

'Ρόος, stream, &c. — R. ῥέω, ἔῤῥοα.

'Ρόπαλον, a club. — R. ῥέπω, ἔῤῥοπα: As thicker at one end, and inclining that way. Some from ῥέμβω, to whirl. And some compare 'Ράπις, a rod.

'Ρόπαλον, a knocker on a house-door, as being a club or hammer. — Above.

'Ροπὴ, verging, gravitation; that which makes the scale turn, weight, importance, gravity, avail. — R. ῥέπω, ἔῤῥοπα.

'Ροπτρὸν, the same as 'Ρόπαλον. Also, the trigger of a trap, being a stick; — or as inclined downwards, immed. from ῥέπω.—And a tambourine or kettle-drum; here from ῥέμβω, to whirl.

'Ρούσιος, 'Ρουσσαῖος, reddish, *russus*, *russet*. From ἐρεύθω, fut. ἐρεύσω, 'ρεύσω, to redden. Steph. says: 'A color as of the Sinopian red lead, as some say.' O, as 'Εθνος, 'Οθνεῖος; κέρας, cOrnu; pEndo, pOndus.

'Ροφάω, -έω, to suck or sup up. — 'Akin is 'Ροθέω, 'Ροχθεω, 'Ροιζέω, 'Ροιβδέω;' Dnn.

'Ρόχθος, 'the same as 'Ρόθος, as Μόθος and Μόχθος:' Dr. Jones. See other derivv. in 'Ρόθος.

'Ρύαξ, ακος, a mountain torrent. — R. ῥέω, to flow, as ῥΥτὸς is flowing. (2) R. ἐρύω, ῥύω, ῥυστάζω, to drag down.

'Ρυὰς, a flow of tears ; — flowing or falling off of hair in disease; &c.—Above.

'Ρυάχετος, the unstable crowd of the Athenians.—R. ῥύαξ, ακος. But the readings vary.

'Ρύγχος, snout, muzzle, beak, bill.—Mrt. from ῥύγχω, to snore: 'For with it the pig snores.'

'Ρόζω, -έω, the same as 'Ράζω.

'Ρύη, for ἐῤῥύη, a. 2. of ῥύω, ῥέω, to flow. So 'Ρυτὸς is flowing

'Ρυθμὸς, 'Ρυσμὸς, an easy flow of sound or motion, from ῥύω, ἐῤῥύθην, ἔῤῥυσμαι, ῥέω, as above:—measured movement, as of the feet in dancing, or of the voice in singing;— harmonious measure and arrangement of words, *rhythm*, proportion, harmony, metre. And 'Ρυθμίζω, to modulate, arrange, regulate, control.

'Ρυκάνη, 'Ρυγκάνη, a joiner's plane, *runcina*.— Schneid. from ῥύσσω, ῥάσσω, ῥαίω, ῥήσσω, ῥήγνῦμι, to break, i. e. break away inequalities. (2) Better allied to 'Ρύπτω, 'Ρύμμα, 'scrapings', (Dnn.) Simply from ῥύω, ἔῤῥῦκα, to draw off (inequalities). Compare Βυκάνη.

'Ρῦμα, a river.—R. ῥύω, ῥέω, as 'Ρεῦμα. See ῥΥτον.

'Ρῦμα, drawing of a bow; — towing-line; — pole of a carriage; — drawing out of danger, deliverance. — R. ῥύομαι.

'Ρύμβος, Att. for ῥόμβος.

'Ρύμη, force, violence, rushing or rush. — R. ῥύομαι, to drag.

'Ρύμη, a street, Fr. *rue*, our *row*. — As Tractus, a Tract of road, so 'Ρύμη from ῥύομαι, traho. 'Tractus in urbe:' Mrt. So

'Ρυμὸς, the pole of a carriage, as 'Ρῦμα, from ῥύομαι, to draw; — trace in harness; — furrow, row, line, as Tractus. Above.

'Ρύομαι, to draw to oneself, draw out of danger, rescue, shield; — draw back; — draw down the scale. — R. ῥύω, ἐρύω, to draw, whence 'Ρυστάζω.

'Ρύπος, dirt, filth; — sordidness, meanness. — R. ῥύπτω, to remove dirt.

'Ρύπος, sealing-wax. Ewing identifies this and the former thus: 'filth, dirt, wax'. Thus *Rhypōdes*, 'Ρυπῶδες, was a kind of plaster, 'à similitudine *sordium* appellata', Forcell.

'Ρυππάπαι, an exclamation exciting rowers, yoho! From the supposed sound. Possibly founded on ῥύω, to draw on.

'Ρύπτω, to remove dirt, cleanse, wash. — As Δύω, Δύπτω, so 'Ρύω, 'Ρύπτω, 'Ρύομαι, to draw away.

'Ρύσιον, ' prey, booty, seized and dragged away ; — what is seized as a pledge or security, pledge, hostage; —what is seized by way of reprisals; claims to persons or things so seized;—(drawing from danger,) deliverance:' Ldd. — R. ῥύομαι, ῥύσομαι.

'Ρύσκομαι, as 'Ρύομαι.

'Ρυσμὸς, the same as 'Ρυθμός.

'Ρυσὸς, drawn up, shrivelled, contracted. — R. ῥύομαι, ῥύσομαι.

Ῥυστάζω, to drag; Lat. *ruo*, Gr. ῥύομαι, ἔρρυσται to draw. ' Ceteros *ruerem*, prosternerem :' Cic.

Ῥυτήρ, ' a drawer as of a bow ; — strap by which a horse draws ; — by which one holds a horse, a rein ; — strap to flog with, (draw a horse on):' Ldd.— R. ῥύομαι, ἔρρύται.

Ῥυτίς, a wrinkle. See Ῥυσός.

Ῥυτὸν, ' a drinking-horn, running to a point, where was a small hole, through which the wine ran in a thin stream: From ῥυτὸς, flowing, running, from ῥέω :' Ldd. or †ῥύω, whence Ῥύη: so

Ῥυώδης, flowing;— abundant, which is from Unda, as Undanti cruore, Virg. — Above.

Ῥωγὰς, and 'Ρὼξ, a cleft, rent; 'Ρωγὰς πέτρα, a cloven *rock;* the word *rock* being allied to these and to Ῥωχμὸς a cleft. — R. ῥάσσω or ῥήσσω, ἔρρωγα, to rend. So

Ῥωγμὴ, a kind of fracture. — Above.

Ῥώθωνες, the nostrils.—'R. ῥέω, ῥῶ, to flow or run :' Dnn. As Nasus from †νᾶσις, a flowing.

Ῥώμη, strength, vigor, *robur.* — From

Ῥώννυμι, †Ῥώω, ῥώσω, to strengthen: ἔρρωσθαι, to be strong; ἔρρωσο, be strong, farewell, Vale. 'Ρώμη above. — As Ἐρωὴ is ' force, strength of a man', (Dnn.) so †ῥωὴ and †ῥώω, to give strength, make strong.— Dnn. allies these to Ῥύομαι 'to move with force and vigor, rush for-

ward: akin to Ῥώννυμι and 'Ρώμη, but more remotely to 'Ρύω, Lat. *ruo*'. Perhaps too compare Ὀρούω, Ὀροθύνω, to rouse up, give tone to.

Ῥὼξ, g. ῥωγὸς, as 'Ρωγὰς, ' a cleft ; — the narrow entrance of a room; acc. to some, a side-door or a window ; — also as 'Ρὰξ, a grape or olive; — also a venomous spider, something like a grape:' Ldd.

Ῥύομαι, *ruo*, to rush, rush on, run, move fast: allied to 'Ρύομαι, to draw oneself on. See also Ῥυστάζω, and 'Ρώννυμι.

Ῥῶπος, small wares, toys, trumpery. — As 'Ράσσω makes 'Ρῶγὰς, and Ἀνάσσω Ἀνῶγω, so 'Ράπτω could make ῥῶπος: Things ῥαπτὰ strung together, as on a string or stick, and carried about. So σκῶληξ.

Ῥῶσις, strength, 'Ρώμη.

Ῥῶσταξ, ' a prop, stand : R. ῥώννυμι, ῥώσω (ἔρρωσται):' Dnn. Making things firm.

Ῥωτακίζω, to make a wrong use of the letter ρ, rho.

Ῥωχμὸς, the same as 'Ρωγὰς, a cleft, gutter, — wrinkle.

Ῥωχμὸς, 'Ρωγμὸς, the same as 'Ρόγχος, 'Ρόγκος.

Ῥὼψ, g. ῥωπὸς, a low shrub, bramble. 'Ρῶπες, twigs, branches. — ' Ῥὼψ, allied to, or rather another form of 'Ριψ:' Dnn. (2) R. ῥέπω, as Παρα-βλὼψ from βλέπω : Not towering, but verging to the ground. (3) For θρψ, ὠρπός: R. ἔρπω, ὅρπα. As ΑΡΠΑΖω, ΡΑΡ'io.

Σ.

Σὰ μὰν, broad Doric for Τί μήν; Σ and Τ, as in Σὺ and Τύ.

Σαβάζω, to break to pieces, shatter. — Perhaps from the Σαβοὶ Bacchanals' cry. ' The modern Greeks still call a madman Σαβός :' Ldd. (2) Hesych. explains by Δια-σαλεύω. Whence R. σάω, σείω, σαίνω, σαφάζω. As -θον, ὤθον, ὦθον.

Σαβακὸς, shattered, enervated, effeminate. Above. Also, rotten, putrid : but here it might come from σήπω, σαπῶ, †σαπακὸς, as σαπρός.

Σαβώτης, ' a shatterer ;— esp. a mischievous goblin who broke pots :' Ldd.— R. σαβάζω.

ΣΑΒΑΝΟΝ, a linen napkin. ' Arab. *saban :* ' Mrt.— A late word.

ΣΑΒΒΑΤΟΝ, the *Sabbath.* A *Hebrew* word.

ΣΑΒΟΙ, a cry like Εὐοῖ at the feast of the *Phrygian* god Σαβάζιος, whose mysteries resembled those of Bacchus, who was therefore so called. Βοῶν (crying out) Εὐοῖ Σαβοῖ, Demosth. ' Hebr. *seba*, to drink hard :' Wr.

ΣΑΓΑΡΙΣ, an Amazonian battle-axe. — ' Reland says it is *Persian* :' Jabl.

Σάγη, equipment, baggage, harness, armour. — R. σάττω, ἔσαγον. (2) ' Hebr. *sek*, to protect :' Wr.

Σαγήνη (as σεΛΗΝΗ,) *sagéna,* ' a large sweep-net for taking a large quantity of fish at once. — R. σάττω

ἔσαγον :' Dnn. ' Dragging with it whatever comes to it : R. σάττω, as laden with fish taken :' Schleusn. Well, for in St. Matth. 13. 47 this net is spoken of ' as gathering of every kind.'

Σαγὶς, a wallet. — R. σάττω, ἔσαγον, to equip : as Σάγη.

Σάγμα, a saddle, pack-saddle ;—large cloak,—covering of a shield ; — pile 'of arms.— R. σάττω, σέσσαγμαι.

Σάγος, a coarse cloak. ' Certainly akin to Σάγη, Σάγμα :' Ldd.

Σάθη, = πέος. Quidni à σάω, ἐσάθην, σαίνω, ut Σάκος, Σάλος, &c.? Simpl. à motu: æquè ac Penis simplic. à Pendendo, secundùm Forcellini.

Σαθρὸς the same as Σαπρός.—' Ernesti from σήθω, [ἔσαθον: as Dr. Major, ' full of chinks like a sieve':] Riemer from σάω, [ἐσάθην,] σείω :' Dnn. Shaky, ' tottering to decay', says Goldsmith.

Σαίνω, to wag the tail, fawn.—Allied to Σείω, to shake, through Σάω, (as †Βάω, Βαίνω,) found in the sense of shaking through a sieve, sifting. So Σαλος, *salum*, is the tossing of the sea. And Σήθω is to shake, and to sift.

Σαίρω, to draw back the lips and show the teeth, grin at, mock; grin in mockery. — Perh. from the sibilant letter Σ, as Ernesti observes that Σαίρω implies

147

'that particular conformation of the mouth whence that *Sibilus* HISS proceeds which Hermogenes had in view'.

Σαίρω, to sweep, clean. — 'R. σάω, to move about :' Lenn. As Ψάω, Ψαίρω, to rub : and indeed Σαίρω may be short for Ψαίρω. As Σέχω for Ψέχω.

Σακάδιον, 'a stringed instrument named from the musician *Sacadas* :' Ldd.

Σάκανδρος, 'ἡ σάκος, σάκκος, barba, et ἀνὴρ ἀνδρός : vox Conica pro τὰ αἰδοῖα γυναικεῖα :' Ldd.

Σακκέω, to strain through a σάκκος cloth, *sack* or bag. (2) 'Hebr. *tzek*, to press out :' Wr.

Σάκκος, Σάκος, 'a coarse cloth of hair, *sack-cloth* ;— anything made of this cloth, a *sack*, bag : — sieve, strainer ;— coarse garment ; — also, a coarse beard, like rough hair-cloth :' Ldd. — Brought by Dnn. from σάττω, σέσαχα, like Σάγη, Σαγὶς, Σάγμα. So Σάντας, Σακτήρ, a sack. Κ, as φυλακή. (2) 'It is observable of the word *Sack* that it is found in all languages :' Todd.

Σάκος, a shield. — Valck. from σάω, σέσακα, prop. to shake. Homer has Σακέσ-παλος, shield-shaking. (2) R. σάω, σώζω : As preserving the body from wounds. (3) 'Hebr. *sek*, to protect :' Wr.

Σάκτας, Σακτήρ, like Σάκκος, a sack.

Σάλα, 'perturbation. R. σάλος :' Dnn.

Σαλαγέω, Σαλάσσω, (as Παταγέω and Πατάσσω,) Σαλεύω, to shake, roll as a ship in the σάλος.

Σαλοῖς, a cry of Σάλα, distress.

Σαλάκων, one who rolls about in his gait and walk, swaggers, and so Σαλεύω is to swagger. See Σαλαγέω.

Σαλμύθη, 'aperture, window to afford issue to smoke :' Ldd. Thought by Hesych. to be †Σελάμθη from σέλας and †βάω. This would mean a window for the 'light to come' in at. Thus 'φραΕὶ for φρΕσὶ, mAneo from μΕνω', &c.: (Maitt.) — Only in Lycophr. 98.

Σαλμακίδες, a name for ἑταῖραι, courtesans. — Called from *Salmacis*, who 'inhabited some Carian lake, where, on seeing Hermaphroditus swimming, she so closely embraced him that they became one body:' Forcell. (Only in the Anthology.)

Σάλος, *salum*, any tossing motion, swell *salis* of the sea, — the open sea, — sea-sickness ; — restlessness, perplexity. Also, anchorage. — R. σάω, prop. to shake. As †Ψάω, Φάλος.

Σάλπιγξ, a war-trumpet ; — the trumpeter-bird. — R. σάλος, as μέλΠω, πόρΠη. From its tremulous rolling sound.

Σάμαινα, a ship of *Samian* build.

Σάμαξ, a mat. — Made from the ΣΑΜΑΞ the flowering-rush : which perb. from σάω, σέσαμαι, to shake, as Δόναξ from δονέω. (Used only by Chionides.)

Σαμάρδακος, a mountebank, called by St. Augustin *Sarmadacus*; and so perb. from σαρμὸς, a heap of sweepings, from σαίρω, but used also for a heap of earth, whereby it would answer to Mountebank. (Rare.)

Σάμβαλον, Æol. for Σάνδαλον.

ΣΑΜΒΥΚΗ, a triangular stringed instrument. Also

148

a warlike engine, of like form. — 'Chald. *sabbeca* :' Mrt. 'And Hebr.:' Wr.

Σαμπῖ, a numeral for 900; being in the form of a σὰν or Ξ, (which was formerly C turned round,) covering a πῖ or Π : Thus ϡ. This was formerly one of the letters and came after Ω, which marking 800, this letter marked 900. This ΣΑΝ is Hebr. *Sin*.

Σαμφόρας, a horse branded with the σὰν : φέρω. — Above.

Σάνδαλον, a *sandal*. — 'R. σανὶς, σανίδος, σανίδαλον, a board, plank:' Hemst. (2) 'The Syrian *sandal*': Mrt.

ΣΑΝΔΑΡΑΚΗ, *sandarach*, a red sulphuret of arsenic — Q. ?

Σάνδυξ, a bright red color, prepared, says Pliny, from the Σανδαράκη ; but it is 'the juice of a plant called ΣΑΝΑΥΣ :' Dnn.

Σανὶς, ίδος, a board, plank, tablet. — The Etym. M. well for ταυὶς, as Σὺ, Τὺ ; Σήμερον, Τήμερον ; Σῆτες, Τῆτες ; Σαργάνη, Ταργάνη ; Σηλία, Τηλία. R. ταίνω, ταινύω : Stretched out.

Σάννας, a fool. — 'R. σάω, σαίνω, σανῶ, from his gesticulations :' Scheide. See Σαννίον. The Lat. *sanna* is a scoff. Observe βλέΝΝα. (2) Our *zany*. 'The barbarous Greek Τζαννὸς, a fool :' Todd.

Σαννίον, a tail. — R. σαίνω, σανῶ, to wag the tail.

Σάος, Σάος, Σῶος, Σῶς, safe, unharmed. — Dnn. well allies it to Ζάω, Ζοὸς, Ζωὸς, alive : 'safe and sound.'

Σαπρὸς, rotten, putrid. — R. σήπω, σαπῶ, to rot.

ΣΑΠΦΕΙΡΟΣ, the *sapphire*. — 'The Hebr. *sappir* :' Mrt.

ΣΑΠΩΝ, *soap*. — 'Sax. *sape*, D. *zeep*, G. *seife* :' Wbst. 'Of Celtic or German origin :' Schneid. *Sapo* Lat.

ΣΑΡΑΒΑΛΛΑ, -βαρα, -πάραι, loose *Persian* trowsers. Dan. 3. 21. So ΣΑΡΑΠΙΣ is a *Persian* robe.

Σαργάνη, the same as Ταργάνη.

Σαρδάνιος, Σαρδόνιος, Σαρδωνικὸς, said of a horrid grin. — R. σαίρω, σαρῶ, σάρδην, (like Ἄρδην,) to grin. (2) From a plant of Σαρδὼ *Sardinia* which was said to screw up the face. 'Sardois amarior herbis,' Virg.

Σαρδίνη, 'a species of anchovy, the Fr. *sardine*, found abundantly near *Sardinia* :' Ldd.

Σάρδιον, the *Sardine* or *Sardian* stone. — 'Prob. as having been orig. brought into Greece from *Sardinia* :' Dnn.

Σαρδόνια, occurring only in Xen. Cyr. 6. 9, 'balls annexed to the extremity of a (hunting) net to buoy it up,' Jones : 'edges raising a net up,' Leunclav. — Perhaps for †ἀρδόνια, from ἄρδην, lifted up, aloft, whence *arduus*. Σ, as in Σαυκὸς, Σαυσαρός.

Σαρδόνυξ, the *sardonyx* : 'a species of the *onyx* Ὄνυξ found chiefly in *Sardinia* :' Dnn.

Σαρδὼ, 'a precious stone, prob. = σάρδιον or σαρδόνυξ :' Ldd.

ΣΑΡΙΣΣΑ, a Macedonian spear. 'Macedoniáque *sarissâ* :' Ov. Yet Sturz says it is a Persian or Median spear, and from Hebr. *saris*.

Σαρκάζω, to tear σάρκα flesh from the bones ; to show the teeth as dogs do when tearing flesh : to sneer at.

Σαρμός, sweepings.— R. σαίρω, σέσαρμαι.

Σάρξ, σαρκὸς, flesh.—As the Æolians and Dorians said σΤρκα, σΤρκας, &c. (Maitt.), so σὰρξ for σὺρξ from σύρω, σέσυρκα : What has been, or can be, drawn off from the body. Compare Σισύρα. (2) 'R. (σαίρω,) σαρόω, to scrape, polish. Thus the Jews called flesh ' à nitore rasili '. Hesych.: Σάρματα: καλλύσματα :' Valck.

Σάρος, a broom to sweep with : — sweepings. — R. σαίρω, σαρῶ.

Σαρωνίδες, oaks with gaps from age.— R. σαίρω, σαρῶ, to open the mouth : Dnn.

ΣΑΤΑΝΑΣ, Satan, N. T.—'From Hebr. satan, adversari :' Mrt.

Σατίνη, a war-chariot.—'Usu. deriv. from σάσαι, Paphian for καθίσαι (to sit) :' Ldd. and Dnn. Then for Σασίνη, as Σήμερον, Τήμερον. (2) ' R. σάττω, onero. As Waggon, Wain, from Weigh, Weight :' Grogan. ' Weigh from Sax. wag, weg, wagan :' Wbst.

ΣΑΤΟΝ, a Jewish measure of wheat, N. T. —' From the Syrian :' Schleusn.

ΣΑΤΡΑΠΗΣ, a Persian satrap. ' A Persian word :' Mrt.

Σάττω, to stuff, pack, load : — to equip, accoutre, harness. — ' Affinity may be traced to "Αδην or "Αδην, and Lat. satio, satis :' Schneid. Nearer to "Αται or "Α- ται, whence "Α-ατος, in-satiable. Σ, as in Σειρά, and Σέλας from "Ελη. (2) R. σάω, σείω, to shake. As Luk. 6. 38 : ' Good measure pressed down and shaken together (σεσαλευμένον) and running over.' Schleusn. explains σεσ., ' concutiendo REPLETUM.' Note κρὰΤΤΩ.

Σατυρίασις, ' a disease in which the bones near the temples are elongated, so as to be like Satyrs' horns;— priapism :' Ldd. — From

Σάτυρος, a Satyr, a wanton Sylvan god;—a dramatic piece in which they appear. — For Σάθυρος from σάθη. So Becm. from ' σάθυ, salacitas.'

Σαυκὸς, dry. — ' Σ for the aspirate from αὔω, αὖω, (αὖκα,) to dry :' Dnn.

Σαυκρὸς, the same as

Σαῦλος, conceited, affected. — Allied to Σαλάκων, swaggering. ' Prob. from σάλος, a tossing :' Dnn. As Jacto, i. e. to throw oneself about.

Σαυνίον, a javelin. — Supposed to come from its use by the Samnians, Sannians or Saunians. (2) R. σάω, to shake. Compare Ἐγχέσπαλος.

Σαυνὸς, the same as Σαῦλος: from σάω, σάλος.

Σαύρα, a twisted-finger case: long as a ΣΑΤΡΑ, lizard. ' A lizard lean and long.'

Σαυρωτὴρ. from σάος, safe: ' An iron sock to make the point of the spear safe and unhurt :' Portus. (2) From Σαῦρα above.

Σαυσαρὸς, dry, parched. — R. αὔω or αὖω, αὔσω, ' Σ prefixed,' Ldd. See Σαυκός.

Σαφὴς, certain, manifest. — As †Ξίω, Ξίφος, and

149

Ψάω, Ψῆφος, Ψαφαρὸς, so Σαφὴς from σάω, σείω, σήθω, to sift, as Certus, certain, from Cerno, to sift. ' Si te diligenter ex-cusseris', Seneca : i. e. from Quatio. We say, To sift it to the bottom. So to Dis-cuss a matter, from Quatio, is to sift it out.

ΣΑΩ, ΣΕΙΩ, †ΣΙΩ, to shake, allied to †ΣΥΩ, †ΣΟΩ, ΣΕΥΩ, which Ewing explains ' to shake, move rapidly, rush'. All primitive words. Mrt. from ' Hebr. sua, to move, agitate.' Some bring the sense of ' making to move fast' from the sound σσσσ used in urging animals on.

†Σβέω, Σβεννύω, -ὐμι, to quench, put out, dry up, drain. — Allied to Βύω, to stop up, through †Βέω, †σβέω. And to Μύω, †Πύω in Πύλη, †Πίω in Πιέζω, &c. Σ, as Σμικρός.

Σέβομαι, ' to revere, respect, worship, to be awe-struck or abashed. Σέβω [i. e. σέFω,] and Σεὸω and Σείω, to agitate, terrify, are plainly akin in form and sense:' Dnn. and Lenn. Σέβω as Φίβω. (2) ' Hebr. tsebi, glory :' Wr.

Σειρά, a cord, rope, chain. — Allied to Lat. sero, to join, and to εἴρω or εἵρω, as Ἑξ, Sex, and as Σέλας from Ἑλη. So nearly all.

Σειρὴν, a Siren, hence used for a fascinating woman, and any fascination. — Usu. derived from σειρά, a band, and so a chain: Enchaining, captivating. — Or, like σειρά, from εἴρω, to weave; thus ὑφαίνω δόλους is used. (2) ' Hebr. seer, to sing :' Wr.

Σείριος, Sirius, the dog-star: from

Σειρὸς, hot.—' Suid. from ΣΕΙΡ, the sun. Or from Σέρος, heat: Θ and Σ interchanged, [as loveΣ, loveTH] :' Dnn. (2) For †ζειρὸς, †ζεερὸς, from ζέω, to be hot. As Zidon, Sidon; Zion, Sion; Ζιβύνη, Σιβύνη. (3) ' Hebr. serak, to shine :' Wr.

Σεισμὸς, an earthquake, and

Σεῖστρον, sistrum, a clapper: from

Σείω: in ΣΑΩ.

Σελαγέω, to enlighten. — R. σέλας, formed as Χαλαγέω.

Σέλας, splendor. — As Ἑξ, Sex, so Σέλας from ἕλη, heat or light of the ἥλιος sun. So Σειρά.

Σελάχη plur., fish with cartilages for bones. — Aristotle from σέλας, ' as most fishes of this kind emit a phosphorescent light.' Galen says they glitter at night.

Σελευκὶς, ' a garment from Seleucia in Syria: — a drinking-cup from the same place :' Ldd.

Σελήνη, the moon: R. σέλας.

Σελήνιον, bald crown of the head, appearing round and shiny like the σελήνη moon.

Σεληνίτης, the selenite or moon stone: σελήνη.

Σελὶς, ' the void space between lines in writing. Some from σέλας, brightness, with much probability. — Also, the void space between benches of rowers or at a theatre: — the space between the paragraphs in writing, and the two columns of a page; — a page:' Dnn.

Σελλοὶ, priests of the oracle of Dodona.—' No doubt Ἕλλην is from Ἕλλος whence was Ἑλλὰς a city built by *Helle*. Now Ἕλλος and Σίλλοι were the same word, as Ἕλη and Σίλας, Ἕξ and Sex. The *Helli* then or *Selli* were a part or shoot of the Pelasgi in ancient *Hellas*, dwelling about Dodōna and Achelōus;' Hemsterh.

Σέλμα, bench for rowing :—any bench or seat :—long platform or standing-place behind parapets for the defenders of walls, and in the upper part of a ship as a deck. Said also of logs of building-timber: from the length, as of benches. — 'Σελὶς and Σέλμα have a close affinity:' Dnn.

ΣΕΜΙΔΑΛΙΣ, *simila*, *similāgo*, the finest wheat-flour. — 'From the Punic *semid*:' Voss.

Σεμνὸς, venerable, august. — R. σέβω, σέσεμμαι, σεσεμμένος. And

Σεπτὸς, as σεμνός. — R. σέσεπται.

Σεύω, pf. p. ἔσσυμαι, to put in quick motion, set on, drive: passive, rush on, speed. — Allied to Σείω, to shake. See ΣΑΩ. (2) 'From the sound σευσυ made in urging on dogs:' Scheide.

Σήθω, to sift : R. σάω, ἐσήθην.

Σηκὶς, a porteress, housekeeper. — Attendant on a Σηκός.

Σηκὸς, a pen, fold, stable;—chapel, shrine, dwelling, tomb, sepulchre—R.†σέω, †σέσηκα, σείω, σεύω, to drive: A place to which cattle are driven. (2) R. σάω, σώζω. (3) 'Hebr. *sag*, to hedge: Chald. *sach*, to cover:' Mrt.

Σηκὸς, from the sense of anything interior, was used for the hollow trunk of a tree, spec. the hollow trunk of an old olive-tree. — Above.

Σηκὸς, a weight. — R. σάττω, σέσαχα, 'to press down'; (Dnn.) K, as φυλακή.

Σηκόω, to weigh, balance. — Above.

Σηλία, Τηλία, 'any flat board or tray with a raised rim or edge; — a stand on which flour, &c. was set out for sale; — a gaming-table; — a stage whereon gamecocks were set to fight; — a chimney-board:' Ldd. These senses point to Τηλία as allied to Τῆλε, marking extension: An extended surface, one stretched out. — Dnn. thinks Σηλία the original, as 'a sieve, a baker's trough, the wooden circumference of a sieve, a chest for containing corn', and from σάω, σήθω, to sift: †σαέλη, †σήλη, σηλία.

Σῆμα, Σημεῖον, a signal, sign, token, mark, seal;—gravestone, tomb, barrow, sepulchre.—R. σάω, σέσημαι, orig. to shake, as Σείω. 'Shake the hand that they may go:' Is. 13. 2. 'Beckoning (κατα-σείσας) to them with the hand to hold their peace:' Acts 12. 17. 'Her husband she espies, Shaking his hand . . . : She took the sign, and shook her hand again:' Dryden. (2) Ldd. for Σῆμα, allied to Σησαίατο for Σεάομαι, to see; 'That by which something is seen.' So Σημὼν is Lacon. for Θημών. And our loveS, loveTH. (3) 'Chald. *simmen*, signāre:' Mrt.

Σημαίνω, to give a σῆμα sign, indicate.

Σήμερον, Σῆτες, = Τήμερον, Τῆτες.

Σήπω, to corrupt, putrify. — 'Allied to Σαπρὸς, perhaps to Σαθρὸς:' Dnn. See Σαθρός. Σήπω is allied to

150

σάω, (σαθρὸς,) as Θήπω to Θάω, Θάομαι. (2) 'Hebr. *saph*, to be finished, consumed. Chald. *seebaz*, putridity:' Mrt. 'Hebr. *sep*, to be hollow:' Wr.

Σὴρ, a silk-worm; from the *Seres*, an Asiatic nation who prepared silk, and introduced it into Greece. Thus, 'Serica vestis,' 'Serica toga.'

Σήραγξ, cleft, rent, cave. — R. σαίρω, ἔσηρα, to open the mouth.

Σὴς, g. σητὸς and σεὸς, a moth :—also a book-worm. —R. †σέω, σείω, σεύω, 'to agitate,' i.e. to 'fret'; this explained by Dr. J., 'to agitate violently by external action.' 'A moth *fretting* a garment.' See Σητάω. (2) Hebr. *sas*, tinea.

Σητάνειος, said of corn, some say 'sifted,' from σήθω, σέσηται, to sift. Others 'of this year,' from σῆτες.

Σητάω, to eat, fret, said σητῶν of moths.

Σῆτες : in Τῆτες.

Σὴψ, g. σητὸς, a serpent whose bite causes putrefaction. — R. σήπω.

Σθένω, to have strength or power, to be able. — As †Γένω and Γάω, Μένω and †Μάω, †Φένω and †Φάω, so Σθένω is deduced by Mrt. from †στάω, to stand, and by Lenn. from Θέω, to run; Σ in the latter as in Σμικρός. With the deriv. from στάω compare 'Α-στηνος ' from Ἵστημι', (Dnn.). Strength then as shown by standing or by running: but better than these as shown by striking, (fighting, boxing, &c.) from Θένω, whence the part of the hand by which we strike is called Θέναρ.

Σιᾱγὼν, the jaw-bone.—As Wachter derives Mentum the chin from Movimentum, so from σίω == σείω, to move, may be Σιᾱγών. Compare Πάγων and Θιαγών. And

Σίαλον, spittle. — 'R. [σίω,] σείω: because it moves to and fro in the mouth:' Schrevel., Lenn., and Mrt. — But Ldd. allies Σίαλον to Ὕαλος, glass, as Σέλας from Ἕλη.

Σίαλος, a fat hog;—fat, grease. Σίαλος and Σίαλον agree in the notion of shining or glistening. Σίαλος is 'also a blockhead: compare Pinguis Minerva, Pingue ingenium: while others explain it a driveller, from σιαλὸς spittle:' Dnn. See above.

Σίδλωμα, and Σιγάλωμα, 'an instrument of smoothing or polishing; — the polished metal rim of a shield:' Ldd. — Allied to Σιγαλόεις, Σίαλον and Σίαλος.

Σίβυλλα, a *Sibyl*.— 'Acc. to the old deriv., from Διὸς βόλλα (or βύλλα), Dor. of Διὸς βουλή: That tells the will of Jupiter:' Ldd. and Dnn.

Σιβύνη, 'from σῦς, συός, a spear for killing boars, a hunting spear: also Σιβύνη:' Ewing. For συβίνη, as μΙστΥλη and μΤστΙλη, μΙττλος and μΤτλος. Thus: συὸς, συβίνη, συβίνη.

Σιγαλόεις, thought by Valck. to be σιφαλόεις, foaming σιάλῳ with spittle: 'Hence, as soft things are called Δροσόεντα as like dew, so soft tender garments are Σιγαλόεντα.'—Ldd. deduces it from σίαλος, grease: 'Shining, with the gloss on, fresh;—fat and oily.' (2) R. σιγή. 'Producing silent admiration by its excellence:' Damm.

Σιγή, silence. — R. σίζω, σέσῖγα, to hush.

Σίγλος, the same as Σίκλος.

Σίγμα, the letter S: the hissing letter, as below. (2) ‘ Hebr. sin, or rather samech:’ Dahler.

Σιγμός, a hissing. — R. σίζω, σέσιγμαι.

Σιγύνης, ‘ seemingly a dialectic form of Σιθύνη:’ Ldd. So Βάλανος and Γάλανος.

Σίδηρος, iron, steel. —‘ R. σίζω, ἴσιδον: from the hissing sound made by hot iron dipped in water:’ Damm. And well, for ″Ὡς τοῦ ΣΙΖ' ὀφθαλμὸς are the words of Homer's simile the eye of Polyphemus cracking, to the effects ΣΙΔΗΡΟΣ of iron tempered in the fire: Od. 9. 393, 4. See Σίζω.

Σίζω, to hiss, making the sound σσσσ, as hot iron plunged in water.

Σίζω, to say Hush hush! — from the sound S, or rather SH, just as we pronounce SHugar for Sugar. Ldd. represents Σοῦ Σοῦ by SHoo ! SHoo ! And see Σίττα.

Σικελίζω, to imitate the Sicilians.

ΣΙΚΕΡΑ, sicera, old Fr. cisere, whence ciere, softly cidre, our cider: prop. strong drink. Σίκερα, Luk. 1. 15, is translated by Wicliffe ‘ sydyr.’—‘ The Hebrew in Greek letters :’ Valck.

Σίκιννις, a dance of Satyrs ‘ named from its inventor Sicinnis, a nymph of Cybele :’ Ldd. (2) Forcell. from σείω, σέσεικα, or σίω, σέσικα, from the immodest movements in it.

ΣΙΚΛΟΣ, a shekel, a coin and a measure. ‘ Hebr. SKL :’ Ewing.

Σικύα, a gourd ; a cupping-glass in its form.— From ΣΙΚΤΟΣ, a cucumber.

Σικυωνία, women's shoes, esp. made at Sicyon in Achaia.

ΣΙΚΧΟΣ, loathing food, squeamish, morose ; Σικχαίνομαι, am disgusted at, ‘ am sick at,’ Blomf. So Ldd. compares sick. ‘ D. sick, Sw. siuk, Icel. syke :’ Wbst. ‘ In Chaucer seke :’ Todd. ‘ The Greek word does not occur earlier than Callim.:’ Lobeck. ‘ Hebr. tzuk, to press, straiten’: Wr.

Σιληνὸς, Silēnus : in Σίλλος.

Σιληπορδέω, ‘ oppēdo alicui, treat one with rudeness. — R. πέρδω, and perh. the Dorians had a form σιλὸς for σίλλος :’ Ldd.

ΣΙΛΙΓΝΙΣ, fine wheaten flour.—‘ From the Lat. siligo, inis :’ Schrevel.

Σίλλος, ‘ gibe, mockery, satirical poem, sillus. Gen. derived from ἴλλω, ἴλλος, Σ added : and so a rolling of the eyes in mockery, as Σιλλόω. — Schneid. says, one who has a cocked nose, flattened towards the root, of the form attributed to Silēnus and the Satyrs, such being a mark of mockery: allied to Σιμός :’ Dnn.

Σιλόδουροι, ‘ devoted friends or retainers, the Lat. soldurii, Cæsar : a Celtic word :’ Dnn. Our word Soldiers, from Solidus, the pay of the Solidarii. And Solidus from ὅλος, Sŏlus, as Vivus, Vividus.

Σίμβλος, bee-hive. — R. σιμαί, bees, as snub-nosed, from σιμός : σίμλος, σίμβλος, as μεσημβρία.

151

Σιμὸς, flat- or snub-nosed, bent in or down, hollow, uphill. And Simia, an ape.—Well supposed by Scheide to be for ϯἱμὸς, (See ϯμᾶς,) as Σέλας from ″Ελη : R. ἵζομαι, ϯμαι, to sink : Depressed.

Σινάμωρος, mischievous. — All from σίνομαι. Some add μωρός : Madly injurious. Some say μόρος.

ΣΙΝΔΩΝ, ‘ fine Indian cloth : prob. from ᾽Ινδὸς. Sind :’ Ldd.—‘ The Coptic tchentoo :’ Class. Journ. 9. 156.—‘ Hebr. seden, a loose garment :’ Wr.

Σινίον, a sieve. — R. σίω, σείω, to shake, as σάω and σήθω are to sift.

Σίνομαι, to ravage, plunder, injure, lacerate, wound. — As Σώχω for Ψώχω, so Σίνομαι for Ψίνομαι, used not in its accepted sense, but as derived from ψίω, ‘ to bruise, break, diminish', (Dnn.) (2) Lenn. from σίω, σείω, quatio, con-cutio, ex-cutio; per-cutio. N, as ϯπίω, πίΝω. (3) R. ϯἰῶ, ἵημι, to hit, smite : then ϯσίω, as ″Ελη, Σέλας. N, as πίΝω. (4) ‘ Chald. sena, to hate :’ Mrt. and Becm.

Σινωπίζομαι, to be utterly dissolute, like the courtesan Sinōpe.

Σινωπικὴ, red ochre brought from Sinōpe in Pontus. Σιδὶ, Lacon. for Θεός. As loveTH, loveS.

Σιπαλὸς, (as χθαμαΛΟΣ,) Σιφλὸς, deformed, maimed, purblind. — With Σ prefix as in Σίλλος, Σειρά, from ἵπτω, ἴσον, to injure, which Σιφλόω means.

ΣΙΠΑΡΟΣ, the fore-sail, in Arrian.— Perh. from the Latin Supparum, Suparum, Siparum. ‘ Suppara veldrum': Lucan. Scheide suggests ὑπέρ: the Greek ῾Υπέρα. But the A ?

Σιπύη, a coffer for keeping meal, flour, or bread ; — a bag, as also Σιπύς.—‘ Akin to Σίββα, and ᾽Ιπύα omitting Σ :’ Dnn. (2) Suid. for ϯσιθύνη, ϯσιτο-βύη. R. σῖτον, βύω : Full of flour. As ᾽Αμφι-φορεὺς, ᾽Αμφορεύς : Idolo-latry, Idolatry. Better from obs. ϯνύω, whence Πύλη, Πυκάζω, Πυκνός.

Σίραιον, new wine boiled down. — Allied to ϯΣιρὸς, Σειρὸς, hot, of which the form Σιριάω occurs according to some. Even Dnn. says : ‘ Σειριάσις or Σιριάσις'. So σκΕΙρων and σκΙρων.

Σιρομάστης, a pit-searcher, a probe with which tax-gatherers searched corn-pits :— hence a barbed lance.— R. σιρὸς, μάομαι, whence Μάσμα, &c.

Σιρὸς, a pit for σῖτος corn.—For ϯΣιτερὸς from σῖτος or σῖτον. As Φόβος, Φοβερός ; Φλογὸς, Φλογερός. So that ϯΣιτερὸς is prop. an adjective.

Σισύρα, Σίσυρνα, a shaggy goat-skin.—‘ The Schol. at Aves 122 says it is prop. a akin with the hair on. R. σύρω, [σύρσω] :’ Dnn. By redupl. as ΑΙλαίομαι : Torn off. (2) ‘ Hebr. sear, pilus :’ Mrt.

Σιτεύω, to feed with σῖτος.

Σῖτος, wheat, corn, food.— R. σίω, σείω, to shake, sift. ‘ Satan hath desired to have you, τοῦ σινιάσαι that he might sift you as σῖτον wheat :’ N. T.

Σίττα, Σίττε, Ψίττα, a shepherd's or drover's cry, from the sound σιτ, ψιτ, by Ldd. represented as ‘ st ! sht !’ (2) ‘ Hebr. soot, to instigate :’ Wr.

Σίττη, a kind of wood-pecker.—Prob. from the sound σίτ, much as above.

Σιττύβη, a leathern garment : allied by Ldd. and Dnn. to Σιούρα. Σιτύρα, Τιτύρα, (as Σὺ, Τύ,) whence Τίτγρυς.

Σιφαῖος in Lucian, thought by Dnn. = σιπναῖος from σιπύη, a meal-jar : ' of fine flour.'

Σιφλὸς, maimed, &c. : in Σιπαλός.

Σιφλὸς, Σιφνὸς, hollow, empty, hungry. — Mrt. from ' Hebr. sapha, DEFICERE.' And Dnn. makes Σιφλὸς prim. to mean DEFECTIVE, which agrees with this. But it may mean prim. ' injured', and so ' defective' : see Σιφλὸς in Σιπαλός.

Σίφων, a reed, tube, pipe, siphon.—Allied by Ldd. to Σιφλὸς, Σιφνὸς, hollow. Perhaps †Σίφος existed. Hesych. explains ἐκ-σιφωνισθείη by ἐκ-κενωθείη.

Σιωπάω, to be silent.—Like Σιζω, Σιγάω, imitative of a hushing sound. An extended form, much as Εἰλυφάω, Θεραπεύω, 'Ερωτάω. Some may add ὠψ, ὠπός.

Σκάζω, to limp.—'Akin is Σκαίρω :' Dnn.

Σκαιὸς, sca Vus, on the left, unlucky, oblique, awkward. —' Akin to Σκάζω :' Dnn. The left, the limping hand, Eustath. But Σκαιὸς is also oblique, not direct, and tallies with our word Right, prop. direct, but which sim. took the sense NOT LEFT (Dr. Johnson).—Hemsterh. supposes a word †Σκάω. So

Σκαίρω, to skip, frisk about.—' Σκαίρω and Σκάζω from †σκάω, †κάω, †χάω, caVo, χαίνω, χάσμα : To curve, incline, bend the body, so as 1. to limp, 2. to frisk about :' Lenn. Σ, as Σμικρός. (2) Skirr in Shaksp.

Σκαλαθύρω, to rake, rake up, as Σκάλλω ; — explore subtlely or over-nicely, as Rake in Johnson: '.To search with eager and vehement diligence,' as Swift : ' The statesman rakes the town to find a plot.'

Σκαλεύω, to stir up, hoe, poke a fire. — R. σκάλλω.

Σκαληνὸς, like ΣΚΑζων, limping ;—uneven, unequal, odd in number. See Σκαμβός.

Σκάλλω, to scratch, scrape, rake, grub, hoe : scalpo, scabo.—As Σ in Σμικρὸς, and as Ψάω, Ψάλλω, so Lenn. deduces Σκάλλω from †κάω, χάω, caVo, χάσμα : To make a gap or hollow. And so Dnn. allies Σκάπτω to Σκάλλω and to Lat. caVo. (2) Mrt. from κέλλω, to move. (3) ' R. ξέω, i.e. κσέω or σκέω, to scrape :' Greg. So Dnn. allies it to Ξέω, Ξαίνω.

Σκαλμή, ' a knife, sword : said to be a foreign word, but at all events connected with Σκάλλω :' Ldd.

Σκαλμὸς, a thowl, one of two sticks or pins driven into the edge of a boat for the oar. — R. σκάλλω, to grub into.

Σκάλοψ, a mole : i.e. the grubber: σκάλλω.

Σκαμβὸς, crooked, bent, bent asunder, of the legs.— Allied to Σκάζων, Σκαληνὸς. Or to †Γαμφὸς, Καμπτός.

Σκάμμα, a trench, pit.— R. σκάπτω, ἔσκαμμαι.

Σκανδάληθρον, the stick in a trap, the trap-string. So Σκάνδαλον is a snare laid for an enemy: hence a stumbling-block, which proves a scandal or offence by

152

which another falls.—R. σκάζω, ἔσκαδον. N, as in χαΝδάνω. Making halt or maimed.

Σκαπάνη, a spade, shovel : σκάπτω.

Σκάπετος, a trench, pit, as Σκάμμα, from

Σκάπτω, to dig, hoe, trench. —Allied to Σκάλλω, scabo, scalpo. (2) Our scoop.

Σκαρδαμύσσω, to blink, wink. — R. σκαίρω, σκάρδην, to spring up, and, says Ldd. it is difficult not to connect –μύσσω with μύω.

Σκαρίζω, like Σκαίρω, ἀρῶ.

Σκάριφος, a pencil, pen, straw, reed, κάρφος. Σκαρίφῶ, †σκριφῶ, scribo. Σκαριφάομαι, scarifico, scarify, scratch an outline, &c.— Allied to Χαράσσω ; Σ, as Σμικρός. ' A form of, or from Κάρφος :' Hemst.

Σκατὸς, gen. of Σκώρ.

Σκάφη, anything dug or scooped out, a trench ; — a boat, scapha, skiff ;—a trough, tub, cradle. — R. σκάπτω, ἔσκαφα.

Σκάφιον, a little Σκάφη ;—any hollow vessel, a night-stool ;— a concave mirror ;—' cutting of hair so as to leave only that on the crown, which then looked like a bowl ; — the crown :' Ldd.

†Σκεθδω : in Κεθδζω.

Σκεθρὸς, ' tight, exact, careful : from σχεθεῖν, σχεῖν, from ἔχω :' Ldd.: Held close. (2) Ξέω, Ξεθρὸς, Σκεθρὸς, as Ξίφος, Σκίφος : Planed, polished, made to the nail. (3) For †κεθρὸς = κεστὸς, cut : as Precise from Præ-cisus.—Others from ἀσκέω, or from σκέπτομαι.

Σκείρων, Σκίρων, a wind blowing from the Scironian rocks in the Isthmus of Corinth. Σκειρωνίδες πέτραι, Eurip.

Σκελέαι, leggings, long trowsers. — R. σκέλος.

Σκελετὸς, dried up, whence Skeleton.—R. σκέλλω.

Σκελὶς, haunch, ham. — Allied to σκέλος.

Σκέλλω, to dry up.—'R. κέω, καίω, to burn ;' Lenn. As Ψάω, Ψάλλω. Σ as Σμικρός. (2) R. ξέω, κσέω, σκέω, to scrape, rub, and so to dry. (3) Allied to Σκάλλω, as βδάλλω, βδΕλλα : To make hollows and furrows. (4) ' R. ΚΕΛ, (Keil,) ΣΚΕΛ (Germ. Schell in zerschellen) :' Thiersch.

Σκέλος, a leg. — ' R. σκέλλω, σκελῶ, to make dry and hard, whence Σκληρὸς, hard. — So called from the hardness of the bone :' Valck. See Κνήμη.

Σκεπανὸς, covering, covered, shaded : σκέπω. Hence a flat fish, Lat. umbra, gliding rapidly by as a shadow.

Σκέπαρνον, a carpenter's axe. — ' Perhaps from σκάπτω :' Ldd. and Dnn. As βάλλω, βΕλος. — Or for Σκήπαρνον from σκήπτω, to let fall hard upon. As κΕδνός.

Σκέπαρνον, ' from some likeness in the shape, a surgical bandage :' Ldd. Above.—Rather, from σκέπω, to protect, guard.—Also a sheep-skin: 'as if Σκέπ-αρνον :' Ldd. That is, from σκέπω, ἀρνός. Perhaps however from σκέπω only, as the last sense.

Σκέπτομαι, to look or examine carefully, consider. — ' R. σκέπω: To cover the eyes with the hand in looking at an object :' Hemsterh. (2) R. κέω, κεάζω, κεστὸς, *cœdo, cœsum, præ-cīsum* : To look at a thing ΣΚΕθρῶs accurately and *precisely*. As †Βάω, Βάπτω. Σ, as in Σμικρόs. (3) ' Hebr. *skeph*, to look:' Wr.

Σκέπω, Σκεπάζω, to cover, shelter, protect. — 'For †Κέπω, (Κῆπος,) allied to Κεύθω:' Lenn. Or σάκος, a shield, †σακέω, †σκέω, σκέπω, as †βλέω, βλέπω. Compare Σκηνή. (2) ' Heb. *sao*, to cover :' Mrt. (3) Our *keep*, Sax. *cepan*. Todd: ' A bee-hive is called a *skep* in some parts of England :' as in Norfolk.

Σκερθόλλω, to insult, abuse. — Σ as in Σμικρός. For κερθόλλω, from κέαρ cor, θόλη a throwing, like Κερ-τομέω : To hit and wound the heart. (2) R. σκὼρ, dung, βάλλω, †βολέω.

Σκεῦος, any instrument or utensil; Σκεύεα, implements, furniture, tackle, baggage, clothes, armor. Σκεύαζω, to furnish, prepare, &c. — ' Prop. α covering; allied to Κεύθω, to hide, cover. Allied to Σκέπας; perh. to Σκηνή and Σκιά:' Dnn. (2) ' R. σάκος, (σακέω,) †σκέω, then σκεῦος, a covering against the injuries of the air:' Valck. (3) ' Germ. fot-*schu* is the apparel of the foot:' Wacht. (4) ' Chald. *scheva*, to be useful:' Mrt.

Σκηνή, a tent, booth, camp, cover of a waggon, covered place or bower for representations, *scena*, theatre, stage for actors; — tent-entertainment. — ' The same origin as Σκεῦος:' Dnn. ' R. σάκος, (σακέω) †σκέω : To cover with a shield:' Valck. ' R. κέω, κεύθω :' Lenn. Σ, as Σμικρός. (2) ' Hebr. *sken*, to dwell in:' Wr.

Σκῆνος, a tent, tabernacle; — the human tabernacle, the body. — Above.

Σκηπάνιον, Σκῆπων, = σκῆπτρον.

Σκηπτὸς, a squall of wind; — thunderbolt; — any visitation or calamity. — R. σκήπτω.

Σκήπτω, to let fall on, press on, urge; — rest or lean on; — midd. prop up one's cause by excuses or pretences. Σκῆπτρον, *sceptre*, staff to lean on. — ' From †κάω, χαίνω, cavo, in curvo:' Lenn. ' From κήπτω, (κάμπτω):' Greg. These have caught the idea of the word : but evidently Σκήπτω is for Σκηρίπτω, though by a strange obliquity Σκηρίπτω is brought by all from Σκήπτω. Σκηρίπτω then, or †Κηρίπτω, seems to descend from κέρας, κορωνὸς, &c. and to have the notion of curving, bending down, or stooping on a prop or support. Thus Κυφὸς is explained by Ldd.: ' bent, bowed forwards, stooping.' Σ as Σμικρός.

Σκηρίπτω : in Σκήπτω.

Σκήψις, a pretext : σκήπτω, ψω.

Σκιὰ, a shadow, shade. — Allied to Σκηνή, Σκέπω, Σκεῦος. (2) R. κίω; As going along with an object. Σ as Σμικρός. (3) ' Hebr. *sekee*, to cover:' Wr.

Σκιάδειον, an umbrella. — R. σκιά, umbra. So Σμικρός.

Σκιαδεύς, Σκιαθίς, the fish called ' umbra' mentioned in Σκέπανός. — R. σκιά.

Σκίδνημι : in Κεδάζω.

Σκιμαλίζω, to feel with the little finger for eggs in hens; — also to hold out the middle finger to, to insult, abuse, and with ποδὶ to kick. Steph.; ' Medio digito

153

tentare an gallinæ ova conceperint, *immisso eo in podicem: adeoque eo podicem fodicare.*' — The long syllable of ΜΑΛ seems to point to μήλη, Dor. μᾶλα, a probe, and Σκιμαλίζω (as Σμικρὸs) to be for Κιμαλίζω from κίω, Lat. *cio*, κινέω, to move, and this μᾶλα: To move with a probe.

Σκιμβὸs, halt, limping, σκαμβός. — ' R. σκίμπτω :' Dnn.

Σκίμπους, a small couch, low bed. — R. σκίμπτω, to lean upon. Dnn. adds πούς: So as to rest the foot upon.

Σκίμπτω, the same as Σκήπτω. ' From it, or a different form:' Dnn. As πΛΕκω, plIco. So σκίναρ, σκίρτάω, σκινδαῖος.

Σκίμπων, Σκίπων, a staff, from σκίμπτω, as Σκῆπτρον a staff from σκήπτω.

Σκίναξ, moving, active; — a hare. — As Μίκρὸs, Σμικρὸς, so for Κίναξ, from κίνῶ to move. As Κίναθίζω.

Σκίναρ, the body. — ' Prob. akin to Σκῆνος the body :' Ldd. and Dnn. See on σκίμπτω. — Or a *moving body* : Above.

Σκινθαλεθίζω, to search narrowly, 'akin to Σκιμαλίζω in its proper sense :' Dnn. — Or rather to

Σκίνδαλμος, Σκινδαλμὸς, *scindula*, a splinter, lath, shingle: — a minute or subtle quibble. — Allied to *Scindo*, Σχίζω, ἔσχιδον. N, as χαΝδάνω.

ΣΚΙΝΔΑΨΟΣ, 'a four-stringed musical instrument: also a tree like ivy: a thing of no value:' Dnn. The Schol. on Apol. Rh. says the tree grew at Nysa in *India*.

Σκίπων, the same as Σκίμπων.

Σκίραφος, a dice-box; — trickery. ' Some from σκῖρος, in the sense of a die:' Dnn.: and this from σκῖρος, 'a chip or fragment of marble,' Dnn, or from the general notion of any hard matter. See Σκῖρος. Petronius speaks of 'crystal dice.' — Others from an abandoned neighbourhood of gamblers and prostitutes at Athens, called τὸ ΣΚΙΡΟΝ.

Σκιρῖται, ' the *Scirites*, a distinguished division of the Spartan army: orig. named from the Arcadian town Σκῖρος :' Ldd.

Σκῖρον, ' like ΣΚΙάδιον, a white parasol borne by the priestesses in a festival of Minerva Σκιρὰs, which was thence called τὰ Σκιροφόρια, giving name to the month. Σκιραφορίών. — Others from Σκῖρος, a Salaminian seer who built a temple to Minerva under this name: and a promontory of Attica was called Σκιράδιον :' Ldd.

Σκῖρον, the hard rind of cheese. — From

Σκῖρος, ' gypsum, stucco; — any hard coat or covering, a tumor, *scirrhus*. The form Σκίρρος arose from ignorance:' Ldd. — Dnn. allies it to Σκηρὸs, Ξηρὸs, dry. See σκίμπτω.

Σκιρτάω, like Σκαίρω, ἔσκαρται, to skip, spring, leap. ' Only another form of Σκαίρω:' Dnn. As Σκεδάω, Σκιδνάω; Πετάω, Πιτνάω. (2) Shaksp. has '*SKIRR* the country round.'

Σκίταλοι, wanton deities, patrons of licentiousness.

X

Toup hither refers *skittish.* Todd: ' *Skit,* a light wanton woman; *skittish,* wanton.'— R. κίω, κέκιται, *citus,* fast, just like "Ιτης 'Ιταμὸς, headlong, from †'Ιω, Εἶμι, to go. Σ, as Σμικρός. The quantity of the A is variously represented.

Σκίφος, for Εἶφος, a sword.

†Σκλέω, Σκλῆμι, the same as Σκέλλω.

Σκληρός, hard, rigid, cruel.—Above.

Σκληφρός, 'Att. for Σκληρός: contr. for Σκελιφρὸς, thin :' Ldd. Explained by Timæus 'dry and gone by,' applying it to 'one older in age, but younger in look.' See above.

Σκνιπαῖος, like Κνεφαῖος, in the dark. See on σκιμβός.

Σκνίπτω, to nip, pinch; met. to be pinching or niggardly: and Σκνιφὸς, like Κνιπὸς, stingy. And

Σκνίψ, the same as Κνίψ.

Σκόλιον, 'neut. from Σκολιός: i. e. μέλος, a banquet-song, sung to the lyre by the guests one after the other. Most derive it from the irregular zig-zag way it went round the table, each guest who sung holding a myrtle-branch, which he passed on to any one he pleased :' Ldd. — From

Σκολιὸς, crooked, distorted, perverse; — depraved, knavish. — R. σκέλλω, ἔσκολα: Dried up, rough, uneven. So Valck. Similarly Greg. from σκελὸς, distorted, or σκελλὸς as in Hesych. Properly, warped. (2) 'Hebr. *sebel,* to pervert :' Wr.

Σκόλοψ, οπος, anything pointed, esp. a pale, stake;— dart; — splinter, thorn. — Allied to Σκῶλος.

Σκόλυθρος, a low three-legged stool; adj. low, mean, shabby :—prop. docked, as allied to Σκολύπτω.

Σκόλυμος, 'an eatable kind of thistle, prob. a kind of artichoke. — Akin to Σκόλοψ, Σκόλοπος :' Ldd.

Σκολύπτω, for Κολύπτω, as Σμικρὸς, 'from κόλος, like Κολούω, to dock, crop, lop : — peel, strip :' Ldd.

Σκόπελος, an eminence whence is a view; — rock, *scopulus.* — From

Σκοπέω, ≈ σκέπτομαι.

Σκοπὸς, an observer, scout;—mark at which we look or aim, *scope,* object or purpose.—Above.

Σκορακίζω, to reject: i. e. send to the κόρακας crows. Σ, as in Σμικρός.

Σκορδίνάομαι, to stretch and yawn, to feel heavy and sick. — Σ added as in Σμικρός; †Κορδινάομαι from κόρυς the head, and δονέω or δίνέω: To have the head whirling. Compare Κραιπάλη. (2) From excessive use of

Σκόροδον, Σκόρδον, garlic. — 'R. σκὼρ, dung, ὄζω, [ὄδον, ὄδα,] from its strong smell :' Ewing. Compare the Latin Nas-turtium, i. e. Nasi-tortium.

Σκορπίζω, to scatter, disperse. — Mrt. from σκαίρω, σκαρῶ, facio saltre, facio dis-silire, to make to spring asunder. — as πόρος, πορΠΑΩ. — But perhaps there was a transposition thus : Σπορὰς, dispersed, †σποράζω, †ἐσπόρακα, †σποαρκίζω, †σπορκίζω, then σκορπίζω, as Σφάγανον, Φάσγανον; ἐκΠΛΑγλος, ἐκΠΑΓλος; Μορφὰ, Forma; ‡σΚεΠιῶ, sPeCio.

154

Σκορπίος, a scorpion. — Nearly all refer to σκορπίζω; σκορπιῶ, to scatter i. e. its poison; some indeed adding ἰὸς poison. Also a thorny plant and fish, ringlet of hair, pointed whip, the scorpion-stone, and an engine for flinging darts, so called, says Vegetius, 'quòd parvis subtilibusque *spiculis* inferant mortem.'

Σκότος, darkness. — 'Of the same origin as Σκοὰ, [in Hesych.], Σκιά :' Dnn. (2) ' Hebr. *seket,* to be quiet :' Wr.

Σκύβαλον, refuse, dung. — For Κύσβαλον, as Σφάγανον, Φάσγανον: Thrown to the dogs, κυσὶ, βάλλω, βαλῶ.

Σκυδάω, and Σκύζομαι, are both referred by some to ΚΥων: ' the latter as prop. to snarl, — the former, to be at heat, of dogs :' Ldd. But these words seem to be the same as

Σκύζομαι, Σκυδμαίνω, to be angry, to growl.—Allied to Σκιὰ and Σκοὰ and Σκότος, as we say To take Umbrage from Umbra: To have the countenance overcast. So Steph. explains Σκύθομαι, 'vultu tristi et obnubilo incedo.' (2) Dnn. approves a deriv. from an angry lion contracting the σκύνιον skin over the brows, as Hom., 'Επι--σκύνιον ξυνάγων. Then for Σκυνιάζομαι. (3) Lenn. from κύω, turgeo (irâ). Σ as Σμικρός.

Σκύθαινα, a maid-servant from *Scythia.* So

Σκύθης, a policeman, as being a *Scythian.*

Σκυθίζω, to drink deep, and to clip the hair, like the *Scythians.*

Σκύθος: the same as Σκύφος.

Σκυθρὸς, angry, sullen. — Allied to Σκύζομαι.

Σκύλαξ, ακος, a whelp, puppy. — ' It has a common origin with Σκύμνος :' Dnn.

Σκύλαξ, an iron chain, — chain for the neck. — As belonging to a Σκύλαξ (above): A whelp's chain. So Plautus uses Catellus from Catulus. : ' Te feriam, cum *CATELLO* ut accubes: FERREO ego dico.' Some read *Canis* in this sense in Plaut. Cas. 2. 6. 37.

Σκυλεύω, to strip or spoil a slain enemy of his arms: and Σκῦλα, spoils. — Allied to

Σκύλλω, to pull about, mangle, rend, skin, flay;— trouble, annoy. — Allied to Σκάλλω, to scratch, scrape. Thus Dnn. allies Σκῦφος and Σκάφος. (2) R. ξύω, κσύω, σκύω, to scrape, and so lacerate: — both Valck. and Hemst. asserting this σκύω. (3) Some from σκύλον a hide, allied to σκύτος : as we say To *wing* a bird, To *bark* a tree. Some ally this σκῦλον to ΣΚέπω, to cover, and to ΣΚΥνιον.

Σκύλον: See in Σκύλλω.

Σκύμνος, a whelp, cub;—child.—Schneid. for Κύμνος, (as Σμικρὸς,) κυόμενος from κύω, to be pregnant : just as 'Εμ-βρυον is used both for an Embryo and a New-born animal. (2) Allied to ΣΚέπω, ΣΚιὰ, ΣΚοὰ, ΣΚιάζω, ΣΚΥνιον : Covered, guarded, protected.

Σκύνιον, 'Επι-σκύνιον, 'the skin above the eyes, Ldd. 'the eyebrow,' Dnn. — Allied to Σκιὰ, Σκοὰ, ΣΚέπω, Σκότος : As overshadowing the eyes. Compare Σκύζομαι, Σκυθρός. (2) Lenn. from κύω, to swell out:

The arch above the eyes. (3) Allied to Σκύλον (in Σκύλλω,) and Σκύτος, a skin.

Σκύρον, chippings from hewn stones: allied by Dnn. to Σκῖρον, hard. (2) Rather from ξύω, κσύω, σκύω, to scrape.

Σκυρωτὸς, paved with stones. — Above.

Σκυτάλη, a staff, mace, club; — slip of a tree for planting; a roller or windlass;—'a serpent of uniform roundness and thickness,' Ldd.;—'a little staff with paper or (σκῦτος) leather rolled round it, for sending private orders to generals:' Forcell. Thus some derive it from σκῦτος. And this seems most natural. But Damm from ξύω, κσύω, σκύω, (as ξυστὸν, a javelin): 'such staffs being carefully polished and adjusted for the purpose'.

Σκῦτος. perh. also Σκύτος, and Κύτος, cutis, hide, skin, cuticle: — whip, made of leather. Lat. scutum, leathern shield. — See Κύτος. (2) 'R. ξύω, σκύω: Skin from which the hair is shaved off: and besides leather ξύεται in various ways:' Damm. (3) Allied to ΣΚέπω, ΣΚιά, ΣΚοά, ΣΚΎνιον: A covering.

Σκύφος, scyphus, a cup, bowl. — 'From κύω, to contain, allied to Κύπη, cup, Κύπελλον:' Ldd. Note that Σκύθος also is found. Σ, as Σμικρός.

Σκώληξ, a worm:—thread from the distaff:—worm-shaped cake; — long wave beating against the shore. — As 'Ράσσω, 'Ρωγὰς, 'Ανάσσω, 'Ανάγω; so Σκάλλω, Σκώληξ : The grubber, as our Grub.

Σκῶλον, an obstacle. — Prop. of thorns, briers, or stakes, from

Σκῶλος, like Σκόλοψ, a pointed stake,—thorn, prickle. —The Homeric σκῶλος πυρί-καυστος, a stake burnt in the fire, would lead to σκέλλω, ἔσκολα, to dry up. (2) 'R. κόλος, clipped:' Dnn. Σ as Σμικρός. (3) All Σκώληξ.

Σκῶμμα, scoffing, raillery. — R. σκώπτω, ἔσκωμμαι.

Σκωπαῖοι, 'dwarfs kept by the Sybarites for their amusement:' Dnn. I.e. to sport and jest at them. R. σκώπτω.

Σκώπτω, ἔσκωφα, to scoff, gibe, Teuton. schoppen.— Lenn. from κόπτω. 'Κόπτω ῥήμασι, to abuse, revile:' (Dnn.). Σ as Σμικρός. (2) 'R. σκαιὰ (ἔπη) ὗπα:' Mrt. Σκαιώπτω.

Σκῶρ, g. σκατὸς, (as Ὕδωρ, ὕδατος,) dung. — Jones compares To scour. But just as well from κορέω, to brush, clean, as Λῦμα from Λύω. Σ, as Σμικρός.

Σκώψ, g. σκωπὸς, an owl. Bochart from σκώπτω, ψω : 'Owls imitating the actions of men.' Passow from σκέπτομαι, ἔσκοπα, as Κλέπτω, Κλώψ: From its staring eyes. — Also a dance in which they mimicked the gait of an owl.

Σμάραγδος, smaragdus, an emerald, or some such: In Μάραγδος.

Σμαραγέω, to roar as the sea, crash, scream. 'From the sound:' Ldd., Dnn., Lenn. Note that Μαράσσω (fut. μαραγῶ,) is used by Erotian, prob. put for †Σμαράσσω.

Σμάραγνα: in Μάραγνα.

Σμάω, Σμήχω, to wipe off, wipe clean; — wipe over, anoint, besmear. — R. †μάω, μάσσω, to squeeze, ἐπιμάομαι, to grasp. Σ, as in Σμικρός.

Σμερδάλεος, Σμερδνὸς, terrible to look at. — Like Σμικρός. Prob. from μέρδω, according to the Homeric 'Οσσε δ' ἄΜΕΡΔεν αὐγή: The brightness blinded the eyes. As said prop. of brass, &c.; then used generally, as Σμερδνὸν βοόων, Hom.

Σμῆνος, 'a bee-hive:—mostly like ἑΣΜΟΣ, a swarm of bees, &c.:' Ldd. 'R. (ἑσμὸς,) ἑσμήν:' Dnn. (2) Σ as Σμικρός. (3) R. σμάω, †σμαεινός: From the gummy substance with which bees smear or line their hives, called ΣΜΗρίον.

Σμικρὸς, the same as Μικρός.

Σμίλη, a scalper, graving-tool, chisel, pen-knife.—Like Σμικρός, for †Μίλη, allied to Μικρὸς, Mica, Μινύθω, Μιστύλλω to mince, &c.: As chipping into micas, fragments. So

Σμινύη, an axe, mattock or hoe. — Allied to Minuo, Μινύθω. See above.

Σμυγερός, 'poët. for Μογερός :' Ldd. Σ as Σμικρός. So Dnn.: 'laborious, grievous.' As ὄντμα.—But rather 'consuming,' 'wearing,' from σμύχω, ἔσμυγον.

Σμύρις, 'emery, a mineral substance, polishing precious stones. Prop. σμῆρις as in Hero. R. σμάω, σμήχω:' Dnn. Υ: as σχΎρος.

Σμύρνα, like Μύρρα. And Ldd. from Μύρρα. Say an adj. μυρρίνα, μύρνα, σμύρνα, as Σμικρός.

Σμύχω, to consume, consume by fire. — 'Akin to Σμάω, Σμήχω, Σμάχω: Passow:' Ldd. So Schrevel. explains Σμύχω, 'to WEAR, consume.'

Σμῶδιξ, a weal. — 'R. σμάχω:' Dnn.

Σμώχω, 'a form and in the sense of Σμήχω, to wipe off, clean, pound, beat, grind:' Dnn.

Σοβαρὸς, strutting, pompous. — From

Σοβέω, and Σόεω, (whence Σοῦσθε,) the same as Σεύω, to put in motion, drive, drive off, scare; — to be off, as Σόβει πρὸς 'Αργυς, get away with you; —' pass. to move with the rapid, hurried air of a man of consequence, pompously and haughtily:' Dnn. 'Σεσοβημένος πρὸς δόξαν, (pushing on to,) all in a fever for glory; σοβούμενος ὀφθαλμὸς, a wild roving eye:' Ldd.—Σοβέω is prop. σοβέω = σεύω: though some senses might seem to point to Σέβω, σέσοβα, and Σεμνός.

Σόβη, 'a horse's tail or horse-hair fan, to σοβεῖν keep off flies:' Dnn.

Σόβος, a Satyr: 'Either from their σόβη horse-tail, or σοβῶ to strut, be insolent:' Ldd.—Above.

Σόλοικος, an inhabitant of Soli in Cilicia founded by the Athenians and speaking a corrupt dialect: whence Σολοικισμὸς, a solecism.

Σόλος, a spherical mass of iron like a quoit. — For ὅλος, sōlus, solidus. 'Massa ferri solidi:' Lenn. As Ἕλη, Σέλας. (2) Hemsterh. 'from σέλειν or σέλλειν, to extend far and wide': These words seeming to come from εἰλέω, ἔολα, to roll. Round.

Σομφὸς, ' porous, light, soft, empty, hollow :' Dnn.— Probably from the same root as Ψόφος, called by Dnn. ' a HOLLOW sound, an EMPTY sound.' (2) Cognate with our *soft.*

Σόος, a strong rapid motion. — R. σοέω, in Σοβέω.

Σόος, safe and sound : in Σάος.

Σορὸς, a cinerary urn,—deduced by Damm from σόος unhurt, unharmed: As keeping unhurt the ashes of the dead. So Gray, 'Their bones from insult to protect.' Or from the verb σόω to preserve.—Then a coffin. (2) ' Very likely, as Passow, from σωρὸς a heap, i.e. a receptacle for bones collected together:' Dnn.

Σὸς, thy. — Σὲ, σὸς, as ἐμὲ, ἐμός.

Σοῦ σοῦ, ' shoo! shoo! a cry to scare away birds:' Ldd. Σ similarly represents SH in Σίζω, to command silence.

Σουδάριον, the Lat. *sudarium*, ultim. from ὕδωρ.

ΣΟΥΚΙΝΟΣ, 'made of amber, from *Succinum*, amber:' Dnn. And this, Pliny from *Succus;* i.e. *sugo, sugicus,* allied to ὑγρός.

Σοῦμαι, to rush: in Σοβέω.

Σοφιστὴς, an ingenious inventor;—aft. in a bad sense, a *sophist.* — From

Σοφὸς, intelligent, clever, knowing, learned, wise. — ' Akin to Σαφής:' Dnn. and Lenn. As Σαφής is 'clear, perspicuous, distinct,' so Σοφὸς, ' clear in his thoughts, perspicuous in his ideas.' See the deriv. of Σαφής. (2) R. σέβω, σέσεφα, σέσοφα: Worthy of reverence. (3) ' Hebr. *sopheh,* speculator':' Mrt.

Σπαδίζω, to tear off: R. σπάω, σπάδην.

Σπάδιξ, a branch plucked off, esp. of the palm : — of a bright red color, like the palm. Above.

Σπάδων, cui testiculi sunt evulsi.—R. σπάω. See above. (2) Angl. *spay.*

Σπαθάω, 'to strike the woof with the σπάθη; hence λίαν σπαθᾶν, to weave at a great rate, to go fast;— throw away money; — weave, devise:' Ldd.

Σπάθη, 'any broad blade of wood and metal; 1. broad flat piece of wood used by weavers in the upright loom for striking the threads of the woof home, so as to make the web close [from κατα-σπᾶν τὴν κρόκην, Etym. M.]; 2. a *spaddle, spatula,* for stirring anything; 3. *paddle* or blade of an oar ; 4. the shoulder-blade; 5. broad blade of the sword; 6. currying-scraper; 7. stem of a palm-leaf, also the *spathe* i.e. sheath of the flower in many plants, esp. of the (σπάδιξ) palm. Lat. *spatha,* our *spade, paddle:'* Ldd.—R. σπάω, ἐσπάθην : What is drawn out.

Σπαθίνης, a red deer two years old : ' from the shape of its horns: Σπάθη :' Ldd. ' From the appearance of the horns:' Dnn.

Σπαίρω, spiro, to breathe hard, pant, gasp with convulsive agonies or *spasms,* from σπάω, as Ψάω, Ψαίρω.

Σπαλίων, ' a machine in a siege to protect the sappers. Prob. from σπάλιον, for ψάλλιον:' Schneid. (Only in Agathias.)

156

Σπανὸς, Σπανιὸς, rare, scarce, lacking. — ' R. σπάω: Con-tracted:' Mrt. ' Attenuated by drawing out:' Scheide. See Σπίζω. (2) Contr. from Σπαρνός.

Σπαράσσω, to tear, rend: from Σπάω, to pluck off.— So †Χάω, Χαράσσω. ' Through the form Σπάρω in the Gramm. Vett.': Dnn.

Σπάργανον, a swaddling-band: 'anything which reminds of one's childhood, the marks by which one's birth is discovered :' Ldd. — R. σπάργω.

Σπαργάω, to swell, teem, burst forth with fulness;— swell with desire. — R. σπαίρω, ἔσπαρκα, to gasp, struggle. (2) Schneid. from σπέρχω. (3) R. σπάω: To be drawn out, distended. (4) R. σπαρδάσσω.

Σπάργω, to wrap, swathe, allied to Σπεῖρα a band, and Σφαῖρα a *sphere;* (Σπεῖρον indeed is the same as the derivative Σπάργανον:) and allied by Vulck. to Σπάω, traho, con-traho, draw or roll together, as Μάρπτος to †Μάω. See Σπάρω in Σπαράσσω. ' Liberorum corpora *con-stringunt*:' Cic.

Σπαρνὸς, 'prop. scattered, rare, few. Prob. from σπείρω, ἔσπαρον, to scatter:' Dnn.

Σπάρτη, a rope, as Σπάρτον:—' a cord, with a plummet at the end, used by carpenters for marking straight lines:' Dnn.

Σπαρτίον, the tongue of a balance, allied to Σπάρτη. So Σπάθμη is a plummet, and Σταθμὸς a balance.

Σπάρτον, ' a rope, cable, strictly made of ΣΠΑΡΤΟΣ. Homer's cables could not be made of the ΣΠΑΡΤΟΣ, [Spanish broom,] as it was not known to the Greeks till long after. Pliny thinks they were made of another *spartum,* a kind of broom, *spartum scoparium*:' Ldd.— After all, Σπάρτον may perhaps be allied to Σπεῖρα a cord.

Σπαρτὸς, sown : σπείρω, ἔσπαρται. Σπαρτοὶ, the Sown-men, Thebans who claimed descent from the Dragon's teeth sown by Cadmus.

Σπάσμα, Σπασμὸς, rent, convulsion, *spasm.* — R. σπάω, ἔσπασμαι, to draw asunder.

Σπατάλη, wantonness, luxury, riot. — For Σπαθάλη, from σπαθάω, to spend one's money fast.

Σπατάλιον, a bracelet, as also Σπατάλη: and ' the hair braided and forming a crown on the head : — from σπατάλη, as being an object of luxury:' Dnn.

Σπατίλη, thin excrement; gen. human dung.—Ldd. and Dnn. take it (as λύκος, Æol. λύπος, luPus,) for σκατίλη, from σκατὸς gen. of σκῶρ, dung, and τιλῶ to dung. (2) R. σπάτος, skin or leather, and τίλλω to pluck. So σπατίλη is explained also ' parings of leather.'

Σπάω, hide plucked off: From

Σπάω, to draw, draw out or forth ;—draw tight, drag, pluck, tear, wrench. — Σ as in Σβέω and Σμικρός: and the obsol. †σάω, to press, whence παύω, πάζω, allied to †πέω, πέμπω, †πάω, πιάζω, πιέζω, to press tight.

Σπεῖρα, spira, (*spire,*) a twisted fold, coil, band ;— twisted rope, cord, net, thong ;— band of soldiers, troop. — Allied to Σπάω, ' to haul or drag along', (Dnn.): or to draw (together, close, or tight). See the obss. on Σπείρω.

Σπεῖρον, a cloth for wrapping round, as Στάργανον: — a shroud : — canvass ; — coat of onions.— See above.

Σπείρω, to scatter, strew, scatter seed, sow.—As Σπαράσσω (Spargo) to pull to pieces, is referred by Dnn. to σπάω, so may σπείρω be, in form as Φθείρω, Ἀγείρω, Μείρω : Dis-traho, di-duco : So Σπίζω. There were Σπάω, †Σπέω, †Σπίω.

Σπεκουλάτωρ, the Lat. speculātor, a guard ;—others for spiculātor from spiculum : a javelin-man.

Σπέλεθος, the same as Πέλεθος.

Σπένδω, fut. σπείσω as from †σπείω or †σπείδω, to pour or offer a drink-offering, pour libations ; make a Σπουδή, treaty. Spondeo, pledge one's word by treaty. — Mrt. allies †Σπείω to †Πίω, Πιπίσκω, Ποτίζω, to make (the earth) to drink, as Anacreon : 'Η γῆ μέλαινα πίνει. —Lenn. compares Σπείρω, to scatter.— And Σπεύδω, Σπέρχω, to urge, propel, may be noticed.

Σπέος, a cave.— R. σπάω, σπαράσσω, traho, dis--traho : Dis-tractum, dis-ruptum, di-vulsum. 'Ruptura montis vel terræ :' Lenn. Compare Σπάσμα. See the formation of Σπείρω.

Σπέρμα, seed, sperm.— R. σπείρω.

Σπέρχω, to drive or hasten forward;—midd. to haste, speed, as ΣΠΕύΔω to which it is allied. — Σπῶ εἰς τὸ ἔρχεσθαι was the old idea. ?

Σπεύδω, to propel, urge on, SPEED, Teuton. spoeden, Germ. spuden.—'R. ἔπω, ἔσπον, σπεῖν : Gramm. Vett.:' Dnn. : To make to follow. In form as Ψεύδω, Εὕδω. (2) 'R. †πέω, πίω, πιέζω, to press tight :' Lenn. Compare ΠΕίθω, ΠΕμπω.

Σπήλαιον, Spelæum, Σπήλυγξ, Spelunca, a cave.— R. σπέος.

Σπίδης, Σπίδιος, extended. — R. σπίζω.

Σπίζα, Σπίνος, 'a small piping bird, a kind of finch :' Ldd. From the sound owl, whence Σπίζω, to pipe, chirp. Σπίνος σπίζων, Arat.: A finch piping. 'Akin is Πιπίζω, Pipio : prob. imitative :' Dnn. And our piping bird.

Σπίζω, to extend.—'Akin seems Σπάω :' Dnn. I.e., to draw out at length. See Σπείρω.

Σπιθαμή, a span.—' R. σπίζω: From the end of the thumb to the end of the little finger extended :' Dnn.

Σπιλάς, Σπίλος, 'a rock, cliff : they have a common origin with Σπέος, Σπήλυγξ. Σπιλάς γῆ, argillaceous earth, is akin to Πηλός :' Dnn. — The Etym. M. says, Λίθος ΕΣΠΑΣΜΕΝΟΣ ὑπὸ κυμάτων: i. e. from †σπίω = σπάω. See Σπίζω, Σπείρω. Torn, rent.

Σπῖλος, a spot, stain.—Jones compares to spoil, ' i.e. corrupt, mar, properly SPILL, spillan Sax.:' (Dr. J.) — Hemst. from σπίζω: Extending itself on a surface. (2) R. †πίω, πίνω, to drink in, imbibe. Or †πίω, πιέζω, to press firmly. Σ, as Σμικρός. (3) Mrt. for σφίλος from σφάλλω a defect.

Σπινθήρ, a spark. — Hemstsrh. allies it to Σπίζω, to draw out, Σπείρω, scatter. ' Claras scintillas dissupat ignis :' Lucret. For Σπινθὴρ, and so like Σπιθάμη.

157

N as λαΝθάνω. (2) Orig. σκινθήρ, whence scintherula, scintilla : from σχίζω. 'Silici scintillam excudit Achātes :' Virg. See Π in σΠατίλη. — Or allied to κῖναθίζω, to be in rustling motion. See Σκίναξ.

Σπλάγχνα, pl., the bowels, entrails.— Σ as Σμικρός : for ΠΛάγχνα from πλάζω, γέσω, πέπλαγχα, to wander about : As being in continual motion. So Ilia from Εἴλέω. Lenn. explains it Tortuous.

Σπλαγχνίζομαι, to yearn in the bowels, have compassion on.— Above. 'My bowels ! my bowels ! I am pained at my heart :' Jer. 4. 19.

Σπλεκόω, coëo : 'ἀ πλέκω,' Hemst. Σ, ut Σμικρός.

Σπληδὸς, ashes. †Spledeo, spleNdeo.—Σ as Σμικρός. For σφληδὸς, (as ἀσΠάραγος, ἀσΦάραγος,) allied to Φλέω, to break forth in eruptions, to Φλέγω, &c.

ΣΠΛΗΝ, the spleen. — Dnn. allies it to Σπλάγχναν. But ?

Σπογγὸς, a sponge. — From †γόω, πόσω, to imbibe. Σ as σπλεκόω. In form as Φθόγγος, Φέγγος, Σφίγγω. (2) Damm from σπάω, as attracting moisture. (3) 'R. saphog, safanga, Arab., a sponge :' Mrt.

Σποδέω, 'to knock off σποδὸς ashes or dust ;— gen. knock, smite, beat, dash ; — also = βινέω : — and like Παίω, Φλάω, &c. to eat greedily, devour, gulp down :' Ldd. The last sense from beating to powder, consuming, devouring.

Σποδίζω, to roast in the σποδὸς ashes.

Σπόδιος, ash-colored. — From

Σποδὸς, hot ashes, ashes, dust. — Soft for Σεοδὸς, from †Σέω, †Σέσοα, σθέννυμι : Extinguished fire.

Σπολὰς, a leathern garment : thought by Dnn., &c., the same as Στολὰς, and Lat. Stola. Thus σΤάδιον, σΠάδιον, sPatium: Τέσσαρες and Πίσσυρες: Ταφῶνος, Pavῶnis. (2) R. σκύλον, a coverlet, dress. As λύΚος, luPus. Ο, as μΥλη, mOla.

Σπονδεῖος πούς, the spondee, agreeing well with Σπονδεῖον μέλος, a SOLEMN melody used on occasion of σπονδαὶ libations.

Σπονδὴ, a libation, drink-offering in making treaties ; — agreement. — R. σπένδω.

Σπόνδυλος, Σφόνδυλος, knuckle or turning-joint of the spine ;—whirl of the spindle ;— counter or pastern bone used in voting.—The sense of whirl of the spindle, and the word σφονδυλο-ΔΙΝΗΤΟΣ, point the origin to Σφεδανός, Σφόδρα, Σπεύδω, &c., as words implying quick motion.

Σπορά, a sowing, &c.— R. σπείρω, ἔσπορα.

Σπουδὴ, haste, quickness, diligence ;— earnestness, attention, seriousness, and Σπουδάζω, to be serious.— R. σπεύδω, ἔσπουδα.

Σπυρὰς, Σπύραθος, dung of goats or sheep.—' Orig. perh. any round mass, from σπεῖρα : Ball-dung :' Ldd. and Dnn. Æolic form. Much as Σφύρα and Σφαίρα. Even in Latin were lIbens, lUbens ; and Gr. βίβλος, βΥβλος. So

Σπυρίς, allied to Σπεῖρα, as above : A round plaited basket, fish-basket

Σταγὼν, a drop : στάζω, ἔσταγον.

Στάδιον, a fixed distance : — a *stadium*, race-course, race. — From

Στάδιος, *standing* erect, firm. Also, of a close battle, *Stataria* pugna. — R. στάω, στάδην: (2) Our *stoyed*, *steady*.

Στάζω, to drop, distil. — Evidently from †στάω, to stand, as †Δάω, Δάζομαι ; †Τάω, †Τάζω, Τεταγών. Thus Dr. J. explains To Stand ' to stop, halt ; to stagnate, not to flow'; and A Stand, 'a stop, halt ; — stop, interruption', — exactly agreeing with a figurative sense of To Drop in Dr. J., ' to intermit, to cease.'

Σταθερὸς, steady, firm, &c., as Στάδιος. Σταθερὰ, the noon, when the sun is stationary. — R. στάω, sto, ἐστάθην.

Σταθεύω, to burn, roast, fry. — Either as done by a steady fire, or it is taken from the burning heat of noon: both of which in Σταθερὸς. Some say, from στατὸς = σταθερὸς, and εὔω, to burn.

Σταθμάομαι, to weigh, consider. — See the two below.

Στάθμη, a carpenter's plumb-line or level, standing straight ; — a rule or line ; — rope for a goal or limit, whence the butt-end of a spear ; — some say, the hilt of a sword. — R. στάω, ἐστάθην. So

Σταθμὸς, a pillar, door-post. From standing straight. As above. — Also a station, halting-place for men or animals to stand : — a *stable*, as *Sto, Stabulum*, στατὸς ἵππος. — A steel-yard, as Lat. *statēra*, — also weight of the balance, scale, balance. Here †Στάω is to weigh, i. e. to make to stand or set in the balance.

Σταῖς, dough. — R. στάω : from its consistency. As Horace of ice : 'Flumina *constiterint*' So Στέαρ is dough.

Σταλάζω, Σταλάσσω, the same as Στάζω. So Ψάω, Ψαλάσσω.

Σταλὶς, a stake or pole set up erect for nets : — a small pillar : στάω.

Σταμίνες, the ribs of a ship standing up from the keel. — R. †στάω, ἔσταμαι.

Στάμνος, a jar, bottle. — R. ἱστάμενος or στάμενος. ' *Stetit* urna,' Hor., and, ' *Ad-stat echīnus*.' ' *Stat* ductis sortibus urna,' Virg.

Στάσιμος, stationary, fixed, steady : and

Στάσις, position, posture ; — standing up or together of the people, revolt, &c. — R. στάω.

Στατὴρ, a weight ; a coin — R. στάω, ἵστημι, to weigh, as in Σταθμός.

Σταυρὸς, an upright stake or pale. R. στάω, †σταερός : Standing up. And Σταυρόω, to impale, crucify.

Σταφὶς, a dried grape, raisin. — Allied to Στύφω, to condense. As γλΑφυρὸς and γλΤφω. Prop. from †στάω, sto, con-sto. — Ldd. allies it to Σταφυλῆ.

Σταφυλὴ, Σταφυλὶς, a grape, a bunch of grapes. — Ewing from στάζω. 'As distilling its juice :' Schrevel. Rather, allied to it, through †στάω. Compare Ψάω, Ψῆφος, Ψαφαρός. (2) Allied to Στείβω, &c. : as trampled on in the vats. See Στέμφυλον. So A in

στρΑγγός. (3) Seemingly from στᾰφίς. But how as to the sense ?

Σταφυλὴ, ' the uvula in the throat when swollen in the lower end so as to resemble a grape on the stalk :' Ldd.

Σταφύλη, the plummet in a carpenter's level. — Like ΣΤΑθμη, and from †στάω, as Ψῆφος from Ψάω. And so

Σταχύνη, a balance, as the last Σταφύλη.

Στάχυς, an ear or spike of corn, from its standing erect ; — from †στάω, †ἔστακα. ' A spike in any plant, and a plant in general : met. the fruit, produce, — a child, offspring :' Dnn.

†Στάω, Στήσω : in 'Ιστάω.

Στέαρ, ατος, dough ; — tallow, suet. — From the consistency. R. †στέω, †στάω, sto, con-sto. So Σταῖς.

Στέγη, a covering, roof, house. — R. στέγω.

Στεγνὸς, Στεγανὸς, covering, enclosing ; — covered in, close, firm, solid. From

Στέγω, to cover, protect, hide. — Prop. to make close or compact, from †στέω, †στάω, to make to stand firm. Allied to Στέφω, Στείβω. *Stipo*, Στύφω. Γ as ψέΓω. (2) ' Hebr. *tech*, to overlay :' Wr. Note Τέγος and *Tego*.

Στείβω, to press down, tread or stamp on; — tread close in the footsteps of another, follow close upon. *Stipo; constipo*. To *stive*. — See above. In form as 'Αμείβω, ΘΛΙβω.

Στειλειὰ, the hole into which the handle of an axe στέλλεται is sent.

Στειλειὸν, the handle of an axe fitted in the Στειλειά.

Στεῖρα, ' the στειρὰ stout beam of a ship's keel, esp. the curved part of it, the cutwater :' Ldd. See Στερεός.

Στεῖρα, a barren cow, *sterilis*. — R στερέω. But Dnn. says : ' Prop. hard, hence sterile.' See Στερῤός.

Στείχω, to go on in a row or order ; — gen. to go, journey. And Στὶξ, στιχὸς, a row. — Σ as in Σμικρός. R. †τέω, τείνω, to stretch out in order, as †Τάω, Τάσσω. (2) From the idea of standing close upon one another, allied to Στείβω, Στέφω, *Stipo*, Στύφω.

Στελγὶς, Στλεγγὶς, a flesh-brush, scraper, — a band of gilt leather for the head, ' R. στέλλω, to adorn (the limbs) :' Mrt., as Ldd. explains στέλλεσθαι ' to be dressed, decked.' Or from στέλλω, ' to constrict,' (Dnn.) Also ' something used to draw wine from a cask, but the form not explained' (Dnn.). Q. ?

Στελεὰ, Στελεὸν, a handle, as Στειλειά.

Στέλεχος, ' the crown of the root whence the stem or trunk springs ; — gen. a trunk, log, akin to *stalk* :' Ldd. ' Trunk, stem, log :' Dnn. — Σ as Σμικρός. R. τέλλω, ' to arise or be produced', (Dnn.) : From which the trunk *springs*. Mrt. and others say, ' What στέλλεται is sent from the root.' — In form, much as τέμΑΧΟΣ στόμΑΧΟΣ.

Στέλλω, to set in order, fit out, equip, dress ; — get ready in order to send, then to send, despatch ; — send or take down, contract, shorten the sail ; — wrap up. — Dnn. makes the proper sense to be, ' to place, fix, set up :' whence (like Στήλη,) Στέλλω may be from †στέω, (as

Ψάω, Ψάλλω,) to make to stand, a word which Schneid. recognizes. And see στΕγω, στΕίβω, στΕφω, &c. (2) R. †τέω, τείνω, as τάω, τάσσω, to set in order. (3) Lenn. allies it to Τελέω to perfect, finish.

Στελμονίαι, ' prob. a local form for Τελαμῶνες:' Ldd.

Στέμβω, to shake by stamping: allied to Στείβω Also to insult, i. e. trample on. (2) Our stamp, and its Northern affinities.

Στέμμα, a wreath, chaplet. — R. στέφω, ἔστεμμαι.

Στέμφυλον, olives or grapes already stamped or pressed. — R. στέμβω.

Στενός, close, narrow. — Allied to Στείβω, to make close; Στέφω, Ἐπι-στέφω, to fill; Στύφω, to condense, constrict, Στύω, &c. Formed much as Γένος, Μένος.

Στένω, Στενάζω, Στενάχω, to groan, sigh, from στενός, as feeling pent up, reduced to straits, oppressed. ' From the stifled sound emitted through pent or contracted bodies:' Dnn. 'From the choking, stifling sensation which produces sighs:' Ormst. 'So Γέμω and Gemo:' Ldd. (2) Thiersch allies Germ. stein, 'stone', as 'close, hard.'

Στέργανος, dung, stercus. — R. στερεός, firm, hard, stiff. Compare Γ in στέργω. (2) As 'dried' from τέρσω, to dry, whence Lat. tergo.

Στέργω, to love tenderly, as parents and children; said also of kings and people, of country and its colonies, less freq. of husband and wife; — gen. to fall in with the wishes of, acquiesce in, am contented with; — to ask in a loving manner, as Plautus: 'Scin' quid te amabo ut facias?'—From στερρός, firm, strong: Am firmly attached to. So Στοργή is natural affection.

Στερεός, Στεῖρος, Στερρός, Στέριφος, solid, firm. — R. †στέω, †στάω, to stand firm, as Στέφω, Στείβω, Ὀ- -στέον, Στύω. (2) 'Or Hebr. tser, to bind close:' Wr.

Στερέω, to deprive, bereave.— 'From the sense of deprivation, laying waste, it may be akin to Στερεός, Στερβός, barren:' Dnn. I.e. to make †στερὸν barren. (2) 'Chald. STR, destruo :' Mrt.

Στέρνον, the breast, ' prop. the anterior bony part of the chest: allied to Στερεός, Στερρὸν, firm:' Dnn.

Στέρομαι, to lack, want, lose: allied to Στερέω, to deprive.

Στεροπή, the same as Ἀστεροπή.

Στερρός, 'stiff, firm, hard, strong;—of lands, stony, barren, sterilis:' Ldd. See in Στερεός.

Στέριφος, a hide, skin, husk. — R. στέριφος, hard. ' Strictly anything firm or tight:' Ldd. See Ἔθνος.

Στεῦμαι, to stand on the spot: — to stand to it, affirm, declare, promise, boast, threaten. 'To stand up and promise:' Dnn. The Latins say ' stare promissis,' to stand to one's promise.— R. †στέω, στύω.

Στεφάνη, a crown, wreath, peak, battlement, helmet, &c.: Στέφανος, crown, victory, battlement, fortified wall crowning the city. — From

Στέφω, to encircle closely or thickly, encompass, cover, as Στέγω, crown, wreath: — fill up to the brim. —

159

Allied to Στέγω, Στείβω, Στύφω, &c. through †Στέω, Στύω, †Στάω.

Στῆθος, the breast; — 'a breast-shaped hill or bank of sand or earth in a river or the sea, as Dorsum (immane in Virg.): — prob. from †στάω, (ἐστήθην,) That which stands up :' Ldd. and Dnn. Or which stands firm, as Στέρνον. So ' Στῆναι, a breast, from στῆναι, firmum stare:' Greg. The breast bone, as Στέρνον.

Στήλη, an upright stone, pillar, slab, monument, boundary-post. — R. στάω, σταέλη, στήλη: Standing up. Στήλην στήσω, Aristoph.: I will raise a pillar. Plautus: Statuam statui. Horace has Stantem columnam. See Is. 46. 7.

Στηλιτεύω, to publish any one's infamy by placarding it on a public column. — Above.

Στήμων, the warp in the upright loom at which the weaver stood; — a thread spun. — R. †στάω, ἵστημαι. Lat. stamen.

ΣΤΗΝΙΑ, a festival at Athens in which the women indulged in gross jests and gibes. Στηνιόω, so to indulge. — Q. if from Στήνιον below : ' Breasts,' as being indecently exposed. ?—There was a place at Athens so called.

Στήνιον : See in Στῆθος.

Στηρίζω, to set up fast, fix up firm; — confirm, establish.—R. †στάω, †σταερὸς, †σταερίζω : To make to stand. So Στερεός.

Στήτη, a woman.— ' Let us bring it from Τήθη :' Mrt. Σ, as Σμικρός. So Scheide compares it with Τιτθός. — Very rare. In Il. 1. 6 for διαστήτην some curiously read διὰ στήτην.

Στία, Στεία, a small stone, pebble.—' Only diff. from Ψιὰ by a dialectic variety :' Dnn. That is Σπιὰ, Στιά. As Σπολὰς for Στολὰς. So sTudeo from σΠεύδω, ἐσΠυδον, †σΠυθέω.

Στιβαρός, packed close; ' and so, thick, strong, stout, sturdy :' Ldd. — R. στείβω, ἔστιβον: allied to Στιφρός, stout, strong, and our Stiff.

Στιβάς, a bed of straw or rushes prop. stuffed into a mattress. — R. στείβω: as Soph. στειπτὴ φυλλάς.

Στίβη, frozen dew, rime: like Στιβαρός. So Παχὺς, Πάχνη.

ΣΤΙΒΙ, ΣΤΙΜΜΙ, black oxide of antimony. — Q. ?

Στίβος, a trodden or beaten path, track; — going, gait. — R. as Στιβάς.

Στίγμα, a stigma, brand of infamy. — And

Στιγμὴ, a puncture, point of time, moment; — point of stop. — From

Στίζω, to prick, goad, brand, make marks or spots. — Prop. to brand with a hot iron by way of punishment, from τίω, †τίζω, στίζω, as Σμικρός. Dr. J. explains a Brand ' a mark made by burning a criminal with.'

Στίλβω, to glitter, shine. — R. στίλη, a drop, as μέλος, μέλΠω. Waller has 'Those little drops of light.' So Pope uses drops for diamonds. — Or στίλη, viewed as a small bit, — comparing Mica, a morsel, and Mico, to glitter.

Στίλη, a very little bit, a drop, *stilla:*—a moment, Στιγμή. Indeed Στίλη seems allied to Στίζω, as Punctus, a point, to Pungo.

Στίξ, g. στιχὸς, and Στίχος, a row, line, order. — R. στείχω.

Στιπτὸς, Στειπτὸς, trodden down, close, firm, solid: tough. —R. στείβω.

Στῖφος, a body of men in close array, close column; and of ships. — Above. (2) Our *Stiff, Stuff, Stifle.*

Στιφρὸς, close-packed, *stuffed,* compact, stout, strong: στιβαρός. — Above.

Στλέγγις: in Στελγίς.

Στοὰ, Στωὰ, a porch, portico, gallery;— roof or shed to protect besiegers; — 'and, (as prob. of a long shape, and supported by pillars,) a storehouse, magazine, warehouse:' Ldd. Hence the Στωϊκοὶ, Stoics, from the painted portico where Zeno taught. — 'Prop. a pillar, but usu. a gallery, porch. R. prob. †στάω, στὼ, ἵστημι:' Dnn. Like Στήλη, Στῦλος. Standing up as a tent.

Στόβος, abuse, insult.—R. στείβω, ἔστοβα, to trample on.

Στοιβὴ, a herb used in making beds, and in stuffing pillows or cushions; — a stuffing into compositions by way of fill-up. — R. στείβω, ἔστοιβα.

Στοιχεῖον, an element or constituent principle, 'from the arrangements of which other things proceed,' Jones: but Schneid. 'from the letters of the alphabet in a row whence words are formed.' So it means a letter, first elements, rudiments. From στοῖχος, a row. Στοιχεῖον is also the pin of a sun-dial, by the shadow of which the hours are marked. In this sense Dnn. allies it to Στοῖχος, an upright stake.

Στοῖχος, a row, rank, Στίχος. Also an upright stake for supporting hunters' nets: as being in στοίχοις rows. 'Series plāgarum:' Steph. — R. στείχω.

Στολὴ, Στολμὸς, dress, robe, *stola, stole.*—R. στέλλω, ἔστολα.

Στολίδες, folds in a garment and in the forehead: i. e. contractions, as in the next.—R. στέλλω, to contract.

Στόλος, preparation, equipment, armament, band of troops, people; — dress, as *stola, stole;*—journey, voyage. R. στέλλω. Also, the projecting part of the prow, beak of a vessel, i. e. says well Hesych., as contracted to a narrow point; for Στέλλω is to bring together, to contract.

Στόμα, the mouth; — 'the whole face:— the foremost part, front, of weapons the point, the edge, point of a sword:' Ldd. — As Σμικρός. R. τομὴ, a cutting, opening. Dnn. gives Στόμα the senses 'orifice, aperture, entrance,' and Ldd., 'a chasm or cleft in the earth.'

Στόμαχος, an orifice,—throat,—orifice of the *stomach,* the *stomach.* — R. στόμα, as Μόναχος, Τάραχος.

Στόμιον, small mouth or aperture;—bridle-bit for the mouth. — R. στόμα.

Στομόω, to block up the Στόμα mouth, muzzle, gag; — furnish with a mouth or opening: — furnish with an edge or point, (See Στόμα,): 'met. give an edge to the

160

tongue, impart wit or eloquence, or render sharp of intellect, —strengthen, invigorate:' Dnn.

Στόμφος, 'strictly a full mouth; hence lofty phrases; bombast; —scoffing, abuse:' Ldd. So Jones: Loud-mouthed. — 'From στόμα:' Ldd. Compare Στωμύλος. (2) From Στέμβω, and allied to Στόβος.

Στόνος, Στοναχὴ, a groan. — R. στένω.

Στόνυξ, anything brought to a στενὸν narrow point, point of a spear, edge of a rock. — R. στενός.

Στοργή: in Στέργω.

†Στορέω, Στορέννῦμι, †Στρέω, †Στρόω, strow or strew, Lat. sterno, to spread, level, lay prostrate, prosterno:— lay the wind, make tranquil, as ' Straverunt æquora venti,' Virg. — Σ as in Σμικρὸς, and in the two next. For τορέω, from τείρω, τέτορα, tero, to rub away, wear away, hence to make smooth and level, 'square' as Forcell. says of *Sternere:* and as is seen in Τορέω, Τόρνος, Τορνόω, Τορνεύω, to round off. Thus *Sterno* viam, to lay or floor with stone; and *Sterno* lectum, to make a bed, &c., carry the idea of making things equable and level. So gen. to lay out level and flat, to strew or stretch out at length. Thus Ldd. makes Στορέννῦμι 'to spread smooth, level.' (2) Our *strew, strow, strawan* Goth., *stroyen* Du., *stroe* Dan., &c. But the O in στορέω marks out the Greek as prior.

Στόρθη, the point of a weapon. Στόρθυγξ, the point of a stag's horn. Στορύνη, a pointed surgical instrument.—All these (as Σ in Σμικρὸς) from τορέω, to pierce, ἐτορέθην, †ἐτόρθην. So

Στόρνη, a girdle. — As Σμικρός. For Τόρνη. *Tórvos* is 'that which is *turned,* a circle, round:' Ldd. (Rare.)

Στόχος, a mark or object, aimed at in a straight line.—R. στείχω, ἔστοχα: said of things moving in a straight line.

Στόχος, a guess; Στοχάζομαι, to conjecture.—Above. We say, I made a good hit. So an Aim is explained by Dr. Johnson 'conjecture, guess,' quoting Shakspeare: 'A man may prophesy, With a near aim, of the main chance of things.'

Στραβὸς, Στραβὼν, who has a twist in the eye, a squint. — R. στρέφω, †ἔστραβον.

Στραγγάλη, a twisted cord, halter. Στραγγαλία, noose, snare; —artful question. And

Στραγγεύω, to twist, turn about, hesitate, waver, tarry. — From

Στραγγὸς, twisted, crooked.—As στέφω and στεῖ'ω, so στρέφω and †στρέΓω, στραγγός. So Ἀ-στράγαλος, Στρογγύλος.

Στράγγω, stringo, to draw tight, squeeze, squeeze out. — Prop. to make tight by twisting: compare Στραγγός. (2) R. στερεὰ or στερὰ, ἄγχω: †στεράγχω, †στράγχω. (3) 'Akin to *stringo,* Germ. *strangen:*' Dnn.

Στράγξ, g. στραγγὸς, a drop, fluid running by drops. —Above: Squeezed out.

Στράπτω, like Ἀστράπτω.

Στρατὸς, an encamped army, a host; prop. 'exercitus *strātus*,' a number scattered over the plain. As our Strewed. Allied to Στορέω, †Στρόω, †Στράω, Stravi, Stratum. The Etym. M. has a form Στρωτός.

Στρεβλὸς, twisted, bent, crooked, squinting, wrinkled : — froward.— R. στρέφω, †ἔστρεβον.

Στρέμμα, a strain, sprain.—R. στρέφω, ἔστρεμμαι.

Στρεπτὸς, bent, twisted, easily twisted, pliant. Subst., a collar of twisted or linked metal ; — a twist, twisted cake, as our Tart from Torta. — R. στρέφω.

Στρεύγομαι, short for Στραγγεύομαι, ' to be squeezed out in drops ;— to be gradually drained of one's strength, worn out, wearied, distressed :' Ldd. Wear away little by little.

Στρέφω, to turn, twist, bend, change.—' Στρέφω and Τρέπω are only different forms:' Dnn. From pf. τέτρεφα. Σ, as Σμικρός.

Στρηνής, rough, harsh. See in

Στρῆνος, ' luxury, and so asperity of manners, ferocity, insolence. R. στερέω to deprive, ἡνία, a bridle: from a horse bursting its reins:' Schleusn. ' The life of such as have shaken off every rein or restraint:' Ewing, Mrt., Pkh. As Lat. ef-frenis. (2) Yet perhaps, with Στρηνής, rough, from τρᾶνής, sharp, Ion. τρηνής. Σ, as Σμικρός.

Στρίβος, ' a weak fine voice, the root of Στριβιλικιγξ, ' a fraction,' ' the very least,' acc. to the Schol. Aristoph. Ach. 1034, though he expressly distinguishes it from Λικιγξ, a bird's voice:' Ldd. Στρίβος seems allied to Στρίζω, and Λικιγξ to Λιγύς. †Στριβιλιγίγξ.

Στρίγξ, a screech-owl. — R. στρίζω, γξω.

Στρίγξ, the fluting of a pillar, mentioned by Vitruv. 10. 15, but Steph. tells us that another reading there is Σύριγξ, which Turnebus supports.

Στρίζω, to cry shrilly, scream: allied to Strideo, Stridor.—' For τρίζω :' Mrt.

Στριφνὸς, = στιφρός. Through Στέριφος.

Στροβέω, to turn, whirl. — R. στρέφω, †ἔστρεβον, †ἔστροβα. So Στροφέω.

Στρόβιλος, a top ;—whirlwind ;— cone of the pine-tree ; conical ear-ring : and

Στρόβος, a whirling round, top.— R. στροβέω.

Στρογγύλος, round ; — well-rounded, neat, terse. — Allied to Στραγγεύω, ' to twist, wind,' Ldd., and Στραγγὸς, twisted.

Στρόμβος, ' a body rounded or spun round, a top ;— snail-shell ; —whirlwind ; pine-cone ; — spindle :' Ldd. —Like Στρόβος.

. Στρουθὸς, a small bird as a sparrow. Ὁ μέγας στρουθὸς was the *avis-struthia* or ostrich. — I believe from †στρόω, as Passer from Pando, Passum : Strewed (passim) everywhere about the ground, i.e. common. Hence Pope says, And envies every sparrow that he sees. See Matth. x. 29, 31. Compare Στρωτός.

Στροφάλιγξ, whirl, whirlwind, orbit, hinge ; — Στροφὴ, turning round of the Chorus to the audience ;— Στροφεῖον, twisted chord ; — Στρόφιγξ, vertebre, pivot,

161

cock of a pipe ; — Στρόφιον, a band ; — Στρόφος, cord, girdle, braid ; &c.—All from στρέφω, ἔστροφα.

Στρυμονίας, a violent wind from the Strymon in Thrace.

Στρυφνὸς, as Στριφνὸς, stiff ;—stiff in temper, harsh, austere ;—harsh in taste, rough, astringent.

Στρῶμα, what is strewed or strown, or spread out to lie on, mattress, couch ; — covering for a bed, coverlet ; —' plur. patchwork, such as these coverlets were often made of ;— hence the name of a miscellaneous volume ; —also piles for laying bridges on :' Ldd.—R. στορέω, †στρόω, to strew. Stratus lectus, strata.

Στρωτῆρες, ' the rafters laid upon the bearing beam ; — the laths nailed across the rafters:' Ldd.—Above.

Στρωφάω, to turn ; — midd. to turn up and down in a place, keep turning in it, and so abiding in it, as Lat. ' versor,' ' conversor,' ' conversant.'—R. στρέφω, ἔστροφα.

Στυγέω, to hate ; — to make hateful and horrid.— R. στύω, to stand stiff i.e. with horror at, to *stand* amazed. Στύζω is mentioned by the Gramm. Vett. See Στύφω.

Στῦλος, as Στήλη, a pillar, column, support ;—a *stylus* for writing with, whence *style*.—R. στύω, †στάω, to stand erect.

Στὺξ, g. στυγὸς, the river Styx ; prop. the Hateful or Hated, and used for hatred, abomination. Also a fatally cold well in Arcadia : hence Αἱ Στύγες, piercing frosts. As horrid : R. στυγέω.

Στύπη, Στύππη, tow, stupa, stuppa.—' Composed chiefly of the rind next the stalk of hemp or flax, hence R. στύφω. Others from στείβω, [στύφω,] as used in *stuffing* :' Dnn.

Στύπος, stipes, a stem, stalk, stock, stump, stake, stick. — Like Στῦλος, from a stake standing straight and erect. (2) Dnn. says : ' R. στύφω, akin to στείβω.'

Στυρακίζω, to stab with a

Στύραξ, the spike at the butt-end of a spear-shaft.— Ldd. allies it to Στόρθυξ, a spike. We may add Στορύνη. (2) Scheid from στύω, †στάω, sto : As making the shaft stand firm in the ground.

Στυφελίζω, to treat harshly, roughly : — From

Στυφελὸς, Στυφλὸς, close, solid, hard, rough ;—rough to the taste, astringent, sour ; — harsh, severe. — See Στύφω.

Στυφοκόπος, soft for Στυπο-κόπος, κόπτων striking with a στύπος stick: Ldd.

Στύφω, ' to constrict, condense ; — to be astringent ; — to steep wool in an astringent mixture ;— to have a sour taste, (make astringent). — Akin to Στείβω. R. στύω, akin to στάω, Hemst. :' Dnn. Sto, con-sto. ' Gelu Flumina con-*stiterint* acuto.' (2) Our *stuff*, *stiff*, so Dnn. Stif, Sax. *styf*, Swed., *stifur*, Icel.

Στύω, tentigine laboro : = †στάω, sto, erectus. ' R. ἴστημι :' Dnn.

Στωϊκός : In Στόα.

Στωμύλος, active with the στόμα mouth, loquacious, fluent.

Y

ΣΥ, ΤΥ, *Tu*, *Thu* Sax., *du* Dutch, and our *thou*. —
Q. ? — Is it possible that Σὺ can be allied to Σύν? As
it always supposes one present WITH another. So Νυν
and Νυ. We find τύΝη for ΣΥ or ΤΥ.

Σύβαξ, lustful, ruttish, in the manner συὸς of a hog :
σύϜαξ. So Lat. *subāre*.

Συβαρίζω, to live like the luxurious people of *Sybaris*
in Italy.

Συβήνη, a flute-case. — Jones and Mrt. from σῦς,
συὸς : 'As made of hog's skin.' †Συήνη, συϜήνη, as σύ-
Βαξ. Συηνὸς, swinish, is found.

Σῦκον, a wart, and hemorrhoidal tumor or piles. —
So called from ΣΥΚΟΝ, a fig.

Συκο-φάντης, 'an informer against persons exporting
figs from Attica, or plundering sacred fig-trees ; — informer, false accuser ; — also, a false adviser :' Ldd.
Hence our *Sycophant*. — R. σῦκον, φαίνω πέφανται.

ΣΥΚΧΟΣ, *soccus*, a *sock*, 'socc Sax., socke Teut.,
sockr Icel., a very ancient and *Phrygian* word : See
Wachter and Serenius :' Todd. 'A *Phrygian* shoe :'
Hesych.

Συλάω, to strip off, drag off, plunder, pillage. — Here
Λ and Ρ agree, as in γλάφω, γρ́άφω ; κλίβανος, κρίβανος ; and συλάω is allied to σύρω, to pull, drag along,
&c. (2) R. σύω, σεύω, 'to chase, drive away', (Dnn.)
Then σύλη, συλάω. (3) 'Hebr. *sel*, to strip off :' Wr.

Συλλαβή, a *syllable*; from λαβή : i.e. where two or
more letters are taken σὺν together.

ΣΥΝ, ΞΥΝ, with, along with, together with, in con-
formity with. — Jamieson allies it to Goth. *sam*.

Σύν-εσις, the power of putting together ideas, com-
-prehension, ap-prehension, judgment, understanding. —
R. ἵημι, †ἕω, ἕσω : as Com-mitto, to join. So

Συν-ετὸς, understanding, sagacious ; — easy to be
understood. — R. †ἕω, ἕται, as in the last.

Συν-ήμων, put or joined together, united ; — a companion. — R. †ἕω, ἥμαι, as above.

Συνωρὶς, a pair, mate. — For συν-αορὶς, from ἀείρω,
ἄορα, as εἴρω, to join.

Συοβαύβαλος, belonging to a pig-sty. — R. σῦς, συὸς,
βαυβάω to fall asleep.

Σύρβη, Τύρβη, *turba*, a noise, row : 'the same sense as
Σύρμα, Συρμὸς, Σύρφαξ. Compare Συρφετὸς. R. σύρω :' Dnn.

Σύριγξ, any pipe or tube, our *syringe* ; — a shepherd's
pipe, whence Hemsterh. from σύρω, 'from the pro-
longed notes of the pipe :' — or from a common pipe
drawing water along. — Also a whistle, and the mouth-
piece of it : — 'anything like a pipe, a spear-case ; — box
or hole in the nave of a wheel ; — hollow part of a hinge ;
— vein, artery ; — a fistula ; — a mine, vault, covered
gallery or cloister :' Ldd. (2) 'Or from Hebr. *serek*,
to hiss, whistle :' Wr.

Συρίζω, to pipe or whistle ; — to whistle at, hiss at.
Lucretius has 'calamorum sibila.'— Above.

Σύρμα, a robe with a long drawing train. — R. σύρω,
σέσυρμαι.

162

Συρμαία, an emetic, as Συρμός. 'They compounded
it, says Erotian, of the juice of the radish and salt-
water ; hence the radish itself is called Συρμαία :' Ldd.
Some think it *Egyptian*. (New Steph. Vol. 1.)

Συρμὸς, track of meteors ; trail of a serpent : — a
drawing off from the stomach, vomiting, emetic. — See
Σύρμα.

Σύρτης, a rope to draw with. — R. σύρω.

Σύρτις, the *Syrtes* on the African coast, banks of
drifted sand. The waves there, says Sall., '*trahunt*
limum et arēnam.' Aviēnus : 'Latè *trahit* æquora
Syrtis'. R. σύρω, σέσυρται.

Συρφετὸς, what is drawn or swept together, as Σύρτις, rubbish, litter, dregs, filth ; — a huddled together,
confused mob, as Σύρβη, refuse of the people. So Σύρφαξ. — From

Σύρω, to draw, drag, force or sweep away. — Allied
to Σαίρω, to sweep, and Σεύω, Σύω, ἔσσυτο, to urge
forward. So ΞΥΡΩ, σΥΥΡΩ. (2) 'Hebr. *soor*, to turn
aside, remove :' Wr.

Σῦς, g. συὸς, *sus*, *suis*, *sow*, hog, boar, pig. — 'R. σύ-
ομαι, ἔσσυτο, to move impetuously, prop. of the wild
sort :' Damm. 'Ὁρμητικὸν γὰρ τὸ ζῶον, says Et. M.

Σύφαρ, the cast-off skin of a serpent, or shell of a
fish ; — a wrinkled skin ; — an old man. — Scheide well
suggests ὑπὲρ, *Super* : The *over* skin. Φ, as σΠόγγος,
σΦόγγος ; ἀσΠάραγος, ἀσΦάραγος. The Gothic *UFAR*,
'*over*,' curiously agrees.

Συφεὸς, Συφὸς, pig-sty. — R. σῦς, συὸς, συϜεός.

Συχνὸς, thick, crowded, numerous, many, much, long.
— R. σύω, σέσυκα, σεύομαι, to hurry, rush on (in
crowds). (2) R. συν-εχὴς, con-tinuous : †συγχὴς :
transp. †συχνὴς.

Σύω : in Σεύω. — Another (supposed) Σύω see in
Κασσύω.

Σφαγή, slaughter ; — the throat, the part cut open
when animals are slaughtered. R. σφάζω, ἔσφαγον.
And Σφαγεῖον, a bowl for catching the blood of sacrifices.

Σφάγιον, a victim. — Above.

Σφαδάζω, to struggle, plunge, writhe. — Aspir. from
Σπαδάζω, (as σΠόγγος. σΦόγγος,) from σπάω, σπάδην,
whence Σπασμὸς, like Σφαδασμὸς, convulsion : — allied
to Σπαίρω, to gasp, struggle *spasmodically*.

Σφάζω, to slay, slaughter. — As Σμίκρὸς for Μίκρὸς,
so Σφάζω for †Φάζω from †Φάω, to kill, as in ἀρεί-φα-
τος, slain in war, πεφάσθαι, to be killed, &c. The Σ
is confirmed by δια-Σφάξ, any opening.

Σφαῖρα, a ball ; — *sphœra*, a *sphere*, globe ; — 'a
weapon of boxers, prob. an iron ball worn with padded
covers :' Ldd. — 'Obviously akin to Σπεῖρα :' Dnn. R.
σπάω. Eustath. well : 'διὰ τὸ συν-εσπάσθαι,
συν-εστράφθαι εἰς ἑαυτήν.'

Σφαιρεὺς, a Spartan youth between an ephēbus and
a man, 'prob. from his then beginning to wear the box-
ing-gloves, or play at foot-ball :' Ldd. — Above.

Σφάκελλος, Φάκελλος, Φάκελος, a bundle, fagot. —

For Σπάκελος, as Φ in σφαῖρα. R. σπάω, (as Ψάω, Ψακὰς,) i.e. συ-σπάω, to draw together. See Next. (2) Mrt. from Lat. *fascis*.

Σφάκελος, like ΣΦΑδασμὸς, spasm, convulsion ;—convulsive fury. R. σπάω, ἔσπακα, †σπάκελος. Also, (consequent) mortification, the highest state of gangrene, and so rot in a tree's root.

Σφάλλω, to upset, make to fall, throw down, trip up ;—disappoint the expectations of, deceive, *fallo*.—As σΠόγγος and σΦόγγος, for Σπάλλω, and this for Πάλλω, as Μικρὸς, Σμικρός : ' To move or *shake* from its place ', explains Dnn. The Σ disappears in Φηλόω. (2) R. σπάω, as Ψάω, Ψάλλω : To drag (aside). Compare ΣΦΑλσάζω. (3) Our *fall*, Germ. *fallen*. (4) ' Chald. *schephal*, (*schphal*,) prosterni :' Mrt.

Σφάραγος, a bursting with a noise, cracking, crackling :— Σφαραγίζω, to stir up as dust with a noise :— Σφαραγέομαι, to burst ;— to be ready to burst, teem, as Σπαργάω, to which it is allied.— R. σπαράσσω, ἐσπάραγον, to rend, cleave. Φ, as ἀσΦάραγος. (2) ' The Gramm. Vett. from φάρυγξ, the throat, [or ἀσφάραγος,]. Most prob. allied to Σμαραγέω' : Dnn.

ΣΦΕ, ΨΕ, him, her ;— them, as also Σφᾶς.— Q. ?

Σφεδανὸς, Σφοδρὸς, vehement, violent, eager.—Aspir. for Σπεδανὸς, Σποδρὸς, from σπεύδω, σπουδή. So σΠόγγος and σΦόγγος.

Σφέλας, ' a hollow wooden body : allied to Σπέος, a cave, and Σπήλαιον :' Dnn. For Σπέλας, as σΠόγγος, σΦόγγος.

Σφέλας, ' a joint-stool, low form or bench, rower's bench :' Dnn. This is ' a hollow wooden body', as above.

Σφενδόνη, a sling for throwing stones or bullets ;— the stone or bullet ;— bezil of a ring to receive a stone, as Lat. *funda* ;— bandage in form of a sling ;—a headband ;— an elliptical figure ;— arched way. — Allied to Σφεδανὴ, vehement, Σφόδρα, and Σφόνδυλος.

Σφέτερος, his, their,— thy, your, and even ' our.'— R. σφὲ, as 'Ημέτερος.

Σφηκίσκος, a piece of wood pointed like a wasp's sting, pointed stake, pile for building.—And

Σφηκόω, to pinch in at the waist, in the manner σφηκὸς of a wasp ;— bind tight, make narrow.

Σφὴν, a wedge, cone. And Σφηνόω, to cleave with a wedge, which shows the deriv. from φαίνω, ἔφηνα, (Σ, as Σμικρὸς,) from ' the old word †φάω, †φάζω, σφάζω, *cædo*', (Valck.). Compare Δια-σφὰξ, an opening.— 'Akin to Σφίγγω, Σφὴξ, Σφηκόω:' Dnn. See

Σφὴξ, σφηκὸς, a wasp. — ' Damm derives Dor. σφὰξ from σφάζω, ξω, [compare Δια-σφάξ] from its appearing cut in the middle. Others from σφίγγω :' Dnn.— Or from σπάω, συ-σπάω : Contracted :—for σπήξ. ' In the middle they are very slender :' Valck. Both the Σφὴξ and the Σφὴν taper down.

Σφιγγία, penuriousness. — And

Σφιγγίον, a band, bracelet. — From

Σφίγγω, ξω, to bind tight, squeeze, shut close,

163

straiten, narrow in. — Βp. Blomf. from σφῆνα ἄγω, σφὴν' 'γω : To drive a wedge in.—But better allied to Φιμός, which see. Σ as Σμικρός, and disappears in Lat. *figo*. ΓΓ : compare φέΓΓος.

Σφίγξ, the *Sphinx*, ' prop. the Throttler :' Ldd. — Above.

Σφίδη, a gut : — cat-gut.—Prob. for σπίδη, allied to σπίδιος, *long* : ' The *long* pipe from the stomach to the vent,' (Dr. J.)

Σφοδρός : in Σφεδανός.

Σφόνδυλος, like Σπόνδυλος, a vertebre, joint ;—' any round body, as Verticillus, the round weight which whirls the spindle ;— a round stone, voting pebble ;— head of an artichoke ; then gen. the whorl of a plant :' Ldd.

Σφραγὶς, a seal-ring, signet ;— impression, mark, spot. Σ as Σμίκρός. Φράσσω, πέφραγα, φρᾱγὶς, σφρᾱγὶς : Enclosing, securing. Σφραγῖσι φυλάσσει, Eurip.

Σφριγάω, to be full and swelling like udders, plump and in good health ;— swell with pride ;— swell with desire.— R. φρίσσω, πέφρῐγα, †φρῐγέω, ῥῐγέω, *rigeo* : To shudder, quiver. Σ as Σμῐκρός.— Dnn. allies it to Σπαργάω and Σφαραγέω.

Σφύζω, ξω, to beat, thrill, throb, palpitate. —'Akin to Σφαδάζω, Σφάκελος :' Dnn. As Σφύρα is allied to Σφαῖρα, and Σπυρὰς to Σπεῖρα, so Σφύζω to Σπάω, Σπασμὸς, whence Σφαδάζω. (2) Allied to Φυσάω.

Σφῦρα, a hammer, — mallet. —'Akin to Σφαῖρα, *sphæra* : from its rounded head :' Ldd. and Dnn. See σπΤρὰς, σπΤρίς.

Σφυρὸν, the ankle, is compared to Σφῦρα above, and to Σφαῖρα : the notion of roundness being common to them all. And they all compare Malleus, a hammer, and Malleolus, an ankle.

Σχαδὼν, the cell of a honey-comb, and the honeycomb itself, from the divisions and separations. R. σχάζω 1, ἔσχαδον :—' the maggot of bees, but more prob. the cells in which they are deposited :' Dnn. — Or from χανδάνω, ἔχαδον, to contain. Σ as Σμίκρός.

Σχάζω, άσω, to *scarify*, cut open, divide, separate. And Σχασμὸς, a scarifying i. e. opening ; both allied to Χασμὸς, a *chasm* i. e. opening.

Σχάζω, to let go, let fall, drop ;— cease from :—' to let a joint go and then pull it back again, set it by a wrench :—bring the hand back to its former position :' Ldd.—As Σμίκρός. For †χάζω, allied to χαλάω: and to †χάω, χάσμα : For to cause to retire or let go is to make a *chasm* or gap. (2) Σχέω, Σχέθω, Σχάω, Σχάζω, Σχάθω, the same sense as 'Εχω : Damm :' Dnn. For σχάζω is not only ' to let fall', but ' to check, hold back, withhold :' (Ldd.)

Σχαλὶς, ' a ladder, *scala* :— a forked stake for supporting hunting-nets :— a two-pronged mattock :' Dnn. —The sense of ' forked stake ' is compared by Lenn. to Σχάω, (See in Σχάζω,) Σχέω, to hold up. And so may the sense of ' ladder ' be. But the other sense of ' mattock' points the whole Root to σχάζω, to lay open.

Then as to 'ladder,' Ldd. says : 'a *forked stick* used as a *ladder*.' Or called from the χάσματα holes between.

Σχαστηρία, 'a rope for letting down ; — rope running round a pulley, — the pulley itself :' Ldd. — R. σχάζω, ἔσχασται.

Σχάω, the same as Σχάζω.

Σχέδη, 'a tablet, leaf ; prob. borrowed from the Lat. *scheda* :' Ldd. And this perh. from σχίδη, cleft wood.

Σχέδην, gently, thoughtfully. — R. σχέω, to hold, hold back.

Σχεδία, a light raft, boat, scaffold or bridge made on the sudden. See Σχέδιος. — Also, a cramp or holdfast : from †σχέω, to hold. Compare Σχεδόν.

Σχεδιάζω, to do a thing in a hurry. — See Σχεδία and Σχέδιος.

Σχέδιος, close, hand to hand, of a fight : sudden, i.e. close in point of time to something else. — From

Σχεδόν, near, hard by ; — nearly, all but, almost ; — near the truth, perhaps. — R. σχέω, to hold on, to be contiguous, as Ἔχομαι. So Ἀμφαδὸν from †φάω.

Σχέθω, to hold or have, hold back, as †Σχέω.

Σχελίς, the same as Σκελίς.

Σχενδύλα, 'perh. a pair of pincers or tongs, from σχεῖν, to take hold of :' Ldd.—R. †σχέω, σχέθην, σχέδυλα, σχένδυλα, as μαΝθάνω.

Σχερὸς, used in ἐν σχερῷ, in a continuous line, uninterruptedly. — R. †σχέω, as Teneo, Con-tineo, Con-tinuus.

Σχέτλιος, holding up, enduring, resolute ; — much-suffering, wretched ; — hardy, hard-hearted, cruel, a 'wretch.'— R. †σχέω, ἔσχεται.

†Σχέω, to hold. — R. ἔχω, †ἔσχω, †ἔσχέω, σχέω. Ἔσχον is common.

Σχῆμα, from †σχέω, ἔσχημαι : Lat. quo more res se habent, habitus, — form, figure, manner, condition ; — outward form or appearance ; — And Σχηματίζω, to form, fashion : midd. to make outside show, appear, feign.

Σχίδη, -αξ, Σχίζα, a cleft piece of wood, a splinter, *scindula* : — a torch, — arrow, — cleft, gap. — From

Σχίζω, sciNdo : to split, cleave, divide. — Σ as Σμικρός. 'Allied to Κέω, Κείω, Κεάζω, Σχάζω. Germ. *scheiden* [Note a. 2. ἔσχιδον] :' Dnn. So Κείρω. 'R. χάω, χαίνω, to open :' Lenn.

Σχινδάλαμος, Σκινδ..., = σχίδη.

Σχίσμα, a cleft, division, *schism*. — R. σχίζω.

Σχοῖνος, a rush ; — rush-rope, rush-basket ; — land-measure taken by a rope, 'Fr. corde de bois :' Dnn.— R. σχέω, ἔσχοα, σχοῖνος : As holding or tying things together. So Jungo, †Jungicus, Juncus.

Σχολή, relaxation, leisure ; spare time ; esp. for philosophical or literary pursuits, (as Vacare is 'to have leisure for, hence attend to, occupy ourselves in,') — place for such, *schola*, a *school*, Lat. *ludus*. Cic.:

'Dionysius Corinthi dicitur *LUDUM* aperuisse.'— R. †σχέω, ἔσχοα: To hold back, remit, relax.

Σχολῇ, slowly, with difficulty, hardly, not at all, 'vix et ne vix quidem.' — Above.

Σχόλιον, a learned inquiry or comment, a *scholium*. R. σχολή.

Σχῦρος, = χῆρ, χηρός. Υ: see σμΤρις.

Σώζω, to make safe or sound, save, preserve. — R. σῶος, σωΐζω, σώζω. So σόω.

Σωκέω, to have strength or power, am able to do. — From

Σῶκος, stout, strong : allied to Σῶος, sound, whole.

Σωλὴν, a channel, pipe, gutter, — syringe ; — fold in a garment ; — grooved tile ; — 'a shell-fish, perh. like the razor-fish. — Said to come from Αὐλός :' Ldd. Then Ὀλὸς, as ΑΤλαξ and Ὀλαξ, a furrow ; cAUdex, cOdex; then aspirated Ὀλὸς and Σωλὸς, as Ἀλὸς, Salis. (2) R. σελίς, space between lines in writing and benches in rowing. As δΕμω, δΩμα: ἀρΗγω, ἀρΩγός.

Σῶμα, the body, in Homer a dead body ; — a person, a freeman, but esp. a slave, as Ovid uses Corpora. — Plato did not suppose that Σῶμα originally signified a dead body, for he derived it from σώζω, σέσωμαι (as σέσωται in σωτήρ): The case or casket preserving the inner soul or spirit. Death of course cuts short that office. 'They found him dead, An empty casket, where the jewel life Was robb'd and ta'en away :' Shaksp. So Hawker: 'When the hour cometh that the casket in which that precious jewel my soul now dwells, is opened for the soul to take her departure',&c. See Σκῆνος, the body. (2) As Σῶος is the same as Σῶὸς, so Σῶμα for Σῶμα, as girding round and enclosing the interior. Dr. J. explains to Gird (inter alia) ' to cover round, enclose, encircle.' See spec. on Κόμβος. (3) R. ζωὸς, living : A living body. Or σῶς, sound, 'integer.'

Σῶος, Σῶς, *sospes*, safe and sound, = σάος, saNus.

Σωπάω, for Σιωπάω.

Σώρακος, a chest, barrow, basket, in which a Σωρὸς heap of things is placed or carried.

Σωρείτης, a syllogism, *cumulative* argument.— From

Σωρὸς, a heap, pile. — As ἀνΑσσω, ἀνΩγω; ἀρΗγω, ἀρΩγός; ῥΑσσω, ἔῤῥΩγα; so Σωρὸς from σαίρω, σέσαρα, σέσηρα, to sweep: Sweepings.

Σῶς: for Σῶος or Σάος.

Σῶστρον, a reward for saving a life. — R. σώζω, σέσωσται.

Σώτρον, the wooden circuit of a wheel, felloe.— 'Schneid. from σούμαι, to move rapidly. Others more prob. from σῶς, entire : the felloe forming one with the cartwheel, as still in Russia and Poland:' Dnn. Or as keeping and securing the whole : much the same as Σωτήρ.

Σώφρων, opposed to Ἄφρων. R. σῶς, φρονῶ.

Σώχω, soft for Ψώχω.

Σώω, the same as Σόω.

Τ.

Ταβλίζω, to play at Τάβλαι *tables* or dice: the Lat. *tabula*. *Tabula* being for *tanibula* from †τανὸς as in τανύ-γλωσσος.

Ταγγή, rancidity:—rancorous tumor.—'perh. from τήκω ['to become decayed, perish': Dnn.]': Mrt. Τήκω, τήξω, †έταΐον, as in τάΓηνον, τήΓανον. ΓΤ as φέΓΓος.

Τάγηνον, like Τήγανον.

Τᾰγὸς, a general, chief. — R. τάσσω, τέταγα.

Ταινία, a band, fillet; — streamer; — strip or tongue of land, — tapeworm; — a long thin fish. — R. †ταίνω, τιταίνω, τείνω.

†Ταίνω: See Τείνω.

Τάλαντον, a balance; — a certain weight, *talentum*, a talent. So Pendo, Pondo, a Pound. — R. †ταλάω, τλάω.

Ταλαὸς, Τάλας, Ταλαίπωρος, enduring toils or evils, miserable. — R. †ταλάω. So Τάλασις is endurance. See for -πωρος on †Παθέω.

Τάλαρος, a basket, cage.—R. †ταλάω: 'That which bears or holds:' Ldd.

Τάλας: in Ταλαός.

Ταλασία, wool-spinning. — R. †ταλάω, †ταλάσω, whence Τάλαντον a weight: 'The weighing out of wool to be spun:' Ldd: As Pensum from Pendo.

†Ταλάω, Τλάω, Τλῆμι, ἐτάλασα, to bear up, sustain, endure. 'Bear to do, notwithstanding danger or shame or pride or grief or pity :' Bp. Monk: have the heart to do good or bad.—With †Ταλάω are connected τΕλαμών, τΟλμάω, τΟλλο, τΟιεro: so that these words seem allied to Τέλλω, 'Ανα-τέλλω, to cause to rise up, to bear up. (2) R. †τάω, †τέω, τείνω, ἀνα-τείνω, 'to hold up, lift, raise, elevate,' (Dnn.) As †Βάω, Βάλλω, Βέλος, †Βολέω; Ψάω, Ψάλλω. (3) 'Chald. *tal*, tolle:' Mrt.

Τάλις, a marriageable maiden.—'Prob. from Θῆλυς, (Θᾶλυς,) a female. Some connect it with the Syriac *TALITHA*:' Ldd. 'damsel,' in Mark 5. 41. Or allied to Ταλασία: A spinster.

Ταμίας, distributor of stores and victuals, dispenser, manager, steward. R. τάμνω, ταμῶ, to cut up, divide. So Ταμιείον and Ταμείον is a storehouse, magazine.

Τάμισος, runnet, 'the concreted milk in the stomachs of sucking quadrupeds;— and not only the runnet, but the stomach curdles milk. The common method is to take the inner membrane of a calf's stomach,' &c. Enc. Br. Hence from ταμῶ, to cut out. As Τόμια.

Τάμνω, τέμνω, to cut, cut asunder, cut through, &c. — Allied to †Δάω, Δαίω, to divide. †Τέω is called by Dunb., 'the attenuated form of †Δάω, Δαίω.' So δέΜω from Δέω in another sense. (2) 'Hebr. *dam*, succido:' Mrt.

Τὰν or Τᾶν, 'Ω τὰν or 'Ω τᾶν, Sir, or Friend. 'Some write 'Ω 'τὰν, as Voc. of ἐτὰν, (ἔτης companion,) as

165

Μεγιστὰν; some 'Ω 'ταν, as Voc. of ἔτης. Passow makes it = τῆνος, (τᾶνος,) as Οὗτος, This man here: or = τύνη, τύ, (Ο you !):' Ldd.

Τάναγρα, a copper kettle. Made, says Ldd., in the city of *Tanagra* in Bœotia. — (Only in J. Pollux.)

Ταναὸς, stretched out, long, slim. — R. ταίνω, τανῶ, τείνω; *tenuis*, thin.

Τανθαρύζω, only in Ammonius, and seems put for Τανταρύζω, a corruption of

Τανταλίζω, 'like Ταλαντίζω, to move to and fro like a Τάλαντον scale. Allied to *Tantalus*, in relation to the story of his hanging balanced over water:' Ldd. But Τανταλίζω may be a mere transp. of Ταλαντίζω.

Τανύω, the same as Ταίνω, τανῶ.

Τάξις, arrangement, array, squadron, band ; —assessment of tribute, *tax*; — position, order, rank. — R. τάσσω, ξω.

Ταπεινὸς, low on the ὁδάπος ground, for Δαπεινός; as Humi, Humilis. Or low like a τάπης carpet. See on †Δάπος. Comp. ὁρΕΙΝΟΣ.

Τάπης, Τάπις, Δάπις, a carpet, rug, *tapes, tapētum, tapestry:* carpet as placed on the †ὁδάπος ground.

Ταραντίνιον, a fine garment of a *Tarentine* woman.

Τάραξις, Ταραχὴ, confusion: from

Ταράσσω, ξω, to stir up, trouble, disturb, agitate; — alarm, confound. — R. τείρω, ἔταρον, to molest, distress.

Τάρβος, terror, alarm, fear: allied to Ταράσσω.

Ταργάνη, Σαργάνη, plaited work, cord, basket. — R. ταργαίνω, ταργανῶ, explained by Hesychius ΤΑΡάσσω, to jumble up; here to jumble together, intermix. Called also ΤΑΡπάνη. (2) 'Syr. *serig*, a net:' Dahler.

Τάργανον, bad wine, vinegar. — 'Perh. from [ταργαίνω =] ταράσσω: Thick troubled liquor. As οἶνος τεταργανωμένος, thick wine:' Ldd.

Τάρες, for Τέτταρες.

Τάριχος, what is preserved, embalmed, as a mummy; — what is salted, dried, smoked, as fish. — 'R. τείρω, [as ΤΑΡάσσω,] to dry: Dried meat :' Mrt. and Greg. 'R. τείρω or τέρσω:' Schrev. 'Some derive Τέρσω from †τέρω, τείρω, to rub, i.e. wipe dry :' Dnn.

Ταρμύσσω, to frighten. — As Τάρβος, Ταρβύζω.

Ταρπάνη, Τάρπη, as Ταργάνη.

Τάρροθος: See in 'Επιτάρροθος.

Τάρσος, Τάρρος, Τερσιὰ, a hurdle or crate for drying cheeses on; — mat, basket;—anything in a broad form like that of a hurdle, as the broad part of an oar, the flat of the foot, the *tarsus*;—the flat of the wing when stretched out. — From

Τέρσομαι, to dry, dry up, allied to Θέρω, Θέρσω: and to *Tergo, tersi*. All connected with Τείρω. See in Τάριχος.

Τάρταρος, Tartarus, Hell. —Many from ταράττω.

Better from τείρω, τέταρται, ' to oppress, distress, torment', (Dnn.) See 'Α-ταρτηρός. (2) ' Some, as Passow, make it imitative of shuddering through terror:' Dnn.: ταρ ταρ.

Τάρφος, thickness, closeness. — R. τρέφω, ἔτραφον, ἔτραφον, to coagulate. See Τραφερός.

Ταρχύω, to embalm. — R. τάμιχος, ταριχεύω.

Τάσσω, ξω, draw up in line, put in order, arrange;—order, enjoin, command, as Paro, Impero: — midd. arrange or agree with another. — R. †τάω, †τέω, τείνω, tendo, to stretch out. As Θάω, Θάσσω.

Τάτα, = τέττα.

ΤΑΤ, the letter Τ: — Hebr. thau.

Ταύλη, = τάβλα, the Lat. Tabula. As ναῦλα, νάβλα. See Ταβλίζω.

Ταυρέα, a bull's hide; — anything made of it, as a scourge, whip; — drum. — From

ΤΑΥΡΟΣ, a bull. — The Syriac and Arabic TAUR.

Ταῦρος, spatium inter scrotum et anum: et pro Πέος. Pro ταερὸς à τάω, τείνω: Extensum, protensum aliquid.

Τάφος, a tomb. — R. θάπτω, ἔταφον, to bury.

Τάφος, wonder: allied to Θάμβος and Θήπω. 'R. †θάφω:' Dnn.

Τάφρος, allied to Τάφος a tomb, grave, — and means a ditch, trench.

Τάχα, quickly. R. ταχύς. Also ' readily, easily:' Dnn.: and this sense seems to have led to that of ' perhaps, probably,' i.e. it may readily and easily follow or be believed. Often joined with Ἴσως, perhaps: Τάχα δ' ἂν ἴσως οὐκ ἐθέλοι, Aristoph.

Ταχύς, swift. — R. †τάω, τέτακα, τείνω, tendo, intendo (cursum). Τέτατο δρόμος, Hom. So Τανύοντο Il. π. 375, ' perniciter currebant,' Cl. And Τιταίνετον ψ. 403. Observe our in-tense, in-tensely. (2) Dnn. from θέω, to run.

ΤΑΩ, †ΤΕΩ, ΤΙΩ, †ΤΟΩ, †ΤΥΩ, Primitive words, to stretch out, like Ψάω, Ψέω, Ψίω, Ψόω, Ψύω. Τάω is acknowledged by Eustath., and produced Τάζω: †Τέω produced Τείνω: †Τόω is asserted by Heyne, Pind. P. 4. 43.

Ταῶς, Ταὼν, a peacock.—R. τάω: As expanding the tail. ' Pictâ pandunt spectacula caudâ,' Hor.

Τε, and. — Dnn. from δέω, to bind, as Δὲ is often used for Τε. — Better from †τέω, τείνω, to extend. An adverb of extension: ' Peter AND John.'

Τέγγω, tingo, to tinge, wet, wash, soften. — Allied to Δεύω, to wet: compare κλᾶΓΓω, φέΓΓος, φιΓΓω.—' Allied closely to Τήκω, and both prob. from †τάω, †τέω, [to expand.] Germ. tünchen:' Dnn.

Τέγος, a covering, roof;— covered part of a house, hall, room, chamber;—' vault:— place for prostitutes. — R. στέγω, Lat. tego. (2) ' Heb. tech, to overlay:' Wr.

Τεθμὸς, as Θεσμὸς, a law, custom.—R. †θέω, ἐτέθην, τίθημι, to lay down a law, ' ponere leges.'

Τέθνημι, the same as Θνήσκω.

Τεινεσμὸς, a tenesmus, straining to evacuate.—From.

166

Τείνω, to stretch, stretch out. — R. †τάω, †τέω, as Γείνω, Κτείνω.

Τείρας, a wonder, like Τέρας: Τείρεα, stars, ' wonderful things.' As the Song: ' Little star, How I wonder what you are.'

Τείρω, tero, to rub, rub or wear away, wear out, harass, afflict. — Allied to Δέρω, from †τέω = †δέω, δαίω, and to Τέμνω. ' Τέω is the attenuated form of Δέω:' Dnn. Τείρω, as Φθείρω, 'Αγείρω, 'Ιμείρω. (2) Compare our Tire. (3) ' Chald. thera, destruc:' Mrt. ' Hebr. tereh, to weary:' Wr.

Τεῖχος, a wall, fortified city, fort.—From obs. †τείχω, whence Τέκτων, a builder, archi-tect. Allied to Τεύχω, Τοῖχος. †Τέκω is, generally to produce, create, invent. See Τέκτων. (2) ' Hebr. deek, a battery:' Wr.

Τεκμαίρομαι, to conjecture from certain signs, judge likely;— mark out a line of conduct for myself, determine, intend; — mark out a line of conduct to others, appoint, enjoin, ordain. — From

Τέκμαρ, Τεκμήριον, Τέκμωρ, well derived by Parkh. from †δέκω or †δείκω, †δέδεκμαι, δείκνῦμι, to show forth: A sure mark, sign or token, a proof, pledge. Also, a constellation in the heavens, which was a sign in foretelling events :—also, a mark or boundary shown and declared, a goal or end. Τ for Δ, as Δαῖδα, Tæda. (2) R. †τέκω, to bring forth, i.e. bring to light: A sign which brings to light what is coming. (3) ' Hebr. tegmer, end :' Wr.

Τέκνον, Τέκος, an offspring, child. — R. †τέκω. Homer: Ἡ τέκε τέκνα.

Τέκτων, a craftsman, carpenter, builder, archi-tect, planner: which last seems the original, from †τέκω, to bring to light, produce. See †Τέκω and Τεῖχος.

†Τέκω, †Τιτέκω, †Τίτκω, Τίκτω, Τέξομαι, to bring forth, beget, produce: much as †Πέτω, †Πιπέτω, Πίπτω.— †Τέκω seems the same as †Δέκω, †Δείκω, ' to show, make appear, betray to view,' (Dnn.) See on Τέκμαρ.

Τελαμών, a belt, band, strap, bandage. — As ΒΑΛΛω, ΒΕΛος, so for Ταλαμὼν, from ταλάω: ' For bearing or supporting anything:' Ldd. Comp. κΕλυφος, κΕλεμίζω.

Τελέθω, to end in being, come to be, become, am. — R. τέλος.

Τέλειος, perfect, complete, absolute, accomplished;—act. making complete; — the last. — R. τέλος.

Τελετὴ, religious rite, τέλος.

Τελευτὴ, end; Τελευτάω, to end; Τελευταῖος, the last. — R. τέλος.

Τελέω, to finish, accomplish;—pay a τέλος, tax, toll, duty, &c.; — to be reckoned in a τέλος class of citizens, to belong to it;— to consecrate, initiate : See the end of Τέλος 2.

Τέλος, a tax, toll, debt.— R. τέλος.

Τέλλω, much as Τελέθω, to end in being, come to be, turn out at last, come forth, rise as the sun. (2) R. †τέω, τείνω, to stretch upwards, rise. As Ψάω, Ψάλλω.

Τέλλω, in comp., to tell one to do, enjoin, as Στέλλω.

(2) R. †τέω, †τάω, τάσσω, enjoin. Above. (3) Our *tell*.

Τέλμα, 'a pool, pond, marsh, swamp;—mud or slime of a swamp;—mud for building with, mortar;—the space pointed with mortar between the courses of masonry:' Ldd., who derives from τέλλω, τέτελμαι, 'as water which has run together:' Jones better as the τέλος or τέλσον ἀρούρης, boundary separating one's land from another's.

Τέλος, the end.—R. †τέω, τείνω, to extend: (Compare Σάλος, Χέλυς, Ἑλος:) The point to which a thing can be extended, the furthest extent, as Πέρας from Περάω. Dr. Johnson defines End 'the *extremity* of anything *extended*.' We say, That was the *extent* of my journey.—Allied to Τῆλε.

Τέλος, the accomplishment, completion, or fulfilment, as of purposes, wishes,—of marriage;—an end proposed;—completeness, maturity, full growth, end of life.—Also, the highest rank or station in civil life, magistracy, office Also, a *limited*, fixed body of troops, cohort, company, squadron;—a fixed *toll* or tribute to the Government;—class and order of citizens as settled by payment of such tribute. 'Consummation of being initiated into the sacred mysteries, esp. the Eleusinian, which were thought the consummation of life;—hence any religious ceremony or solemnity, as of marriage:' Ldd.—Above. In some senses it may seem to belong to †Τέω, Τάω, Τάσσω, and Τίω.

Τελχίν : in Θελγίν.

Τελώνης, farmer or collector of the τέλεα *tolls* or taxes. Some add ὠνέομαι.

Τέμαχος, a slice cut off, esp. of salt fish.—R. τέμνω, τεμῶ. So

Τέμενος, a piece of ground cut or marked off, assigned to men or to the gods, as Lat. *templum.*—Above. Τέμενος τάμον, Hom.

Τέμνω : in Τάμνω.

Τέμπεα, any beautiful vale, called after the famous vale of Tempe in Thessaly.—'*Rupta* loca, R. τέμνω:' Mrt. Note *Templum*.

Τέναγος, a swamp, marsh.—R. τείνω, τενῶ. '*Extenta* visentur Lucrino STAGNA lacu:' Hor. 'Where wild Oswego SPREADS her swamps around:' Goldsmith. Comp. as to form, Γλάγος, Πέλαγος. (2) R. τέγγω, †τέγγος.

Τένθω, Τενθεύω, to gnaw, nibble, eat daintily.—Ldd. compares Tenuis, to *Attenuate*: allied to Tαναός, thin. Or it is allied to Τέμνω, to cut. (2) 'Hebr. *tehen*, to grind:' Wr.

Τενθρήνη, Τενθρηδὼν, a kind of wasp.—'R. τένθω [or τενθεύω]:' Mrt. : What eats only, and does not work. Like Κηφῆν, a drone, which see. Above.

Τένων, a tendon, sinew.—R. τείνω, τενῶ. Its principal action consists in *tension*.

Τεὸς, thy.—R. τὸ acc. of Τύ.

Τέραμνον, Τέρεμνον, 'what is closely shut fast or closely covered, a room, chamber, as οἴκων τέρεμνα;— from τέρεμνος = στίρεμνος, στερεὸς, firm, close :' Ldd.

167

(2) Jones for Κέραμνον, from κέραμος a tile. As Τῆνος and Κεῖνος are the same

Τεράμων, as Τέρην, soft, tender;—made soft by boiling.

Τέρας, Τεῖρος, a sign, wonder, prodigy, miracle.—R. †τέω, τείνω, tendo: answering to *Os-tentum*, *Portentum*. So Ξέω, Ξερός. Ending like Πέρας. (2) R. τείρω, τερῶ, 'to distress, torment, having perh. the same origin as *terreo*', (Dnn.). 'By signs and wonders . . . . . and by great *terrors*': Deut. 4. 34. 'With great *terribleness* and with signs and with wonders' 26. 8.

Τέρεμνον: in Τέραμνον.

Τερετίζω, to twitter, chirrup:—to quaver, of men.—From the sound, says Ldd.: i. e. from the sound τερετ. (2) 'Perh. from τερέω to pierce: from the shrill sound:' Dnn.

Τέρετρον, a gimlet, *terebra*.—From

Τερέω, *terebro*, to bore, pierce, make a hole.—R. τείρω, τερῶ, *tero*, to rub, wear a hole.

Τερέω, to turn round on a lathe: whence Lat. *teres* is round or rounded, i. e. worn smooth, from τείρω, τερῶ, *tero*.

Τερηδὼν, a wood-worm; a caries of the bones.—R. τείρω, τερῶ, to rub, wear.

Τέρην, soft, tender.—R. τείρω, τερῶ : Rubbed down, worn smooth.

Τερθρεία, jugglery, trickery.—R. τεράζω, to declare prodigies: ἐτεράθην. Or †τερατήρ, †τερατηρεία, †τερτρεία. See Τέρας.

Τέρθρον, an end;—end or point of a sail-yard.—Allied to

Τέρμα, Τέρμων, an end, boundary, goal, mark aimed at;—highest point, *terminus*. Like Τόρμη, a turning-post, round which the chariots turned, and so by Damm is derived from τρέπω, transp. for τρέμμα. (2) Τέρμα for Τέλμα viewed as Τέλος: P and Λ interchanging, as γλάφω, γράφω; &c. (3) Reimer from τέρας, a sign: but that is rather a sign in the heavens. (4) 'Hebr. *terem*, to fill up: A limit:' Wr.

Τερμέρειον κακὸν, a misfortune we bring on ourselves. —'Said to be derived from one *Termerus*, a highwayman:' Ldd. 'From one *Thermerus*:' Dnn.—Or perh. allied to Τερμία, which is applied to a spot 'where one is destined to end life:' Ldd. Which ends one's life, fatal, a 'settler.' See above.

Τέρπω, 'to fill, satiate, satisfy, gratify, delight, amuse. Compare Τρέφω to nourish, as also Θεραπεύω to take care of. The R. may be Θέρω, Θέρπω, as Τέρπω, as Θάλπω :' Dnn. (2) Transp. from τρέπω, as ἀτΑΡπὸς for ἀτΡΑπὸς; Τέρχνος, Τρέχνος. Thus to Di-vert and Di-versions are from Verto. (3) Lenn. from τείρω, τερῶ, to rub (the body gently), tickle, gratify.

Τερσιὰ, the same as Ταρσός.

Τέρσω, to dry, dry up, allied to Θέρω, Θέρσω, and to *Tergo, tersi*. 'From τείρω, τερῶ, to rub, i. e. wipe dry': Dnn. (2) Germ. *dörren*, to dry.

Τέρφος, the same as Στέρφος.

Τέρχνος, Τρέχνος, a twig, branch. — Allied to Lat. *TERMES*, and both from τέρυς, *teres*, tapering, as 'Virga *teres*.' See Τερέω 2. (2) Τρέχνος the original word, from τρέχω, to run. 'Whose branches RUN over the wall:' Gen. 49. 22.

Τέσσαρες, four. — As Πέσσυρες is found, perh. from πεσσὸς, a cubic mass. Indeed Ldd. compares Πεσσὸς with *Tessera*, a die. (2) Τέτταρες: Sanskr. *chatur*, Lat. *quater*, *quatuor*.

Τεταγών, having taken; formed from †τάω, †τάζω, †ἔταγον, †ταγῶ, *taNgo*, to touch. Prop. to stretch out the hand.

Τέτανος, a stretching, straining; — convulsive stiffness of the body, *tetanus*. — R. †ταίνω, τανῶ, †τετανῶ.

Τέταρτος, fourth. — R. τέτταρες, τέταρες, τέσσαρες, four.

Τετίημαι, to be sorrowful, to mourn : 'akin to (Τίομαι,) Τίνειν, to be punished, and so made sad:' Ldd. Perhaps, struck with remorse, sorry for an offence.

Τέτμον, ἔτετμε, to come upon, find;—receive by fate or lot, partake of. — Prop. 'to get by a short cut,' ἐν ἐπι-τόμῳ καὶ συν-τόμως. R. †τέμον, †τέτεμον, τέτμον; as †φένω, †τεφένω, πέφνω.

Τετρα-, for Τέτταρα.

Τετράδων, Τέτραξ, Τετράων, Τέτριξ, a bird prob. of the grouse kind : 'said to utter a loud cry, τετράζειν:' Dnn. This Τετράζειν is explained by Ldd. to cackle as a hen on laying an egg.—All these seem fanciful imitations of the sounds made : τετρ. Or as Τέττιξ (2).

Τετραίνω, to bore through : allied to Τερέω, Τρέω, through †Τράω, †Τραίνω. (2) 'Germ. *drehe*, to turn :' Thiersch.

Τέττα, 'like Ἄττα, Τάτα, Ἄππα, Πάππα, a friendly or respectful address of youth to their elders :' Ldd.

Τέττιξ, a kind of winged grasshopper: — a figure of one worn in the hair. — 'Prob. formed in imitation of its note:' Dnn. and Ldd.—Or from τερετίζω, to chirrup, whence †τερετιξ, †τέρτιξ, τέττιξ.

Τετυκεῖν : a. 2. redupl. of Τεύχω.

Τευμάομαι. = τεύχομαι. (Rare word.)

Τευτάζω, 'for ταυτάζω (τὰ αὐτὰ,) to say or do the same thing, dwell upon a thing, be constantly at it :' Ldd. and Dnn. Allied to Ταυτολογία, *tautology*.

Τεῦχος, anything made, utensil, tool, vessel, urn ;— the human frame;—a book, as *Penta-teuch*. Τεύχεα, armour; — tackle, rigging. — From

Τεύχω, to work, make, construct, build, forge, form : — τέτυκται, has been formed, exists, is. — Allied to †Τεύκω, whence †Τέκτων a builder, and Τέχνη which see.

Τέφρα, ashes. — 'From τύφω:' Ldd. Allied by others to Θάπτω, ἔταφον, prop. to burn: and to Lat. *tepeo, tepidus*. (2) Sanskr. *tapa*, (Lat. *tepor*,) and *tapitum* to warm.

Τέχνη, art :—an art. — R. τίκτω, τέξομαι, to produce: Creative art. (2) R. τεύχω, to work, form.

Τέως, so long. See in Ἕως 2.

Τῆ, take. — For τάε, from †τάω, †τάζω, †ταγῶ, *taNgo*, τεταγών: Stretch out your hand. (2) For Τῇ, there, there it is for you. But pl. τῆτε is found.

Τήβεννα, -ος, a dress worn by great men. — 'From one *Tebennus* an Arcadian:' Steph. Like our Spencer, Wellingtons, &c.

Τήγανον, a frying-pan.—R. τήκω, ξω, a. 2. prop. ἔτηγον.

Τήθη, a grandmother : and also a nurse. —Allied to Τίτθη, a teat, and also a grandmother. (2) Allied to our *Teat*.

Τηθίς, an aunt.—Of the same class as Τήθη, a grandmother.

Τήκω, to melt, dissolve, pine away. — 'Akin to Τέγγω:' Dnn. 'Perh. from τάω, [τέτηκα,] to extend', Lenn. Or to expand. Thus Ταινστὸς is 'extension, expansion', (Dnn.). Or even to make *thin*, as Tenuis from Τανάος.

Τῆλε, far off. — Buttm. from τέλος. Or †τάω, †ταελὸς, †τήλος: Extended far. As Τανάός.

Τηλεθάω, to flourish. — R. Θάλλω, ἔθηλα, θηλεθάω, τηλεθάω.

Τηλία: in Σηλία.

Τηλίκος, answ. to Ἡλίκος.

Τηλύγετος, born afar off: R. τῆλε, †γέω, γενάω, γίνομαι.—Also, as some say, 'born when his father was far away, or met. born far off in time, born late.' Buttm. compares it with Τελευταῖος, which he makes 'the last child, one followed by none,' even though none went before, as in Μοῦνος τηλύγετος.

Τημελὴς, careful, needful.—R. μέλει, it is a care to : but τη is unexplained; prob. from τῇ = ταύτῃ : 'Attending upon this very thing :' Rom. 13. 6. Or τῆνο.

Τήμερα, Τήμερον, Σήμερον, to-day. So Τῆτες, Σῆτες.—R. τῇ ἡμέρᾳ, on this day : and Σ, as Σὺ, Τύ.

Τῆμος, then : answering to Ἧμος, when. — Also, to-day : this answering perh. to Τήμερα: from Τὸ ἧμαρ.

Τηνάλλως, i.e. τὴν ἄλλως (ἄγουσαν ὁδὸν), by the way leading ἄλλως otherwise than what is right, i.e. in a vain way, to no purpose. (2) 'R. τῆνο ἄλλως, hoc frustrà :' Mrt.

Τήνελλα, a word invented ('ficta', says Bergler,) by Archilochus to imitate the twang of a guitar-string at the beginning of a triumphal hymn to Hercules :- Τήνελλα ὦ καλλί-νικε, &c.

Τηνίκα: answ. to Ἡνίκα.

Τῆνος, Κῆνος, = Κεῖνος.

Τηρέω, to watch attentively, guard carefully and narrowly.—Like Τῇ, from †τάω, †ταίνω, τείνω, *intendo* (animum), *intentus* sum, am *intent* on, attend to, as Ἀ-τενίζω : consider Τεταμένως. †Ταερὸς, †τηρὸς, τηρέω. Compare Τῆλε.

Τητάω, to bereave, deprive. — Damm makes it a redupl. from τάω, explained (ζητέω by the Etym. M.: τάω (as in Τῆ) being prop. to stretch out the hands to take, to desire, long for: act. to make to long for, cause to want, and so bereave. — Or, as Τεταγών, to lay hold of, appropriate, take away.

Τῆτες, Σῆτες, this year.—From ἔτος, a year, and Τ as in Τήμερον.

Τηθσιος, empty, vain, foolish, hurtful. — Like Διαπρύσιος in form; and from τῇ, like ταύτῃ, 'thus,' as Horace 'SIC temerè,' where Forcell. says that SIC seems to mean 'lightly, carelessly, negligently.' So Αὗτως, 'even so,' means 'in vain, without effect.' (2) R. τάω, explained (ζητέω by Hesych., as Μάτην, in vain, from Μάω.

ΤΙΑΡΑ, a Persian turban.

ΤΙΒΗΝ, 'as if Τριβήν, tripus, tripod :' Steph. But the P?—Only in Lycophr. 1104, so a barbarous word.

ΤΙΓΡΙΣ, a tiger.—Varro says, an Armenian word.

Τίζω, am always asking Τί, Why ?

Τίη, the same as Τί, why ?

Τιθαιβώσσω, 'to build, make a nest ; — make honeycombs ;— to nourish, foster, tend. Akin to Τίθη, Τίτθη, (a teat and a nurse,) Τιθήνη, &c.:' Ldd. †Τιθάω, †Τιθαιάσσω, as Καπρώσσω ; Τιθαιβώσσω, as ὠβὸν Dor. (2) Damm for Τίθημι βόσιν, to lay up food.

Τιθασὸς, Τιθασσὸς, tame, domesticated, — reared in gardens, of plants ;—domestic, of broils.— Prop. nursed, reared, tended, as in Τιθήνη and Τιθαιβώσσω. (2) R. Θάσσω, to sit (quiet).

Τιθῆ, the same as Τίτθη.

Τίθημι : in †Θέω.

Τιθήνη, a nurse ; — a mother. R. †Δάω, †Τιθάω, Τιθήνη, as Εἰρήνη : Giving suck. Τιθηνὸς adj. is used of nursing, tending, rearing, and in the masc. is used of a tutor. Ldd. allies Τιθήνη to Τίτθη, a TEAT.

Τιθὸς, the same as Τιθασός.

Τίκτω : in †Τέκω.

Τίλαι, things pulled to pieces, as flocks, motes in the hair, 'riff-raff flying from plucked rags :' Steph. — R. τίλλω.

Τιλάω, to dung ; esp. in a liquid manner : and Τίλος is dung in general, and esp. liquid dung. But it seems to be prop. riff-raff, refuse ; then, as Excernimentum, Excrementum, excrement, from τίλλω, to pluck. As Τίλαι.

Τίλλω, to pluck, pull, pick out ;— midd. pull the hair in grief, mourn.—It seems allied, through the affinity of Τ and Δ, to Δὶς, Δίχα, Διὰ, and to mean separation and excision. As Ψάω, Ψάλλω. (2) Scheide allies it to Τέλλω, to cause to rise up, as Dnn. makes 'Κίλλω a form akin to Κέλλω.' Hesych. explains Τίλλει by 'Ανα-σπᾷ, draws up. (3) Allied to our Till.

Τιμή, honor, &c.—R. τίω, τέτιμαι.

Τίμησις, valuation, census. — R. τίω.

Τιμωρὸς, 'honoring, valuing ; but usu. helping, aiding ; — avenging, punishing. R. τιμὴ, ἀείρω (ἄορα) αἴρω ;' Ldd. 'R. τιμὴ, ὅρω :' Dnn. For Τιμάορος.

Τινάσσω, to shake, brandish. — Allied to Δινέω, (as Δαῖσα, Τᾶδα,) to whirl or roll about ; or (as Σὺ and Τὺ,) to Σινίον a sieve, Σινιάζω to sift. — But Dnn. explains it prop. to hold forth, and derives it from τείνω. Nearer, τίνω. So Lenn. ' from τίω, pro-tendo.'

Τινθὸς, Τινθαλέος, boiling-hot. — 'Of comm. origin

169

with Θιβρὸς from a form Δίπω, τέθιππαι, τέθιπνται, τέθινται, whence Τινθός. So Τύφω to burn:' Dnn. (2) 'Τινθαλέος, perh. for Τιθαλέος, for Δαλέος from Δάλλω, [whence Δάλπω, to warm]': Lenn. (3) Our tind, tinder, Sax. tendan.

Τίνυμαι, to punish, Τίομαι. And Τίνω, to pay a penalty, as Τίω.

Τιὸ Τιὸ, imitation of a bird's note.

Τίπτε, = τί ποτε, why ever . . . ?

Τὶς, gen. τίνος, who ? Τίνος is prob. from τείνω or τίνω, to stretch out the hand to point to. 'Digito monstrabitur', Hor. — So Τις, some one.

Τιταίνω, as †Ταίνω, Τείνω, Τανύω, to stretch, spread out ;— draw along, as a chariot ;— midd. strain or exert oneself ; — strain, tend or move towards.

Τίτανος, 'gypsum, chalk, marble-scrapings. — Perh. from the Thessalian town or hill Τίτανος, Il. 2. 735, (Τιτάνοιό τε λευκὰ κάρηνα,) as Creta, chalk, from Creta, Crete :' Ldd. (2) Mrt. from τιταίνω, τιτανῶ : 'From its being drawn out in plastering.'

Τίταξ, a king ; Τιτήνη, a queen. Hence Ldd. derives the Τιτᾶνες, Titans, a race of gods : i.e. kings. —' R. perh. τίω, [τέτιται] :' Dnn. So Greg.: 'Τιτάνη, honorāta'. Compare Lat. titulus.

Τίτθη, a TEAT, nipple ;—a nurse. And Τιτθὸς a TEAT; — a nurser, rearer. 'Akin to Τιθ. R. Δάω, to suckle :' Dnn. (2) Our TEAT.

Τιτίζω, 'like Πιπίζω, to cry ti ti, chirrup like a young bird :' Ldd. To Twitter.

Τιτλάρια, 'a kind of writing-tables : others write Τιλλάρια, pens :' Ldd., i. e. from τίλλω : Plucked out from birds. Titulus is 'a ticket, scroll or tablet', Forcell. Τιτλάρια then from

Τίτλος, the Lat. titulus. And this from τίω, τέτιται : prop., a scroll or title or mark of honor.

Τιτραίνω, = τετραίνω.

Τιτρώσκω, to wound, prop. to pierce, Τιτραίνω. Formed from Τρόω, like †Τορέω, Τερέω, and allied to Τραύω, whence Τραῦμα a wound. (2) 'Hebr. tor, to cut :' Wr.

Τιτυβίζω, 'strictly of the cry of partridges: also, like Τιτίζω, of swallows, &c., to twitter, chirrup :' Ldd. — From the sound τιτ, twit.

Τίτυρος, Dor. for Σάτυρος, a Satyr, companion of Bacchus. Also, like Σάτυρος, a tailed ape. And the goat or ram that leads the flock. The Satyrs were represented with goats' legs : And the Satyr Pan had his nose flat like an ape.— But rather Τίτυρος is for Σίσυρος, (as Σὺ, Τὺ,) from σισύρα, prop. a goat's skin.

Τιτύσκομαι, to prepare, make ready, allied to Τεύχω, †Τύκω, †Τύσκω.

Τιτύσκομαι, to aim, i. e. as above, prepare the bow to strike.—Schultens compares through †τύω Lat. in-tueor, to look at, i. e. aim with the eye : and so both are allied to †τάω, †τέω, τείνω. 'Telumque tetendit :' Virg. 'Doctus sagittas tendere :' Hor. ΤΕΙΝΑΙ τὰ Δεῶν βέλη, Soph. So 'Ορεξάμενος Il. π. 314. See Τυγχάνω.

Z

Τιτώ, the day. — Allied to Τιτὰν, Titan, the god of the Sun. And to Τίταξ, which see.

Τίφη, a water-spider, supposed to be a marsh-spider, from Τῖφος. Also, a kind of small boat made for the marshes. And a kind of grass or straw, growing in or about the marshes. 'Herba palustris,' Steph. — From

Τῖφος, a marsh, pool; — marshy woodlands. — Much as Εἶφος, Ψῆφος. From τείνω, τίω, τάω, to extend, stretch out. Compare Τέναγος.

Τίω, to pay 1. an honor to a person, 2. a price: allied to Τάω, Τείνω, to stretch out the hand to pay: 1. To honor, esteem, value, rate. 2. To pay a compensation or retribution. Τίομαι, to punish, recompence, Ἀντι-τείνω. Compare Τῆ.

Τλάω: in Ταλάω.

Τλήμων, enduring, miserable,—bold, patient.—Above.

†Τμέω, Τμήγω, to cut, divide. — R. τέμνω, †τεμέω. Τόθεν: answ. to Ὅθεν.

Τοι, the old dat. τῳ or τωι, (as οἶκΟΙ for οἶκῳ,) from obs. †τος = πος, any. In any or some manner or respect. And, like Quidem for Aliquiddam, is 'indeed, truly,' &c. I.e., I must allow to a certain extent, in some degree. 'It is so indeed, but' &c.

Τοι, therefore : for τῷ, τῶι, i.e. τούτῳ, 'on account of this.'

Τοιος, of such a kind, of that kind.— R. τοῖ, τῷ, 'in this way', 'so'. See Οἷος.

Τοῖχος, the wall of a house or court: side of a ship. — Allied to Τεῖχος.

Τόκα, Dor. for Τότε, as Ὅτε, Ὅκα.

Τοκεὺς, a father.—R. τέκω, τέτοκα, τίκτω. So

Τόκος, gain produced by money at interest.—Above : as †Φεο, Φύω, Fenus.

Τολμάω, like Τλάω, †Ταλάω, to bear, endure, hazard, undertake, undergo, tolero, &c. Τόλμα, boldness. — See †Ταλάω.

Τολύπη, a clew or ball wound up for spinning : Τολο-πεύω, to wind up, hence to finish, as Τελέω, accomplish, achieve. And to wind off for spinning, — spin, devise. As Τολύπη is the ball wound up, and this is the 'finishing', then from τελέω, τέτολα, to finish. As πόρΠΗ, ἀγαΠΗ. (2) 'R. ταλάω, as Ταλάσιον :' Mrt. Compare ΤΟΛμάω.

Τομή, a cutting, cut, &c. — R. τέμνω, τέτομα.

Τόμια, as Ἔν-τομα, entrails of victims cut out for sacrifices on taking oaths.—Above.

Τόμουρος, Τόμᾶρος, priest at Dodōna.—'As these were Egyptian rites, prob. from τομὴ, οὐρά : from the priests being circumcised :' Hemst. 'A eunuch. — Some from Mount Τμᾶρος in Epirus : Jupiter Tmarius in Claudian. The mount is called Τόμαρος by Strabo :' Ldd.—'From the τομαὶ sections or Templa (as this from Τέμνω,) into which they divided the sky :' Scheid. — Or from τόμος, a book, (= τομή : Separate part of a book,) οὖρος, a guard. As guarding the sacred books containing the laws.

Τονθορύζω, to mutter, babble. — 'Formed prob. to re-
170

present the sound :' Dnn. and Lenn.— ' R. τόνος :' Mrt. Allied to Lat. tono, to thunder.

Τόνος, tension.— R. τείνω, τέτονα ; — strain or tone in music ;—accent, measure, &c.; intensity, vehemence ; — a rope, cord, to strain or tighten, or which may itself be stretched.

Τόξον, a bow ; plur. bow and arrows, and the arrows only. — 'Τάζω, τάξον, τόξον :' Etym. M. As Ἄγκος, Ὄγκος ; Ἀγμὸς, Ὄγμος ; λΑγχάνω, λέλΟγχα ; &c. 'Doctus sagittas Tendere :' Hor. Or the obs. †τόω, τάω, whence ἐκ-έτοσσε in Pindar, 4. 4. 43. (2) R. †τέκω, †τέξω, whence Τέκτων, Τεύχω, and Τεῦχος, an implement, weapon, &c.

ΤΟΠΑΖΙΟΝ, a topaz.—Pliny says, from Topazos, an island in the Red Sea.

Τοπάζω, to conjecture, suspect. — R. τόπος. I. e. to give a place to a conjecture. Somewhat as Hammond : 'There is no PLACE of doubting that.' ' To figure out in one's fancy :' Schrev. — Others thus : to attempt to put into a place by aiming at,—to aim at by conjecture, as Στοχάζομαι.

Τόπος, a place, spot : place or passage in a book. — R. †τόω, (like †τάω,) to extend, (a word asserted by Heyne, Pind. P. 4. 43): Extent of place. — Greg. from †τάω, τῶ, as meaning to take, receive, like Τάζω, Τεταγών. See Τῆ. And compare Χώρα, Χῶρος. (2) 'Chald. tephas, comprehendo :' Mrt.

Τόργος, a vulture.—R. τορὸς, 'sharp, said of the sight, the Lat. torvus', (Dnn.) ꙮ τορΓός. Or †τοριχός.

Τορεύω, in the same senses as Τορέω. Also, 'to grave as a sculptor, hollow out; engrave, carve, form figures in alto or basso relievo, emboss ;— polish or give the last finish with the chisel :' Dnn.

Τορέω, as Τερέω, to bore, pierce :— utter in a loud and piercing tone.

Τόρμα, -μη, the same as Τέρμα, a turning-post.

Τόρμος, a hole or socket, nave of a wheel, the socket in which a door turns. — R. τορέω, to bore.

Τόρνος, ' a carpenter's tool for drawing a round, like our compasses ;— a turner's chisel, lathe-chisel, — a carver's knife or chisel;— that which is turned, a circle, round. The same with Τόρμος, Τόρμη, akin to †Τορέω, Τείρω :' Ldd. That which wears away or chases in turning. So Τορνεύω, -όω, torno, to turn, work with a lathe and chisel, to round.

Τορὸς, piercing, sharp, clear, audible ;— intelligible, explicit, accurate :—sharp, active.— R. τορέω, to pierce.

Τορύνη, a stirrer, ladle for stirring liquids on the fire. R. τείρω, τέτορα, to rub : As rubbing and bruising substances in a pot. So from †τορύω, τρύω, to rub, is Τρυήλης a ladle for stirring with. Hence Τορυνητὸν, panada or stir-about.

Τόσος, so great: answering to Ὅσος.

Τόσσαις : in Ἐπέτοσσε.

Τότε, i. e. τῷτε, 'and at that (time),' 'then,' answering to Ὅτε.

†ΤΟΦΟΣ, tuff, sandstone, rotten-stone, töfus, Germ.

tof. Τόφος is not found: only Τοφεὼν, a quarry, in Tab. Heracl. — Q. if allied to Τέφρα ? Loose crumbling stone like so much burnt ashes ?

Τόφρα, for so long; — for such an object, so that. — Answering to Ὄφρα.

Τραγανὸν, a callosity; — cartilage. — R. τρήχω, ξω, †έτραγον, 'to be rough or stiff,' (Dnn.). Thus Aristotle says of sponges, that one kind are ' very hard and τραχεῖς rough, called Τράγοι.'

Τραγάω, ' to be over-luxuriant and so unfruitful: as buck-goats high in flesh are unfit to produce:' Dnn. R. τράγος.

Τράγημα, and Τρωγάλια, 'what is eaten for eating's sake, dried-fruits, as figs, almonds:' Ldd. — R. τράγω.

Τράγος, a he-goat, from τράγω, έτραγον, to gnaw. As in Ovid: ' RODE, caper, vitem.' But some from τρήχω, to be rough. Also, the smell' of the arm-pits, like that of a goat;— lasciviousness, as of the goat:— and the first period of the sensual appetite, whence Τραγίζω to change the voice at the time of puberty.

Τραγ-ῳδία, tragedy, the prize for which was a goat. — R. τράγος, ᾠδή. ' Carmine qui tragico vilem certavit' ob HIRCUM,' Hor.

ΤΡΑΚΤΟΝ, white-bleached wax; Τράκτωμα, a sticking plaster made of it. — A Latin word, if Stephens rightly explains τράκτος κηρὸς 'cera quæ tractando inalbuit.' And Τράκτα is a kind of paste, (Steph.) *tracta*, mentioned by Cato, and expl. by Forcell.: 'manibus bene subacta, et in longum *tracta* in modum membranarum.'

Τραμπη, Τράμις, the line dividing the scrotum and passing on. Allied by Ldd. to Lat. *trames, tramitis*. But perhaps from †τράω, τετραίνω, to perforate, and so to divide. Moreover, Τράμις is also the hole τὸ Τρῆμα of the breach, says Photius.

Τραμπὶς, a ship. — For τραπὶς, (as ΛαΜΘάνω,) allied by Ldd. to *Trabs, Trabis*, and Τράπηξ, which see. (Rare.)

Τρανὴς, piercing, shrill; — clear. — As Τορὸς from τορέω, †τρέω, so from †τράω, τιτραίνω is Τρανής.

Τράπεζα, a table, bench, tablet; — counter, bank : Τραπεζίτης, a banker.—For τετρά-πεζα, having four feet. As Avunculus, Uncle.

Τραπέω, to tread or trample on grapes. — Jones from τρέπω, τραπῶ: To TURN about as in treading. Damm: ' To tread so as to TURN into wine.'

Τράπηξ, Τράφηξ, *trabs, trabis*, a beam : but it really means the handle of an oar, (Hesych.) R. τρέπω. ' Perhaps because in rowing it is *turned* hither and thither:' says Steph. Or, with Dnn., 'as with it a boat is *turned* or moved.' See St. James 3. 4. — Or properly a curved beam : Τράπηξ meaning also the keel of a ship, like Τρόπις, which see.

Τρασιὰ, for Ταρσιὰ like Τάρσος, a hurdle to dry cheeses on. So Πέρθω, έπαρθον, έπραθον.

Τραυλὸς, lisping, mispronouncing.—'R. Θραύω to break: Θραυλὸς :' Ldd. Or even †τραύω, to wound, ('clip the Queen's English,') whence Τραῦμα. Compare Κωφὸς and Ψελλός.

171

Τραῦμα, a wound. — Allied to Τρόω, Τιτρώσκω, to wound, through obsolete †Τραύω.

Τραφερὸς, fat, well-fed; — fattening. — R. τρέφω, έτραφον.

Τράφηξ: in Τράπηξ.

Τραχηλίζω, ' to take by the throat; — to bend the neck back or grip by the throat; — bend back the victim's neck, so that the throat gapes when cut; hence to expose to view, lay open:' Ldd. — From Τράχηλος, the neck, throat. — Hemsterh. from the roughness of its joints, from τράχὺς, or rather τρήχω, †έτράχον to be rough. 'From the processes of the cervical vertebræ :' Dnn. (2) R. τρέχω, from the circular form. Compare Θόλος from Θέω, Ίτνς, and Περί-δρομος a circular gallery.

Τράχὺς, rough, rugged.—R. †τράω, τιτράω, τιτραίνω, τετραίνω, to pierce.

ΤΡΕΙΣ, ΤΡΙΑ, *tres, three*. — ' Dre Sax., dry Du., tri Welsh and Erse :' Dr. J. — Suppose, as 5 is thought called in Greek from the *five* fingers, so 3 called from the *three* WORKING fingers, i.e. the thumb and the two next : from δράω, i. e. δρέες, δρεῖς, τρεῖς, as D is found in the Sax. and Dutch, and ΔΡΕμω and ΤΡΕχω are allied. ?

Τρέμω, to tremble, *tremo*, τρέω.

Τρέπω, to turn.—' The old Lat. *trepo*. The radical Τρέω to tremble:' Dnn. I. e. to make τρέειν to fear, to terrify, rout, turn. As †βλέω, βλέΠω; δρέΠω.

Τρέφω, to make thick, curdle, coagulate; derived by Parkh. from τρέπω, τέτρεφα, to turn i.e. into curd: then, to make compact, firm, or solid, to fatten, nourish, feed, rear up. So Dalzel makes it prop. to coagulate. (2) R. Θέρω, †Θερέω, †Θρέω, to warm, cherish, nourish. (3) ' Hebr. *tereph*, to feed:' Wr.

Τρέχνος, in Τέρχνος.

Τρέχω, to run.—Like Τρέπω, from τρέω, to flee. Thus ' Τρέχω with ψυχῆς and περὶ έωντοῦ, to run for his life: met. to hazard, risk:' (Dnn.) The fut. †τρέξω was softened into Θρέξω. (2) ' For ΔρΕχω allied to †Δρέμω, Δρόμος. (3) ' Hebr. *derek*, to go forward:' Wr.

Τρέω, to fear, tremble, flee.—' R. τείρω:' Mrt. Future τερῶ, †τερέω, τρέω: Prop. to be distressed, tormented, allied to Ταράσσομαι, to be agitated.

Τρέω, to bore: for Τορέω.

Τρῆμα, a hole; pl. the holes or pips of dice. — R. τράω, τιτραίνω, or τορέω, †τρέω, to pierce. What is pierced through.

Τρήρων, fearful, from τρέω: also 'the fearful dove.' Τρήρωσι πελειάσι, Hom.

Τρηχύς: Ion. of Τράχὺς.

Τριάκοντα, 30. — R. τρία, and -κοντα formed perh. from είκοσι, είκοτι, †είκοΝτι, Lat. vigiNti. So Πεντή-κοντα, &c.

Τριάζω, to conquer, i. e. to throw one's adversary τρία three times. ' This is one of my THREE conflicts,' has Æschylus. So Τριαγμὸς a victory, and allied seems (†Τρίαμβος,) Θρίαμβος, *Triumphus, Triumph*.

Τρίαινα, a trident. — R. τρία, tria.

Τριβακὸς, rubbed, worn, fine; — inured, practised, hackneyed, crafty, as Τρίβων, Τρίμμα. — R. τρίβω.

Τριβαλλοὶ, 'the Triballi, a people on the borders of Thrace; hence a Comic name for barbarian gods:— a slang term for young fellows who lounge about taverns, like the Mohocks of Addison's times;' Ldd.

Τρίβολος, 'like Τρι-βελὴς, three-pointed, three-pronged; hence subst. a caltrop;— a thing of like shape on a horse's bridle; — from the likeness of shape, a prickly water-plant, water-caltrop, tribulus, and a land-plant; — plur. smart sayings, gibes, Fr. pointes:' Ldd. — R. τρία, βολή.

Τρίβος, a beaten path; — practice, exercise; — delay. — R. τρίβω, τρῖβῶ.

Τρίβω, to rub, wear, bruise, wear out, exhaust, ener-vate; — wear the time, protract, delay; — become trite and common;— mid. to wear away the time on anything, exercise oneself in, inure oneself to. — 'Allied to Τείρω, and Trivi, Tritum:' Dnn. Thus : τερῶ, †τερίω, †τρίω, τρύω. So Θλάω, ΘΛΙΒΩ. And see Ἀμφι-τρίτη. (2) 'Hebr. tereph, to tear:' Wr.

Τρίβων, well-versed or skilled, &c., as Τριβακὸς. Also, a worn thread-bare cloak. — R. τρίβω.

Τρίζω, to squeak, chirp, — creak, grate, jar. — Allied to Στρίζω, Strido. 'Τρίζω and Κρίζω prob. formed to imitate the sound :' Dnn. Or for Τερετίζω. Or even allied to Τρίβω, to rub, scrape.

Τρίμμα, a practised knave, as Τριβακὸς, Τρίβων : τρίβω, τέτριμμαι.

Τρίναξ, a trident. — R. τρία.

Τριξὸς, for Τρισσὸς, as Δισσὸς, Διξός.

Τριοτὸ, 'a sound imitative of a bird's voice :' Ldd.

Τριοττὶς, ear-ring with three eyes or drops: τρία, †ὔττε, ὄσσε, eyes.

Τριπέμπελος, childish from age. — From τρία, πέμπελος, which see. (2) Dr. Jones from τρία, πέμπω: 'Who sends himself on with three legs.'

Τριπλάσιος, Τριπλόος, triple. As Διπλάσιος, Δίπλοος.

Τρί-πους, Τρίπος, g. τρί-ποδος, tripod :—τρία, ποῦς.

Τρὶς, thrice, as Δὶς, twice : R. τρισὶ dat. of Τρεῖς.

Τρισσὸς, Τρίτος, Τρίτατος, third. — R. τρίς.

Τριτογένεια, Minerva, born at the Lake Tritōnis in Libya. 'Pallas Libycis Tritonidos edita lymphis :' Sil.

Τριττὺς, the third of a tribe, &c. — R. τρίτος.

Τρίχα, Τριχθὰ, in three ways. — R. τρία, as Δίχα, Διχθά.

Τριχὶς : in Τρίσσα.

Τρόμος, trembling. — R. τρέμω.

Τροπαῖον, tropaeum, a trophy raised at a Τροπῆ.

Τροπάλὶς, Τροπηλὶς, a bundle, bunch. — R. τρέπω, as Τροπός, a twisted thong. See Τροπός.

Τροπὴ, turning of the enemy : τρέπω.

Τρόπηξ, handle of an oar, 'by which a boat τρέπεται is turned or moved :' Dnn. See in Τράπηξ.

Τρόπις, a ship's keel. All from τρέπω. 'As made

172

of timbers turned': Greg. Compare Τράπηξ. Hence metaph. the commencement.

Τρόπος, the turn, disposition, character, temper of the mind ;— the manner of doing anything, as marking the turn of mind, as Κατὰ τὸν Ἑλληνικὸν τρόπον, After the Greek fashion. Also a trope or figure, change from the ordinary to a figurative meaning. — R. τρέπω.

Τροπὸς, 'a twisted leathern thong, with which the oars were fastened to the thole: called also Στρόφος, stroppus, (a strap). Also a beam: see Τράπηξ :' Ldd. — R. τρέπω, verto, volvo.

Τρουλλίον, trulla, a trowel, shovel: allied to Τρυήλη, a ladle. (2) From the Lat. trua, trulla.—Very rare.

Τροφαλὶς, fresh cheese. — R. τρέφω, to curdle.

Τροφὴ, food. — R. τρέφω.

Τροχαῖος, a trochee, - ∪. All derive from τρόχος, cursus. Terent. Maur. calls the Iamb 'pedem raptim citum,' and adds of the Trochee: 'Nec minùs CURRIT Τροχαῖος lege versâ temporum.'

Τροχαλέα, a roller, wheel, pulley, windlass. — R. τρέχω, to run.

Τροχίλος, a wren;— a wagtail, sandpiper, or such like. — R. τρέχω. So Currūca, the hedge-sparrow, seems to come from Curro.

Τροχὸς, a wheel, hoop, &c. And Τροχάω, to revolve. — R. τρέχω.

Τρύβλιον, a cup, bowl, dish. — 'I think it is that in which are put τὰ τρυόμενα, intrita, tritæ escæ :' Mrt. Or R. θρύπτω, †ἔτρυβον, as ἐκάλυβον. Compare Τορύνη.

Τρύγη, 'ripe fruit gathered in for keeping, fruit, corn, from τρύγω, to dry, as the notion of ripeness includes that of dryness; Τρύγη means also dryness :'Ldd. — See in Τρύξ.

Τρυγονάω, Θρυγανάω, to tap at the door.—' To make a hollow murmuring sound : from τρύζω :' Dnn.

Τρύγω, Τρύσκω, to dry. — ' R. Θέρω, [Θερύω,] τερύω. Or τείρω, τέρω :' Schneid. Compare Τέρσω.

Τρυγῳδία, comedy. — ' Called from the prize which was a cask of (new) wine :' Bentl. ' Because the singers smeared their faces with lees as a ludicrous disguise : Hor. A. P. 277 :' Ldd. — R. τρὺξ, τρυγός.

Τρύγων, turtle-dove, from its cooing. — R. τρύζω, τέτρῦγα.

Τρύζω, 'like Τρίζω : Τρύζω referring to duller, Τρίζω to sharper, shriller sounds :' Ldd. ' Doubtless formed to imitate the sense :' Dnn.

Τρυήλα, -ης, 'a cook's ladle or pestle. Comp. our trowel, [and trulla]. R. τρύω :' Dnn.

Τρυλλίζω, to cry, esp. used of the quail. —' Formed from the sound, as Τρύζω :' Ldd. and Dnn.

Τρύμη, Τρυμαλιά, a hole. — R. τρύω, to rub a hole.

Τρύμη, like Τρίμμα, a knave. — R. τρύω. See Τρίμμα.

Τρὺξ, gen. τρυγὸς, 'new wine not yet fermented and racked off, wine with the lees in it, — hence new bad wine ; — the lees of wine or oil, dregs, dross, metaph. of an old man:' Ldd.—'R. τρύγη, or the same origin:' Dnn., who adds the sense of '*wine*' to the meanings given by Ldd. of Τρύγη. So Schrevel. of Τρύγη, '*wheat, corn, fruits, vintage.*' (**2**) 'Hebr. *tirosch*, mustum:' Mrt. ?

Τρυπάω, from τρύω : to bore a hole, pierce with an auger called Τρύπανον.

Τρυσσὸς, easy to be rubbed, friable.— R. τρύω, σω.

Τρυτάνη, a balance, and the tongue, *trutina.* — All derive from τρύω. ' Eustath. as it τρύεται [is much worn, *trita*, opp. τὸ ἄ-τρυτος,] by the weight of the things weighed. If it is prop. the *hole* of the balance, within which is the tongue, then rightly from τρύω = τράω, to perforate, as Τρύμη [and Τρύπα]:' Greg.

Τρυφάλεια, ' a helmet with a φάλος projection to receive the plume. Τρύω:' Buttm. Τετρυμένη. (**2**) For Τρι-φάλεια, as Τετρά-φαλος is also used. ?

Τρυφαλλὶς, a small piece or slice.—And

Τρυφὴ, effeminacy, luxury, insolence, wantonness.— R. θρύπτω, ἔτρυφον: As breaking down, dissolving, weakening the strength or corrupting the morals.

Τρύφος, a morsel, fragment.— R. θρύπτω, ἔτρυφον.

Τρῦχος, a rag, shred.— R. τρύχω, to wear out,—as in Τρύω, Τρύχω, to wear, rub, wear a hole ; — wear the spirits, fatigue, vex, molest, afflict.— R. τείρω, τερῶ, †τερύω, σω. So Hemst., &c.

Τρωγάλια, ων : in Τράγημα.

Τρώγλη, a hole, hollow, cave.— R. τρώγω: As eaten through, exēsa.

Τρώγω, to gnaw, eat.— R. τορέω, †τρώω, τρώγω, as Τμήγω : To pierce with the teeth. — Or τείρω, to rub, as Τρύχω.

Τρώκτης, a devourer : R. τρώγω, τέτρωκται. —' In Homer, Phœnician traffickers are called Τρῶκται, greedy knaves : some however take it as a proper name :' Ldd. ' In vulgar language, a bite:' Dnn. ' A devourer of others :' Damm. ' To *truck*, traffick by exchange, Fr. *troquer*, Span. *trocar*. Deduced by Salmas. from τρώγω to get money :' Todd.

Τρώξ, a caterpillar ; i.e. gnawer.— R. τρώγω, ξω.

Τρώξανον, what falls from the manger while cattle are eating. R. τρώγω, τρώξω. Also, dry wood, brushwood: allied to Τρύγη, dryness, which is allied to Τρύξ.

Τρωπάω, Τρωχάω, formed from Τρέπω, Τρέχω.

Τρώω, to woand, hurt : in Τιτρώσκω.

Τὺ, *tu, thou :* See in Σύ.

Τυγχάνω, through †Τυχέω, †Τεύχω, to strike upon, hit or light upon, chance upon, find, obtain : — happen to do, or to be, prop. τυγχάνω ἐών. Ὁ τυχὼν, one who happens upon you, any chance or common person. Allied to Τιτύσκομαι, to aim at, hit; which see : And to Τύπτω. Dnn. allies Τιταίνω.

Τύκος, Τύχος, 'from τεύχω: an instrument for working stones with, mason's hammer or pick : — from the likeness of shape, a battle-axe:' Ldd. So

Τυκτὸς, wrought, made, well-wrought, Τευκτός.— R. τεύχω.

Τύλη, Τύλος, any swelling, lump, bunch, nail, knot,

peg, spindle ;—pad, bolster, cushion.—As γΤνη, βΤθὸς κΤθηλις, ρΤμβος, νΤμφη, so τΤλη is allied to Τέλλω, Ἀνα-τέλλω, to rise up: for †Τόλη, †Τόλος : and allied to Tollo, Tuli, Sus-tuli, to raise up. (**2**) R. †τύω, †τάω, †τέω, to extend, expand. Tumeo, Tumor, must be noticed.

Τυλίσσω, to roll up, prop. in the form of a Τύλη, bolster.

Τυλόω, to make callous : — R. τύλος in Τύλη.

Τύμβος, ' strictly the place where a dead body τύφεται is burnt : usu. a (*tumulus*) mound of earth heaped over the ashes ; — a tomb, — tomb-stone ; — old man just going to the tomb :' Ldd. Comp. στρόΜΒΟΣ. (**2**) Some compare *tumeo, tumulus.* ' Welsh *twm* mound : Ir. *tuoma* :' Wbst.

Τύμμα, a blow.—R. τύπτω, τέτυμμαι.

Τύμπανον, a kettle-drum ; — drum-stick, or gen. a stick to beat with : *Tympanum*.—R. τύπτω, †τύπανον, τύμπανον, as λαΜΒάνω, στρόΜΒος.

Τύνη, = τὺ, *tu*, thou.

Τυνὸς, Τυννὸς, small.—' These sound like the Latin *Tenuis* :' says Mrt. And *Tenuis* is Ταναὸς, extended, long, thin. Τυνὸς seems an Æolic form, as γΤνὴ, βΤθὸς, &c. Compare Ἐλαχύς. (**2**) Our *tiny*, Dan. *tynd*.

ΤΥΝΤΛΟΣ, ' mud and confusion :' Phot. ' In Aristoph. P. 1148 Τυντλάζω is to grub round a vine's roots, i. e. by going in the mud or mire :' Ldd. Τύντλος is explained by Schrevel. ' clay, trifles.' And Τυντλώδης is silly, frivolous. — Perhaps all from τυνὸς, small, and so frivolous, trifling ; then earth reduced small, mire, &c. : †τύνελος, †τύνλος. See Κόπρος from Κόπτω. The Dan. *tint, tynd*, small, is still nearer.

Τύπος, stamp, figure, impression, mould, pattern, form, rough sketch, &c. — From

Τύπτω, to strike, beat. — Allied to Τυγχάνω, to hit a mark ; Τιτύσκομαι, to aim at or hit : and perhaps Ἀ-τύζω. Comp. θρΤΙΠΩ, θΤΙΠΩ, βλάΠΤΩ. (**2**) Mrt. from Hebr. Rab. *thaph*, to beat. Our *top*, Fr. *taper*, Dan. *tapper*. See Δοῦπος. All from the sound.

Τύραννος, a king, tyrant.—Gen. thought the same as Κύριος and Κοίρανος, as Τῆνος and Κεῖνος. (**2**) Mrt. from τείρω, τέτορα, to oppress, torment. Τ Æolic, as γΤνὴ, βΤθὸς. (**3**) As lord of Τύρος, Tyre. (**4**) Allied to τΤΡσις, a tower, TURris. See Τύρσις.

Τύρβη : in Σύρβη.

Τυρὸς, cheese. Βού-τυρον, *butter*.—' Some from obs. †τύρω akin to †τάρω, the assumed R. of Ταράσσω, to stir up: Hence Τυρόω, to stir up, disturb:' Dnn.—This last suggests †τύρω as = σύρω, (like Τὺ, Σύ; Τῆτες, Σῆτες ; Τεῦτλον, Σεῦτλον,) whence Σύρβη, Τύρβη, *Turbo, Dis-turb*. (**2**) Mrt. from τείρω, τέτορα, to rub, wipe dry, whence Τέρσω, to dry. Τ Æolic, as γΤνὴ, βΤθὸς, νΤμφη.

ΤΥΡΣΙΣ, ΤΥΡΡΙΣ, *turris*, a tower, Sax. *tor*.—As Θύρσος from θύω, Βύρσα from βύω, Τύρσις might flow from †τύω, †τέω, τέλλω, to rise.—Dnn. allies TURgeo.

Τυτθὸs, 'young, or small. Allied to Τιτθὸs, Τίτθη :' Dnn. ' Yet under the Τιτθός :' Mrt. (2) Our *tit* in *Tit*-mouse, Tom-*tit*.

Τύφη, 'a plant used for stuffing bolsters, our cat's-tail :' Ldd.—Allied to Στύφω, to draw together, and our *Stuff*. (2) Our *tough*.

Τυφλὸs, blind.—' Prob. τυφελὸs from τύφω : Smoky, misty, darkened :' Ldd. Or having τῦφον smoke cast in the eyes, a mist thrown over the eyes. (2) R. τύπτω, τέτυφα, as from Κωφὸs from Κόπτω is Κώφωσις ὀφθαλμῶν in Erotian.

Τῦφοs, smoke, mist, cloud ;—met. conceit, vanity, as all smoke ;—folly, silliness ;—stupor as clouding and darkening the mind, arising from fever, *typhus*. And

Τύφω, to raise a τῦφος smoke, to smoke, to consume in smoke.—' Τύφω is certainly akin to Θύω, Θυμὸs, Æolic

Φυμὸs, *Fumus* : also to Θάπτω, Τέφρα, *Tepor* :' Dnn.

Τυφὼs, a furious whirlwind, whirling clouds of dust, from Τῦφος, smoke, cloud. (2) ' Because it was held to be the work of the giant *Typhus* :' Ldd.

Τύχη, chance, luck, fortune.—R. †τυχέω, τυγχάνω to light on.

Τωθάζω, to taunt, mock.—From the obs. †τόω, †ἐτάθην, as in 'Επ-ετόσσε, Τόσσας, Τόσος, allied to Τάω, †Τέω, Τείνω, to stretch out, then point i.e. the hands in derision. In form, compare Ψόθιον, 'Ρώθων, Κλόθω. (2) As Taunt from the ancient Tand, a tooth, so Τωθάζω allied to our *tooth*, Sax. *toth* : To show the *teeth*, snarl at. Or in the sense, ' to cast in the *teeth*', Matth. 27. 44.

Τὼs, so : answering to 'Ωs.—Prop. τοῖς i.e. τούτοις, ' his modis.'

Υ.

"Υ ὒ, sound to imitate a person snuffing a feast. ' Ηυ hu !' Plaut.

'Υάγων or Συάγων, = Σιάγων.

'Υάδεs, the *Hyades* or *Rainers*, a constellation supposed to bring rain : hence Virgil, ' Pluvias *Hyadas*,' the rainy *Hyades*.—R. ὕω.

"Υαινα, a sow, from "Υs, ὑός : —the hyena, with a bristly mane like a hog. Αἱ θαιναι, the women dedicated to Mithras, the men being called Lions.

"Υαλος, "Υελος, alabaster, crystal, amber, glass.—R. ὕω : from the watery or rainy color of glass. Salmas. says it is ' prop. *humectum*, dein pro *lucido*.' ' From the transparency of glass', Dnn., who adds, ' R. ὕω, for χύω, to melt.' As Γαῖα, Αἶα ; Λείβω, Εἶβω. In form as κρύσταΛΛΟΣ.

'Υβὸs, hump-backed.—' Υβὸs and Κυφὸs are prob. the same word. Compare *Gibbus* :' Dnn. And Germ. *Hübel*. So Λείβω, Εἶβω : Γαῖα, Αἶα. (2) R. ὑπό : Bent under. So Συνὸs, 'Αντίοs. B as in ὕβρις.

'Υβρις, proud insolence, outrage, violence.—R. ὑπὲρ, ὑπερὸs, ὑπερὶs, ὕπρις, ὕβρις : as Super, Superbus. The setting oneself above others.

'Υβρις, ιδος, a mongrel, *hybrid*.—Perh. allied to the above : as an injury or outrage to Nature.

'Υγιὴs, healthy, vigorous, sound.—Allied to 'Υγρὸs, which, says Damm, often means ' bene valens.' Dnn. gives the sense ' nimble, agile ', to 'Υγρός ; and ' agility' to 'Υγρότης : and refers 'Υγιὴs to ὕω, ' from the intimate connection betw. moisture and growth.'

'Υγρὸs, wet, moist ;—pliant, tender, soft.—R. ὕω, to wet, ὕκα, †ὕκρὸs, ὑγρός.—Or from †ὕζω, †ὕγον.

'Υδέω, 'Υδῶ, "Υδω, to tell of, celebrate, sing, as "Αδω. —'From ὕω. The notion of singing flows easily from irrigation. All poets are said to have *watered* their gardens from the fountain of Homer :' Valck. (2)

174

Perhaps "Υδω is only "Αδω Æolicised. As γΥνὴ, βΥθὸs, "Υδνον. (2) ' Hebr. *hodah*, celebro :' Mrt.

"Υδνον, = οἶδνον, a puff-ball : Æolicè.

'Υδρία, a water-pot ;—any vessel.—And

"Υδρωψ, ωπος, dropsy for *hydropsy*.—R. ὕδωρ. Horace: ' Aquosus humor.'

"Υδωρ, water.—R. ὕω, as 'Ιδρὼs from †ἱέω, †ἱῶ, Ἱημι. Herod.: 'Υσαι ὕδατι λαβροτάτῳ.

'Υειος, belonging to 'Υεs, *sues*, swine : — 'Υηνέω, to be like a hog.

'Υετὸs, rain.—R. ὕω.

'Υηs, 'epith. of Jupiter, like 'Υέτιος: Jupiter pluvius. Also of Bacchus : prob. as the god of fertilising moisture : hence his mother Semelé was called 'Υη, and the nymphs who reared him 'Υάδες :' Ldd.

'Υθλος, idle talk, nonsense : also "Υσλος.—R. ὕδω, ὕθαι, ὕσαι, to talk of, to sing : Sing-song. In 'Υθέω. (2) ' Hebr. *hithul*, derisio :' Mrt.

'Υὸs, 'Υιεὺs, 'Υὶs, a son.—' R. ὕω, φύω :' Dnn. See in 'Υλη. 'Ο φὺς is a ' son ' in Eur. Ph.—But perhaps ὕω in *its own* sense, much as 'Αρόω and Σπείρω are used ' de generandis hominibus.' 'Υὶs would thus answer much to the same use of Σπόρος or Σπέρμα: An efflux. (2) R. φύω, †φυιὸs, υἱὸs, as Γαῖα, Αἶα, and Φεῦ, Heu.

'Υιωνὸs, a grandson : R. υἱὸs, as Οἷος, Οἰωνός.

'Υλάω, 'Υλακτέω, to HOWL, YELL, ululo, bark, bark at. Icel. *yla*, Germ. *heulen*, Hebr. *helil*. All from the sound.

'Υλη, †ὕλϝα, *Sylva* or *Silva*, wood, a wood, under-wood, wood cut down for fuel, fire-wood :—the raw un-wrought material, whether wood, stone, metal, &c.—matter, of which a thing is made—subject-matter, matter treated of.—' R. ὕω in the sense of φύω : A place where trees or plants grow :' Dnn. As Γαῖα, Αἶα:

Φεῦ, Heu: Φέρβω, Herba. — Or ὕω in *its own* sense, as from this Dnn. elsewhere derives Ὕλη, 'from the intimate connection between moisture and growth.' So Greg. 'from ὕω, as timbers require much rain [or moisture].'

Ὑλίζω, to cleanse, strain, filter.—Schleusn. from ὕλη, 'thick matter, sediment.' See Ὕλη, 'matter.' So Dnn. also, who adds: 'From ὕλις for ἰλὺς accord. to the old Gramm.'

Ὑμέναιος, *hymenæus*, wedding song, marriage: also *Hymen*, Ὑμὴν, the god of marriage. Ὑμὴν δ᾽ Ὑμέναιε. Eurip.— Ὑμὴν, ὑμένος is in this sense gen. derived from ὑμένος which produced Ὕμνος, *hymnus*: The marriage song. (2) A sequenti ὑμὴν, ut dictum puta de virgineâ *membranâ*.

Ὑμὴν, a skin, membrane. ' By Ὑμένες physicians meant the thin skins, covering the eyes, from their moisture, for they were always moist except in sleep:' Valck. That is, from ὕω, ὕμαι, to wet. (2) Some from ὑφῶ to weave. A web.

Ὕμνος, *hymnus*, a song, hymn.—For ὑδόμενος or pf. ὑμένος, sung. Compare Σεμνός.

ΫΝ, ᾿ΙΝ, a *hin*, a *Hebrew* measure.

Ὕννις, Ὕνις, a plough-share. — 'Plutarch from ὕς, acc. ὕν, from the hog's nozzling and rooting;' Ldd.

Ὕννος, the same as Ἴννος.

Ὑοσ-κύαμος, ' strictly Hog-bean, answering to our Hen-bane, which causes giddiness and madness : Ὑοσ-κυαμάω, to be raving-mad :' Ldd.

Ὕπαρ, a real visible appearance, opposed to Ὄναρ; whence Homer's Οὐκ ᾿ΟΝΑΡ ἀλλ᾽ ΫΠΑΡ. — Scaliger from τύπέω, ὕπ-ειμι, as Ὑπό-στασις, 'a real existence,' ' substance.' In form as Εἶδαρ.

Ὕπατος, for ὑπέρτατος, most above, highest, from ὑπέρ. Much as Inferissimus, Infimus: Optatissimus, Optimus.

ΫΠΕΡ, *super*, Ang. Sax. *ofer*, our *over*, above;— *over*, across, beyond;—like *super*, on or about, concerning; — over, so as to defend, in defence of; — on behalf of, in the room of. ' Mœs. Goth. *ufar*, Scotch *war*:' Dunb. (2) R. τύπτω, ἅπτω, to join, connect. Compare Ὑπό and Ἐπί.

Ὑπέρα, the UPPER rope, i. e. the brace attaching the sailyards to the mast. — R. ὑπέρ. Properly *Supera*.

Ὕπερος, -ον, a pestle. — Prob. as simply being used ὑπὲρ over the mortar. See Ὑπέρα, Ὑπερφά.

Ὑπερφίαλος, ' most huge, exceeding in power;— overbearing, arrogant.— 1. Βία, ὑπέρ-βιος, †ὑπερθίαλος;— 2. Changed from Ὑπερ-φυὴς, from φυὴ, growth, stature;— 3. Running over the φιάλης cup's brim : This is very far-fetched; — Breaker of truces made by libations from [over] φίαλαι cups : This is hardly worth notice :' Ldd. Or ὑπερ-φίαλος, i. e. ὑπερ-ιὼν, trans-grediens, transgressing.

Ὑπέρφευ, 'like Ὑπερ-φυῶς :' Ldd. Nearer, for Ὑπερφυέα neut. pl. of Ὑπερφυής.

Ὑπερφά, the UPPER part of the mouth, palate;

175

Ὑπερῷον, the UPPER part of the house. — R. Ὑπέρ.

Ὑπήνη, ' the UNDER part of the face on which the beard grows, hence the beard:' Ldd. — Clearly from ὑπὸ, under, as Εἰρήνη. (2) Dnn. ' from ὑπὸ, †ἡνη, ἡνίον, the part of a bridle in a horse's mouth: the part under this is Ὑπήνη. (3) Some say that which is both under and above, i. e. ὑπὸ and ἀνά.

Ὑπηνήτης, a young man with his first beard. — Above. Homer: Πρῶτον ὑπηνήτης.

Ὑπηρέτης, an under-rower, inferior servant, helper, &c. — R. ὑπ᾽, ἐρέτης, a rower.

Ὕπνος, sleep. — *Supinus* is allied; and both are from ὑπὸ, from under, *up*: 'A lying on the back,' says Liddell : i. e. so as to look *upwards*. See Ὕπτιος. (2) For Ὑποπνος from ὑπο-πνέω: A breathing gently.

ΫΠΟ, Ὑπαί, under, close under; — near; — under the power of; — near such a time. — ' *Uf* Mœso. Goth:' Dunb. — Perhaps †ὙπΤω was used Æolicè like Ἅπτω, to join, connect. See Ὑπέρ and Ὑφάω. Ὑπὸ and Ὑπὲρ seem allied not only in sound, but in the sense of junction or connexion of one thing with another.

Ὑπο-, in an underhand manner, secretly, insensibly ; — from under, up, ὑπ᾽. So Sub-spicio, Suspicio, is to look ' from under,' *up*.'

Ὑπόγυος, -γυιος, close under or by the hand, near, like Ἐγγὺς, Μεσηγὺς, which see: — near in point of time, recent, late.

Ὑπόδρα, casting an under look, so as to look suspiciously or grimly. — Short, as Δῶμα, Δῶ, for Ὑπο-δρακὼν from ὑπο-δέρκομαι. Nicander has Ὑποδράξ. (2) R. ὑπό, ὁράω : Acting in an underhand manner. (3) Some from ὑπὸ, ὁράω : D, as proDest, proDit, and somewhat as Θ in Ἰφθῖμος.

Ὑπόνομον ἕλκος, a sore feeding under the surface: νέμω, νένομα. Hence the sense of Ὑπόνομος, an underground passage, mine, water-pipe.

Ὑπόσχεσις, a promise. — R. ἔχω, †σχέω: A holding oneself under an engagement.

Ὕπτιος, flat on one's back, with the face UP. — As Sub is ' from under, UP,' in Suspicio, so ᾽Ὕπτιος from ὑπὸ, ὑπ᾽, like Supinus from Sub:' Ldd. and Dnn.

Ὕραξ, a shrew-mouse. — R. ὕς, ὑὸς, from the snout resembling the swine's. For Ὕραξ from a form ὑερὸς, as Ἱερὸς, Ἱέραξ.

Ὑράξ, confusedly,—thought as †Συράξ, from σύρω, as Σύρμα and Συρφετός, are things dragged, thrown, or swept together. So Ὗς and Σῦς.

Ὑρρίσκος, Ὑρρίχος, a basket, ἄρριχος.—An Æolic form, as it seems, from εἴρω, ὅρα, to weave, whence †Ὀάρις, †Ὑρρὶς, as γΥνὴ, βΥθὸς, Ὕσδος. See Ὀρχή. (2) Æol. for Ἀρρίχος.

Ὑρχή, a pickle-jar, *urceus*, *orca*: allied to Ὁρκάνη and Ἕρκος, an inclosure generally. See in Ὑρρίσκος.

Ὗς, the same as Σῦς.

Ὑσγῖνον, ' a vegetable dye-stuff, made from the insect on a tree or shrub called ΫΣΓΗ :' Dnn.

"Υσδος, Æol. of Όσδος, Όζος.

Ὑσμίνη, a conflict, battle.— Prob. Æolic for †Ἐσμίνη from ἐσμὸς, 'a crowd, multitude,' (Dnn.) Compare Ύῤῥίσκος and Ὑρχή. See Ὑσσός.

Ὑσπληξ, ηγξ, a rope drawn across the bounds in a race-course. It seems clear that it must have meant orig. a whip or lash to drive swine with, or a whip of swine's hair to scourge with: from ὗς, πλήσσω, ξω, like Βουπλήξ. It then seems to have meant the whip to give the start with at the games : and, when a rope became used for this purpose, as let down at the starting, the old word was still retained : much as Transenna, the cross-barred starting-place, was used also for the rope, by which it was let down. Dnn. says : ' Prop. a rope serving as a bar.'—Also a rope or noose used by bird-catchers. — It meant also the catch in a trap which FALLS when touched, perhaps from the FALL-ING of the rope in the course, of which Lucian says ΈΠΕΞΕΝ ἡ ὕσπληξ.

Ὑσσακος, Ὑσσαξ, = τὰ αἰδοῖα γυναικεῖα. Ab ὗς, ut Porcus et Porca apud Varronem et Catonem: et sic Χοῖρος. Forsan ultima pars -σάκος = σδκανδρος, ut vult Ldd.

Ὑσσός, a javelin.— Much like Ὑσμίνη. Probably Æol. for †Ἐσσός, formed as Ἐσσὴν and Ἐσμός: What is sent or thrown, as Jacio, Jaculum. (2) R. ὔω, ὔσω, metaph. as Gray's 'arrowy shower', and Pope's 'showers of stones.' (3) From the sound of its HISS or WHIZ through the air.

Ὑστέρα, the womb.—R. ὕστερος : 'As the lowest of the viscera:' Dnn.

Ὑστερέω, am ὕστερος too late.

Ὑστερος, later, the latter :—too late: Ὕστατος, the last. — R. ὑπό, ὑπέστερος, ὕστερος, as Ὑπέρτατος, Ὕπατος. More under, more after.

Ὑστριξ, Ὑστθριξ, hedge-hog. — R. ὗς, θρίξ: Hog's-bristles.

Ὑφάω, Ὑφαίνω, to weave.—Ldd. thinks ὑφ-, (Ψυφ,) Weave allied. So Woof. The Su. Goth. waefwa. (2) Perhaps an Æolic word for Ἀφάω from ἅπτω, to join, connect: To insert one part within another. And so perhaps is Ὑφεαρ the mistletoe. Compare Ὑπέρ, Ὑπό. And Ὑ as εὔντα, γἴνὴ, βΥθός. (3) Mrt. from Hebr. aphah, to cover. ?

Ὕφεαρ: in Ὑφάω.

Ὑψηλὸς, high : from

Ὕψι, Ὕψοῦ, on high. — All compare Ὕψ or Ὕπσὶ with Ὑπ, up, as in Ὑπ-είδομαι to look up,—and also with Ὑπὲρ, above. Compare Ἁψ and Ἁπό.

Ὕω, to wet, water : Ὕει, it rains; Ὑετὸς, rain.— The same as †ἔω, †ἴω, to send down. Thus compare Ἰδρὼς and Ὕδωρ. (2) For Χύω, as Γαῖα, Αἶα. And much as Φεῦ, Heu. We say, How it is pouring down ! Ὑώδης, swinish: R. ὗς, ὑός.

Φ.

Φαάντατος, most bright. — As Φδανθεν, from φαίνω, †φααίνω.

Φάγαινα, Φαγέδαινα, an eating ulcer : from

Φαγεῖν, Φάγομαι, to eat.—Allied to Πδομαι, Πατέομαι, to feed on. Γ as in τμῆΓω, τεταΓόν. (2) ' R. †φάω, findo :' Lenn. As in Ἀρηΐ-φατος, Σφάζω, &c. (3) ' Hebr. pheh, the mouth ; or Chald. phaga, the jaw :' Mrt.

Φαέθω, to shine. And

Φαεινὸς, Φαίδιμος, Φαιδρὸς, bright, gay, illustrious. — R. φάος.

Φαικὸς, 'explained by Hesych. φαιδρὸς, λαμπρός. So from φάω, φαίνω :' Ldd. —And Φαικᾶς, -άσιον, certain white shoes.

Φαινὸνδὰ παίζειν, to play at ball so that, when you φαίνῃ seem to be going to throw it to one person, you throw it to another.

Φαινόλης, a thick upper garment, pœnula. 'According to some, R. φαίνω, ὅλος :' Dnn. ' As appearing whole: as it is the outermost vest:' Greg. — See on Φελόνης.

Φαίνω, to show.—R. φάω, as †Βάω, Βαίνω.

Φαιὸς, grayish, dusky, dun ;—dull.—For Ὑπό-φαιος, somewhat shiny, something between light and dark.

176

So by Φαλὸς Hemsterh. understands Sub-albus, shiny. Dnn. explains Φαιὸς ' resembling the dawning of day.' R. φάω.

Φάκελος, -λλος : in Σφάκελλος.

ΦΑΚΟΣ, 'the lentil ; — lentil-shaped vessel : lentil-spot : Φάκ-οψις, freckle on the face:' Ldd. - Q. ?

Φάλαγξ, a phalanx, line of troops, battle-array ; — the three joints of a finger, disposed in a line ; a spider, from the long joints of its legs ;—anything long, as a log, pole, beam of a balance, lever, roller under ships.— R. φαλὸς, bright. Φάλαγγες, the shining ranks, glitter-ing with armor. Κεκορυθμένος αἴθοπι χαλκῷ, Hom. (2) Aspir. for †πάλαγξ from πάλλω, to wield a spear. See Πήληξ. (3) ' Hebr. pheleg, to divide :' Wr.

Φαλακρὸς, bald-headed.—R. φαλός: As having a white appearance. Some add τὸ ἄκρον, the top.

Φάλαρα, 'from φάλος : parts of the helmet, prob. the cheek-pieces :—later, the cheek-pieces of horses and mules, adorned with embossed straps, Lat. phaleræ:' Ldd.

Φαλαρίζω, to imitate Phalaris, tyrant of Agrigen-tum, in cruelty.

Φαλαρὶς, a coot, from its white bald head : and Φα-λαρὸς, having a patch of white. — R. φαλός.

Φαλῆς, Φαλλὸς, penis coriaceus seu ligneus. Comparatur à Ldd. cum Lat. *palus*, *i*, et Angl. *pale*, *pole*. Comparat Dnn. cum 'Φάλος 2., prominens aliquid.' (2) Jablonski makes it *Egyptian*.

Φαλλός : in Φαλῆς.

Φαλὸς, bright, shining, shiny. — R. φάω.

Φάλος, 'a part of the helmet, but what it was, is very hard to say :' Ldd. The metal ridge, says Buttm., in which the plume was fixed. Prob. from φαλὸς, bright, as Homer has Κόρυθες λαμπροῖσι φάλοισι. Dnn. says : 'Φάλος, a stud, a projecting knob in the front of a helmet : the same word as Φαλὸς, bright, with the additional sense of something prominent or projecting :' Dnn.

Φανερὸς, clear, manifest.—R. φαίνω, φανῶ.

Φανὸς, bright : Φανή, a torch : Φαναί, torch-processions. — R. φάω.

Φάνης, the sun, Apollo : — the first principle of all things. — Above.

Φαντάζομαι, to show oneself ; place before one's mind ; — Φαντασία, appearance, image in the mind, *fancy*. — R. φαίνω, πέφανται.

Φάος, φῶς, light : τὰ φάεα, the lights of the body, the eyes. — R. φάω.

Φάραγξ, a chasm, ravine, valley, precipice — R. φάρω, to split, sever, which verb is acknowledged by Schneider and Ldd., ' of which the affinity with Πείρω is very probable.' See in Φάρσος. (2) R. φέρω, †φαρέω as in Φαρέτρα, answ. to Κατω-φερὴς, prone, steep. (3) ' Hebr. *pherek*, to break :' Wr.

Φαράω, to plough. — R. φάρω, to cleave. See above. (Rare.)

Φαρέτρα, *pharetra*, a quiver. — R. φέρω, †έφαρον : Arrow-bearer. So ἰσο-φΑρίζω.

Φαρκὶς, a wrinkle, fold. I.e. having clefts, as Φάραγξ.—' R. φάρω, πέφαρκα, to split :' Dnn. (Very rare.)

Φαρμάσσω, to dye, color, adulterate, poison, bewitch with drugs. Φάρμακον, (as Φυλάσσω, Φυλακὴ,) a drug, medicine, poison. — ' Reimer from φάρω or φύρω, to mix.—Others prefer μάσσω :' Dnn. If the latter, then for Μαρμάσσω, as Μαρμαίρω : M and Φ, as Μύρμηκα and Formica. But Dnn. explains Φάρω, ' to cut, divide', and thence it could well mean ' to mix, adulterate', as Κεράω from Κείρω. We may add that Homer has πεπαρμένος from πείρω, and from πέπαρμαι could be †Παρμάσσω (as 'Αλλάσσω) and for euphony Φαρμάσσω : To penetrate, then (as Δεύω), to soak, steep.

Φάρος, Φάρος, ' an ample robe of state, mantle, large veil, linen covering for a corpse, sail-cloth :' Dnn.—' Hebr. *PAR*, an ornament :' says Mrt. But better in this way from φάω, †φαιρὸς, as Φαειρὸς, Φαιδρὸς.— Greg. from φέρω, φορέω, to wear, as dress. A, as in φΑρέτρα, ἰσο-φΑρίζω.

ΦΑΡΟΣ, a light-house : ' from *Pharos*, orig. an island near Alexandria, (connected aft. with the continent,) celebrated for its lighthouse :' Dun.

Φάρος, the same as Φάραγξ.

177

Φάρσος, a part, piece. — R. φάρω, πέφαρσαι. Allied to Πεπαρμένος in Homer, and Lat. *PARS*. (2) ' Hebr. *pheres*, to divide :' Wr.

Φάρυγξ, the gullet, swallow, throat. — ' Of the same origin as Φάραγξ :' Dnn.

Φάρω : in Φάραγξ.

Φάσγανον, a sword, knife. — R. σφάζω, ἔσφαγον, to kill : for Σφάγανον. ' Slaughter-weapon,' Ezek. 9. 2.

Φάσηλος, a canoe : from the shape of the ΦΑΣΗΛΟΣ, kidney-bean.

Φασιανὸς, a pheasant, from *PHASIS* in Colchis.

Φάσις, appearance, *phase* : R. φάω, φαίνω.—Saying, rumor : R. φάω, φημί.

Φάσκαλος, Φάσκωλος, a wallet, sack, coffer.—Transp. from Σφάκελλος, a bundle, much as Φάσγανον for Σφάγανον.— (Very rare.)

Φάσμα, a spectre, Φάντασμα : — R. φάω, πέφασμαι, φαίνω.

Φάτνη, a manger, crib. — ' The common form was Πάθνη,' Ldd. And Πάθνη from πάομαι, ἐπάθην, to feed. ' R. πατέομαι :' Dnn. (2) Φαγεῖν, Φαγεδάνη, †Φάθνη, Φάτνη, as Ἔγνος, ἀΤμήν.

Φατνόω, to hollow out like a Φάτνη : Φατνώματα, panels, compartments in a ceiling, like stalls in a stable.

Φατρία, = Φρατρία.

Φαύζω, Φάζω, Φώγω, to roast, toast. — R. φάος, φῶς, a fire, in Callim. See Φαῦσιγξ. ' R. φαύω, φάω :' Dnn.

Φαῦλος, bad, worthless, *vilis*, *vile*, mean, common, trifling : — light, as To bear φαύλως lightly. — Probably Φλαυρὸς (which see,) was transp. to Φραυλὸς, then softly Φαυλός. (2) The Etym. M. from φάω, φαύω, φαύσις : Of mere outside show.

Φαῦρος, ' same sense and origin as Φαῦλος :' Dnn.

Φαῦσιγξ, blister from burning. — R. φαΰζω, σω.

Φαῦσις, light, splendor. — R. φάω, φάσις.

Φάψ, g. φαβὸς, allied to Φόβος, fear : A fearful wild dove or pigeon, as Τρήρων from Τρέω. So Φάβα is ' fear' in Hesych., whence Lat. *faba*, a bean, the object of superstitious fear. Some from Φάψ deduce ΦΑΣΣΑ, a larger kind of dove. Thus Φαβὸς, Φάβασσα, (as μέλιΣΣΑ,) Φάσσα.

ΦΑΩ, †ΦΕΩ, whence Φέγγος, Φίνω, †ΦΙΩ, Lat. *fio*, †ΦΟΩ, whence Φώσκω, Φωστὴρ, ΦΥΩ, seem original words, prim. meaning to open or bring out, then to appear, show, produce, shine forth : — make an opening, stab, kill : — open one's mind or thoughts, speak out, unless this came from the sense ' show', as †Δείκω, Δείκνύμι produced the Latin *Dico*. — Φάω may be nevertheless aspirated from the obsolete ΠΑΩ, which see. Mrt. derives Φάω, to shine, from Chald. *opha*, to shine : and Φάω, to speak, from Hebr. *pheh*, the mouth.

Φέβομαι, to be terrified : †Φέδω, Φοδέω, to terrify, put to flight.—Allied by Dnn. to Φεύγω. Allied also to σΦΕΔανὸς, σΠΕύδω, σΠΕρχω. Φέω as Σέδω, Τρέδω.

Φέγγος, light, splendor. — R. φάω, φαίνω. ' The ancients said †Φέω, †Φένω, †Φένγος, [or †Φέναγος as

A A

Τέναγος,] Φέγγος :' Hemst. So †Γάω, †Γένω. So the Φένω in actual use. And Φθέγγομαι.

Φείδομαι, to restrain, abstain, spare. — ΦΕΙΔομαι is allied to Φιμόω, and without the Aspirate to Πιέζω, Πιλέω, &c. (2) Allied to Φεβομαι, to flee from, Φεύγω, &c.

Φελλός, the cork-tree, bark. — The whole tree is 'bark'; Φελλός therefore is allied to Πέλλα, a hide, Lat. pellis. So Φολίς is a skin. (2) Voss from φηλῶ, fello, Æol. of Δηλῶ, to suck up. (3) Our fell in fell-monger. Shaksp. has 'Flesh and fell.' Sax. fell, Celt. pil.

Φελλός, Φελός, stone, rock. — Φίλος is transp. from †Λεφός, (see Φολίς,) as Σφάγανον, Φάσγανον, Μορφά, Forma : answ. to Λεπάς, a rock. (2) Our fell. The fells in Northumberland. 'Flood and fell': Byron. Fels Germ. Fiaell Su. Goth., a ridge of mountains.

Φελόνης, Φενόλης, Φαιλόνης, 'a covering, in general : — from φελός, the bark of a tree : a cloak or frock, the Lat. pœnula :' Dnn. Φενόλης may belong to Φαινόλης ; see that word.

Φενάκη, false hair, wig. — R. φέναξ, ακος. (2) The same as Πηνήκη.

Φέναξ, ἄκος, an impostor. — R. φαίνω, φανῶ, and †φενῶ as in φΕγγος ; Φαίνομαι, to appear : Who has all show. So ΒΑΛΛω, ΒΕλος.

†Φένω, to kill, from †φάω, as in 'Αρηί-φατος. So †Γάω, †Γένω.

Φέρβω, to feed, nourish. — R. φέρω, to bear, produce, as fruits. B, much as ΘΑΛΠω, μέλΠω, sylVa.

Φέρετρον, a bier, feretrum. — R. φέρω, fero. As Bier from Bear.

Φέριστος, Φέρτατος, best, as being most bearing or productive; — or as most enduring, strong or brave, as Fortis is from Φέρω; or φέρω = προ-φέρω: προ--φερέστατος.

Φερνή, what is brought by the wife, as Dos, a dowry, from Do. — R. φέρω, fero.

Φερρέφαττα, Περσέφαττα, Περσεφόνη, Persephoné, Proserpine. 'R. πέρθω, φόνος, φόνος. She is death itself who wastes all with slaughter. Ov. Epist. : Persephone nostras pulsat acerba fores :' Forcell. and Steph. — Then -φαττα formed as in 'Αρηί-φατος.

Φέρω, fero, to bear, bring, carry, carry off. — Aspir. from Πείρω, περῶ, to make to pass on. (2) Our bear, beran Sax., bairan Goth., fahren Germ. Pheres Hebr., &c.

Φεῦ, heu, alas! — 'From the sound:' Lenn. (2) For Φεύγε, Φεύγ', like 'Απ-αγε, Apage! So Δῶ for Δῶμα, Μᾶ for Μᾶτερ.

Φεύγω, fugio, to flee, run away; — flee one's country for a crime committed, go into exile;—to be prosecuted, accused, 'for voluntary exile was permitted, before the final sentence was pronounced.' Dnn. — 'Akin to Φεβομαι :' Dnn. And σΦΕδανὸς, σΠΕύδω, σΠΕρχω. As τμΗΓΩ.

Φεύζω, to cry Φεῦ, alas!

Φέψαλος, a spark. 'Ψάω, to rub; †ψάλος, redupl.
178

†ψέψαλος, softly φέψαλος : From the sparks emitted from iron while forged :' Damm : Rubbed off. Φεψαλόω, to consume by producing smoke and sparks.

Φηγός, 'a kind of oak : not the Lat. fagus, (Æ. Φāγὸς,) our beech, though the names are identical :' Ldd. 'Having a round ESCULENT nut : from φάγω :' Dnn.

Φηγός, = νέος. 'Nam pars quædam ejus dicitur βάλανος glans :' Scap. Vid. supr.

Φήληξ, a wild fig which seems ripe when it is not so. — From

Φηλός, deceitful : Φηλῶ, to deceive: allied to Σφάλλω, fallo, ἐσφηλα.

Φήμη, Æ. φāμα, fama, saying, report, fame, oracular voice, &c. : from

Φημί, φάσκω, (as †Βῆμι, Βάσκω) to say, affirm; and φάσκω to say to oneself, think. — Allied to Φάω, Φαίνω, to show, as Πιφαύσκω is both to show and to tell; and Δίκω, to tell, is †Δείκω, Δείκνῡμι, to show.

Φήνη, the osprey or bone-breaker. — Scheide well from †φένω, to kill.

Φήρ, fera, a wildbeast, Æol. for Θήρ : — a Centaur: — a Satyr.

Φήρεα, swelling of the parotid glands, as giving the face the appearance of that of Satyrs. — Above.

Φήτρη, Φάτρα, = φράτρα.

†Φθάω, Φθάνω, †Φθῆμι, used often with πρὶν, to get before others, do before others, anticipate, 'præ-venio,' prevent;—do or come quickly, with a participle, as Λέγε φθάσας, Speak quickly.—R. †πτάω, †πτάμαι, Ἵπταμαι, to fly, get fast to, πρὶν, before, &c. See †Φθάω. (2) R. ἅπτομαι, ἅφθην, †ἄφθάω, †φθάω : To touch, reach, tango, attingo, contingo, πρὶν, before &c.

†Φθέγγομαι, to utter a clear sound, speak loud, shout, &c. — As χθαμαλὸς, πΤόλεμος. R. †φάω, φημί; like Φέγγος from †φάω, to shine.

Φθείρ, a small shell-fish which fixes upon and φθείρει consumes the bodies of other fish. Also, a louse, of such kind perhaps orig. as I have seen in myriads devouring the inside of a yet living stag-beetle. The lousy disease is called Φθειριάσις.

Φθείρω: in †Φθέω.

†Φθέω, †Φθίω, Φθείρω, Φθίνω, Φθινύθω, to cause to decay, ruin, destroy. — †Φθέω (acknowledged by Matthiæ) is aspir. for †πτέω, †πτετέω, †πτέτω, πίπτω : To fall off. Thus Dnn. explains Φθίνω 'to fall, fall away'. So ἀγΕΙΡΩ, ἐμΕΙΡΩ. (2) As χθαμαλὸς and φΘέγγομαι. R. †φάω, †φένω, to kill. (3) Dnn. allies Φθείρω to Τείρω. Θ, as Φρίσσω and Frango. ?

Φθογγή, the voice : φθέγγομαι.

Φθόη, consumption : †φθέω, †ἔφθοα.

Φθόϊς, φθοῖς, a cake ;—pastil.—R. ἐφθός, cooked : or †ἐφθέω, †ἔφθοα: compare Φθόη. So Πόπανον from Πέπτω.

Φθόνος, envy.—R. †φθέω, †ἔφθοα, φθείρω: As pining and wasting away. 'Envy is the rottenness of the bones.' Prov. 14. 30. 'Suffer them φθινύθειν,' Hom.: 'tabescere,' Cla.: 'view with envy:' Pope. So Epigr. :

Ὁ φθόνος .. τήκει φθονερῶν ὄμματα καὶ κραδίην. And our Poet : ' Or jealousy That inly gnaws the secret heart.'

Φθύζω, in 'Επι-φθύζω, from πτύω, †φθύω : To spit upon.

Φιάλη, an urn, bowl : Φιαλὶς, small bowl, *phial*, *vial*. —' R. [πίω,] πίνω, as in Athen. p. 501 :' Dnn.

Φιαρὸς, shining : aspir. for Πιαρὸς, fat, like Πίων.

Φιβαλέοι, a kind of early fig. — ' Said to be called from *Phibalis*, a district of Attica;' Ldd.

Φιλέω, to kiss, to love. Φίλημα, a kiss. — Allied to Πιλέω, to squeeze, to press, Πιέζω to squeeze, Φιμόω to muzzle. The I is long in ἐφίλατο, φίλε Il. 5. 359. (**2**) Damn from †πίω, πίνω, to drink (with the lips).

Φιλήτης, ' a thief : same sense and R. as Φηλήτης,' Dnn. i. e. from φηλῶ to deceive. (**2**) Allied to Πιάζω, to seize, to Πιλόω, to squeeze tight, Φιμόω, &c. Compare Lat. *pilo*, *com-pilo*, our *compile*.

Φιλομήλα, *philoměla*, *philomel*, a nightingale.—Prob. from φιλῶ, μέλος.

Φίλος, dear, a friend. — R. φιλέω.

Φίλτατος, dearest. — R. φίλος, †φιλώτατος.

Φίλτρον, love-potion, charm.— R. φιλέω, †φίλητρον.

Φιμὸς, ' a band, or anything which constricts or binds, — thus, a muzzle, — a goblet used in dice-playing, [with some *restrictive* arrangement, suppose, like the reticulated cover of ballot-boxes, (another sense of Φιμὸς), so arranged, says Steph., 'ne immissa suffragia dilaberentur',] the nose-band of a bridle:' Dnn.—Allied to Πιέζω, Σφίγγω, Πῖλος, &c. through obs. †πίω or †πιῶ, to squeeze : for †Πιμὸς. See †ΠΑΩ.

Φιτρὸς, a trunk, log. — Allied to Φιτύω. ' For from it spring the branches:' Damm.

Φῖτυ, a shoot, branch, offspring. — From

Φιτύω, to sow, plant; pass. am begotten. — Allied to Lat. *fio*, Φύω, Φυτεύω. Dnn. from φύω. But evidently there was an obs. †φίω, = φύω. We find φαΐδδω and φαῖδδω.

Φλάζω, am rent in pieces : from φλάω = θλάω, as Φὴρ = Θὴρ. (**2**) Allied to the next word.

Φλάζω, to boil up, swell; —hence storm, stutter, speak unintelligibly. And hence Παφλάζω. Allied to Φλέω, Φλύω, to gush out, teem.

Φλαττο|θραττο|φλαττο|θρὰτ, ' formed to ridicule a pompous phraseology :' Dnn.

Φλαῦρος, trivial, bad, evil, foul. — ' R. φλυάρος :' Mrt. (**2**) R. φλάω : Easy to crush, fragile.

Φλάω, as Θλάω, to bruise, crush : ' to break with a kind of crack :' Bp. Blomf.

Φλάω, ' to bruise with the teeth, eat up, swallow greedily :' Ldd. — Above.

Φλεγύας, fiery, red-brown: epith. of the eagle.—From

Φλέγω, to 'burn up, scorch. — R. φλέω : To make wood or other things to swell out and burst with fire. See Φλοιδάω. (**2**) R. φαλὸς, shining, ' for †φαλέγω', Mrt. Much as ὀΛΕΚΩ.

Φλέδων, an idle talker. — R. φλέω, Hesych., to overflow with talk, φλύω.

179

Φλὲψ, -εϐὸς, a vein. — R. φλέω, to teem, swell : Swollen with blood.

Φλέω, to teem, gush, overflow. So Φλύω. Allied to Βλύω, to bubble out, and to †Βλέω, to throw out. Thus Βρέμω, Fremo.

Φλέως, φλοῦς, a marsh or water plant. — R. φλέω. ' Growing in a moist place :' Dnn.

Φλήνω, to talk idly : Φλήναφος, idle talk.—R. φλέω, whence Φλέδων, an idle talker.

Φλιὰ, a door-post, — vestibule. — ' R. φλάω, θλάω :' Mrt. Allied to Θλίϐω. Homer says, Ὅσ πολλῆσι ΦΛΙΗΣΙ παρα-στὰς ΦΛΙΨΕΤΑΙ ὥμους. And Horace : ' *Postes* et heu *Limina* dura quibus lumbos et *IN--FREGI* latus.' ' The vestibule', says Greg., ' from its being often knocked and thumped.' Some add ' the threshold', which would still better agree with φλάω, but this sense seems unsupported.

Φλίϐω, = Θλίϐω. As Θὴρ, Φὴρ.

Φλιδάω, as φλυδάω from Φλύω, ' to overflow with moisture or fat; hence to putrefy :' Ldd. *Flow* away, *diffluo*. Thus Φιτεύω, Φυτεύω.

Φλοιά, epith. of Proserpine. —'Prob. from Φλόος : Verdant, blooming :' Ldd.

Φλοιδιάω, to make to swell, ferment. R. φλέω, ἔφλοα. Also, to scorch, burn. So Φλέγω, to burn, is allied to Φλέω.

Φλοιὸς, peel, bark, rind of trees. Φλοΐζω, to strip off the bark, flay. — ' Another form of Φλόος :' Dnn. ' R. φλέω :' Ldd. Thus Blomf. says : ' From φλέω came a large family of words having the notion of lightness or emptiness or tumor'. And so Φλοιὸς is metaph. ' empty pride'. And Φλοιώδης is ' spungy, puffed out.' Just as Persius : ' Nonne hoc *spumosum* et *cortice* pingui ?' (**2**) R. φαλὶς, a scale : φλοῖς.

Φλοῖσϐος, murmur, din. —From the *flow* and dash of waters : φλέω, ἔφλοα, φλύω, *fluo*, βλύω. See 'Α-φλοισμὸς. And

Φλοίω, as Φλέω, to teem.

Φλὸξ, g. φλογὸς, a flame. — R. φλέγω.

Φλόος, the bloom, the blooming, healthy state of a plant, Lat. *flos*:' Ldd. From φλέω, ἔφλοα, to teem. Also ' Φλόος is said for Φλοιὸς :' Steph.

Φλύαρος, an idle or silly talker; — silly talk, FLUM. — R. φλύω.

Φλυδάω, to over-*flow* with moisture, to be soft or flabby. — R. φλύω.

Φλύκταινα, Φλυκτὶς, a blister, pustule. — R. φλύω, φλύζω, πέφλυκται, to swell. So Φλύσις is a breaking out, eruption.

Φλύω, like Φλέω, to Φλάζω, to swell over, teem, bubble: over-*flow* with words, talk idly, talk FLUM.—R. βλύω, as Βρέμω, Fremo.

Φνεῖ, ' Comic imitation of the snuffing nasal sound, *phin* :' Lnn.

Φόϐη, locks, mane, hair; — foliage, as Lat. *coma*. — Pindar has δρακόντων φόϐαι, whence Damm from φοϐῶ : Used spec. of grisly locks inspiring awe or terror.

'Long hair was thought to strike terror in battle :' Ormst.

Φόβος, fear. — R. φέβομαι.

Φοιβάζω, to cleanse, purify : Below.—To inspire by Φοίβος, *Phœbus :* and Φοιβάs was his priestess or prophetess.

Φοῖβος, bright, pure : whence *Phœbus* is called by Homer Φοῖβος 'Απόλλων : ' not in the character of the sun, but of the purity and radiant beauty of youth ;' Ldd. — R. φόως, φῶς.

Φοίνη, for Θοίνη, as Θήρ, Φήρ.

Φοινίκls, a red cloak, &c.— From

Φοῖνιξ, ικος, a purple red, ' from the *Phœnicians* who were celebrated for dyeing purple-red :' Hemst. (2) R. φόνος : φοινὸς, blood-red.

Φοῖνιξ, the palm-tree, the date, branch of palm.— Bland (' Lat. Hexain.') makes *Phœnicia* ' the land of *palms*'. See above.

Φοῖνιξ, ' a musical instrument of *Phœnician* invention :' Dnn.

Φοινίσσω, to make red : φοῖνιξ 1.

Φοῖτος, a frequent coming or going, roving about, rambling, rambling in mind. — As Φοξὸς from Φοξὸς, R. οἴω, †Φοίω, Φοῖται, (as in Οἶτος,) to carry oneself about, as 'Υπ-άγω, &c.

Φολὶς, a scale of a reptile, ' often interchanged with Λοπίς :' Dnn.: and thus perh. transp. for Λοφὶς, whence Λοφνίς : — but gen. thought allied to Φλοιός. Φελλὸς, *pellis,* a skin, has also its claim.

Φολὶς, a scale, is also a fleck or spot on the skin.— Above.

Φολκὸς, with distorted eyes.—R. ἕλκω, ὅλκα, Γόλκα, Γολκός. Buttm. makes it bandy-legged. (2) R. ἐφ--ολκός. (3) Some from φάη, the eyes, and ὅλκα.

ΦΟΛΛΙΞ : the Lat. *follis.* And

ΦΟΛΛΙΣ, a piece of money :—like the Lat. *follis,* which was not only a purse, but a coin. ' Centum *folles* æris :' Lamprid. See Φόλλιξ.

Φόνος, murder. — R. †φένω.

Φοξὸς, pointed, peaked.—R. ὀξὺς, Φοξύς. (2) Buttm. for φωξὸς, from φώγω : Warped by burning.

Φορά, a bringing or bearing ; — ʀ being carried ; — that which is borne or produced ; — vast produce. — R. φέρω, πέφορα.

Φορὰς, fœmina prægnans. As above. Lat. *Forda,* from acc. φοράδα.

Φορβή, pasture : — φέρβω.

Φορβειά, ' a feeding-string, by which a horse is tied to the manger ; mouth-band put like a halter round the lips and cheeks of fifers to soften the voice :' Ldd. — Above.

Φορειά, dung.—R. φορὸς, bearing downwards ; whence Φορὰ γαστρὸς is diarrhœa. Hence Φορὸς is Podex ; *Forio* is Caco ; *Forica* is the Public jakes.

Φορεῖον, a sedan. — R. φέρω.

Φορέω, == φέρω.

ΦΟΡΙΝΗ, hide of swine, thick hide ;—want of feeling. —Very rare.—Q. from φορέω : What swine wear ?

ΦΟΡΚΟΣ, *Orcus,* Erebus. Q. for Φόρκος, ῎Ορκος, as being sworn by. ' It was a great matter of conscience to swear by Pluto and by Στύξ :' Forcell. *Orcus* is allied by Riddle to ῎Ερκος. — Also white, gray, whence *Phorcus* an *old* sea-god, and his daughters Φορκίδες. (Rare.) — Q. ?

Φόρμιγξ, ' the *portable* lyre *carried* on the shoulders by a belt :' Ldd. — R. φέρω, πέφορμαι.

Φορμὸς, a basket : some say, a hand-basket, as carried in the hand, from φέρω as Φόρμιγξ. So a bundle, fagot, ' tied up so as to be conveniently carried :' Ldd. (2) Some derive it as Φορμὸς 3.

Φορμὸς, a corn-measure : perhaps as much as would fill a basket. — Above.

Φορμὸς, a mat. I. e. Φορμὸς (as Φολκός,) from εἴρω, ὅρμαι, to weave : A woven mat. — And a sailor's dress, of wicker-work. ' Φορμοὶ is transl. *vitilia* by Pliny :' Dnn.

Φόρος, tribute, as brought in by foreigners. Φόρον φέρειν, Herod.: and Φόρου ἀπ-αγωγή.

Φορτικὸς, burdensome, troublesome, unpleasant, vulgar, low, coarse. — And

Φορτὶς, a ship of burden. — From

Φόρτος, a burden, freight. — R. φέρω, πέφορται. ' *Onus quod fertur,*' Ov.

Φορύσσω, Φορύνω, Φορύω, to mix up, stir together, knead : to adulterate, defile, spoil. — ' R. φύρω :' Dnn. and Mrt. Yet rather Φύρω from Φορύω. ΦΟΡύσσω seems allied to ΦΑΡμάσσω. Compare ῎Αγω, ῎Ογμος : ῎Αγκος, ῎Ογκος : ῎Ακρις, ῎Οκρις, &c. (2) Æol. of Μορύσσω, as Μόρμηκα, Formīca.

Φορύτος, ' whatever the wind (φορεῖ or φέρει) carries along, rubbish, sweepings, refuse, chaff, chips ; — mish-mash :' Ldd.

Φραγέλλιον, the Latin *Flagellum.*

Φραγμὸς, a hedge. — R. φράσσω, πέφραγμαι.

Φραδὴς, shrewd, cunning. — R. Φράζομαι, ἔφραδον, to ponder, perceive.

Φράζω, to tell, speak, give to know or understand, point out, show. Φράζομαι, to talk to oneself, soliloquize, consider, ponder, come to know, perceive. — From †φράρέω, †φράδω, φέρω, as in φΑρέτρα, ἰσο-φΑρίζω : To carry a message, as ῎ΕΡΩ μῦθον Il. o. 202. So Re-*fero,* Re-*late,* Re-*porto,* to Re-*port.* (2) ' Hebr. *pheres,* to explain :' Wr.

Φράσσω, to fill quite full, block up, hedge close in, enclose, secure.—As ῎Εμ-φορτος is loaded, full of, and 'Εμ-φορέομαι to overcharge oneself, so φράσσω is from †φαρέω, †φράω, φέρω : See in Φράζω. Thus Con-*fero,* Con-*gero,* Ag-*gero,* Con-*geries,* Con-*gestion,* &c. The compound is often omitted, as in ῎Ιτυς, Βῆμα, ῎Οχα, &c.

Φράτρα, Φρήτρη, Φρατρία, Φατρία, Φήτρη, Dor. Πάτρα, ' orig. the descendants of the same *father,* a band of persons of the same race :—a sub-division of a tribe, grounded on certain degrees of consanguinity : — assembly of a family at a religious festival. R. πατήρ :' Dnn. (2) ' R. φρέαρ, φρέατος, a well, which the ward used in common :' Scal. (**3**) Allied to Lat. *frater*, Sanskr. *bhratara*, Pers. *broder*, our *brother*.

Φρέαρ, a cistern, reservoir ; — large oil-vessel : — also a spring or well, hence referred to *πρό-εαρ* from *πρό*, †*ἔω* = *ἵημι*: As sending forward water. Much as Fons, Fontis, à Fundendo. Compare Φροῦδος from *πρὸ ὁδός*. (**2**) R. Φλέω : P for Λ. Thus we have βΡύω, φΛύω. (**3**) 'Hebr. *beer*, a well :' Dahler.

Φρενῖτις, fever of the brain, *frenzy* : φρήν.

Φρέω, Φρῆμι : for Φορέω.

Φρήν, *g.* φρενὸς, the mid-riff, *diaphragm*, heart, seat of life, the soul, mind. — As we find εὐ-φρΑίνω, Passow is justified in deriv. from †φράω, φρΑσσω, whence Διά-φραγμα, the *diaphragm*, a partition dividing the heart and lungs from the liver and spleen. †φραίνω supposes †φράω, then Φρενὸς much as Μένος, Γένος, &c. (**2**) R. φράζομαι, to reflect. ?

Φρίκη, rustling, shivering. — R. φρίσσω.

Φριμάσσομαι, to snort and jump about, wanton. — Allied to Βρέμω, Βριμάομαι, Lat. *fremo*. (**2**) Allied to Φρίσσω, Φρίκη, thrilling with delight.

Φρὶξ, much as Φρίκη.

Φρίσσω, ξω, am rough and bristly ; bristle, rustle, bristle up, stand on end ; — am in a shiver or chill when the hairs stand on end, shudder with fear and fright ; — thrill with delight.—An imitative word. (**2**) Allied to Θρὶξ, Æolic Φρὶξ : i. e. to be hairy, bristly. (**3**) Some think Φ not original, and compare our *rise*, Belg. *rijzen* : Gr. ῥῖγος, rigeo. 'Hebr. *rigo*, to be stiff :' Wr.

Φροίμιον, for Προ-οίμιον, prelude. — R. οἴμη.

Φρονέω, to have or exercise φρένας, have good heart or sound mind, to be high-minded or spirited, reflective or prudent and wise, to ponder, think. — Allied to Φρὴν, -ενός.

Φροντὶς, thought, reflection, care, &c. — Above.

Φροῦδος, vanished, gone : prop. gone on one's way, from *πρὸ, ὁδός*. Homer : 'When they were gone and *πρὸ ὁδοῦ ἐγένοντο*.' (**2**) R. *πρὸ οὐδοῦ*, Before the threshold. As Φροίμιον.

Φρουρός, a guard, watcher. — R. *πρὸ, ὁράω, ὁρῶ* to observe ; or *πρὸ, οὖρος* a watcher, as Φροίμιον.

Φρυάσσομαι, to snort and prance, to be wanton or arrogant.—As Βρέμω, Fremo : R. βρύω, to burst forth, i. e. with spirit and high bearing, exult, be proud. Or R. φΛύω, to overflow, as †Lagellum into φΡαγέλλιον. See on Φρύγω.

Φρύγανον, dried sticks for burning.—R. φρύγω. As Cremo, Cremia.

Φρύγω, *frigo*, to broil, roast, toast, *fry*. — Ldd. says of Βρύω, to swell, burst forth, 'allied to ΒΛύω, ΦΛύω.' So Βρύω may be also †Φρύω and φρύγω (as τμηγΩ,) prop. to make the juice of meat burst forth. (**2**) 'To *fry*, Lat. *frigo*, Welsh *ffrio*, Erse *frijck* :' Dr. J.

Φρυκτὸς, roasted, dried ; — a burning torch, firebrand ; — signal fire, beacon ; — toasted bean, voting counter.— R. φρύγω, πέφρυκται.

Φούνη, Φρῦνος, 'a toad ; — a nickname of many
181

Athenian courtesans, from their (bloated) complexion :' Ldd.—From φορύνω, says Mrt., to pollute, defile. 'Et' *uncta turpis* ova ranæ sanguine :' Hor.

Φῦ, 'a word of grief or of discontent : the same as Φεῦ :' Dnn. See Φεῦ. — Or agreeing with our *Faugh*.

Φυγγάνω, = Φεύγω.

Φυγὴ, Φύζα, *fuga*, flight. — R. φεύγω.

Φυὴ, the natural form or disposition. — R. φύω.

Φύκης, a fish living in sea-weed. — From

Φῦκος, *fucus*, sea-weed ; — paint prepared from a red sort of it. — Like Φύτον, a plant. From φύω, πέφυκα. (**2**) 'Hebr. *phuc*, antimony :' Dahler.

Φυλάσσω, to watch, guard. — Aspir. from *πύλη*, for πυλάσσω, as 'ΑλλΑσσω : Am at a door, watch. Πύλας φυλάσσετε, Eurip. We say a Porter from Porta. Φ, as Φιάλη from †Πίω, Πίνω.

Φυλὴ, a tribe or clan. R. φύω : As being born or growing up together in the same town or country. So Φῦλον is a race, people, nation, as Nation from Natus, and Genus from Gigno, Genui. (**2**) 'Hebr. *bel*, to mix :' Wr. ?

Φύλλον, *folium*, a leaf ; — also a plant, 'esp. like *folium*, of savoury herbs :' Ldd. — R. φύω. The product of trees. Homer has, ΦΥΛΛΑ ὕλη ΦΥΕΙ.

Φύλοπις, battle-cry. — R. φῦλον, ὂψ ὀπός : Confused shout of tribes or nations meeting in battle.

Φῦμα, a growth ; and, as Φυτὸν, a grown or growing swelling or boil, as Cresco, Excrescence. — R. φύω.

Φύρω, Φυράω, to mix, to mix and knead ;—adulterate, defile ; — put into disorder. — As Πτύρω, Ευρω from Ξύω. Aspir. from †Πύω, ΠυκΑζω, Βύω, Μύω, allied to †Μάω, Μάσσω. So Im-*buo*, from 'Εμ-6ύω, is to steep one thing with another. (**2**) Shortened from Πορφύρω. (**3**) Contr. from Φορύω, Φορύσσω. — Some ally it to ΦΑΡμάσσω, as περΑω, †πρΑω whence διαπρΤσιος : &c.

Φυσαλὶς, a pipe, as blown upon : φυσάω. 'Calamos *influre* leves :' Virg.

Φύσαλος, a toad ; as puffing itself out. 'The swelling toad :' Dryd. —Above. — Also, a whale, like Φυσητήρ.

Φυσάω, to blow, puff ; — blow through the nose, snort, snuff. Φῦσαι, bellows. — Prob. from the sound. Compare our *fizz* : 'Icel. *fis*, a puff :' Todd. (**2**) Allied to Βυκάνη, a trumpet, from βύω, as filling the mouth. So Βρέμω, Fremo.

Φυσητήρ, a whale.—Above : As puffing and blowing. Forcell. from its throwing out water from pipes placed in its neck. See Φυσαλίς.

Φῦσιγξ, prop. a bladder, but used for 'the outer inflated coat of garlic :' Dnn. — R. φυσάω.

Φυσικὸς, natural, &c. Οἱ φυσικοὶ, magicians who pretended to special knowledge of Nature : , Φυσικὰ φάρμακα, magical remedies : — *physic*. — From

Φύσις, from φύω, φύσω, as Natura from Natus : Nature, as producing all things ; — the particular nature, disposition, form, kind, &c.

Φύσκη, a blister, bladder :—the stomach and large intestine; — a black pudding stuffed in it. — R. φυσάω.

Φυστή, a barley-cake, of which the dough was lightly mixed. — Ldd. and Dnn. from φύρω, to mix : but this would be Φυρτή. Rather from φυσάω, φυσητή, φυστή : Puffed. Φυστήν μᾶζαν, Aristoph.

Φυτὸν, a grown plant or tree; — growth in the body, tumor, as Φῦμα. — From

Φύω, to bring forth, produce: pass. am born, am formed by nature. And Φῦμι, to be born; and, for Συμ--φύω, to grow to as an excrescence, to stick to.— Allied to †Φάω, Φαίνω, to bring to light, bring forth. Other forms existed, †Φίω, †Φίω: as appears from Fio, Φῖτυ, Φιτύω, Fetus, Fecundus. Hence Fuo, Fui.

Φώγω, Φώζω, to roast, toast, parch.— 'Akin to Φάω, Φῶς, Φαύω, Φαύσκω :' Dnn. In form as τμήΓΩ.

Φωΐδες, Φῷδες, a burn, blister caused by a burn.— Allied to Φάζω, †Ἔφωδον: (as χαράδρα from χαράσσω, ξω,) from φόος, φωΐζω, like Φαῦσιγξ, a blister, from φάω, φάος.

Φώκη, a sea-calf or seal. Φώκαινα, a whale. — R. βῶξ, βωκὸς, a sea-calf.

Φωλεὸς, a den, lair : — a school.—'Akin to Γωλεός', says Dnn. But Φ and Γ? Better the old deriv., from φάος ὀλέω, ὄλωλα: Where the light perishes : φα-ολεός. —But Φωλὰς is, lurking in a den. Perhaps then †Φῶλος, φόλολος, from φάω, whence σφάζω, as Σφὰξ was a chasm of the earth (Steph. 8918.) And note Ἀρηΐ-φατος, killed i. e. cleft in battle.

Φωνή, sound, voice. — R. †φάω, †φαονὴ, φωνὴ, φημί.

Φώρ, g. φωρὸς, fūr, fūris, a thief.—R. φέρω, πέφορα, to carry off.

Φωράω, to search after a φώρα thief, trace; — detect, discover.

Φωριαμὸς, chest, coffer.—Eratosthenes : 'They called it Φωριαμὸν, because it contained Φώριον ἄγρην furtive prey.' Damm from φέρω, πέφορα, to bear, carry, contain. — Some read Χωριαμὸς from Χωρέω, to contain.

Φῶς, g. φωτὸς, light, for Φάος.

Φὼς, a man. — R. †φάω, †φῶ, φημὶ, to speak.

ΦΩΣΣΩΝ, Φώσων, a coarse linen cloth; a coarse sail. — Pollux makes it an Egyptian word.

X.

Χάζω, Χάζομαι, to give way, draw back, decline, refuse. — Prop. make a χάσμα chasm or vacuum, retire, from †χάω, χαίνω.

Χαίνω, to open the mouth, gape : — gape at, greedily desire, 'in-hio :' in Lat. cano, to sing. — As Βαίνω from †βάω, so Χαίνω from †χάω, κέχασμαι, χάσμα, a chasm or opening. So χάνος is an aperture.

Χαῖον, a shepherd's crook. Hesych. explains it, a bent stick, i. e. crooked : and so allied to Κάμπτω, Γάμπτω, Γαυσὸς, Γύαλον, Κοῖλος, Γυρὸς, &c.

Χάϊος, good, honest. And Χάος the same, — also illustrious. — As Γενναῖος, noble, is from γέννα, †γενέω, and Generosus from Genus, so †Γάϊος from †γάω, γέγαα. Then Χάϊος, as Χαίρω allied to Γαίω. (2) Allied to Ἀ-γαυὸς, Ἀγαθὸς, &c.

Χαίρω, to rejoice. — Allied to Γαίω, to exult in, and Γηθέω. (2) Our cheer.

Χαίτη, flowing hair, long mane. — Hesych. explains Χαῖται by κεχυμέναι τρίχες, and thus nearly all derive from χέω or χύω: nearer the obs. †χάω, whence χαλάω, laxo, which see. Χυτὴ χαίτη, Nicand. 'Effusâ jubâ,' Ov.

Χαλάζα, hail.—'R. χαλάω : That which is let fall :' Ldd. : χαλασθεῖσα, Greg.

Χαλαρὸς, slack. — R. χαλάω.

Χαλαστραῖον, a mineral alkali found at Chalastra in Macedonia.

Χαλάω, to make loose or slack, loosen, let go. — As

Ψάω, Ψαλάσσω, so Χαλάω from †χάω, χάζω, χέω, χύω. 'Χαλάω from χάζω': Schneid. and Herm.

ΧΑΛΒΑΝΗ, galbanum, a resinous gum. — 'Hebr. chelbanah :' Mrt.

Χαλεπαίνω, to be χαλεπὸς hard-tempered, morose, severe, angry. And, as Χαλέπτω is also, to make angry, vex, &c. See the next.

Χαλεπὸς, hard, hard to bear, hard to bear with, hard to do;— hard to deal with or be dealt with, morose, severe, cruel, &c. So some: but Ormston arranges the senses thus: ' Pernicious, injurious;—dangerous, perilous; — arduous, difficult;—awful, terrible;—hard, grievous, — troublesome; — fierce, harsh, angry, hard to please. From χαλέπτω, to hurt.' And Χαλέπτω from χαλάω, to loose, dissolve, undo, &c.

Χάλιμος, drunken, frantic: R. χάλις.

Χαλινὸς, bridle, bit. — All from χαλάω to loose. Xen. χαλαρὸς χαλινὸς, a loose bit: Ov. 'frænaque laxa.' Virg. 'laxas habēnas.' But much better, with Damm : 'As it relaxes the mouth of the horse.'—Or as it slackens its pace: the verb being 'opposed to ἐπι-τείνεσθαι,' Ldd. : intendere. — Or as causing the horse χαλᾶν 'to yield to, give way to' (Dnn.) the driver.

Χάλιξ, calx, pebble, flint-stone, lime-stone. — 'Akin to Κάχληξ, Κάχλιξ, Κόχλαξ :' Dnn.

Χάλις, sheer wine. — 'As Λυαῖος, Bacchus, is from λύω, so Χάλις from χαλῶ, to dissolve the mind or the body :' Ldd. and Dnn.

Χαλκεὺς, a brazier: χαλκός.

Χάλκη, = κάλχη.

Χαλκίς, a black mountain-bird.—R. χαλκός. 'Some from its copper color: others from its clear-ringing voice:' Ldd. — A female slave, 'as purchased by brass or money, or as brought from *Chalcis*:' Dnn.

Χαλκὸς, copper, brass. — 'Prob. from χαλάω, (κεχάλακα,) for the ductibility of metal was first observed in copper, and that in a very high degree :' Ldd.

Χάλυψ, υβος, steel. — 'From ΧΑΛΤΒΕΣ, a people of Pontus, through whom the Greeks became acquainted with it :' Dnn.

Χαμαί, on the ground. Χαμόθεν, from the earth. Χαμαλὸς and Χθαλαμὸς, low, as Humi, Humilis. — As 'from χάω, to contain, comes Χάορος, Χῶρος', (Dnn.) so from χάω, κέχαμαι, is †Χαμά and †Χαμός. (2) If Θ in χΘαμαλὸς is original, then χαμαί or †χΘαμαί might be allied to Χθόν.

Χαμηλὸς, low, dwarfish: — χαμαί.

Χανδάνω, †Χαδέω, to hold, contain, receive.— R. χάζω, ἐχαδον, from †χάω, whence *cavus*, hollow. N, as ἁΝδάνω. (2) Goth. *henda*, to lay hold of, with the *hand*.

Χανδὸν, gaping : χαίνω, χανῶ.

Χάος, chaos, chasm, Χάσμα; — the vast abyss or void of elements floating in infinite space. — See †Χάω.

Χαός: the same as Χάιος.

Χαρά, joy. — R. χαίρω, χάρῶ.

Χαράδρα, a furrow, channel, bed of a torrent, ravine. — R. χαράσσω.

Χαραδριὸς, some bird inhabiting the χαράδρας ravines.

Χάραξ, ακος, a pointed stake, palisade. — From

Χαράσσω, ξω, to make sharp or pointed ;—exasperate, as this from Asper; — to scratch, furrow, grave. Χαρακτὴρ, impression : *character*. — The first sense seems to be 'to make a notch, groove or hole', (Dnn.) and so from χάω, *caVo*, as Σπάω, Σπαράσσω. Then to make fit for making such incision, to sharpen. (2) 'Chald. *charath*, sculpo:' Mrt.

Χαρίζομαι, to confer a Χάρις favor, to pardon, give.

Χάρις, delight, satisfaction, pleasure, Χαρά; — what gives satisfaction, as a kindness, favor, gift, praise, fame ; — a charm, attraction, loveliness : — thanks for favors. (Κατὰ) χάριν, for the satisfaction or sake of.

Χάρμα, joy, delight. — R. χαίρω, κέχαρμαι.

Χαρμή, conflict, fight : i.e. χάρμα joy of battle : 'The stern joy that warriors feel,' quoted by Ldd. from Scott.

Χάρτης, charta, paper. — R. χαράσσω, or †Χάρω, like Φάρω. Note χαράδρα. 'To be scratched or graved with a pen, ex-arandus :' comp. χαρακτὴρ, impression. See Γράφω.

Χάρυβδις, the celebrated whirlpool *Charybdis*. — 'Passow from ροιβδῶ:' Dnn. Better Mrt. from χάος, ροιβδῶ. But best allied to Χαράδρα, a torrent.

Χάρων, un eagle and a lion: from χαρά, whence Χαροπὸς, 'glad-eyed, bright-eyed, light-blue or grayish :' Ldd.

Χαρώνειον, a gate through which culprits passed to execution, — and a deep pit for them. — As leading to *Charon* in Hell.

Χαρωνίτης, 'coming from *Charon* or the nether world : — used also to translate Lat. orcini, the low persons whom Cæsar brought into the Senate :' Ldd.

Χάσκω, to gape; from †χάω, χαίνω, as †Βάω, Βάσκω. Χάσμα, a gaping, *chasm*. Above.

Χατέω, Χατίζω, to want. — As Χάσμα, a gaping or *chasm*, from †χάω, χαίνω. 'No craving void left aching in the breast :' Pope.

Χαυλι-όδων, with outstanding teeth: i.e. with open teeth, as Anacr. has Χάσμ' ὀδόντων in regard to lions. — From a word †Χαῦλος, formed like

Χαῦνος, slack, loose, flabby, hollow, empty, puffed, puffed up, proud. — Allied to Χαίνω, Χάος.

Χαύνωσις, a making useless, deceiving. — Above.

†Χάω, Χάσμα : See in †ΓΑΩ.

Χεδροπὰ, pulse plucked with the hand, as Legumina from Lego. — For Χερί-βροπα, (Compare Ὁλέκρᾶνον,) from δρέπω, δέβρυπα and χερί dat. of χείρ.

Χέζω, κέχεκα, oaca.—R. χέω, fundo.

Χειὰ, a hole, cave. — Allied to Lat. *Hio*, and from †χείω, χείσομαι, to contain, as in Χείρ. — Ewing from †χάω, *cavus*: see Valck. in the next.

Χεῖλος, a lip.—Boз thinks it transp. for †λείχος, (as Μορφά, Forma,) from λείχω to *lick*. — But better from †χείω, χείσομαι, to hold, as Labrum and Labium from λαβεῖν to lay hold of. — Valck. from †χέω, †χάω, to gape, open.

Χεῖμα, a tempest, and so Χειμών: — the winter. — R. χέω, χείω, κέχειμαι, to pour down: A pouring storm of rain, and the pouring season. Ormst.: 'Downpour of rain or snow.' Homer: 'When Jupiter χεῖ pours violent rain.' Amos 9. 6.

Χειμάζω, to agitate by a χεῖμα, tempest.

Χείμαρος, a plug in a ship's bottom. 'Hesiod so calls it facetiously, as thence flows the bilge-water as through a Χείμαρρος, drain, conduit :' Steph. And Χείμαρρος from χεῖμα, ῥέω: What flows down by a tempest.

Χείμετλον, Χίμ-, chilblain in Χεῖμα winter.

Χειμών, a tempest, Χεῖμα.

Χεὶρ, the hand, Lat. *hir*. — R. †χείω, χείσομαι, χανδάνω, to contain.

Χειρὰς, a chap in the χεῖρες hands.

Χειρίζω, to take in χειρί hand.

Χειρὶς, glove for the χείρ.

Χειρόομαι, to reduce under one's χεῖρες hands.

Χείρων, Χερείων, worse: Χείριστος, worst.—R. χείρ. One who works at handicraft trades, low, inferior. (2) Ldd. from χῆρος, deprived of.

Χειρώναξ, 'one who is ἄναξ τῶν χειρῶν master of his hands, an artisan :' Ldd.

Χειρωνὶς, a medical book. — From Χείρων, *Chiron*, the Centaur.

Χείσομαι, fut. of †χείω, †χάω, χάζω and χανδάνω.

Χελιδων, 'the frog in the hollow of a horse's or a dog's foot, being forked like the tail of the ΧΕΛΙΔΩΝ swallow: the hollow above the bend of the elbow :' Ldd.

Χελῦνη, a lip, Χεῖλος.

Χελύνιον, the jaw-bone. — Like Χέλυς, the arched breast.

Χέλυς, a tortoise ;—a lyre, ' as Mercury made the first lyre by stretching strings on the shell of a tortoise serving as a sounding-board : — the arched breast, from its likeness to the back of a tortoise :' Ldd.—' Prob. from obs. †χέω allied to χάω, cavo :' Dnn. From its concavity or convexity. See Χεῖλος, Χειά.

Χέλυσμα, sheathing to cover the keel of a ship, like a χέλυς.

Χελύσσω, to expectorate. — R. χέλυς, pectus.

Χελών, a fish with a long snout. So Lat. labeo from ' labium ' = χεῖλος or χελῦνη.

Χελώνη, a tortoise ;— shields of soldiers held together to make a covering, as ' Subter densâ testudine,' Virg. : — ' a frame or cradle on which heavy weights were moved by means of rollers underneath ; — also a stool, foot-stool :' Ldd. : ' a joint-stool :' Dnn. And a coin with the impress of a tortoise. — R. χέλυς.

Χελώνιον, arch of the back, — spherical mirror : χελώνη.

Χεράς, gravel, shingle.—' Allied to Χέρρος, dry, hard :' Ldd. (2) ' Χερμάς is a stone which fills the χέρα hand ; Χεράς is somewhat less :' Bp. Blomf.

Χέρνης, who lives by the labor χερὸς of his hand, laborer, poor.

Χέρης, worse, as Χείρων, Χερείων. Ldd. makes it = ὑπο-χείριος, under another's power, inferior.

Χέρσος, Χέρρος, dry land as opposed to water ; — firm, hard, sterile, barren. —' Akin to Ξερὸς, Ξηρὸς, Σκερὸς, Σκηρός :' Dnn.

Χέω, Χύω, Χεύω, Χάω, to pour, pour out ; — pour earth on earth, heap up. —We have seen Χέω allied in sense to †Χάω, Χαίνω or Χάζω, in Χείσομαι, Χειά, Χεῖλος, Χέλυς ; — so here Χέω is allied to Χάω, whence χΑλάω, ' to let down, free from tension, slacken, free, open :' (Dnn.) Compare also χΑίτη.

Χηλή, a cloven foot, claw, hoof ; — a forceps ; — cleft notch of an arrow ; — needle, divided or cleft in two points for making nets and mats ; — semicircular pile with arms extended into the sea like crabs'-claws, mole, pier.—R. †χάω, †χαελή, χηλή, χαίνω, to open wide. So Χηλὸς, a chest. —' R. χάω, [χάζω,] χανδάνω, to contain :' Dnn. †Χαελὸς, Χηλὸς. See above.

Χηλόω, to net, to bind together. — R. χηλή, a needle for making nets.

Χήμη, ' a yawning ; — the cockle, from its gaping double shell ; — a measure of about the size of such shell :' Ldd. — Origin like Χηλή. So χυλὸς and χυμός.

Χὴν, gander, ganza, hansa Sanskr., goose. — R. χαίνω, ἔχηνα : From its wide gaping mouth. Παρὰ τὸ ΧΑΝΔΟΝ ἐσθίειν : Eustath.

Χὴρ, g. χηρὸς, Her Heris, a hedge-hog. So Eres, Ericius, Erinaceus. —' Χὴρ, Χοῖρος, Σχῦρος seem allied :' Dnn. And Σκῖρος, hardness. (2) For †'Εχῆρ,

184

(ending as Αἴθὴρ,) allied to 'Εχυρὸς, secure. (3) For †'Αχὴρ, allied to 'Ακὶς, a thorn.

Χηραμὸς, a gap, hole, cleft.— R. †χάω, †χαερὸς, χῆρος, χηραμός : allied to Χειά, Χήμη, a yawning, and Χηλή.

Χήραψ, g. χήραβος, = κάραβος, a small crab.

Χῆρος, bereft, destitute. — R. †χάω, †χαερὸς, χῆρος, allied to Χατέω to want, and Χητεύω.

Χηρωστὴς, an heir-at-law in default of issue.—Above.

Χητεύω, like Χατέω, to want ; Χῆτος, want.

Χθαμαλὸς, for Χαμαλὸς, as πΤόλεμος for πόλεμος : Low χαμαι on the ground. So Humi, Humilis.

Χθὲς, for 'Εχθὲς, yesterday. And Χθιζά.

Χθὼν, g. χθονὸς, earth, ground, region.—The Etym. M. for Χῶν, capiens, from χῶ, capio. Just as Χῶρος. Θ, as in χΘαμαλὸς, and Τ in πΤάλις, πΤόλεμος. (2) Lenn. for †ἐχθὼν from ἔχω, ἔχθην, to hold. (3) For Κτῶν, R. κτάομαι : A possession, territory, as Regio from Rex.

Χιάζω, to mark anything as spurious in the form Χ, chi ; to place transversely ; — to imitate the Chians.

ΧΙΔΡΑ, ων, a dish made of unripe groats 'of wheat toasted. But Hesych. makes it also meal of pulse, as we say bean-meal, &c.: so that Χίδρα may perh. be a corruption of Χέδροπα, pulse. — Mrt. allies it to Χόνδρος. ?

Χίλιοι, Χείλιοι, Χέλλιοι, a thousand. — As χΕΙὰ, χΙτὼν and χΙὼν are referred to Χείω, Χίω, Χέω, so Χείλιοι : Χέω, Χείω, viewed either as fundo, and so Χείλιοι agreeing with Μυρίοι from Μύρω to flow,— or as capio, this number being, says Damin well, ' capacissimus.' See Δέκα.

Χῖλος, fodder, forage. — Perh. for †Σχιλος, from σχίζω, to cut. As Τέγος and Στέγω, Fallo and Σφάλλω.

Χίμαρος, ' a young male goat: Χίμαιρα, a female yearling goat. R. χεῖμα, (as χίμετλον,) i. e. born [or dropt] in winter :' Dnn. and Mrt.

Χίμετλον ; = χείμετλον.

Χῖος, an unlucky throw of the dice, taken from the proverb Χῖοι κακοὶ, the Chians are bad. In Aristoph. is Οὐ Χῖος ἀλλὰ Κῖος or Κεῖος : where Brunck thinks there is no allusion to dice, but that it is an attack on versatile minds who are always changing to the most advantageous side. ' It is a contrast between the dishonest Chians and the honest Ceians :' Ldd.

Χιρὰς, the same as Χειράς.

ΧΙΤΩΝ, a woollen shirt or smock ; — any covering, coat, coat of mail. —' It may be from χείω, to contain, χείσομαι :' Dnn. So Χίλιοι. ' Capacious'. Plut. uses κολπωτὸς of it ; Philo has κόλπους χιτώνων. (2) ' Hebr. cetoneth, tunica. Chald. kethan, linteum :' Mrt. ' Our cotton :' Gesen.

Χιὼν, snow. — Allied to χέειν to pour. ' Χεῖν is said of snowing, ll. 12. 281 :' Ldd. And Euripides has Βορέας χιόνα χέει, pours down snow. Thus also Dnn. See above.

†Χλάζω, Κεχλάδω, to gush, bubble, sound with a gurgling noise ;—gush out, teem, am full of. Allied to

Καχλάζω, to murmur, splash. In Pindar κεχλάδὼs is said of a song 'sung:' and allied by Heyne to Κλάζω, (Κλαγγή,) and Κράζω.

Χλαῖνα, læna, 'an outer garment, gen. of a thick woolly texture for winter.—Hemst. rejects the old deriv. from χλιαίνω [χλίανα, χλαῖνα,]: A more prob. one is from λᾶνος, λῆνος, wool. Γ and X are prefixed to Λ, as Γλήμη, &c.:' Dnn. See Χλαρόν.

Χλαμὺς, chlamys, a cloak. mantle, chiefly military.— 'Of the same orig. with Χλαῖνα:' Hemst., Ldd. and Dnn. And Χλανίς. (2) Better R. χαλάω, †χλάω, to let fall. (3) 'R. [χλιάω,] χλιαίνω:' Mrt.

Χλανὶς, 'an upper-garment of wool, like the Χλαῖνα, but of finer make:' Ldd. 'Of the same orig. as Χλαῖνα:' Dnn.

Χλαρὸν γελᾶν, 'only in Pind. Py. 9. 65:— acc. to Hermann the Dor. for Χλωρόν: To laugh fresh and loud: but some for Λαρόν:' Ldd. Πρᾶτος is said for Πρῶτος. See Χλαῖνα. (2) R. χαλαρὸν, loosely. Or χλάζω.

Χλευή, joke, ridicule.— '†Χεῖλος, Χεῖλος, †Χελευή, Χλευή: Moving the lips in ridicule, as 'Επ-ιλλίζω to roll the eyes in ridicule:' Valck. So Χελυνάζω, says Ldd., from χελῦνη a lip.

Χλῆδος, sand and slime rolled by a torrent.— R. χλάζω, κέχληδα, to gush.

Χλιδὴ, delicacy, luxury; Χλιδὼν, ornament, from Χλίω, to become warm, dissolve;— to be delicate or luxurious:—Χλιαίνω, to warm, melt;—Χλιαρός, warm. —Ruhnken: 'Χαλάω, †Χαλίω, Χλίω.'

Χλόα, Χλόη, Χλοίη, a young green shoot or verdure. — Lenn. from χαλάω, which Dnn. allies to χλίω, χλιαίνω, to warm. Thus Θάλλος from Θάλλω, allied to Θάλπω, to warm. As Ruhnk. joins 'Χαλάω, †Χαλίω, Χλίω,' so we may join 'Χαλάω, †Χαλόω, †Χλόω.'

Χλούνης, epithet of a wild boar,—some say as sleeping or having its εὐνὴ bed in the χλόα grass: †Χλο--εύνης, as Χαμαι-εύνης;—others say, as living εὖνις bereaved i.e. solitary in the χλόα grass. Some understand εὖνις here spec. 'castratus,' εὖνις (ὀρχέων).

Χλωρός, pale-green, light-green, fresh and blooming, —also pale. — R. χλόα, χλοερὸς, χλωρός. Called from young shoots.

Χναῦρος, dainty : i. e. nibbling.— From

Χναύω, 'strictly == κνάω, to scrape; [which see:] gnaw, gnaw off, gnaw at, nibble:' Ldd. Χναῦμα, a titbit, piece cut off.

Χνόη, prop. that which makes a scraping noise, ' from κνάω, κνῶ, (as χναύω.) to scrape:—the iron box of a wheel in which the axle turns, the nave ;— hence the axle :— Χνόαι ποδῶν, the joints on which the feet play, as the wheels on the axle:' Ldd. Κνόη Bp. Blomf. thinks would be more correct.

Χνόος, Χνοῦς, prop. that which can be scraped off, as in ΄όη: small dust, down, bloom, foam, froth.

΄άανος, -νον, crucible, furnace. R. χέω, κέχοα, to pour out, melt. 'A funnel : by which anything is poured in :' Hemst.

Χοὴ, libation to the dead ; Χόος, earth heaped up or thrown together, bank, mound ;—also a liquid and corn measure : οἱ Χόες, 'the Pitcher-feast,' Ldd.— Above.

Χοῖνιξ, a dry measure. For Χοῖνιξ, like Χόος a corn-measure. 'And, from the likeness of shape, the box or nave of a wheel : and a kind of shackle or stocks for fastening the legs :' Ldd.

Χοιρὰς, the scrofula. — From Χοῖρος. Swine being subject to it. So Scrofula from Scrofa.

Χοιρὰς, a rock just rising from the sea, like a hog's back. So Lat. porca. The 'back' is like Virgil's 'Dorsum immane mari.'—R. χοῖρος.

Χοιρίνη, a muscle-shell.—Q. as sticking to the rocks, from χοιράs.

Χοῖρος, a hog, pig. — Some ally it to Χὴρ χηρός, a hedge-hog, and to Σχῦρος the same. But perh. from the sound Κοῖ Κοῖ of little pigs in Aristoph. Χοῖρος, says Ldd., is prop. a young swine.—Hippōnax says, Χοῖροι are what are still 'tender and humid', whence Scheide from χέω, ἔχοα, fundo: As but lately dropt.

Χοῖρος, pudenda muliebria. Sie et Porcus et Porca dicitur. 'Quia,' ait Varro, 'initio nuptiarum antiqui reges ac sublimes viri, novus maritus et nova nupta, Porcum immolant.' — Supra.

Χολάδες, the bowels. — 'Perh. allied to Κοῖλος, hollow:' Dnn.

Χολερὰ, the cholera: derived by Alex. Trall. from Χολερὰ, the gutter of a roof, down which the rain is discharged. So the contents of the body, by purging. From χέω, ἔχοα, to pour.—But gen. derived from

Χολὴ, Χόλος, gall, bile;— anger, choler.— Damm allies Χόλος to Χυλὸς, juice.— But Dnn. and others refer Χολὴ to Χόω, Χώω, to cause anger or displeasure, Χόομαι to be angry; so that Χολὴ should be thus explained: 'anger, and then the seat of anger, bile, gall.' (2) 'Hebr. gol, to loathe:' Wr.

Χόλικες, the bowels of oxen, tripe: as Χολάδες.

Χόνδρος, 'the cartilage of the breast-bone, and cartilage generally ;— groats of wheat or spelt, porridge ; prob. from the form of groats, a grain, any small grumous concretion, a pill, &c. Groats, macerated in water, are soft on the outside, but harder in the middle: hence the other senses :' Dnn.—'Cartilage : from the white viscous appearance of gristle, which is something like groats when washed :' Ldd.—For χόδρος, (N as ΙΝΔάλλομαι,) as Μυδ-χοδον from χέζω, κέχοδα: prop. 'dung,' hence any round or grumous substance.

Χόος, χοῦς, a heap of earth thrown up, bank : χέω. Dust; κόνιν χεύατο, Hom. A certain measure, from χέω, χείω, χείσομαι, to receive, contain. Or even from things being poured into it.

Χορδεύω, to make χορδὰs sausages ;— chop up.

Χορδὴ, a gut; — string or chord of a lyre;— bowstring:—sausage. Dr. J. defines Gut 'a long pipe with many convolutions.' So that Χορδὴ is allied to Χορὸς, Κέρας, Κορωνὸς, Κυρτὸς, Γυρὸς.

Χορεῖος, Χόριος, a foot marked _ ◡, 'and so called as verses composed of it were fitted for Χοροί dances ; the foot being also called Τροχαῖος from τρέχω :' Steph.

Χόριον, ' a skin, leather; but espec. the membrane which wraps the fœtus in the womb. Χόρια, a preparation of milk and honey, Theocr. 9. 19; but some interpret it entrails. R. from χάω, χάζω, to contain:' Dnn. Rather, from the curve or round, as in Χορὸς, Κέρας, Κορωνὸς, Κυρτὸς, Γυρός.

Χορὸς, ' dance in a ring, round dance ; — a dance with song, a choral dance; — a chorus, choir, band of dancers and singers; — gen. a troop, band:' Ldd. Allied to Κορώνη, Corona, Κορωνὸς, Κέρας, Κόραξ, Κυρτὸς, Γυρός: 'from the circular movement:' Dnn. See Χόριον. (2) Wr. from the Hebr. ker.

Χορτάζω, to feed with χόρτος provender; — feed so as to satisfy, — simply, satisfy, as Matth. 5. 6.

Χόρτος, 'strictly an enclosed place, but always as a feeding-place, straw-yard;—met. the expanse of heaven: —then food, fodder, provender. Allied to Hortus, and our Court:' Ldd. ' Akin to, or from Χορὸς:' Dnn. I.e. a round place. And compare Κυρτός. Or even from ' containing', as compared with Χεὶρ, χερὸς, &c. (2) But the order of the senses from ' an enclosed place' to ' fodder' seems unnatural: — rather first fodder, hay, straw, then a place for it, straw-yard, inclosed place. For Κορτὸς from κείρω, κέκορται, to shear, clip. So δέκομαι, δέΚα.

Χραίνω, to touch lightly, — hence to smear, daub, stain, anoint, —allied to Χράω, and to Χρίω to anoint.

Χραισμέω, to be of use to, allied to Χράομαι, to use ; —to help, defend;— help by driving off a foe, as 'Αρκέω has both these senses.

Χράομαι, to make use of, i. e. apply the χέρα hand to: for †Χεράομαι.

Χράομαι, to have intercourse with friends, have to do with, as Utor: ' Nihil te UTOR,' Plaut. And to negotiate, transact business with.—Above.

Χράομαι, to need, want. I. e. to put out my Χέρα ` hand for: †χεράομαι. See Χράομαι 1.

Χράομαι, to consult an oracle, i. e. to use, as Tacitus: ' Apollinis oraculo UTI': and Herod. 1. 47, χρῆσθαι χρηστηρίοισι. — Or from wanting and needing the aid of the oracle: Above.

Χράω, for †Χεράω, to touch or brush χερὶ with the hand, scrape, GRAZE, which Ldd. thinks allied: — also, in a further sense, to lay the χέρας hands on, ' to lay violent hands on, attack,' Dnn., harm, hurt, harass: as Eurip. has ἐν τέκνοις βαλεῖν ΧΕΡΑ: and Nehem. 13. 21, ' I will lay hands on you.' (2) In the sense of scraping, from †χαράω, χαράσσω, to grave.

Χράω, Χρείω, to give an answer or oracle, simply, to put χερὶ in the hand. Thus Mando is Manui do. So

Χράω, to lend, i. e. to give χερὶ with or to the hand
186

in loan. As above. (2) Prop. to be of use to, allied to Χρεία.

Χρεία, use, usefulness, utility, service, benefit. Allied to Χράομαι, to use. As Ovid: '.Malo fuit USUS in illo.' —Also, the having use or necessity for, the need or want of. — Also, a request for service or help, as dictated by the want of it. — Also, any necessary business or employment, matter, affair, as Χρέος is used and Χρῆμα.

Χρεμέθω, Χρεμετίζω, to neigh, i. e. to spit out from the nose. — Allied to

Χρέμπτομαι, to hawk and spit. — ' From the hoarse tremulous sound accompanying coughing:' Dnn. Perhaps orig. with Σ, †Σχρέμπτομαι, as the Latin SCREO, so that ΣΧΡ is the leading sound.

Χρέος, as Χρεία, necessity, want, need ; — necessary business, office, charge, affair.

Χρέος, a debt, i. e. ' what one must needs pay,' Ldd. Above. — Also a debt of service, — debt of death, as in Horace : ' DEBEMUR morti nos nostraque.'

Χρέος, use, profit, as Χρεία.

Χρεών, what one must needs come to, fate : — the debt of death we must all pay, as Χρέος; — what is needful or expedient, as Χρέος, Χρεία.

Χρῆ, need, necessity, Χρέος, Χρεία. And Χρὴ, it is needful, necessary, behoving, it behoves.

Χρηΐζω, Χρήζω, from χρεία: I need, lack; — long for, desire; — beg, ask for. — Μὴ ἔχρηζες θανεῖν ? O that thou hadst not died ! properly, Didst thou need to die ? Shouldest thou have died ?

Χρῆμα, anything that one χρῆται uses or that one needs; — anything fit for use, and generally, anything; —necessary business, occupation. Χρήματα, necessaries of life, effects, goods, property. We find Χρήμασι χρῆσθαι.

Χρῆμα, oracular answer.—R. χράω, to give an oracle.

Χρηματίζω, to carry on a χρῆμα business, traffic;— make χρήματα money; — carry on business with the gods, consult them and get an answer; or at once from χράομαι, κέχρημαι, as before.

Χρηματίζω, to be called, as ' It came to pass that the disciples χρηματίσαι Χριστιανοὺς,' Acts 11. 26, were called Christians. Erasmus says from χρήματα business or professions. ' To assume a denomination:' Dnn. To have a name given to a χρῆμα thing.

Χρήσιμος, much as Χρηστός.

Χρησμὸς, an oracular answer.— R. χράω, to give an answer, or χράομαι to consult the gods.

Χρήστης, a debtor, and a creditor. R. χράω to lend, or rather χρηΐζω, χρήζω.— And a prophet: from χράω, to give an oracle.

Χρηστὸς, useful, serviceable, good and useful;—much used, &c. — R. χράομαι, κέχρησται, to use, as above. So Utilis from Utor.

Χρίπτω, Χρίμπτω, like Χράω and Χρίω, is to pass or skim lightly over, graze, scratch; — nearly touch, come near to, approach, keep closely along the coast.

Χριστὸς, ὁ, The Anointed (King), Jesus *CHRIST*: from

Χρίω, like Χραίνω.——R. χερὸς, †χερίω, χρίω, to touch with the hand. So from Τείρω, Τερῶ, is †Τερίω, †Τρίω, *Trivi*, Τρίβω. 'Χράω, Χρίω, Χρόω have a comm. origin :' Dnn.

Χροιὰ, Χρόα, Χρῶμα, the surface, as Χράω and Χρίω are to graze the surface: — hue or color or complexion on the surface: made by Ldd. the original sense, and then the 'surface' as 'the seat of color,' as Χρίω is to color.

Χροΐζω, to give a χρόα color to: — and like Χράω, Χρίω, to touch, and so to be in contact with, lie or sleep with.

Χρόμαδος, a grating, jarring noise. — 'Formed from the sound :' Ldd. (2) Allied to †Κρόω, Κέκρομαι, Κρότος, a noise: (3) Allied to Χρόμος, neighing of horses, through Χρεμέθω, to neigh, Χρέμπτομαι, to hawk and spit.

Χρόμιος, a sea-fish: allied to Χρόμαδος: 'Said to utter a jarring sound :' Ldd.

Χρονίζω, to spend a long χρόνος time on, loiter.

Χρόνος, time. Forcellini defines Tempus 'an interval in which anything *is done*:' so that Χρόνος is not ill allied by Dnn. and Ewing to Κραίνω, to accomplish. It takes time to do everything, and time accomplishes all. 'There is a time to every purpose under the Heaven.' Napoleon said: '*Time* enters into every thing : it is the element of which all things are composed :' Enc. Brit. x. 157. Note the K in Κρόνος. (2) As Κλάω, Κλόνος; Θράω, Θρόνος; Φάω, Φόνος, so have been proposed 1. Χράω, Χρόνος; Time laying its hand on everything; 2. Χράομαι, Χρόνος. Time being given to be used. '*Utendum est* ætate.'

Χρυσαλλὶς, the *chrysalis* or Aurelia, as this from Aurum.'— From

Χρυσὸς, gold. — As Χράω, (Χραίνω,) Χρίω, Χρόω, so also †Χρύω, to color, whence Χρυσὸς, THE color, gold. T, as ξΤω, ψΤω, τρΤω. (2) Bochart from the Hebrew : '*cherootz*, gold', (Wr.)

Χρώζω, = χροΐζω.

Χρῶμα: in Χροιά.

Χρὼς, g. χρωτὸς, like Χροὰ, Χροιὰ, the surface; — skin; — body.

Χυδαῖος, common.——R. χύω, χύδην: 'Poured out in streams or masses, abundant:' Ldd. 'Overflowing: Dnn. 'Fusè et copiosè,' Cic.

Χυλὸς, 'juice, moisture, drawn out by *infusion*, from χύω, χέω, fundo: — juice by digestion, *chyle*; — the flavor, taste of anything, as this lies in the juices:' Ldd

Χύμα, a fluid, stream, flood : χύω.

Χυμὸς, like Χυλὸς, juice, *chyme*: — taste.

Χυτὸς, poured, shed; — melted, fluid. — R. χύω.

Χύτρα, a pot into which liquids, &c. are poured. — Above.

Χύω: in Χέω.

Χωλὸς, lame. — The same as Κόλος, mutilated. And Κυλλός. (2) 'Χάω, hisco, Χαολὸς, Χωλός:' Lenn. 'R. χάω, hisco, deficio :' Valck.——And Dnn. compares Χαλάω.

Χωννύω, to melt, smelt.——R. χέω, κέχοα.

Χώομαι, am angry. — Hesych. explains Χώσασθαι by ' συγ-ΧΥΘῆναι, ὀργισθῆναι, λυπηθῆναι.' I.e. from χύω, συγ-χύω, χέω, *fundo*, *furun*: To be con-*fused*, agitated, *confounded*: or to be suf-*fused* with anger, suf-*fundor* rubore.

Χώρα, Χῶρος, space, room: allied to Χάζω to contain, through †Χάω, †Χαόρα.

Χωρέω, to make χώραν place, give way, go: — have room for, contain, hold. See above.

Χωρίζω, to part χωρὶς asunder.

Χωρὶς, asunder, apart, separately, differently.——Allied to Χωρέω to give way, retire.

Χωρίτης, inhabiting the χώρα country, used in opp. to the town: a rustic.

Χῶρος, the N.W. wind, Acts 27. 12. — 'R. χωρεῖν, explained by Suidas πορεύεσθαι, ὁρμᾶν: As violent and stormy :' Schleusn. (2) 'Acc. to others, Κῶρος, from καίω, [καύσω,] to burn' [i.e. to nip,] :' Schrev. *Caurus* is Virgil's word. (3) 'From Hebr. KR, cold :' Pkh.

Χωστρὶς, 'that is fit for or used in making mounds or entrenchments. R. χόω, (κέχωσται):' Ewing.

Ψ.

Ψαγδάν, an Egyptian ointment. — Jabl. says it is *Egyptian*; but Schrevel. from Ψάω, to rub (on the face). Like Ἀπο-ΜΑΓΔΑλία in form.

Ψαθυρὸς, friable, crumbling, loose.——R. ψάω, ἐψάθην.

Ψαίνυθος, good for nothing, vile, false. — R. ψάω, †ψαίνω, as Σάω, Σαίνω: Prop. (like Ψαθυρὸς,) easily friable, light, &c. Or as Ψεύδω. — Only in Lycophr.

Ψαίρω, as in Ψάω, (as †Δάω, Δαίρω,) to graze or touch gently :—also a dialectic form of Σπαίρω, Πσαίρω.

Ψαιστὰ, ῶν, cakes of *ground* barley, mixed with honey and oil. — R. ψάω, ψαίω.

Ψάκαλον, a new-born animal: 'from Ψακὰς, a drop, as Ἔρσαι and Δρόσοι were also used :' Dnn.

Ψακὰς, Ψεκὰς, Ψιὰς, a small piece rubbed off, crumb; — small drop. — R. ψάω, ἔψακα, ψέω, ψίω.

Ψαλάσσω, = ψάλλω.

Ψάλιον, Ψέλιον, Ψέλλιον, 'a bridle; but prop. the curb of a bridle, or a nose-band to which a rope was fastened, of the kind used in training horses: — Ψάλια,

187

bands, chains, armlets:' Dnn. — 'R. ψαω: As rubbing the mouth of the horse :' Steph. See Ψαλίς.

Ψαλίς, a razor, shears, scissors,—and, from the semicircular form of the handle of the shears, an arch or bow. — Ldd. from ψάω, to graze, scrape off.

Ψάλλω, to touch, feel, move, twitch, pluck; — twang with the fingers the bow-string, strike a harp, or sing to it. — R. ψάω, as †Βάω, Βάλλω.

Ψαλμὸς, a psalm sung to a harp. — Above.

Ψάμαθος, Ψάμμος, sand. — R. ψάω, ἔψαμαι: As rubbed by the sea.

Ψὰρ, Ψὴρ, a starling : — hence Ψαρὸς, spotted like a starling, and also rapid, just as Βαλιὸς has both senses. — Dnn. identifies Ψὴρ, g. ψηρὸς, with αἱΨΗΡΟΣ, λαυΨΗΡΟΣ, rapid, 'from ψαίρω, to touch gently, graze.'

Ψαύω, to touch, feel, handle, either lightly or heavily. — R. ψάω.

Ψαφαρὸς, like Ψαθυρὸς, friable, crumbling, loose; — dry, as easily friable; — sandy, dusty, i.e. rubbed, crumbled, as Ψάμαθος is sand; — ἡ ψαφαρά, the shore. — R. ψάω, †ψάπτω, †ἔψαφα, much as Ψῆφος.

Ψάω. Valckenaër says: 'Every Greek word, beginning with Ψ, springs from one of these five forms Ψάω, Ψέω, Ψίω, Ψόω, Ψύω: Primarily, to scrape, then rub, attenuate, — make warm.' Bp. Blomfield: 'I would translate Ψάω to scrape; Ψαύω to touch; Ψαίρω to graze or raze.' The first meaning however is to touch; so Ewing, 'to touch, touch lightly, stroke, wipe, graze', &c. And Ψάω is for 'Αψάω, from ἅπτομαι, ἅψομαι, to touch.

Ψέγω, from ψέω, ψάω, (as Λάω, Λέγω,): prop. to make smaller by rubbing, — to lessen, disparage by evil report, censure, as Hor. 'laudes de-terere,' 'urbem de-fricuit,' Pers., ' radere mores:' So Ψίθος is De-traction (de-traho).—Note τμηΓΩ.

Ψεδνὸς, rubbed off, bare, bare of hair, &c. So Ψηνὸς and Ψιλὸς. — R. ψέω.

Ψεθυρὸς, '= ψιθυρός :' Dnn.

Ψεκὰς, = ψακάς.

Ψέλιον, = ψάλιον.

Ψελλὸς, speaking imperfectly or obscurely, stammering, &c. — 'R. ψέω. I. e. frittering away syllables or words, as Τραυλὸς from Θραύω :' Ldd. Much as we say, Clipping the Queen's English.

Ψεύδω, to cheat; Ψεῦδος, a lie; Ψευδὴς, false. — As Σπέω, Σπεύδω, so Ψεύδω from ψέω, ψάω, to lessen, curtail, i. e. clip the truth; or lessen by fraud. 'Curtailed of this fair proportion, Cheated of feature:' Shaksp. 'Nothing extenuate', &c.: Id. Compare Ψαίνυθος, Ψίθος, Ψύθος. — Or even from ψέω, to smooth, and so gloss over.

Ψέφος, Ψέφας, darkness, vapor, gloom. Ψέφος, smoke, in Hesych. Now Hesych. explains Ψέφω by λυπῶ, so Ψέφος is what distresses and annoys: Scheide referring Ψέφω to Ψέω, to graze, &c. And Ψαύω is 'to touch as an enemy, lay hands on', (Ldd.) (2) Allied to Ζόφος, Ζέφυρος. Or Ψέω, ' to make warm,' Vlk.

188

Ψῆγμα, scrapings, chips, gold-dust. Prop., rubbings off. —And

Ψήκτρα, a scraper, currycomb. — R. ψήχω.

Ψηλαφάω, 'a rare instance [as Δυσπαλίζω] of one verb compounded of two : ψάω, (ψαελὸς, ψηλὸς,) ἀφάω: Prop. to feel or grope in the dark :' Valck. ' Prop. to touch by scraping, as we do horses;— then to feel one's way as the blind:' Lenn.—But some from ψάω, ψάλλω, †ψαλάπτω, &c. Ending as Εἰλυφάω.

Ψὴν, the gall-insect living on the fruit of the wild-fig. — R. ψάω, †ψαίνω, †ἔψηνα, to scrape, rasp.

Ψηνὸς, like Ψεδνός.

Ψῆφος, a small round worn stone, pebble; — pebble used in draughts and voting, a counter. — R. ψάω, †ψήπτω, †ἔψηφα. So Ψάμαθος. See ψαφαρός.

Ψήχω, to rub down, smooth down a horse. — R. ψέω, as Νέω, Νήχω.

Ψιὰ, a pebble, as Ψῆφος, from ψίω, ψάω, ψέω: Rubbed by the sea on the shore. — And 'a pebble used by children in certain juvenile games, play, sport:' Dnn.

Ψίαθος, a rush-mat. — As Ψάμαθος. R. ψίω, ψάω: As that we rub our feet upon. See Ψιά.

Ψιὰς, the same as Ψακὰς, Ψεκάς.

Ψίθυρος, whispering, — slanderous; — Ψιθυρίζω, to whisper.—Valck. from the sound ψιθ. (2) R. ψίω, ἐψίθην, allied to Ψαίρω, to whisper as the wind among the leaves. — Or as compared with Μινὸς and Μινυρός. (3) R. Ψίθος, detraction, slander, which from ψίω, as in Ψέγω.

Ψιλὸς, rubbed bare, made bare,—stripped of feathers, — bare of clothes, said of light troops; — bare, mere, alone. R. ψίω, ψέω, as Ψεδνὸς, Ψηνός. Ψιλὸς meant also bare of or without the aspirate, i.e. having only the soft breathing. 'The letter υ is called υ ψιλὸν, upsilon, to distinguish it from υ serving instead of the Æolic F Digamma, or υ used to denote aspiration:' Dnn.

Ψίμυθος, Ψιμύθιον, Ψιμίθιον, 'white lead, used to whiten the skin, and used even for the hair:' Ldd.— Much as 'Ορμαθὸς, Ψάμαθος in form: R. ψίω, ἔψμαι: As rubbed on the skin and hair. So Ἐν-τρίμμα.— Or as made of very thin filings of lead.

Ψίνομαι, to shed the fruit before ripening.—' Perh. akin to Φθίνομαι :' Ldd. (2) Or from ψίω, as Ψιλὸς, bare.

Ψὶξ, g. ψιχὸς, a crumb, morsel.—R. ψίω, ἔψικα, to rub to pieces.

Ψίττα, like Σίττα.

ΨΙΤΤΑΚΟΣ, psittacus, a parrot. — An Indian word, thinks Voss.

Ψὸ, ' our pshaw:' Ldd. From the sound.

Ψόαι, the muscles of the loins, the loins. 'Ψόα, Ψοία, the loins. Some from †Ψόω, Ψάω :' Dnn. ' R. ψάω, mulceo. As animals are fond of rubbing that part:' Mrt.

Ψόγος, blame. — R. ψέγω, ἔψογα.

Ψόλος, soot, smoke, fire. 'Ψόθος, blackness, filth, foulness, may be from Σποδὸς, Ψοδός. Ψόλος and Ψόθος seem akin, and may be compared with Ψόα. Photius says that Ψό was an exclam. of disgust at anything filthy:' Dnn. See Ψόα.—In form as Θόλος: and perhaps, through Ψόω and Ψέω, allied to Ψέφος, smoke.

Ψόφος, 'any inarticulate sound, noise. — Akin to Ψόθος, Ψύθος, Ψίθος:' Ldd. And to Ψίθυρος, whispering. — Or, as Ψῆφος from ψάω, so Ψόφος from †ψόω: Noise of things· rubbed, much as Κτύπος from Τύπτω, Κόμπος from Κόπτω. See Ψαίρω in Ψύχω.

Ψύδραξ, 'a white blister on the tip of the tongue, prop. a lie-blister:' Ldd. — From

Ψυδρός, lying : allied to Ψεύδος a lie. So Ψύθος is a lie.

Ψυκτήρ, a wine-cooler. — R. ψύχω.

Ψύλλα, -ος, a flea. — R. ψύω, ψάω: Radens, scratching the skin.

Ψυχή, breath, life;—the breath of the soul, the soul, (as Anima, Animus): — a butterfly, a beautiful emblem of the immortal soul by its apparent death in the chrysalis. — R. ψύχω, to breathe.

Ψῦχος, εος, cold. — From

Ψύχω, to breathe, blow ; — blow upon, cool, dry, refresh. — R. †ψύω, (as ψΥλλα,) ψάω, ψαίρω : Said here of the wind grazing or sweeping any surface. Thus Ψαίρω is 'to emit a sound as the whispering or murmur of wind among the leaves of trees', (Dnn.) Compare Ψίθυρος.

Ψόα: 'from Ψό, pshaw ! putrid stench, rottenness :' Ldd. and Dnn. See on Ψόλος.

Ψώθιον, a small Ψωμός.

Ψωλή, the prepuce, 'pars circumcisa.' — From

Ψωλός, circumcised. — Ψάω, †ψαολός, ψωλός. 'Derasus,' Hemst.

Ψωμίζω, to feed, prop. infants by putting ψωμούς into their mouths :—also to distribute food, &c., to give it away in bits and scraps.

Ψωμός, a crumb, bit. — R. ψάω, ψῶ, or ψόω, to rub into bits.

Ψώρα, the itch, scurvy. — Ψάω, †ψαόρα, ψώρα : As causing the rubbing of the skin.

Ψώχω, to rub in pieces, crumble : from Ψάω, like Ψάω.

Ω.

Ὦ, ὦ, oh ! From the sound.

Ὦα, for Οἴα from ὄïς, οἴς : — a sheepskin with its wool ; — wallet ; — edge of a garment, 'prob. as edged with sheepskin :' Ldd.

Ὦας, = ὄθας, οὖς.

Ὠδή, a subdivision of the three Spartan clans, 'distributed according to certain οἴας = οἴμας districts :' Dnn. I. e., οἴα, ὀα, ὦα, ὠβὰ or ὠβή : as ὠὸν, ὠβὸν, oVum. (2) 'Others for οἴα, the political unit :' Ldd.

Ὠγενὸς, like Ὠκεανὸς, which see.

Ὠγύγιος, of the times of Ogyges, an ancient king of Attica and Bœotia : primeval.

Ὧδε, in this way, in this place. — R. ὅ-δε, the proper dative φ̄-δε.

Ὠδή, a song, ode, Ἀοιδή. So Ὠδός, a singer.

Ὠδίς, g. Ὠδῖνος, pains of childbirth : and other pains : allied to Ὀδύνη pain. And Ὠδίνω to be in pain. 'Ὠδίνων ὀδύνησι, Hom.

Ὠέ, ohe, oh ! Like Ὦ.

Ὠζω, to cry ὦ oh ! to lament. As Οἴζω, or Ὀΐζω.

Ὠή, oh there, holloa ! as Ὠέ.

Ὠθέω, †Ὦθω, fut. ὄσω, to thrust, push, drive, push away. — R. †οἴω, οἴσω, †ὄω, †ὄθην, as in Οἶστρος, impulse. So Φέρομαι, is 'to be hurried along or impelled', (Dnn.)

Ὠκεανὸς, the ocean.—Usu. derived from ὠκὺς, ὠκέος, rapid. As οὐρΑΝΟΣ. Some say ὠκέα νῶ, to flow rapidly. ? (2) 'From the oriental OG, circuit : whence 'Ὠγὴν the most ancient word for ocean': Ormston and Bochart. See Ὠγενός.

189

Ὠκὺς, quick, swift, sharp. Lat. ocyor. — R. ὠθέω, fut. ὄσω, †ὄκα, to push on. (2) Some compare Ὀξὺς and Ἀκή.

Ὦλαξ, Ὦλξ : in Αὖλαξ.

Ὠλένη, the elbow, arm, armful. †Ὤλνα, ulna : Sax. eln, our ell. — R. ἔολα, ἔωλα, pf. of εἴλω, ἑλίσσω, to turn or bend round.

Ὠλέκρᾶνον, for Ὠλενό-κρᾶνον, point of the elbow. As Idolo-latry, Idolatry. Above.

Ὤμιλλα, a game in which different persons put nuts, birds, &c., within a circle, and each endeavoured to strike out from the circle the stake of one of the others. — As Ἅμα, Ἅμιλλα, a contest, so Ὁμᾶ, †Ὁμιλλα, Ὤμιλλα. So Ὅμιλος.

Ὦμος, the shoulder. — R. †οἴω, to carry, οἴμαι or ᾤμαι, as Isocr.: φέρων ἐπὶ τὸν ὦμον. Aristot., βαστάζειν ἐπὶ τῶν ὤμων. 'I shall bear upon my shoulder', Ezek. 12. 7.

Ὠμὸς, unripe, raw, undressed ; — cruel, as Crudus, Crudēlis. — Lenn. from †οἴω, οἴμαι, as said of fruit which the tree must yet bear. See Ὦμος. (2) But perh. from ὄζω, ὄμαι : 'What makes us ὄζειν': Mrt. : i. e. raw. So Nasturtium for Nasi tortium, Μυττωτὸς, Κρόμυον.

Ὦν, Ion. for Οὖν, therefore.

Ὦνος, a buying ; — payment, price, value : — things for sale, and the place. — Ὠνέομαι, to buy. — The price and value of a thing as depending on its Ὄνησις, utility or advantage. (2) R. νέω, to heap ; †ὀνέω, (as Ὀ-κέλλω,) whence Onus : As Auction from Augeo, Auctum ; prices at it being increased at each bidding. —The

Etym. M. very curiously, though absurdly : ' As from
Ἄρνες is Ἀρνυσθαι, and from Πῶλοι is Πωλέω, so
Ὠνέομαι, from the sale of Ὄνοι asses.'

'Ωὸν, an egg : — poet. a bald head. — Mrt. ' would
derive this from αὔω to shine, as white and shining :'
i.'e. αὔον neut. particip. As τρΩμα, Ὠλαξ, cOda, cO-
dex, cOlis, sOdea. (2) The Et. M. says ·it should be
written ᾠὸν or ὠιὸν, that is Οἰον, as it is always dropt
single. But Turton derives Unio, a pearl, from Unus,
' As there is never more than one found in the same
shell :' and there is only one embryo in the egg. (3)
Scheide from †οἴω, †οἴον, bear'ng, i. e. a chicken in it, as
Webster explains Egg, ' containing an embryo.'

'Ωὸν, a word used in encouraging rowers or sailors.
— From the sound. Schrevel. compares our ho up.

Ὤπις : in Οὖπις.

Ὤρ : for Ὄαρ.

Ὤρα, allied to Ὅρος and Οὖρος a bound : ' a season
fixed by the laws of Nature or the customs of man : —
any one of the four seasons ; — time of meals, as breakfast, &c. : — an hour of the day, hora : — the season of
youth, as limited ; — beauty :' Lenn. And the particular
age of any one. (2) ' Hebr. aur, light : Time, &c.:' Wr.

Ὤρα, care, attention. — R. ὁράω, to look to. — ' Akin
to Οὖρος :' Dnn. (2) R. ᾦ. Anxiety. (3) ' Hebr.
or, to raise [rouse] :' Wr.

'Ωραῖος, in season, ripe : — beautiful, &c. — R. ὥρα.

'Ω–, or Ὠρακιάω, to faint, swoon away i. e. from ὥρα
anxiety. Eustath. says it means also φροντίζω. We
must suppose a word ὡράω, ὥρᾱκα.

'Ωρεῖον, a barn for the fruits of the ὥρα season,
horreum.

Ὧρος, time, — a year.—As Ὤρα.

Ὧρος, for Ἄωρος.

'ΩΡΙΩΝ, the constellation Orion. — From the giant
so called, who, the Fable says, sprang from the Οὖρον of
190

Jupiter, Neptune, and Mercury. . Hence Ovid says :
' Perdidit antiquum litera prima sonum.' As Orion
should be Urion.

'Ωρύω, to howl, roar. — Lenn. and Pkh. from the
sound. — But as we find Ὠρυγμὸς and Ἐρυγμὸς, Ὠρυ-
γὴ and Ἐρυγὴ, Ὠρύω is well allied by others to Ἐρεύ-
γω, ὁρευγα, ὥρευγα, whence a bull is Ἐρυγμηλὸς,
vomiting forth, roaring.

'Ὡς, for Οἷς, Ὧις : by what means or ways, quibus
modis, how : — also, at what times or seasons, when : —
how that, that, as He said how that or that . . . — Also,
how I wish that.— By which means it may, i. e. so that,
in order that. — And ' as,' i. e. ' He did so in the way in
which I did.'

'Ὡς τὸν ποταμὸν, for 'Ὡς (πρὸς) τὸν π. Thus : ' He
went as towards the river.'

Ὧς : in Οὖας.

'ΩΣΑΝΝΑ, Hosanna: Made up of Hebrew words
meaning ' Save, I beseech Thee.'

'Ωσία, as Οὐσία.

'Ωσις, impulse. — R. ὠθέω, ὥσω. So 'Ωστίζομαι, to
push.

'Ω τᾶν : in Τᾶν.

'Ωτειλὴ, a wound.— R. οὐτάω, to wound. Οὐταμένην
ὠτειλήν, Hom.

'Ωτὶς, a bustard with long ear-feathers. — R. ὦς,
ὠτός.

'Ωφελέω, I help : ὀφέλλω.

'Ωφελον, I wish that ! Prop., how I ought to have
done so ! 'Ωφελε, how it ought to have been so !—
From ὀφείλω.

'Ωχρα, yellow ochre : from

'Ωχρὸς, wan, pale, yellow. — R. ὄζω, ὄχα, to wail.
(2) R. ὠοῦ χρόα, the color of egg.

'Ωψ, g. ὠπός, the eye, face, countenance. — R. †ὄ-
πτομαι, †ὦπα, ὄπωπα, to see.

FINIS.

ADDITIONS AND CORRECTIONS.

'Αβρός. Add βλάπτω, έδλαβον.
'Αβροτάζω. 'Misled night-wanderers:' Shaksp.
'ΑΒΥΡΤΑΚΗ. Add the Æolic Βανά for Γυνή.
Ἄγχω. (2) R. ἔγχι. To move near and close.
'Ακανθίς. For 'flour' read 'seeds.'
Βαμβαίνω. For 'N as μαΝθάνω' it ought to be 'M as λαΜβάνω.'
Βραχύς. We say, I'll do it in a crack.
Γρόνθων. Perhaps better allied to Κροαίνω in the sense of beating the time. See Κρουπέζαι.
Διάζομαι. At the end add 'as in Δι-φάσιος, Δι--αυλος, &c.'
'Εναίρω. (3) R. ἴνω = φένω, as γερΑΙΡΩ. See Ἐνύω.

ἘΩ 2. We say 'I have never BEEN TO such a place.'
Καινός. (2) R. καίω. 'He was a καιόμενος burning and a shining light', John 5. 35.
Μιμέομαι. 'Less than the reality.' Thus Pliny says : 'Quem imitati sunt multi, æquavit nemo.'
Πέντε. Thus Πεμπάζω is to count on the FIVE fingers.
Σάθη. (2) Ut Σάχω pro Ψάχω, sic Σάθη pro Ψάθη à Ψάω, frico.
Στοά. (2) Σ as Σμικρός. From †Τόω to stretch out, as in Ἐσ-έτοσσα, Τόξον, Τόπος. Like Latin Tentorium from Tendo, Tentum.

ADDITIONS TO THE LATIN ETYMOLOGY.

Acipenser. As osPray for osFray, osaiFraga.
Anus, an old woman. (3) R. ἄ-νους. Γραωδεῖς μύθους 1 Tim. 4. 7 : silly.
Arbor. (3) R. ἀερο-θάσα, ἀεροθᾶσ', ἀεροθάρ, as honoS, honoR. Ἀν-έθησαν, of the seeds, Mark 4. 7.
Aruspex. Riddle 'from ἱεροσκόπος, for the Italian Greeks said ἰΑρὸς for ἱΕρός.' Transp. as sPeCio from σΚεΠιῶ.
Buteo. For βου-ωπέων.
Cerritus. (3) Cerebrum, cerebritus, as Entêté.
Crux. (4) R. χάραξ.
Damnum. Ldd. has δαμία Cretan for ζημία.
Ergò. (3) R. ὀρεγυία.
Filius. In (2) add Φίλε τέκνον, Hom.
Flos. Ldd. from φλόος. Bailey from θάλος Æol. φάλος.
Focus. In (2) add Foχεὸs, a holder.
Frequens. Observe vice versâ aiGle from aQUila.
Olobus. (3) R. κόλπος, κλόπος, globus. (4) An old Dict. says 'Γήλοφος, γλόφος, globus.'
Gradivus. Add ' Or gradiens Divus', μακρὰ βεθηκώς.

Hariolus. As in French Hors from Foris. — James Bailey brings it from ἰΑρὸς as in Aruspex above : then ἀρὸς, hariolus.
Hispidus. From ὗς, as HIStrix. Much as Σῶς, Sopitis, in termination.
Inchoo. From χοή say ἐγ-χοάω, ἐγχοῶ.
Inde. (3) For im-do : im acc. of is. As vice versâ Ad-eò, abl. after Ad. See Unde.
Infit. As φατὶ was an Æol. 3d person, suppose ἔμ-φατι, ἔμφατ'. As ἐν-έπω.
Is. Liddell has the Greek word *Ἴς in this sense.
Locus. The Rev. P. French refers it to †λέλοχα, λέλογχα, †λαχέω, λαγχάνω : That which is allotted or assigned to us.
Malus. Old Dict. from μάχλος, as Χλαῖνα, Læna.
Masturbo. Voss. : 'SUI IPSIUS leno esse'. As we say 'Felo DE SE'. Still the 'DE SE' is sadly wanting.
Menda. Job 31. 7. We say, That spot will ever remain.
Mænia, line 1. Vice versâ, cReperus from κΝέφας, ocioB from ὠκίωΝ.

191

Mollis. (**2**) R. μῶλυς.

Mugmor. In (**2**) compare Μιν and Νιν.

Mulier. In (**1**) compare Odyss. 7. 104 : 20. 105. Matth. 24. 41. Exod. 11. 5. Isa. 47. 1, 2.

Necto. (**3**) R. νάσσω, νένακται.

Nuntius, Nuncius. Riddle for *novum-cius*, from *novus, cio, cieo.*

Obba. R. ὄλπα, †ὄππα.

Olla. Ὄλλιξ is in Liddell.

Parma. Liddell has Πάλμη.

Patagium. Steph. and Ldd. have Παταγεῖον.

Posthumus. For *posthumātus*, as Servātus, Servus.

Rabulus. Compare Ῥαβάζω in Ldd.

Re-pudio. Mr. St. John Parry compares *tri-pudium*, and derives both from ποὺς, ποδός. *Re-pudio*, to push back with the feet : ἀπο-πυδίζω.

Rivalis. See Gen. 26. 20, 21.

Sape. In (**1**) compare ἤσαν ἴσαι πως, Eur. Hec. 130. A friend wrote to me unconsciously in a letter : ' Thus is it with me *ALMOST EVER*'.

Saltem. In (**1**) compare our '*SAVE* that . . . .'

Saltus. In (**2**) add : Yet Virgil has ' *Saltibus* in VACUIS '. See the meanings of Νέμος.

Scateo. (**2**) R. σκεδάω, dispergo.

Secūris. (**2**) *Se* for *semi, curis*, a spear.

Sella. For *Sedēla*, as Tutēla.

Semis. ' *Semi-as* ', says Bp. Colenso.

Si. In (**2**). ' *Be it* that I have erred ', Job 19. 4.

Sibilus. Add : Or σιπάλος, ugly, deformed.

Sitis. Add to (**3**) Ovid, ' *arida* facta *situ*'.

Sodālis. ' Perh. from *sodes*, amicus :' Ridd.

Sonus. Add to (**1**): So Σεῦτλον, Τεῦτλον.

Tempora. Mr. Hensley of Bath says, because age first shows itself on the temples by the hair becoming grey there first.

Testis. We say, Further than this the DE-PONENT sayeth not.

Truns. A Latin Grammar says, for *Trahens*.

Ventus. Ἀέντες is said of the winds, Il. 5. 526.—Add to the second part, ἐλθὼν ἄνεμος Iph. T. 1394. Ζέφυρος ἐλθὼν Il. 2. 147. Νότος ἐλθὼν 2. 395.

Vergo. (**3**) Γοργύω, Γόργω. As vOster, vEster.

Vestigium. (**4**) *Vestigo* : ve, στείχω?

Vigeo. Lyttleton from Φυγιής, Φυγιέω.

Vinco, vici, from Fίκω, to come down upon, Lat. *ico*.

Vita. (**2**) Βιοτά, βιτά.

Vitium. Οὐδὲν εὑρίσκω AITION, Luke 23. 4.

Vulgus. Key says : *Volvo, volvicus, volcus* : Circular assemblage.

Uxor. In (**1**) compare particularly 1 Sam. 25. 40, 41.

LONDON ·
PRINTED BY SPOTTISWOODE AND CO
NEW-STREET SQUARE

Milton Keynes UK
Ingram Content Group UK Ltd.
UKHW021912091023
430259UK00004B/148